THE PUPPET THEATRE IN AMERICA

PUPPET BOOKS BY PAUL McPHARLIN

A Repertory of Marionette Plays (Edited) 1929

Puppetry, an International Yearbook of Puppets
and Marionettes (Edited) 1930-1948

Puppet Heads and Hands and their Making 1932

A Producer's Guide to Plays for Puppets, Marionettes,
and Shadows 1932

Marionette Control 1934

A Plan for a Folding Stage Adaptable for Puppets,
Marionettes, and Shadows 1934

Posters, Playbills, and Publicity for Puppet Shows 1934

Animal Marionettes 1936

Puppets in America 1739 to Today 1936

Punch: his Life and Adventures, by Octave Feuillet
(Translated) 1946

PUPPET BOOKS BY MARJORIE BATCHELDER

Rod-Puppets and the Human Theatre 1947

The Puppet Theatre Handbook 1947

Hand-and-Rod Puppets (with Vivian Michael) 1947

Puppets and Plays, A Creative Approach (with Virginia Lee Comer) 1956

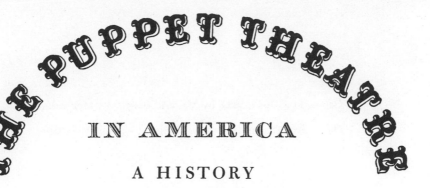

THE PUPPET THEATRE

IN AMERICA

A HISTORY

1524-1948

BY PAUL McPHARLIN

WITH A SUPPLEMENT
PUPPETS IN AMERICA SINCE 1948

BY MARJORIE BATCHELDER McPHARLIN

Boston   PLAYS, INC.   *Publishers*

NOTE

The Puppet Theatre in America: A History 1524–1948 by Paul McPharlin has been a standard work on American puppetry and puppeteers since it was first published in 1948. The book has been out of print for several years, but because the material and scholarship are still authoritative and valid and the demand for it continues, the present publishers feel that it merits reprinting.

This volume makes available again Paul McPharlin's unique book; also, to bridge the gap between 1948 and the present, I have prepared a comprehensive Supplement and a Bibliography, and these are included here with the unabridged reprint of the original book.

M.B.McP.

Contents

vii

SUPPLEMENT

PUPPETS IN AMERICA SINCE 1948

by Marjorie Batchelder McPharlin

Foreword

When was the first puppet show seen in America? Where was it and who was the puppeteer? People of an inquiring turn kept asking me such questions. What course had puppetry followed before its revival as an artistic medium in the United States about 1915? I myself wondered. So I took time from producing and performing puppet plays to look up what could be found.

Information was not plentiful. The theatre annals generally passed over puppet shows as too insignificant for mention. There was one notable exception, the *Annals of the New York Stage*, by my old teacher at Columbia College, George C. D. Odell. He chronicled every kind of show, no matter how minor, and puppet shows were painstakingly included along with the rest. Thanks to his all-encompassing scheme I was able to find more puppets in New York than anywhere else. In fact, by taking a New York appearance as a point in the itinerary of a company, I could sometimes trace its previous and subsequent engagements throughout the country.

Occasionally the section on theatricals in a local history would have a word on puppets. The accounts of travelers and the reminiscences of old-timers yielded a delightful description of a show now and then. But it was too vast a task to comb every American autobiography, or even the early ones. I looked into as many theatre memoirs as I could, and for the rest skimmed through whatever came my way, developing an ability to spot "puppet" or "Punch" in deserts of words.

When I had a clue about the time and place of a show I could turn to newspaper files for a notice or an advertisement. This stage of the search would have bogged down without the many reference librarians who gave me more assistance than their professional duties required. Even when puppet items were hidden in microscopic sizes of type, much came to light through their co-operation. I suspect that they grew inadvertently fascinated.

I cannot mention them all, but I wish to thank them for the patient checking that would have taken me many an hour and travel from coast to coast.

Impetus was given my project, which had started slowly and casually, when I decided to work on it as a doctoral thesis in the Institute of Fine Arts at the University of Michigan. Professor J. G. Winter was the chairman of my committee; I am grateful to him for sharing my enthusiasm for what must have seemed a rather strange subject. Dr. Randolph G. Adams, who also served on the committee, was constantly helpful in suggesting treasure troves of information. I wish that I might have been able to look for puppet references in all the source material in the William L. Clements Library over which he presides. James M. Plumer, another committee member, was so flattering as to foresee the thesis as a published book. It was submitted in 1940; save for additional material which has since appeared and been incorporated, and considerable re-writing to spare the reader from unwarranted dullness, this book is the thesis. The chapter on contemporary puppets brings it up to date; I had broken off the study at 1915 as a logical stopping place. Some of my master's thesis, *Esthetic of the Puppet Revival* (Wayne University Teachers College, Department of Art, 1938), done under the chairman-ship of Professor Jane Betsey Welling, has been worked into that chapter and the first one.

Many of my friends among puppeteers, hearing of my quest, came to my aid with information that they found in the archives of their own cities. I hesitate to begin naming them for fear I may leave some out unintentionally; the more complete my list of acknowledgments, the more serious will an omission be; if I forget someone, may I be pardoned.

Felix J. Smyth found information about Philadelphia shows for me; he was a conscientious and rapid researcher. Catherine Reighard turned over to me her findings about puppets in the New York codes and laws. Nathan R. Berke, whose wife Miriam was one of the talented puppeteers in my company, exhumed some Michigan puppet laws and gave advice on getting hold of the documents of the Royal Marionettes law suits. Marjorie Shanafelt traced the engagement of the Deaves marionettes in Lincoln, Nebraska. My old friend, Victor A. Lemaitre, gave me a hand in writing letters to South America and translated many passages in Spanish relating to puppetry.

Puppeteers of the older order were especially gracious in furnishing information. Mme Pinxy of Chicago told me of Punch and Judy men in the Chicago region. Mr. and Mrs. George Middleton recounted events in their own early career. Edwin Deaves wrote me a good deal about the globe trotting of his puppeteer family. But I wish particularly to thank David Lano for allowing me to retell parts of his unpublished memoirs, which I hope may someday appear in print as they deserve.

The pioneers of the revival, Ellen Van Volkenburg (and Louise M. Martin who was one of her puppeteers at the Chicago Little Theatre), Remo Bufano, Helen Haiman Joseph, and Tony Sarg, have told about the first-beginnings of modern puppetry in America in many pleasant conversations. Others of the newer order—I think I have met most of them, or at least heard from them by letter—have indulged my demands for history, taking time out from their work to do it.

I am very grateful indeed to Marjorie Batchelder, who has since become my wife, for compiling the list of puppeteers, a chore she has undertaken with her usual care and thoroughness. I hope that I may presently be allowed to show my appreciation by making an index or glossary for a book of hers.

A word about the illustrations in this volume: because line cuts only are used, I have made versions of some subjects, prints or photographs, in pen-and-ink; these are designated as after an original. Where a source is not indicated, the item is in my own collection.

There are of course many puppeteers and performances that have escaped me. I shall appreciate hearing of them so that this story may eventually be made more complete.

P. McP.

Murray Hill, New York City
8 May 1948

This book was in press when the author died on September 28, 1948. He had read all the proof and had made layouts for 350 pages of text and illustrations when he was forced by illness to put aside the scissors and paste pot. The work was completed by his wife, who also added the index. Every effort has been exerted to make the book as he would have wished it.

 THE PUPPET THEATRE IN AMERICA

I

Origins

The puppet, a theatrical figure moved under human control, has held an agelong fascination for mankind. Wherever detailed records survive there are evidences of it. It differs from all those articulated images, dolls, and automata which are not theatrical, not animated by human control. First and always it is a player, whether it be a three-inch cardboard Thespian or a thirty-five-foot telescoping clown such as Remo Bufano built for Billy Rose's production, *Jumbo*. It can play any character, cowboy, horse, enchanted tree, flying rug, ghost, or gremlin. Unlike the human actor, it is not limited to an opaque body and more or less transparent disguises; it has its own proper size, shape, and qualities made to order. It is, of course, a projection of the human being who controls it. Those who watch identify themselves with it, soaring when it vaults, accelerating to its frenetic pace, and exulting in its defiance of physical obstacles. Because its scope is so much wider than that of the human actor, it affords a wider release.

Charles Nodier, writing in *La Revue de Paris* in November 1842, stated that an audience feels protective toward puppets as if they were dolls banished from the nursery. Charles Magnin, in the classic history which will be mentioned again presently, said that the audience felt religious awe, as if puppets were divine images in the dusk of a temple. Spectators may experience both emotions. But when puppets come alive and the play is on, the overwhelming appeal is that of the theatre. One ceases to think of wood and wire; one is absorbed in the action. One loses a sense of proportion; a three-foot proscenium encloses the vastness of Aladdin's cave. All life is encompassed in the miniature stage realm; the puppeteer is the hand of destiny. The audience, accepting the convention of puppets, projects itself into them with the same empathy that it feels for any other actors.

When man wanted to invoke the spirit world he made images as intermediaries between him and it. He wore a mask and was himself an image. His spirit so entered the spirit world; when he played scenes of the chase he drew game to him by sympathetic magic; when he re-enacted the lives of heroes he became possessed of their strength. This mystic masquerade came to be the theatre. It was only another step to animate the image and create the puppet.

1

But to document the beginning of puppet history is difficult. Little jointed figures of sun-baked clay, some of them with loops on the head to suspend them by, have been dug up in Greece and Italy; if they were puppets they were only children's toys. The ancient Egyptian string-operated figurines which have come to light from tombs were probably models of workmen. The allusions to puppets in classic literature are tantalizing in their brevity. Father Mariantonio Lupi, an Italian scholar so obscure as to elude the biographical dictionaries, was first to point some of them out in his *Dissertazioni*, which were translated in *Le Journal étranger* of January 1757, and then in Gordon Craig's *The Marionnette* in 1918. There are, for example, metaphors of string control in Marcus Aurelius (VII, 3) and in *De Mundo* (VI), a work attributed to Aristotle but actually by another. Xenophon's *Symposium*, supposed to have transpired about 420 B.C., has (II, 1) a Syracusian showman who remarks that fools support him by seeing his neurospasta—string pulling; but there is no description of a puppet show. In the *Deipnosophistae* of Athenaeus, written about A.D. 230, it is mentioned (I, 19) that Potheinos, a neurospastes or puppeteer, had played in Athens on the very stage of Euripides. What the puppet theatre of the ancients was like, however, can be inferred from the book of Hero of Alexandria on water-power automata and mechanical scenes, which were elaborately articulated and contrived.

Father Lupi's citations were repeated by Johann Beckmann, whose work was translated from the German as *A History of Inventions and Discoveries* (London, 1797). They were used again by John Payne Collier in his erudite but inventive introduction to *Punch and Judy* (London, 1828). Charles Magnin, who had made his mark as a theatre historian with *Les Origines du théâtre moderne* (Paris, 1838), began the serial publication of his *Histoire des marionnettes en Europe depuis l'antiquité jusqu'à nos jours* in *La Revue des deux mondes* in 1848; in 1852 it appeared in book form and in 1862 in a revised edition. The chapter on puppets in England—the only one ever to be translated into English—ran in Volume 14 of *Sharpe's London Journal*, 1848-1849. But though Magnin added further classic allusions, and no one has ever covered the period so well as he, his conclusions are not too firmly grounded, and very little is still known of how puppets began.

Their early course must be reconstructed from what we know of them today. They probably played in suburbs of towns and in out-of-the-way places for humble audiences, giving simplified or burlesqued versions of what had been popular in the big theatre a few seasons before. Their booths or stages were light enough to ride in a cart or on the showman's back. The delight of the common folk who had no other theatre, they

were, however, not unknown to aristocrats who liked parody or had
seen too much of the big theatre.

When the theatre of ancient Rome crumbled, if any actors survived
they were forced to throw in their lot with that of the traveling entertainers—jugglers, acrobats, and puppeteers. A whole variety program
came to be performed by a small troupe or a mere team. The jongleurs
who wandered from castle to castle could sing, tumble, and work a
puppet. Little by little a new sort of theatre emerged, that of the Church,
enacting miracle and morality plays suitable for the sacred precincts.
Now it happened that the Church had images; the actor again bethought
himself of animating them. A well-loved grouping of images was that
about the manger at Christmastide. St. Francis of Assisi is credited with
its inauguration. It was not too startling to make these images into puppets
to speak the words of the Nativity scene. The little figure of Mary in
the center, little *little* Mary or marionette, gave her name to all the
puppets in Italy and France, though they have been known by various
other names as well.

At the time of the first voyages of discovery to America, puppets in
Europe were either part of the bag of tricks of the mountebank, who
showed them in courtyards, marketplaces, or halls, or fixtures in certain
shrines, brought out at holiday season. When the first explorers and
settlers were crossing the Atlantic, mountebanks, aware of the new life
in the theatre, ventured more elaborate shows. They made puppet
Pulcinellas, Arlecchinos, and other characters of the improvised mask
comedy which was sweeping from Italy throughout the Continent. They
salvaged scraps of religious drama, poked fun at the literary stage, and
gave stock puppets such as Punch all the leading roles. Had a court
performance featured a poetic Hero who swam the Hellespont? Well,
then, a puppet comedian would swim the Thames.

When there was a chink of stowage in the tightly laden ships sailing
westward, puppets made the voyage. Of course the Puritans who landed
in New England abhorred the theatre, though puppet shows had managed
to play during the enforced closing of the theatres in England. Puppets
were to be the harbinger of the theatre in the New World—they needed
less equipment than live players. But their story has been so little known
that one finds people under the impression that in America they were an
innovation of the present century.

In Helen Haiman Joseph's *A Book of Marionettes* (first edition, New
York, 1920), a delightfully written account of puppets all over the world
and a pioneer history of modern puppetry, there are only a few references
to American puppets of the nineteenth century. Margaret Jean Mac-
Claran's unpublished thesis, *The Revival of Puppetry in America*

(Northwestern University, 1931), lists but a dozen performances in the eighteenth and nineteenth centuries. My own *Puppets in America, 1739 to Today* (Detroit, 1936) merely touches upon early history, the concern being contemporary examples.

When it was not assumed that puppets were comparatively recent newcomers, it was thought that they had never been sufficiently popular in the old days to be of any importance in America's entertainment life. In the introduction to a reprint of the Collier-Cruikshank "Punch and Judy" (*Harper's Monthly Magazine*, May 1871) S. S. Conant, little knowing what perennial favorites Punch and his spouse had been and were to be, said of the play, "It was exhibited for a short time at a popular place of amusement in this city [New York] about a year ago, but did not take sufficiently with the audience to induce the manager to go on with it."

"We are too busy a people," wrote F. J. Ziegler ("Puppets Ancient and Modern," *Harper's Monthly Magazine*, December 1897), "to squander time on the puppet show, and too practical a people to see anything heroic in the fantoccini." Granted that Americans were both busy and hardheaded, still they were flocking, at the turn of the century, to dime museums, vaudeville, circus sideshows, and Sunday-school parties, at all of which puppets were an accepted feature.

Elva McFie, in her thesis, *Opportunities for Diversified Creative Experiences in the Field of Puppetry* (Colorado State College of Education, August 1938), declared, "There was almost a complete lack of interest in any form of puppetry in America up through the 1800's." But she based her statement on the paucity of magazine articles about American puppets in the nineteenth century!

Puppet shows, unless they were unusually affluent, seldom advertised in the newspapers. And the newspapers almost never took any critical notice of them. That is still the case today. Yet almost the only records of early shows are to be found in advertisements in the papers. Until recently few puppeteers wrote their memoirs; their diaries and account books have not been saved in public collections. Fortunately, it has been possible to draw upon the recollections of many old-time puppeteers to enrich this history. Observers of the American scene such as Dickens and Mrs. Trollope, both of whom were interested in things theatrical, managed to miss seeing puppet shows. But a few travelers and diarists noted them, often shows of which there is no other record. Together with other stimulants, puppets have frequently been frowned upon in America. They were itinerant and they were small; if they escaped suppression they risked oblivion. It is possible that many an early showman has disappeared without leaving a trace.

The history of local theatres in America has just begun to be studied extensively. But where the major theatres have been chronicled, the casual ones have been overlooked. Regional accounts have yielded little—with the monumental exception of George C. D. Odell's *Annals of the New York Stage*.

The sparse data having been gathered, at least in part, a picture of puppetry in America takes shape. The puppeteers who are active today will see it in a sympathetic light, for they can understand how much their predecessors accomplished. The stranger to puppets may glimpse, through the figures in the foreground, the wide American scene.

This stranger may wish to ask a question at this point, What is the difference between a puppet and a marionette?

Puppet is the older word in English. It comes from *pupa*, Latin for "girl" or "doll" or "small creature." The *-et* makes it diminutive, a *small* small creature. It has been spelled *poupette, poppit,* and *poppet*. Shakespeare uses it several times. In his day a puppet show was called a *motion*. Thenceforward, it being in the nature of English to keep changing words and word uses, puppets and puppet shows were variously designated, as the reader of this history will discover. The word *marionette*, of Italian-French origin, "little *little* Mary," does not differ from *puppet* in basic meaning, though it has a double diminutive ending. A comparative newcomer to English, it has struck showmen as having a more elegant look than plain old *puppet*.

At the start of the puppet revival in the 1920's the string-operated sort was popular and the word *marionette* was preferred. Hence *marionette* differentiated string-puppets, and the distinction still prevails. But to make himself quite clear, the puppeteer must say *string-puppet, hand-puppet,* or *rod-puppet* to identify a type.

Puppets may be operated from above, from below, or from the plane of action. They may be operated over the hand, by strings or wires, or by sticks or rods. It is difficult to be sure what kind was used in many early American shows. It seems that hand-puppets and string-puppets were both in use from the sixteenth century onward. To know which was the type one must surmise how the showman traveled: if he had a cart or a pack horse he may have had string-puppets and their comparatively bulky equipment; if he went afoot he must have carried simple hand-puppets. As specific shows are recorded more will be said of modes of operation.

Early Spanish Puppeteers

Among the mimes and minstrels who brought the traditions of the theatre into the Middle Ages were *bastaxi* who worked puppets, carrying a few in their knapsacks along with their dancing pumps and conjuring tricks. They wandered from court to court giving their entertainments after the last of the Roman theatres had fallen into disuse. A few of them settled down as musicians and jesters to serve one prince. Thus they gained security and a respectable place in society, for a wandering player was no more than a rogue and vagabond, while the servant to a noble house, no matter how humble his work, was established in the feudal hierarchy. As a matter of convenience the English traveling puppeteers of the sixteenth century styled themselves, on the model of the actor companies, as "Her Majesty's" or the "Lord Chandos'" men; this sanctioned their enterprise; under Tudor law they could have been jailed as vagrants. Feudally attached puppeteers existed so late as the eighteenth century, when Prince Esterházy had a troupe for which Haydn composed operettas.

In conformity with the practice of the period, Hernando Cortés had a puppeteer among his servants when he set out on 12 October 1524 from Tenochtitlan, which is now Mexico City, on a six months' march to rumored gold fields in Hibueras (Las Higueras, Honduras). He took along with him, according to Bernal Diáz del Castillo, the diarist of the expedition (*Historia de la conquista de Mejico*, XIV, 174), "five players on the oboe, sackbut, and dulcimer, and an acrobat and another—*otro que jugaba de manos y hacía títeres*—who did sleight-of-hand and worked puppets." That these entertainers were personal servants is indicated in Cortés' own account, sent to the Emperor Charles V of Spain, in which he reported that he had traveled "with some persons both mounted and on foot, but no more than those of my household and some friends and relations."

The first European play to be done with human actors in America was not performed until 24 June 1538, fourteen years later. Joaquin García Icazbalceta recounts, in the introduction to his edition of *Los Coloquios de Gonzáles Eslava*, that four sacred dramas were then presented in Mexico for the edification of the Indians. Puppets have always been in the vanguard as the theatre has followed explorers to the frontiers of America.

What sort of puppets were used by this man of Cortés, this Spanish master of legerdemain, to while away the uncanny night beside the campfire in the Tehuantepecan jungle? One can only speculate. They may have been no more than a pair of light hand-puppets animated above a blanket stretched curtainwise to mask the operator. What interlude did they perform? Spaniards of the time would have applauded the deeds of a martyr, the miracles of a saint, or the chronicle of a Biblical king. And they would have roared at the re-enactment of a droll mishap of the march, or a caricature of one of the company. They would have enjoyed the slapstick antics which still rouse a chuckle today. One must be content with the meager mention of this initial puppet show.

Since the Spaniards explored and settled in America before others, and since they were fond of puppets, as references in *Don Quixote* and other seventeenth-century literature indicate, it must be assumed that they continued to bring puppet shows to the New World. Only scattered records of them have so far come to light. In 1569 Juan de Samora petitioned the authorities for permission to play during the Lenten season in the town of Tezcuco, Mexico, "three puppet shows, which would give the gentry no cause to blush." On 15 July 1597, in Lima, Peru, a mountebank, El Doctor Julio and another, Jusepe Hernandez, proposed to show the public, upon the payment of an entrance fee, "an invention called the Castle of Marvels." Was this a puppet booth? Also in Lima, in July 1629, in the cloisters of the Convent of St. Francis, upon the occasion of the festival for the martyrs of Japan, a puppet show was given, as Father Juan de Ayllon records in Canto III, folio 69, of the *Poem on the Festival* which was published in Lima the next year.

The first woman puppeteer in America makes her appearance in Peru at the end of the seventeenth century. Her name, according to *El Correo* of Lima for 1 February 1840, was Leonor de Goromar; under her direction plays with large puppets (string-puppets, perhaps) were given in the Teatro Principal at Lima in 1699. The entry in Mendiburu's *Historical and Biographical Dictionary of Peru* lists her as Leonor Godomar, Spaniard, who gave puppet shows in 1696. It is likely that she was a widow carrying on her husband's work. While women were allowed to do this to support themselves, they would not ordinarily have entered such an enterprise at that time of their own choice.

Within a few decades, with the coming of the eighteenth century, there would be permanently housed puppet theatres in Spanish, French, and English America. But a digression is necessary to find what puppets there had been in America before the coming of the Europeans.

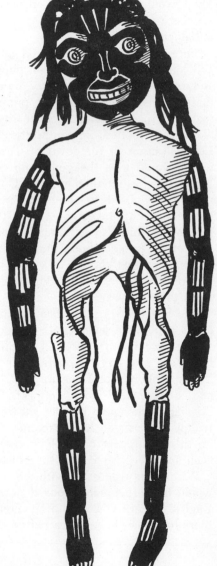

Skeleton figure from the Haida tribe, Northwest Coast. Wood, hair, and cloth. In the United States National Museum, Washington, D.C., No. 89039. After a drawing by R. Bruce Inverarity interpreted by a silk-screen print in his Movable Masks and Figures of the North Pacific Coast Indians.

Figure of wood, cloth, and fur, seated in a fur-lined swing; strings raise its arms; Northwest Coast. Affectionately known as "Susie" by the staff of the Royal Ontario Museum of Archaeology in the collection of which it is preserved. After a drawing.

Puppets of the Aborigines

Whereas the puppets which came from Europe were presented as mere entertainment, those already in America were used by the Indians for religious ceremonials. The method of their manipulation was concealed, not as a showman's secret but as a sacred mystery. The two sorts of puppetry were as far apart as the late Roman theatre, devoid of spiritual significance, and the early Greek choral devotions which grew into drama. All that they may have had in common were manipulative similarities. It is just possible that European and Indian techniques might have influenced each other had they met. But the European shows were confined to large settlements out of the Indian's range and the native mysteries were not enacted for profane eyes.

How ancient is the use of puppetry in Indian ceremonials? In the absence of chronicles, none can say. But at the beginning of the sixteenth century it was noted by Bernal Díaz, who of course knew the puppeteer of Cortés, in Mexico; the Indians there, he observed, understood conjuring and working puppets, "saben jugar de mano y hazer títeres." He may not actually have seen Indian puppets in operation, for he described no performance. He must have taken them on hearsay. They would have been holy figures, not to be shown to the white strangers.

Fray Bernardo de Sahagún, who died in 1590, actually saw a minor sort of puppet worked by a Toltec medicine man in Mexico. In his *Historia de las cosas de la Nueva España* (facsimile of MS., Mexico, 1905-1938) he wrote, "Another trick of the said necromancer was this: seating himself in the middle of the marketplace at Tianquiztli, he announced that his name was Tlacavepan, otherwise Ocexcoch, and proceeded to make a tiny figure dance in the palm of his hands. Seeing this, the Toltecs all arose and went to watch him. . . . The necromancer then questioned the Toltecs, saying, 'What manner of trick is this? Ha, why do you not understand it?'" A puppeteer would have looked for the thread on this little figure, or speculated whether it might have been of some light papery substance animated by the heat of the hand.

A century later, in 1655, a Jesuit in Lower Canada saw a brief Indian miracle play. According to the *Jesuit Relations for 1655-6*, a medicine man of the Onontagué, an Iroquois tribe, demonstrated that his magic herbs were so potent that they could bring the dead back to life. He took what was apparently a dead squirrel from his pouch and held it by "a cunning attachment to the end of its tail." Applying the drugs to it, he so pulled the string that it hopped back into the pouch of its own accord. Withdrawing it again, he made it move "as the jugglers of France move their puppets." The good priest, though he had seen puppet shows at home, was probably as mystified by this performance as any of the on-lookers. His description leaves one in doubt whether the puppet squirrel was moved by strings, by a hand inside its body, or by a combination of the two. It was rarely that such a puppet was worked in the broad light of day, where its mechanism might be detected, and more rarely still that it was shown to a European, religious man though he might be.

While few Europeans were able to see Indian puppets, four Indian chieftains, "sachems, or kings of the five Indian nations," were shown a puppet performance in London as one of the sights of town, between 20 and 29 April 1710/11, when they came to offer their services to Queen Anne against the French in Canada. Just a few years before, the first English puppets had found their way to the West Indies in America. Narcissus Luttrell recounted, in his *A Brief Historical Relation of State Affairs* (Oxford, 1857), that "her Majestie ordered them presents, the Lord Chamberlain to entertain them at her charge, and that they be shown what is remarkable here." And so they were conducted to Punch's Theatre, at the upper end of St. Martin's Lane, joining to Litchfield Street, where they witnessed a performance of *The Last Year's Campaigne,* fittingly military. Their names were set forth in the playbill that day:

A) The Emperor Tee Yee Neen Ho Ga Row
B) King Sa Ga Yeau Qua Rah Tow
C) King E Tow oh Koam
D) King Oh Nee Yeath Tow no Riow

and these were keyed to portraits, or simulacra, in a rough woodcut illustration which showed them on a stage, very much like puppets themselves. In No. 50 of *The Spectator* what pretended to be their impressions of London was published, but no description of Powell's puppets was put into their mouths. If these noble savages had been initiated into the occult art of Indian puppetry, they must have been amazed to see what had become of it in the land of the white man. Their sight-seeing schedule was a busy one, however, and it is unlikely that they were given a few minutes backstage to observe the workings for the benefit of their tribesmen back home.

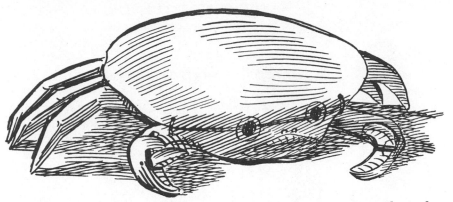

Wooden crab from the Tsimshian tribe, Northwest coast, 24 inches wide; its legs and claws are articulated. In the Museum of the American Indian, Heye Foundation, New York, No. 1/8928. After a photograph.

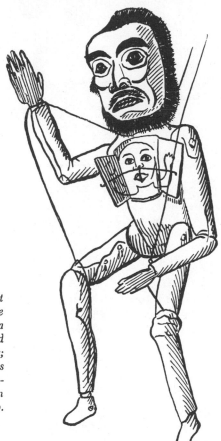

"Nonlemgila" or puppet with doors that open and close to show the white face of its spirit, from the Nishka tribe, Skeena River, British Columbia; wood covered with buckskin dyed brown; wig of fur; 30½ inches tall. One set of strings works the doors, the other lifts both limbs together. In the Museum of the American Indian, Heye Foundation, New York, No. 8/2606. After a photograph.

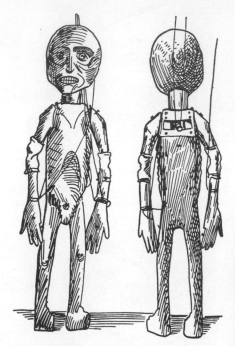

Two skeleton figures, wood, with articulated heads and limbs, used by the Northwest Coast medicine man as an evocation of the dead in a performance half magic, half religious. In the Royal Ontario Museum of Archaeology, Toronto. After a photograph.

Front and back of a skeleton figure from the Kwakiutl tribe, Northwest Coast. A set of strings to the peg at the back of the neck turns the head; others raise the arms. Cedar with cloth tubes at elbows. The feet were probably once attached to a base. Height 28 inches. Collected 1912. In the Milwaukee Public Museum, No. 17373/4615. After a photograph.

Toward the end of the nineteenth century Indians occasionally saw a frontier puppet show of the white man—Dave Lano's, for example, as will be recorded in the chapter on his work—but by that time their own culture had been crowded practically into oblivion. It may be noted that in the 1930's puppetry in the European-American style was taught at such Indian schools as the Escuela del Estudiante Indigena, Mexico City, and the Haskell Institute, Lawrence, Kansas, without concern for aboriginal methods.

Indian puppetry is practically extinct and little has been recorded of it. Franz Boas studied the secret masking societies of the Kwakiutl tribe on the Northwest Coast; puppetry was included in their rites; his notes appeared in the 1895 *Annual Report of the United States National Museum* (Washington, D. C., 1897). But few others investigated the subject. About a dozen actual Northwest Coast puppets are in the collection of the Museum of the American Indian, Heye Foundation, New York; others are in the National Museum, Washington, the Chicago Museum of Natural History, the Milwaukee Public Museum, the Royal Ontario Museum of Archaeology, Toronto, and the Provincial Museum, Victoria, B.C. Further attention should be given these examples.

In 1932, prompted by a desire to learn how these coastal puppets had been used, R. Bruce Inverarity, artist and puppeteer, visited the Queen Charlotte Islands. He gained the confidence of the Haida tribe by sketching for them and was granted three interviews with the octogenarian chief, Gidanst, who told about the ceremonial puppets he remembered from his youth. These were seen by firelight in a ritual house. The thick brown spruce and fern root strings that pulled them, visible enough in daylight, disappeared in the flicker of fire glow. The puppets represented such awesome things as a spirit in human form, an otter totem, and a decapitated man whose head rejoined his body. The puppets were hidden in a trench in the ground until the time for their appearance, when they arose, controlled by strings passing aloft over the rafters or out through the roof; the medicine man and his confederates were the puppeteers. Inverarity's notes were published in *Puppetry 1933* and in *Movable Masks and Figures of the North Pacific Coast Indians* (Cranbrook Institute of Science, 1941). The articulated masks of the region, seen in the same firelit performances as the puppets, for the same purpose of showing the bonds between the human and spirit worlds, were also string controlled.

The puppets are not unlike European string-puppets. They are carved of wood with simple tongue-and-groove joints, or bending places of a tube of cloth. They are dressed in scraps of cloth and fur or left uncostumed. Their stringing depends upon the motion they are to make. One figure has cords attached first to the knees, then to the wrists, so that arms and legs lift together. In another the strings pass through the body and come out at the back. Maximum action is obtained by a minimum number of strings—a virtue admired by all puppeteers.

Northwest Coast handicraft came to flower after contacts with the European trader. Tall totem poles, in the numbers that were carved, would have been impossible without axes and knives from Birmingham and Connecticut. Now it happens that Northwest Coast puppets are almost the only Indian ones available for study today. They look surprisingly like European puppets. Could the Indians, seeing some traveling Russian show in the nineteenth century, have assimilated its technique? But if a Russian puppeteer had strayed that far afield he would have been traveling light; he would have had hand-puppets. Hand-puppets are more typically Russian, anyway, than string-puppets; they penetrated into Moscovy from Germany in the seventeenth century. But there were string-puppets in Persia and India which may have wandered up to Siberia and then— This is all speculation, however. Suffice it to say that the Indians had puppets, had them certainly before the coming of any European. What they brought with them from Asia when they came over the Bering Straits, centuries before they met the white man, is another matter. That leads into even vaguer speculation. Perhaps it is wise, for the moment, to attribute Indian puppetry to spontaneous and independent invention.

There were puppets until quite recently, and some may still exist, among the Southwest Indians. The Hopi saw them in firelit huts, as did the Indians on the Northwest Coast. Jesse Walter Fewkes gave a detailed

Two "nonlemgilas" of wood and hair which rise from a mystic coffer at the pulling of a string; Northwest Coast. The wooden coffer is painted with symbolic masks of totem animals. In the Royal Ontario Museum of Archaeology. After a photograph.

A puppet screen with birds and corn maids from the Hopi tribe in the Southwest. Made by a man named Totci sometime before 1899. The corn maids, mythical personages who brought seed corn to mankind in ancient times, are honored at planting time in a performance that re-enacts their age-old grinding of corn. Kneeling in their feather kilts before a miniature grinding stone placed before the screen, they raise their arms as if to grind meal. On the top pole of the screen painted with rain-cloud symbols hop two twittering birds. After an Indian drawing, Plate 27 in J. Walter Fewkes: Hopi Katchinas.

account of *A Theatrical Performance at Walpi* which he witnessed before 1900 (*Proceedings of the Washington Academy of Sciences*, Vol. 2, p. 606 ff.). Here serpents four or five feet long, their bodies made of a stick and hoops covered with painted cloth, their heads of gourds or carved cottonwood, crawled out of holes in a screen to cavort and eat corn offerings. In *Hopi Katchinas* (*21st Annual Report of the Bureau of American Ethnology*) the same author speaks of figures of maids grinding corn and birds which were probably worked by strings or rods. Also at Walpi, in the March festival with its sun-deity serpents, he saw masked men with puppet serpents over their arms like sleeves; false arms hung at their sides to mystify spectators about the animation of the puppets.

Not only in America but on the islands of the Pacific, the stepping stones by which Mongolians came to the continent, where they became the Indians, puppetry was practiced. Wooden marionettes that performed

In the first act of a planting-time mystery play at Walpi, Arizona, as it was performed about 1899, six serpent-deities poked open the sun-emblem discs in the puppet screen, steadied by naked attendants in mud-head masks, emerged, twisted about, and snapped at the offering set out before them in the pattern of a cornfield. A bowl of meal was also proffered them. The screen was painted with rain clouds and other symbols. After a drawing by Mrs. M. Wright Gill, Plate 32 in Fewkes: A Theatrical Performance at Walpi.

ceremonial dances descended to the Maori, according to their legends, from a blond aboriginal forest people (James Cowan, *Journal of the Polynesian Society*, June 1921). J. Macmillan Brown, in *The Riddle of the Pacific* (Boston, 1924, p. 142), mentions that there was a tradition of puppetry on Easter Island. The *Bounty* mutineers, poking into old graves on Pitcairn Island, found crude jointed figures similar to those placed with the dead on Easter Island.

The Hawaiians used *hula kii*, or "dance images," (six of them, hand-puppets, are in the National Museum, Washington, D.C.) as late as the reign of Kalakaua in the 1880's. They had arms loosely jointed to the body and were costumed in bark cloth. The performer stood behind a screen to work them while he recited their lines. The plays depicted Hawaiian life and had passages sung to the accompaniment of the *ipu*, or calabash drum. It was at first thought that these puppets were imitations of the European, but upon study of the play texts it was found that

*In the fifth act of the same play, another screen surmounted by rain-cloud motives,
lightning symbols painted on its slats, and covered with pine boughs, two sun-emblem
flaps encircled by turkey feathers were pushed open by larger serpent deities. They
snapped at the miniature cornfield set out before them and intertwined. Then mud-
head maskers wrestled with them. A youth rode one of them as if on horseback but
was thrown. All the maskers were overcome. The entire performance took place in
a ceremonial house, or "kiva," illuminated only by firelight. To darken the room while
the screen and puppets were installed, blankets were held around the fire. After a
drawing, Plate 33, in the same work by Fewkes.*

there were obsolete words and other evidences of the antiquity of the
form. Since the plays were for entertainment and not religious celebration, they had doubtless undergone long evolution.

So there were puppets along the Northwest Coast, among the Eastern
woodland tribes (the resurrected squirrel), in the Southwest, in Mexico,
and in the Pacific islands, a distribution which would indicate that
they were generally to be found throughout the Western Hemisphere.
It is a pity that the independent art of the aborigines remains so little
known.

Act six of the serpent-deity play at Walpi showed two serpent puppets which popped open the lappets on jars and rose, swaying and dipping, to partake of the miniature cornfield offering. Then they sank back into the jars. They were controlled by strings running over the rafters of the "kiva," one at the top and a pair at the sides of the head. From a drawing, Plate 34, in the work by Fewkes.

IV

Eighteenth-Century English Puppets

1. How Puppet Shows Were Given

There is a dearth of evidence how puppet shows were given in the English colonies in the eighteenth century. But, since they were, like the colonists, transplanted bodily from Europe, what is known about them in the old country will throw light upon their appearance in the new.

Shows were advertised in three ways: by the noise of trumpet, drum, and public proclamation; by the showing of playbills, written or printed, posted or distributed; and by the insertion of notices in the newspapers. These methods were identical with those used by the larger theatre. Except for the obsolete trumpet and drum—crying survives in the patter of the ballyhoo man—they are still in force.

A pamphlet describing the appearance of Bartholomew Fair about 1650, quoted in Samuel McKechnie's *Popular Entertainments* (London, 1931), says "Here a knave in a fool's coat with a trumpet sounding, or on a drum beating, invites you and would fain persuade you to see his puppets; there a rogue like a wild woodman, or in an antick shape like an incubus, desires your company to view his motion." In No. 16 of *The Tatler* it is described how, to announce Powell's performance of *The Creation of the World* at Bath in May 1709, "the puppet drummer, Adam and Eve, and several others who lived before the flood, passed through the streets on horseback." The ingenious showman who devised this cavalcade, we are told in No. 372 of *The Spectator*, gave the proceeds of his performance on the evening of 7 May 1712 to the poor of the parish—a good way to advertise, too—of St. Paul's, Covent Garden, London, to make up for the racket he had occasioned "by the constant rattling of coaches, drums, trumpets, triumphs, and battles" in and around his theatre. A scene in the second act of Henry Fielding's *The Author's Farce* is done in the style of the proclamation of a puppet show, with a drum. The central figures in Hogarth's *Southwark Fair*, where *Punch's Opera* is playing, are a pretty girl drummer and a blackamoor with a trumpet; this is dated 1733.

19

By the King's Authority.

From my House, in Dean's Court, in New Round-Court, in the Strand.

WHEREAS by Virtue of Letters Patents, under the Great Seal of *Great Britain*, Made and Granted unto me *JOHN SHORE*, Esq; Serjeant-Trumpeter to his Majesty, there is a Power given for the better regulating and keeping in Order all *Trumpeters, Drummers,* and *Fifes* within this Realm, or that shall Sound, Beat, or Play, at any *Play, Dumb-Shew, Models, Rope-Dancing,* or to *Mountebanks, Prize-Players,* or any other *Shews* or *Plays* whatsoever in any City, Town-Corporate, Market, Fair, Village or Hamlet, within his Majesty's Realm of *Great Britain,* (His Majesty's Play-Houses excepted) that they shall not presume to Sound, Beat, or Play, without License under the Hand and Seal of Me, Serjeant of all *Trumpeters, Drummers,* and *Fifes,* first had and obtain'd.

And whereas by Warrant and Grant, there is given and granted Power and Authority, (paying Me the said Serjeant an ancient and customary Fee in the said Grant specified) to License all and every Person and Persons that shall so Sound, Beat, or Play, at or to any *Plays, Dumb-Shews, Models, Rope-Dancers, Mountebanks,* or *Prizes,* with full Powers to suppress, as I the said Serjeant shall see Cause. I do therefore, pursuant, and by Virtue of the said Grant, authorise and appoint you *Thomas Smith, Merchant & Burgess from Jedburg* to make Use of any *Trumpet, Drum,* or *Fife,* at and for your *Shew of Puppets* within his Majesty's Realm of *Great Britain,* until the *first* Day of which shall be in the Year of our Lord, One Thousand Seven Hundred and *Thirty One* at which Time this Licence shall end.

And whereas by the said Warrant and Grant, there is an ancient Fee of Twelve Pence a-Day, due and payable to me the said Serjeant, for every Day whereon any *Trumpet, Drum,* or *Fife,* shall Sound, Beat, or Play, at any *Plays, Dumb-Shews, Models, Rope-Dancing, Prizes,* or to *Mountebanks,* or *Prize-Players,* without License from me first had and obtained; I do therefore hereby Order and Direct you to apply your self to the several Magistrates and Officers, (in the several Cities, Towns, and Villages, where such Person not so Licensed, shall or may come) who are hereby impower'd and desir'd, to levy and take of such Person or Persons, who have not my License, the said Twelve-pence a Day, for the Use of their respective Poor, unto whom I freely give the same. And in Case of Refusal of Payment thereof by any Person who shall so Sound, Beat, or Play, without such License from Me, as aforesaid, I desire you to make Oath thereof before such Magistrate, Justice of the Peace, or Officer impower'd thereunto, and return up the same unto Me, in Order to his being taken into Custody (as is usual) by one of his Majesty's Messengers, for Contempt of his Royal Authority, and the farther Prosecution of such Person as a Vagrant, pursuant to the several Statutes in that Case made and Provided: No License from the Master of the *Revels* being sufficient to acquit or discharge them from the said Due. And for your so doing, this shall be your Authority and License. And whereas I am sensible of the Power which justly belongs to all Magistrates and Civil Officers, in their respective Cities, Towns and Villages, I do (notwithstanding the Authority of my Patent) in a most friendly Manner, desire the said Magistrate and Officers, that as they will not suffer any of the abovesaid Persons to Sound, Beat, or Play, without my License first obtain'd; so likewise to assist and further those Persons that have it, without any of your Letts or Molestation, they behaving themselves orderly, and according to the Laws and Constitutions of this Realm, Given under my Hand and Seal this *First* Day of *Au.* in the *4th* Year of the Reign of our Sovereign Lord *GEORGE* the Second, by the Grace of God, of *Great Britain, France,* and *Ireland* King, Defender of the Faith, One thousand seven hundred and *thirty*.

All Mayors, Bailiffs, Sheriffs, Justices of the Peace, and other His Majesty's Officers, are desired to take Notice, That this *License* endeth upon the *First* Day of *August* One thousand seven hundred and *Thirty One*.

John Shore

License for Thomas Smith of Jedburg, England, to use a trumpet to advertise his puppets, issued 1 August 1731. Original sheet 12 x 15 inches.

A license, the original now in the possession of the writer, was granted by John Shore, Serjeant-Trumpeter to George II, on 1 August 1730 to a showman otherwise unknown to history: "Thomas Smith, merchant and burgess from Jedburg, to make use of any trumpet, drum, or fife, at and for your show of puppets within his Majesty's realm of Great Britain, until the first day of August which shall be in the year of our Lord, one thousand seven hundred and thirty-one, at which time this license shall end." The fee received by Shore, according to the stamps on the document, was one shilling and six pence, plus the paper tax of eight pence a quire. (There were nuisance taxes then, too!) The license warns that "the ancient fee of twelve pence a day" for every day on which "trumpet, drum, or fife shall sound, beat, or play at any plays, dumb-shows, models, rope-dancing, prizes, or to mountebanks or prize-players," is payable to the sergeant-trumpeter by those without a license, on refusal to pay which fee the offender would be taken into custody for contempt of royal authority.

The humbler shows would have had only a written playbill; the more prosperous ones indulged in printed announcements. Several Bartholomew Fair puppet bills have survived. One of them, for John Harris's booth, offers *The Court of King Henry II, The Death of Fair Rosamond, with the merry humors of Punchinello,* and *The Lancashire Witches*; it is preserved in the Harvard College Library theatre collection. Bills were sometimes thrown in at the doors of coffee houses, as is attested in Jean Dumont's *Les Soupirs de la Grand Bretaigne* (London, 1713).

Powell, of Bath and London, canny showman that he was, advertised frequently in *The Spectator* (in Nos. 295, 297, 302, 304, 312, 319, 325, 329, 331, 335, 337, 339, 343, 345, 347, 349, 353, 368, 534, 546, and 550, and perhaps others). Though he had been mentioned by Addison and Steele before he paid for notices his co-operative spirit helped to win him an undying place in literature: allusions to his shows were charmingly woven into the text of these essays. Puppet-show advertisements in American newspapers contain a large part of the information to be found about performances in the New World.

When most communities had but one playhouse, puppets were unable to play in it unless it happened not to be occupied by a company of live players. They had to find whatever assembly room, improvised hall, or barn they could. The size of their stage allowed them to fit into small quarters. And they could afford to play to small audiences. The long room of an inn, familiar to townsfolk for all sorts of gatherings, was a preferred spot. Barns (in which the American frontier theatre was born) were sometimes far from comfortable. In one at Newmarket, England,

*Puppet shows, like other perambulating entertainments, were announced by trumpet
and drum. Here a Negro boy and a pretty young woman drum up business for a
show at Southwark Fair, England. Detail from an etching by William Hogarth, 1733.*

114 persons of an audience watching a puppet show perished in a fire on
8 September 1727; the terrible event was reported in news pamphlets
and furnished a subject for widespread fulminations against the theatre
from the pulpit.

In the English colonies puppet shows generally began at seven o'clock
in the evening, the doors opening an hour earlier. Toward the end of the
eighteenth century a few shows were billed to start at six or half-past.
Powell's shows were advertised at six; they lasted till eight or half-past.
On days when he had special subscription performances they were arranged either at noon or at five o'clock; in the latter event the regular
evening show was moved forward to seven.

Powell charged two shillings for box seats and one for pit; sometimes there was a sixpenny advance on both. In America during the eighteenth century the most expensive puppet-show seats were five shillings; at premières the usual two-shilling rate for the best seats was doubled, along with the whole scale of prices; two shillings, one shilling sixpence, and one shilling. At this time the regular prices for the Haymarket Theatre, London, were 8 shillings for box seats, 5 for pit, 2s. 6d. for the first gallery, and 1s. and 6d. for the upper gallery. Admissions to the humbler puppet shows at English fairs, or to strolling puppets in the colonies, were but a few pence.

Hand-puppets and string-puppets were most generally seen; shadow figures came into vogue toward the end of the century. It is difficult to distinguish between hand- and string-puppets as they are announced in the advertisements unless identifying particulars of size or action be given. Naturally the mode of operation was kept a secret insofar as possible, for the old-time showman felt that mystery was one of his chief assets. It would seem that string-puppets were the type most often advertised; perhaps they were, as they are today, the most popular sort.

There are few pictures of eighteenth-century English hand-puppets, the sort worked by hands thrust into their hollow bodies, their arms and heads controlled on the fingers. One is in Hogarth's *Southwark Fair*. Under the banner that shows Adam and Eve and *Punch's Opera*—Punch is about to dump Dr. Faustus from a wheelbarrow into hell mouth—at the right of the scaffolding, is an open-topped booth out of which three-hand-puppets are thrust. Their action is meant to rouse interest in the show inside. While one puppet stands by (it doesn't look like the lady fair who caused the fight) the others cross sticks in a longstaff bout. Later on, in Punch and Judy shows, there is only one cudgel, and Punch as its possessor has unfair advantage. This simple "come-on" for the more elaborate puppet show, which was probably done with string-puppets, indicates that hand-puppet technique was the same then as it is today.

There is no verbal or pictorial evidence to show in detail how string-puppets were controlled. Artists usually omitted the strings, just as the eye of the spectator does when it is intent on the action. What they saw and drew, if they drew any attachment at all, was the rod or wire that was fastened to the top of the puppet's head to suspend it. The earliest European puppets that survive intact, such as the Italian eighteenth-century sets in the Museo Correr, Venice, and the Victoria and Albert Museum, London, are hung from a central wire ending in a turnip-shaped handle, to which the limb strings are attached with tabs of leather. Puppets so suspended are to be found in the twentieth century in

Hand-puppets cross sticks over the top of a screen on a platform outside a puppet-show booth at Southwark Fair, London. Detail from an etching by William Hogarth, 1733.

the change-resisting folk theatres of chivalrous combat in Flanders and southern Italy. *A New English Dictionery* by Thomas Dyche (London, 1768) defines puppet as "the representation of a man or woman, boy or girl, by little babies [dolls] that are moved by wires, etc., in shows." It has become customary, in using puppet metaphors, to say "moved by wires."

Punch's tall hat, as shown in the frontispiece to *A Second Tale of a Tub* (*The History of Robert Powel the Puppet-Show-Man*, an anonymous work by Thomas Burnett satirizing Robert Harley, London, 1715), would seem to span the distance between his short stature and a rod of the usual length for other puppets. Such a tall-hatted Punch, a performer at French fairs, was illustrated in the *Magazin pittoresque* of 1834. The traditional conical headgear seems to have degenerated into a limp stocking cap by the mid-nineteenth century; it was still erect and grenadier-like in Cruikshank's etchings for *Punch and Judy* (London, 1828).

In Hogarth's *A Medley* (1762) the symbolic puppets are all suspended by the head with heavy wires. In *England's Remembrancer* (London, (1756/7) the row of puppets is similarly suspended from twisted-wire rods; the hook—probably going through a loop—in Punch's head is plainly visible. Puppeteers who have used a rod-suspended puppet can attest its qualities: its weight resting on the stage, its head can be turned by a slight twist of the rod without moving the body; or the whole puppet can be turned or whirled with a more definite twist. There is a direct control and instantaneous response lacking in string-suspended puppets. But of course the rod is conspicuous, and sometimes clinks and rattles. Such rod-hung puppets have strings to control the limbs in the usual way. In the hands of a skilled manipulator they have a delicate and natural action. The rod may have been discarded in the latter half of the nineteenth century when puppet companies came to be great globe trotters, and its weight and length, with increasingly high puppet proscenium openings, made it inconvenient to pack. In some of the old Lano family puppets, now string suspended, broken-off eyes and wires may be seen in the top of the head. Toy puppets suspended by a wire, with no strings at all, are still to be found in Italy and Mexico.

In No. 44 of *The Tatler* Isaac Bickerstaff pretends to be angry with Powell and writes, "I can look beyond his wires, and know very well the whole trick of his art, and that it is only by these wires that the eye of the spectator is cheated, and hindered from seeing that there is a thread on one of Punch's chops, which draws it up, and lets it fall at the discretion of the said Powell, who stands behind and plays him, and makes him speak saucily of his betters."

From this passage W. J. Lawrence guessed, in *Immortal Mr. Punch* (reprinted from the London *Times* in *The Living Age*, 22 January 1921), that "what Powell really did was to cover the proscenium opening of his little stage with open-meshed wire lattice-work, a very effective method of hiding the shining wires with which he worked the puppets." This

John Harris's *BOOTH*,

in Bartholomew-Fair *between the* Hospital-gate *and* Duck-lane-end, *next the Rope-dancers, is to be seen,*

THe Court of *King Henry the Second*; And the Death of Fair *Rosamond*: With the merry Humours of *Punchinello*, and the *Lancashire*-Witches. As also the famous History of *Bung*, and Frier *Bacon*: With the merry Conceits of their Man *Miles*. And the brazen speaking Head; wherein is represented the manner how this Kingdom was to have been walled in with *Brass*. *Acted by Figures as large as Children two years old.*

☞ *Mistake not the Booth*; *you may know it by the* Brazen Speaking Head *in the Gallery.*

Perhaps the earliest English playbill extant, advertising the puppets of John Harris at Bartholomew Fair, London, before 1660. After the original (in which the woodcut is 5½ inches wide) in the Harvard College Library theatre collection; size of sheet 6¼ x 8 inches; bottom right corner torn off. Dr. William Van Lennep, curator of the collection, in an article, "The Earliest Known English Playbill" (Harvard Library Bulletin, Vol. 1, pp. 382-385, Cambridge, 1947), indicates that the paper, style of typography, and lack of the flourish, Vivat Rex, *date it as from the Interregnum, when theatres were closed but puppet shows allowed. Punchinello had very recently come to England.*

would seem to be a farfetched conjecture were it not that such a mesh on a puppet proscenium is actually shown in an engraved illustration by Harrewyn for *Don Quixote* (Bruxelles, 1706). Suppose that such a wire screen were used, would it serve to camouflage the puppet wires? If the stage lights were within the screen, they would nullify it, and if they were outside they would make it difficult to see beyond the screen at all; anyone who has seen lights on a scrim drop curtain on the stage recognizes this. It is unlikely that the forged iron wires of the eighteenth century, exposed to British weather, would long remain shiny. Then what were the wires for, if Isaac Bickerstaff means that they were woven into a screen? Perhaps to keep the audience from coming up and touching the puppets? Well, they didn't prevent Don Quixote from wrecking the puppets—or Isaac Bickerstaff from seeing the string that moved Punch's jaw!

The frontispiece to *A Second Tale of a Tub* shows that Powell's scenery was of the usual sort used in the big theatre of his day. Consisting, in this view, of four pairs of wings and a backdrop and four sky borders, it was painted with pilasters, niches, and balustrades to suggest architecture, and with clouds. The puppets are between the first and second wings and borders, near the audience. They were limited to sideward movement in this plane. If it was required for them to appear further upstage they would have had to go off at the side and reappear between the next strips of scenery. Perhaps they followed the conventional mode of placement for all players of that day, the principal characters downstage near the audience and the minor ones further upstage; crowds of supers were at the very back, and could be smaller than the leading puppets, to get more of them on, to suggest diminishing perspective, or to symbolize their relative lack of importance. The opera stage today still observes this arrangement.

George Speaight, in *A Reconstruction of Powell's Stage* (*Puppetry 1944-45*), noting that the wings in this view are drawn slightly out of alignment, advanced the interesting theory that the front bridge from which the puppets were worked was placed at an angle to the footlights so that a character might enter or exit at one side both before and behind the second wing, thus permitting a certain variety in its gambit. The engraver of the view was not too precise; he shows no rods or strings on the puppets; and it is unlikely that he was permitted to peep backstage. But even if this diagonal bridge were not used, it is worthy of Powell's ingenuity.

Powell's stage is shown to be lighted by footlights; six tongues of flame emerge from wicks that may float in a trough of oil. Footlights were

By AUTHORITY.
AT
FAWKES, PINCHBECK, and *TERWIN's*
GREAT THEATRICAL BOOTH,
Oppofite the Crown - Tavern *in* Weft - Smithfield,

DURING the Time of Bartholomew-
Fair, the Town will be agreeably Diverted by
Mr PUNCH's Celebrated Company of COMEDIANS,
Formerly Mrs. Charke's, *from the Theatre in the* Hay-Market;
And by them will be prefented a New Play, call'd
BRITONS STRIKE HOME;
Or, *The* Englifh Sailor's Triumph.
The Part of Briton Strike-Home, by Mr. Lyon; Sir John Free-
born, Mr. Englishman; Lieutenant Meanwell, Mr. Bays; Export,
Mr. Merchandize; Boatfwain, the facetious Mr. Punch; the King
of Spain, Mr. Fearful; Don Guarda Cofta, Mr. Pyrate; Don Su-
perbo Hifpaniola Piftole, Mr. C——r; Father Dominique, Fryar
Bacon; Queen of Spain, Mrs. Termagant; Donna Americana, by
Mrs. Cl—ve, the Favourite of the Town.
With feveral ANTIC DANCES between the ACTS.
To which will be added, a Lively Reprefentation of the Taking of
The TOWN of *CHAGRE.*
With the Bombarding of the Forts and Cafle of St. Lorenzo,
by Admiral VERNON.
LIKEWISE
Mr. PINCHBECK's famous MUSICAL CLOCK,
And feveral other Entertainments.
To begin each Day at Ten o'Clock.
N.B. The Booth will be diftinguifh'd from the reft by
bearing ENGLISH COLOURS.

An illustrated advertisement for a puppet show, probably from the London Daily
Post *of 31 August 1740. A clipping mounted in the same 1835 scrapbook about
Bartholomew Fair, kept by George Daniel and now in the Harvard College Library
theatre collection, which contains the John Harris playbill. Two of the showmen
were the younger Fawkes and Pinchbeck—who gave his name to imitation gold
jewelry; Charlotte Charke is mentioned.*

not then the rule in the larger theatre. Overhead lighting from chandeliers is conspicuous in pictures of the stage. But a chandelier over the apron of a puppet stage would have interfered with strings and wires. Extra lighting may have been provided by lamps placed behind the wings; it would have been necessary to use them if the depths of the scene were to be visible.

There was considerable scenic elaboration in Powell's shows. For a special performance on 18 March 1711/12, advertised in No. 329 of *The Spectator*, he gave *The False Triumph, or the Destruction of Troy*. "All the Greeks," he announced, "will be exactly drest after the ancient manner of that country, and the Trojans the same. At Paris's triumph, the stage is to be beautified with trophies, the side scenes representing elephants with castles, in which are Syrians holding forth splendid banners, with Indians on horseback, bearing of curious trophies. The part of Jupiter to be performed by Signior Punchanella who in a chariot drawn by eagles descends and sings to Paris, with a prospect of the city of Troy in flames, concluding with a piece of machinery." The machinery would have been one of those aerial contrivances popular in the eighteenth-century theatre, on which were lowered divinities seated on painted clouds. It was probably much easier to manage with wooden actors on wires than with human ones on ropes! Powell was not to be outdone by the scenic or mechanical effects of opera; and if his contrivances did not work smoothly, they added to the parody of the big stage, which was notably vexed by wires that stuck and set pieces that collapsed.

In his production of *The Beauteous Sacrifice* there were portrait puppets of Queen Anne and her suite, a liberty of representation which could not now be taken by a showman in England (save in Tussaud's waxworks). Similar portraits of an English reigning monarch and his family were to be shown in Quebec by Daddy Marseille toward the end of the century, as this story will duly recount. Powell's advertisement in No. 319 of *The Spectator* offered the enticement of "her most serene Majesty of Great Britain in her royal robes, attended by her peers and officers of state, under their feet . . . the trophies taken from the French and Bavarians by her Majesty's arms this war." It was evidently a tableau, not a moving picture.

In his *King Bladud* the puppets were costumed as ancient Britons but the scenery showed Bath and its "walks, groves, and the representation of the King's Bath and new Pump House," with "the figures of gentlemen, ladies, and guides, all moving in real water," according to the advertisement in No. 304 of *The Spectator*. If this was anachronism it was meant to be funny.

By way of parody of the spectacular effects at the Haymarket Opera, Powell introduced live creatures among his puppets. "The sparrows and chaffinches at the Haymarket," writes a correspondent to *The Spectator* No. 14, "fly as yet very irregularly over the stage, and instead of perching on the trees and performing their parts, these young actors either get into the galleries or put out the candles; whereas Mr. Powell has so well disciplined his pig, that in the first scene he and Punch dance a minuet together. I am informed, however, that Mr. Powell resolves to excel his adversaries in their own way, and introduce larks in his next opera of *Susanna, or Innocence Betrayed*."

It is likely that Powell stood before the stage as a presenter or master of ceremonies, explaining the action and serving as a human link with the audience, as well as trying to keep it in order if it were unruly. Such a functionary was usual in puppet shows of earlier times, and survives (when there is one) in the outside man for Punch and Judy, who carries on dialogue with the puppets and collects money. However, the hunchbacked figure standing before the stage in the frontispiece to *A Second Tale of a Tub* should not be taken as a portrait of Powell. The face is Robert Harley's, from the portrait of him by Godfrey Kneller. Even the white wand of the Lord Treasurer, paralleling the showman's pointer, which makes the whole thing pat, is from the portrait. Perhaps Powell used no pointer; Thomas Burnett's "little crooked gentleman, that holds a staff in his hand, without which he must fall," is a jibe against Harley. When puppets enacted a dumb show or appeared in a battle piece or diorama, there was need for a presenter. In a play with dialogue he would have been superfluous unless, like the outside man for a Punch booth, his duty was less to be Punch's "stooge" or "straight man" than to pass the hat and keep order among riotous young spectators.

Audiences at puppet shows conducted themselves no differently than they did in the bigger theatre; that is to say, adults as well as children could be noisy and obstreperous. Don Quixote's behavior when he made an assault on Master Pedro's puppets and slashed them to pieces may have been aped by saner (though inebriated) gentlemen. Powell seems to have kept order in his theatre, however; perhaps pranksters were awed by the presence of fashionable ladies and their escorts. Mary Granville Pendarves Delany, in the second letter of her *Autobiography*, speaks of having been taken to Powell's theatre as a child in a party including Lord Bolingbroke, Sir John Stanley, Vice-Chamberlain Cook, and others of the court circle. Popular puppet shows had been frequented by the "carriage trade," in fact, since Charles II saw a puppeteer who called himself "Signor Bologna, alias Pollicinella" and gave him a medal worth £25 in November 1662, as a token of his appreciation, and since

Rod-supported puppets of a witch, devil, Mrs. Veal, Julius Caesar, and George Villars, held by Harlequin in a minister's gown and pegged up around a pulpit; detail from William Hogarth's satirical etching, A Medley, 15 March 1762.

the king's mistress, Lady Castlemaine, had attracted a crowd (noted by Pepys) when she went to see a puppet show of *Patient Grisell*.

What was the attitude of the eighteenth century toward puppet shows? The Puritans, lumping them with all things theatrical, considered them vanities and devices of the devil. John Rowe of Boston, Massachusetts, upon seeing a model or diorama such as puppet theatres sometimes included for scenic effect, wrote in his diary (*Proceedings of the Massa-*

Puppets hanging on display from heavy single cords while Charlotte Charke bally-hoos them; a satirical etching against her extravagance and things French from England's Remembrancer, London 1756-7, Plate 37.

chusetts Historical Society, Vol. 10) under the date of 26 October 1764, "an afternoon show at the White Horse [an inn in Boston] which was a very faint representation of the city of Jerusalem, in short, 'tis a very great imposition on the publick." Though this show may have been an unsatisfactory affair to the eye, Rowe sounds a little like one who expected more in the way of religious edification and regretted the money he had been tempted to spend. The puritanical attitude was still strong in the nineteenth century. "Should a Christian, a child of God, be seen standing to gaze at a puppet show . . . ?" asked a devout writer in *The Watchman of the Prairies*, Chicago, 9 September 1851. The inference, though unintended here, was that he might see the show so long as he himself was not seen doing so; and many Americans, whether for this reason or others, have gone furtively to puppet shows.

Even to the more liberal, puppets were sometimes a deplorable frivolity. A disgruntled writer looked with jaundiced eye upon Powell's success in *Les Soupirs de la Grand Bretaigne* (London, 1713): "On enquiry into the matter, I find this has long been a noble diversion of our quality and gentry, and that Mr. Powell by subscriptions and full house has gathered such wealth as is ten times sufficient to buy all the poets in England. . . . This, I confess, is such an argument of fine taste, that I believe no age or nation can parallel from Lapland to China. It is so much below ridicule, that the bare recital is a satire upon all who frequent this fantastick and childish entertainment." But, save for such peevish envy, it is plain from Powell's success that most people liked puppets and were neither prejudiced nor incensed against them.

One of the first Americans to make his living by the pen in London, James Ralph, a Philadelphian who crossed the Atlantic in the same ship with Benjamin Franklin when he sailed for England as a journeyman printer, was one of the first, also, to compose a defense of puppets. In his collection of journalistic pieces, *The Touch-Stone* (London, 1728), he glows in Spectator vein: "I confess, I cannot view a well-executed puppet show without extravagant emotions of pleasure: to see our artists, like so many Prometheuses, animate a bit of wood and give life, speech, and motion, perhaps to what was the leg of a joint-stool, strikes me with a pleasing surprise and prepossesses me wonderfully in favor of those little wooden actors and their *primum mobile*.

"These portable stages," he goes on, "are of infinite advantage to most country towns where playhouses cannot be maintained; and, in my mind, superior to any company of strollers; the amusement is innocent and instructive, the expense is moderate, and the whole equipage easily carried about; as I have seen some couples of kings and queens, with a suitable retinue of courtiers and guards, very well accommodated in a single band-box, with room for Punch and his family in the same machine. The plans of their little pieces do not barely aim at morality, but enforce even religion; and it is impossible to view their representations of Bateman's ghost, Doctor Faustus's death, or Mother Shipton's tragical end, but that the bravest body alive must be terribly afraid of going to the d——l."

2. Programs

More is known about Powell than of any other English showman of his period, and since the popularity of his plays influenced other puppeteers in choosing themes, it will be interesting to see what he presented; some, but not all, of his types of pieces were echoed in colonial shows in America.

Serious and comic elements were present, in varying intermixtures, in each of his plays. "Mr. Powell has melted a whole audience into pity and tears," says the introduction to *A Second Tale of a Tub*, "when he

THEATRE
DES PIGMÉES,

Theater der Zwerge,
unter der Direction des Herrn Verdant.

Headings from the two sides of a bilingual playbill of Sieur Verdant's puppets, which played in the Great Pavilion opposite St. Peter's Gate, Vienna, 24 April 1804. The transformations shown in the woodcuts are a come-apart hussar, a lady-into-balloon, a windmill into a chariot, and clouds into shepherds and a shepherdess into a chariot. Such trick puppets were to be found in America at the same time.

has made the poor starved children in the wood miserably depart in peace, and a robin bury them." Laughter was roused by parody of high-flown opera, such as *Venus and Adonis, or the Triumphs of Love, a*

Mock Opera (listed in *Biographica Dramatica*, London, 1812, as an octavo printed in 1713—no copy seems to exist in American libraries or the British Museum). Guffaws were evoked by lampoons of human players, as when Punch fought with a pig, as Mrs. Delany recalled it, in imitation of the singer Nicolini's battle with the lion in *Hydaspes*. And smiles accompanied the commedia dell' arte *lazzi*, or "gags," of Punch "and his merry companions," traditionally flippant, introduced at the most unexpected and unlikely moments. The light gas of their foolery bubbled up to make sparkling wine of every dramatic drink.

Five sorts of plot material are distinguishable. There is the old Biblical story, popular in dramatizations since the Middle Ages, but at this period obsolescent on the large stage, represented in Powell's *The State of Innocence, or the Fall of Man* (advertised in *The Spectator*, No. 302) and in his *Susanna* (in the same, No. 14). There is the folk tale—one may not yet at this time call it the nursery tale—such as *The Children in the Wood*, mentioned previously, and *Dick Whittington and his Cat* (*The Spectator*, No. 14). There is the adaptation of popular drama, such as *Doctor Faustus* (*The Second Tale of a Tub*) or *The Blind Beggar of Bednal Green* (*The Spectator*, No. 534). There is the mock-heroic tragedy or opera drawn from the lore of classic antiquity, such as *Orpheus and Euridice* (the same, No. 295) or *Heroic Love, or the Death of Hero and Leander* (performed on 7 and 12 January 1713/14), perhaps a travesty similar to that in Jonson's *Bartholomew Fair*, a puppet piece wherein a Bankside Hero tempts a Cockney Leander to swim the Thames. And finally there is the piece of timely import or commentary, such as *The Vices of the Age Displayed, or Poor Robin's Dream* (played from 1711 to 1713), or *The Beauteous Sacrifice* (*The Spectator*, Nos. 319 and 353), a kind of set piece or pageant in celebration of the prowess of Queen Anne's military forces. Plays in the folk-tale category were most numerous, not only in England but in America.

As in the operas of the period, or the plays too, for that matter, songs, dances, and specialty numbers might be interpolated wherever there was a pause in the action, or between scenes. An advertisement for a theatre subsequent to Powell's, set up in connection with a coffee house in a great room in Panton Street, London (Panton being a coincidental pun on *pantin*, French for jumping jack; toy Punches were sometimes *pantins*), stated that "the company will be entertained gratis with the plain old puppet show of *Bateman*, who died for love, with the comical humors of Punch and his wife Joan, with all the original jokes, f-rts, songs, dances, battles, kickings, &c."

At the close of the eighteenth century these specialties began to include transformation figures, hoop-skirted ladies that turned inside out

At Punch's Theatre in the Little Piazza, Covent-
Garden, to Day and to Mor ow, being the 18 h and 19 h of this in-
ftant February, will be prefented an Op ra call'd, King Bladud the
Found r of the Bath: The Figur s being in he Drefs of the anci nt
B itcins, with the Walks, Groves, and the Reprefenta ion of the
King's Bath a d new Pump houf : The Figures of Gentlemen, La-
di s and Gu des, all m ving in real Water. Beginning exact'y at 6
a Clock. Boxes 2 s. Pit 1 s. Note, No Perfons with Masks are to
he admitted   1712

By the Defire of feveral Perfons of Quality.
AT Punch's Theatre Covent-Garden, this prefent
      Tuefday will be prefented, By Subfcription at 12 at Noon
(half a Crown Tickets tak n from the Tneatre) the New Opera called
The Falfe Triumph, Or the Deftruction of Troy. All the Greeks will
be exactly Dreft after the Ancient Manner of that Country, and the
Tr jans the fame. At Paris's Triumph, the Stage is to be Beauti-
fi d with Trophies, the fide Scenes Reprefenting Elephants with Ca-
ftles, in which are Syrians holding forth Splendid Banners, with Indians on Horfe-Back, bearing of Curious Trophies. The part of Jupiter to be perform'd by Signior Punchanella who in a Chariot
Drawn by Eag'es, defcends and fings to Paris; with a Profpect of
the City of Troy in Flames; Concluding with a piece of Machinary.
To be acted at Night as ufual. B xes 2 s. 6d. Pit 1 s. 6d. No Mony
to be return'd after the Curtain is Drawn up; Nor any Entrance
at the defcending of the Machines without P ying the full Price. 1712

*Advertisers today would protest very understandably if such broken and unreadable
types were used for their messages! Two of Powell's notices in* The Spectator, London, *1712, for showings of* King Bladud the Founder of the Bath *(in No. 304, 18
February) and* The False Triumph *(in No. 329, 18 March), a subscription performance
at noon.*

and sailed off as balloons, or hussars or skeletons that came apart like
unstrung beads and reassembled in a wink, and all sorts of rope dancers,
contortionists, and jugglers imitated from the fair and circus. String-
operated figures could do this sort of thing by the very nature of their
suspension. While there is no clue to the existence of such trick puppets
in the seventeenth century, they were closely akin to the "effects" popular
on the Restoration stage, dismembered bodies whisked from chimneys,
or Faustuses torn to pieces—surely human-size puppets worked on
cords or wires. In Ravenscroft's *Dame Dobson* (1683) there is a stage
direction in Act IV, "Parts of the body fall down the chimney. . . .
Thunder and lightning redoubles, during which the parts of the body
approach and join together. The body rises and walks to the middle
of the stage. . . . . The body vanishes." In Mountford's *Faustus* (1686)
at the finale Faust is disclosed torn asunder; the scene changes to Hell;
the limbs come together; there is a song and dance. In Thurmond's
Harlequin Dr. Faustus (1724), when Faust's leg is cut off and taken
by a money lender, Mephistophilus gives a command and an assortment
of legs files in; Faust chooses a new one and dances away. At the end

AT Punch's Theatre in the Little Piazza, Covent-Garden, this present Thursday, will be presented the late New Opera that was by Subscription, called, The Beauteous Sacrifice, where Punch performs the part of Captain. All the Figures being New, and their Dresses agreeable to their Characters. With a new Piece of Machinery after the British Manner, contrived and just finished by Powell, which reprefents a Paradice wonderful Surprifing. At the breaking of the Clouds arise several Triumphal Arches, which form several most agreeable Prospects; beautify'd by her most Serene Majefty of Great Britain in her Royal Robes, attended by her Peers and Officers of State; under their Feet are reprefented the Trophies taken from the French and Bavarians by her Majefty's Arms this War. And a new Prologue spoken by Powell by way of Ænigma, which gives a Defcription of Punches Family. Beginning exactly at fix, concluding half an hour after eight. Boxes 2 s. 6 d. Pit 1 s. 6 d. No Mony to be return'd after the Curtain is Drawn up; Nor any Entrance at the d fcending of the Machines without Paying the full Price. 1712.

AT Punch's Theatre in the Little Piazza, Covent-Garden, this present Saturday, will be prefented an Opera called, The State of Innocence, or the Fall of Man. With variety of furprizing Scenes and Machines, particularly the Scene of Paradife in its Primitive State, with Birds, Beafts, and all its Ancient Inhabitants, The Subtilty of the Serpent in betraying Adam and Eve, with feveral other Diverting Interludes, too many to be Incerted here. Beginning exactly at fix. No Perfons to be admitted with Masks, or Riding Hoods. Boxes 2 s. 6 d. Pit 1 s. 6 d. No Mony to be return'd after the Curtain is Drawn up. 1712

Two more of Powell's advertisements in The Spectator, *1712, for* The Beauteous Sacrifice *(No. 337, 27 March), in which Punch played a comic captain and there was as much mobile scenery as in a big opera house, and for* The State of Innocence, *a Biblical piece with a spectacular scene of the Garden of Eden. No masks, no rioting!*

of the play he is torn apart by devils. This seems to have been a stock conclusion. If the property men who devised these effects shared their secrets with puppeteers—or were indeed puppeteers working in the big theatre—there has been a long tradition of trick puppets, for this type is still in evidence to the day when this is being written.

3. The First English Show in America

Like Columbus, the first English puppets to sail for America did not reach the mainland; let us call them the first, since no record of earlier ones has come to light so far.

John Oldmixon, a historian worthy of Hakluyt's mantle, in *The British Empire in America* (London, 1708, Vol. 2, p. 127), recounts, "There was once a Company of Poppet Strowlers in this Island [Barbadoes]; they came from *England*, and set up their Fairy Drama at the *Bridge*, where, for the Novelty of the Matter, they found a good Market: From thence they went to the Leward Islands, and thence home. We wonder their Example has not been follow'd by some of the young Fry of Poppet

Players at *London,* who would do better to go over, and either play or work at *Barbadoes* voluntarily, than rake at home till they are sent thither by the Magistrate against their Wills."

Well, puppet players, whether they were young fry from London or not we shall never know, knowing so little of the pioneers, did try their fortunes in the American colonies from time to time thereafter—let us hope not to evade the arm of the law at home, which had a way of deporting convicted criminals to the transatlantic wilderness.

So from Oldmixon we know, if not their names, that a troupe of English puppeteers played successfully at Bridgetown sometime before 1708, touched at the Leeward Islands, and then circled back to their starting point. What if Powell, whose beginnings are obscure, should have been one of these adventurers? We do not even know his given name. How then can we presume to guess it was he—or who it was?

4. Did Henry Holt's Show Include Puppets?

Puppet shows that followed these visitors to the West Indies may have got to the seaboard towns of the colonies to the north, but in the absence of newspapers or other chronicles all trace of them has been lost. Certainly it was known what puppets were and there was an interest in them, for an item in the Virginia *Gazette* of 22 December 1738 reported that a dog had seized Punchinello at a puppet show in Southwark Fair and torn him to pieces. If those who read of this incident had not seen a puppet show in Williamsburg, they recalled nostalgically the ones they had seen in the homeland.

Interesting, if for no other reason than that it is one of the earliest existing advertisments for a theatrical entertainment in New York, is a notice in the New York *Weekly Journal* of 11 February 1738/9 (there were notices of the same tenor in the New York *Gazette* of 29 January, 6 February, and 13-20 February that year). It reads, "At Mr. Holt's Long Room, on Monday 12 February, will be performed a New Pantomime Entertainment in Grotesque Characters, called the *Adventures of Harlequin and Scaramouch,* or *The Spaniard Tricked,* to which will be added an Optick, wherein will be presented in perspective several of the most noted cities and remarkable places both in Europe and America . . . the epilogue to be spoken by Master Holt. Tickets to be had at Mr. Holt's at five shillings each, nobody to be admitted after six, nor anyone behind the scenes. N.B. The scenes, habits, and decorations proper to the occasion are entirely new. Vivat Rex."

Henry Holt was not a puppeteer but a dancing master. Upon arriving in Charleston he inserted a notice in the South Carolina *Gazette* of 2-9

November 1734, saying that he would open a dancing room in Church Street, "having served under Mr. Essex jr. [translator of Rameau's *Dancing-Master*, London, 1728; Hogarth portrayed him in the second scene of *The Rake's Progress*], the most celebrated master in England, and danced a considerable time at both playhouses" in London. To show the proficiency of his pupils, no doubt, he organized a ball which he advertised on 8-15 November 1735. But on 8-15 February of that year he had advertised the production of "the opera of *Flora*, or *Hob in the Well*, with the dance of the two Pierrots, and a new Pantomime Entertainment in Grotesque Characters, called *the Adventures of Harlequin and Scaramouch*, with *the Burgomaster Tricked*."

By the time it had reached New York, Holt's new pantomime was, then, at least four years old. Having moved north and begun dancing classes afresh, the master organized a ball which was announced in the *Weekly Journal* of 4 July 1737. This took place at a house at the southeast corner of Broad and Pearl streets; it had been built in 1719 by Stephen de Lancey, was bought in 1762 by Samuel Fraunces and operated as the Queen's Head Tavern, and was called Fraunces' Tavern after the Revolution; there Washington, in the long room that became the meeting place of the Social Club, the Society of the Cincinnati, and the Sons of the Revolution, took farewell of his officers in 1783; for that reason chiefly, the building, which deteriorated to a tenement and warehouse in the nineteenth century, was restored by the Sons of the Revolution in 1905, and may still be seen to this day. Holt's long room, as it was called in the notice of the 1738 entertainment, was naturally the one at de Lancey's where he was accustomed to teach and give balls. The house was then in the heart of town, conveniently located a block from the West Dock for people who might come by water from their country places on upper Manhattan or Long Island.

The long room is one flight above the street, at the street-crossing corner of the house. It is a big room for a private house, 19 feet 10 inches in width, 39 feet 3 inches in length, and 9 feet 7 inches high. But it is not too large a place for a stage entertainment.

What kind of a pantomime was Holt's? Something similar had been played at James Miles's booth in Bartholomew Fair in 1699, according to Edward Ward's *The London Spy*, published that year, "a new entertainment between a Scaramouch, a Harlequin, and a Punchinello, in imitation of *Bilking a Reckoning*," which sounds like slapstick antics—Harlequin and Punchinello tricking Scaramouch out of a bill they owed him. Rich, the phenomenally successful producer of pantomimes, staged *Daphne and Apollo, or the Burgomaster Tricked* in 1726; the vocal parts were published. It consisted of alternate scenes: serious, in which the classic

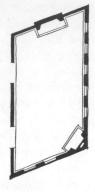

Plan of the long room where Henry Holt's entertainment was given in New York, 1738. The lozenge shape is caused by walls which follow the obtuse angle of the meeting of Broad and Pearl streets. The corner fireplace is an unusual feature in an early eighteenth-century colonial building. The two sets of double doors afforded separate entrances for audience and performers.

TOmorrow (being *Wednesday* the 21th of of *February*) will be performed in Mr. Holt's Long Room, the New Pantomine Entertainment in Grotesque Characters, called, *The Adventures of Harlequin and Scaramouch,* or *The Spaniard Trick'd.* To which will be added An *Optick,* wherein will be Reprefented, in *Perspective,* several of the moft noted Cities and remarkable Places in *Europe* and *America,* with a New *Prologue* and *Epilogue* addrefs'd to the Town. To begin precifly at fix o'Clock. *Tickets to be had at Mr.* Holt's *at* Five Shillings *each.* This is the laft time it will be acted.

Advertisement for the last performance of Holt's entertainment from Bradford's New York Gazette of 20 February 1738/9. Original 3 inches wide and even more illegible, in the New-York Historical Society.

myth was treated in dancing, song and dialogue; and grotesque (that is, comic or character), in which extraneous fun was inserted. It was rather like the masque of Ben Jonson, with contrasting graceful and weird parts. John Weaver, who wrote a *History of the Mimes and Pantomimes* (London, 1728), accredits himself with the invention of English dance mime "carried on in grotesque characters after the manner of the modern Italians." Holt's pantomime was in the current London fashion, a dancing offshoot of the commedia dell' arte.

Suppose that it was performed by human dancers, there would have been two difficulties. If the stage were at one end of the long room, raised a minimum of three feet from the level floor so that all could get a better view, and equipped with such rudimentary scenery as a backdrop and narrow wings, it would have been only about ten feet square, with a foot headroom for a short man. And there was the difficulty of assembling even a small group of trained dancers. Though ladies and gentlemen of the period might act in amateur theatricals they would never do stage dancing; it wasn't proper. Holt would have had to rely on apprentices, if he took any, or upon members of his family. If he had children he would have trained them, of course, and they would have fitted on the tiny stage better than adults; indeed, Master Holt spoke the epilogue.

Since he was not distinguished by Christian name, he could have been the only boy in the small family troupe. Holt himself may have done Scaramouch, his son Harlequin. But what of the optick that rounded off the program?

At a later period this term was applied to peep shows. They were boxes with one or more peep holes for spectators, a slot at the top to admit light, and painted views that the showman could change by pulling strings. The peep show with changing photographic views is still to be found in penny arcades and is a direct precursor of the movies. Frank Weitenkampf has treated prints showing peep shows in the *Bulletin of the New York Public Library* for June 1921. But such a show could be seen by only two or three. The description of Holt's optick indicates that it consisted of perspectives of notable cities and places, in short, dioramas perhaps with backdrops, wings, and lighting changes, like stage scenery. A 1749 New York show, indubitably played by Punch's company of comedians, was advertised as the "optick tragedy of the Babes in the Wood" (*Journal*, 19 September). This indicates that opticks were thought of as miniature stages. Puppet shows, when they had panoramic scenic effects, were in fact opticks. These spectacles might have rounded figures in the foreground, the painted figures of the background continuing them in perspective, but since the figures were not moved under human control for dramatic effect, the opticks were not puppet shows.

How could Holt have set up a miniature stage for opticks after the eyes of his audience had just grown accustomed to the scale of human dancers? It would have created a shock of incongruity. But, impossible as it is to prove that his show included puppets, it is impossible to prove that it did not include them. So early as 1879, W. J. Judd, in his edition of *Punch and Judy*, pointed out that this entertainment had an air of puppetry. Just to be on the safe side, the Puppeteers of America, meeting in June 1939, for the fourth American puppetry festival, foregathered at Fraunces' Tavern to toast the first puppeteer to play in New York, whoever he was, and to celebrate "the probable two-hundredth anniversary of a possible puppet show."

5. Along the Atlantic Seaboard

On 30 December 1742 this advertisement appeared in the Pennsylvania *Gazette*:

At the sign of the Coach and Horses, against the State House, in Chestnut Street, Philadelphia, every evening, at seven a clock precisely, will be acted, in several scenes, viz. An agreeable comedy or tragedy, by changeable figures of two feet high.

A sight of the sea and ships.
A merry dialogue between Punch and Joan his wife. With several other pleasing entertainments.
The prices, two shillings, eighteen pence, and sixpence.

The name of the proprietor, the titles of the repertory of plays, and other details that would fill out the picture are not given. The figures two feet tall were probably string-puppets; "changeable" was another way of saying movable. The "sight of the sea and ships" was a diorama like Holt's optick. It would have been as simple as the rocking ships on the face of a grandfather's clock, but if the showman were worth his hire, it had moving ground strips scalloped into white-capped waves, ships that sailed in cardboard splendor from one side to the other, and a lantern that was darkened, to the whistling of a wind machine and the rain pelt of peas in a box, to give the effect of a storm. Since Punch and his wife did not head the bill, they seem to have been reserved for an afterpiece, along with the "other pleasing entertainments," perhaps trick and variety numbers. No diary or letter has come to light to indicate what some Philadelphian may have thought of this show. The Coach and Horses was an inn that survived into the nineteenth century. In it the signers of the Declaration of Independence, crossing the road from the State House, refreshed themselves.

On 7 September 1747 this advertisement was in the columns of the New York *Gazette revived in the Weekly Post-Boy*:

To be seen at the house of Mr. Hamilton Hewetson, at the sign of the Spread-Eagle, near Whitehall Slip, Punch's opera, *Bateman, or the Unhappy Marriage*, with a fine dialogue between Punch and his wife Joan, acted by a set of lively figures late from Philadelphia.
. . . By Richard Brickell & Richard Mosely.
Every evening.
Tickets to be had at any time, at 2s. 6d., at 2s., at 18d. or 1s. according to situation. To begin exactly at seven o'clock.

The wording of this notice is too similar to that for the 1742 show to be a coincidence; no other puppet show had been advertised in Philadelphia in the intervening five years. Where had these puppets been all that while? Had they traveled along the seacoast (by ship, then the only feasible mode of transportation) to Annapolis, Charleston, and the Indies and back? Or had they gone home to England for a while? Was this a small provincial company or was it the troupe that had played on Panton Street, London, in 1745-1746? More of these transatlantic connections will be considered presently.

The Coach and Horses, an inn behind the State House, Philadelphia, where the first recorded puppet show within what is now the United States took place. From old prints of an unlocated original view. A corner of this inn may be seen in the more familiar eighteenth-century view of the State House from Chestnut Street.

In later years Richard Brickell was to be heard of again in New York as a showman of an electrical demonstration (2 May 1748), of slight of hand (4 May 1752), and of "a curious musical machine" (29 December 1755). Odell, in his *Annals of the New York Stage* (Vol. 1), supposes him to have been "a clock-man, and therefore naturally an exhibitor of clock-work." He may have been a partner in the show but not the puppeteer; certainly he was inclined toward the stage and could have lent a hand in working puppets. Who then was the other Richard? Was Mosely the man who had brought the puppets from Philadelphia? Was it he who had given the 1742 shows in the Quaker City? No trace of Mosely is to be found among puppeteers in England. And after this single appearance he vanished.

Hewetson's was a public house in the vicinity of Bowling Green. The spread eagle of his sign antedated the official American eagle by some thirty-five years. Did he have a long room or a loft large enough to justify a gradation of four prices for different seat locations? Or was it merely the distance of his benches from the stage that gave them decreasing value?

The folk tale of Bateman was poignant and well-known, full of possibilities for puppet action. Bateman, a dashing young fellow, rode through Clifton Town and made a conquest of the fair Isabella, a farmer's daughter. Upon his departure she fell ill; he returned in a physician's habit, disclosed himself, and cured her. The young lovers wished to marry but Isabella's father withheld his consent, preferring a rich old man named Jermain for his son-in-law. Jealous of Bateman, Jermain attempted to kill him but was himself wounded; Bateman escaped. Isabella put on a disguise and searched the woods till she found him. Exchanging vows to be faithful to each other, they broke a coin in two and each kept half. When Isabella got home her father locked her up and would give her no rest until she consented to take Jermain. At length she was forced to give in and marry him; she sent back her part of the coin to Bateman. Brokenhearted, he came and hung himself before her door. She saw his ghost, was overwhelmed with remorse, gave birth to a child, and was carried off by a spirit. After these harrowing scenes the tomfoolery of Punch was a decided relief.

A puppet theatre was housed in a specially built room from 25 July to 27 November 1749, a run which later Broadway shows would not despise. The players, said the *Journal* of 25 July, were "Punch's Company of Comedians . . . thought to be the compleatest of the kind ever seen in Europe." The auditorium was "a large theat[r]ical room next to the sign of the Dolphin (built on purpose) near the Work-House of New York City." This was on the northerly outskirts of town, above Wall Street. The first show was "the whole play of *Princess Elizabeth, or the Rise of Judge Punch*; showing the cruelty of Queen Mary and the intrigues of Bishop Garner, with entertainments of dancing." This should probably be classed as a folk-tale play rather than a historical one. An added feature, not puppets, was an "admirable piece of mechanism" with "sundry histories beautifully represented by moving figures." This was a diorama, or *theatrum mundi*, with figures animated by clockwork. Perhaps Richard Brickell had something to do with this part of the show. The doors opened at six, the show began at seven, and front seats cost four shillings, middle-gallery ones three, and upper gallery two. It would appear that the theatrical room was a complete playhouse if the galleries were not mere raised benches. Advertised weekly, *Princess Elizabeth* ran for a month.

On 29 August the company offered "the play of *Whittington and his Catt*, showing how he was rise [*sic*] from a poor sculling [*sic*] boy, to be Lord Mayor of London, with the cruel usage he received from Marg the cook maid, when sculling under her." Cruelty was evidently a saleable spectacle! The show continued to include the entertainment of dancing and the *theatrum mundi*, labeled the "Athenien [*sic*] Temple of Arts and

Sciences," offered to "gentlemen, ladies, and others" at prices cut to the more usual scale of two shillings, one shilling sixpence, and one shilling.

On 19 September the tearful cruelties of Marg the cook maid were exchanged for the lachrymose "optick tragedy of the *Babes in the Wood.*" The dancing and the Athenian Temple continued. On 9 October the play was changed to "the Tragedy of *Fair Rosamond.*" Finally, on 17 October, "the tragi-comedy of *Maudlin the Merchant's Daughter of Bristol*" began its run with a benefit performance for the "poor debtors now under confinement in the prison of New York," scarcely a stone's throw away.

Dick Whittington had been a popular puppet play since 1668 at least, when Pepys, visiting Southwark Fair on 21 September, wrote the classic remark that it "was pretty to see: and how that idle thing do work upon people that see it, and even myself too!" It has already been noted in the repertory of Powell. *The Babes in the Wood* was also a Powell piece. *Fair Rosamond* had been done with human actors at Bartholomew Fair in 1734 and by puppets in Panton Street, London, in April 1748. *Maudlin the Merchant's Daughter* was played by flesh-and-blood actors at Bartholomew Fair in August 1729.

This season consisted of five major plays. Suppose that the puppets for certain minor characters were reused from play to play, there was still a fair number of special ones for the leading roles, upon the whole a good-sized set. Whose puppets comprised this company, "the compleatest of the kind ever seen in Europe"?

Now the daughter of Colley Cibber, the ill-fated Charlotte Charke, had a puppet theatre at the Old Tennis Court in St. James's, near the Haymarket, in 1737-1738. In her autobiography (London, 1755) she wrote that it "was allowed to be the most elegant that was ever exhibited. I was so very curious, that I bought mezzotintos of several eminent persons, and had the faces carved from them. Then, in regard to my clothes, I spared for no cost to make them splendidly magnificent, and the scenes were agreeable to the rest. This affair stood me in some hundreds." Illness and an unlucky venture with her puppets in Tunbridge Wells—she had none of Powell's skill at making money in a watering place—made her decide to give them up. "I resolved to make the best use I could of my figures without fatiguing myself any further, and let my comedians out for hire to a man who was principally concerned in the formation of them: but business not answering his ends and my expectations, I sold, for twenty guineas, what cost me near five hundred pounds."

Because she felt that she had been taken advantage of, she did not mention the name of the purchaser, which would be an interesting one to know. Her narrative, hastily scribbled in her pressing need to make money, now has a difficult passage: "I gave him the privilege, as I had a license," she wrote, "to make use of that and my name; which now, whenever I think proper . . . shall always employ Mr. Yeates, who is a skilful person, and one who has made it his business from his youth upwards." This probably means that Yeates, the puppeteer who had the Old Tennis Court for the seasons of 1739-1740, took over Mrs. Charke's license and used her puppets. The only other show in London in 1739 was Russel's, in Hickford's Great Room, Brewer Street, in which she wrote that she was employed at a guinea a day "to move his Punch in particular." She mentioned that these puppets were small and that, after Russel's death, she wanted to buy them, no longer having any of her own. Meanwhile her own fine puppets would certainly have continued in use by someone.

After the burst of activity in Punch's Theatre, London, from January to March, 1740, there are records of puppet shows in Norwich, Kent, the Isle of Thanet, and Canterbury, but of none in London again until 1745-1746 when Mme de la Nash was the incumbent in Panton Street. Could her production of *Fair Rosamond* have been the one that was seen in New York a year and a half later? There happen to be no records of puppet shows either in London or the provinces from July to November, 1749. Could not the Panton Street company, possessor of what survived of Mrs. Charke's equipment, refurbished and put together with other puppets new and old, have gone across the Atlantic to try its fortune? Richard Charke, Charlotte's ne'er-do-well husband, had gone to Jamaica in 1735 as a violinist and singer; Mrs. Harman, her daughter, went to Jamaica in 1758 and died in New York in 1773, to be buried in Trinity churchyard. If these members of her family came to America, could not her puppets have made the voyage too?

Before taking leave of Richard Brickell we may see how his "curious musical machine" presented the tragedy of Bateman; the theme had charmed him since he took part in its puppet presentation and he had redone it for clockworks. "Two folding doors fly open," said the account in the New York *Mercury* of 29 December 1755, "a curtain draws itself up, and exhibits a company of gentlemen and ladies with knives and forks in motion, sat down to a wedding dinner. The bride having promised marriage to young Bateman proves false, and marrying old Jermain, Bateman hangs himself on her wedding day. Four cupids fly down and carry Bateman away. The bride still enjoying herself at dinner, she at last falls from the table, dead; and her rosy color changes to a deadly paleness: after which the devil comes up and carries her away. Here the curtain falls and ends the first act. The curtain drawing up a second time, instead of the wedding, exhibits young Bateman laid in state with the mourners about him, dressed in black cloaks and white hatbands; the room hung with escutcheons, and six ringers, in their shirts, ringing the bells. The representation of a carpenter's yard, with people at work, with several other moving figures." One had to know the story in order to be able to recognize it as interpreted by these automata! This is quite different, by the way, from *The Loving Ballad of Lord Bateman*, which struck the funny bones of Cruikshank, Dickens, and Thackeray in the next century. (See *The Colophon, New Graphic Series*, No. 1.)

The next New York puppet show occurred in 1767, unless there were others before that left no trace. On 2 April of that year, as announced in the *Journal* of 26 March and 2 April, Mr. Punch begged leave to inform the public that "his merry family and company of artificial commedians [*sic*] near three feet high" would perform "several diverting drolls, burlettas, &c. &c. With the curious performances of his artificial posturemaster; and a grand court of twenty-eight figures, or old maids' and bachelors' assembly. To conclude with a view of the sea, with ships sailing, fish &c. &c. swimming." Ladies and gentlemen were promised that "the strictest decency and modesty will be observed in the performance." This took place "in a commodious room which is now fitted up in a theatrical manner . . . at the sign of the Orange Tree, on Golden Hill." This hill, later to win fame as the spot where the first Revolutionary blood was shed, was what is now John Street, east of William Street. The city's playhouse was on John Street at this period. The announcement in the *Journal* went on to say that care had been taken "to divide the seats properly according to their different prices. Front seats 3*s*., boxes 3*s*. 9*d*., second seats 2*s*., back seats 1*s*. Performances to continue every Monday, Tuesday, Thursday, and Saturday evening for a few weeks." Were Wednesdays and Fridays set aside for subscription performances?

As it worked out the performances were perhaps not so frequent. The 2 April show was done for the benefit of those imprisoned for debt. On 14 April a benefit was announced for Mr. Bayly—who may or may not have been a puppeteer; he was credited specifically with "dexterity of hand" only—at which Mr. Punch was to give his drolls and burlettas as well as "a new farce, the Enchanted Lady of the Grove, also his views of the sea, with fish and sea monsters swimming &c." But this was put off because of bad weather to 30 April and again to 5 May. Performances were still advertised, meanwhile, for the regular four evenings a week; a different piece and good music were to be given each evening; Punch was not mentioned; this went on till 18 May, when Bayly made a last attempt at a benefit by presenting a play with human actors, recruiting local interest by gathering amateurs from town. These details are noted in April and May numbers of the *Journal*.

The names of the professional actors in the afterpiece of this program were given as Messrs. Shaw, Martin, and Tea, and Mrs. Bayly. Did any of these double as puppeteers? The diorama of ships at sea is already familiar. Puppets nearly three feet tall would be, by their size, string-puppets. The "artificial posture-master" was the forebear of many puppet tumblers and acrobats. This program would seem to have been made up altogether of short pieces, a variety offering that sounds scrappy and a little dull.

In 1764 a diorama or model of the City of Jerusalem had been exhibited, to the dudgeon of John Rowe, in Boston. On 14 March 1768 Boston's first definite puppet show was recorded. The *Chronicle* of that date announced, "For the entertainment of the public, Monday, Wednesday, and Friday nights, a compleat set of artificial figures representing of divers Masquerade Characters will be exhibited by Joseph Gibbes at the house of Mr. John Moore, to which will be added the tragical story called *The Babes in the Wood*. Tickets to be had at said house, at three shillings, lawful money. N.B. Any gentlemen and ladies that chuse to have a private night are desired to apply to the said Gibbes."

At this time stage shows were prohibited in Boston. An attempt had been made by its citizens in 1767 to have the 1750 Massachusetts act against plays repealed, but the effort was in vain. In fact, when Boston's first playhouse, the New Exhibition Room, was opened with tight-rope dancing a quarter of a century later, on 10 August 1792 (a playbill is preserved in the Harvard College Library theatre collection), the performance was surreptitious. Hence the puppet show flaunted the law, even daring to advertise openly. It probably got around the prohibition by claiming that it was not a full-sized stage show and hence exempt. Those whose puritanical conscience prevented them from being seen at such an entertainment at least could book a private show!

Punch and his merry crew were euphemistically referred to as masquerade characters, lest their very names might sound wicked. *The Babes in the Wood* was probably felt to have a strong enough moral to justify it. This program bears no resemblance to the one in New York the year before; it could not have been done by the same showman.

But the perennial *Babes in the Wood* cropped up in Williamsburg a year after the Boston show. The Virginia *Gazette* of 13 April 1769 carried the announcement:

By permission of his excellency the Governor, for the entertainment of the curious,
On Friday 14 April will be exhibited, at the theatre in Williamsburg, by Peter Gardiner, a curious set of figures, richly dressed, four feet high, which

shall appear on the stage as if alive; to which will be added a tragedy called the Babes in the Wood; also a curious view of water works, representing the sea, with all maner of sea monsters sporting on the waves. Likewise fireworks, together with the taking of the Havannah, with ships, forts, and batteries, continually firing, until victory crowns the conquest; to which will be added a curious field of battle, containing the Dutch, French, Prussian, and English forces, which shall regularly march and perform the different exercises to great perfection. . . . Tickets to be had at the Raleigh Tavern. Box 3s. 9d., pit 2s. 6d., gallery 1s. 3d. The doors to be opened at four o'clock, and the entertainment at six. None can be admitted without tickets, nor any admitted behind the scenes, as the inconvenience must be obvious. N.B. None of the above is represented by way of an optick box, or peeping through glasses, but shall appear publick on the stage, conspicuously to the view of the spectators, without confusion.

The omitted section states that Peter Gardiner would lay his head on one chair and his feet on another and let a 300-pound rock be broken on his breast with a sledge hammer. This display of muscle was not vouchsafed in Boston. Yet here are the babes, and even the sea monsters, of New York in 1767.

If Gardiner were newly connected with the puppets, or a puppeteer who had just come into the open in the advertisements, his play and diorama may still have been the ones previously seen in the northern colonies. The representation of the puppets as four feet tall—inconveniently large for any puppeteer but a strong man—may have been, like the 300-pound rock, a showman's exaggeration. In New York the puppets were described as a little less than three feet—and even that may have been stretching them—though string-puppets of this size are usual on large stages in twentieth-century America.

The fireworks (how they were done without fire will be indicated presently) and battle pieces on land and sea seem to be new presentations, though the incidents in the Seven Years' War which they illustrated were not; the siege of Havana took place in 1762; the peace was concluded in 1763. It will be noted that the puppets were able to get possession of Williamsburg's regular playhouse (a building which is to be rebuilt) and strut in the place of human actors. Because of the care with which the show was described to distinguish it from a mere peep show, it would seem that this may have been the first visit of a puppet company to Virginia's capital. Certainly it was the first time that one was advertised in a Virginia newspaper.

The warning that none was to be admitted behind the scenes was usual for all theatres when members of the audience could not be seated on the stage during the performance. This troublesome custom, prevalent since the seventeenth century, would have been particularly trying to puppeteers. As today, the curiosity of the uninitiated in how the strings were pulled would have delayed work and destroyed illusion. The same warning was issued for Holt's show because seating anyone on a ten-foot-square stage space was out of the question. If this was Virginia's first puppet show, it was the first in a long line. Gardiner was to return to Williamsburg in 1772.

A magician-puppeteer again took up his stand in New York near the location of the 1767 show at the sign of the Orange Tree on Golden Hill. The New York *Mercury* of 24 and 31 December 1770 published his announcement. A little less than a year before had occurred the Battle of Golden Hill; the people and the British soldiers had engaged in a fracas about the cutting down of a liberty pole on the common (now City Hall park) and citizens had been shot. The neighborhood was therefore tense with remembered emotion. The advertisement said:

To every admirer of real curiosities.
The noted William Patridge begs leave to acquaint the ladies, gentlemen, etc., that he has taken a large and commodious room at Mr. McDougall's, at the sign of Lord John Murray, in Orange Street, Golden Hill, fitted up in a genteel manner, where he proposes to divert the company every Monday, Wednesday, and Friday, by his art of dexterity of hand. . . . Likewise he will make it his chief study to divert the company by introducing Mr. Punch and his merry family, with new alterations every evening. Likewise his Italian Shade, so much admired in Europe. . . . N.B. Gentlemen and ladies that choose to have a private performance, by giving timely notice will be waited on.

Patridge, however noted he might be by his own proclamation, eludes identification in other records. Whether he had just arrived from Europe —which seems likely, because he introduced the new fashion of shadow-figure plays, of which this is the first mention in America to be found— or served an apprenticeship with the 1767 group or with Gibbes in Boston, is not known. Perhaps he used hand-puppets, for he altered his program from night to night and hand-puppets lend themselves to improvisation, needing few set words so long as they are lively. Because he would "wait on" gentlemen and ladies, he probably took his theatre to private houses; hand-puppets and shadows both are portable.

By 16 November 1776 Peter Gardiner was again in Williamsburg. On that day George Washington made this entry in his account book:

By Cost of seeing Wax Work 7/6
By Ditto Do. Puppit Shew   11/6

His diary for that day mentions only that he dined and spent the evening at Mrs. Ambler's; it was there that Martha Washington and her two children, then in their teens, were lodged with him during a visit to town. This does not preclude the possibility that Washington took his family to the show rather than buying tickets, in a generous mood, for others. His usual dinner hour was at three in the afternoon; only on state occasions was it delayed till four. The evening was that after-dinner span of November twilight before the puppet show at six o'clock.

How many admissions did his eleven shillings sixpence purchase? The prices for Gardiner's show were, as in 1769, 3s. 9d. for boxes, 2s. 6d. for the pit, and 1s. 3d. for the gallery. A box would have been uncomfortable for Washington's long legs; besides, he could have had only three box seats for 11/3. For the same amount he could have had four pit seats, enough for the whole family, and one in the gallery for a Negro footman besides. But what of the extra three pennies? Washington was not apt to make a mistake in recording a sum; he spent the full 11/6. Why, then, he must have given the pennies as a tip to the theatre doorman.

From Washington's record it appears that Gardiner was playing at the Williamsburg theatre a week before he advertised his performance of 23 November in the *Gazette* of the 19th. He announced "a curious set of figures, richly dressed, four feet high, they are to appear on the stage as if alive, and will perform a tragic performance called *Bateman and his Ghost*. Likewise a set of water works, representing the sea, and all manner of sea monsters sporting on the waves." The diorama of the victory of Havana was repeated and there was a new spectacle, "a magnificent piece of machinery, called *Cupid's Paradise*, representing seventy odd pillars and columns, with the appearance of Neptune and Amphitrite, and music suitable thereto. The whole to conclude with a magnificent set of fireworks, such as Catherine wheels, Italian candles, sea fountains, and sunflowers with the appearance of the sun and moon in their full lustre." Mr. Gardiner would still suffer any of the audience to break a stone of 200-weight (that was only 224 pounds; how about the 300?) on his bare breast. But the puppets were still four feet high! With a patriotic "Vivant Rex & Regina" the advertisement concluded, but there was a footnote, "Between the acts will be instrumental music, consisting of French horns and trumpets."

It has long been known, from the account-book entry, that Washington spent money on a puppet show; this announcement now tells what he must have seen and heard. After the cannonades in the military piece, the horn and trumpet music, and the fireworks, the Washingtons must have left the theatre with tired ears and eyes. The theatre was Williamsburg's second, erected on the street back of the Capitol in 1751; it disappeared about 1780; Gardiner's show is the last on record in it.

Front and back of eighteenth-century Italian giuoco di luce for producing fireless fire-
works effects. In the Cooper Union Museum for the Arts of Decoration, New York.
The paper wheel is turned by sand which pours through a funnel from a reservoir in
the top of the box and collects in a scoop at the bottom for reuse. A candle reflects
against the silver foil lining of the box to light the revolving spokes. A number of
paper slides with opaque and transparent patterns of sunbursts, fountains, and
illuminated palaces and gardens may be placed in the slots before the wheel, which
gives them a sparkling and flickering movement. From photographs.

A simple but effective imitation of flowing water or fireworks, popular
as a sort of moving picture in the eighteenth century, was called in
Italy a *giuoco di luce*, or play of light. A fine example of a small one
is to be seen in the Museum for the Arts of Decoration, Cooper Union,
New York. This consists of a flat oblong cabinet or box, standing ver-
tically, the inside covered with white metal foil to intensify the light
from a candle placed in it. On the face of the box, over an opening, is
placed an opaque paper disc with transparent arcs radiating from its
center; through these the light of the candle shines. Before this disc,
which is turned by the weight of falling sand in the box, are placed
paper slides, the most translucent sections of which are cut into a
pattern of sparks and rays. Given an effect of glimmer by the turning
lights and darks of the disc, the Catherine wheels or sunflowers, rockets
or Roman candles, fountains or flowerpots seem to move and flame. A
giuoco di luce makes no smoke and sends out no tinder; it is altogether
as lovely as real fireworks to watch; it is just the right size to place either

in the proscenium frame or at the back of a vista of wings in a puppet stage. By varying the light stripes in the disc and the subject painted and pierced on the slide, a number of effects of playing water or fire could be obtained. The eighteenth century much preferred the controlled patterns of fireworks to a haphazard sunset sky, the jets and rills of a Versailles fountain to a woodland cataract. Natural landscape it considered wild, unartistic, and decidedly formless.

Torpedoes, crackers, and red and blue fire were necessary adjuncts of the spectacular pieces in the Victorian theatre; doubtlessly they were used in the puppet theatre too; but real fireworks, not uncommon in the big theatre (the normal end of theatres was by fire), would have been out of scale for puppets. Until the introduction of electricity and recorded sound effects, puppet shows supplemented their ordinary lighting with colored chemical flame and added to the din of battle pieces with gunpowder.

In the last quarter of the eighteenth century puppet shows became more and more obsessed by lighting effects. For a while it seemed that shadow-figures, introduced by William Patridge in New York, might supplant three-dimensional puppets altogether in popular favor.

One more show ventured to come to America before Europe heard of the increasing unrest in the English colonies which was to lead to the Revolution. On 12 May 1773 was advertised in the Pennsylvania *Journal:*

This is just arrived from London and to be seen at the Theatre in Southwark [outside Philadelphia], on Mondays, Wednesdays, Fridays, and Saturdays, to begin at seven o'clock in the evening, the beautiful and unparalleled new prospective theatre, which the Sieur Mercier has brought over. . . . It contains a great variety of pleasing and inimitable representations, among which is one that entirely represents the late Italian fantoccini in Panton Street.

Sieur Mercier is not to be traced in Europe. Was he French or an Englishman who had taken a foreign-sounding name for professional use? His "inimitable" imitation of the Italian fantoccini would suggest that he was given to imitations. The word "fantoccini," which is to remain in the playbills for the next hundred years, appears for the first time in America as a synonym for "puppets"—what would now be called string-puppets, to be specific. For purposes of ballyhoo in the eighteenth century puppets were seldom called by their simple name. Lest people think that they were too small and unimportant they were designated as Mr. Punch's comedians or his merry family; they were lively or changeable figures or artificial comedians; they even presented the fairy drama. And in the coming years they were to be called not only fantoccini but marionettes, manikins, and a small thesaurus of other names to make them as mysterious and exotic as possible. Perhaps at the bottom of all this was a vestige of the Puritan attitude; if one called a playhouse a museum, lyceum, opera house, or what it was not, conscience was appeased and the hold of the devil weakened.

Sieur Mercier's perspective theatre, another diorama, showed views of Paris, Greenwich, Rome, Florence, and Amsterdam, as his advertisement expatiated; there was "a sea storm, with a view of several ships cast away; the reports of the guns; the thunder and lightning; the rain and hail; all which will be exhibited in a very curious and natural manner." Naturalism is invading the eighteenth century; formalism is about to become old-fashioned. Tickets, the notice went on to say, cost 5s., 3s. 9d., and 2s.—not excessive in view of the fact that colonial currency was not on a par with English and bought less; eventually the shilling, which continued as a name in the United States well into the nineteenth century, was valued at 12½ cents. The advertisement concluded, "If any ladies or gentlemen are desirous to see it at any time of the day or night, the Sieur Mercier (willing to obtain the favor of the ladies and gentlemen) does inform them, that by giving notice to Mr. Bossio, at the place of performance, two hours before, they may depend upon being waited on. Vivant Rex & Regina." How soon the loyal formula was to be anathema!

Mr. Bossio, the guardian if not the operator of the puppets, had an Italian-sounding name. Can it be that these fantoccini were more than a mere "representation," in fact an offshoot of the company in Panton Street which Oliver Goldsmith had seen? It reflects on the obtuseness of Boswell, who tells the anecdote under the record of 1763 in his *Life of Johnson*, that he seriously says Boswell boasted at the puppet show that he could excel a puppet at tossing the pike and later broke his shin trying to repeat the acrobatics of a puppet jumping over a stick. Those who knew Goldsmith would know how waggishly he would have said, with the most naive air, that he could do it better than a puppet. Joseph Cradock vindicates Goldsmith of any stupidity about the puppets in his *Literary Memoirs* (London, 1826).

The storm at sea has a familiar ring. "Perspective theatre" is a good name for this sort of spectacle. Popular again after many periods of being in fashion, these shows were seen on a lavish scale at the Chicago 1933 and New York 1939 world's fairs, where they were rather loosely called dioramas, a term that has been adopted in this narrative for want of a better. "*Theatrum mundi*" and "moving picture" were also once applied to vista stages with changes of lighting and scene and sometimes moving figures, either mechanical or operated by a showman

A slide for the giuoco di luce *in Cooper Union. A palace illuminated for a fête of the House of Savoy, with rockets, pinwheels, and fountains. A wonderful finale for a puppet show! From a photograph.*

—which made them puppets. Delighting in obfuscation, the presenters of dioramas may even have passed off as automatic what was not; machinery was more marvelous than wires in the human hand.

Joseph Strutt described such diorama gods-from-a-machine as Washington paid his shillings to see in Williamsburg. In his *Sports and Pastimes of the People of England* (London, 1833) Strutt wrote, "The heathen deities were manufactured from pasteboard and seated in rows one over the other upon clouds of the same material; at least I have seen them so fabricated and so represented, about 1760, at a show in the country [in England], which was contrived in such a manner that the whole group descended and ascended with a slow motion to the sound of music."

For the next few years the colonists were in no mood to see dioramas or puppet shows of any kind. A writer in the Virginia *Gazette* of 13 January 1776, deploring bad conditions, exclaimed, "And in the midst of this crash of ruin, this great man [King George III] can go composedly to see a puppet show or laugh with a buffoon. O wretched England!"

Tunes for shadow-figure scenes from The Favourite Airs . . . in the Ombres Chinoises, *London, 1780.*

V

Chinese Shadows Reach America

It is the hypothesis of Georg Jacob, indefatigable historian of the shadow-figure, that this type of puppet, which is first recorded in China, came to Italy in its Westward travels by way of Tunis, Asia Minor, Persia, India, and elsewhere in the Orient; the silhouette, a blacked-in outline form of representation, also of Eastern origin, followed a similar route; somewhere along the way shadow-figures, which had been translucent and colored in China, took on the appearance of silhouettes and became opaque and dark. Jacob's researches are summed up in his *Geschichte des Schattentheaters im Morgen- und Abendland* (Hanover, 1925). Colored translucent shadow-figures were brought to America only at the end of the nineteenth century, from Greece by way of Turkey; but silhouette shadow-figures had arrived a century earlier, coming from Italy through France, Germany, and England.

, Europeans had known of Chinese shadow-figures at least as early as 1735, when J. B. du Halde mentioned them in his *Description . . . de l'empire de la Chine* (Paris, 1735, Vol. 2, pp. 96-97). There was a tendency to call them Italian, however, because Italy was their immediate source. Shadow-figures had been exhibited in Naples and Rome in 1674, according to the records found by Georg Jacob. Italian showmen exhibited them at the Easter fair in Frankfurt in the year 1686. Jacob thinks that the shadow showman in Goethe's *Jahrmarkstfest zu Plundersweilern (Junkdump Fair)*, first played in 1769, which was of course inspired by the one in Frankfurt, is made to speak with an Italian accent. However, the Frenchman Audinot was exhibiting shadow-figures at the Foire St. Germain, Paris, in 1760, and another Frenchman, Ambroise, took his shadow-figure show to Frankfurt in 1774 and to London in 1776. A shadow-figure play, *L'heureuse pêche*, was published in Paris in 1770; it had been played privately in 1767. Ambroise's season in London made such an impression that the music of his songs had a ready sale in published form (see *A Favorite Song, sung with applause in the Broken Bridge scene at the Ombres Chinoise [sic] in Panton Street, Haymarket*, shown in facsimile in *Puppetry 1939*, pp. 62-63) and two of his pieces, *The Duck Hunt* and *The Broken Bridge*, were to become shadow showmen's stand-bys for over a century.

Les Ombres chinoises.
He! l'Ami!___quelle heure
est-il?

im Verlag von G.Morino & Compl. Königl. Acad. Kunsthändler in Berlin.

Orchestra and audience for The Broken Bridge, *from an etching by Carl Christian Glassbach after a Berlin scene by Wilhelm Chodowiecki, one of a series published in Berlin, 1790. From a print in the Harvard College Library theatre collection.*

William Patridge's "Italian shades" heralded the vogue for this sort of show in America. During the Revolution most theatres were closed, but when it was over shadow-figures resumed their sway. On 17 March 1785, announced the Pennsylvania *Packet* of that date, "that much admired entertainment called les grand omber Chinoes" [*sic*] was given as a curtain raiser for some "lectures moral and entertaining" at the Theatre in Southwark, near Philadelphia. The lectures were dramatic scenes in disguise; a new blue law, passed 30 March 1779, prohibited theatrical performances in Pennsylvania. The 1742 Philadelphia puppet show had been quite legal, since a theatre interdiction of the Quaker Assembly in 1711 had been repealed in 1713 and no other had been enacted until 1759. W. S. Dye goes into all this in his study, *Pennsylvania versus the Theatre*, in the Pennsylvania *Magazine of History and Biography* for October 1931.

The actors, or rather the lecturers, who followed the shadow-figures on this bill were, according to G. O. Seilhamer's *A History of the Ameri-*

can Theatre (Vol. 2, p. 165), Hallam, Mr. and Mrs. Allen, and John and Caroline Durang. But since the lecture season had been some months under way before the shadow-figures joined it as an extra attraction, it is probable that they were manipulated by someone else.

The *Packet* of 29 March again advertised "the celebrated entertainment of Les Grands Ombres Chinois [*sic*], with additions of a pleasing variety of shadows"—a bit of tautology. The 2 April announcement said, "In the shades will be introduced a favorite dance called La Fricassee; the whole of the shades are entirely new." The tag to advertisements is now "Vivat Respublica." On 9 April the shadows performed once more.

But on 9 May either the showman or the figures had changed. They were then announced in the *Packet* as "Les Petites Ombres Italienes; the machinery of these shades are [*sic*] entirely new." Perhaps it was only a change of name, though the difference between "grands" and "petites" would be hard to account for in that case. This show was repeated on 11, 16, 18, and 26 May and 6, 8, and 13 June 1785.

In an exhibition room at 14 William Street, New York, "adjacent to where the Speaking Figure is exhibited," a shadow show was given on 21 and 27 January 1790 and advertised in the *Daily Advertiser* of the 20th and 27th. Its numbers were listed. On the first night there was an introductory prologue, followed by "mechanical artificers in the Chinese shades: shoemakers, barbers, coopers, taylors, etc."—a sort of *theatrum mundi* in silhouette. The third number was "a sailor's prologue"; this began the show in its second performance. Then came a pantomimic representation in Italian shades of *Robinson Crusoe*, with transparent scenes adapted, appropriately enough, from illustrations to Cook's *Voyages*. Between the acts in the second performance, songs from *The Poor Soldier* were placed; but in the first one they followed *Robinson Crusoe*. Next came a representation of *The Broken Bridge and the Drunken Carpenter*. Then a view of Passaic Falls; in the second perform-

The theatre in Southwark, Philadelphia, built of brick in 1766 (the first such structure in the English colonies), rather like a religious meeting house. From a view after an unnamed original in the New York Public Library theatre collection.

Theatre, Water Street.

MONDAY Evening, March 11, 1799.
And Every Evening this Week.
At Mr. G R A N T's, No. 242, Water Street,
Between Beekman and Pecks Slip
Will be prefented a GRAND MEDLEY of ENTERTAINMENTS in 5 Parts,
P A R T I.
Comic Scene between the Old Beggarman & the Termagant Landlady
P A R T II.
By the much admired

Ombres Chinoifes,

Willl be prefented the

BROKEN BRIDGE,

Or the Difappointed Traveller. With the Downfall of

The Impertinent Carpenter

P A R T III.
The ingenious fcene of the SPORTSMAN and his faithful DOG,
Which has never failed of giving univerfal fatisfaction.
P A R T IV.
A Grand Collection of Wax-Work Figures, reprefenting the ancient Court of

Alexander the Great,

Their graceful moyements have never failed of giving univerfal fatisfaction.
The Performer has fpared neither pains nor expence in the richnefs of their.
drefs.
By the curious Pruffian Fanticina will be performed the following Figures:
The Merry, Humours of Old JONATHAN and his WIFE,
A Figure in the character of a Country Girl, will dance a J IG, as
natural as Life,
A Hornpipe by a fmall Figure in the character of an American Tar.
The aftonifhing Lapland Lady will dance a Jig, and change her Face
three times imperceptible. Likewife a brilliant Collection of FIGURES,
Being the richeft of the Kind ever exhibited.
A Curious ITALIAN SCARAMOUCH will dance a Fandango,
and put himfelf into twenty different fhapes, being one of the greateft
Curofities ever prefented to an American audience.
☞ In the courfe of the Performance Mr. Maginis will fing the folfowing
" The HOBBIES", alfo " The Country Clown's Defcription of

Playbill of a variety show including shadow figures, waxworks, and puppets. From the original (7½ x 11½ inches) in the Harvard College Library theatre collection. The bottom of the bill is missing, and has been trimmed off in some reproductions.

ance the mechanical artificers had this spot. Then a favorite hunting scene (probably the perennial *Duck Hunt*), with songs adapted. Then *Bucks Have at Ye All*. The closing piece in the first performance was a view of Broadway from St. Paul's in transparency.

There is no clue to the showman. The final clause was, "No person whatever, on any pretense, will be admitted behind the scenes at the time of performance." Backstage interlopers would of course have ruined a scene with extraneous shadows. What was the distinction between Chinese and Italian shades, since the two terms were used together? Was it a difference in size, in manner of manipulation, or perhaps even in color? Or was this merely a press agent's way of suggesting a variety of things on the bill?

It seems probable that this show was the same one that had played at the Theatre in Southwark in 1785, for thither it returned in July 1790, being advertised in the Pennsylvania *Packet* to perform from the 3rd to the 7th of the month. This time it was "Les Petite Ombres Chinoise"— further confusing the matter of size and continuing to mangle French— and they offered nautical scenes with a fight between two vessels, a sportsman and his faithful dog duck hunting, a boat and sailors swallowed by a whale, *The Broken Bridge* complete with tavern, windmill, a miller and his jackass, the same or another miller jolly with his bottle, the miller's maid, an old cow, a goat, "&c &c," besides the central dramatis personae of the insulting carpenter and the traveler.

On 1 and 5 August 1790, at Kingston, Jamaica, the *Daily Advertiser* stated that Mr. Mahon the singer would offer "A miscellaneous entertainment of music, scenery, and machinery, selected from the favorite entertainments of the Eid[o] sphusikon [some sort of a *giuoco di luce*], fantoccini, and les ombres chinoises." While the Southwark shadow showman might have reached Kingston in time for these performances by fast ship, it was most probably another, as the added feature of fantoccini attests. Mr. Mahon organized and managed the show and perhaps rendered vocal numbers behind the shadow screen. The program consisted of *The Broken Bridge*; a rural prospect with a mill, carts, horses, etc.; the public gardens at Paris with different companies, attendants, etc., in motion, equal to life; a thunderstorm; a hornpipe in the English taste; a dialogue by a French gentleman; a foreign robbery with the detection of the thieves by a faithful dog, with sundry curious figures of moving animals, etc.; a view of the coast of Africa, with the method of taking the lion in the toils; and a transparency of Lord Rodney. A patriotic conclusion!

A company of French rope dancers, headed by Moullin, as his name was spelled in the New York billing, or DuMoulain as Philadelphia had it, arrived from St. Domingo and began an engagement in New York in August 1791; by September, according to the *Daily Gazette* of the 2nd, "transparent shades of men" were added; a shadow-figure showman, whoever he was, had joined the troupe. He followed it to Philadelphia where it played in the Theatre, Northern Liberties, from 26 November 1791 to 11 February 1792, according to Dunlap's *American Advertiser* of those and intervening dates. But only on the last night was it advertised that the show was "to conclude with large Italian shades, representing men, women, and children at different occupations."

At the assembly room on William Street, New York, Signor Falconi, a magician who had appeared previously (New York *Advertiser*, 25 June 1787), though without offering puppets or shadow-figures, opened a season on 22 June 1795 (*Advertiser* of that date) and added Chinese shades by 7 July, together with "the artful contrivance of Punchinello, and the thunderstorm, with the sea in tumult and waves rolling." By speaking of "the" thunderstorm the advertiser reveals that it was a pretty familiar number. This sounds like some old performer in a new partnership.

By 18 November 1795 the rage for shadow-figures seems to have waned, for on that date John Anderson, as he wrote in a MS diary now in the library of the New-York Historical Society, went to a room in Courtlandt Street, New York, and saw a variety show by Gonoty which included the exploits of Punch and his family and "an imitation of fireworks, without powder, fire, smoke, &c.," worked into views of parks and buildings in England—but no shadow-figures. "The music," commented Anderson, "was dealt out by two tolerable fiddlers, one a degree better; and now and then a tune from a hand-organ by one of the managers of the entertainment. The puppets caused a great deal of laughter from every part of the room." The diarist concludes with a note that he spent two shillings for his ticket.

On 21 January 1796, according to the *Gazette* of that date, Gonoty's entertainment had removed to Mr. Martling's long room, 87 Nassau Street; besides the fireless fireworks, diorama views, and humors of Mr. Punch and his merry family, there were "Chinese shades representing above 350 different figures, as natural as life." If they were losing popularity, the shadow-figures were not to disappear altogether. Gonoty remained in his new location until mid-February.

The New York *Minerva* of 19 May and 21 June 1796 advertised, as part of an equestrian dramatic show at Ricketts' Amphitheatre, Broadway at Exchange Alley, both Italian and Chinese shades, "or the art of magic, forming figures from 5 to 10 feet high, with other surprising metamorphoses." The second performance was given "with alterations."

Shaped boxes and a package, covered in blue paper, for shadow figures of the Séraphin theatre, about 1810. Stenciled labels. In the Cooper Union Museum for the Arts of Decoration.

Were figures so tall as this an exaggeration, or was the light source sufficiently far behind the screen so that when a figure was drawn away from the screen toward the light, it cast a lengthening shadow that overtopped a man?

An eighteenth-century American playbill featuring shadow-figures has survived. It is now in the Harvard College Library collection. It announces, "Monday evening, 11 March 1799, and every evening this week, at Mr. Grant's, No. 242 Water Street, between Beekman and Peck's Slip [New York], will be presented a grand medley of entertainments in 5 parts." This improvised playhouse, either in an inn (for Water Street was then lined with public houses frequented by seafarers as well as citizens) or in a warehouse, was only a short walk from Fraunces' Tavern; the amusement district had remained in this part of town for nearly a century, but it was soon to start uptown with the expansion of the city northward on Manhattan.

The second part of the program at Mr. Grant's consisted of ombres chinoises in *The Broken Bridge*; the third was "the ingenious scene of the sportsman and his faithful dog," the recurrent *Duck Hunt*, of course. But the fifth part offered "the curious Prussian fanticina" in the merry humors of Old Jonathan and his wife (had Punch become Americanized?), a country girl dancing a jig, an American tar executing a hornpipe, "the astonishing Lapland lady" who jigged and changed her face "three times imperceptible," an Italian Scaramouch dancing a fandango, who "put himself into twenty different shapes, being one of the greatest curiosities ever presented to an American audience," and "a brilliant collection of figures, being the richest of the kind ever exhibited." Here were trick and changing puppets in a group of numbers innocent of drama, a variety bill that may have had no dialogue save the jokes passed between Old Jonathan and his wife. With the wordless puppet show any

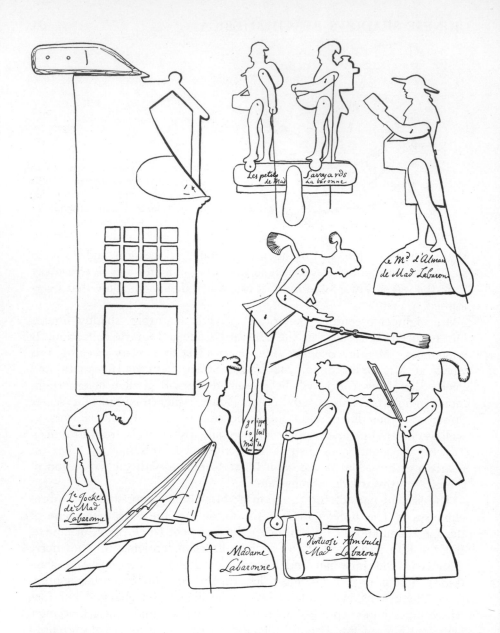

Wing and shadow figures for Madame la baronne *of the Séraphin theatre, about 1810. The dormer and window afford look-outs for characters; the wing is clamped to the shadow screen by a wooden cleat at the top. Note the little Savoyards with their magic lantern, the vender of almanacs, Grippe Soleil the comic servant, the page, Madame with her fanning-out train, and the blind street musicians. One-third actual size. In the Cooper Union Museum for the Arts of Decoration.*

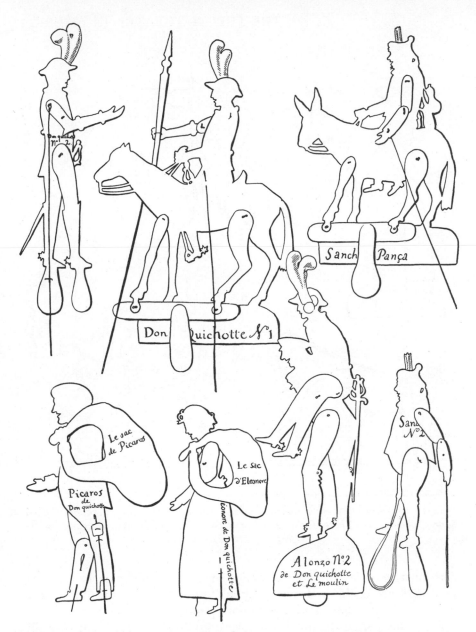

Séraphin shadow figures for the windmill episode of Don Quixote, about 1812. The figures are of cardboard; feathers and ruffs are of translucent paper watercolored. The joints are pivoted on fine wire or knotted thread. Parts are sometimes weighted with lead-wire rods or cardboard tabs control the action. One-third actual size; the figures average 6 inches in height. In the Cooper Union Museum for the Arts of Decoration.

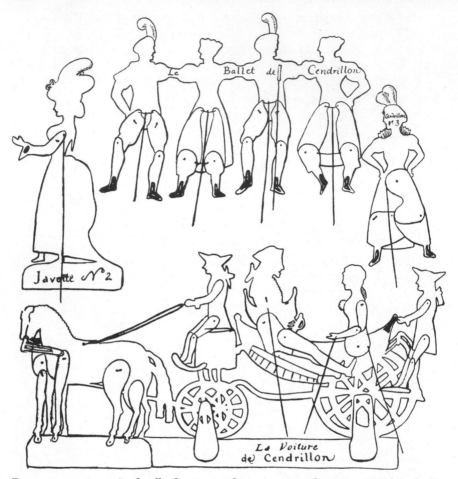

Dancers, step-sister, Cinderella dancing, and in carriage with prince, Séraphin shadow figures, about 1812. Three-tenths actual size. In the Cooper Union Museum for the Arts of Decoration.

performer, even lacking a smattering of English, could play in America, as Americans could in future play all around the world. In dances, tricks, transformations, and pantomime, puppets were international.

From this period shadow-figures were gradually to drop out of sight, although never altogether, until their revival at the end of the nineteenth century. Then they were to have a brief glow of glory, and marine battles and the duck hunt were again to be seen, before they were supplanted as a commercial entertainment by the wonderful infant kinematograph.

In the Water Street playbill fantoccini were called Prussian—as a guaranty of excellence rather than nationality—for the first time in America. In England, which seems always to have had misgivings about its own artistic rank, there had long been an impression that German puppets excelled. In *The Second Tale of a Tub* it was stated that Powell outdid "the Dutch, the most expert nation in the world for puppet shows." In 1737 a puppet troupe playing in Canterbury had styled itself the "Saxonian novels." In Kent in 1742 "German" puppets played the very English *Virtue Rewarded,* adapted from Richardson's novel, *Pamela.* Perhaps it was the same company that called itself "High German" in 1743. In Canterbury once more, one Thompson presented a "Prussian Punch and his family" in 1761. Two years later, puppets that had given "general satisfaction to the Duke of York, Marquis of Granby, and most of the nobility and gentry of Scarborough Spaw, and at York," called themselves Prussian. Sybil Rosenfeld mentions these provincial shows in *Strolling Players and Drama in the Provinces* (Cambridge, 1939).

But toward the end of the eighteenth century, most puppets that cried their virtues in terms of the exotic acknowledged Italian extraction. It is not unlikely that wandering German puppeteers got to England. But from what scant indications there are, it seems that most of the eighteenth-century puppeteers in the English colonies in America were British; a few may have been French or Italian. Perhaps even the "Prussian Fantacina" puppeteers were Italian, considering the Italianate trend at the close of the century. John Bernard, a visiting English actor, in his *Retrospections of America, 1797-1811* (New York, 1887, p. 52), wrote of Italians with fantoccini who lived in his New York boarding house in 1797. Lack of knowledge of the language was no barrier when actors with trained voices could be instructed to say the lines for the puppets, as they frequently did in Italy. Particularly in musical pieces it was impossible to expect a performer to sing beautifully while going through the gymnastics of operating a heavy puppet. The jigs, hornpipes, Lapland lady with changing faces, and contorting Scaramouch—despite the curtsy to America in Old Jonathan and the American tar—sound like something out of the bag of tricks that Italian puppeteers have always taken abroad with marked success.

Shadow-figures were ideal for the traveling showman. All the equipment for a show could be packed flat in a comparatively light bundle. A large repertory of numbers could be carried if need be. The frame of the screen was made of sticks or poles that could be demounted or even found at each new place; its covering was a linen sheet (the Chinese used paper) that could be folded. The shadow-figures were cardboard; their controls were simple wires; they could be repaired or replaced easily. The only light necessary was a single lantern, preferably with a bull's-eye lens, to given even illumination on the screen when placed behind it. Of course shadow-figures had to be seen after dark or in a room with curtained windows, but they were all the more awe inspiring, like the ceremonial puppets of the Indians, for the mysterious darkness in which they lived.

A shadow-figure theatre set up in a more or less permanent stand could indulge in such elaborations as a number of screens, each painted for one scene, parades and defiles of figures fastened to base sticks, and colored and dimming light effects. Despite the cheap and elementary materials required, there was a possibility of great flexibility of atmospheric effect. But even the crudest shadows, from their beginnings in firelit caves of primitive man, had a hypnotic fascination. This was not lost in the refinements of the shadow-figure of China and in the mechanized movie.

VI

Eighteenth-Century Spanish Puppets

1. In Mexico

Today it is easy to forget what an important part the theatre once played in the life of every community. Before the distractions of suburbanism and travel, everybody in town might have been seen at the playhouse. In America, though the theatre was often frowned upon, it was the meeting place of the laborer and the professional man, the immigrant and the old settler; those who were divided at social gatherings, at church, and at politcal rallies, were united before the stage. This was particularly true where puritanical scruples were absent. Strait-laced though the Spanish were, and insistent upon the etiquette of public assemblies, they regarded theatregoing as a continuation of an old-country custom.

They recognized that the puppet theatre appealed to all classes, to young and old. It was the most widely popular of theatrical entertainments among them. Charles Magnin recorded, in his *Histoire des marionnettes en Europe* (Paris, 1862), that "for many years, every Spanish town of importance had a permanent puppet theatre set up in an auditorium, ordinarily of sufficient size and convenience, where an audience of the most diverse society came together. In a country of extreme social inequality, one cannot help but notice the true human equality which exists."

He cited as an example of such a civic puppet theatre the one in Valencia. There in 1808 a public of the highest to the lowest boisterously applauded *The Death of Seneca*, a piece with timely overtones in a day of opposition to imperialistic aggrandizement. Had not Seneca been born in Cordoba? He was a Roman, but also a Spanish, hero.

It is natural, therefore, that Spaniards not only supported traveling puppet shows but endeavored to set up permanent puppet theatres in the towns of New Spain.

In Mexico there was a puppet show in Morelia in 1734. There was a skilled puppet maker in Pátzcuaro in 1740; he figured in a lawsuit against the maker of a powder that was represented as having properties to win a cockmain. In 1764 the actors of the Teatro Principal, Mexico City, petitioned the city council that the unfair competition of the puppet shows be removed; they complained that they were suffering from the neglect of the public that flocked to see the miniature players.

Such a complaint had parallels in Europe when live actors objected to the presence of more popular wooden ones. But the attraction of the puppet theatre in Mexico City seems to have been so potent that it even weaned actors away from their own stage to become puppeteers. On 18 November 1786, Don Silvestre Díaz de la Vega, Comptroller of Hospitals and Theatre, issued an order to Don Mariano de Zepeda, Clerk of the Theatre. It is transcribed in *Reseña del teatro en Mexico* by Enrique de Olavarría y Ferrari (Mexico, 1895, Vol. I, p. 60). The order runs, "It being understood that various members of both sexes of the dramatic company and corps de ballet and others attached to the Theatre in the Capital, on nights when they do not perform, as well as on those nights when they do, go after the performance to take part in puppet plays in those houses where such may be found; with the result that, staying up till all hours of the night, they lack time the following day to study those roles which they are expected to act; to which it must be added that the disorder and drunkenness which follow bring about illnesses and indispositions which prevent them from attending the Theatre, thus gravely interfering with its interests and those of the public.

"To remedy all this the Clerk, Don Mariano de Zepeda, is hereby commissioned to inspect with due caution the houses where such puppet plays are given and, upon finding therein any actors, dancers, or singers, to place them forthwith under arrest and at the disposal of the Director of the Theatre, without exception. He will further ascertain how long such employees of the Theatre have been attending these places. He will also request the government license under which such puppet plays may be performed. Should no license be produced, he will proceed against these puppeteers in the same manner as the Theatre Bureau does on similar occasions. He will warn license holders that they may not take into their companies any employee of the Theatre, and that upon failure to comply, they will be proceeded against. All this done, the Clerk will furnish an immediate report."

What sort of actors were these, to take a busman's holiday playing in a puppet theatre? Zepeda carried out his orders and got in touch with the alleged offenders. The first to appear was "a man who said he was Francisco Javier Alcantara, born in Puebla, Spain, and a resident in this city since childhood. He stated that he was 35 years old, unmarried, and living in Venero Street beyond the wine shop and the ditch. I took

his oath by Our Lord and the Holy Cross to tell the truth. Asked what
he did for a living, he replied that he eked out an existence from the
performance of puppet plays under the license obtained from His Excellency the Viceroy, which he showed me. I hereby attest to having
seen it, read it, and returned it to him. It was granted in this city on
15 December of last year, 1785, with the proviso that performances
commence exactly at dusk and end at ten o'clock; that neither food nor
drink be served; that the place be well lighted; that the audience be
properly separated by sex [it was the oriental custom in Spain that
men and women be separated at the theatre; on 17 April 1630 the Viceroy
of Peru proclaimed that they must enter the Corral de las Comedias
in Lima by separate entrances and sit apart]; and that the selectman
of the district be charged with the enforcement. I then returned the
license to him, warning him to follow its provisions and not to allow
any participation by the actors and actresses of the Theatre. He asserted
that none such came to his place and that the house where they go is
that of another troupe, located in the Calle del Portal de Tejada and
operated by a man named Estrada."

The second person to appear before the investigator was "a woman
who said that her name was Francisca Tomasa Montoya y Gadena, of
gentle blood, spinster, native of the city of Puebla, resident in this city
for 18 years, aged 48, and at present living in the Puente Colorado in
the house called the Playhouse." Puebla, it seems, was a fountainhead
of puppetry in old Spain. One is gratified to find that a gentlewoman
of certain years could manage a puppet show as a means of livelihood.
Having been sworn, she was questioned and said that, "because of her
infirmities and increasing age, after having acted in the Theatre here,
as well as in those of Puebla and Veracruz, she is reduced today to the
small income from the puppet shows which she has presented since 13
May of this year. On that day His Excellency the Viceroy granted her a
license, which I attest to having seen, with the condition that performances be given in the outlying districts but not in the center of town."
For the rest, the testimony of Francisca Montoya y Gadena was similar
to Alcantara's, and so were the admonitions of the clerk.

"From the above declarations," he went on, "I gathered that there
was a puppet theatre in the Calle del Portal de Tejada in the house
at the corner of Polilla Alley above the wine shop. I therefore went
there this afternoon, 24 November, and having inspected the theatre I
inquired after the owner from a woman who happened to be there.
She stated that she lived in the house and that the owner was sick
with spotted fever. Going into the farthest inner room, I found a man in
bed, apparently ill. When asked for his name and other facts, he stated

that he was José Estrada, Spanish, married to Augustina Morales, and that he was a gold worker by trade, 25 years old. He said he is the proprietor of a puppet theatre with which he seeks to supplement his wages, and in which he takes the leading part.

"He claimed that the theatre and puppets are the property of Don Felipe Manjarrés, from whom he rents them for eight pesos a month, under the guaranty of Don José Ponce de León; that his assistants are Francisco Coca, who takes the second lead, José Cano, who takes the third lead, José Romero and Mariano Zanca who play the old men, and Mateo Cevallos the clown. The leading lady is Ana la Zanca, the second woman Ana García, and two servants, Maria and Pepa, are the singers. He stated that it is true that Francisco Carreño, Miguel Alanís, Teresa Acosta, and José Viguera, called 'the Little Teacher,' have taken three or four parts for fun and without compensation; that only Alanís has had an occasional benefit night. Asked under what license he gave these performances, he replied that he had none; only for this reason had he agreed to let Carreño and the others take part once in a while, in the belief that they could protect him against prosecution. I then demanded that he surrender the puppets to me. He complied by delivering twelve puppets which I then put in charge of the Auditor. I enjoined him against giving similar performances ever again."

It is a little hard to see how four stage actors could have done any harm by reading the lines in a puppet show for fun. Perhaps they were victims of a typical green-room cabal. On the other hand, why had Estrada not applied for a license? Was sanction to play puppet shows given only to the elderly and destitute? Or was he without money to pay the fee after having reimbursed Don Felipe and Don José for the use of the puppets? These gentlemen should at least have been sufficiently cautious to safeguard their property and risk. Strange to find a Ponce de León underwriting a show that was a sort of fountain of youth for the spirit!

If Estrada surrendered all his puppets, he must have had more people than puppets backstage. Certainly the variety of lines of actor would have allowed the interpretation of almost any kind of drama. From the location of all these puppet theatres in the *banlieues* of town it is evident that they were the resorts not of fashionable but of common people. Because of the injunction against serving food and drink it may be supposed that such theatres had once provided refreshments and were, in fact, a sort of cabaret. Estrada, being unlicensed, may have made bold to regale his audience with drink; in any event the wine shop was downstairs. Perhaps both puppeteers and public, like many unhappy laborers, forgot their cares in inebriation.

A clue to what plays were performed lies in the stock parts taken by the members of the company. They would indicate a repertory parallel to that of the bigger theatre. The type of puppet used—the text has the word *muñeco* throughout, rather than *títere*, though both mean puppet—was probably supported by a rod to the head and supplementary strings from above, which was usual in the civic puppet theatres of the eighteenth century.

The fourth theatre to be investigated by the assiduous Zepeda was properly licensed, so that he was not detained by looking into the details of its operation. On 1 December he summoned "a woman who said her name was María Petra Aguilar, Spanish, married to José Meléndez, over 35, a native and resident of this city, at present living in the Portillo San Diego." After the administration of the oath and the observance of formalities, she stated that "she obtains her livelihood from puppet shows, which take place at the said Portillo in her house called the Workshop, under license obtained from His Excellency the Viceroy Don Matías de Gálvez . . . which she showed me. It is dated 22 October 1783, and was granted by virtue of her petition that she was overburdened with family and that her husband was unable to work at his trade of tailor because of failing eyesight. She further stated that she had never taken any role herself, nor allowed anyone from the Theatre in her house, and that most of the time the performances were given with the approbation of Don José Iglesias, selectman of the quarter. She also asserted that she has always obeyed the conditions imposed by the license."

These provincial showmen, little people hard pressed by want and sickness, are a far cry from the successful Powell of Bath and London, who was wont to drive, according to contemporary report, in his own coach.

It is likely that there had been a succession of small established puppet theatres in Mexico City during the eighteenth century, as well as wandering puppeteers throughout the country. The traveling shows may even have crossed the Gulf of Mexico and worked their way up the Mississippi during the brief rule of Spain in Louisiana. One of them, perhaps, was that described by Lyle Saxon in his *Fabulous New Orleans*; he found mention of it in a court record that eluded him when he wished to refer to it later for verification. In 1771, the record stated, Temba, a Negro slave in the household of a Spanish nobleman, murdered his master and was condemned to be executed in the Place d'Armes (now Jackson Square). When the throng arrived with the man to be hung, they found a puppet show in Spanish going on before a rapt audience. The scene can be pictured: the onrush of the rabble around the executioner's cart, the alarm and scattering of children and nurses, the folding up of the showman's *castella*, and the erection in its place of the gallows for the playing of a grimmer drama.

2. In Peru

From the days of Jusepe Hernandez and Leonor Godomar in the seventeenth century onward there had probably been a scattering of puppet shows in Lima and elsewhere in Peru. But there is no record of one to be found until 1761. In the *Acts* of the Cofradía of the Hospital de San Andrés for that year is a note of the sum of 3000 pesos delivered to the "authors and musicians" for a "Máquina Real de Munecos"—royal mechanism of puppets—in the Dramatic Coliseum. This was Lima's regular theatre, the revenue from which went to the order of the Hospital de San Andrés. The show may indeed have been of regal scale. It appears that the money given the "authors and musicians" was the performers' share after the hospital had deducted its own from the takings.

More light is thrown on arrangements for playing in the Dramatic Coliseum by a document signed by Silvestre Bravo, notary and assistant to Don Ambrosio Cerdan y Pontero, special judge in charge of this theatre. It is dated 1 June 1786. It asserts that Don Ambrosio granted "a license to Pasqual Calderon to exhibit, on regular nights when there were no other plays, puppets, juggling, sleight of hand, and such other entertainments as he presented, in the Dramatic Coliseum by contract; performances to begin at seven and half past nine promptly; no suspicious looking people to be allowed in the playhouse; no riot or scandal to prevail; nor should the puppets dance improper dances; no placards to be put up on the Coliseum as they usually are; no drum or trumpet to be played in the streets or at the entrance to the place of entertainment. I, the notary," concluded Bravo, "shall keep myself posted in order to inform His Lordship of what comes to pass."

This license seems to have been taken as full sanction by Pasqual Calderon to play during the next half-year, even during Lent and after disturbances in the crowd had caused the Superintendent General of Peru to forbid performances. On 27 February 1787 José Maria de Egaña apprised the Superintendent, "Your Excellency was pleased to give me a verbal order to forbid any performances of mountebanks or puppets at night, in order to prevent the unseemly offences which are committed in these assemblies. Your Excellency took this measure since such shows are not controlled by the presence of an officer of the law and the spectators, being nothing but rabble, indulge in flagrant disorder and licentiousness. Having learned that this sort of thing went on at the ball court during these nights of Lent—and all the more reprehensible at so inappropriate a time—I proceeded to do my duty and forbid it. But I was unable to accomplish my purpose because of the license issued by Don Ambrosio Cerdan, the original of which I enclose." Then he showed Pasqual Calderon's permit. Regretfully he pointed out that it would have been all right if the rabble had behaved, and referred obscurely to the entertainment as obscene, mentioning "the shameful dances in the ridiculous nonsense."

On 1 March 1787 the whole affair came to the ears of the Viceroy Don Teodoro de Croix in a letter from Jorge Escobedo:

Most Excellent Sir:
Guided by what I am accustomed to hear, by informal advice, and by news from the godfearing, I sought to avoid the nuisance of the mountebanks or puppets which are carried on as a personal enterprise of some who give themselves to this idle occupation, eschewing others to which they could give themselves with greater usefulness to themselves and the state. Thus I have denied such permits when they were requested of me and charged the Lieutenant of Police, in whose province in the civil management of the city it is, to do likewise; but I have just been informed that a certain Pasqual Calderon, charged with maintaining this sort of entertainment at the ball court on nights in Lent, has produced a license given him on the first of June last year by Don Ambrosio Zerdan as special judge for the Royal Dramatic Coliseum. Though I do not believe that this office implies so much jurisdiction, since rules for that house were established the previous year and the said judge may have been given such powers, I bring this to Your Excellency's attention in order to obviate confusion and jurisdictional disputes. I await your superior resolve and enclose a copy of the aforesaid license and the report from the Lieutenant of Police whom I have warned to take no action until Your Excellency shall communicate his pleasure.

Then the matter was thrown back to Don Ambrosio—he himself spelled his name Zerdan—who explained to the Viceroy, in a long letter of 4 March 1787, "When through Your Excellency this court was placed in my charge I found that it had been the practice of my predecessors to license these entertainments, within the Coliseum and outside it. So I granted a permit to Pasqual Calderon on 30 May of last year and a similar one to Josef Ignacio Cantos on 18 October, limiting both to two months. The notary, who is now dead, ignored this clause. He should have given the mountebank a faithful copy of the well-meditated resolution which I set down in my own hand, without making additions or inventions.

"The basis of this court's concern outside the Coliseum has been that performances in the street interfere with the theatre, whether it has bills scheduled or not, and divert its revenues from the original owner, the Royal Hospital of San Andrés, or its tenants or agents. Therefore the right to decree the proper measures for fulfilling the desired objectives has been reserved to your conservator judge in the event that permission is requested for any such performances."

After a prolix paragraph on jurisdiction Don Ambrosio again shifted the blame to his notary. "On two occasions only have I given such licenses, limited to two months. At the expiration of this time I took care to retrieve the license from Josef Ignacio Cantos, but if Pasqual Calderon retained his it is undoubtedly due to the forgetfulness or negligence of the notary Bravo, whom I ordered to get it back last year." Bravo was dead and couldn't deny this. In a final flourish of self-vindication Don Ambrosio wrote, "The above brings my report to an end. I must close by declaring to Your Excellency what I think of these entertainments. They seem to me to be ridiculous and fit only for children and low people, even when done with skill and dexterity. In consequence of my firm resolution not to allow them, or comedies, interludes, and other pieces outside the theatre, because of the disorders which may result . . . I last month denied to this same Pasqual Calderon permission, which he requested, to play the above sort of entertainment in the theatre during Lent, whose days and nights deserve to have worthier observance from all Christians."

And so it comes out! The judge turned the showman away and disorders ensued when he played at the ball court. Whose fault was it? Well, Calderon was the one who suffered. The Viceroy wrote the Superintendent of the Treasury that all licenses were to be revoked, and that in future whatever permit the judge for the theatre issued was to be validated by another civil court. The final document in this formidable dossier is dated Lima, 12 March 1787, and directs, "Append this to the foregoing and warn the Lieutenant of Police that, continuing his zeal in the prevention of disorder and the stopping of assemblies offensive to God and the public good, he is not to permit puppet shows under any pretext without express license from the Superintendence of the Treasury." The memo is signed by Escobedo.

How long, one wonders, was it before Peruvian puppets again got into trouble?

3. In the Argentine

Puppets were the harbingers of the theatre along the Rio de la Plata as well as in Mexico and Peru. They existed in Montevideo before 1800, according to Ruth Richardson's *Florencio Sanchez and the Argentine*

Theatre (New York, 1933, pp. 32-34). Vincente Rossi said of the puppets in the region (*Teatro Nacional Rioplatense*, Cordoba, Argentina, 1910, pp. 161-162), "A títere or puppet is a bit of wood which is carved generally with a good penknife or *navaja*. The wood, chosen for its softness and pliability, was often the stem or sprout of the *agave* or century plant, which combines these qualities to a marked degree. Once completed the face of the puppet had the form of a large hollow cardboard mask put on over the head."

A document in the archives of colonial Buenos Aires gives a hint of the presence of puppets. "In the name of his Majesty the King," it reads, "at San Ildefonso, 7 August 1795. . . . On the part of the civil government of the city of Montevideo, a plea has been entered that measures be taken to redress the vexations, humiliation, and lack of respect with which the Governor, Don Antonio Olaguer y Feliu, of that city, has treated its people. The complaint is made that he arbitrarily, without notice or consultation with the City Council, allowed plays to be given in 1793 when hitherto there had been none, at least only puppet shows and tight-rope walking, which were attended by the Council and regular Councilmen."

Recent findings, according to Alfredo S. Bagalio, a student of Argentine puppet history, show that the first theatre building in Buenos Aires was one put up in 1757 by Don Pedro Aguiar, a native of Spain and shoemaker by trade, on a lot adjoining the house of Top Sergeant Pinedo which belonged to Doña Maria Tomasa de Arze. Two years after it was built the Bishop of Buenos Aires ordered its closing. The reason? Don Pedro, it seems, had a wife back in Spain. He was ordered by ecclesiastical authority to return dutifully to her side. A decree of the governor, Lieutenant General Don Florencio A. Moreyra, dated 17 May 1759, explained the nature of the entertainment in this theatre.

"The shows," it stated, "are nothing but a Máquina Real, by which is to be understood puppets, figures, or costumed mannequins, managed as they customarily are during Lent in the theatres and inn-yards of Madrid, playing parts as if alive, in prose, verse, and with music, behind curtains. Until now there has been no evidence of the slightest disorder in the course of these shows, and I can say that I have been informed, by persons of good judgment who have attended, that care is taken to separate the sexes in the audience and follow the other regulations pertaining to assemblies."

Puppets, then, held forth in the first theatre in Buenos Aires between 1757 and 1759, until the Bishop ordered its closing to reunite a reluctant husband with his spouse. The shows recalled by the indignant citizens of 1793 were perhaps these of the first theatre, perhaps others that had played subsequently. Could not the Buenos Aires Máquina Real have been the one that played in Lima in 1761, after a journey including a loop to Spain? If so, did the deserted wife come along with the puppeteer, or was she again left behind? The Governor's decree reinforces the position of Pasqual Calderon who, in asking for permission to play during Lent, was merely following the custom of Madrid. Even in Rome Lent was the liveliest season for puppets, when scores of little theatres were open to take the place of the closed opera and playhouses. Lima was naturally more sanctimonious than Rome!

4. In Chile

In La Serena, in the northern part of Chile, an *entreme*, or short dramatic piece, was played in 1796. It may and may not have been a puppet show, but at least the principal character was El Moroco, the black one or devil. This is mentioned in Francisco A. Machuca's *Escenas historico-militares Coquimbanas* (Valparaiso, 1938, pp. 204-205). In other parts of Latin America there could well have been eighteenth-century puppet performances. With the brisk activity of the puppet theatre in twentieth-century Latin America, local historians will be on the lookout for indications of its past.

VII

Eighteenth-Century French Puppets

As in Spain, so in France were there many fixed puppet theatres during the eighteenth century. Bienfait, Nicolet, the Prévosts, and Séraphin had established theatres in Versailles and Paris; there were others in the provincial cities. It is therefore not surprising to find a puppet theatre in Quebec, one that was to stay entrenched in the life of the town for over half a century and to pass into the hands of a third generation of a puppeteer family.

According to the testimony of Philippe Aubert de Gaspé in his *Mémoires* (Ottawa, 1866, p. 544), this theatre began in the city of Quebec in the mid-eighteenth century. When Gaspé was a boy, in the 1790's, it was already well rooted in the Rue d'Aiguillon near the Rue des Glacis in the Faubourg St. Jean. It played from the day after Christmas until the beginning of Lent, opening its doors every night at six o'clock. For a child the entrance fee was six sols, a small sum. When the storm door stood open, as it generally did, one saw a life-size grenadier painted in striking colors on the inner door. (By a curious coincidence, in the small Danish town in Theodor Storm's *Puppeteer Paul*, a work of fiction based upon the author's boyhood memories, the Militia House, where puppet shows were wont to play, had just such a guardsman painted on the door.) The Quebec auditorium was small; when all the seats were filled latecomers had to wait patiently out in the snow for two hours until the second show. Sometimes there were three shows a night.

The old puppeteer of this theatre was lying dead when Gaspé, a schoolboy, had his first glimpse of him. "It was a Friday during the fine summer season," he remembered, "and all the joyous band of the Quebec boarding school pupils had gone to its summer house, the Canardière to spend the day, when, turning into the poplar-bordered road which led to the old Dorchester bridge, we came upon a group of women before a house of poor appearance on the east side of the Royal Highway. One of them, the wife of an innkeeper in the vicinity named Frederick, told us that Daddy Marseille, the old puppeteer, was dead.

"Daddy Marseille was little more than a myth to me. I had heard my parents speak of the shows which he and his wife had given when they were children. I had often heard complimentary remarks about this distinguished pair of artists when their theatre was compared with that of their successor, Barbeau; and I was seized with the desire to see the remains of this man I had heard talked about, but who I thought was long since dead.

"Although I was the wildest boy in the school, or perhaps because of it, our master, M. Bedard, had a weakness for me. I often profited by it in soliciting favors when others would not have dared ask him.

" 'I've never seen a dead person,' I told him. 'Please let me see Daddy Marseille.'

" 'If I thought it would have a good effect on you,' replied M. Bedard, 'I'd gladly consent.'

" 'It surely will, sir,' said I, looking sweet as an angel and winking to my companions.

"The master pursed his lips. 'Those who wish to go into this house, follow me.'

"Only a dozen of the younger scholars entered the funeral place. M. Bedard uncovered the face of the deceased and told us, 'Regard death and reflect solemnly, for some day, which may not be distant, it awaits you all.' "

The narrator must have had a twinkle in his eye when he recollected this remark some seventy years later! He continued, "Today it is difficult for me to recall what I felt upon my first view of death. Twenty years later I should, perhaps, like Hamlet holding the skull of Yorick, have tried to distinguish in that earthen face, the large aquiline nose, the long chin bound with white to keep the huge mouth closed, some trace that marked it as that of a puppeteer.

" 'Well, Gaspé,' said the master, 'you who are so wild, perhaps to-morrow you will be as quiet as this old man . . .'

"Trying to console myself, I retorted, 'But I'll never be so ugly!' "

Daddy Marseille had received his sobriquet because of the city of his origin. His name was Jean Natte; he was a soldier and a painter by vocation. On 6 February 1758, he married Marguerite Duchesneau in Quebec. Becoming a widower, he married Marie Louise Fluet, the widow of Joseph Barbeau, on 5 May 1781; she died in 1795. Jean Natte was buried on 30 July 1803. These facts are to be found in E.-Z. Massicotte's detailed article, *Les Marionnettes au Canada* (*Bulletin des recherches historiques*, Vol. 28, Quebec, 1922, pp. 12-13).

In the opinion of Pierre-Georges Roy, archivist of the Province of Quebec, Daddy Marseille's theatre did not actually come into being during the French regime; he believes that it began about 1775 or even later. The parents of Gaspé, who was born 30 October 1786, could not in that case have remembered it since their childhood. His statement that "this brilliant theatre . . . was the delight of several generations of children for more than a century" is an exaggeration.

At any rate, this old resident of Quebec put many details about it into his lively reminiscences. "Marseille and his wife," he wrote, "so long as they were able, took the personnel of their theatre to the homes of the heads of the best Canadian families who wished to entertain their children and those of their friends, for the sum of eight piastres [worth about $25 in 1940 purchasing power]. These parties, to which the parents of the younger set were invited, always ended with a supper and often with a ball as well.

"The Marseilles, like all celebrated actors, had their night of great triumph, the memory of which they cherished to their death. His Royal Highness, the Duke of Kent, father of our gracious Sovereign [Victoria], deigned to honor their theatre with his presence one night. [The Duke was in Quebec from August 1791 to January 1794.] It was necessary to get up something new and extraordinary for so great a personage, and the genius of the Marseilles did not fail them on this momentous occasion. As the Prince had engaged the theatre for himself and his party several days in advance, our artists had time to prepare everything for the surprise they planned for him.

"The Marseilles had already been able to amuse the Prince with their puppets, but they meant to follow up their comedy with touching drama and to move him as well. The curtain fell; Mrs. Marseille, who had been seated before the stage during the show as usual, next to the orchestra—one violin and drum, augmented for the occasion by a flute—the mistress of ceremonies for her worthy spouse, arose, made a deep curtsey to the Duke of Kent, and said, 'My Prince, this is the end of the puppets; the devil has taken them all away.' As a matter of fact his Satanic Majesty, in the form of a prairie partridge, had just swept the stage clean of Punch and his companions at the climax of a more than animated dance, and Mother Marseille had drawn the curtain.

" 'But, my Prince,' she added, 'we are going to idemnify your realm for so great a loss by giving a spectacle of the siege of Quebec by the Americans in 1775, and of the signal beating which the English and Canadians gave them in consequence, to teach them to live properly with their cousins.'

"And, having delivered herself of this bellicose harrangue, Mother Marseille, doubtless to the Prince's amusement, sang *Malbrouk s'en va-t-en guerre, mirliton, mirlitaine,* from the first line to the last. [Punch sang this in the 1828 text of his play and the tune, known to us by the words, "He's a jolly good fellow," is still traditional with him.]

"The curtain rose, and with surprise the spectators saw the city of Quebec, made in miniature of cardboard, no mistaking it in any detail: at the summit of the high citadel floated the British ensign, troops and citizens lined the ramparts, cannoneers were at their posts, matches burning, the American battalions mounted to the assault, the ordnance boomed, a sharp fusillade could be heard, the besiegers took flight, and the city was saved.

"The orchestra played *God save the King* and the whole English royal family filed across the stage; King George III headed the procession, mounted on a blooded charger, with Queen Charlotte seated acroup behind him, and the two crowned sovereigns were followed by their numerous [thirteen] offspring of princes and princesses on brave steeds. But let us have Mother Marseille, to lay her spirit, recount the scene which was so flattering to her self-esteem.

" 'When the Prince recognised his dear pa and ma that he hadn't seen for so long, he reined in to hide his feelings, but when he set eyes on his little brother Rudolph, his heart just bust, and he buried his face in his hanky.'

"Telling the story, Mother Marseille would find her eyes filled with tears and she would take a big snuff of tobacco to clear her view."

But was it for sorrow that the Duke had to hide his face?

"Since Master Barbeau, son-in-law and successor of the Marseilles, refused to take the puppets around," continued Gaspé, "one of us—I was then a pater familias [his first child was baptized in 1812]—would rent the theatre and he would give, at five in the afternoon, cutting the fee to four piastres, an extra show for our private company. It was understood that, after the show, we'd pass the evening at the house of whoever had rented the theatre. Laughter is contagious, and I've seldom seen a whole crowd laugh more heartily than we did at Master Barbeau's.

"Having bespoken the theatre one particular year, I invited Mme. Pierre de Sales Laterrière, née Bulmer, a young Englishwoman recently come to Canada, who had no idea of what sort of a show she was going to see. We were watching, rather casually, the pranks and doings of Mr. Punch and his company, which we had seen a hundred times. She restrained herself as long as she was able, even pinching herself to keep a sober face, but finally, writhing in her seat, she had to burst out and cried, 'It's so ridiculous!' Laughter is catching, as I observed before. Never did Master Barbeau play to such gales of it. As for our young Englishwoman, every time she thought of the play during the evening at my house with my other friends, she exploded anew, 'It's so ridiculous!' "

Outside of the exhibition of a staid Bulmer disintegrating into risibilities before something strange and new to her—the English had a hilarious time in Victoria's reign, tittering at everything incomprehensible, from Jabberwocky and the Ahkond of Swat to Darwin and Wagner —this account holds several points of interest.

The fee for a private show is about what a modest puppeteer would still ask, in current purchasing equivalents of money, in 1948.

Mother Marseille acted as a presenter before the stage, just as had In-and-In Medlay in Jonson's *A Tale of a Tub* (Act V, scene vii), Master Pedro's boy in *Don Quixote* (Part 2, chapter 26), and Powell, if he stood where he was shown in the frontispiece to *A Second Tale of a Tub*. The outside man, when there is one, still occupies this position in a Punch and Judy show.

Barbeau was probably Daddy Marseille's stepson rather than son-in-law.

The battle piece of the siege of Quebec belongs to a familiar genre. The four American Indian chieftains, in London in 1710/11, had been regaled with *The Last Year's Campaign,* which, according to the playbill, showed "the famous battle fought between the confederate army (commanded by the Duke of Marlborough) and the French in the woods near Blaguiers, with several comical entertainments of Punch in the camp. Also a variety of scenes, with a most glorious prospect of both armies, the French in their entrenchments and the confederates out, where will be seen several regiments of horse and foot engaged in forcing the French lines." George Washington had seen a noisy interpretation of the storming of Havana at Williamsburg in 1772.

Such panoramic action could be effective on the smallest puppet stage so long as the figures were in scale, whereas the deepest stage in a big theatre, with actors handicapped by human size, would fail to convey the magnitude of clashing armies on a field of battle. It was only with the invention of the motion picture that the flexibility of the puppet stage for "close-ups" and "long shots" was equalled.

The cavalcade of George III and his family was probably accomplished with flat figures cut from cardboard and painted. They may not have been articulated. Mounted to a lath which could be cantered up and down as it passed along, the procession would have had a fair resemblance to a parade on horseback. Daddy Marseille, even with a few days' warning, could not have made a set of three-dimensional puppets in honor of the Duke of Kent; that would have taken weeks. His piece of the siege of Quebec was probably a stock item in his repertory.

It is significant, from the point of view of the place of the puppet theatre in the life of the community, that both the ordinary citizen and the leading family of Quebec enjoyed it; both children and grownups were in the audience; and since the regular shows were given at night, there was no special catering to children or people of leisure; it was for all ages and classes. It speaks well of the trust placed by parents in the theatre that they allowed their young daughters to attend it unaccompanied in the evening; indeed, it speaks well for the content of the bills. Gaspé tells an anecdote of three young girls who went to the puppets one night between 1812 and 1814:

"It was during the continental war, and passwords were so strictly demanded that one might have thought the French encamped on the Plains of Abraham. From nine o'clock at night it was necessary to answer to the 'Who goes there?' of sentinels posted in every corner of the city of Quebec. They even tell lamentable stories of persons upon whom the sentries fired because, not knowing English, they had not replied with 'Friend.'

"Three Canadian sisters, aged from 12 to 15, were coming gaily home from Master Barbeau's theatre toward nine at night when the sentry posted at the Porte St. Jean bellowed to them in stentorian voice, 'Who goes there?' Either through fear or ignorance of what reply to make, the girls kept going. But at a second order in an even louder voice, the eldest, trembling, replied, 'Trois petites Dorionnes comes from ze marionettes.' The sentry, seeing the youngsters, laughed and said, 'Pass, trois petites Dorionnes come from ze marionettes!'"

In 1837 a faction of French Canadians sought to break away from the British and set up an independent republic. Everything French was consequently suspect at this time and the puppet theatre, whether guilty of voicing rebellious sentiments or not, succumbed. Gaspé gives a rather hazy account of its end:

"The hand of a despot made a clean sweep of them [the puppets] during the troubles of 1837 and 1838. It was feared, I suppose, that Punch and his troupe would swell the ranks of the rebels. There were, as a matter of fact, some very redoubtable fighters among the puppets. 'Bring on the Germans!' manager Barbeau would cry, and straightway there entered a dozen Teutons of both sexes. Having danced with naked swords in their hands, the men finished by falling to blows, to the great alarm of the lady Germans, until two or three of the warriors were strewn on the ground.

"The police, after having demolished and looted the theatre of Sasseville, who had succeeded Barbeau, paraded in the streets for some time with their opima spolia on their shoulders, shouting, 'Here's rebel A,' or rebel B or C, giving the names of the imaginary leaders of the rebellion, who certainly did not exist in the district of Quebec."

Were these puppets the first in America to meet destruction as political martyrs?

The fixed theatre in Quebec therefore flourished from about 1775 to 1837 under the proprietorship of Daddy Marseille (Jean Natte) and his first and second wives, Marguerite Duchesneau and Marie Louise Fluet, the latter the widow of Joseph Barbeau; then of her son; and finally of his successor, Sasseville, who may have been a relative, for the enterprise was a family one.

There were too few big towns in Canada to attract French puppet showmen in the eighteenth century; and the French were never wanderers, like the English, for the mere fun of it. Therefore, there were few French puppets in the New World, either at this time or later; they could find so few who understood their language that they were forced to play in pantomime if they did venture across the Atlantic; and then they might assume almost any foreign-sounding name—most Americans were unable to pronounce their French ones. For a French community such as Quebec, where the audience was stable, an established theatre was a possibility. It is a pity that this traditional puppet playhouse did not survive to this day, or that others did not follow in its pattern.

VIII

Fantoccini and Variety Bills

In the first half of the nineteenth century, if any form of puppet show may be said to have predominated in the United States—for there were all kinds—it was the variety show done with string-puppets, abounding in acrobatics, dancing, and transformations. While these elements were present from the beginning of the eighteenth century, they were generally subordinated to (or ran riot over) a dramatic theme. After the middle of the nineteenth century the tricks, always one of the most effective features of a puppet show, were used in the mimicry of the minstrel show, spectacular extravaganza, and vaudeville of the big stage. But at first they were presented simply as themselves. The audiences that enjoyed these amusing turns were a cross section of the public, both children and adults; the naïveté of the program was not tailored consciously to the youth of the spectators. Adults were thought of as the chief patrons of puppet shows, for nineteenth-century advertisements kept urging them to bring the children. Special entertainments for children, like special clothing styles and food, are a comparatively recent development. Look at any old picture of a street puppet show; among the onlookers the majority is shown as grownups.

The spell of the shadow-figure, which lingered on though the vogue for it had passed, is seen in the protestation of the showman Maginnis who, offering his "artificial comedians who will walk, speak, and move as natural as life" (in the New York *Daily Advertiser*, 11 June 1799), at Ricketts' Circus—the first recorded instance of puppets in a circus in America—on that date, advertised that the performance was not to be done "by shades, but by real figures and machinery." The show included a topical patriotic scene, *The Launch, or Huzza for Adams' Frigate*, concluding with "a beautiful launching of the frigate," a distant prospect of part of New York, a country German dance, the Sultan's House [*sic*] Guards going on parade, and Venus, drawn by turtle doves, ascending and descending. Among "a hundred different figures as large as life, in the brightest colors," were Mr. Cedar, Mr. and Mrs. Beech, Mr. Pitch Pine, Mr. Live Oak, and Mr. Sugar Maple—American puppets all, to the very core. What fervor the young nation had for its own! Independence was as exciting as first long pants to a boy.

The circus, an intimate one-ring show, as it remains in Europe to this day, before Barnum had swelled it to a hippodrome, was for equestrian feats and whatever else could be found to pad out the bill. It was not the best home for puppets save in their frenetic pace. Curiously, they still cling to the circus side show, almost overpowered by gorillas, fat ladies, and cotton candy. The misalliance may have been even earlier if Blanchard's exhibition of automata at Boston in June and July of 1795, at an amphitheatre also managed by Ricketts, meant puppets or included them.

The chance preservation of the playbill of a wandering showman among the papers of Benjamin Cummings, selectman of Dartmouth, Massachusetts (whose great-great-grandson, Lawrence B. Cummings, discovered it and helped decipher its hand-written part), shows what a country puppet performance was like about the year 1800.

TO THE CURIOUS.

Exhibition of Puppets.

The first kind of Arabian SPEAKING PUPPETS (thirty-six in number) will in the course of their performance dance reels, jigs, hornpipes, and country dances. Mr. Nodle and Mr. Duncan will show themselves above the screen, at the same time will blow out a candle and take a mug and drink to the ladies. A lady will appear on the stage holding a sick child in her arms, discoursing with the Doctor, which will be very curious. Capt. Davis will walk out with his crutch and dance with a very beautiful lady. Capt. Punch and his Wife will appear on the stage and perform many curious feats. Jack Tar will also appear on the stage with great activity. Priest Williams will appear on the stage and address the audience. Peter Gimblet and Little John will be seen to stride the screen and fight a very severe battle. Mr. Emery and his wife will be seen above the screen, in order to convince people how they should behave after marriage. Also Pomp and Phillis will appear on the stage with poor Quash. Belsemy is employed in carrying the dead from off the stage.

The scene will conclude with the battle of the seven devils.

Admittance for grown persons, nine pence, small children half price.

Written in the space at the bottom of this printed broadside are the particulars, "At 6 O'clock in the Evening of the 11th Instint the above performance will Commence at Shadrache Shearmen's, Innh[ol]d[er], in Dartmouth at a place call'd Russell's Mills. Richd. Hoyt." Russell's Mills, a settlement in the center of the township of Dartmouth, had a meeting house which Ralph Geddis and Francois Martin made into a puppet theatre in the mid-1930's.

Puppets that appeared above the screen and bestrode it could have been only hand-puppets, the kind with legs dangling from the cloth tube

TO THE CURIOUS.

Exhibition of Puppets.

THE firſt kind of Arabian SPEAKING PUPPETS thirty-ſix in number) will in the courſe of their performance dance reels, jigs, hornpipes and country dances. Mr. *Nodle* and Mr. *Duncan* will ſhow themſelves above the ſcreen, at the ſame time will blow out a candle, and take a mug and drink to the ladies. A lady will appear on the ſtage holding a ſick child in her arms, diſcourſing with the Doctor, which will be very curious. Capt. *Davis* will walk out with his crutch, and dance with a very beautiful Lady. Capt. *Punch* and his Wife will appear on the ſtage, and perform many curious feats. *Jack Tar* will alſo appear on the ſtage with great activity. Prieſt *Williams* will appear on the ſtage, and addreſs the audience. *Peter Gimblet* and *Little John* will be ſeen to ſtride the ſcreen, and fight a very ſevere battle. Mr. *Emery* and his Wife will be ſeen above the ſcreen, in order to convince people how they ſhould behave after marriage. Alſo *Pomp* and *Phillis* will appear on the ſtage with poor *Quaſh*. *Belſemy* is employed in carrying the Dead from off the ſtage.

The ſcene will conclude with the battle of the ſeven devils.

☞ *Admittance for grown Perſons, NINE PENCE, ſmall Children half price.*

At 6 O'clock 'In the Evening of the 11th Inſtant the above performance will Commence at Shadracha Shurmen's Inn Lr. in Dartſord at a place Calld Roſula Mills Nine Days

After a playbill, circa 1800, in the possession of Lawrence B. Cummings. The space at the bottom was left for writing in local particulars. The original, 7½ x 9½ inches, has been folded in eight and is split along some of the folds.

over the operator's arm. Did the difference between appearing "above the screen" and "on the stage" mean anything? Probably not; it was only a simple booth, apparently, without so much as a curtain or background to the stage, and there could not have been another space for another kind of puppet. The hand-puppets may have been varied, however, with hand-and-rod puppets and rod-and-string puppets like jumping jacks. The crutch of Captain Davis, a one-legged sailor man, could have extended below the screen as a stick to work him by. Jack Tar and the other dancers could have been of the jumping-jack variety, which was a familiar sight in the London streets of the early nineteenth century. Called fantoccini to distinguish them from puppets like Punch, they were depicted by George Cruikshank—a Joey clown (in Hone's *Every-Day Book*, p. 1113) and a dancing skeleton (from the company that called itself the Original Fantoccini, which had played at Vauxhall) —and by T. H. Shepherd (*London in the Nineteenth Century*, 1829), who showed a Highland-fling figure in a booth in Russell Square. Richard Hoyt, the Dartmouth showman, could have had this kind as easily as not.

His show seems to have had a thread of plot through it. After Mr. Noodle or Mr. Noddle (he should have been spelled with another letter) and Mr. Duncan had drunk their toast and extinguished the candle by way of prologue, the lady with the sick baby, undoubtedly Joan, holding Punch's infant, called the Doctor and gave Punch reason for being on edge and launching into his career of manslaughter. Belsemy— short for Beelzebub—was kept busy thereafter cleaning up after him. This drama of struggle and carnage was divided by interludes of dancing, mock preaching (who was Priest Williams but the embodiment of the controversial Roger Williams?), knock-about love making (one wonders how much Mr. Emery and his wife were permitted to exhibit), and perhaps bathos (Pomp and Phillis suggest Negro characters and poor Quash an animal, a recalcitrant mule).

The local color was so much of New England that the showman must have known the region well. Sailors and sea captains, dour characters whom he took off as Mr. Duncan and Mr. Emery, fighters muscular and spiritual, were all drawn from native life. Even Punch, in deference to the most glamorous of New England occupations, was a ship's captain. One wonders how Hoyt avoided getting his show suppressed, since he dealt with such delicate subjects (for the puritanical) as drink, love, combat, and religion—and boldly brought up the devil! He may have been a puppet showman all his life, though there is only this glimpse of him, and trained his son to be a puppeteer after him. In 1838 one G. W. Hoyt presented a Punch and Judy show in Brooklyn.

Hoyt played at an inn, probably in its largest room, as had the show-men of the preceding century. Hand-puppet booths were often set up out of doors, however, as they were in Italy and England. A stage direction in William Dunlap's play, *Wife of Two Husbands*, produced at the Park Theatre, New York, on 4 April 1804, calls for an open-air puppet booth. Act IV includes a scaffolding with a Merry Andrew and a puppet show, men, women, and children gazing at it. Dunlap may not have bothered to have the booth constructed by a property man and an actor trained to fake the show; he may merely have transplanted a real puppeteer from the street.

Coming from Saddler's Wells Theatre in London, a player or show-man named Maginnis, according to the *Columbian Centinal* of 12 January 1796, presented a variety bill in Boston. The broadside announcement (reprinted in Harper's *Literary Museum*, New York, 1927, p. 390) states, "To the curious! Tuesday and Thursday evenings will be exhibited at a commodious room in Mr. Dearborn's new building, at the south entrance of the narrow lane leading from the Theatre to Milk Street . . . a grand medley of entertainments." Act I consisted of a transparency, the Unfortunate Beggarman, the Broken Bridge, and the Sportsman and his Dog. Act II offered "Prussian Fantoccina by a grand set of artificial wax-work comedians from Rome, in Italy," with the Babes in the Wood, Roger de Coverly (had puppets in *The Spectator* led to its characters being in puppets?), the Lancashire Witch, a country girl who danced a jig, and an Italian Scaramouch who executed a fandango "and at the same time put his body in twenty attitudes." Act III had a sea engagement with fishes sporting in the waves, Neptune, tritons, and a beautiful mermaid. The broadside concludes with the details, "Doors to be opened at half past 5 o'clock and performance at half past 6. Front seats 3s., second seats 1s. 6. Tickets may he had at Maj. Forbes's tavern, Baker's hotel, the Orrery Printing Office, and the place of performance. Children half price. Vive la Republique!"

These were certainly the same puppets that played in an almost identical bill at the Water Street Theatre in New York in 1799. But the program of Maginnis' "artificial comedians" at Ricketts' Circus, New York, in June 1799, seems to have been another one, unless *Huzza for Adams' Frigate* was just a variation of the sea diorama. Maginnis could have been a manager rather than a puppeteer, engaging first one puppet company and then another. The Water Street show, which did not carry his name, may have been the company of the contorting Scaramouch on its own.

When Maginnis opened at Mechanics' Hall, Broadway at the corner of Park Place, New York, on 19 April 1804 (New York *Chronicle* of that

Richard Hoyt's booth, with puppets that appeared above and bestrode the screen, may have been a simple affair of cloth hung from a framework of crossed sticks, like this detail after an etching, circa 1810, Le grand charlatan, *published by the Widow Chereau, Rue St. Jacques No. 10, Paris. The nostrum-seller is saying, "Break your arms, your legs—with my cure it's a mere nothing!" while Punch poises his stick to belabor the devil and the charlatan's dog sits at attention.*

date), he showed the "Eudifocican, an evening's entertainment of philosophical experiments and theatrical amusements," a potpourri that could have included puppets, though they were not mentioned. A week later in the engagement (New York *Post*, 26 April) he added to the "Eudifocician, or mysteries of Mechanism" (was it a diorama or magic-lantern show?)—perhaps because the puppets had been playing elsewhere or had been omitted inadvertantly—"a rich group of figures representing the ancient Egyptian court, four feet and a half high," the Olympic castinet dance by a figure in the character of the Empress of Morocco, a fancy dance by a lovely village maid, rendered with "native elegance and simplicity," and "a small figure (in imitation of the celebrated Little Devil)" which performed all manner of tumbling; also the Lapland sisters dancing a jig and an automaton figure in the character of an American tar, footing a hornpipe with a variety of steps. This sounds very much like Maginnis's Boston show. He may have had the same puppet company right along; he may not have thought it important to put his name on the Water Street playbill.

At Boston, in the lower hall of the Columbian Museum, Peter Blancan presented his "Pittoresque & Mechanique Theatre" on 26 September 1808 (*Columbian Centinal* of 24 September). Then he brought it to

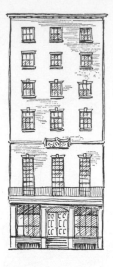

Mechanics Hall at Park Place and Broadway, occupied by the General Society of Mechanics and Tradesmen, an educational service for young workmen, 1801-1810. After a lithograph in the Annals of the Society, *New York, 1882.*

New York, opening in a new building on the east side of Broadway, opposite the hospital, between Duane and Worth Streets, on 27 December of that year (New York *Commercial Advertiser*, 26 December). The New York advertisement is headed by a device of Pierrot opposite Punch, with the name of the theatre encircling them; Punch wears his hat with a conical crown. This is remarkable for being the first illustrated advertisement for a puppet show in America. The device was probably brought from France, but it was copied either in engraved boxwood or type metal by Alexander Anderson, America's first engraver in the style of Bewick, for a proof of it was saved by Anderson in his scrapbooks (Vol. 3, p. 18, No. 1076), now in the New York Public Library.

Blissfully ignorant of his predecessors, Blancan respectfully informed the public "that he came to this city with a kind of amusement entirely unknown in this country. His exhibitions consist of Fontoccini or Artificial Comedians, Arabesk Fires, small Chinese Shades, and animated pictures, imitating those of the celebrated Vetor in Paris." Boxes cost $1, the pit 50¢, and children under the age of ten were admitted at half-price. A gallery was provided for people of color. Blancan stayed in New York about a month, until late January 1809. Then he decamped, not to be heard of again. Who was the celebrated Vetor? Perhaps it should have been Victor, but I have found no Parisian showman of that name. Blancan's variety show included string-puppets, fireless fireworks, shadow figures, and dioramas—all familiar to American puppet-show audiences. He probably assayed no dialogue, not knowing English, and the comic relief of Punch's patter was absent. The building opposite the hospital

The first illustrated American puppet-show advertisement that has so far come to light, from the New York Commercial Advertiser of 26 December 1808. The cut was engraved by Alexander Anderson; the proof of it from one of his scrapbooks has been substituted for the somewhat blurrier impression in the copy of the newspaper in the files of the New-York Historical Society. The original cut is 2 inches in diameter.

MR BLANCAN,

RESPECTFULLY informs the Public that he came to this city with a kind of amusement entirely unknown in this country. His exhibitions consist of *Fontoccini* or Artificial Comedians, Arabask Fires, small Chinese Shades, and animated pictures, imitating those of the celebrated Vetor in Paris. These four kinds of amusements will be exhibited on Tuesday evening next, the 27th inst. in a very convenient new building in Broadway, opposite the Hospital.

Prices of admittance—Boxes one Dollar, Pit fifty cents—children under the age of ten years, half price. A gallery will be provided for people of color. Particulars in future advertisements.

dec 24   3t*

was still called the Theatre Pittoresque et Mechanique when it burned down 20 April 1812 (*Columbian Centinal*, 1 May).

Could it have been one of the puppeteers of Blancan's troupe who found his way out to Detroit in 1811? This showman sent a note to Col. Jacob Kingsbury, dated Detroit, 22 January that year, "I, Moreau, will perform within the Fort this evening and will represent the Great City of Marengo in Italy and Bonaparte on horseback in front of the City with French Colors in one hand and sword in the other Holding his bridle in his mouth.

"If the Colonel pleases to send his Children they will be admitted gratis; in addition to the above there will be exhibited French Puppets—with Music during the performance."

Though the British had taken possession of Detroit in 1760, it still had a French-speaking group of citizens, mostly farmers who lived along the river. It was natural for a French puppeteer to seek out such an audience, which might be presumed to have a quickening of the heart at the sight of Napoleon in a diorama. The manuscript note is in the Kingsbury Papers in the Burton Historical Collection of the Detroit

Public Library, and was located by Elleine H. Stones, the Librarian of the collection.

Sometime before 1814 another Frenchman, a seaman held by the British as a prisoner of war on Melville Island, Halifax, Nova Scotia, made a few pennies by exhibiting, in a bazaar where his fellows had scrimshaw and other handiwork for sale, "a kind of puppet show with vocal accompaniments." (This is mentioned in Beamish Murdoch's *History of Nova Scotia*, Halifax, 1867, Vol. 3, p. 350.)

But for a prisoner turned puppeteer the most fabulous was Henry More Smith, alias Henry Frederick Moon, alias William Newman, a young Englishman of twenty-three who said he had come to Canada to get away from the war. He gave a lot of trouble to Walter Bates, Sheriff of King's County, New Brunswick, who wrote *The Mysterious Stranger, or Memoirs of Henry More Smith*, and had it published at New Haven in 1817; it has since gone through many editions. While awaiting trial as a horse thief at Kingston, New Brunswick, Smith escaped and did a little burglary; sentenced to hang, he whiled away the time in jail by making lifelike effigies and costuming them in his own clothes—at least as a change from filing off his shackles, sawing his bars, ripping down the wall, and giving every indication that he was unhappy locked up.

Then he was struck by an idea. Refusing food for seven days, starting 13 June 1815, he set to work and disclosed at the end of the period a show he had been making. Few puppeteers could own to his zeal! Sheriff Bates was so impressed that he wrote a letter to the *Royal Gazette* of 11 July, couched in the hyperbole of a veritable press agent. Reading it, the public flocked to the prison to see Smith and his show. "The most extraordinary, the most wonderful of all," wrote Bates, "is that in this time he had prepared, *undiscovered*, and at once *exhibited* the most striking picture of genius, art, taste, and invention that ever was and I presume ever will be produced by any human being placed in his situation, in a dark room, chained and handcuffed, under sentence of death, without so much as a nail or any kind of thing to work [with] but his hands, and naked." The Sheriff should have expected cleverness from a young man so handy at making saws from old knife blades and cutters from watch springs. The figures were made of straw, "curiously twisted and interwoven," and features were indicated with charcoal from a burned timber; they were dressed in rags of the denuded maker's clothes.

"The exhibition," continued the Sheriff, "consists of ten characters, men, women, and children, all made and painted in the most expressive manner, with all the limbs and joints of the human frame, each performing different parts; their features, shape, and form all express their different offices and characters; their dress is of different fashions and suitable to the stations in which they act. To view them in their situation they appear as perfect as though alive, with all the air and gaiety of actors on the stage. Smith sits in his bed by the side of the jail—his *exhibition* begins about a foot from the floor and compasses the whole space of [to] the ceiling. The uppermost is a man whom he calls the tambourine player, or sometimes Dr. Blunt, standing with all the pride and appearance of a master musician, his left hand akimbo, his right hand on his tambourine, dressed in suitable uniform." Below him was a lady in a swing, a servant and a gallant to either side of her to propel it; below them a young man and girl playing at tilts; and below this pair a Harlequin figure called Bonaparte, beating music and surrounded by children.

"The first operation is from the tambourine player, or master, who gives two or three single strokes on his tambourine that may be heard in any part of the house, without moving his body. He then dances gracefully a few steps; then the two below tilt a few times in the most easy, pleasant manner; then the two children dance a little, holding each other by the hand; after this Smith begins to sing or whistle a tune, to which they are to dance, at which the tambourine strikes and everyone dances to the tune, with motion, ease, and exactness not to be described."

In a postscript the enthusiastic Sheriff noted that a drummer had been made to stand beside the tambourine player on Wednesday 28 June, and that a gentleman from Boston had come to see the show and said, in the words of the Queen of Sheba, "The half has not been told!" An editorial note reinforced the matter by saying, "Those who are acquainted with the Sheriff know him to be incapable of stating falsehoods." One almost suspects that the gratuities from visitors were shared between prisoner and jailer.

This was a very rudimentary kind of puppet show, only once removed from the automata exhibited, by report of Richardson Wright in *Hawkers & Walkers in Early America* (Philadelphia, 1927, p. 179), at Henniker, New Hampshire, in 1814; figures two feet tall that held hammers and struck bells at the turning of a crank; or the dancers, soldiers, and black girl seen by Nathaniel Hawthorne at North Adams, Massachusetts, on the top of a hand organ. Smith's group of figures could be controlled separately, probably by pulling strings, or all together by a master string. Their vertical arrangement made this possible with a minimum of friction. Smith could lie in bed, play a musical instrument, and work his "family" by the movement of a toe or knee, much as a showman works jigging puppets on a string between his knee and a fixed point.

This exhibition was notable more for its circumstances than its quality. As the crowds came to see it they brought Smith thread and needles, calico and ribbons, and even a small pair of scissors which he was permitted to use. Pleased with the attention, he seemed content not to break jail. By 10 August he had a fife which he could play left- or right-handed, and had learned the fiddle; his puppets numbered twenty-four, and he took up telling fortunes with tea leaves. And it came out that he had preached for the Methodists in England. On 17 August he carved his first wooden puppet head for a Scotch sentry. Now a celebrity, he of course had to be pardoned. He seemed almost reluctant to leave, but packed up his puppets in a box and set off for St. John. Sheriff Bates saw him aboard a ship; he skipped off before it sailed, leaving the puppets.

But that was not the end of him. He got to the United States, stole some spoons from a hotel in New Haven, was apprehended in New York, and clapped into jail at the place of his depredation. There in New Haven, locked up till 12 January 1817, of course he made another puppet show, this time carving the figures out of the timber of his cell with a tool made of a piece of horseshoe whetted against the stone wall. Sheriff Bates came down to see him. It would not be too much to suppose that he made a bargain with Smith to write and sell his memoirs. The last that the Sheriff heard of him, he was confined in Simsbury Mines, Connecticut, a model prisoner. Thanks to his side line of crime, we have a detailed description of this puppeteer.

He was 5 feet 9 inches, slender, large boned, well jointed, with strong wrists and long fingers; his complexion was light but sallow; he had abundant dark brown hair that stood up in front in waves; bright, quick, and piercing light gray eyes; a prominent nose, a thin face, and scars on his right cheek and left chin. Always neat, he was brisk and deft in movement (handcuffed he could catch a mouse), liked to smoke, sang and whistled well, and played any instrument. He had the skills of blacksmith, shipwright, tailor, and farmer, "the strength of a lion and the subtlety of the devil."

With the alarums of 1812 giving way to peace both in Europe and the United States, Dominique Vitali, "recently from Italy," came to play in Washington Hall, 598 Broadway at Reade Street, New York, 9 August 1819 (New York *Post* of that date). The advertisement said, "The figures act, dance, eat, drink, smoke, and in everything imitate persons." Living likenesses indeed! These puppets offered *The Triumph of Washington*, either a transparency or a diorama, evidently as a compliment to the visited country and a fitting show for Washington Hall. They also presented a variety of "beautiful metamorphoses," the magic art of Harlequin, the Spanish fandango with castanets, an Indian dance (surely not

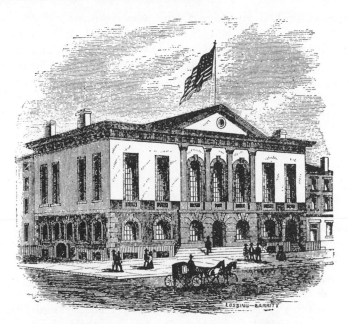

Like most theatre buildings, Washington Hall, at Broadway and Reade Street, New York, underwent many changes; this is how it looked in 1828, after alterations and repairs; presumably it was not too different when Dominique Vitali's puppets played there in 1819 or Hannington's in 1850. From a wood-engraving in the Harvard College Library theatre collection.

American), the grand conflagration of Spolito's forest (out of *Orlando Furioso*, of course), and the Grand Temple of Apollo. These were all in pantomime, no doubt, so there was no difficulty about a foreign language, though at home Vitali would have supplied dialogue, or at least recited the poetry of Ariosto for the forest fire.

In 1824, according to Hugh Lindsay's *History* (1859, reprinted Macungie, Pennsylvania, 1883), a puppeteer who may have been of German extraction was playing in Pennsylvania. "When [Miller] came to Philadelphia in the spring, to start his menagerie on a traveling tour through the country," wrote Lindsay, "I got in with Myers and Mestayer, to help on the stage as supernumerary and hand Myers his puppets while he performed with them. From him I learned how to handle puppets." Lindsay was one of the first to use a Pennsylvania-German type, Peter Honse, as a puppet; his work will again be mentioned in the chapter on German puppets.

Maelzel's mechanical chess player was presented as an automaton; Edgar Allan Poe, in his celebrated exposé of the figure, deduced that its motion was controlled by a dwarf concealed within it. If this were the case, the chess player may be classified as a puppet. And it should therefore be mentioned here that it was shown at the National Hotel, 112 Broadway, opposite the City Hall, New York, from 21 April to 5 July 1826, and that it reappeared in town every year until 1830, with intervening tours to Boston, Philadelphia, New Orleans, and Nashville. It cropped up in New York in 1834, 1840, and 1842, always astonishing spectators with its uncanny skill. The dwarf puppeteer was a champion chess player.

Another Mechanical and Picturesque Theatre appeared under the direction of Joseph LeMonier at Washington Hall, New York, for a run beginning 11 July 1826 (New York *American*, that date). It presented a diorama of the "battleground at New Orleans, with infantry and cavalry evolutions and General Jackson, with suite, commanding. Also the pantomime of Orpheus entering the dominions of Pluto in search of his wife. Likewise the metamorphosis of a female to a balloon and two misses seat themselves in the car of the balloon, which ascends." This bill was repeated until 20 July, when the Battle of Lake Champlain was added, to continue until 2 August (again the *American*). The War of 1812, like its predecessors, furnished a plenitude of noisy spectacles for the miniature stage. The lady-into-balloon trick, here specifically mentioned for the first time in America, was a natural outgrowth of the 1780 popularity of ballooning and hoop skirts. The bell skirt resembled an inverted balloon bag. Good! Why not turn it inside out over the lady's head, reveal a passenger basket where her legs should have been, pop a couple of little puppets into it (they could be her sleeves turned inside out), and have the balloon sail off? No sooner thought of than done. The lady-into-balloon transformation persists to this day. The Lano family used it; Dave Lano performed it; so did Carl Schichtl. It never fails to amaze. It is illustrated in a Viennese playbill of 1804 (partly reproduced in *Puppetry 1936*, p. 126); for Schichtl's version see *Puppetry 1935*, p. 15; if you want to know how it's managed, refer to Nelson and Hayes, *Trick Marionettes* (Detroit, 1935, p. 5).

At New Orleans, after having been repeatedly promised, a French puppet show was announced once more in *Le Passe-Tems* of 29 February 1828 by Mr. Alexis, a former actor in the Théâtre d'Orléans company, to play at the Salle St. Philippe. It was to be like the show of the ventriloquist Comte in Paris, presenting vaudeville and short comedies. Whether it eventually materialized the records do not show. A previous New Orleans puppet show had been the Spanish one in the Place d'Armes, which was terminated by the hanging of the slave Temba, back in 1771.

Device for the entertainment hall in the Chatham Museum, New York, a cut by Alexander Anderson (No. 655 in his proof scrapbooks in the New York Public Library).

The year 1828 is notable in puppet annals for the publication of the text of *Punch and Judy* in London. That very year the play was produced from this text, or an adaptation of it, in New York. But all this will be treated presently in a chapter on Punch and Judy.

Beginning with the second quarter of the nineteenth century, puppets, so long interlopers in playhouse and inn room alike, found a home in that particularly American institution, the dime museum, which gathered every attraction: drama, freak, zoo, art and science, under one roof for a single admission fee. There had been small museums with pictures and stuffed specimens in New York and Philadelphia at the end of the eighteenth century. Scudder set up a museum of this sort which moved into the New York Institute, an old almshouse to the north of the City Hall, in 1810. Natural—and mythical—curiosities were added to these collections until they grew into sizable shows. A small hall was set aside for lectures. Here puppets held forth when the lecturer was off duty. Eventually the lecture hall became a regular variety theatre. I can remember a dime museum on Woodward Avenue in Detroit, its ground floor housing vaudeville and cases of coins and arms, its second floor freaks, glass blowers, magicians, and a Punch and Judy, and its top floor a menagerie—admission to everything ten cents.

In the Spectaculum of the Chatham Museum, New York, from 8 January to 13 February 1829 (New York *American*, those dates), an unnamed puppeteer presented the merry humors of Old Jonathan and his wife, along with "Italian Fantocina, by artificial figures near the size of life," and "Punch and Judy in a superior style." Punch had been running since 22 December 1828 (the same paper). Admission was 25¢, children half-price. On 16 February (still the *American*) the show was augmented by a "representation of the sea, where vessels will pass and repass, saluting each other; also, a variety of sea animals. The scene to conclude with a view of that monster called the sea serpent." Moreover, Jonathan was carried off by Old Nick in the shape of a horse, and these "automatons" appeared: a Moorish princess, a country girl, Jack the Sailor, the Irishman with his shillelagh, tumbling by two figures, and an Italian Scaramouch who puts his body into a variety of wonderful postures, and at the same time swallows his own head. These tricks hark back to Maginnis; the puppets may have been the ones he presented.

Both Mrs. Trollope and Dickens, not looking in the right places or arriving at the right season for puppets, commented on their absence in America. Frances Trollope, speaking of American glumness in 1830 (*Domestic Manners of the Americans*, reprint, New York, 1927, p. 175), wrote, "They have no fêtes, no fairs, no merry-makings, no music in the streets, no Punch, no puppet shows." Had she seen Punch, she would of course have commented on his American vulgarity. Charles Dickens, arriving in New York in April 1842, observed, "But how quiet the streets are! . . . By day, are there no Punches, Fantoccini . . . ? No, not one." (*American Notes*, Nonesuch Press, London, 1938, p. 84.) April is apt to be rather inclement for street shows in New York, and even Dickens, a theatre enthusiast, would have disliked Punch's nasty American habit of spitting. But puppet shows and Punches there were in America, if these travelers had sought them.

About 1830, having come to America from Italy by way of Spain and England, Alberto Lano joined the Thayer circus with his puppets. More of the Lanos anon.

On 7 August 1830 a belated shadow-figure show found its way to Nashville, Tennessee; puppets were going West. A certain Mr. Dumilieu (Nashville *Republican and State Gazette*, that date) appeared at the Summer Pavilion, opposite the old theatre in Market Street, with his eight "Chinese views, or pyric and hydraulic transparencies, after the manner of those represented in the Palace Royale by the celebrated Séraphin." Séraphin's ombres chinoises were a landmark in Paris; they were even to get to New York for a brief engagement in 1865.

Had Dumilieu been part of a show that played in Louisville the month before? That indomitable traveler, Anne Royall, wrote in her *Southern Tour* (Washington, 1831, Vol. 3, p. 205 ff.), "There was no [theatrical] company at Louisville; I merely went to the theatre to aid a poor foreigner who was exhibiting the *Conflagration of Moscow*, a Mr. Maelzel, the proprietor. It was truly sublime: soldiers marching—the whole city, with its hundred steeples—the moon—the people setting fire to the city with torches—people flying in all directions—drums beating —alarm bells—and the roar of cannon. In the height of the fire a mine explodes and fills the spectators with terror. But the best of it was two little speaking figures, one a boy and the other a girl. The latter was handed to my friend Price who beau'd me to the theatre and was sitting by me. As soon as he took it in his hand it looked him in the face and said, 'Papa, papa'; and, handing it to me, the little witch said, 'Mama, mama,' as plain as I could, and set the house in a roar. The figure speaks by moving the arm."

The automaton speaking figure was a separate item on the program, not part of the *Moscow* spectacle.

This entertainment, the *Daily Louisville Public Advertiser* recorded on 30 June 1830, was scheduled to play on Wednesday, 30 June, and the following Friday; its last night in town, announced in the same paper, was on 17 July.

The *Burning of Moscow* had been seen in Philadelphia in 1830 together with Maelzel's chess player and automata of a trumpeter and oyster woman. The show was given in a hall on Fifth Street between Prune and Walnut streets, where it was seen by a little girl who grew up to write *A Book of Remembrance* by Mrs. E. D. Gillespie (Philadelphia, 1901, p. 61). The combination transparency and shadow-figure spectacle of the conflagration was the final number in the performance. "The city was before us, closely built up and the houses all aflame. We quivered at the sight; saw men, women, and children making their escape from the burning buildings with packs of clothing on their backs."

Perhaps en route to Spanish America, Señor Valencin and his company from Spain stopped off in New York to play at the New York Museum, Broadway and Anthony Street, 7-11 December 1830 (New York *Post*, those dates). They brought fantoccini, a drop scene representing the Goddess of Liberty (anticipating Bartholdi's statue), a diorama of Naples with Vesuvius in eruption and "the arrival and departing of ships of all nations and description, in full sail, firing salutes, which are returned by the castle," and "beautiful Chinese views," including temples, waterfalls, gardens, palaces, the Emperor Napoleon, Washington, and Lafayette. What was Señor Valencin doing with that diorama of Naples? Was he, like Columbus, an Italian sailing under Spanish colors?

From 4-11 January 1832 "Gray's celebrated fantoccini or mechanical figures from Vauxhall Garden, London," appeared at Peale's Museum, Broadway (New York *Post*, those dates). This company had followed the engagement of Ramo Samee, a clever Indian juggler, at Vauxhall in 1822, and had emulated him in its "celebrated Indian juggler," performing with golden balls, a trick that is among the classics of puppetry. (See Nelson and Hayes, *Trick Marionettes*, Detroit, 1935, p. 13.) It also had a puppet counterpart of Joe Grimaldi, the famous clown, who had retired in 1828. Its trick figures included "the old soldier who disengages from his body

Diagonally across Broadway from Scudder's American stood the rival Peale's Museum, long a home for puppets. On the floors above a bookshop, its quarters were modest. After a drawing in the Harvard College Library theatre collection.

the whole of his limbs" (Nelson and Hayes, p. 4, the same in operation as the come-apart skeleton; in the Viennese playbill of 1804 is pictured a come-apart hussar whose head transforms into a small figure of a girl); "the mechanical skeleton: this figure was got up during the time the celebrated Living Skeleton was in England"; Ben the sailor who danced a hornpipe; Mother Shipton, a fortune-telling Mother Goose kind of a character who generally smoked a pipe (Nelson and Hayes, p. 27), as in an old Clunn Lewis puppet in the Leopold Dor collection; and the Grand Turk (Nelson and Hayes, p. 8) who tumbled apart and turned into a whole family of little Turks. Admission to Gray's lively show was 25¢ and 12½¢. It evidently went over so well that "the amusing and wonderful exhibition of the fantoccini, or mechanical theatre of automatons," was engaged at Peale's Museum for holiday week, 24 December—1 January 1835-1836 (New York *Commercial Advertiser*, 25 December 1835).

The Mechanical Theatre of Arts was in evidence at George Colon's Hall, 98 Wooster Street, New York, 18 March—15 April 1836 (New York *Sun*, 18 March 1836). The performance started off with "the laughable pantomime scene taken from *Mother Goose*, with all the tricks and transformations." Here was a downright imitation of the big stage. Thomas

Dibdin's *Harlequin and Mother Goose,* produced in London, 29 December 1806, had changes of the principal characters into Harlequin, Columbine, Clown, and Pantaloon; of a rum puncheon into a fruit barrow; a wheel into the Goddess Fortune; benches into a steel trap and a spring gun; trees into statues; hats into bells; a letter box into a lion's head; tea chests into a heaped-up sideboard; a grocer's parlor into a farmyard; and a sideboard into a beehive stand, according to the scenario, published in C. W. Beaumont, *The History of Harlequin* (London, 1926, pp. 133-147). Such harlequinade tricks were often done quite simply. Painted flat representations of an object were toppled face down upon the stage while other painted flats were drawn up in their place. The toy paper theatre managed the tricks very neatly with cut-out cardboard properties. Victorian pantomimes liked transformations to be puns: a pear into a pair, a gooseberry fool dessert into a clown, and so forth.

After all this—if the Mechanical Theatre was true to its word in following every trick—the puppets represented Ramo Samee the Italian (*sic*) juggler, the melodrama of *The Children in the Wood* (absent from the boards since 1796), the Polander who went through a variety of astonishing tricks, and "a much admired quadrille by a group of garland dancers." Admission was only 12½¢ and the front seats were reserved for ladies. The juggler, whether Indian or Italian, had made an impression and was in the puppet bag to stay.

At the American Museum, Broadway and Ann Street (which was to become Barnum's in 1841 and go up in well-publicized flames in 1865), Maillardet's automata happened to be on exhibition when Herr Schmidt's "pyric fires, or mechanical and optical firework," together with "a grand display of the dissolvent tableaux or aerial visions," were on view in the lecture room, 3-9 January 1837 (New York *Commercial Advertiser*, 3 January).

Hanington, a showman who was to reappear in New York eight years later, offered Italian fantoccini at Peale's Museum, 25 September—14 October 1837. The notice in the *Commercial Advertiser* of the initial date gives no further details.

These piddling and repetitious variety shows were put in the dark when, at the beginning of December 1837, under the management of Bragaldi and Palmo, the latter a restaurateur, a season of musical plays and ballets was presented at the Apollo Theatre, 410 Broadway, New York, with Italian marionettes—the first instance of the use of this word in America for string-puppets. "The popular melodrama of *Blue Beard, or Female Curiosity,*" was played from 4-13 December (New York *American,* 4 December 1837). On 14 December two more numbers were added to the bill: "the tragic opera of *Bombastes Furioso,*" by William

At the Apollo the first American puppet performance of La Sylphide, *now a ballet classic, was given; for the run of the puppets the term "marionettes" was first used in America. Erected in 1837 or a little before as Euterpean Hall, by the time the Bragaldi and Palmo company arrived it was called the Apollo Saloon. Derived from a wood-engraving of Dent's Ale Vaults, 400 Broadway, in the Eno Collection, New York Public Library.*

Barnes Rhodes, first played by humans in 1810 and printed in 1813, a burlesque in the style of Henry Fielding's *Tragedy of Tragedies*; and the ballet, *La Sylphide* (*American*, that date). This, the first romantic ballet, which replaced the figures of classic antiquity in its dramatis personae by fairies, nymphs, and sprites, crystalizing the form of fairies for the whole Victorian era as creatures with ballet skirts, low décolleté, hair parted in the middle, and starry diadems, was first danced in Paris by Taglioni, 14 May 1832, and in New York by Celeste, 15 April 1835. While it was therefore familiar to New York theatregoers, it was only a little more than two years old in town, and the novelty of seeing puppets —puppets by the new name of marionettes—enact the *jeune premier* Scot and the soaring sylph must have been piquant to no small degree.

On 20 December (according to the *American*) *Blue Beard* gave way to *The Swiss Cottage, or Why Don't She Marry*? On 27 and 28 December the bill was made up of *The Forty Thieves*, "a grand coronation dance [Victoria had been crowned 28 June] in imitation of the style of Lecomte, Augusta, and Celeste," and *La Sylphide*. On 29 December *The Swiss Cottage* and *Bombastes Furioso* were back with the ballet. On 31 January 1838 there was inaugurated, "with entire new scenery, dresses, music, properties, etc., the grand spectacle of *Lurline, or the Revolt of the Naiades*;" *La Sylphide* concluded the fay, aerial entertainment, which ran until 10 February, when the company was heard of no more in New York. (The *American* affords these data.)

These puppets were the first to gain critical acclaim in the papers in America, albeit the constant warmth of approval (which was shown later companies in the 1870's as well) suggests the pen of the press agent. In the New York *Mirror* of 16 December 1837 the show was called "the greatest curiosity ever offered the American publick . . . the whole of the drama went off with considerable *éclat* . . . the machinery was perfect . . . the coryphées drew down batteries of applause. . . . Some of the first families of New York were present, and we are fully convinced that this little mechanical theatre will become the resort of beauty and fashion during the winter." This repertory formed an oasis in the desert of trick fantoccini.

Bragaldi was the manager who had brought the troupe from Italy, recruiting it, if he followed the methods that were advertised in the London *Illustrated News* of 10 January 1852, when he took a similar company to England, from "the theatres of Naples, Rome, Genoa, &c." That is, he chose the best puppeteers from the permanent puppet theatres in those cities, with perhaps a few of the singers and musicians who had worked with them. Italy was full of established puppet theatres, accustomed to present ambitious programs of opera and ballet. Their puppeteers were well trained, for they were generally scions of puppeteering families and had operated puppets from a childhood apprenticeship. The musicians in such theatres may not have been maestros and prima donnas— spectacular talent was brought by the opera houses—but they were disciplined in a collaborative performance, and may have included some fresh young voices and hardy old fiddlers who knew the operatic repertory by heart. Since the puppeteers were not expected to sing or speak lines, but took their cues from the readers and music, the nucleus of the voices could be augmented by English ones, trained to synchronize in delivering the lines of the English plays. The troupe was necessarily large, making for a grateful degree of polish. Yet New York admission prices were only 50¢ and 25¢ for children.

For his London season in 1852, Bragaldi was to form a partnership with Simpson and launch a successful six-months' season, presenting *Bombastes Furioso* as an opening piece on 12 January, and following with *The Swiss Cottage* (called *The Chalet* later in the year, said the London *Illustrated News* of 6 December) in the third month of the run. The fluidity with which puppet companies combined and split was indicated by another troupe, the "Ebony Minstrels," joining the Italians during their London engagement, leaving them for three weeks, and coming back to play with them again until they quit England. Bragaldi's earlier "hit" in New York makes his London acclaim understandable. In the British capital he was content to let Simpson's name alone be connected with the company, perhaps because Simpson was known to Londoners as the lessee of the playhouse in Adelaide Street where the puppets appeared. But on the tour of the English provinces that followed, his name emerged.

To return to New York, during the week of 1 July 1838 there were "Italian fantoccini, or mechanical theatre," at Peale's Museum (New York *Commercial Advertiser*, 5 July). The museum had the same, or other Italian fantoccini from 26 February—4 May 1839 (the same paper for those dates). The program probably varied somewhat from week to week, but had a standard basis of trick puppets. Fantoccini were an expected part of the museum.

From a random note in Isaac J. Greenwood's *The Circus* (2nd ed., New York, 1909, p. 135), it may be learned that Dan Rice, later to be known as "king of the clowns" and a circus manager, got his first job in a traveling puppet show near Reading, Pennsylvania, in 1840—was this Hugh Lindsay's company?—at $4 a week. Considering the value of money in those days, this was not ungenerous for the work of a novice puppeteer.

At the American Museum, New York, from 30 March to 4 April 1840 (as noted by the *Commercial Advertiser* of the initial date), appeared the "grand Italian fantoccini, the most surprising exhibition of animated mechanism ever adapted to excite a pleasing interest among juvenile visitors, and cannot fail to give effect to the risable faculties of an adult" —a statement in Barnumesque hyperbole without Barnumesque felicity.

Barnum was, however, manager of the American Vauxhall Gardens, an imitation of London's, when on 21 July 1840 they numbered among their entertainments the "grand Italian fantocinna, which has been the theme of unusual admiration and applause throughout Europe"—weak puffery, if Barnum wrote it. (The notice appeared in the New York *Post* of that date.) Vauxhall Gardens were on the northern outskirts of town; one drove out Broadway to reach them from the west, or the Bowery from the east. Here on ground higher than that at the foot of Manhattan one could get cool evening breezes and sniff the country greenery after the dusty heat of town. The Gardens were between Astor Place and Great Jones Street, Fourth Avenue and Broadway; when Lafayette Place was cut through it bisected them. Were all these Italian fantoccini the same ones? It seems likely.

On 16 November 1840, again at the American Museum (just before Barnum took it over), continuing to the last day of December, the evening's entertainment concluded with "Mr. Macezel's beautiful and unrivalled mechanical figures," according to the *Post*—Maelzel's automata, of course, and one of them almost a puppet if the chess player was there.

At another summer garden, the Colonnade, Brooklyn Heights (New

Barnum's American Museum, thanks to the ballyhoo of the great showman, remains vivid in memory. It carried on the tradition of puppets among an assortment of attractions. Standing at Broadway and Ann Street, it was a couple of blocks south of Peale's and around the corner from the Park Theatre. From a drawing after a contemporary print.

Yorkers took the Wall Street ferry to get there), T. White had first place on the bill of 1 and 2 July 1841 "with his elegant fantoccini so highly spoken of in French and English papers," said the New York *Herald* of those dates. "For particulars of his performance see small bills." Had one of these fragile handbills survived we might know which of the classic tricks his puppets performed. White's earlier transoceanic shows have not been traced.

On 22 December 1841 Italian fantoccini once more began an engagement at the American Museum (New York *Post* of that date), which Barnum took over five days later, coming in on their run and seeing that they were an established Christmas-week feature. In his autobiography, *Struggles and Triumphs* (New York reprint, 1927, Vol. 1, p. 195), he called them "exceedingly successful"—and this was genuine praise, for there was no immediate need of beating the drum in their behalf when he wrote. On big holidays, the showman recounted, he put on as many as a dozen shows in his lecture hall. Though each number must have been cut pretty short, that would have been hard work for the puppeteers.

In the fall of 1843 a puppeteer variously spelled Vinaldi, Rinaldi, and Grimaldi, was active in the museums. As Vinaldi he showed his "far famed mechanical figures" at the American Museum, 4-6 September (New York *Daily Tribune*). As Signor Rinaldi he made his "mechanical figures go through their laughable performances performing many feats never executed by a human being,"—not even such a human being as Oliver Goldsmith—at Peale's Museum, 23-27 October (as noted in the same paper of those dates). As Mr. Grimaldi he introduced his "automaton performers" in the drama of Punch and Judy, also at Peale's, on the customary Christmas week, 25-30 December (again the *Daily Tribune*).

Every afternoon and evening of the week of 29 March 1844, Peale's Museum presented "Signor Montivedo with his grand mechanical exhibition of nine performers" (*Daily Tribune* of those dates). Admission was a shilling, or 12½¢, nearly the same as that for the later dime museums.

At the Elysian Fields, a plaisance in Hoboken (one took the ferry across the North River from Manhattan), Signor Garcia showed, from 21-25 July 1844, said the New York *Herald*, his "laughable and pleasing Italian fantoccini, representing life." The characters were Monsieur Moulette the Polander, Scaramouch or Somebody-Nobody (evidently a contortionist), Jack Junk who danced a hornpipe, Signor Ballasandra the chain balancer, Monsieur Blanc the Diamond of Dancers, the Grand Turk who transformed himself into a balloon (instead of coming apart in the proper way into a swarm of little Turks), Conrad Hassan the ball tosser, a *pas de deux* by Monsieur de Stella and Madame Jordan, and as a finale a grotesque chase of a clown after a butterfly. Pleasant diversion for the Elysian Fields!

For the week of 16 September 1844 Barnum presented "automatons from Paris, including a superb mechanical rope-dancer and juggler," at his museum (New York *Daily Tribune*).

Starting on Christmas Day, 1845, at the building previously known as Peale's Museum, appeared Hannington's Grand Theatre of Arts, a moonlight view of Melton Abbey, a thrilling representation of a storm and shipwreck, a magnificent fairy grotto with a rising palace of jewels, and a splendid display of Chinese artificial fireworks, as well as "Italian fantoccini by Signor Montano, including the Sable Serenaders," who entertained the company with several melodies of the sunny South (New York *Herald*, 25 December). Together with this somewhat old-fashioned show of transparencies and dioramas is the first puppet Negro minstrelsy

The Philadelphia Museum on Chestnut Street, a counterpart of New York institutions, housed fantoccini and perhaps Punch too. It was in an arcade running to the next street. After a drawing by C. Burton, 1831, published by L. T. Hinton and Simpkin & Marshall, London.

I have found on record. It was, of course, a copy of the big-stage minstrel show, then in its first burst of popularity. The genre was ready made for puppets with its stylized blackface, its exaggerated costumes, its line-up of seated singers, and its specialty numbers for which they were a background.

For the two weeks of 23 February—5 March 1846, "les fantocinis italiennes, or life [*sic*] moving figures," played at the Philadelphia Museum and Gallery of Fine Arts on Chestnut Street, coming after a performance of *The Fairy Sibyl, or the Lady Magician*. This is recorded in the Philadelphia *Public Ledger* of these dates. The same paper for 7 December 1847 heralds the coming to Temperance Hall, Third Street below Green, on 9 December, of Monsieur Metayer, the famous ventriloquist, with "nine speaking automata," probably the dummies into which he threw his voice. The Italian fantoccini of 1846, to judge by the near-English of the announcement, were in the hands of a Frenchman.

For the week of 4 October 1847 at his American Museum, Barnum "engaged for the especial amusement of the juvenile portion of General Tom Thumb's friends, Signor Vito's Fantoccini, or dancing figures, the most beautiful and interesting ever seen in America." Superlative, naturally! The New York *Daily Tribune* of 5 October says that there were shows at 11:30 A.M. and 3:00 and 7:30 P.M. The famous midget shared the bill with puppets that may have been his very size. "Interesting" had supplanted the tired, overworked, eighteenth-century word "curious" as a modifier of "puppet"—and has now, in the twentieth century, become equally worn itself.

At Washington Hall, on Broadway, Hannington reappeared on 1 June 1850 (New York *Herald* of that date) with his "beautiful moving dioramas" of the creation of the world, the ruins of Tintern Abbey, the River Rhine, the deluge, the Arctic region, and the "highly amusing Italian fantoccini, or mechanical figures. N.B. This is an exciting exhibition and differs from all panoramic displays from its truly life-like appearance imparted by the aid of the mechanism, painting, and optics." Were audiences growing a little weary of this sort of thing, that they had to be assured it was exciting?

It is here inserted, for the chronological record, that a German-language puppet show, calling itself the "erstes deutsches Marionetten-Theatre in Amerika," played at another Washington Hall, this one at the Bowery and Hester Street, New York, on 26 October 1852; the drama was *Don Carlos*. It was the first of a number of German performances for immigrants from the Rhineland, performances that were to continue through the next sixty years; they must be distinguished from the Pennsylvania-German puppet shows, which were mostly in English because the showmen who, from the time of Hugh Lindsay, wandered through Pennsylvania's German-settled regions were not themselves of the local stock.

Faithful to their custom of arriving among the foremost, puppets got to California at the very beginning of the gold rush. A Punch and Judy show played at Sandy Bar, near San Francisco, in a rough building of pine poles covered with canvas, about 1850; it will be described more fully in the next chapter. And a Chinese show, not unlike the rod-puppet ones still to be seen in 1930 in the streets of Peiping and described by Benjamin March in *Puppetry 1930* (Detroit, pp. 36-42), cropped up one August afternoon in Portsmouth Plaza, San Francisco, in 1853. Here were puppets converging from West and East! The Chinese show was humorously described at considerable length in the *Daily Alta California* of 2 September 1853; this passage is quoted *in toto* in George R. MacMinn, *The Theatre of the Golden Era in California* (Caldwell, Idaho, 1941, pp. 493-495).

"About ten minutes past two Tuesday afternoon," begins the anonymous reporter, "a Celestial planted himself in the middle of the Plaza and commenced beating a gong. Another by his side had an ordinary table and upon this was a light framework, 3 or 4 feet high, lined with blue cotton and surmounted by a little stage, provided on one side with curtains.

"In precisely one minute and 13 seconds after the first beating of the gong, 60 persons had assembled about the table. This select party increased in five minutes to number at least 215 men and children, so that by 2¼ the Plaza, from being a cleared space, became a scene of excitement to which persons were hurrying from all sides, and the more they came the more they wondered what they were coming for.

"Presently the performance commenced. A celesial but by no means heavenly symphony, sounding like a penny trumpet and a hoarse tin pan, was struck up inside the little framework on the table, though the space

This is not the kind of a Chinese puppet show that was seen in Portsmouth Plaza, but the gong, table, and puppeteer are very like. After a lithograph published by Mlle. Formentin, Paris, from a drawing by Schaal, 1825. This Chinese street showman pulls the strings to jiggle his music-box figures while calmly smoking his pipe.

inside was but little more than 3 feet cubic. After the teeth of the crowd had been sufficiently set on edge, and their feelings had been properly worked up by the admirable squeaking and rattling of the music, a very grave and reverend little Chinese automaton stepped upon the stage from behind the curtains, and made his reverences to the crowd with all the gravity and politeness of a Chinese mandarin; and then addressed the assembled company in excellent Chinese, in a very small voice. He tells them that they are about to behold a Chinese puppet show, for their instruction and amusement, and for the benefit of the manager, if they (the crowd) shall vouchsafe anything to the hat when passed around. The morals of this performance, he says, are unexceptionable, being in strictest accordance with the revered precepts of Confucius. The scene about to be presented will show to the old, symbolically if not literally, a part of life as they have seen it, and to the young it will teach how they should live. The subject is the pursuit of love under difficulties, and the moral that true love and dauntless energy must succeed at last. He then retires and the play commences."

Now the action is minutely described. Fuh, the heroine, with a voice like the pouring of a liquid from a small-necked bottle, is set upon and eaten by a monster. Chang, who loves her, slays the beast like a celestial St. George, but overcome with grief for his beloved, he "determines to get her remains and give them a Christian burial." Thereupon he pulls her feet-first from the dragon's maw, restores her to life, marries her, and is made a mandarin by her grateful father. "The pantomime of the performance," the reporter continues, "was very intelligible and cleverly managed, and a continued conversation is kept up that adds a great deal to the interest of the play for those who understand Chinese. Between the scenes the infernal music is never omitted. The energy of the performance never permits the interest to flag, and frequently it 'brought down the house.' For instance, when the monster had swallowed Fuh and came to the edge of the stage and smacked his lips over the delicious morsel, he was rapturously applauded. The crowd was very anxious to see the whole performance, and several lifted boys up so that they could see the stage. This, however, shut off the view for those at a distance and Chang several times turned upon the intruders with his trident, and shook it at them to the great amusement of the audience. When the performance was closed the plate was passed round, but the majority seemed to think that a Chinaman had no right to expect pay for furnishing fun."

While round puppets from the East have always been something of a rarity in America, Oriental shadow-figures have been frequent visitors, either by the indirect route from Europe or directly across the Pacific from Cathay.

From 19-26 November 1855 Signor Gallavotti's Italian marionettes—they were called marionettes and not fantoccini—played at the Adelphi Theatre, Dupont Street near Clay, San Francisco (*Daily Alta California* for those dates). They enacted "an elegant comedy" and appeared on a bill with views of the Crimean War. The paper remarked, on 21 November, "The exhibition is a peculiar one in California, and cannot fail to interest and please the curious." "Interest" and "curious" together! In McCabe's *Journal*, preserved in the Sutro Library, this show was noted as the first exhibition of Italian marionettes in California; more important, it states, "D. C. Anderson, W. Barry, and Mrs. J. B. Booth doing the speaking." American actors were of course brought in to read the lines—and one of them was the mother of the man who was to shoot Lincoln a decade later.

The Pacific Museum, San Francisco, added to its variety of entertainments on 29 June 1857 (San Francisco *Daily Evening Bulletin* for that date), "an exhibition of marionettes or puppets." The newspaper commented, "The Museum seem [*sic*] determined to keep up with the times." This amusement hall offered the marionette show of *The Children in the Woods, The Sea Fight between the Constitution and the Guerrière*, and other pieces on 7 November of that year (says the *Daily Evening Bulletin*); two days later it was also offering *Perry's Victory on Lake Erie*; and the show of 18 November is not specified. These naval spectacles of a war-before-last may have been a little hoary, but perhaps they pleased the entertainment-hungry Californians.

Oliver Lano, whose work will be chronicled presently, joined the Dan Rice circus (back East) in 1856. By then puppets were a recognized part of the traveling hippodrome under canvas. During the Civil War he was to play in army camps on both sides, for North and South impartially.

In the darkness of a Séraphin shadow-figure show accidents could happen—a soldier might sit down beside an attractive nursemaid and squash a child! This incident during a performance of Puss in Boots *was drawn by Eugene Fouet, or Forest, or whatever his name was, and printed by the Bertauts lithographic shop about 1850.*

There were a few more shows before the outbreak of hostilities restricted the puppet gambit. Thiodon's Mechanical Theatre of Art (perhaps there was something of puppetry about it) came over from Southampton to play at Barnum's American Museum 14 August—November 1858; it was at Mozart Hall 18 October 1859; Barnum mentions it in Chapter 33 of his *Struggles and Triumphs*. Jeronelle's Italian fantoccini and a Punch and Judy show ran for the week of 18 July 1859 at an uptown picnic place on Manhattan, Jones' Wood (New York *Herald*, 15 July). And there were other Punch and Judies. But it was not until the Civil War was over and the United States began to recover from mourning for Lincoln that puppets launched forth again. Then they were to enjoy two decades of ubiquitous activity and popularity.

Its arrival badly timed, one of the most important companies since Bragaldi's came to the Stuyvesant Institute, 659 Broadway, New York, on 19 June 1865. It was the Théâtre Séraphin from Paris, perhaps under the management of Mme Paul Royer. Its repertory (as recorded in the New York *Herald* of 18 June) consisted of "grand fairy extravaganzas, grand ballet, and brilliant harlequinades." The show began with an explanatory address by Mr. Punch; after a musical interlude, *Beauty and the Beast* was presented. There were changes of program, said the *Herald*, on 25 June and 2 July, although the plays were not specified. The July bill consisted of a "new musical burlesque, new grand ballets, new transformations, trick figures of life-like quality, and new and wonderous effects. Notice: The marionette company can be engaged for private family sources."

This visit to America has not been included in the brief published history of the theatre, *Feu Séraphin: Histoire de ce spectacle* (Lyon, 1875). Séraphin, founder of the theatre, started out with shadow-figures (then at their fountainhead of fashion) and was patronized by the family of Louis XVI at Versailles. Moving to Paris, he died in 1800 and was succeeded by a nephew who added string-puppets to the show and maintained the theatre to the time of his own death in 1844. Paul Royer, a son-in-law of this nephew, inherited the theatre. Being energetic, he moved it from the cramped quarters in the Palais Royal, where it had been housed for over half a century, to a larger room in the Boulevard Montmartre and gave it a new lease on life by producing spectacular pieces with noteworthy scenery, costumes, and music. He died in 1859 and his widow and partner continued the theatre with diminishing success. It was during the period of their struggles to recoup the fortunes of the theatre that the trip to America was undertaken.

But how were Parisians to know that June in New York is too hot for theatregoing; how were they to divine that Lincoln would be assassinated two months before their opening date? The ill-starred run lasted only till 5 July. Returning to Paris poorer than it had started out, the theatre limped along for a few more seasons and closed its doors forever on 15 August 1870, just before the city was to suffer siege and famine.

Beauty and the Beast, by Maillé de Marencourt, was one of the repertory of sixty-five plays done with string-puppets by the theatre; it also had ninety-five shadow-figure plays and a great number of *divertissements* and tricks such as the Italian fantoccini performed; probably some had been brought to New York, as they were understandable to audiences of all tongues. Recognizable as common to the fund of fan-

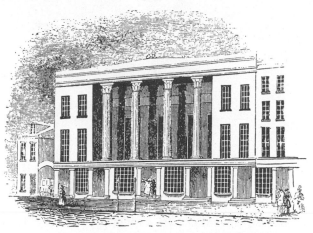

Stuyvesant Institute, 659 Broadway, north of Bleecker Street, was a monumental granite Greek revival building which served a variety of uses; it contained three halls which could be used for lectures or entertainments. At the time this wood-engraving appeared in A Picture of New York in 1846, *by Edward Ruggles (C. S. Francis & Co., New York, 1846, opposite p. 55), it was occupied by the University Medical School; the New-York Historical Society also was lodged in it for a while. The Séraphin shadow figures must have played in one of the halls.*

toccini were these Séraphin tricks: the Five-in-One (a sort of Grand Turk), Mère Gigogne (a female counterpart, also prone to decompose into progeny), the lady-into-balloon, Chinese dancers, quadrille dancers, Jack Tar of the hornpipe, and Polichinelle in a butterfly chase.

Much of the stock of this theatre, puppets, shadow-figures, manuscripts, and playbills, was kept together, passing into the possession of Arthur Maury, director of the New Séraphin Theatre, Passage de l'Opéra, Paris, about 1902. After his death it was dispersed by auction in 1908. (The puppet items from the catalogue were listed in *Puppetry 1939*, Detroit, pp. 55-56.) Some of the shadow-figures and musical parts for orchestra are now in the collection of the Cooper Union Museum for the Arts of Decoration, not too far from the site of Stuyvesant Hall.

Trick puppets and variety programs are perennial in their fascination. But without the more sustained dramatic matter that makes puppetry memorable they are apt to be dismissed as trifling. A trick puppet well operated requires a skillful puppeteer and a precisely adjusted mechanism; it is one of the most difficult things in the puppet theatre. A smoothly accomplished trick, taken for granted by children, marveled at by grownups, is often forgotten as soon as it is done. A stirring drama leaves its effect and the puppets enacting it are described by old men to their grandchildren.

IX

Punch and Judy

It is sometimes supposed that Punch originated in dim antiquity. True, ancient figurines of hook-nosed hunchbacks have been found in Italy, but this proves only that certain comic types are recurrent. Pulcinella (perhaps from *pulcina*, "little chicken," because of the cockerel-like beak, squawk, and strut he affects) was first given a part in the scenario, *La Trappolaria*, by J. B. della Porta (1538-1615), and gained prominence about 1600 from Silvio Fiorillo's playing of the character. He rapidly won a large public, and like public figures today, was made into a puppet. While human Punches have continued to perform, their puppet parallels have put them in the shade.

Polichinelle is found as the leading character in a puppet theatre in France in 1649; he is supposed to have written the *Lettre de Polichinelle à Jules Mazarin* which was published as a pamphlet in Paris that year. Coming to London in 1662—Pepys saw him there on 9 May—he played before Charles II at Whitehall on 8 October and was duly given a medal worth £25 as a reward, as the Lord Chamberlain's records attest. He was the tail that wagged many a puppet show, gaining prestige from the wit of Powell and other showmen. Only in the twentieth century have Punch and Judy shows grown banal through uninventive repetition.

Punch appeared in the news in America when the Virginia *Gazette* of 22 December 1738 printed an item about his destruction by a dog at Southwark Fair. He carried on a merry dialogue with his wife Joan in a 1742 Philadelphia show. As a string-puppet he appeared in a considerable repertory of plays throughout the eighteenth century. There is no certainty of when he assumed hand-puppet form in America. As Captain Punch in Hoyt's Dartmouth show of about 1800 he was certainly a hand-puppet and a naturalized New Englander, too.

But when "Mr. Mathews of the Surrey Theatre and Royal Gardens, Vauxhall," presented "the much celebrated and highly amusing tragical comedy and comical tragedy of Punchinello, or *Punch and Judy*," at the Park Theatre, opposite City Hall Park, New York, 4-9 September 1828 (New York *American* for those dates), the hand-puppet play in which Punch cudgels his triumphant swath over every obstacle, a play

116

Two views of an Italian Punch booth with peep holes below the stage opening, Rome,
1809 and 1815. Reduced details from etchings by Pinelli.

known by its classic text as arranged by J. P. Collier, was introduced
to America. Mathews evidently availed himself of this text because his
announcement used the very words from its title page. He may have
got hold of the first pirated American edition that was rushed out in
1828; but if he had just come from England it is more likely that he
would have brought an authentic edition with him; if he had the first
edition (the second was better, being more complete) he could even
have picked up a copy from S. Prowett, the publisher, in December 1827
(coming out at the end of the year, it was dated 1828). All these
bibliographical points have been set down, by the way, in my article,
"The Collier-Cruikshank Punch and Judy," in *The Colophon* (N.S., Vol.
1, pp. 371-387).

A complete copy of the first American edition of the play has just
come to light. Hitherto only the imperfect Harvard College Library

THEATRE.

First Appearance in America of

☞ *Mr. Mathews.*

From the Surry Theatre and Royal Gardens Vauxhall London who will introduce in the highly popular Burletta of

PARIS AND LONDON,

The Tragical Comedy or Comical Tragedy of

☞ **Punchinello,**

OR

Punch and Judy.

As performed at the different Theatres in Europe. and at the Masquerades, Italian Opera House, London.

The first advertisement for Punch and Judy in an American paper. From the New York American, 4 September 1828. The theatre was the Park. Original 2⅜ inches wide.

copy was known; this consisted of six leaves and lacked the frontispiece. When the popularity of the Collier-Cruikshank book was attested by brisk sales in London, copies of it were rushed to New York by clipper ship. There were no international copyright laws and the first to come out with an American edition was the first to profit. Because the Collier introduction and notes were dropped and certain scenes cut, and only two of Cruikshank's small vignettes were copied, Neal & Mackenzie (a canny, Scotch-sounding firm) were undoubtedly first in the field. They issued a 6x3½ inch booklet with two twelve-page signatures and a separate frontispiece leaf, all sides stitched together with a bit of thread in unprinted gray paper covers—at least in the copy that is before me.

The frontispiece, an etching, shows Punch seizing the Devil by the tail and belaboring him with a stick, with Punch and Judy imbibing hot punch in a scene below it. Why were these two small spots, wood-engraved tailpieces in the London edition, chosen rather than the head of Punch, a more impressive frontispiece subject, which faced the original title page, for reproduction? Did the etcher, who was probably D. C. Johnston, prefer their scale for a little chapbook? Or did he have only the letterpress part of the English book to work from, without its etched plates? As the agents who supplied American pirates were sometimes inside workers who had access to sheets before they were bound, the transference may have been effected by a nervous thief who overlooked the plates, or by one too much in a hurry to wait for them.

S. King, another New York publisher, seeing that the Neal & Mackenzie edition lacked so much, found a complete copy of the book and turned out a reasonable facsimile of it. It may have taken some months before this edition was ready; no date appears on it, committing it to ulteriority. There were even copies with colored plates, evidence of leisurely going. S. King could not have sold out this edition (something must be said for firstcomers), for it was turned over to G. G. Sickels, who reissued it with his name on the title page, also without a date.

"All the great theatrical stars from Europe," wrote Edward Ruggles in A Picture of New York in 1846, "make their first appearance here. The fact of coming from this theatre stamps them at once with character." New York's best theatre in 1828 was just the right size for puppets. The interior of the Park Theatre with Charles Matthews (not the Punch man) and Ellen Johnson on the stage and a gathering of distinguished citizens in the auditorium. A drawing in the Harvard College Library theatre collection after a watercolor by John Searle in the New-York Historical Society. Having burned in 1820, the Park was rebuilt in 1821 (this view was drawn 7 November 1822), to be burned again in 1848.

THE

TRAGICAL COMEDY,

OR

COMICAL TRAGEDY,

OF

PUNCH AND JUDY.

EXTRACTED FROM THE LONDON EDITION.

With a design, by G. Cruikshank.

Pub.d by Neal & Mackenzie 4 Chamber S.t N.Y.

NEW-YORK.

Neal & Mackenzie.

at the Circulating Library, and Dramatic Repository,
4 Chambers-Street,
And 201 Chestnut-Street,
Philadelphia.
1828.

From a perfect copy of the first American edition of Punch and Judy.

Even the Neal & Mackenzie edition suffered vicissitudes. Sheets must have remained on hand unsold, for they were acquired by Elton & Perkins of 323 Broadway and 65 Canal Street, and issued at 12½ cents with an imprinted wrapper but with the old title page. On this wrapper the title was *Punch and Judy, a Whimsically Queer, Tragically Operatical Comedi* [*sic*], by "Rev. J. Humbug'em." On the back of the wrapper is a cut of a dandy who says, "You want Comic songs, eh! go to Elton's Canal Street, that's all." A copy of the play in this state is in the Grosvenor Library, Buffalo, New York.

Before 1828 Punch's adventures had followed no set pattern. In a children's book, *Pug's Visit to Mr. Punch,* published by William Charles

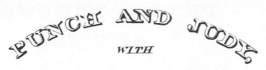

PUNCH AND JUDY

WITH

ILLUSTRATIONS

DESIGNED BY

GEORGE CRUIKSHANK.

ACCOMPANIED BY THE DIALOGUE OF THE PUPPET-SHOW,
AN ACCOUNT OF ITS ORIGIN, AND OF PUPPET-PLAYS
IN ENGLAND.

From the first London Edition

NEW YORK.

Published by S. King

The title page of the S. King edition, 1828 or shortly thereafter, is engraved.

in Philadelphia, 1821, no detail of the familiar plot appears: Punch
sends his dog Towser to invite Pug, a monkey, to "have supper and
crack a good bottle or two." Punch's wife (without a name) prepares
a jolly spread and, after the repast, she has to put Pug to bed. While
Mr. and Mrs. Punch are asleep, Pug dresses himself in Punch's clothes.
Mrs. Punch is so charmed with him in them that she runs away with
him, leaving Punch still asleep. When he wakes to find himself alone,
he rushes to Pug's house and finds his wife dancing a minuet with the

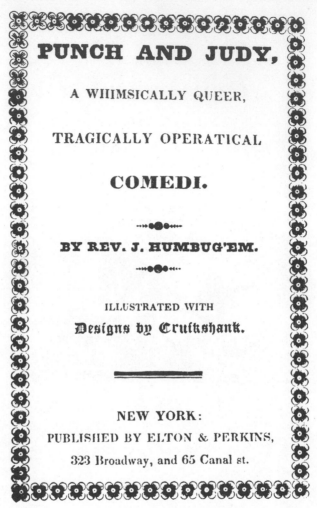

The cover on the reissue of Neal & Mackenzie's edition.

monkey. But in later children's books about Punch, of which there are scores, the Collier version of the story is repeatedly followed.

Punch's wife was known as Joan until the end of the eighteenth century. A Covent Garden Theatre playbill of 11 April 1798 includes a "modern dance by Punch and Joan." Sir Walter Scott writes of Punch and Joan in 1818 in *The Bride of Lammermoor* (in Chapter 1, made a preliminary chapter in the 1830 and later editions). But in *The Sketch Book* of Geoffrey Crayon, Esq.—nom de plume of Washington Irving—

(2nd ed., New York, 1820), it is said that Master Simon could imitate Punch and Judy. And in *The English Spy*, by Bernard Blackmantle (London, 1826), the couple is also Punch and Judy (Vol. 2, p. 73). It appears that Collier's text may have helped to crystalize them so.

The dialogue for the play was taken, Collier stated, from the performance of Piccini, an Italian showman in London; how much polishing and augmenting is from the editor's hand one can only guess. But in its printed form the play became standard. A few new characters were added by certain performers; topical allusions were worked in; but the basis of almost every Punch and Judy show from 1828 to this day is in this text. By reading it one may find more or less what Mathews played at the Park Theatre.

Seven London reprints (called "editions") appeared during the nineteenth century. O. B. Hubbard brought out an almost original version at Lawrence, Massachusetts, in 1874. Thomas A. M. Ward published an adaptation at Janesville, Wisconsin, in 1874; W. J. Judd another in New York in 1879. While the Collier-Cruikshank book was hardly intended for an acting script, it has always been available in one form or another and has helped many a showman.

From the Park Theatre, usually the home of human actors in legitimate drama, Mathews took his Punch and Judy further up the street to the Chatham Museum, Park Row between Duane and Worth streets, New York, where he played on 27 September 1828 (New York *Post* of that date). In the Spectaculum of the same Museum, on 22-30 December of that year (New York *American* for those dates), Mr. Henry, "lately from Europe," proffered the "comic, laughable scene, Punch and Judy, in a style far superior to any exhibited in this city." Here was competition for Mathews! During the week of 2-7 January 1829, Mr. Henry's Punch played on at the Spectaculum (New York *American*); and though the showman is not mentioned thereafter, it is likely that the same Punch and Judy stayed on through 16 February and even 14 April (as reported in the *American*).

For the benefit of the Fire Department, G. W. Hoyt, perhaps the son of Richard Hoyt of the Dartmouth show, gave Punch and Judy at Haworth's Institute, Brooklyn, 19 February 1838 (Brooklyn *Star* of that date). It will be seen that Barnum's statement, in his *Struggles and Triumphs* (New York reprint, 1927, Vol. 1, p. 195), that he brought the first English Punch and Judy to the United States to his American Museum, is mistaken.

During Christmas week, 1843, Grimaldi—or Rinaldi or Vinaldi— played "the laughable farce of Punch and Judy" at Peale's Museum. The

THE TRAGICAL ACTS,

OR COMICAL TRAGEDIES

OF

PUNCH AND JUDY,

WITH TWENTY-THREE ILLUSTRATIONS,

FROM ORIGINALS BY

GEORGE CRUIKSHANK

AND OTHER PLATES,

ACCOMPANIED BY THE DIALOGUE OF THE PUPPET-SHOW, AN ACCOUNT OF ITS
ORIGIN, AND OF PUPPET-PLAYS IN ITALY, ENGLAND AND AMERICA,
WITH INSTRUCTIONS CONCERNING THE CHOICE, SELECTION
AND ACTING OF THE PUPPETS.

BY PROF. W. J. JUDD.

NEW YORK:
HAPPY HOURS COMPANY, PUBLISHERS,
No. 5 BEEKMAN STREET.

Judd, a Punch man and puppet maker, brought out an edition of the classic in 1879, adding some speculations of his own to Collier's imaginative history of Punch. Whenever the text of Punch and Judy seemed about to become hard to get, someone obliged by reprinting it. Its bibliography is therefore long and not a little puzzling.

New York *Daily Tribune* for 25-30 December goes on, "The mirth and fun which this play produces for the children of all ages is immense. Punch is a real fighter; he beats the Negro, kicks the Doctor out of doors, knocks down the Constable, whips his own dear Judy, hangs the Hangman, and is finally carried off by Old Nick." Except for the outcome of this last encounter, the version tallies with Collier's, wherein Punch, it will be recalled, triumphs over even the devil.

In pre-Collier forms of the play Punch sometimes does escape his just reward, as does Casper in the German puppet play of *Faust*. A ballad, dating supposedly from the 1790's, is quoted by Collier in the introduction to the text of *Punch and Judy*—if "quoted" is the right term for something he probably wrote himself; he started out on his career of literary forgery in a small way, inventing points in the history of puppets—and in it Punch puts an end to the Prince of Darkness:

> The Devil with his pitch-fork fought,
> While Punch had but a stick, sir,
> But killed the Devil, as he ought,
> Huzza! there's no Old Nick, sir.

Advertisement by a Philadelphia lawyer who was also a puppeteer, from his edition of Punch and Judy, *printed at Janesville, Wisconsin, 1874. This edition has an original text, instructions for performing, and advertisements of a rival Punch man, Signor Blitz of 1831 Wallace Street, and of George Doll & Company, 10 North 6 Street, F. Eberhardt, 928 Arch Street, and G. A. Schwarz, 1006 Chestnut Street, all in Philadelphia, who sold Punch and Judy puppets and stages.*

In an article purporting to come from the London *Morning Chronicle* of 22 September 1813 (Collier was dramatic critic on the paper) an instance is cited, in a version of the Punch play, of Punch killing not the Devil, but Death. To Dr. Johnson, who laughed at the killing of the ghost in Fielding's *Tragedy of Tragedies*, this anomaly might have been funny. But Punch's worsting the Devil, after a sinful career as assiduous as Faust's or Don Juan's, was not only funny in its surprise, but rather satisfactory in a vicarious way to audiences of the early nineteenth century.

The Collier plot bears a relation to medieval morality plays and, indeed, to American gangster movies of the 1930's. In a fit of temper Punch commits a murder that he must cover by a succession of further killings; finally he is confronted by the Devil. Eugene O'Neill's *Emperor Jones* has a gripping scenario of similar pattern. Film producers would not dare to let a gangster go unpunished. Puppeteers faced this delicate situation boldly. To satisfy morality, they knew, Punch should be sent to hell. But with insight worthy of a later day, they knew that an audience identified itself with Punch, not his victims, and had a glorious time helping him whack. It would have thrown cold water over the audience after this to have a "proper" ending and show that the audience had been in the wrong. As the nineteenth century went on and Punch and Judy were dressed in clean pinafores for parlor and Sunday school presentation, Punch no longer went his wicked way with impunity. At the same time it became indelicate for the devil to appear at all. Thus it became necessary for Nemesis to overtake Punch in the form of a crocodile, which gobbled up Punch's stick and then Punch himself. Luckily for Victorian parents, they did not foresee what Freudians would have made of this; eager for "oral aggression," the children forthwith switched to identifying themselves with the crocodile, and with a bellyful of stick and Punch, enjoyed naughtiness redoubled!

For the week of 18 July 1859, Punch and Judy shared the bill with Jeronelle's fantoccini at Jones' Wood, as has already been recounted, in a "grand musical festival and fête champêtre" (New York *Herald* of that date); citizens still liked to escape the pavements and go to bosky dells for relaxation. Punch was to become a regular feature of the church and fraternal picnic; he was to appear in the city streets and parks, as he did in London; he was to inhabit the circus sideshow and the gallery of curiosities in the dime museum; he was to appear on the boards of the variety theatre, whether it was called music hall, vaudeville, cabaret, or night club. He was to become the plaything of amateurs and of fathers turned showman in the nursery. He had a busy career before him in the forthcoming years.

A pleasure garden without Punch was hardly a pleasure garden at all. He was to be found at Hoering and Hennie's People's Garden, on Harrison Street between Second and Third, in Davenport, Iowa, on 7 August 1858, presented by Monsieur de Rathsckoff, late of Paris (Joseph S. Schick, *The Early Theatre in Eastern Iowa*, Chicago, 1939, p. 273). One may doubt that Rathsckoff was originally from Paris, but not that the potation in this garden was malted.

Punch's noisy goings-on seemed an appropriate part of the cheerful hubbub of clinking glasses and conversation at beer gardens, which made immigrants forget their homesickness for the old country. At the Central Park Garten, "Punch and Judy with Captain Jenks" enlivened the Christmas season of 1868 (New York *Herald*, 16 December); the ad-

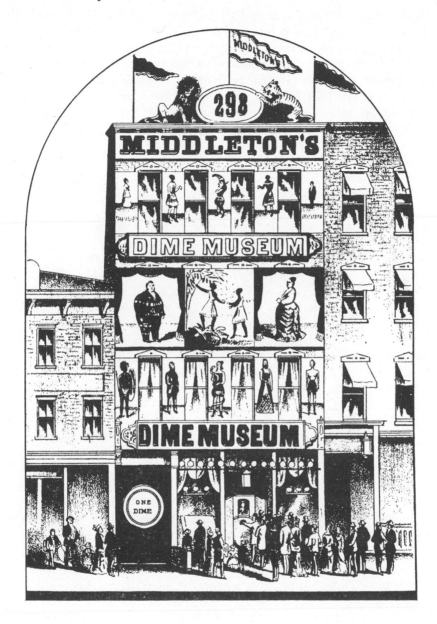

No doubt that Punch played in Middleton's on Broadway, New York—his portrait is in the center top row of the pictured attractions. From a colored lithograph of about 1885 in the Harvard College Library theatre collection.

mission price of 25¢, children 10¢, and boxes $2 extra, was probably representative for all such places. For those who wanted puppet shows in German, John Rach and other showmen played at the Bowery Garten, Held's Hamilton Park, and elsewhere, as will be seen in another chapter. Punch paused in his wayfaring at Brooklyn Terrace Garden, 198 Court Street, 8-15 July 1873 (Brooklyn *Eagle* for those dates). He moved on to a tent at Jamaica and Jagger avenues, Brooklyn, sharing the Independence Day program with orations, on 4 July 1874 (Long Island *Times* of that date). He was at the National Garden, 104 Bowery, in August 1874 (Odell, Vol. 9, p. 448). He was presented by Eugene Blitz at Aberle's Tivoli, New York, 21-26 July 1879 (the playbill is in the Harvard College Library). In short, he was at all such convivial places.

Though Dickens commented on the absence of Punch from the streets of America, two Punch men claimed that he had seen them. The *History of O. B. Hubbard's Celebrated London Punch and Judy as exhibited by him throughout the United States and England for the past fifteen years, with a Full Explanation How to Work it*, Lawrence, Massachusetts, 1874 (a copy is in the Harvard Library), maintained, "When Charles Dickens visited this country a few years ago—he was stopping in New York while I was playing at Brooklyn—he came to see me. The next day there came out, in the New York *Times*, a whole column telling the public the pleasure that would be derived from this innocent amusement." This story has not been located as yet; Hubbard quoted from it. Dickens was in New York in December 1867 and January, February, and April 1868. E. Beck told a reporter of the Frankfort, Pennsylvania, *Register* in May 1896 that he and his brother, who had been acrobats in England, "first introduced Punch and Judy to the American people in the streets of Brooklyn" in the spring of 1866, when Dickens had seen them and declared that "the American eagle would shelter with its wings many more such shows," which sounds too benign for Dickens in America.

The Frankfort *Register* article indicated that the Becks moved to Boston shortly after their debut in America and set up their booth on the Common. There for three years, they hired Samuel Murdoch as musician—presumably to play the traditional drum and pan-pipes as outside man. Though they tried to keep the use of the reed that produces Punch's skirling voice as a secret from him, he mastered it and, when the Becks departed, took over their stand for himself. He was there for a quarter of a century. An old Bostonian who died in 1940 at the age of 101 recalled that it was on the Tremont Street Mall, near the Park Street Church, and always attracted an appreciative crowd. Kate Ryan the actress, who was born in 1857, saw it when a child; she knew just

MISTER PUNCHINELLO!

A CELEBRATED GLEE,

Composed & Arranged for

FOUR VOICES

with an Accompaniment for the

Piano Forte,

And Dedicated to the Murphy Club

By

I. T. NORTON R.A.M,

Composer & Director of the Music to the Chesnut St. Theatre.

Philad? Published & sold by Geo. Willig N.º 171 Chesnut Street.

Oh mamma I must be mar_ried to Mister Pun_chi_nel_lo,

Punch and Judy inspired some lively music on both sides of the Atlantic. Here is a four-part glee by the composer and director of music to the Chestnut Street Theatre, Philadelphia; from the ladies' style of costume it is about 1835. Engraved sheet from the Bella C. Landauer collection. A comic song much sung in music hall and parlor was Thomas Hood's The Lost Child, whose frantic mother found it watching Punch.

PUNCH *and* **JUDY'S WALTZ**

NEW-YORK Published by Firth & Hall Nº344. Pearl $1

Waltzes and galops, and a schottische or two, were composed on the Punch and Judy theme, from this one, about 1835, an engraved sheet in the Bella C. Landauer collection, to Victor Herbert's familiar Punch and Judy *(copyright in a Harold Sanford arrangement by Carl Fischer, 1926) from the operetta* Naughty Marietta. *Even Martha Graham's theatre dance,* Punch and The Judy, *with its spoken passages quoted from Gordon Craig's* The Marionnette, *derives from the classic "bustle and tussle" of the play.*

enough about puppets by hearsay to know that they were worked by strings, and tried very hard to see them (Ryan, *Old Boston Museum Days*, Boston, 1915, p. 10). In the summer of 1943 the Boston *Herald-Traveler* revived the institution, engaging Ralph Geddis and Francois Martin to play Punch on the Common Saturday mornings; their booth was set up by the Parkman Bandstand (*Puppetry 1942-1943*, p. 8). On this occasion, to quote from Irma Kierman in *Puppetry*, "The papers printed letters from old Bostonians about their memories of Punch. These were clipped, together with the 1943 publicity, and placed among the records of the Bostonian Society in the Old State House. And the swan boat man in the Public Gardens was entranced. His Saturday intakes trebled."

Punch was in other city parks. Randolph G. Adams remembers him in Fairmount Park, near Strawberry Mansion, Philadelphia, about 1905. An old resident of Detroit, his memories stirred by the opening of a Grosse Pointe movie theatre called the Punch and Judy, wrote to the Detroit *News* (2 February 1930), "It was in the early 70's. The 'show-house' was a wooden frame covered with picturesque calico on a two-wheeled hand cart with a stage cut in the front.

"The manager or operator was an Englishman; the season was during the winter months. . . . The Englishman gave his exhibition at the south-west corner of Grand Circus, East. . . . After the second performance of

4   VARIETY BOOK.

OSCAR BRUCE.

This little boy with a tremendous big head has been permitted by his parents to go and see the performance of Punch and Judy; his name is Oscar Bruce, he is a very bad boy, and a very ignorant one—see how he laughs at the comicalities and drolleries of Punch. Now, as I am speaking of Oscar Bruce, I will give you a little of his history. He cultivated an acquaintance with a very bad boy by the name of Thomas Nan, who used to swear, steal, and disobey his parents; and Oscar soon got as bad as his profligate companion. His mother moved into another city, for the purpose of separating him from his deluded comrade, and opened a little grocery store for the purpose of supporting him; she put Oscar in it to take charge of it, but he used to steal all the sugar and cakes, and candy from his poor mother and eat them. He is a lazy, bad boy; he gets up very late in the morning, and does nothing all day. No good boy will go with him.

American children's books tried to pump goodness into reluctant little children through every story, even such a piece of implausibility as this tale of wicked Oscar Bruce. From The Variety Book for Children, *a colored chapbook published by Illman & Sons, Philadelphia, about 1825.*

bad old Punch batting Judy around, we welcomed the wooden dummies with a storm of snowballs and drove them out of sight. . . .

"Well, then, the operator stuck his 'cocoanut' up to the stage opening and began, 'Ladies and gentlemen, Hi ham doing this for a liveli'ood—' when, wow! Jim Ulrich slammed him with a snowball and the gang chased him down Miami Avenue to Grand River."

If this performer gave up Detroit as a bad job there was another active in the town in 1875 or 1876. My father remembers him. His show arrived in a light wagon; the booth was unloaded and erected on Jefferson Avenue near Meldrum, where a setback in the row of buildings gave extra width to the sidewalk. At sight of the preparations all the neighborhood children ran home to get pennies and were back with them in good time for the show. The Punch man himself passed the hat to collect his fee, working alone as had the hapless showman in Grand Circus Park. He should have teamed with an outside man to take the collection and keep inquisitive and mischievous boys from the booth.

Punch performed on the beach at the seashore, as he was accustomed to do in England. A description of Coney Island in 1878 (*Harper's Weekly*, 10 August, p. 631) numbers its attractions, among them don-

Punch was to be found on the beach at Coney Island, just as if it were an English seaside resort, in the summers of the late 1870's. He is to be seen there in a detail of a wood-engraving after a drawing by W. A. Rogers in Harper's Weekly *of 10 August 1878, p. 632.*

keys to ride, "but these appeal chiefly to the little ones, who are also the main patrons of the candyman, the peanut vendor, and Punch and Judy, all of whom flourish blandly on the sands." An illustration drawn by William A. Rogers shows the veritable booth in a panorama of beach activities.

On the testimony of W. J. Judd (*Punch and Judy*, New York, 1879), "Punch came into special favor about the year 1866, as may be gathered from the reports in the English newspapers of that time, Manvers and others of England's best Punch and Judy players having left its shores to try their fortunes in America's more favored channels. In 1874 the demand for puppets was so great that it became difficult to meet the wants of the many professors that had decided to become performers. Notwithstanding the growing number of actors, in the fall of 1876 not one unemployed Punch and Judy performer could be found in New York City." There was a postwar boom in the United States and English Punch men flocked to the young and prosperous country. Among them were Richard Codman, whose family is still in Liverpool, Daisey and Collins, Davies, Heller, Irving, Logrenia, Mercer, Morley, Pidgeon, Rodgers, Walton, Webber, and doubtless many others whose names are lost.

Punch and Judy at Rockaway Beach, from a drawing by H. P. Wolcott in Scribner's
Monthly Magazine, July 1879, p. 480.

When inclement weather set in, Punch men who were wiser than the
one in Detroit sought the shelter of halls and dime museums. Thus
we find Punch at Bunnell's Dime Museum, Fulton Street, Brooklyn, 23
February—1 March 1879 (Brooklyn *Daily Eagle* for those dates). And
there were hundreds of other such places for him. But with spring, the
sap rose in his walnut veins and he hankered once more for the out-of-
doors and the road. Showmen such as Theodore Lyman Webber, unwilling to face the hazards of barnstorming by themselves, threw in their
lot with a traveling circus; Harry Houdini was engaged as a young
man by John and M. H. Welch's circus in the spring of 1895, and also
for the season of 1898, to work in the sideshow and play Punch and
Judy, doing magic in the concert part of the program (Harold Kellock,
Houdini, his Life Story, New York, 1928, p. 72).

But it was in the music halls, as a turn in the variety program, that he
found himself best publicized. He played during Christmas week, 1861,
at the Canterbury, 585 Broadway, New York (New York *Herald*, 19
December). He was on the program with Professor E. Andrews, a
magician, who may have doubled in working him, at Military Hall,
Schols and Leonard streets, Williamsburgh, New York, 1 February 1866
(Odell, Vol. 8, p. 119). He shared the stage with stereopticon views at
St. Julien Hall, Staten Island, New York, 4 February 1867 (Staten
Island *Gazette* of that date).

Alternating Punch and Judy *shows, like dance bands in the better places today, kept up the gaiety of Tammany Hall when it opened entertainment concessions in its new quarters, 14 Street between Irving Place and Third Avenue, New York, in 1869. The Academy of Music, then New York's opera house, was in the building adjoining to the west. From a wood-engraving in* Harper's New Monthly Magazine, *April 1872, p. 685. Proof from the original boxwood block.*

At Harry Hill's dance hall on Houston Street near Broadway, New York, Punch and Judy had "a box to themselves" and alternated with a ventriloquist. (Matthew Hale Smith, *Sunshine and Shadow in New York*, Hartford, 1868, p. 440.) Hill's was notorious in its day. "It is not a bar-room, not a concert saloon, not a pretty waiter-girl establishment, and not a free-and-easy. . . . It is all . . . at once," wrote John J. Jennings in *Theatrical and Circus Life* (St. Louis, 1882, p. 393). Today it would cause little remark; it was like our night clubs (though less expensive) such as the French Casino at Seventh Avenue and 50 Street, New York, in 1935, where one found "a brightly salacious marionette show, and the most enticing little lighted windows, let into the walls aquarium style, displaying Russell Patterson's naughty, alluring puppets, cavorting statically in their natural habitats (Peggy Bacon, *Stage*, June 1935, p. 68).

The Tammany Society removed to its new hall on 14 Street between Irving Place and Third Avenue, New York, in 1869. To help defray maintenance expenses of the building, the political club installed two auditoriums where shows might go on simultaneously, in the style of the big London music halls. Advance publicity promised Punch and Judy (New York *Evening Post*, 29 December 1868) but at the opening there was actually a pair of shows, Gardner and Brewer's, "from Windsor Castle and the Crystal Palace," and Manley and Brewer's—did Brewer, perhaps acting as outside man, divide his loyalty between Gardner and Manley? Manley and Brewer had a dog Toby and probably played their turn in

This little boy, playing in the attic on a rainy day, has been so fortunate as to find a set of puppets in an old trunk. Note the memorial wreath and Civil War swords. Improvising a stage from a cloth and a chair back, holding the book of words on his knee, he plays Punch and Judy for his patient spitz. A lithographed trade card by Buek & Lindner for the Palais Royal, a department store on 14 Street and Fifth Avenue, New York. About 1880.

PALAIS ROYAL,
Nº 4 E. 14ᵀᴴ ST. N.Y.

the auditorium on the top floor, the theatre proper, with a stage "forty feet wide between the proscenium—the largest in the country," as the description in the New York *Times* of 3 January 1869 ran, while Gardner and Brewer held forth in the basement promenade hall, 90 x 33 feet, "where a band of music, a Punch and Judy performance, and other light recreations" were to be enjoyed. There was a continuous round of activity from 7 P.M. to midnight for a 50¢ general admission charge, and through playing in duplicate, Punch may well have grown tired.

Punch started Walter E. Deaves off on a long career of puppeteering in San Francisco in 1869; Deaves was then fifteen. Punch had arrived in California almost before San Francisco was built.

"One Sunday," wrote Carlisle S. Abbott in *Recollections of a California Pioneer* (New York, 1917, p. 114)—the year was about 1850—"a ventriloquist made his appearance at Sandy Bar and secured the use of a store which had just been completed (pine poles and canvas-covered top and sides) for an evening performance. . . . The big room was literally packed with miners, all standing, while the pile of goods in the rear was covered with men, among whom was our friend Dr. Woodward, sitting upon a sack of Sandwich Island potatoes.

"The performance was a Punch and Judy affair, and wound up with a production of the devil, horns and all, who looked terrifying enough.

The rather bored children at a well-to-do family holiday party of the 1870's were willing to do anything for a little amusement, even look at a Punch and Judy show.

So, at least, the artist depicted them for a wood-engraving in Harper's Weekly of 6 January 1872, p. 5. The text attributed their attention to a love of the horrible.

A playbill of Tony Pastor's, 10 June 1871, featuring Johnny Daisy's Punch and Judy. From the original in the Harvard College Library theatre collection.

The head and shoulders of his Satanic Majesty appeared just above the curtain, and by means of some wire attachment he was made to move his lips and chin as in talking. He made quite a speech, saying, among other things, that in this wild region where there were no infernal laws to bother, no society, no ladies, and no churches to make a great fuss about nothing, it was perfectly proper and commendable to get drunk on Sunday and have a good time. Meantime Dr. Woodward, with a few jolts under his belt, had been busy cutting open a sack of potatoes, from which he selected a large one (worth a dollar, by the way), and threw it over the heads of the crowd below him, striking the devil squarely in the face. The devil dropped behind the curtain and remained out of sight until the yells and swinging of hats had ceased; then he came cautiously

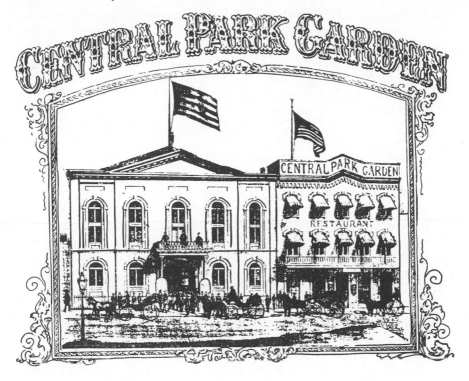

The scene of concerts and Punch and Judies for the poorer and less bored American
was this lush beer hall on 59 Street facing Central Park, New York. From a lithograph
on a sheet of music in the Harvard College Library theatre collection.

into view above the curtain and, with a long, bony finger pointed at Dr.
Woodward, solemnly said:

"'Doc, Doc Woodward, I have a lien on you.'"

In the second half of the nineteenth century Punch's performances
proliferated. He played in so many variety programs, and was so often
advertised without a showman's name or other particulars, that such
facts as have been gathered are put in the index of puppeteers at the
back of this book. He continued to haunt the music hall to the days
when a new form of entertainment, the cinematograph, appeared—
eventually to take over the whole program, like the horse that got its
nose into the tent. He shouldered part of the show in some of the
dingy little made-over-store theatres where films were first exhibited.

Nicola Seraphine, who was still working in a theatre in the Bronx in
1947, first operated a Punch and Judy show, according to a letter from
Arthur W. Schwaikert in the New York *Sun* of 11 April 1947, in a heat-

less corner store at 89 Street and East End Avenue, diagonally opposite the Gracie Mansion, in New York, about 1905. Then he opened a movie house on the east side of Third Avenue, between 84 and 85 streets. It was installed in what had been two stores, and was fireproofed to the extent of having metal sheeting on its walls. Next he had a theatre at 49 Street and First Avenue, as another oldtimer recalled in a letter to the *Sun* of 22 March 1947. In it there was a movie screen to the right and a Punch and Judy booth to the left. The neighborhood children were drawn to it as by a magnet, not only for the "moom pictures" and puppets that swept thrillingly on and off in their stage, but for the games and prizes that Nick—as Seraphine was called—devised for audience participation.

The amateur Punch and Judy showman sailed along in the wake of all this interest in professional shows. He found eager audiences in the parlor, nursery, Sunday school room, and social gathering place. He did not have to be handy at making things; it was possible to buy puppets from various dealers. W. J. Judd's edition of *Punch and Judy* was perhaps no more than a promotional piece for his business at 131 Henry Street, New York. He offered the principal characters for the play, "handsomely dressed," with carved wooden heads, at $1.25 each; the dog and horse were $1.50 each; properties ran from 50¢ to $2.00; a booth cost $12.00. This was in 1879. His competitors were Peck and Snyder of 124 Nassau Street, New York, as Professor Hoffman disclosed in *Parlor Amusements* (Philadelphia, n.d., footnote on p. 192), and Theodore Mack & Sons of Chicago, whose business, founded in 1880, was continued by Frank Marshall, maker of Bergen's Charlie McCarthy; this is mentioned in Marshall's 1931 catalogue. Peck and Snyder sold such trick puppets as the come-apart Turk (Hoffman, p. 217). These sources of supply were called upon by the professional Punch and Judy man too, who was more often skilled at histrionics than handicrafts.

Although the method of manipulating Punch and producing his twangling voice was kept a deep secret of the trade, initiates would occasionally lead a hierophant into the mysteries for a consideration. A Punch man interviewed by Henry Mayhew, as he recorded in *London Labor and the London Poor* (London, n.d., Vol. 3, p. 53), said of the reed, which was placed between the tongue and the palate to produce the vibrato tones, "These calls we often sell to gennelmen for a sovereign apiece, and for that we give 'em a receipt how to use them." The Pinxys of Chicago, who sell reeds as this is being written, go so far as to tell one that, in case the squeaker is accidentally swallowed, one should hasten to eat as much bread as possible, which will form a bolus about the intruding metal and help it outward along the usual channel. Charles Nodier, a devotee of the theatre in France who haunted puppet shows

Advertisement pages from Judd's edition of Punch and Judy, *New York, 1879.*

at the fairs, once asked for lessons in the use of the reed, and was not satisfied till he had one of the difficult little instruments in his mouth. After experiment he asked his teacher, "But don't you sometimes swallow it?" Affably the showman replied, "Oh, yes; I've swallowed that one three times."

The reed consists of a taut piece of silk tape or other vibrating material held between two bowed pieces of metal, generally silver. As it is balanced on the tongue, the breath of the performer carries his falsetto through it and gives a buzzing overtone like comb-and-paper music. Punch uses this voice but other characters speak without the reed; as they say their lines the reed is slipped off the tongue but not out of the mouth. With practice it can be used without cramping enunciation altogether. But what Punch says is recognizable more by his intonation and gesture than by his distinctness.

The traditional Punch booth consists of a portable and demountable framework of wood covered by cloth curtains. At the bottom of the proscenium opening, which should be just above the head of the stand-

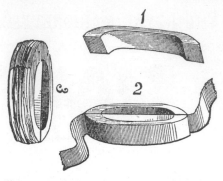

"Get two small pieces of clean white pine, and with a sharp knife cut them of the shape and size of the diagram marked 1. Then put these two pieces together as represented in Figure 2, having previously slipped between them a piece of common tape. . . ; then wind some thread round the whole thing lengthwise (to keep the bits of wood together and the tape taut) . . . as represented in Figure 3. . . . The instrument must be placed well back in the mouth near the root of the tongue, in such a position that you can blow through it and at the same time retain free use of your tongue. A little practice will enable you to do this, and to pronounce many words in a tolerably understandable manner." From Frank Bellew, The Art of Amusing, New York, 1866, p. 39. Most Punch men prefer bowed strips of silver and silk tape for the reed.

Playing Punch and Judy on a stage improvised in a doorway. From Bellew, The Art of Amusing, opposite p. 40.

ing puppeteer, is a shelf that projects outward toward the audience; on it properties are placed and the dog Toby sits. Sometimes there is a flap below the main opening, out of which the devil may make a surprise appearance. Scenery is painted on cloth drops or board cutouts; for the purposes of the average Punch play, a single street or garden will serve. Such furniture as chairs and tables is seldom used. The gallows is set up by pegging its base into a hole in the shelf.

On a row of hooks at a convenient height inside the booth the puppets are hung upside down by loops in their skirts. The showman plunges his hand into the hollow costume, wriggles his thumb into one arm and his second finger into the other, and brings the puppet up. Entrances

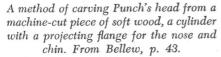

A method of carving Punch's head from a machine-cut piece of soft wood, a cylinder with a projecting flange for the nose and chin. From Bellew, p. 43.

The heads of the Constable, Judy, and Punch made from painted cylindrical wooden boxes with applied putty noses. From Bellew, p. 42.

and exits are always vertical. The figures are held over his head at arm's length; he steps about as they turn and walk. In Piccini's booth as Cruikshank drew it, the puppets hung head up, their necks wedged tightly enough between pegs so that they could be slipped on without aid from the other hand. Punch is always on the right hand if the operator is right-handed, his left arm lower than his right because it is moved by the thumb. The other characters give way to each other on the left hand while Punch holds the stage.

The properties, particularly sticks, bells, pots, and other weapons, are more important than the scenery. Hand-puppets grasp them between their arms; it is one of the features of hand-puppet action. The showman's wrist makes the puppet's supple waist. In such stage business as chopping wood, rubbing clothes on a washboard, or shaking out a rug, where waist flexing is the feature, hand-puppets are convincingly human. Some puppets have legs sewed to the dark bag that conceals the puppeteer's arm. These dangle on the shelf to approximate walking; they are particularly useful for a kick or a jig. But puppets without legs can strut, limp, hobble, polka, and waltz even more effectively than those that have them, for their body motion suggests the presence of legs without the impediment of legs that co-ordinate sketchily.

Two puppets, one on each hand, are as many as a puppeteer can manage at once, though others may be propped in seats or lie prostrate on the shelf for the purposes of the plot. Sometimes an army or a mob is held on a forked stick. Of course there can be additional operators, each holding two more puppets. The Punch and Judy man was almost always a solo performer.

In 1854 a shorter and simpler text than Collier's was made available in England for "ambitious young gentlemen aspiring to give private

representations. . . . By a careful study of the dialogue and stage directions, coupled with a diligent and frequent rehearsal of the squeak (which is not difficult, and may be practiced at the top of the house), a youth of average abilities may, in a comparatively short time, acquire such a proficiency in the art of performing Punch, as to render an apprenticeship to a regular professor (to which most parents, on its proposal, would be found to object) wholly unnecessary." This was *Punch and Judy* by Papernose Woodensconce (London). In 1866 Frank Bellew's *Art of Amusing* was published in New York, with an illustrated chapter on how to make puppets and a Punch reed, and a partly developed scenario of the play, involving Punch, Judy, the Baby, the Ghost, and the Constable. Bessie Alexander, later to become Mrs. Ficklen, author of *A Handbook of Fist Puppets* (in which she mentions it on p. 37; her book was published in New York, 1935), was one child who learned puppetry from this delightful volume. In 1868 a new edition of *Every Boy's Book* by Edmund Routledge contained a section on making Punch and Judy, with illustrations taken from the Woodensconce edition of the play (London and New York, pp. 746-749). A still later edition, called *Every Little Boy's Book,* added the play text from the same source. Similar books, all basing their information on Bellew and Routledge, followed: *Parlor Amusements* by Professor Hoffman (Philadelphia, n.d.); *What Shall We Do Tonight?* by Leger D. Mayne (New York, 1873); and comparatively recent ones such as *The Boy's Own Book,* about 1910. The knowledge of how to become a Punch and Judy operator was very accessible.

The plot as crystallized by Collier continued to be used in the main, but certain variations came about. Toby the dog, a puppet as Cruikshank pictured it and as an apprentice of Piccini attested (Mayhew as cited before, Vol. 3, p. 53), became a real animal. Perhaps Piccini had merely broken the tradition of Powell, who introduced live creatures among his puppets, though Pike, Piccini's successor, is credited (again in Mayhew) with the innovation of the live dog. A live dog is seen in another engraving in *Cruikshank's Comic Almanac* for July 1836, entitled *Dog*

After one-quarter of a penny cut-out woodcut sheet of Punch and Judy published by H. C. Clarke & Company, London, in the 1870's; copies probably were sold in America.

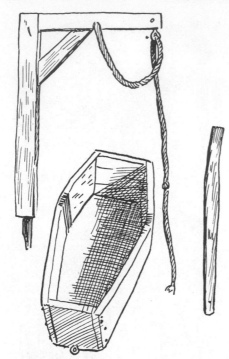

Necessary properties for the classic play: gallows, coffin, and stick. These were used by George H. Irving (1858-1936) of Haverhill, Massachusetts. From the Michigan Art and Craft Project, WPA, Index of American Design plate by George J. File.

Days; one appears again, sitting up and holding a pipe, in the anonymous *Sergeant Bell and his Raree-Show* (London, 1839). A Seven-Dials ballad, *The Downfall of Punch*, dating from about 1840, laments, "Toby's got the mange, and can't even crawl on all fours." A veritable dog figures on the traditional cover of the London magazine, *Punch*. Manley, Gardner, and Brewer had a dog at Tammany Hall, but fewer American than English showmen used one, either for lack of time to train one or because of their wider itineraries. Ernest Russell, an amateur, admitted in *The Most Popular Play in the World* (*Outing Magazine*, January 1908, p. 476) that he omitted Toby for reasons of time. Few amateurs would have been patient enough to rehearse him.

In Collier's version, which would have played well over an hour if given in its entirety, there were minor characters: Scaramouch, a Courtier, a Servant, a Blind Man, and Polly; perhaps they had once had larger parts in other plays, or had suffered cuts in action. The puppeteer interviewed by Mayhew said that the Merry Andrew and Blind Man were "quite done with now" in 1852; and explained that Polly was left out because she "wasn't exactly moral." Scaramouch gave way to Joey the Clown, a tribute to Joseph Grimaldi's stage creation; there was a string puppet Joey in Gray's 1832 show. The blackamoor Servant turned into

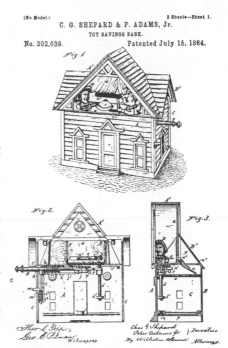

(No Model.)   2 Sheets—Sheet 1.
C. G. SHEPARD & P. ADAMS, Jr.
TOY SAVINGS BANK.
No. 302,039.   Patented July 15, 1864.

The popularity of Punch and Judy caused them to crop up in every form, even in cast iron for a mechanical savings bank, patented by Charles G. Shepard and Peter Adams jr., as recorded on this reproduction of a United States Patent Office sheet. Application for the patent was filed 30 October 1883. As the bank was finally manufactured in Buffalo, New York, the characters were placed in a miniature stage rather than a house. In this form they were to be found in two or three versions. One pulled out the bar g, placed a coin in Judy's pan e, touched the release m, and the coin was flung through the slot into the bank. One had entertainment as an inducement to thrift.

Jim Crow, perhaps soon after 1836 when Thomas Rice, inventor of that singing and dancing darky, came to England. Mayhew's Punch man declared, "Jim Crow sprung from Rice from America. . . . Everybody liked to hear *Jim Crow* sung, and so we had to do it."

And there was a quite new character, the Ghost. Albert Smith wrote in *Comic Tales and Sketches* (London, 1852, p. 19), "The drama of Punch has suffered material change within the last few years. The baby, Jack Ketch, the gallows, and the—(we hesitate to write his name) the—enemy of mankind, have almost disappeared. Their places have been supplied by a clown, . . Jim Crow, . . and a spectre made of wood, with an enormous mouth of red cloth. We do not like these innovations. They look like a taste for spectacle, and where this prevails the legitimate drama must fall." Mayhew's puppeteer expatiated, "This is the Ghost that appears to Punch for destroying his wife and child. She's the ghost of the two together, or else by rights there ought to be a little ghost as well, but we should have such a lot to carry about. . . . The Ghost comes up very solemn and mournful-like. . . . Punch don't see the Ghost till he gets a tap on the cheek, and then he thinks it's somebody else; instead of that, when he turns round, he's most terrible alarmed." In the Woodensconce text of 1854, Joey and the Ghost, but not Jim Crow, are present.

Punch and Judy in the nursery; this time Judy has the stick. An illustration by Edward H. Wehnert for Great Fun for Our Little Friends, *London, 1862, p. 35.*

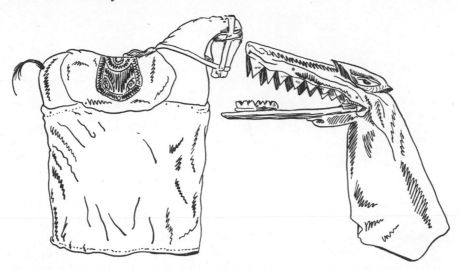

Punch and Judy animals: Hector the horse (with ears, mane, and tail pretty well worn off), George H. Irving's wood and cloth puppet, and the Crocodile, which belonged to John Difenderfer (1866-1933), made of tin, wood, and black oilcloth. From Michigan Art and Craft Project, WPA, Index of American Design plates by James McLellan and Christ E. Makrenos.

In fact, the first published text I have been able to find that includes Jim Crow is the New York one issued by McLoughlin in 1902; it also has the Crocodile.

Russell, the amateur Punch and Judy exponent, believed that the ideal cast would consist of Punch, Judy, the Baby, the Doctor, the Policeman, Jack Ketch, and the Devil, "together with the Darky, the Clown, and the Ghost." "By no means," said he, "sacrifice the Devil to outside opinion; his overthrow quite puts the finishing touch upon the production. In this connection Pollock tells the following amusing story. Pausing in the course of his wanderings to watch the efforts of a puppet showman in a rural English town, he was horrified to see a vile caricature of an alligator take the place of 'the enemy of mankind' in the closing scenes. Lingering about until the operator appeared, Pollock expostulated with the fellow at this violation of most sacred tradition.

" 'I know it, sur,' responded the showman dejectedly, 'I 'ates to do it and it 'adn't ought to be done, but y' see, I cawn't 'elp it, sur, it's all along o' these meddlin' curates, sur.'

"Though the present writer has yet to suffer at the hands of the 'meddlin' curates,' he has, in deference to delicate suggestion and with inward regret, presented at church fairs and kindred functions an expurgated

The mobile Punch, mounted on a bunt-
ing-draped wagon. After a photograph by
M. R. Halladay reproduced in Outing
Magazine, January 1908, p. 472.

edition of the play wherein the puppet Devil, rechristened as the Bogey-
Man, has filled the rôle of his horned relative and received the same
effectual treatment." (*Outing Magazine* cited above.)

Perhaps the most usual ending for the play in America early in the
twentieth century was the swallowing of Punch by the Crocodile. So, at
least, I saw it at the dime museum in Detroit about 1911. The showman,
whose booth was on the second floor of the exhibition building, cheek
by jowl with snake charmers and armless ladies, had provided his scene
with a wall telephone the ringing of which was brought several times into
the action—a sophistication taken by Punch in his stride.

Punch and Judy men had not only professional hazards but the law to
steer clear of. In England they claimed their pitches in the city streets
by customary or squatter's rights, as in the Lime Street, Liverpool, position opposite St. George's Hall, held by Richard Codman's booth; I saw
it there, lashed to a lamp post and vacant, in the spring of 1938. The
London Metropolitan Police Act of 1852, while it abolished dogs as
draught animals—they had sometimes drawn puppet booths as they are
still harnessed to carts in Flanders; a pair is seen hitched to the framework of a fantoccini stage in *The Original* (London, 1832, p. 217, reproduced in *Puppetry 1944-1945*, p. 62)—neglected to prohibit, or forgot
all about, Punch and Judy. In America there were city and state licensing
acts which it was easy to fall foul of.

New York state had an act to suppress common showmen, mountebanks, and jugglers, passed 13 April 1819. "I. Be it enacted by the people
of the State of New York represented in Senate and Assembly that from
and after the first day of July next it shall not be lawful for any person
or persons to exhibit or perform for gain or profit any puppet show, wire
dance, or any other idle shows, acts, or feats . . . in any town in this
state; nor shall it be lawful for any owner or occupant of any house, outhouse, or field to furnish accommodations therefor; and for each and every

Negro, Policeman, and Devil of George H. Irving. After Michigan Art and Craft Project, WPA, Index of American Design plates; Policeman by Dorothy Harris, Devil by George File.

offense against the provisions of this act, the person or persons so offending shall forfeit the sum of $25 with costs of suit to be recovered in an action of debt in any court having cognizance thereof to the use of the poor of the town . . . provided however, that nothing above contained shall be construed to extend to any museum or repository of natural curiosities, wax figures, useful works of art, or to the exhibition of any animal." The second article of the act provided that animals, paintings, and natural or artificial curiosities could be exhibited by obtaining written permission from two justices of the town. By the Revised Statutes of 1829 (Part 1, Chapter 20, Title 8), this law of 1819 was made Section 834 of the Penal Code of the Laws of New York State. It remained in force until 1932, when it was repealed.

Thus the New York legislature went on record as considering puppet shows done for a livelihood as "idle shows," while elephants, mermaids, and waxworks chambers of horrors were sanctioned. The fine line drawn between the permissible (and moral) and impermissible (and immoral) gives an indication of American taste of the early nineteenth century. Had this law been observed to the letter, all puppet shows would have been suppressed for 112 years in New York State. Obviously they got around the prohibition, since the law allowed whatever went on under the roof of a museum or repository of natural curiosities, by staying off the streets and seeking shelter with Barnum and his confraternity. But petty blue laws tend to stay on the books long after the cause for their existence is forgotten, and many a puppeteer and theatre owner must have been unaware that he was a law breaker.

An ordinance adopted by the Board of Aldermen and approved by the Mayor of New York City on 6 December 1884 affords matter for speculation. "No person within the City of New York shall," it went, "from any window or open space situated in any story of a house above the street floor, which window or open space is visible from the street, or from the

George H. Irving's Punch and Judy. From the Michigan Art and Craft Project, WPA, Index of American Design plates by Dorothy Brennan and Ed Strzalkowski.

sidewalk on the opposite side of the street, exhibit to the public upon said street, or upon the opposite sidewalk, any pantomime performance of puppet or other figures . . . or any other entertainment of the stage or dramatic performance, or of that nature, under penalty of $10 for each such offense." Had some Punch and Judy men, debarred from the streets, taken to giving shows in an upstairs window? Or were the aldermen merely forestalling this? There seems to have been no objection to puppet shows in windows on the street level, where they are, indeed, sometimes still given as department-store attractions (though the Fifth Avenue Association frowns upon any moving window display), making a jolly jam of pedestrians, and sometimes even of vehicular traffic, at holiday season.

The 1936 New York Code of Ordinances (Chapter 3, Article 3, Sections 60-62) defined puppet shows as common shows and required them to be licensed at $50 a year, and more when their seating capacity exceeded 600—rather too large an audience for the average puppet show.

A Pennsylvania Act of Assembly of 22 May 1879, P. L. 73, provided that it be unlawful in cities of the first class to show any interlude, tragedy, comedy, or such, without first obtaining a license, the fee being $25 a year. This was held to apply to Punch and Judy shows by a City Solicitor's opinion, dated 20 December 1899 (*Philadelphia Ordinances and City Solicitor's Opinions*, 1899, p. 95). In Boston, on the other hand, where one might expect particularized injunctions, the City Clerk reported to me that "there are no ordinances regulating the licensing of puppet shows or Punch and Judy shows."

Puppets of the amateur Punch and Judy showman, John Difenderfer: Devil, Punch, and Policeman. After Michigan Art and Craft Project, WPA, Index of American Design plates. Punch by Lillian Stahl.

On 12 April 1827 the Michigan Territorial Legislature approved an act "for the prevention of immoral practices," Section 5 of which said, "That if any person or persons shall exhibit any puppet show, wire dancing, or tumbling, juggling, or sleight of hand within this territory, or shall ask and receive any pay in money for exhibiting the same, such person or persons shall for every offence pay a fine of not less than $10, nor exceeding $20, at the discretion of the court." This was quoted in the Detroit *Gazette* of 24 January 1828. Apparently the act continued in force until 1837, when Michigan became a state. It does not appear among any of the state laws.

To judge by these instances, puppet shows were often forbidden, or suffered to play only upon buying a license, in the early United States; and since they did play almost everywhere, and probably wriggled out of the license fee, they were among the illicit pleasures of our forefathers.

Punch's sway extended over land and sea. While there is no record that some soldier showman amused his company with Punch on a troop transport ship, at least not until World War II, when I know puppets went everywhere with the G.I., there must have been instances of improvised shows on shipboard. At least there was a Polichinelle, operated over the canvas side of a horse stall, on a French troop ship which took Zouaves and grenadiers from Marseille to Sebastopol in the Crimean campaign. J. Worms illustrated the show and audience in *L'Illustration* of 15 December 1855 (the picture is reproduced in *Puppetry 1941*, p. 25). Some American soldier or sailor must have been as ingenious.

It is highly improbable that slave traders amused their Negro cargoes on the way to America with Punch and Judy, but P. J. Béranger thought of the possibility and wrote a verse about it that appeared in his *Oeuvres* (Paris, 1840. p. 363). The illustration, drawn by J. J. Grandville, whose

John Difenderfer's Chinaman and Judge.
After Michigan Art and Craft Project,
WPA, Index of American Design plates.
Judge by Beverly Chichester.

fantasies are among the precursors of surrealism, shows Punch confronted by a very dark devil after he has killed the Policeman; to one side of the booth, acting as presenter, stands a portly John Bullish sailor; of the audience one sees six chained Negroes, the front row, intently watching. Translated from the French, the verse goes like this (it was printed in its entirety, along with the illustration, in *Puppetry 1942-1943*, p. 63):

> A slave-ship cargo, bored to death,
>   Was badly on the dwindle.
> The captain yelled till out of breath,
>   "You blackamoors, you swindle!
> You've got to land alive, you know—
> Perk up and watch this puppet show!"
>
> A booth was brought and battened fast;
>   The blacks began reviving.
> Punch popped up—they laughed at last;
>   The cargo was surviving.
> "It's good for you to grin, you know—
> Keep an eye on that puppet show."
>
>   * * *
>
> And so they sailed day after day
>   Until they hailed Nantucket.
> The captain knew that puppets pay.
>   No slave had kicked the bucket.
> His profit share was lots of dough,
> Thanks to Punch and the puppet show.

To summarize the progress of Punch and Judy, the show appeared on the legitimate stage at the Park Theatre, New York, in September 1828; shortly thereafter it was at the Chatham and other museums; it began

its long music-hall and variety-theatre career at Canterbury Hall in 1861;
it had played out of doors at Jones' Wood in 1859, as it was to do in other
pleasure gardens and parks; it was in the city streets and at the seaside
when there was an influx of English Punch men shortly after the Civil
War; its Tammany Hall engagement in 1869 foreshadowed others in
free-and-easies, cabarets, and night clubs; it was in a circus sideshow by
1873; at this time amateurs had taken it up for home and school; and
early in the twentieth century it shared the nickelodeon with the newly
born movies. Because of its portability it had crossed the continent and
got to California about 1850; it played in all sorts of unlikely places,
such as behind the battle lines on both sides in the Civil War, and it may
even have been a shipboard entertainment before that time. Punch was
an Englishman when he came to America, but he soon settled down—
if settled down he ever has been—as a naturalized citizen.

X

The Odyssey of the Royal Marionettes

Lime Street, Liverpool, is distinguished in the annals of puppetry not only for the pitch of Richard Codman's Punch and Judy—that Codman whose family name was made into Codlin for the Punch man in Dickens' *Old Curiosity Shop*, and who himself "crossed the Atlantic twice and gave his show in America where it was as popular" as in England, according to the reminiscences of "Nomad" in *The World's Fair* (Oldham, 14 September 1935)—but as a street bounding St. George's Hall, in which in the last century was the American Bar where showmen met to discuss business. At one time in the 1880's there were all of six rival puppet troupes playing in Liverpool, and the managers would foregather there for an amicable talk, said Harry Wilding (*The World's Fair*, 25 November 1939, p. 10). It is not unlikely that this bar was the scene of the meeting on 5 March 1873 between William John Bullock of 25 Colquitt Street, Liverpool (his address in a power of attorney given by him to Joseph D. McLaren in New York), the successful owner of the Royal Marionettes, which had played the summer before to "splendid and fashionable audiences" at St. James's Great Hall, London (London *Times*, 3 August 1872), and at least one of the partners, John E. McDonough and Hartley A. Earnshaw, American or perhaps Scotch-American theatrical agents, who had managed the St. James Theatre, New York, in 1871 (Odell, Vol. 9, p. 194).

Back in the United States McDonough had presented a spectacular transformation scene some fourteen years before, as was noted in an advertisement in the Philadelphia *Public Ledger* of 17 March 1874, when the scene was used again for the puppet stage. He had just come from America, having promised to bring the citizens of Reading, Pennsylvania, "the most wonderful performance from Europe," the Royal Marionettes (Reading *Daily Eagle*, 21 February 1874). In Liverpool an agreement was reached whereby McDonough and Earnshaw were to act as managers for Bullock's company and take it to America. They signed a contract that was to be in force until 15 December 1873, renewable for another six months thereafter by common consent (McDonough and Earnshaw *vs.* Bullock *et al.*, No. 10 Equity Docket 1874, Motion for injunction and bill, filed 26 February 1874, Court of Common Pleas, Dauphin County, Pennsylvania).

On 5 December 1873, when the three men renewed this agreement in Philadelphia, the original terms were probably repeated. According to the new contract, McDonough and Earnshaw were to provide suitable halls for the marionettes, with a stage at least 20 x 24 feet; they were to heat, clean, and light the hall; hire five musicians, including a pianist; have the ticket seller and take care of coupon tickets; advertise in full in the principal daily and weekly papers a week prior to the opening and throughout the run; issue complimentary tickets to the press and suspend the free list when business urged it; bill themselves as lessees and managers of Bullock's Royal Marionettes; transport the scenery and effects and supply railroad fares for the puppeteers, readers, and singers. Notice of intention to renew or cancel the contract was to be given six weeks prior to its expiration.

Bullock for his part was to furnish the company of puppeteers, readers, and singers, the calcium lights and a man to operate them, the scenery, puppets, wardrobe, properties, and every accessory; he was to give a full performance for each date announced; to provide "illuminated printing," posters, window cards, and programs; to furnish ushers and check takers; to set up and tear down the equipment; and to give six evening and three matinee performances a week, with more for schools if it was mutually agreed upon. The managers were to pay the owner or his representative one-half the gross takings for each performance, half of this sum to be handed over every Saturday and the balance on the following Wednesday morning, for the whole week. Bullock reserved the right to sell books of words and to issue passes.

Gathering a company of perhaps twenty (the advertisement in the Harrisburg *Daily Patriot* of 14 February 1874 announced a band and chorus of twenty-five persons—perhaps to be taken as a total company of that number), including some of his best puppeteers, James Shaw, the man who had built the puppets and properties (who made a deposition before a notary public in Harrisburg during the suit cited), and a key musician, singer, and reader—others could be picked up in America —Bullock and the managers sailed for New York and the land of the dollar. The entertainment they were taking was tried and trusty, essentially the same as that which had run at St. James Hall, 2-31 August 1872, and which had been performed so many times in London, the provinces, and Ireland, that it went fast and trippingly.

The name Royal Marionettes? It had served for the popular Italian company in London in 1852; Americans would be impressed by its sug-

gestion of gold and purple. Little did anyone then know what a surfeit
of royal and imperial marionette troupes there was to be!

Bullock sold the book of words in America for 15¢ a copy. No example
of one with an American imprint has yet come to light, so that one from
the St. James Hall engagement of 1872 will have to take its place: *The
Royal Marionettes, Words of the Songs and the Pantomime of Little Red
Riding Hood, W. J. Bullock, Sole Proprietor.* As therein set forth, Part I
of the program is the Fantoccini, nine turns of trick puppets, most of
them thoroughly familiar:

> Blondin's Tight-Rope Feats
> The Scaramouch
> The Wonderful Contortionists
> The Perfect Cures
> The Compound Turk
> Pat and Biddy in their "rale Irish jig"
> The Pole Balancer
> Tommy and Sarah
> The Celestial Dancers and Bell Ringers

Any puppet tight-rope walker would have to bear the name of the famous
Frenchman who had poised himself over Niagara Falls in 1859. The Contortionists' trick was to jerk their heads "curiously out of their bodies,"
said the London *Daily Telegraph* of 3 August 1872. Tommy and Sarah
were a wooden-legged sailor and his wife who sang a traditional song,
the last stanza of which (from the book of words) went like this:

SARAH. My love he plays the fiddle through all the streets of town,
     And I sing at his elbow, we wander up and down;
     We spend our days in harmony, we very seldom fight,
     Unless that he gets grog on board, and I get gin at night.
         (*spoken*) Eh, Tommy?
TOMMY. Ah, Sarah, you likes your twopennyworth of gin on the sly, you
     knows you does, Sarah.
SARAH. Yes, I does, Tommy. Then chorus, Tommy.

The Celestial Dancers were figures *à la chinoise* with little bells fastened
to their hands and sewed to the points of their costumes. Their limbs had
sidewise jumping-jack movement. Mrs. George Middleton told me that
it was a simple number to do but very effective. She and her husband,
each working a Celestial, held sleigh bells together with the control
sticks. As the puppets bounded lightly to music suggesting the orient,
the little bells were reinforced by the sleigh bells in a pleasant tintinnabu-
lation. The usual turn had three Celestials, though two would suffice.

Part II of Bullock's program was a miniature minstrel show called *The Automatic Christy Minstrels.* The human Christy blackface players had come to England from America in the 1850's, creating such a sensation that their name became a generic one for all Negro impersonators. Bullock's burnt-cork company doubtless included interlocutor, end men, jokes, specialty dances, and songs by the whole group in typical minstrel-show pattern. The songs in the book of words are the robustious *Hunky Dorum* and *We'll All Skedaddle,* and the sentimental *My Gentle Mother Dear,* typical too; perhaps they were the sort of thing a parent might think a child would like.

The minstrel show was, it has been mentioned, perfectly suited to puppet technique. The row of darkies could be strung in two tandem groups, one on each side of the center man; he, Tambo, and Bones, the end men, would be separate so that each could rise and cavort by himself. When a specialty dance took place in front of them all could be hung so that they would sit and watch. Thus two or three puppeteers could animate eleven to fifteen puppets.

At the time of Bullock's London engagement in 1872, it so happened that he occupied the large St. James's Hall while a human Christy company was in the small one. This gave a critic in the *Times* of 2 August occasion to remark, "One painful reflection forces itself upon the mind. Are we about to have a new instance of the collision between labor and capital?" He was thinking of technological unemployment, of five actors replaced by one string puller.

Part III was the main piece, an extravaganza in the style of an English Christmas pantomime. It was "written expressly for the Royal Marionettes, and revised and corrected by the proprietor, W. J. Bullock," said the book of words. The list of dramatis personae indicates how the Little Red Riding Hood theme was elaborated. The characters fall into three groups: mortals, immortals, and gnomes. The mortals comprise Little Red Riding Hood, a forest maiden; Monica, her mother; Dorothy, her grandmother; Ravensburg, a wicked baron; Poggidorff, a foppish courtier; and Hyacinth, a son of King Carnation, disguised as a shepherd. The immortals are Amaryllis, queen of the fairies; her two lieutenants; six belles of the court; Martinette, general of the Pigmy army; and his soldiers. The gnomes are Hobblegobblewitz, king; Howler, Prowler, and Scowler, his retainers; and Jack, "a wonderful jackdaw."

Scene I is in the gnomes' den. After an opening chorus by his horrific band, Hobblegobblewitz explains in verse that he must "grieve some hearts and homes each passing hour"; moreover, that he has bound Duke Ravensburg to a compact, signed Faustwise in blood, whereby the Duke

must fetch him victims in return for gold. The gnomes vanish. The Duke
enters, pleading that he can find no victim anywhere, but that if he were
turned into a wolf he might be more successful. The gnome king assents
to working the transformation and bids the Duke bring him Little Red
Riding Hood. The Duke demurs, offering her grandmother instead, but
finally gives in to Hobblegobblewitz's demand. The dialogue is strewn
with puns in the fashion of the time.

The scene changes to a fairy grotto, as beautiful as the den of the
gnomes was ugly. A lieutenant of the fairy queen summons the ethereal
denizens of the realm. Amaryllis enters singing, then tells of Little Red
Riding Hood's danger. Hyacinth comes in and, with the manly direct-
ness we admire in a hero, states:

> A royal prince, in shepherd's guise I rove,
> To win Red Riding Hood to be my love.

The Queen promises him aid against the Duke who, it appears, is also in
love with Little Red Riding Hood. Thereupon the Prince sings (tenor,
of course) of his constancy, but mixes in several topical allusions:

> I've heard all the news from America,
>   And of Alabama Claims had enough;
> I'm glad that Stanley's found out Livingstone,
>   He's a Yankee who's as brave as he is tough.
> May the Stars and Stripes and dear old British Standard
> Never float but in a friendly sort of way,
>   And may the men who'd mar
>   Two such nations by a war
>   Have their mothers-in-law to love.
> May School Boards all agree
> How to teach the A B C
> If ever I cease to love.
>   If ever I cease to love,
>   If ever I cease to love,
>   May Frenchmen live to see
>   That peace and unity
>   Are the best of things to love.

Such a politico-amorous declaration is what might be expected of a
prince who had read his newspapers in the summer of 1872; the concilia-
tory attitude toward America suggests that the ditty was intended as a
vehicle of timely patter for a transatlantic tour.

As a conclusion of the scene the fairies joined in dancing the Chilperic
Quadrilles.

Scene III is the grandmother's cottage in the wood. In the very first two lines—admirable play writing!—the characters of Little Red Riding Hood's mother and grandmother are made clear:

MONICA. Come along, mother, let us join our neighbors' holiday.
DOROTHY. Ah, they creeps to work, though fast they runs to play.

After grandmother has grumbled about the agitation for the new-fangled nine-hour working day, Red Riding Hood enters and sings of the joys of plucking "the flowers in the greenwood shade." Her grand-mother groans that it's a mercy the wolf hasn't eaten her, whereupon Red Riding Hood retorts, "If he did, Hyacinth would make him rue it," and we know which way the wind is blowing. Now the heroine tells her mother that she has made some cheesecakes; the grandmother says she'd like one; Red Riding Hood is about to start home for them when a storm blows up and the Duke's hunting party is heard offstage; the women take shelter in the cottage. The Duke comes up and is about to burst in on them but Amaryllis intervenes while Red Riding Hood escapes. This causes the Duke and Poggidorff to sing and dance *The Perfect Cure*—already per-formed as a number by the fantoccini—a popular polka of the day; a "cure" was a "caution," slang for an odd person:

> I've burst my pumps,
> I'm black with bumps,
> No more can I endure;
> In all the land
> There does not stand
> Another such a cure.

Scene IV shows the forest in winter—a snow scene too pretty not to use, though rushing the season a little. Amaryllis disposes her Pigmy army in hiding places. The Wolf prowls in. Then Little Red Riding Hood enters, and as she pauses to pick a flower (left over from the summer a few minutes back), he accosts her. Coyly bantering, she tries to cut the encounter short because the wicked Duke lives near by. She ex-patiates on the villainy of the nobleman and uses Nanki-Poo's improve-ment on the line in *Hamlet*:

> Not long ago, this thing of shreds and patches
> Prompted the Chancellor to tax our matches.

WOLF.   Oh, Lucifer, a Lowe trick!

The Wolf offers to accompany the girl to her grandmother's, saying:

> Accept my company.

L.R.R.H.   Oh, you're most polite;
> But granny would declare 'twas shocking quite.
> Good day.

As she leaves him, the Wolf resolves to get to the grandmother's cottage first. Poggidorff enters, unaware that his master has been changed from human form, and calmly delivers the classic line, "My lord, the carriage waits." Then, spying the transformation, he is seized with terror. But he understands what has happened when his master gives him a message to deliver. Now Hobblegobblewitz appears to spur the Wolf on; as the creature heads for the cottage the Pigmy army marches out and follows to the rescue.

There is a shift to the interior of Granny's cottage. Amaryllis posts a talking Jackdaw on guard. When Poggidorff comes with the Wolf's message the bird nettles him with saucy remarks. But Granny believes Poggidorff's tale that her daughter is ill and hurries off to see her. Then the Wolf arrives, disguises himself and, when Little Red Riding Hood comes in with the cheesecakes, almost overpowers her. The Pigmy army rushes in to shoot him and save the day.

Scene VI is the transformation scene. Amaryllis changes Hobblegobblewitz into Clown, the Duke into Pantaloon, Hyacinth into Harlequin, and Little Red Riding Hood into Columbine. Hereupon the harlequinade begins. Since this feature depended almost altogether upon action, the book of words breaks off at this point. But a critic in the London *Daily Telegraph* of 3 August 1872 told what happened. "The Clown and Pantaloon go through a series of droll adventures which keep the audience in a continual roar of laughter, but when the inevitable Policeman, getting in the way of a cannon, is blown to pieces and coolly takes himself up and reunites his scattered fragments, there is a shout of merriment from the juvenile portion of the spectators which would establish the reputation of any pantomime. The ingenuity of the transformations, the startling rapidity with which the scenes are changed, and the incessant bustle and fun of the action, are to be appreciated by elder people quite as much as by younger folk."

The London *Times* of 2 August 1872 supplements the account. "Not only do Harlequin and Columbine execute their 'trips' with wondrous agility, not only do Clown and Pantaloon knock each other about and triumph over the irrepressible Policeman, but in every scene, as in the olden times, some ingenious mechanical trick is introduced. The arrangements of the stage cannot be too highly recommended. When we say that there are twelve scenes in the little pantomime, and that but one of these is in the front groove, all who can understand us will see that a difficult problem is solved."

Like the minstrel show, the Victorian pantomime played into the hands of the puppeteer. Its tricks and transformations, its scenic resplendency, and its stock characters seem to have been made for puppetry. There

During the first New York engagement of the Royal Marionettes the auditorium at 18 East 16 Street in which they played was known as Robinson Hall. Between Union Square and Fifth Avenue, it was in the heart of the entertainment district. The building was erected sometime prior to 1868; in that year it was the Allemania Club. Taken over by the Society of Mechanics and Tradesmen in 1871, it was known as Mechanics Hall till 1875, and as the Parisian Varieties in 1877. After a lithograph opposite p. 169 in the Annals of the Society, New York, 1882.

was nothing that the big stage and human actors could do in this realm that puppets couldn't do just as well or even better. Therefore an audience would not be apt to look patronizingly upon a puppet pantomime as an imitation; it would accept it as a dramatic form in its own right. The delight with which Bullock's triple budget was accepted everywhere, together with its suitability for all ages, made it a money mine for the Liverpool manager.

Upon landing in New York the show was booked into Robinson Hall on 16th Street west of Union Square, an auditorium which has now been pulled down. It opened on 8 September 1873 (New York *Herald* of that date) with "J. E. McDonough and H. A. Earnshaw, Proprietors," advising the public:

The Royal Marionettes, from St. James Hall, London, in their wonderful performance of the Original Christy Minstrels; Part II, the antics of the amusing fantoccini: Blondin of the Tight-rope, Pat and Biddy, the Comic mules, Pete and Barney, Tommy and Sarah, the Celestial Dances by Chang, Bang, and Wa[n]g! concluding with the Grand Fairy Pantomime of Little Red Riding Hood, replete with scenic and mechanical effects, closely following the sad story of that sweet child, who was so dearly beloved by its mother and all the people of the village, closing . . . with a grand transformation of Neptune's Flight to the Enchanted Isle. Prices: sofas in parterre, $1; chairs in parquet, 75¢; general admission, 50¢; children always half price. Performances at 3 and 8 p. m.

Minor changes had been made in the London program. The comic mules were new in the fantoccini. As the George Middletons performed a similar trick (*Puppetry 1936*, p. 11), "Pantaloon rides in seated backwards on a

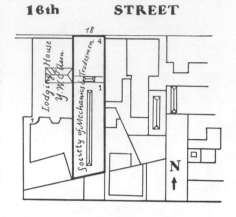

16th   STREET

Detail after an insurance map of 1889 in the New-York Historical Society, showing the plot at 18 East 16 Street. Unlike most New York blocks with their checkerboard regularity, this one has diagonal property boundaries, relics of the farm plots which ran at right angles to the old Bloomingdale Road, now Broadway. No. 18 is therefore an unusually long lot. Behind the four-story club building was built an auditorium 38 x about 120 feet with a long skylight —larger than some of the playhouses off Broadway built in the early 1900's.

donkey. Joey the Clown points out his mistake. But as Pantaloon turns around, the donkey's head disappears and another sprouts out at its tail. He is still seated backwards. He proceeds to sell the beast to Joey, who can never get to its head before it sprouts out at the opposite end. Finally both of them mount the donkey, which sprouts two heads, splits in two, and walks off, each half on two legs with one of them. (The donkey has two heads, which collapse under its belly like the blades of a jack-knife. It has no tail or tails. And its halves are held together with a vertical pin.)"

Little Red Riding Hood had either been changed into a more sentimental play than the London one or the "sad story of that sweet child" was written with tongue in cheek. The grand transformation scene, the subject of which was not specified in London, was certainly a *non sequitur,* what with Neptune's flight; but pantomimes were put together like that. It must have shimmered marvelously, in any event. Rita Lawrence who as a little girl lived near at 58 West 11 Street, may have seen this show. In *Amateurs and Actors of the 19th-20th Centuries* (Menton, France, 1936, p. 10) she recalled that she was taken to the marionettes. "It was such an important event for me that I looked very solemn, my mother said. The transformation scene, a golden rain, I shall never forget, and nothing since has ever surpassed it, no matter how wonderful."

The *World* of 9 September commented, "The ingenuity, the humor, and the flexibility of these performances are something astonishing, and to a community of wire-pullers must open up a vast vista of possibilities. The puppets not only play dexterously upon the bones and tambourine, and execute the sailor's hornpipe and a number of other difficult dances with a grace that is quite supernatural, but they sing and discourse most reasonably and humanly—at least they seem to. A more harmlessly laughable entertainment than they provide, it would be hard to conceive."

The auditorium was turned into library stacks by the Society of Mechanics and Tradesmen in 1878. From a lithograph of the stacks opposite p. 192 in its Annals *the appearance of Robinson Hall may be reconstructed. It probably had a cramped stage at the far end, a level floor, windows and a skylight imperfectly shaded, and all the inconveniences of the average school auditorium in which puppets play today.*

The *Daily Graphic* of 8 September said, "The wooden clown rivals in grotesque contortions the proverbial Fox. The 'Fairy Queen' in gold tissue moves about with as much 'empressement' as the genuine article, and bursts into song after the accepted fashion, but with the great advantage of being furnished with a much better voice than is usual. The minstrels give songs and choruses in true burnt-cork abandon; but perhaps the greatest hit is the duet, 'Tommy,' in Part II, which introduced an energetic old woman and her one-legged husband. The 'business' in the pantomime is very droll, and nothing wanting in elaboration."

A week later the *Graphic* went on, "The Marionettes at Robinson Hall are not to be mistaken for a mere addition to our most sprightly amusements. They are in reality a school for actors, and the enterprise which brings them here is surely a benevolent one. But then, there is little hope that our actors and actresses will ever equal these admirable puppets. If they are not quite as large as life, they are certainly twice as natural as the sort of life which we see on the ordinary dramatic stage." And again, on 20 September, it said, "The leading tragedian never makes the slightest objection to assuming any part that may be assigned to him and the leading lady, from the moment she leaves the stage and has her legs folded up preparatory to being stowed away in her box, never says a word about the hardship of her life or the impossibility of living on her salary. Ah! what wives and daughters, and especially what mothers-in-law, the ladies of the marionette company would make."

The *World* of 27 September reported a visit, the night before, of the great actress Christine Nilsson, who "was in her seat before the performance began, and seemed to enjoy the entertainment exceedingly, being often the first and loudest to applaud. At the close . . . she cordially thanked Mr. Bullock." An accomplished player could appreciate the puppets to the full.

Twelve shows a week were given for seven weeks until 1 November (New York *Herald* of that date), when the company moved to the Brooklyn Atheneum, boasting of "a most successful run in New York of 100 performances" (Brooklyn *Eagle,* 4 November). There it played a like number of shows a week until 15 November. The program was to continue unaltered for almost six months.

From Brooklyn the Royal Marionettes, with McDonough and Earnshaw advertised as proprietors and Bullock not mentioned, crossed the Hudson to the Newark Opera House, beginning a short run on Tuesday evening, 18 November, and playing matinee and evening shows through Saturday (Newark *Daily Advertiser,* 15-22 November 1873). The newspaper critics had nothing but praise for the marionettes; one suspects that they ran "hand-outs" given them by the show's publicity man. This is the sort of thing used in Newark; everywhere else it was to be the same:

The Royal Marionettes from St. James' Hall, London, drew a large audience at the Opera House last evening. The performances consist of representations of Blondin on the tight-rope, sailor's hornpipe by an "old salt," Irish jig by Pat and Biddy, comic mules, Celestial dances, singers and bell ringers, pantomime of Little Red Riding Hood, with songs and choruses, etc.—the only actors appearing to view being life-size wooden figures operated with considerable mechanical skill.

Of course the puppets were not life sized. But the illusion of bigness, which everybody experiences when there is nothing full scale against which to measure the miniature stage, either deceived the critic or allowed the proprietors to foster the idea.

From Newark the company moved back to Brooklyn, playing at Hooley's Opera House from 24 November through 12 December, three weeks lacking a day (Brooklyn *Eagle* for those dates). Money was rolling in.

On 5 December, Bullock, McDonough, and Earnshaw renewed their agreement in Philadelphia, where they were making arrangements for the Royal Marionettes to appear. W. W. Scovern—the signature is not clear; it may be Schaven or Scheven—perhaps a Philadelphian in some way connected with the show business, signed as witness (McDonough *et al. vs.* Bullock *et al.,* Schedule A, 26 February 1874). Bullock was evidently satisfied that all was going well, though he specified in this contract that his name was to be connected with the show. McDonough, who was known in America, may have persuaded him that the marionettes would fare better under a familiar manager's name; the omission of Bullock's name while he was present had not, evidently, seemed consequential to him. He appeared to have no misgivings whatsoever.

THE

ROYAL MARIONETTES.

WORDS OF THE SONGS

AND THE

PANTOMIME

OF

LITTLE RED RIDING HOOD.

PRICE SIXPENCE.

ST. JAMES'S GREAT HALL, REGENT ST.

Two Performances Every Day at Three and Eight o'clock.

W. J. BULLOCK, Sole Proprietor.

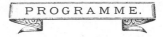

PROGRAMME.

PART I.

THE FANTOCCINI.

1.—Blondin's Tight Rope Feats.
2.—The Scaramouch.
3.—The Wonderful Contortionists.
4.—The Perfect Cures.
5.—The Compound Turk—"Multum in Parvo."
6.—Pat and Biddy in their "rale Irish Jig."
7.—The Pole Balancer. A perfect wonder.
8.—Tommy and Sarah, the Comic Duettists.
9.—The Celestial Dancers and Bell Ringers.

THE CLAIMANT'S SONG *(occasionally introduced)*.

I 'm not so old in appearance or years
  As I am in folly and sin ;
Experience teaches fools to be wise,
  But not till their troubles begin.
I know that in this worldly fight
I 've not been always in the right,
But a different view I 'd keep in sight
  Could I live my time over again.
    But what 's the use of fretting, my boys,
    In this world of folly and pain ;
    But oh, what a different man I would be
    Could I live my time over again.

And now instead of a millionaire,
  And possessed of the baronetcy,
I 'm bound to stump it from town to town,
  With Mr. So-So, M.P.
Think kindly, then, of poor old Roger,
Who really 's not the only dodger,
And in Newgate would be no lodger
  Could I live my time over again.
    Then what 's the use, &c.

Book of words sold at performances of the Royal Marionettes in England; there was an American edition as well. Original page size 8½ x 5½ inches. Cover and first page.

By 12 December, Joseph Dixon McLaren of Edinburgh, Scotland, had arrived in New York, where Bullock gave him power of attorney to collect the proceeds from the show and act as his agent. Bullock then returned to England where he had other irons in the fire. It is just possible that he took back a few puppeteers with him, replacing them with players he had found in New York so that he would have the nucleus of another company to play in England. The number of puppeteers who were to manipulate the Royal Marionettes was not fixed in the contract. So long as the performances were played and the puppeteers felt that they were not overworked, everything proceeded apace.

The renewed contract went into effect on 15 December, when the company opened at Concert Hall, Philadelphia, for a four-week run. The advertisement for the first performance, in the Philadelphia *Public Ledger* of that date, was headed, "John E. McDonough, Manager." Why was Earnshaw left out? It went on, "Something new and entertaining. First appearance in Philadelphia, Monday evening, 15 December, and every evening at 8. Matinees at 2 p. m. on Wednesdays and Saturdays of each week. W. J. Bullock's Automatic Troupe of Royal Marionettes. Pronounced by the New York *Tribune, Herald, World, Home Journal, Times, Sun, Graphic*, Brooklyn *Eagle*, and the entire press of that city to be the most astonishing performance that has ever crossed the Atlantic, and entirely free from any objectionable feature. [This for the reassurance of staid citizens of the Quaker City.] Band and chorus number 25. . . . Secured seats, 75¢; children (secured), 40¢; general admission, 50¢; gallery, 25¢."

As the contract demanded, Bullock was properly mentioned. Business was very good. Advance ticket sales must have shown that a month was all too short a stay in town, for at the beginning of the third week of the run this announcement was added to the regular advertisement, "In consequence of having previously arranged to appear in Washington 13 January, it will be impossible to prolong our stay beyond the time mentioned." This was in the *Ledger* of 29 December. At the start of the last week there was this notice, "Any persons holding tickets who were unable to obtain admission on Friday and Saturday evening of last week, will have their money refunded, if so desired, or their tickets will be received as admission for any evening or matinee during our last week." (*Ledger*, 5 January 1874.) The run closed, as recorded in that paper of the same date, on 10 January.

Then the company went to Washington, D.C., opening at Willard's Hall on 12 January, properly advertised as Bullock's in the Washington *National Republican* of that date. Among the features mentioned in the fantoccini numbers were the usual ones and "the original stilt performer." At the beginning of the third week a somewhat misleading advertisement appeared in the same paper, "Change of bill! First time of the new feature. Compound Turk! The Scaramouch!" These numbers were certainly not new, though it is possible that the puppets, wearing out, had been replaced with fresh duplicates. Notices in the *National Republican* from 12-15 and 17-30 January state that many people were turned away for lack of seats. On Friday, 30 January, the last night of the scheduled run, for some unannounced reason there was no performance.

At this time McLaren, acting for Bullock, must have become suspicious of McDonough and Earnshaw. He asked them to sign an additional clause to their contract, as was brought to light in the McDonough *vs.* Bullock Affadavit of Defense, filed 5 March 1874. "It is further agreed by the undersigned parties," it read, "that the contract signed in Philadelphia 5 December 1873 with regard to Bullock's Royal Marionettes shall be fully carried out without the slightest variation, and that no damages shall be claimed of either for the failure to exhibit last night, 30 January 1874, at Willard's Hall. All this to be in full faith and confidence." Dated at Washington, 31 January, this was signed by McLaren and by McDonough for himself and Earnshaw. Where was *he*?

On Tuesday evening, 3 February 1874, the company opened at the Maryland Institute in Baltimore. Bullock was named as owner. The matinees were Monday, Wednesday, and Saturday at two. The only novelty, apparently, was "the Piccaninni Ballet" (Baltimore *Sun*, 3 February 1874). The name of J. E. McDonough appeared in the advertisements but Earnshaw was still missing. For the first time one finds "the great charm of the household" applied to *Little Red Riding Hood* as an epithet of praise (the same paper, 6 February). Though trouble was brewing, no signs of it appeared. The last Baltimore performance was on 14 February.

Meanwhile, back in London, Bullock had secured an engagement for another company of his at the theatre in the Crystal Palace; it played from 16-28 February 1874. The advertisements in the London *Times* speak of "Bullock's life-size and lifelike marionettes (from America)" and "their unique performance" without mentioning details of the program. Was the assertion that the marionettes were from America a piece of press-agentry, true in the loose sense that their owner also had a troupe in America, or was it to be taken literally? Had Bullock brought back some of his company, who formed the core of this unit? Since the names of puppeteers were never given in billing, this must remain a mystery.

McDonough and Earnshaw—the latter was back again—duly announced that Bullock's Royal Marionettes would open at Odd Fellows Hall, Harrisburg, "on Monday evening, 16 February, for one week, including three family matinees, Wednesday, Thursday, and Saturday at 2 P.M. J. E. McDonough begs leave to inform the citizens of Harrisburg, the members of the Legislature, and public bodies thereto belonging, that having been so successful in the cities of New York, Philadelphia, Baltimore, and Washington in the administration of wire-pulling, thereby giving an entertainment full of fun and fancy," they would offer —we know the details—a band and chorus of twenty-five persons, etc. The company arrived and opened in due course (Harrisburg *Daily Patriot*, 14-16 February 1874). All was deceptively calm during the week. McDonough inserted an advertisement in the Reading *Daily Eagle* of 21 February to herald the coming of the troupe to the Grand Opera House there the following week, "in accordance with his promise made a year ago." But what difficulties he was to have in trying to keep it!

At the end of the run on Saturday night, when Earnshaw was in Philadelphia and McDonough out of town, presumably as advance man for the company, out of a clear sky McLaren announced that the contract between Bullock and his managers had been violated and hence was at an end. He sent a letter to this effect to Earnshaw and gave notice to William Adams, the treasurer for the company, as representative for McDonough (Affidavit for Defense, paragraph 11). McDonough, hurrying back to Harrisburg, wrote a letter to the Reading paper, asking that the people of the town suspend judgment in the case until it could be heard before the proper tribunal, and saying that "the mean and contemptible advantage taken of our absence on Saturday evening" was proof of cowardice.

Convinced of duplicity on the part of McDonough and Earnshaw, McLaren took the strings into his own hands. Until he could arrange for further bookings, he leased the Odd Fellows Hall for another week. Then he ordered a handbill and newspaper advertisements to announce that the marionettes would remain one week longer. They contained the warning, "Caution. The public will please beware of fraudulent imitators and mean traders on the titles, success, and reputation of this entertainment. . . . Messrs. McDonough and Earnshaw are no longer connected in any capacity with Bullock's Royal Marionettes." He signed himself as business manager for William J. Bullock, sole proprietor. A copy of the handbill is preserved as an exhibit with McDonough *vs.* Bullock, Motion and Bill for Injunction, filed 26 February. The advertisement ran in the Harrisburg *Daily Patriot*, 23-28 February. William Adams was ousted and Edward Harvey was made the new treasurer for the show.

"On Sunday," the Reading *Daily Eagle* of 24 February reported, "there was much angry discussion between the contending parties." On Monday morning, when the troupe did not arrive in Reading with its baggage to set up for the show that night, the manager of the Grand Opera House took the train to Harrisburg to find out what was wrong. Meanwhile McDonough had "asserted his right to the scenery and other property of the show by entering the hall and removing it to the depot for shipment to Reading." McLaren armed himself with a search warrant, arrived at the depot with an officer of the law, had McDonough arrested for stealing and malicious mischief, and bore the paraphernalia triumphantly back to Odd Fellows Hall. Hell was let loose with a flood of the denunciatory handbills.

McDonough went before Alderman Edwards to charge McLaren with perjury, and McLaren and Harvey, the new treasurer, with conspiracy. "Before the show went on in the evening the parties were arrested, and at a hearing they conducted themselves in a most shameful and ungentlemanly manner. McLaren and Harvey were released on bail," as Mc-

Donough had been. Manager Steel of the Reading Opera House and manager Mishler of the Reading Academy of Music were on hand to watch the progress of the fight with more than the interest of bystanders.

On Tuesday McLaren went to court, showed his power of attorney to act for Bullock, pointed out that Bullock was the owner of the marionettes, McDonough and Earnshaw only his hirelings, and asked for an injunction to prevent them from seizing the show, which they still threatened to do, to the great monetary damage of the owner. Judge John J. Pearson granted the injunction, upon McLaren's furnishing bond for $300 (Bullock *vs.* McDonough, Bill in Equity, filed 24 February, Court of Common Pleas, Dauphin County).

While Manager Steel saw the possibilities of securing his attraction fade, manager Mishler closed with McLaren to bring the show to his theatre the next week, if all went well for McLaren; the Reading *Daily Eagle* of 25 February gave tidings of their arrival at the Academy of Music on 2 March. Meanwhile McDonough was busy preparing a countersuit. And it was to be observed that he had drawn certain of the better puppeteers aside and had long talks with them; a statement signed by six of the company was dated 25 February but not released till 7 March. Crowds crushed to see the show that was getting so much publicity. "Several persons nightly sleep in Odd Fellows Hall," said the *Daily Eagle* of 25 February, "to repel any invasion that might be attempted by the enemy, and the building is otherwise guarded."

On Thursday, 26 February, McDonough went to court and showed his contract with Bullock, claiming that it had made him a partner in the enterprise. He pointed out that the agreement was to continue to 7 March and that he had already given due notice in writing that he wished an extension for another six months. He was to receive, according to contract, half the gross proceeds; he had expended large sums fulfilling his part of the agreement and making the business profitable to all concerned. He had acepted McLaren as Bullock's agent from 12 December 1873 to 21 February 1874, when McLaren had suddenly interfered with the routine and prevented him from taking the show to the next engagement arranged for. Now McLaren was taking all the receipts without giving an account of them. He was negotiating alone for bookings in Lancaster and elsewhere, and was about to remove the show thither, disregarding the contract and repudiating McDonough and Earnshaw. Proceeds from the enterprise were sizable, averaging $1000 a week for the past nine weeks, $400 of this being net profit; he was ready and willing to adhere to the contract. Therefore he asked that McLaren be restrained from removing the show and exhibiting it, that he be required to hand it over so that the agreement might be carried out in good faith, with provision for indemnification, that the partnership be declared to exist, and that further relief be granted (McDonough *vs*. Bullock, Motion for Injunction, filed 26 February).

As proof that the business was lucrative, William Adams went on record, in the same Motion for Injunction, as having been treasurer for the last week in Philadelphia and those in Washington, Baltimore, and Harrisburg, six weeks during which he had kept account of moneys received to the amount of $8,141.30. To understand the value of these earnings, it must be recalled that the dollar was then worth five times its 1948 purchasing power. This in face of the fact that times were growing hard. Shortly after the arrival of the marionettes from England, postwar inflation had been punctured and the country was sinking more and more deeply into depression week by week. That a show could draw overflowing audiences at such a time was proof both of its entertainment qualities and of the worries from which the public wished distraction. The profits were worth fighting for in any event.

Judge Pearson granted an injunction against McLaren's removing the show until the status of all parties could be determined. This was on 26 February, the same day that the petition had been tendered (McDonough *vs*. Bullock, Bill filed that date). Considering it an initial victory, McDonough joyously telegraphed the news to his friends in Reading, and of course to the *Daily Eagle*.

The show played in Harrisburg to the end of its second week. On the following Monday, 2 March, Manager Mishler began to chew his fingernails, for the baggage was not in evidence in Reading. As the reopening of the court hearing was not to be till two o'clock that afternoon, nothing could be moved until the injunction was modified.

McDonough had prepared an answer to McLaren's charges. He maintained that he and Earnshaw were indeed partners of Bullock and again exhibited his contract as proof. He denied that he had unrightfully attempted to transport the show to Reading and produced a letter proving that McLaren had agreed to go there:

Baltimore, Md.
9 Feby. 1874

John E. McDonough:
Sirs:

Yours of yesterday date to hand. I have voted Harrisburg from 16-21 February and Reading from 23-28.

I decline to go to the places you propose after that date, *viz*: Lancaster, Allentown, and Elmira, having no intention of visiting the small towns only and leaving the large cities for others.

Jos. D. McLaren

This was included in the Answer filed 2 March.

Judge Pearson ordered that the defendants be at liberty to remove the baggage of the show as they saw proper if they deposited in lieu thereof $5000, as the removal of the property would be of benefit to both parties concerned (Order of Court filed 2 March). McLaren was prepared for this; indeed, he had cabled Bullock in Liverpool for that amount the Wednesday before and received it, said the *Daily Eagle* of 25 February. But it was too late to get the show to Reading for the promised opening. The puppets did not arrive at the Academy of Music until Tuesday, 3 March, and there were then so many other troubles that it was announced there would be no performance until the company was thoroughly reorganized.

It burst as a bombshell that McDonough was preparing to open with a marionette show of his own in Philadelphia on 16 March; the *Daily Eagle* carried the news on 3 March.

The next day McLaren betook himself to Judge Pearson to unbosom new griefs. McDonough was continuing to molest him in the exhibition of the show. He had, in fact, just caused the sheriff of Berks County to attach the outfit for a debt which he claimed to be unpaid. Since, because of the $5000 security, the puppets were virtually in the possession of the court, and since the debt would have to be proven, he petitioned that McDonough be arrested for violation of the injunction and for contempt of court (Bullock *vs.* McDonough, Affidavit and Petition for Attachment, filed 4 March).

Upon the description of the sheriff, the boxes of equipment that had called forth so much delight were but sorry things. He stated that he had taken possession of "a lot of puppets, or wooden figures, about 80 in number, scenery and effects thereunto belonging, together with calcium lights and other property." The sheriff's name was Evan Mishler. Was he a relative of the theatre manager, obliged to act against family interest through professional duty?

Judge Pearson ordered that McDonough be arrested and brought before the court to answer for contempt (Bullock *vs.* McDonough, Order of 4 March). On the same crowded day, Steel of the Grand Opera House brought suit against McDonough, Earnshaw, and Bullock to recover damages for the failure of the marionettes to appear at his house the week before, the *Daily Eagle* recorded. He too asked for an attachment of the unfortunate puppets. When Judge Woodward of the Berks County court heard of the complications, he ordered the puppets to remain untouched at the Academy of Music. The sheriff had placed a watchman over the puppet boxes all Tuesday night; McDonough was about to remove them Wednesday when he was prevented by Judge Woodward's order.

Now Steel's writ was dissolved and, upon giving security for them, McLaren got back the puppets. He gathered together what remained of his puppeteers, six having been enticed away by the offers of McDonough, and limped into production at the Academy of Music on Thursday night, 5 March, as the *Daily Eagle* advertised.

McDonough was conducted back to Harrisburg (Bullock *vs.* McDonough, Motion to Commit Defendant for Contempt, filed 5 March). McLaren presented his affidavit of defense the same day. In it he stated that he did not think the contract between McDonough and Earnshaw and Bullock had made them partners; in fact, the show belonged wholly to Bullock, as James Shaw, who had made the puppets on salary for Bullock, attested. The managers had been reimbursed for their work according to contract. But they had violated it in several ways: they had not announced the show as Bullock's, but merely as the Royal Marionettes, hoping later to trade on the name themselves; they had abused the privilege of issuing complimentary tickets to the press; they had not advertised the Reading engagement sufficiently in advance; in Baltimore, Reading, and other places, they had usurped Bullock's prerogative in issuing bills and posters; they had contemplated or offered bookings in small, unimportant towns. The most serious of these charges, that of failing to use Bullock's name, was untrue insofar as the period after the renewal of the contract was concerned; this we have checked. Before that period Bullock himself had been present, and he need not have renewed the contract if he had felt this omission deliberately contrived. The other transgressions may have worked no harm; they would seem to have been minor. However, McLaren could now be certain of the rumors he had heard of a competitive company. Though it violated nothing in the contract, it certainly invalidated the agreement.

In his Affidavit of Defense he stated that "figures and properties of similar character to those used in this entertainment are being prepared in Philadelphia and in England to be used for said McDonough's private use and advantage; that said enterprise has been preparing for a long time, and was so preparing when said McDonough, with intent to deceive the deponent and said Bullock, gave the respondent notice that he would continue said contract for six months from 7 March 1874; and that said McDonough, so far from intending to fulfill that assumed and pretended engagement, has already engaged Concert Hall in Philadelphia for a marionette exhibition which is not this entertainment for a period of six months from 16 March 1874, and has engaged five persons of said Bullock's company to enter his own service and assist in the management of said private exhibition from the said 7 March."

To test the truth of this, McLaren declared, he had offered to go to play in Philadelphia on 2 March at the Concert Hall. But McDonough had pretended that this theatre could not be hired until 23 March. Very well, McLaren had replied, he was willing to play there on 23 March. McDonough had not only failed to arrange for this but had booked the hall for his own purposes. Hence the dissension.

The corroborative evidence throws light upon details backstage.

James Shaw, being sworn before a notary on 27 February, said "that he had manufactured the figures and properties now in dispute for W. J. Bullock at a weekly wage [one wonders how little], except the scenery, and came with them from England to this country; that nothing has been added to them since they came to America, and that they have never been sold to anyone by said Bullock, to the best of deponent's knowledge and belief. And that the scenery was also brought from England and belongs also to said Bullock."

Philip George Clark, being sworn in also on that day, revealed "that on 21 November 1873, at Newark, N.J., John E. McDonough, one of the complainants in said bill, offered deponent, for himself and his wife who are figure-workers in Bullock's Royal Marionettes, an engagement with himself (said McDonough) to begin on 8 March 1874, in an employment in a marionette company with which said W. J. Bullock was not to be connected, offering deponent a larger salary than he now received. That said McDonough then told deponent that he was getting up a new company of marionettes and wanted to employ him for that purpose from 8 March 1874.

"Deponent further says, that one of the present workers for Bullock's marionettes told deponent that he had been employed by said Mc-Donough from 8 March 1874; and deponent has been informed and believes that several other workers have been so engaged by said McDonough and are to enter his service on 8 March 1874." Clark made his mark, not being able to write his name to sign the statement.

So an excellent company was destroyed through the cupidity of its entrepreneurs.

Those who remained faithful to McLaren played matinee and evening shows in Reading on Friday and Saturday, 6 and 7 March. Because another show had already been booked into the Academy of Music for the first part of the following week, it did not play out its week until 12-14 March (Reading *Daily Eagle* of those dates). Then it paused for reorganization.

The legal entanglement eventually worked itself out without determining who was most at fault. Judge Pearson gave this explanation for handing the puppets over to McLaren: "In the present case we are satisfied that to continue the writ would be highly injurious to both parties; that it is for the benefit of all that the figures should be removed from town to town and exhibited; on that depends the whole value of the property and the profits of the concern. Many matters have been averred in the answer filed against the preliminary writ and urged in the argument, which are entirely out of place at present" (McDonough *vs.* Bullock, Order of Court filed 6 March).

The Judge confined himself to the chief point: were these men partners? He said that by their contract they were not. However, McDonough and Earnshaw were entitled to possession of the outfit to transport it, and the charge of larceny and obtaining it by a search warrant were entirely illegal. Neither managers nor owner could maintain an action of replevin against each other, for each had an equal right in the possession and must work out his rights either at law or in equity, under the contract. If there had been a partnership, it would have been the duty of the court to appoint a receiver if the partners could not agree. But since there was none, no action was taken but to dissolve the injunction.

The Judge also declared, in connection with the contempt-of-court action against McDonough, that this contender had unfortunately been misadvised in starting proceedings in another county while the case was within the jurisdiction of Dauphin County; being fully satisfied that no contempt of court was intended, he discharged McDonough upon his paying the costs of making the attachment (Opinion filed 6 March).

McLaren asked that his $5000 deposit be refunded. It was given back to him on 10 April. Judge Pearson gave this opinion on 15 April: "On the argument of the application it is continued that the injunction should not have been dissolved, and if it was, the money should be held as security for what may be ultimately decreed. . . . A party cannot claim on one ground and ask for a decree on another. If other reasons existed on which an account could be demanded, under the partnership, they should have been set forth on the bill amended. The attention of the court cannot be called to a claim on one ground, and when that is overruled and the injunction under issue, urge it on another not then suggested. . . . The defendants . . . are entitled to take the money out of court according to the condition of the deposit."

As for the information made against McLaren and Harvey for perjury and conspiracy, on 30 April a grand jury ignored the two bills in which it had been contained and imposed costs on McDonough (Reading *Daily*

Eagle, 1 May). Recognizing that suits at law were wasteful of time and money, the former collaborators turned their energies from the courts to the project of cutting each other's throats.

On 7 March the Reading paper ran this manifesto:

Harrisburg, 25 February 1874

For good and sufficient reasons, we, the undersigned members of Bullock's Royal Marionettes, from the great St. James' Hall, London, also of Robinson Hall, New York, . . . do most respectfully inform the public that we have most honorably fulfilled our engagements with that gentleman, and will in the future be connected with Messrs. McDonough and Earnshaw's Royal Marionettes, and will have the honor of presenting, for the first time in America, Thomas Holden's great performance of *Robin Rough Head*, originally performed by him in London for 200 nights. Also, the reconstructed pantomime of *Little Red Riding Hood*.

Mrs. Charles Webb
Mrs. Thomas Holden
Miss Elizabeth Hughes
Mr. Charles Webb
Mr. W. H. Lawrence
Mr. Thomas Holden
Formerly stage manager of Bullock's Royal Marionettes

When this proclamation was published in the Philadelphia *Public Ledger* of 16 March, it was dated from Philadelphia, 7 March, and included one more signature, that of Mr. H. N. Cronwell. Perhaps he had remained faithful to McLaren to the end of his Reading engagement and had then gone over to McDonough.

The names of ten of the original Bullock company thus are known, the seven above, James Shaw, who evidently remained with McLaren because McDonough had other puppet makers in Philadelphia and England working for him, and Mr. and Mrs. Philip George Clark. Obviously McDonough had taken the cream of the troupe. The Clarks were probably the only actual puppeteers he had rejected, though he had made overtures to them in Newark when he must have approached each in turn. How had McLaren managed to do shows for the six days in Reading? He must have impressed into service some of the singers and readers who had not hitherto handled puppets, but who had watched the technique and perhaps tried it secretly. The performances could not have been good. But Reading was a provincial town, to be imposed upon with impunity!

With the choruses of puppets strung in tandem, as they probably were, a truncated version of the program could have been managed by the

Clarks, Cronwell, and Shaw. The latter must have been able to work his own puppets, though he traveled in the capacity of property man, to make repairs when necessary. A competent twentieth-century company of five puppeteers would be able to manage a whole program such as this, save perhaps for the singing.

Bullock needed a company of twenty or twenty-five (if his announced strength was not an exaggeration) because of the division of labor in his show. He used perhaps ten puppeteers, one of them the stage manager, another the property man, and one of the women a wardrobe mistress; he had perhaps six singers and readers, a male quartet and two female voices, a lighting man, and three stagehands to set up, take down, and pack the stage, the puppeteers assisting them. That makes twenty. Then there were five musicians, as specified in the contract, who did not travel with the troupe but were hired from town to town.

The "front of the house" crew, ticket seller, ticket taker, and ushers, were of course found locally. McDonough, and McLaren later, acted as advance man, writing and placing advertisements, securing bookings, and managing business in general. The treasurer kept accounts and provided railroad tickets and hotel accommodations. McDonough declared that expenses amounted to $600 a week. The salaries of the company could not have averaged more than $15 a week—perhaps $25 for man and wife. But that was at least as much, in the purchasing power of its day, as a good puppeteer or actor received on the road in 1948.

It is with a thrill of recognition that one sees the name of Holden, member of the important English puppeteer family. After a couple of years with McDonough and Earnshaw, Thomas Holden was to return to Europe and play on the Continent with great success. Edmond de Goncourt, seeing his marionettes in France on 5 April 1879, wrote in his *Journal*, "Holden's marionettes! These wooden creatures have a disquieting spell. There's a ballerina, pirouetting on toe-point in the moonlight, like something out of *The Tales of Hoffmann*, and a clown who goes to bed, snuggles down, and falls asleep, with all the movements of a human being of flesh and blood." There were several Holdens, Thomas's brother John, who had a marionette company in London in 1878 (listed in the *Era Almanach* of that year); his brother James, considered the cleverest manipulator of puppets in the family, "though no talker," according to Harry Wilding (*World's Fair*, 2 December 1939); his sister Mae, who married Jesse Jewell and came to America to live, having brought her own troupe across the Atlantic early in the twentieth century; and his sister Sarah Jane, who married Henry James Middleton, of another important puppeteering family, and came to America soon after her brother, as we are to record.

The Lawrences were still another family who followed puppeteering. Mrs. Thomas Holden had been a Miss Lawrence; James Holden married another Miss Lawrence (as Harry Wilding remembered); hence the W. H. Lawrence in this company was Mrs. Thomas Holden's brother. Perhaps it was he who started a troupe under the Lawrence name in London in 1877 (listed in the *Era Almanach* of 1878). This intermarried and closely related group must have worked with great understanding and co-ordination, its emotional friction more fraternal than professional. Because of Holden's position as stage manager for Bullock, his skill and experience were considered superior. From long practice in teamwork this company must have been a remarkable one.

One wonders why these puppeteers, whose sense of loyalty could have been no less than that of others working under the apprenticeship system, seem to have had no qualms in deserting Bullock and going over to his rival. If they were under contract until 7 March 1874, Bullock apparently did not bother to renew it or to meet the higher salaries offered by McDonough, which McLaren must have heard about before 23 February. So they were quite within their rights in accepting new jobs. It is unlikely, of course, that they had contracts; only important stars could exact a written agreement from a producer. Players were at the mercy of theatre managers, and were often left stranded penniless when an enterprise failed. The puppeteers had worked hard for Bullock. What actor today would consent to do twelve shows a week? They saw that they were helping to make a lot of money. They were not underpaid, but they may have taken a dislike to Bullock or to McLaren for his attitude toward them. McDonough, to judge from newspaper accounts, had a winning personality; he was always smiling and polite. He was the sort of man in whom one placed confidence. His plans may have sounded exciting—a trip across the far-flung continent—new towns in the west—gold-mining camps—buffalo, cowboys, Indians—whereas Bullock may have said nothing at all of the future. Whatever the reasons, the puppeteers went over to McDonough. They had no occasion to regret it. He gave them two years of steady employment and took them half around the world and back.

Bullock was indifferent or tight lipped because he knew he could find plenty more puppeteers in England. He hoped to thwart his competitors by rushing over another big company to crowd them out of all the big cities. At the beginning of the trouble McLaren had cabled him to send such a company. It arrived almost as soon as McDonough's new equipment was ready.

There were delays because of necessary preparation. McDonough's reopening in Philadelphia was scheduled for 16 March but it did not take place until 21 March, a Saturday night (*Public Ledger* of that date). If he had ordered scenery and puppets from England, did they arrive in time? This is to be doubted if a single worker such as James Shaw was entrusted with them; an elaborate show takes several months and a crew to build. Then there was the Philadelphia puppet maker. Who was he? In 1908 there was such a craftsman in town. "If the best grade of puppets are desired," wrote Ernest Russell in *Outing Magazine* (January 1908, p. 479), "they can be had (made to order and of any design) of a gentleman in Philadelphia who has followed this trade for thirty years. His puppets are works of art, beautifully and substantially dressed, carefully painted, and cost from $2.50 to $3.50 each." Was this still the same person? Unfortunately his name has not come to light.

On 17 March McDonough had advertised in the *Public Ledger* "our promised return with the original troupe" to Concert Hall. "Everything new, sparkling, bright. Introducing, for the first time in America, Thomas Holden's sketch, *Robin Rough Head, or Plowman Turned Lord*. Followed by a Grand Variety Fantastique: Blondin of the rope, Zanfretta on stilts, the comic mules, the compound Turk, the Chinese dancers. Concluding with the fairy pantomime of *Little Red Riding Hood*, the Charm of the Household, with new and gorgeous scenery, introducing, for the first time in fifteen years, John E. McDonough's celebrated transformation scene from *The Seven Sisters*, entitled *The Birth of the Butterfly in the Bower of Ferns*. . . . Scale of prices: secured adults, 75¢; ditto children, 40¢; general admission, 50¢; gallery, 25¢. Notice. The stage has been raised and the general condition of seating much improved."

On the opening day another advertisement, with doubled and tripled display lines, a publicity device that had started as a typographical makeshift when large sizes of type could not be held against the drum of early rotary newspaper presses, announced "a new marionette exhibition and the old company, the only ones that have ever appeared in the great St. James' Hall, London. . . . We challenge all Europe to excel it in scenic effect, in mechanical art, in wardrobe and fantoccini. . . . Carriages ordered at 10" (the *Ledger*). In the second week, if the Saturday opening may be considered a first week, the advertisements boasted that 5000 adults and 6000 children had thronged to Concert Hall during the week. By the third week the audiences were computed at 31,000. *Robin Rough Head* was replaced by "The Original Christy Minstrels, full band and chorus, introducing sentimental and comic songs, and Old Uncle Eph." The program was now practically identical with Bullock's. One wonders whether the text of *Little Red Riding Hood* was adapted, "borrowed" as Mark Twain put it, or completely rewritten. It was probably "borrowed," for in the absence of proper copyright protection, anyone could produce

Handbill of the Boston engagement, 16 April-16 May 1874. Original 6 x 9 inches. The playbill of this run, preserved in the Harvard College Library theatre collection, has an initial note, "Mr. W. J. Bullock . . . begs distinctly to inform his patrons that no living person appears on the stage in sight of the audience, but that every artist is a Marionette or Puppet, each being manipulated by an unseen worker. Numbers having been deceived, it becomes necessary to state this, that the novelty, cleverness, and travesty on humanity may be duly appreciated." And he added, "The entertainment never exceeds two hours."

a play if he got hold of the script. This was not honest, but not uncustomary.

The last show in Philadelphia, marked in the *Ledger*, was on 25 April. The names of McDonough and Earnshaw appeared nowhere on the billing. While the managers were trading on the name and fame of Bullock's Royal Marionettes, the public was not being cheated, even if it was being deluded, for it saw the same program, performed by the same puppeteers, which it had so much enjoyed before.

McLaren had gone meanwhile to Lancaster, but did not play there. Heading back to the larger cities, assured that reinforcements were on the way from England, he went to Baltimore and opened again at the Maryland Institute on 26 March. The Baltimore *Sun* announced a two-week reappearance of the Royal Marionettes, with "new songs and fresh attractions . . . and the fair *Loyal* Little Red Riding Hood. . . . W. J. Bullock, proprietor." (The *"Loyal"* is in my italics.) Had some extra puppeteers been picked up, or was McLaren getting along with his reduced forces? During the run, which lasted till 11 April, Bullock's shock-troupe landed in New York and opened forthwith at Hooley's Opera House, Brooklyn, with *Bombastes Furioso* and, of course, *Little*

Red Riding Hood, playing the week of 6-11 April (Brooklyn *Daily Eagle* for those dates). Anyone who did not know the circumstances would think that America had developed a mania for *Little Red Riding Hood*; three separate companies were playing it simultaneously in Brooklyn, Philadelphia, and Baltimore, and all to good audiences.

Hastening to cover the big cities before McDonough and Earnshaw could get to them, Bullock sent his new unit to Boston, advertising it as "from New York and London" in the *Evening Transcript*. It played *Red Riding Hood* and a Negro minstrel show at Horticultural Hall, 16 April— 16 May 1874. McLaren's unit moved from Baltimore to Pittsburgh, playing there at the Academy of Music, 13 April—2 May (Pittsburgh *Gazette* for those dates). The advertisements in that city bore a slogan that Bullock kept using, "Novelty curious! Fun furious! Humanity spurious!" The count of the "band and chorus of 20 performers" was slightly depleted. The critic in the *Gazette* of 14 April wrote, "To see 'manikans' [*sic*] go through all the eccentric maneuvers of a minstrel troupe, sing, dance, play, and talk glibly, is certainly a novelty—and better still, to hear the fresh, hearty laughter of the juveniles, is of itself an entertainment. . . . The fairy play of *Little Red Riding Hood*, with its glittering scenery and comical situations, seems even more than anything to charm all present. These are the same puppets that performed 400 consecutive nights in London, and gave 300 representations in Liverpool, 200 in New York, and ran a month in Philadelphia."

From Boston the Bullock unit went southward to Hartford, playing a week at Allyn Hall, 18-23 May, and receiving favorable reviews (Hartford *Daily Courant* for those dates). The McLaren unit, finding, perhaps, that the only possible Cincinnati booking had been pre-empted by McDonough and Earnshaw, jumped to Chicago, where it held the boards of the Kingsbury Music Hall, just opened six months before, one of the many new playhouses that had mushroomed up after the Chicago fire, from 13-20 May (Chicago *Tribune* for those dates). McDonough and Earnshaw had grabbed the profitable engagement at Robinson's Opera House, Cincinnati, 18 May—13 June, and their advertisements still protested that their company was the only one that had appeared at St. James' Hall (Cincinnati *Inquirer* for those dates).

Bullock came back to Robinson Hall, New York City, 6-13 June (New York *Herald*, 6 June), while McLaren went to DeBar's Opera House, St. Louis, 8-13 June (St. Louis *Republican* for those dates). The last review given him there (the *Republican*, 14 June) comments on the excellence of the performance and—a new note—poor attendance. McDonough finished his Cincinnati run on that fateful 13th. Hot summer weather was closing the theatres. Perhaps Eastern theatre agents were chary of the number of Royal Marionette troupes. What if a rival house ran the same bill when one of them was booked? Bullock may have felt that he had taught McDonough and Earnshaw their lesson. He was too good a businessman to keep two companies in America, with the certainty of diminishing returns, now that the chief cities had been covered and the slack season was at hand. I find no further traces of him or of McLaren. They must have sailed for home, where the likelihood of summer engagements was greater.

They may have left some of the puppeteers behind them, or even lost them before the tour was finished. For the week of 2 May, at 3:30 and 9:00 P.M., concurrent with a diorama of *London by Night*, Fred and Jerome Lubin's Original Imperial Marionettes appeared in the Lectorium at P. T. Barnum's Colosseum, Broadway at 35 Street, New York; this information is from the playbill; they were in a small hall below the rotunda of the impressive circular structure. This company, previously unheard of, may have been an offshoot of Bullock's company which had decided to stay in America to try its fortune. It was at the Colosseum until 4 July.

Further to complicate the record, at Wood's Museum, Philadelphia, on 8 June there emerged an "extraordinary attraction, entire new troupe: first appearance in this city of the Royal Oriental Marionettes, just arrived from the Crystal Palace, London" (*Public Ledger* of that date). On the afternoon of the opening day, "owing to the extensive preparations necessary for the proper production of the Royal Marionettes," there was no show, but every afternoon and evening thereafter during the week was played a program of the "*Children in the Wood*, with beautiful and imposing tableaux; the beautiful oriental spectacle of *Blue Beard*, with entirely new scenery, tricks, transformations, dresses, &c.: opening scene, Crystal Caverns of the Deep Blue Sea; grand transformation scene, Venus and Adonis, or the Golden Grotto of Love. The performance will commence with a complete troupe of Christy Minstrels, with their repertoire of oddities, songs, and breakdowns, followed by the miraculous antics of the Italian fantoccini." This program, so full of echoes of the eighteenth century, ran until 4 July.

No company named the Royal Oriental Marionettes had been playing that spring at the Crystal Palace; in fact, the last marionettes there had been Bullock's in February. One can make two guesses who the Oriental puppeteers were. They may have been people who had worked for Bullock at the Crystal Palace and come over in his shock troupe to succor McLaren, or who had worked for him at Crystal Palace and decided to band together to go to America on their own. With so many English puppeteers going to the New World there must have been a fever to do it. If they were people taken overseas by Bullock, where did they get their puppets? Did they send home for them in the expectation of staying longer in America, or was the "entirely new scenery" something that McDonough had ordered? In any event they opened at an inopportune time at the end of the season, after there had already been marionettes in town for nine weeks. In spite of this they enjoyed a month's run. Why did they make their debut in Philadelphia? Was it considered the best American city for puppets?

George William Middleton, who came to America as a young boy with his parents at about this time, recalled that the puppet company they were with stopped at the Bull's Head Hotel, Market and Eleventh streets, Philadelphia. The troupe brought along a male quartet and four musicians. John Till was the property man; the puppeteers included his wife Louisa, who had been a Miss Sanderson, John Sanderson her brother, Elizabeth Case, and Mr. and Mrs. Henry James Middleton. The latter was the son of a puppeteer of the same name who had flourished in England about 1830; he was probably dead when his equipment was sold to Clunn Lewis about 1860. The marionette company of the Middleton Brothers which played in England in the 1870's was owned by Henry James and William; William never came to America. George William's mother was Sarah Jane Holden. With him were brought his brother, Henry James (1858-1884), known as Harry, and his sister Sarah (1860-1939). George William was born in 1865 and died in 1946. An undated English playbill of about 1880 lists "W. Middleton, only member of the celebrated musical family now traveling, marionette manipulator and speaker." He was the only one left on his native shores.

The Oriental company—perhaps it was the one that included the Tills and Middletons—evidently remained in Philadelphia after it disbanded. It has not been traced elsewhere; there are clues of its members giving shows separately in town; and in the fall it was reorganized for further local performances.

It is possible that McDonough and Earnshaw drew a few puppeteers from this company too. On the strength of it they were to advertise their troupe as from the Crystal Palace as well as St. James' Hall—unless they succeeded in recruiting personnel from Bullock's shock-troupe. Someone in the McDonough and Earnshaw company had a copy of a letter of commendation from the manager of the Crystal Palace; McDonough used it in his publicity in California.

From Cincinnati the schismatic McDonough and Earnshaw company made the long jump—seeing slight possibility for Eastern and Middle Western engagements in the face of competition—to San Francisco. Such a trip would be far too expensive for any traveling theatrical company in the mid-twentieth century, and it was expensive then too. But there was nowhere else to go. Although the easy money of the gold rush was a thing of the past, the West was still booming.

The troupe arrived about 2 July, when its first advertisement appeared in the San Francisco *Bulletin*. It was shorthanded by now and its hastily assembled equipment was in need of repairs and additions. It took advantage of a short breathing spell before its opening to effect improvements. McDonough looked around for a scene designer and mechanician, was told of Edwin Deaves, and went to him for help. This information, handed down as family tradition, I had from the grandson of Edwin Deaves, another Edwin. McDonough was probably surprised to learn that Deaves, Philadelphia-born in 1809 and a Californian since late in 1854, had made and performed with puppets for his own amusement after seeing a puppet company in Boston in 1819 (perhaps Dominique Vitali's which had played in New York that year), and had introduced a puppet specialty into the Virginia Serenaders, an early Negro minstrel troupe, about 1838.

Deaves had had years of experience with portable theatrical equipment. He made suggestions for improvements in the structure of the bridges from which the puppets were operated and showed better methods of packing and crating the equipment, which was cumbersome and ill adapted to travel conditions then prevailing in the West.

McDonough met Deaves's son, Walter E., who had been born in Melodian Hall, Cincinnati, 4 July 1854, and had helped his father work puppets from the time when he was so small that he had had to stand on a box to reach them. Walter had given Punch and Judy shows in the San Francisco streets in 1869, assisted by Ed Mozart (later to become the owner of a chain of theatres in the East) as outside man. Walter was signed up as a puppeteer with McDonough.

"The grandest show in the world, the original troupe of Royal Marionettes, from the St. James Hall, London, and the Crystal Palace," presented its usual program at Platt's Hall, San Francisco, "with band and chorus of 20 persons," opening on Tuesday night, 7 July, and playing through Saturday, 8 August. There were matinees on Monday, Wednesday, and Saturday (San Francisco *Bulletin* for the stated dates). On the last night there was a benefit for John H. Hunter, who may have been a San Franciscan rather than a member of the company. McDonough alone was named as partner, though Earnshaw came back into the partnership in 1876.

In better shape for travel than it had been before, the company was reported in the San Francisco *Chronicle* of 2 August to be headed for Vallejo and Napa, where it probably played 10-15 August. The dates cannot be verified because no newspapers for these towns in that week are known to exist.

From 17-22 August the troupe appeared at Brayton Hall, on the north side of Twelfth Street between Webster and Harrison, Oakland. There were matinees Wednesday and Saturday at 2:30 P.M. This testimonial appeared in the advertisements in the Oakland *Daily Transcript*:

> Crystal Palace, Sydenham
> 11 February 1874
>
> This is to certify that the Marionettes [surely a word qualifying the name has been omitted] fulfilled a fortnight's engagement at the Crystal Palace in February of this year, during which time their performances were witnessed by 40,000 visitors with evident satisfaction.
>
> J. Wilkinson, Manager
>
> Their success in New York, Boston, Philadelphia, and Baltimore, and all cities, has been honored with the same favor.

This letter is peculiar in more than one respect. It is dated five days before the Crystal Palace run of Bullock's Royal Marionettes began; it may have been carelessly copied. Only Bullock's new unit had played in Boston. McDonough seemed to be taking credit for all the three Royal Marionette companies and forging the Wilkinson letter besides—unless he had hired one of the puppeteers from the new unit, who had at least some right to take credit for the Crystal Palace success.

Attendance in Oakland was splendid. A commentator in the *Daily Transcript* of 22 August wrote, "We begin to suspect the great rush of blooming damsels to Brayton Hall is in a measure attributable to the two very handsome and polite men who 'sit at receipt of customs.' One is a blonde and the other a brunette, so you pays your money and you takes your choice." Were these McDonough himself and William Adams, the treasurer dismissed by McLaren?

A practical joke played by the company on the lighting man was the means of preserving his name in the same story. "Presentation. Yesterday afternoon Professor Burke, he who manipulates the calcium lights of the Marionettes, was the recipient of a watch and chain from his brother artistes. It turns out, however, that the aforesaid watch is of wood, and the chain twine 'happily blended together.' All of the articles can be seen at the Golden Star Hotel on Broadway, where they are on exhibition. The Professor should either feel complimented (?) at this token of appreciation or feel like venting the 'vial of wrath' on their devoted heads." The wooden chronometer could have been the handiwork of Walter Deaves.

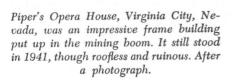

Piper's Opera House, Virginia City, Nevada, was an impressive frame building put up in the mining boom. It still stood in 1941, though roofless and ruinous. After a photograph.

The company next appeared at the San José Opera House, 24-29 August (San José *Daily Patriot*), then went to Mozart Hall, Stockton, 31 August—5 September (Stockton *Daily Independent*), then to the Metropolitan Theatre, Sacramento, 7-12 September (Sacramento *Union*), and then probably to Grass Valley, although no newspaper for this period in that mining town exists for corroboration. The Saturday matinee in Sacramento had brought out an audience of 1450, "the largest ever known in this city," said the *Union*.

Now the marionettes crossed into Nevada. In Virginia City they performed to large audiences at Piper's Opera House, 21-26 September (Virginia *Enterprise*), and there were crowded houses at the Carson City Theatre, 28 September—1 October, save for the last day, when there was bad weather (Carson *Daily Appeal*). At the Wednesday matinee on 30 September there was "called out the most numerous attendance of youngsters we ever saw in Carson City—from babies in arms to lads and lassies of the size and age which entitles boys and girls to the designation of Brook Fish. Even the gallery was filled with ladies and children. A more delightful assemblage never sat before the footlights. The puppets were at their best." The Carson paper summed up, "Take it for all in all, the Marionettes had a remarkably successful season here."

During October, while there was a conference of the Church of Latter Day Saints, the company played at the Salt Lake City Theatre in Utah, evidently on a profit-sharing basis, for the "highly amusing and interesting entertainment gave conference visitors their money's worth and replenished the treasury," recalled John S. Lindsay in *Mormons and the Theatre* (Salt Lake City, 1905, p. 134). The dates of the run were 5-10 and 12 October, as noted in the *Deseret News*. The Salt Lake *Daily Herald* of 9 October said of the Thursday matinee (there were others on Wednesday and Saturday), "Eight hundred children with their faces beaming with joyousness made everyone happy around them. Their merry laughter rang through the spacious auditorium in a delirium of delight. 'So mote it be.' Childhood and innocent amusement belong to each other. On Saturday afternoon the last matinee will be given. Mothers take your children. Husbands take your wives." In another city this invitation would not have sounded polygamous. Advertisements in the *Deseret News* promised, "At the matinee each child will be presented with an illustrated book of Little Red Riding Hood." This bonus had first been distributed in Oakland, as the Oakland *Daily Transcript* of 8 August had said, and was McDonough's improvement over selling the book of words—which was not his to sell.

Rather than return East, where Philadelphia was now being regaled with the Anglo-American Marionette Combination, a reorganization of the Oriental company, McDonough wisely decided to venture to Australia—perhaps hoping to get there before Bullock if he were headed the other way around the world. At San Francisco young Deaves left the troupe, for he was soon thereafter to have his own puppets and travel with them in Mexico. Perhaps other members of the company also decided against the journey to the antipodes, for the next program of the Royal Marionettes was to lose its long-familiar features.

At the Royal Hawaiian Theatre, Honolulu, 5 and 8 December 1874, the offering included "the original Rice's Wooden Minstrels, with songs, dances, etc., and the Charm of the Household, the spectacular drama of the *Babes in the Wood*, with appropriate music," according to the *Pacific Commercial Advertiser* of the first date. Except for the phrase, "the Charm of the Household," pre-empted from *Little Red Riding Hood* (what had happened to the play—was it laid up for repairs or lack of personnel?) one would hardly be able to recognize McDonough. The billing read, "The Royal Marionettes, including the original Rice's Wooden Minstrels," which leads one to suppose that McDonough had joined forces with Rice. The latter was probably the puppeteer and mind reader who played as Professor Rice a year later in Seattle.

At ease in the knowledge that McDonough was to have a warm welcome and prosperous year and a half in New Zealand and Australia—the itinerary is given in the list of puppeteers at the back of this volume—let us see what other troupes were doing meanwhile.

A company starting northwest from Salt Lake City on 13 October could have reached Seattle by Saturday, 17 October, when a combination show opened there at Pavilion Hall, announced in the Seattle *Weekly Intelligencer* of that date. The combination consisted of Dr. Haskell, lecturer, an orchestra with singers and dancers, and the Royal Marionettes. Since no details about the puppet program were published, it is impossible to say what troupe this may have been. In Portland, Oregon, this "Quircuplexal troupe, grand combination, three distinct organizations in one," appeared at Wood's Museum, 9-14 November, with a matinee on Saturday, the last day, at two o'clock, "for little folks, ladies, and families," said the Portland *Oregonian* of 6 November. The marionettes were here called Robert Houdin's—a name appropriated from the famous French magician—"mechanical automata, gotten up at a cost of $5000. These wonderful fantoccini convulse the audience with uncontrollable laughter. The children scream with delight." By Thursday, 12 November, "elegant presents, consisting of provisions, cutlery, clothing, watches, pictures, books, and articles of 'vertu,' and $10 in gold coin," were being given at the end of the show, with a gift for each child as he passed out the door.

The show had been expected in Salem, Oregon, since 20 November, but on 24 November this notice appeared in the Salem *Daily Oregon Statesman*, "We yesterday received a letter from Dr. Haskell written at Roseburg [in southerly Oregon, about 100 miles from the California border], announcing that he considered it suicidal to return on the road and requesting us to withdraw his name from the public for the present. It seems that the mud and rain have made this step necessary and he will probably return to San Francisco as soon as possible. The *Weekly News* [of Portland] of the past two weeks has been making it rather tropical for the Doctor and has placed him in rather an embarrassing position. He will return to Portland at an early day." That copies of the Portland *Weekly News* for these weeks are missing deprives one of seeing the verbal drubbing administered the Doctor; but to understand the difficulties of barnstorming is to know what a tale of adverse weather and skipped debts is implicit in this.

One may only guess that the marionettes beat a retreat to San Francisco along with the Doctor. How had he fallen in with them? Had they been McDonough's company in full strength they would not have consented to join forces with a lecturer. They must have been a section of the McDonough company, unwilling or unbidden to share the Australian adventure, but determined to have a try at the Northwest. It may have included Walter Deaves and other American members of the troupe.

Going backward two months in time, and across the continent in space, we find ourselves once more at the Concert Hall on Chestnut Street near Twelfth in Philadelphia. It is Monday, 21 September 1874. The Anglo-American Marionette Combination, says the *Public Ledger* today, numbering "100 marionettes," is to open with "the pleasing representation of *The Broken Trust* . . . the Carnival of Fun, introducing manifold vagaries and varieties . . . Ethiopian delineations by the celebrated Virginia Minstrels . . . and the grand, comic, romantic, operatic, melodramatic, fairy spectacular pantomime, entitled *Humpty Dumpty and Harlequin's*

Adventures, the whole to conclude with the great transformation scene."
Perhaps this is essentially the Oriental company of the preceding summer.

Playing nightly, with Wednesday and Saturday matinees, it gave
variety to its announcements by adding to the previous features such
numbers as Old Black Joe, the Buffalo Boys (both warranted American),
and *Beauty and the Beast,* perhaps a not altogether different pantomime
from *Humpty Dumpty.* The run closed on 3 October. A review in the
Philadelphia *Inquirer* of 22 September gave these details. "The performance began with the representation of *The Broken Trust,* concluding with
an allegorical tableau. Then followed various carnival performances,
juggling, tight-rope dancing, grotesque dances, &c., after which came
Ethiopian delineations of an excessively comical description, and the
chief feature of the performance, a spectacular pantomime of approved
pattern, though much more amusing than is often done by living actors,
entitled *Beauty and the Beast,* introducing Humpty Dumpty and Harlequin. A beautiful transformation scene was reproduced, representing the
Lagoon Lake by moonlight, Birds of Paradise, Coral Cavern, and Vale of
the Silver Mist."

A review in the Philadelphia *City Item* of 22 September declared, "The
troupe far surpasses anything in the marionette line ever seen in this
country. It is infinitely superior to Bullock's Royal Marionettes." After
this brief resurrection the company is heard of no more until a year
later.

Coincidental with the run of the Anglo-American Combination occurred
the "first appearance of the greatest ventriloquist and fantoccinist, Mr.
Alex Davis, the funniest of folks, with his likelike speaking figures," at the
Grand Central Variety Theatre, 21 September—3 October (Philadelphia
Public Ledger of the first date). In an advertisement for a later appear-
ance of Davis at the Arch Street Opera House, his dummies were named
Sam, George, Little Jessie, and Grandfather Davis (Philadelphia *Item,*
19-31 October 1874).

A puppeteer not untouched by the Royal Marionette infestation was
Professor Wyman, whose "magical, ventriloquial, and marionette seances"
at the Assembly Buildings and Concert Hall, Philadelphia, were stretched
out to long runs by the giving of prizes (*Public Ledger,* 9 March—3 April
1875, 27 March—29 April and 28 August—14 October 1876).

John and Louisa Till struck out for themselves and created their own
Royal Marionettes, which were to have a long career in variety theatres
of the 1880's. They were first heard of on 26-28 May 1875 when they were
listed in the *Public Ledger* for a "re-engagement" at Smith's Island, Philadelphia. Their company comprised "100 mimic artistes"—a good round
number. No advertisement of the first engagement has been found in

1874 or 1875. Smith's Island, which was dredged out of existence to improve navigation in the Delaware River, 1891-1897, extended from Walnut to Arch Street and was a bathing resort as early as 1826. In the 1870's it had a restaurant, a beer garden, and such occasional attractions as balloon ascensions and tight-rope walkers. Since it was a summer resort, it is improbable that the Tills' first engagement was earlier than May in the year 1875. Therefore it must have gone unadvertised in the summer of 1874, when the Oriental company was "resting." Smith's Island offered puppet shows almost every season. In 1877 Henry J. Middleton died of sunstroke suffered while filling an engagement there, and in 1881 and 1882 Professor Pharazyn showed his Royal Marionettes there, when it was renamed Ridgeway Park, having passed out of the possession of the Smiths.

The Anglo-American Marionettes played once more at Concert Hall every evening from 20 December 1875 onward, with matinees on Thursdays and Saturdays, according to the *Public Ledger* of those dates. The puppeteers had evidently gone their several ways, to be brought back together only for a holiday revival such as this. No good for the future of the company was augured by the appearance of this advertisement in the *Public Ledger* on the opening day of its run:

For Sale: The best marionette exhibition in America, known as the Anglo-American. Just the thing for the Centennial. Will be on exhibition at Concert Hall. . . . Will sell with or without engagement. Apply to or address

Joseph Shoemaker
Proprietor

The show continued through the week of 3 January 1876 with the Christy Minstrels, Carnival Fantastique, *Beauty and the Beast*, and a grand transformation scene. On matinee performances and those evening shows in the latter part of the week, *Beauty* was replaced by *Little Red Riding Hood*, the "Charm of the Household," with *The Birth of the Butterfly in the Bower of Ferns*. This was Bullock and McDonough material indeed, and leads one to suspect that one of the *Little Red Riding Hood* shows had been left in storage in Philadelphia.

"The largest and best marionette exhibition in America, known as the Anglo-American," was again advertised for sale in the *Public Ledger* on 23 April 1876, this time, cheap. The owner was to be found at 1722 Green Street. Since the resident at that address is not shown in a property atlas for 1876, it cannot be ascertained whether Shoemaker was still the negotiator. Had he been the prime mover of the Oriental troupe, or was he someone who had come into possession of the marionettes without being connected with puppetry?

The Centennial Exposition in Philadelphia opened to the public on 10 May and closed officially on 10 November 1876. Sometime during its course Henry James Middleton played a puppet show, as George William Middleton, then a boy of eleven, remembered, before the great organ, probably near the United States exhibit in the Main Hall. It may be noted that there have been puppet shows at almost all the great American expositions since. In 1881 "the Original and Only Royal Marionettes" were to play in the Permanent Exhibition Building, Philadelphia, from 25 June to 2 July, and in the Main Centennial Building on 4 July.

At Maguire's Opera House, San Francisco, McDonough and Earnshaw (the latter again billed as a partner), back from a triumphal tour in the Southern Hemisphere, opened on 17 July 1876 with a program almost identical with that of two years before (San Francisco *Daily Evening Bulletin*, 15, 17 July). It included "twenty minutes with the Georgia Minstrels in songs, glees, and duets; twenty minutes with the Italian fantoccini: La Trenka, Hindu juggler, double-headed man, Grand Turk, Zanfretta on stilts, the comic mules, Pete and Barney, and the Chinese bell ringers, Ching, Chang, and Chow; and *Little Red Riding Hood*, or the Charm of the Household, closing with the grand transformation scene, entitled the *Abode of the Fairies*." The advertisement pointed out the "simplicity of language, rapidity of action, and grandeur of scenery." This engagement lasted till 5 August.

Again shorthanded, McDonough had hired Daniel Meader of San Francisco as reader and singer. Born in Vallecitos, Calaveras County, California, 17 April 1856, his father from Nantucket and his mother from Santiago, Chile, he had been apprenticed to Thomas Garsman, considered the best property maker in the West, at the Grand Opera House where Edwin Deaves also was connected. He stayed with McDonough on the tour into the Northwest.

"The readers were never allowed to handle the marionettes," wrote Perry Dilley in *Puppetry 1930* (p. 18), "reading and manipulating being done by two separate groups in the European style. But Meader became so fascinated by the marionettes that he came to the theatre early before performances and taught himself to operate them. One night the chief puppeteer came in too drunk to work; Meader confessed his practice and offered to step into the breach. He was given the opportunity, and later was engaged as operator as well as singer."

A playbill of the sort printed in quantity, with a blank space for imprinting the dates of an engagement, to be used broadcast in any town, was preserved by Meader and came with the marionettes that he later

TO-NIGHT!   TO-NIGHT!

McDONOUGH & EARNSHAW'S, ROYAL

MARIONETTES

WITH FULL TROUPE

English and French Workers.

FULL COMPANY

SOLOISTS SINGERS

AND

GRAND CHORUS

NUMBERING

22 LADIES AND GENTLEMEN

WITH

GRAND SCENERY

GLITTERING PARAPHERNALIA

AND

COSTLY WARDROBE.

BEAUTIFUL TRANSFORMATION SCENE

COSTING IN ENGLAND

THE SUM OF

NINE THOUSAND DOLLARS,

IN GOLD.

....

Nothing like it has been seen in this part
of the country.

Remember the Matinee.

After a handbill for McDonough and Earnshaw's western tour in 1876, found among the Daniel Meader puppet material by Perry Dilley, in whose collection it now is. Original 5 x 8½ inches. The clown was a stock cut used for any theatrical bill.

made for himself into the hands of Perry Dilley, San Francisco puppeteer of the modern era. It is decorated with a wood engraving of a big-headed clown, probably a stock circus cut. In an assortment of display types it proclaims, "Tonight! McDonough & Earnshaw's Royal Marionettes with full troupe English and French Workers. . . . Soloists, Singers, and Grand Chorus numbering 22 Ladies and Gentlemen. . . . Beautiful Transformation Scene costing in England the sum of $9000 in gold. Nothing like it has been seen in this part of the country. Remember the matinee."

When Meader built a show of his own in 1882, he was naturally influenced by the Royal Marionettes; in fact, he followed their style of program, even to *Little Red Riding Hood*, which must have been acted from Bullock's book of words, for the characters were named Hobble-gobblewitz, Duke Ravensburg, Poggidorff, Hyacinth, and so on. Being a property maker, he observed his models well and duplicated them to the last detail. Therefore, though the original puppets may be lost, the copies can show what they were like. Perry Dilley described them in the article in *Puppetry 1930*. "His marionettes average 42 inches in height.

The heads are all carved of wood, most of them with movable jaws, nicely constructed; in some the eyes roll downward as the mouth opens. The heads are well finished and some have good character. The arms and legs are wood, the torsos wood canvas-covered. . . . Punch is very interesting as a type. The Boy and Donkey are excellent. A two-bar controller was used."

As these figures came into Mr. Dilley's possession directly from Mrs. Daniel Meader, there is no question of their provenance or original condition. The Art Project of the California WPA made exact colored drawings of several of the puppets in the group; these Index of American Design plates are now in the National Gallery, Washington, D.C. Among them are a Chinese Minstrel, a Clown on stilts, a Devil, a Minstrel End Man, Mother Goose, Punch, Harlequin, a Tight-rope Walker, and a Turk.

From San Francisco, McDonough and Earnshaw with Meader and possibly other recruits may have gone to San José and Vallejo, where they had played in 1874, but no newspapers from these towns are available for checking their steps. They came back to play in Dietz Hall, Oakland, 21-26 August (Oakland *Daily Transcript* for those dates). On 20 August a writer for this paper prepared the way for them with a story:

"Two years ago when the smiling and courteous McDonough, manager of the Royal Marionettes, called upon us, we naturally inquired who and what in the —— are the marionettes? 'Wait until tomorrow evening and you shall witness a wonderful spectacle.' And we did. The troupe of 'inanimate' figures was invested with as active and, we may add, graceful life as human beings. The performances were witnessed by so many of the families and other citizens of Oakland that the manager waxed jubilant and expressed himself in exhaustive adjectives about the liberality of the amusement-loving people of this lovely city. . . .

"Two family matinees will be given, one on Wednesday and one on Saturday afternoon. These will be visited by the public and private school teachers and pupils; also by students of the State University and ladies and gentlemen of elegant leisure.

"In Australia the Royal Marionettes were enthusiastically received and ovations extended to them in every principal town in which they appeared.

"The journals all over the Dominion compliment them highly. Eulogistic and exhaustive reviews of their entertainments appear in the Ballarat, Hobartown, Sydney, Melbourne, Castlemaine, Sandhurst, Adelaide, Launceston, Geelong, and other newspapers of influence in the colonies. . . ."

The company announced that it was making its last appearance in

After the Royal Marionettes advertisement in the Salem Daily Oregon Statesman, *13 October 1876, from a file in the Bancroft Library of the University of California. The illustration is a stock cut of harlequinade characters, in lieu of anything closer to the marionettes.*

California, as it was on its way back to Europe. The program contained "Four different entertainments each night: *Babes in the Wood, or a Mother's Prayer*, with new and beautiful scenery, closing with one of the most beautiful tableaux ever witnessed upon any stage, *The Ascension of the Lost Ones*; 'Angels ever bright and fair' will also be performed every evening with all the grand scenery and glittering display; *Little Red Ridng Hood*, the Charm of the Household, and the comic Georgia Minstrels; full band and chorus, together with the wonder of all wonders, the Italian fantoccini . . . two hours of constant amusement."

The troupe went to the Stockton Theatre for the week, 11-16 September (Stockton *Daily Independent* for those dates). The marionettes advertised "their final tour, and positively the last appearance in the state." A reviewer enumerated "the great troupe of English and French workers, soloists, choristers, in all, twenty persons." The French puppeteers are a mystery. Were they discovered in Australia, or was this just a bit of pretense to make the show seem more special?

With one of those splits that were characteristic of puppet companies, the Royal Marionettes now went off in two directions. One group boarded the mail steamer for Victoria on Wednesday, 20 September, as the Victoria *Daily British Colonist* of 22 September reported. D. G. Waldron, who had been with the Alleghenians and Bell Ringers the year before, acted as manager. The other troupe went eastward. The Northwest Coast was so alluring that McDonough could hardly bear not to send at least part of his company there. In unit two, as it may be called, were Meader and young Harry Middleton from Philadelphia.

Unit two played at the Theatre Royal, Victoria, British Columbia, 25-30 September, and on 2 October gave half its receipts for the benefit of the local orphanages, as the *Daily British Colonist* noted. "The Marionettes," it said, "during their stay here have enjoyed unprecedented success, having given nine consecutive performances [six evening shows and two matinees the week before] on each occasion to large and fashionable audiences. They leave this morning per steamer *North Pacific* for Puget Sound and we heartily recommend them to the liberal patronage of our friends 'across the water.'"

The unit played at Yesler's Hall, Seattle, 4-6 October (J. Willis Sayre list of *Complete Bookings at Seattle Playhouses*, Seattle Public Library). Earlier in 1876 Professor Taylor's marionettes had occupied the same hall on 9-10 April (E. C. Elliott, *A History of Variety-Vaudeville in Seattle*, Seattle, 1944, p. 71); Professor E. C. Taylor's Royal Italian Marionette Troupe was to crop up at Forrester's Opera House in Denver in 1878. The unit then went to Reed's Opera House, Salem, where it held forth during state-fair week, 9-14 October (Salem *Daily Oregon Statesman* for those dates), taking advantage of the crowd gathered there. The advertisement had a wood engraving of Pantaloon, Columbine, Harlequin, and Clown, a stock cut; McDonough and Earnshaw's Royal Marionettes were billed as "from London." There was the usual program of minstrels, fantoccini, and the "Charm of the Household," with the grand transformation scene that had cost $9000 in London.

A reporter from the Salem paper said, "The songs and choruses were very nicely rendered and the audience being so attracted by the motion of the miniature musical instruments was led almost to believe that the

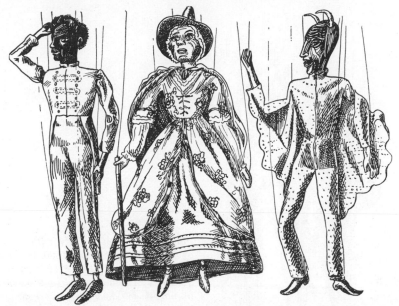

Marionettes made in San Francisco by Daniel Meader about 1880, in the style of the Royal Marionettes with which he received his training. Bell Hop, Mother Goose, and Devil. In the collection of Perry Dilley. After California Art Project, WPA, Index of American Design plates by Emile Cero, Rose Gerke, and Verna Tallman.

figures were living beings. . . . In the comic part of the entertainment, which immediately follows the fairy pantomime, the clown is remarkably mimicked, and with the assistance of the 'old man' character, a peculiar horse with two heads, a most uncomfortable bed, a mad bull, a balloon ascension and the fall of the clown and his companion from the clouds, the piece is rendered quite irresistible. Everything is carried out so naturally and the voices are so suited to the figures supposed to possess them that the illusion is as perfect as is within the reach of possibility."

On Friday, 13 October, there was a change from *Red Riding Hood* to *The Babes in the Wood*; among the tricks newly mentioned were "the wonderful animated skeleton" and "The Old Woman who Lived in a Shoe," a traditional figure, out of whose pockets popped a brood of children. This week there were matinees and evening shows daily. "All children attending the matinee," went the notice in the paper, were "presented by Little Red Riding Hood with her little book." Was a little girl dressed up in a red hood and cape to give out the story books?

On the last day of the Salem engagement the paper became personal about the puppets. "We are sorry that they are going away," it said. "Mr. Dan Waldron, their manager; Mr. Bailey, his assistant; Mr. Warner,

Punch and Clown on stilts (with a bottle) of Daniel Meader, about 1880. In the collection of Perry Dilley. After a snapshot. Meader's marionettes averaged 42 inches in height and had two-stick controllers. The wobbling of the drunken Clown would provide suspense and laughter in the variety part of a program. These characters were in the Royal Marionette tradition.

director of amusements; and Mr. Harry Middleton, master of the figures . . . are all gentlemen of culture and refinement." Was Mr. Warner the conductor of the music, or the master of ceremonies, or both? This is the first appearance of the younger Middleton with the company. He had probably been called to join it in San Francisco, coming from Philadelphia where he must have been helping with the show before the great organ at the Centennial; his brother had no recollection of his having gone to Australia.

In Portland the unit played at the New Market Theatre, opening on 16 October (Portland *Oregonian*, that date). It decided to stay a second week because excursion rates on the railroad were bringing throngs of visitors to town for horse races. On 26 October the marionettes had an ovation when an excursion steamer from Vancouver brought the Twenty-first Infantry band of twenty-two pieces to town and to the theatre, along with "a large and fashionable audience."

Back in Philadelphia, a new arrangement of the kaleidoscopic pieces of the Oriental and Anglo-American companies resulted in "the world-famed Royal Marionettes from Crystal Palace, London." Profiting from the Centennial crowds, they played at the Assembly Buildings, 30 September—25 October, offering "all their charming specialties, the Christy Minstrels, *Humpty Dumpty*, *Babes in the Wood*, *Little Bright Eyes*, *Grand Centennial Tableaux*, and *Beauty and the Beast* (Philadelphia *Press* for those dates). Special matinees were given on the last Monday, Tuesday, and Wednesday, "in consequence of the great desire of strangers to witness this marvelous exhibition." Since the run of Wyman's séances, also in the Assembly Buildings, overlapped that of the Royal Marionettes until 14 October, they must have occupied separate auditoriums.

On 27 October, McDonough and Earnshaw's Royal Marionettes had given their final performance in Portland, Oregon, and tendered the mayor $150 for a worthy charity, the bereaved Mrs. McCabe and her destitute family (Portland *Oregonian*, 28 October). On 30 October they opened at Concert Hall, Philadelphia. To one unaware of the bipartite company this would look impossible, for that was before the day of transcontinental flight. But it was unit two that closed in Portland and unit one that opened in Philadelphia. In self-defense McDonough and Earnshaw had to advertise their offering as "the original Royal Marionettes," for they came in on the heels of the run of the Assembly Buildings Royal Marionettes. Also hoping for the patronage of world's fair visitors, they admonished, "Strangers to the Centennial Exhibition, don't miss it." They proclaimed their "return from New Zealand, Australia, and California, where they have been exhibiting the past 21 months to crowded houses." Presenting Bryant's Minstrels, fantoccini, and *Little Red Riding Hood*, they played till 2 December, past the closing of the fair (Philadelphia *Public Ledger* of that date).

The Assembly Buildings company had broken off its run in the middle of the week. McDonough and Earnshaw, having left part of their forces in the West, opened on the following Monday. Was there not an amalgamation? The Middletons of one crew were related by marriage to the Holdens of the other; the Sandersons were cousins of the younger Middletons, the Cases their uncle and aunt; Till was their cousin by marriage. There would have had to be a family get-together to tell all about Australia and California, even if there were no collaboration. Harry Middleton probably got back from Portland before the Concert Hall engagement had ended. Such a gathering of the clan had not been possible since those meetings at the American Bar in Liverpool three years before.

Then, early in December, the reunion came to an end. Some of the puppeteers went back to England, perhaps to work for Bullock again. Some, like Holden, struck out on their own to tour on the continent of Europe, never to return to America. Some remained in the United States.

Such were John and Louisa Till, who carried on the name of the Royal Marionettes, and Harry Middleton, who teamed with his younger brother William, after the death of their father, to perpetuate the Middleton Brothers style. But everywhere the Royal Marionettes had left their impress. On the West Coast Deaves and Meader were to start companies of similar dimensions. In fact, all marionettes were Royal for a long time. The thousands in America who had seen these competent, large-scale, amusing and dazzling shows were to think well of puppetry and cherish memories of it, in town and hamlet, East and West, to the end of their days.

XI

The Lanos: a Dynasty of Frontier Showmen

The Lano family might have been typical of those scores of puppeteers whose names were allowed to vanish because they were not committed to the print of playbills or newspapers. Three generations of Lanos played from city to frontier settlement throughout the United States, yet practically nothing about them appears in the records. I count myself happy to know David Lano, an affable old-time puppeteer, the last of his line in the hereditary work, who has saved the story of the family from oblivion. He has set down an account of their professional wanderings to the year 1900, upon which he has allowed me to draw. And in several conversations he has added fresh details of bygone theatrical lore preserved in his sharp memory.

David Lano was born at Irongate, a hamlet between Leesburg and Clifton Forge, Virginia, in 1874, while his parents were traveling in a two-mule van with their puppets and rope-dancing act. His mother had been born at Buckhannon, West Virginia, on a stop of Dan Rice's wagon-drawn circus. Oliver Lano, his father, was the son of Alberto Lano, an Italian, and his Danish wife, who had come to the United States in 1825 after playing in Austria, Spain, Portugal, and England. And Alberto was the son of Enrico Lano of Milan, who had trundled his puppet show about the streets of his native city in a handbarrow and died in 1802.

Alberto Lano landed at Norfolk, Virginia, with only four words of English: how much, water, hungry. But he had a dozen serviceable string-puppets and a red plush curtain with a scene from *Orlando furioso* stitched on it. Despite his unfamiliarity with the new country, he began earning his living at once. He would approach an innkeeper and arrange for the use of his large room in exchange for the custom the show would bring in. Then he hung up an announcement board in the common room, a shingle-sized sign on which particulars were lettered in Italian and English. If the community permitted theatrical entertainments there might also be a proclamation by the town crier. The plush curtain was now stretched on a pole across a corner of the room for the performance, a keg or table to stand on was borrowed, and all was ready. The puppets went through their tricks and dances on the floor. In out-of-the-way places where any entertainment was rare they must have struck the audience with delighted wonder. When the hat had been passed the show was packed up, the showman had supper, and asked the way to the next likely place for an exhibition.

After three years in America, Lano had prospered sufficiently to add rope dancing, a trained bear, and a boy and girl apprentice to his show. The European puppets and curtain, rich with hand-beaten gold sequins and bullion fringe, were in use for many years. David Lano saw the curtain and said that he had never seen the like of its handiwork in all the years of his traveling. Puppets and curtain together were lost, like so many appurtenances of the theatre, in a fire.

In 1830 Alberto Lano joined the Thayer circus, playing puppets and doubling on the slack rope. His son Oliver was born in 1832. By 1849 he had acquired a buckboard wagon and a two-mule van. That season he toured six states in the South with a company of six, giving 246 performances. He often met people who said how much they had enjoyed the show because it reminded them of what they had seen in the old country. Nostalgia is not the least of the pleasures of puppet shows in America, which has always had immigrants with tender memories of their homeland. A puppet show would remind them of one they had attended with their parents, their brothers and sisters, from whom they had long since been separated.

When Lano's little caravan came back from its tour that season and put up for the winter it had amassed a tidy sum in gold and silver pieces hoarded from the admission fees. Those who had not been able to pay in money had brought venison, bear meat, turkey, and pigeon; this had kept the showmen's larder well stocked, for the surplus was traded at stores for other provisions.

Oliver Lano underwent a thorough apprenticeship, both in making and manipulating puppets, with his parents, and worked with them till he was twenty-five. He then struck out on his own. One of his outstanding plays was *Faust*. During the Civil War he played in army camps, crossing the battle line from one side to the other. Perhaps he had only a Punch and Judy for this. Later he joined such circuses as Jack Shields', Cole and Coupe's, and George Hall's. He retired in 1900, after trips to Canada and South America and a long career at fairs and dime museums. He died at Panama City, Florida, in 1902.

He apprenticed his ten-year-old son David to his grandparents in 1884. By that time Alberto Lano had bought a small plantation in Virginia with his profits and shrewd trading ability. His company numbered twelve, including Negro mule drivers and canvasmen to put up the tent.

Punch and Judy used by the Lano family. Note the wire rings at the bottoms of the cloth tubes to facilitate the entry of the puppeteer's hand. After Michigan Art and Craft Project, WPA, Index of American Design plates by William E. Kerby and Dorothy Brennan.

For the season when David came to him his Danish wife had decided to produce a play about Erling the Bold, whom she regarded as a sort of ancestor. She wrote the script in Danish and had it translated into English by a friend in Williamsburg. For the Viking ship that was to be used in one scene she found a picture in *Harper's Weekly* to go by. A six-foot-long vessel was built by two sailors from Norfolk, who dubbed it "the rowboat" and Mrs. Lano "the skipper." It proved to be too big to use conveniently on the stage—a shadow in the old tradition of shadow-figure sea pieces was substituted—but "the rowboat" was not wasted. Beautifully carved and painted, filled with figures of fierce-looking Vikings, it was displayed in the post office or other public places of a town as an advertisement for the show.

David's grandparents had already made an impressive number of productions. *David and Goliath*, *Why the Sea Is Salt*, *Dr. Faust*, and themes drawn from Greek mythology were in their repertory, all adapted to performance by a small troupe. David had cause to remember *Dr. Faust* vividly. His first season on the road it was played in Berryville, Virginia, before an audience of mountaineers. When Mephistopheles appeared to bear Faustus off to the nether regions, a tall woodsman rose, unsteady with moonshine, cocked his rifle, yelled "Git back, Devil, git back!" and took a shot at the puppet. This was worse than potato pitching. The bullet went through the backdrop and lodged in the shoulder of a Negro assistant who was hanging the puppets away. Alberto Lano was arrested by the city marshal for inciting the riot that ensued.

The company made its way into West Virginia, playing in wild little coal-mining towns, being guests in the domain of the feuding Hatfields, sharing the collection with ministers who worked *David and Goliath* into prayer meetings in their churches, giving free shows at the expense of a big company that wanted to buy out small mine owners and get their good will in Beckley, opening the new town hall at Marlington, and following the creek beds in the region of Davis because there were no wagon trails.

In the season of 1885-1886 Oliver Lano had toured in Canada. He carried a company of four with a two-mule living van, on top of which the puppet outfit was cradled, and a one-mule cart that served as a harbinger for the troupe. He had played *The Knights of King Arthur*, *The Adventures of Tamlane*, and *Tom Thumb*. In the following season he took David with him to Canada. The other apprentice was Jenny, a young girl of his age. About 3000 pounds of equipment were carried. The new play this season was *Jack the Giant Killer* and their advance agent, "Montreal Jack," translated it into French for them. David and Jenny learned the lines, poll-parrot fashion, by hearing them spoken by two Canadian French children. In January 1887 they played for three weeks in Montreal. Then they went up to Trois Rivières and came back to Lachine, where the show was hired to advertise beer—an early example of puppet entertainment with a commercial tie-in. They visited various towns for a month under this sponsorship, presenting free shows but receiving $1000 from the brewery. From Windsor, Ontario, the Lanos crossed back into the United States and played the week of 14 March in Detroit at Sackett and Wiggins' Wonderland, Eden Musee, Menagerie, Curiosity Parlors, and Mammoth Theatorum in Merrill Hall,

Sambo, from the Lano Punch and Judy cast. The nose and chin of the puppet have been worn almost flat from long battering. The costume is gold velvet with green satin and brass button trimming. After a Michigan Art and Craft Project, WPA, Index of American Design plate by Beverly Chichester.

80 Woodward Avenue, where the puppets were billed as "Winsome Fairy Actors in Miniature" (Detroit *Free Press*, 13-21 March 1887).

Thence they went to Chicago, playing at both the State and Dearborn Street museums; they spent a week apiece in Cleveland and Pittsburgh museums and ended the season at a museum at Ninth and Arch streets, Philadelphia, where a young man named John Schiedler was the lecturer, magician, and Punch and Judy operator. In exchange for helping Schiedler, David received a Punch reed with directions how to use it.

When he got back home to Virginia, he still had not had enough of puppets. He happened to read *Uncle Tom's Cabin*, and though his parents remarked that it was hardly a thing to play in the South, he dramatized it and performed it in the barn with string-puppets made of corn cobs; Little Eva was a small doll and Legree and St. Clair were whittled out of alder wood; admission for the neighborhood children was ten pins.

David's parents made provision for him to enter school, took Jenny, and went off on a South American tour. His grandparents too had played in Latin America. They had gone out in 1849 with *Robinson Crusoe, Tom Thumb*, and *Damon and Pythias*, stopping at Havana, Cartago, San José, Limon, Cartagena, Bogotá, and Guayaquil. They crossed Colombia and

Ecuador by burro and played at small settlements and ranches along the way. They sailed northward to California, where they appeared in the honky-tonks of the mining camps. They worked their way back East by a northerly route in 1851, playing at the Mormon settlement of Cardston, Alberta, where an episode from the life of Joseph Smith was especially prepared and presented with shadow-figures cut from buffalo hide.

About 1858 David's grandparents were again in the West. A carved walnut string-puppet of Goliath was portrayed for the Index of American Design by the Art and Craft Project of the Michigan WPA some eighty years afterward; this recalled to David the circumstances that had brought it into being on that tour.

"That figure," he said in a letter to me, "gave its first performance in a church in South Lyons, Iowa, then just a crossroads post office, blacksmith shop, and stopping point for a stagecoach line from Red Wing, Minnesota, to Des Moines in or about 1858—anyway, it was just after the Sebastapool Indian massacre at a point across Lake Pipin on the Minnesota side. My grandfather was crossing the continent and had just played . . . Frontenac . . . for a Catholic priest in the mission there when the news of the Indian uprising reached him. He took the next stage out for the south and stopped at North Lyons, found no place to exhibit, and drove three miles to South Lyons, where he got the church people to arrange for a marionette production. He used an imported German music box and had to change rolls for each selection. His lights were candles and also flares—little teapot-looking affairs with the wick running down into bear's grease or whatever oil they could get. His stage was heavy and hand-carved. The church insisted that *David and Goliath* be presented. He carved the figures to make up the cast in the hotel and adapted others he had on hand.

"I think he got a reward of his hotel costs and $5 for the two weeks' work in preparing the show. The audience was less than fifty drivers, settlers, and Indians."

Before leaving for South America, David's father had given him a small chest with fourteen string-puppets and seven hand-puppets, to be his very own. He practiced with them all summer long. In the fall, when the money that had been left for his expenses was running low and his parents had not been heard from, David was advised to go to his grandparents. Rather than be a burden to anyone he packed his puppets in a carpet roll and set out to make his own living. He was thirteen; the date was 7 November 1887.

He hiked and rode freight trains to Cincinnati. In the door of a tool car on a siding he gave a show for a railroad construction gang and

Lano trick marionettes: lady-into-trapeze performer and ball juggler. After Michigan Art and Craft Project, WPA, Index of American Design plates by Frank H. Gray and David Ramage.

received $1.90 for it, as well as dinner and a bunk for the night. At Covington he fell in with Holland and McMahon's circus, getting a job as cook's assistant. From this he was promoted to playing Punch and Judy and string-puppet numbers in the sideshow at a dollar a week.

While in Birmingham, Alabama, he visited a variety hall and met the English performers who were billed as Desmond and Desmond. As a finale for their act they had a humanette number; they stuck their heads through holes in a curtain, attached 24-inch rod-controlled figures to their necks, and sang and danced as human-headed puppets. They were going to Australia and the stage they used for this was old and heavy— it took two packing crates—so they gave it to David. He repaired its crudely carved ornaments and was delighted to add it to his assets.

On the last night of the circus engagement in Mobile there was a fight between the town and circus people—"Hey, rube!" was the warning cry of the circus personnel at the outset of such a fracas—and David was slightly injured and one of the tent crew killed. For six weeks the circus played in and around New Orleans, then worked its way by steamboat up the Mississippi, stopping to give shows at plantations along the river.

At Plaquemine, Louisiana, with the circus sinking more and more deeply into difficulties, David left it, together with Oscar, a Swiss who had helped repair the carvings on the humanette stage front. They bought a pair of light buggy wheels, built a cart, and started north along the levee top, as that was much better than the roads. They gave shows in vacant stores, small halls, churches, livery stables, hotels—anyplace they could find. With the coming of warm weather Oscar went off by himself.

But David found Arthur, a Negro boy, who volunteered to be his body servant and pull the cart. They joined forces with Willie Mason's medicine show for a while, then took to fishing and trapping to augment their earnings from the puppets. In the spring of 1889 the New Orleans police found David and delivered a message from his father, still in South America. His mother had been killed in an accident in the Lowanda circus.

David decided to go to St. Louis to sell the furs that he had collected. On the northbound river packet it was discovered that he worked puppets. He was invited to play some scenes from *Huckleberry Finn*, a story redolent of the Mississippi. Among the passengers were a Louisiana teacher who had a copy of Mark Twain's book and a lady from St. Louis who had studied art in Europe. The teacher coached some children to read the lines; the lady, whose name was Clendennin, painted scenery and lent a hand in manipulating the puppets. The pilot had a model of the steamer *Paul Jones* with a smaller carved figure of Mark Twain at the wheel. This was pressed into service for the play. It was fitted with rollers made of spools so that it could cross the stage, the mechanism covered by a blue ground strip representing water. The performance was played somewhere near New Madrid, and a collection of $15 was taken for David.

Miss Clendennin, a well-to-do middle-aged amateur of art, had grown so interested in puppetry that she invited David to stay in St. Louis and use her Olive Street studio as a workshop. Meanwhile he could continue going to school. The offer was tempting and he accepted it. Arthur, his bodyguard, remained with him. Miss Clendennin's circle comprised several local artists, including a red-bearded portrait painter named Holmes, all of whom she inspired with an enthusiasm for puppetry. The group decided that David's next production should be *The Count of Monte Cristo*. Holmes offered suggestions for the heads of the characters. Arthur, taken into Miss Clendennin's employ although still serving David, worked on the puppets in his spare time while David was in school. The money from the sale of the furs and from the shows was shared with Holmes, who was chronically hard up. The humanette stage front was

completely overhauled and enlarged. But the new show progressed
slowly. David's benefactress was taken from her studio by numerous
social engagements.

A letter from his grandparents told David that they had been in Alaska
and were now playing in California. Having gone West with stops in
Chicago, Kansas City, and El Paso, they dipped into Mexico and came
up at Yuma, finally touching San Bernardino and the then tiny communities of Los Angeles, Wilmington, Long Beach, San Pedro, Santa Rosa,
and San Diego; after the Alaskan trip they were in San Francisco and
the surrounding towns once more.

The Count of Monte Cristo was finally produced, but only for a private
studio audience. Next it was decided to essay *The Tempest*. For it Miss
Clendennin had built a portable stage that might be set up in a drawing
room. *Robin Hood* was in production when David's grandparents, his
father, and the Chilean lady, who was his new wife, came to St. Louis
to look him up in 1892. For this family reunion Miss Clendennin arranged
a party to which she invited the mayor and other prominent citizens.
The Lanos combined forces on this occasion to play *Dr. Faust* with the
grandfather's old puppets. There was a good deal of applause. Enthusiasm among the guests ran high. Someone suggested that St. Louis
ought to have a municipal puppet theatre with the Lanos installed as a
permanent company. But the manager of a local theatre objected that
it could not be made to pay; as the excitement died other objections were
found; the project never got beyond the discussion stage. David's family
went off for another South American tour and he was left to be graduated
from high school and receive his teacher's certificate.

But he was not too anxious to teach. He wanted to build a production
of *Columbus Discovers America* for the Chicago World's Fair. After
his graduation he bent all his efforts toward this, carving and discarding
many puppets before he was satisfied with them, and getting a professional costume maker, Madame Cordelia, from the Smith wagon show
which wintered in a suburb of St. Louis, to dress them. The artistic ladies
who frequented the studio were not much help in getting anything
finished. They cut out and basted costumes together but ended by mis-
placing them.

In March 1893 Holmes and Miss Clendennin announced their engagement to be married. They declared that they wished to adopt David but
he was loath to stay. At a final party he was given a check by Miss
Clendennin, a paintbox and brushes by the studio circle, and everybody's
good wishes. Accompanied by the faithful Arthur, he left for Chicago
with his puppets in April. There he found work for a few weeks in a dime

museum before he set up his show in a vacant store shared by several attractions at the Stony Island and 63 Street entrance to the fair grounds, where it was hoped that the crowds coming and going would drop in. He got along during the summer, but the fact that the store had a door connecting it with a saloon, in the back room of which a confidence game was run, caused police raids to make the location undesirable. The variety show, David's puppets with it, then played at county fairs in Muncie, Laporte, and Portland, closing at Vincennes late in October because of poor business. Arthur, who had become entangled in matrimony, had been left behind in Chicago.

Many world's fair attractions, including Fatima the hootchie-kootchie dancer, had secured engagements at an Augusta exposition. Working his way thither, David joined Sig Cannon's variety show. The exposition ran a month, closing with a benefit performance at the Augusta Opera House, for which David's puppets were one of the numbers selected. From the stock in this theatre he bought a velvet masking curtain cheaply to complete his stage. With Cannon he went to Savannah, playing at Turner's Hall, and then to Jacksonville, where the Mitchell-Corbett fight was about to take place. As Cannon had fallen behind in paying salaries, David went over to the rival show of Hurd and Berry, with which he traveled to Mobile and then New Orleans, where he played two weeks at Clough and Thayer's Museum on Canal Street.

While in New Orleans, David called upon Faranta, the manager of the Opera, who knew his father and grandfather. Faranta urged him to produce historical plays and to take them to schools—an idea that was thirty years ahead of the times. The manager had a small collection of Italian and German toy puppets, and puppet plays in French and Spanish.

In Memphis while the Hurd and Berry show was playing in a vacant store, David was engaged to do a special performance at Memphis Kitty's gambling house. The all-male audience wore evening dress and included the mayor and other city officials. Kitty conducted her establishment with the greatest decorum. She told David that she was the daughter of a Tennessee aristocrat by an octoroon, and that she had been educated in a convent abroad, by way of substantiating which she described puppet shows she had seen in France and Italy. She was very kind to David and he felt sorry for her. By way of remembering her he had her name tattooed on his right arm.

The show crossed into Arkansas, making one-week stands at such towns as Jonesboro. At Fayetteville the instructor in drama from the state university came to the show, asked many questions about the puppets, and was manifestly eager to learn the secret of their working. David of course divulged nothing. Hoping to satisfy his curiosity, the instructor engaged the puppets for $5 for a demonstration before the students. After the stage was set up David discovered the instructor and some of his pupils on the catwalk above the flies of the university stage. But the velvet masking curtain he had acquired in Augusta cut off their view. Discomfited, they were obliged to take their places in the audience and learn what they could by peering through opera glasses.

The show worked northward to St. Louis. David found the studio shut up and Mr. and Mrs. Holmes absent on a trip abroad.

In Detroit it played while the Sells Brothers' circus was pitched in a lot on Jefferson Avenue. In the circus David found his old friend Oscar, the Swiss wood carver. He had seen David's grandparents since their last meeting with him; they had been in Bermuda, where they had picked up two puppeteers who were excellent save for their pronounced Cockney accents which made them unintelligible to Americans.

At Mt. Clemens the Hurd and Berry aggregation became the sideshow with the Nelson Family circus and traveled with it across swamp and corduroy road to Ithaca, Michigan, where there was a big turnout of lumberjacks on 5 July 1894 to swell the receipts.

Again by themselves, the Hurd and Berry troupe played at Put-in-Bay, at Forest City Park, Cleveland, and at a country fair in Logan, Ohio. Then it went to other fairs in Portsmouth, Ohio; Lawrenceburg, Indiana; and Warren, Erie, Shamokin, and Danville, Pennsylvania. David played both his version of Punch and Judy and a few string-puppet turns. In the winter of 1894 Hurd and Berry's "Great London Museum" circulated among the towns in the Pennsylvania hard-coal region. In Pottsville, David made the acquaintance of a young girl named Annie Ward, who so impressed him that he left the Museum at Shenandoah in order to linger in her vicinity.

He joined forces with a show consisting of Enoch Wren, his wife, and a comedian, and among them they mustered enough variety acts to keep going through the winter. Then he found work with the medicine shows of "Doc" Spangler and "Doc" DeForrest in turn, visiting the Pennsylvania German settlements. In one Amish community which frowned upon the theatre, as they soon discovered, the owner of a hall over a store collected the rental fee from them in advance, but no audience was forthcoming at the hour set for the performance. They were puzzled to know what was wrong, for it seemed to be a populous and prosperous village. At last, when they had decided to wait no longer, a little boy dressed as a solemn replica of his elders stuck his wide-hatted head in at the door and shouted, "Humbug!"

David had been at pains to rehearse *William Tell*, the only play with a German background within his command, to please them.

Now he went with "Doc" Todt and "Doc" Walter West—none of these medicine shows was doing very well. While he was with West, Annie Ward came to see him. She showed so much interest in the puppets and mended their costumes so beautifully that he was convinced he wanted to marry her.

But there was a living to earn. He had a try at a tent show in partnership with a young actor named Mantell. While it was in Landisburg, Pennsylvania, Miss Ward arrived and became Mrs. Lano. Shortly thereafter Mantell eloped with a nurse and left the young Lanos to do the whole show by themselves. Annie pitched in like an experienced trouper, and together they managed, even playing a simplified version of *Dr. Faust*. When the season of fairs began, they found an engagement with the variety show of J. Augustus Jones, opening at the big Grangers' Picnic at Williams Grove, then going to Center Hall, where they met Harry Houdini with another show. They had a long discussion about what might be done with puppets in magic.

Next they went to Bath, New York. There, billed among the free attractions, they found the Three Lanos and their Manikins—David's father and grandparents; his Chilean stepmother had died. The grandmother was over seventy, but still hale and fine looking, though the aging grandfather was growing uncertain in his puppet manipulation. The young Lanos dropped their work to see their elders' production, which included the adventures of a certain Captain Soup and a bullfight. The familiar old puppets had been repainted and newly costumed. Then the young people disclosed themselves. There was an immediate compulsion, once the greetings and introduction of Annie were over, to put on one more show together, all three generations of Lanos. They furbished up *Why the Sea Is Salt* from their old repertory and performed it.

After this show, perhaps because of the emotional excitement, grandfather Lano suffered a stroke. When it was safe to move him he was taken to Florida by his wife; the old couple never played again. David and Annie helped their father finish the engagement at Bath. Then father and son parted. Oliver Lano was too proud to ask further help, and too independent to form a partnership with his son. Continuing to play at small fairs, David left Jones and joined a company headed by Warfield. When the season closed with the coming of winter, the newlyweds went to Florida to visit their grandparents.

The following season found them still with medicine shows, first around Cincinnati with "Doc" Huddleston, then at Wauseon with "Doc"

Lano "Friday" (dressed as a Negro minstrel with a gardenia on his lapel) and Chinese ball juggler. After Michigan Art and Craft Project, WPA, Index of American Design plates by Elmer Weise.

Hale. At Jasper, Michigan, they found themselves alone for a while, playing *David and Goliath*, circus turns, and *Dr. Faust* with Faust swallowed at the end by a monster, *à la* Punch. They fell in with "Doc" Hazel at Fairfield and continued with him to Plymouth. Venturing into Ohio, they played at the opera house in a sawmill town, where David made a puppet cook grease a stage griddle by skating over it with hams tied to his feet; he did not, however, name the play from its Paul Bunyan theme. "Doc" Hazel was dropped because he was an excessive drinker. A real Doctor of Medicine who was starving in a small town already occupied by two older doctors was tempted to become a medicine showman, but lasted only two weeks at it. Then came Captain Hicks and his Indian wife; then Fred McKinney, an amateur from Coldwater; then Zarmo, a cross-eyed magician; then Jack Shill. Partners came and went like puffs of wind.

In August the fairs began. The first engagement was at Swayzee, Indiana; the next at Elwood, where Lucky McDonald joined the show; other program mates came and went in Indiana and Ohio. The season ended poorly. But before it was up, David's father and grandmother came to help him out, as Annie was nearing the time of her confinement. Together the three played *Pygmalion and Galatea*, an old play in the family repertory, together with *William Tell*.

David's father had been playing in dime museums. He left an engagement at the Clark Street Museum, Chicago, having planned to go to Minneapolis, Superior, and St. Louis. He played *Why the Sea Is Salt* and *Dr. Faust*. For assistants he had a man and his two daughters. He received $60 a week for the act, of which he managed to save $15 for himself after his helpers and all expenses were paid.

In mid-November 1896, the Lanos stored their equipment in Cincinnati and went home to Florida where they stayed for the holiday season. Among the guests who dropped in at the plantation house on their Gulf Coast island were the captain and crew of a Scandinavian lumber schooner. A performance of *Erling the Bold* was put on for them, the old stage being set up and the grandmother delivering all the lines in Danish. The grandfather, paralyzed and bedridden, but retaining the use of his hands and voice, watched the show from a high-backed rocking chair, complimented David's wife on the deftness of her operation, and conceded that David might yet become a puppeteer.

On 10 January 1897 the Lanos' son was born and named Oliver John after his two grandfathers. But he was called Jack. When he reached manhood, crippling neuritis cut him off from following the family vocation.

As soon as David felt he could leave his wife, he picked up his equipment and joined the medicine show of "Doc" Alfredo, an Englishman, in a town about fifty miles from Eau Claire, Wisconsin. Toward spring the blackface comedian in the company objected more and more vociferously that the puppets were detracting from his applause—the first of many instances David found of human actors being jealous of puppets—and David changed to the William circus, which had winter quarters at Medford, Wisconsin. This small circus had no sideshow; David did acrobatic acts but was not able to use his puppets. When the season for fairs began and it was apparent that the circus was breaking up, he advertised for puppeteers to help him. The first to apply was Charles Hansen, who had some ten-inch string puppets of his own, and endeared himself to David at once by admiring the venerable Lano puppets. Then came a telegram, "HIRE NO MORE OPERATORS. ONE COMING. MEET ME AT STATION. YOUR WIFE." And Annie appeared with her seven-month-old son.

"Doc" Alfredo cropped up again to become a partner. He had a girl show which was combined with the Lanos' puppets. At a fair in Iowa the constables, having had complaints of the brevity of the girls' costumes, broke in backstage. They found only Mrs. Lano nursing her baby, but everyone was hailed into court and fined for indecent exposure. Alfredo and the Lanos parted after that, the puppets continuing at fairs in Arcadia, Wisconsin, and Pipestone, Minnesota. There David saw the Indians carving objects out of the soft pipestone, which hardened upon exposure to the air. One of these, not intended as a souvenir for sale to the white man, seemed to him to be a sort of puppet. It was twenty inches tall, had a pipestone head, a basketwork body, loosely attached limbs, and leather hands and feet.

The German and Swedish immigrants in this region paid no attention to the puppet show until signs in their languages were posted and a Swedish ticket seller was hired. Hansen knew Swedish and spoke the lines in that tongue. Then the success was overwhelming. With the coming of winter Hansen went off with a medicine show and the Lanos settled in Red Wing to make preparations for a wagon show to take out in the spring in partnership with Sam Culbertson, a blacksmith with the wanderlust. To collect an odd dollar they played in halls in the neighborhood. One performance in a parish house was arranged by an enterprising Catholic priest to raise funds for local use; he handed over $77 to the Lanos for their share of the receipts. The play was *David and Goliath*. The priest asked why a Passion Play could not be done with puppets; David objected that it would require too many characters.

Snow lay deep over the country that winter. On the way back to Red Wing in a sleigh after a show, the family was followed by timber wolves, which Annie routed by a bombardment of gunny sacks flaming with gasoline from their flares. The baby slept under the lap robe through all the excitement.

When spring came, Culbertson's wife objected to his leaving the certian trade of his blacksmith shop for the hazards of show business. The Lanos set out alone. The new cinematograph was creating a stir, but projecting machines were costly. The Lanos made their own moving pictures: shadow figures cut from tar paper, glued to sticks, and moved against a screen with candlelight behind them. Among other things they showed a sea piece of the sort that had been seen along the Eastern seaboard a century before, with a ship that caught fire, its crew escaping by lifeboat, a lighthouse flashing its beacon, and a bellbuoy tolling as the vessel exploded, split in two, and sank. Few in these audiences had seen the real cinema, and the shadow scene added variety to the puppets.

Now the Lanos contracted to buy a tent outfit and combine with Erling's medicine show, in which they found Hansen and a motion-picture machine with a reel of the Jeffries-Fitzsimmons fight. They were getting along nicely and had just set up in Mazeppa, Wisconsin (a name that recalls an equestrian play rather than the Byronic poem on which it was based), when a cyclone struck and ripped most of the equipment to shreds. Erling left with his projector and the Lanos salvaged what they could; fortunately the puppets had not been unpacked and were safe. With what remained they set out for the fairs in the Dakotas. Another cyclone grazed the wagons as they were proceeding along the road but left them unharmed. They gave shows for the harvest hands wherever they happened to stop at night. At the Wisconsin border the wagons and canvas were stored, the Lanos continuing by train to Elkton, South Dakota. They made one or two other stops on the way to Pierre, where they gave two performances for a church audience. From that point westward to the Black Hills they found the excess baggage costs for their equipment prohibitive and turned back. At a ranch where well water was sold at 25¢ a bucket they gave Punch and Judy for some cowboys, who were so appreciative that they insisted upon the Lanos performing at another ranch twenty miles away.

On the way to this outpost they camped on an Indian reservation. David made friends with the Indians and found that their medicine man had some puppets, which he was persuaded to show. "We saw four images," wrote David, "the faces were carved of pipestone, and as near as I can remember, they represented the four winds. Each was dressed different, and they were worked by what looked like small willow sticks from behind the ceremonial sheet. This was of buckskin, painted with animals and men, and the four figures were placed in the equally divided centers of the painting. The working was crude in the daylight. The figures did not walk, but moved their heads and hands, and as I was not allowed to touch them, I did not get a close inspection, but they were very, very old, and the costumes were beautifully done. I tried hard to get an explanation of the movement of the figures, and the consequent pantomime of a certain number of young braves, who responded only to the action of a certain figure, but I got no information from them. I noticed that the faces of the figures were flatter than the usual Indian's, and that the figures in shape and looks resembled the Eskimo more than the Indians of the Plains."

The next morning, when the Lanos continued their journey to the ranch, the Indians, hearing that David was a white medicine man, broke camp and came along to see the magic. During the three days the Lanos

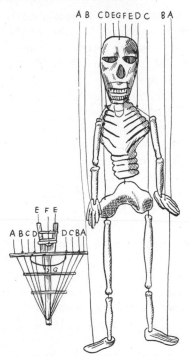

Come-apart skeleton and controller of the Lanos. The letters on the strings and the controller correspond. The parts may be pulled up separately and reassemble when dropped. Wood painted white and black. From a Michigan Art and Craft Project, WPA, Index of American Design plate by George File.

spent at the ranch they rehearsed a piece about Jesse James for the cow-boys and got their trick figures in working order for the Indians. Riders had gone off in all directions to round up an audience; about 200 appeared, and there were that many Indians more. The puppet stage was mounted on a hayrick and the spectators sat on the grass. For lack of gasoline to light the flares, the show was done in the evening twilight. Some of the puppets had been retouched with paint borrowed from the Indians, to play their new parts in *Jesse James*. And when the puppeteers sang the then-popular "Jesse James" as Ford crept in and shot him, the audience joined in and roared out the chorus.

To mystify the Indians there were a tight-rope walker, a juggler, a magician, a clown, a lady-into-balloon, a come-apart skeleton, and the simultaneous working of a witch-into-monkey and a figure that split into six smaller ones. All this, David recalls, really amazed the Indians.

Many of these old puppets are still in David's possession. Their make-up has been retouched from time to time and their costumes have been renewed, but the basic carved-wood figures are the service-worn veterans. The Index of American Design of the Michigan WPA Art and Craft Project has recorded some thirty-four of them, including dog Toby (not a real dog), Punch, Judy, Baby, Negro, Blind Man, Indian,

Policeman, Skeleton, Scaramouch, Sailor, Pretty Poll, Sally, and Devil for *Punch and Judy*—some of the characters from the Collier version of the text may be recognized; and string-puppets of Goliath, Man Friday, Cannibal, Missionary, King Saul, a Chinese Juggler, a Lady-into-Balloon, a tight-rope Walker, a five-pop-out-heads figure, and a Jester. Some of these trick marionettes took part in the North Dakota ranch performance in that summer evening of 1898.

The cowboys passed the hat—a big Western hat, no doubt—and collected over $120 for the Lanos; the Indians loaded down Mrs Lano and the baby with beadwork and a bearskin rug.

The showmen retraced their steps to Minnesota, playing at fairs in Arlington, Granite Falls, and Red Wing, a street fair at Mankato, a vacant store in Des Moines, and so on, working down the Missouri, where at Gentryville they fell in with "Doc" St. John and two Kansas City players who augmented the company. Leaving Mrs. Lano and her father, who had joined them a short while before, in Albany, Missouri, David went to Omaha, Nebraska, to work with the Spencer Brothers' medicine show, but two weeks later it closed for the winter and he was obliged to make his way back empty handed.

With scant earnings, the Lanos got to Quincy, Illinois, and there a second son was born. The next summer they joined a medicine show. They showed their puppets at the fairs as a feature to attract patronage to a cyclorama of Libby Prison shown by Emery. There was a street fair at Trenton, Missouri, and shows in halls followed. The new baby, which had been frail, died. With no heart for their work, the Lanos went about it mechanically. They played in small Illinois towns until they became part of a winter circus at Havana, Illinois, where young Jack, trained by his father, made his first appearance in the ring as an acrobat in December 1899.

The circus saw lean days and the Lanos transferred to "Doc" Smith's medicine show in Iowa. That breaking up, the performers organized their own company and played in churches, an abandoned blacksmith shop, schoolhouses, livery stables, skating rinks, and even in a derelict brewery in a German settlement. Finally they got to the banks of the Mississippi and proceeded eastward at the rate of about a hundred miles a week, playing in three towns a week, "some good, some bad, some terrible," as David recalls. In the spring of 1900 David's grandmother came up to Cincinnati to take Jack home with her, and the Lanos ended their independent wandering by signing as performers with the John Robinson circus.

For many years they followed the circus, taking the puppets with them

Carved walnut heads of figures that pop out of a larger one in a Lano come-apart trick. Wigs of sheep pelt, fur, or paint. After a Michigan Art and Craft Project, WPA, Index of American Design plate by Frank H. Gray.

whenever they could. Attracted to the automobile factories which were springing up in Michigan, David spent his winters there, where his skill in handicraft stood him in good stead. Eventually he built a little house as permanent quarters in Flint. The puppets were always cherished. In 1939 he brought them out to play for the Federal Theatre Project, and later the Recreation Project, of the Michigan WPA. At one time Mr. and Mrs. George William Middleton were his team mates. He proved to be an apt instructor of young puppeteers in the Recreation Project. With the coming of better times, he again found engagements for the puppets in schools and clubs around Flint, and then returned with them to his old familiar place in circus sideshows. With his niece, Caroline Chaney, as an assistant, he has recently traveled the breadth of the United States with Clyde Beatty's circus, the Dan Rice show, and other circuses, and is as active as ever as this is being written.

The Lano puppets and the Royal Marionettes differed in that the first traveled in remote frontier trails and the second only on the highroads. The first played in obscure settlements, often under informal conditions, the second only in big cities in regular theatres. The first advertised themselves fitfully, as best they could, the second had display space in the daily newspapers. The first often improvised programs on a day's notice, and were careless of detail; the second adhered to a set program, with execution on an almost invariably high level. The first teamed with all sorts of other shows and were often only a number on the bill, the second

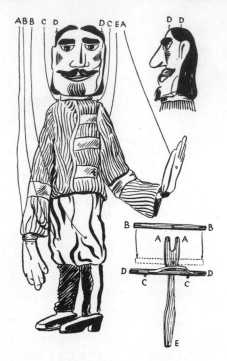

Goliath for the Lano version of the Biblical play. The letters on the strings and controller correspond. Costume of rose corduroy, blue satin ribbon, and dark blue woolen. After a Michigan Art and Craft Project, WPA, Index of American Design plate by Elmer Weise.

were a feature in themselves. The first were casual, leisurely, and unpretending; the second were purposive, hurried, and anxious to have their virtues known. The first gave old plays of merit, albeit crudely; the second, glittering novelty. The Lano puppets were typical of the wandering show before the day of the organized variety theatre. The Royal Marionettes were unique in the size and importance of their operations. They had many imitators whereas the Lanos had few. They left their mark on the course of puppet history; the Lano puppets have narrowly escaped being forgotten. But they were far from unimportant. Like other small shows on the frontier, their value as an entertainment in remote places was implicit in the delight of the audiences that saw them. In the theatre-hungry backwoods they were the theatre.

XII

German Puppetry in America

The Prussian fantoccini that played in the Water Street theatre, New York, in 1799 were Prussian in name only; the performance was of course in English. To call the puppets German was to add glamor— German mechanical ingenuity was thought superior to English—as to call certain sorts of art foreign today is to recommend them. Among the early puppeteers who came to America were Spanish, English, French, and Italian, but there seem to have been no German. Not until 1848, when political and economic troubles in the German states brought an onrush of their people to the new country, did puppeteers immigrate. The Germans had a love of puppetry, fostered by an abundance of companies in the homeland. In the strange and disquieting land of their adoption they were grateful for any show in their own tongue, and especially for puppets with all their nostalgic memories.

The German puppet theatres in America were generally modest affairs, one-man or family enterprises, carried on in the hope of bringing in a little extra income after the regular day's work at some trade was done. Since the appeal was limited to those who understood German (if Americans had a second language it was French in those days), not a moneyed class in their first years over, the earnings of the showmen were small. Like itinerant Punch and Judies, some of the German shows were perhaps too obscure to leave any record. But the few examples that are known will indicate what the others must have been like.

Here are to be considered together the shows that were done in German and those that were done for audiences of German background, sometimes in English by showmen of other antecedents. They were all influenced by what these audiences expected in a puppet show. A stock character, popular in English shows in Pennsylvania-German districts, was therefore suitably named Peter Hauntz (Peter Hans).

Hugh Lindsay indicated in his *History of the Life, Travels, and Incidents of Col. Hugh Lindsay, the Celebrated Comedian* (1859, reprinted Macungie, Pennsylvania, 1883) that he began to show "Old Hons" in 1828. He was later to become famous for the Pennsylvania-German quips of his puppets. Lindsay, as his name would indicate, was not of German lineage. But he lived among the Germans and was able to study their mannerisms and dialect. A tavern keeper in winter, he went on the road in summer as a circus performer, playing as a clown and exhibiting on the tightrope. He had learned how to handle puppets from a certain Myers for whom he had worked as a helper. Had Myers originated Peter Hauntz, or was he already a stock character in Germany? John Weidel was Lindsay's partner when he started out with puppets of his own; he too might have helped create the figure.

Dr. E. Grumbine, in *Stories of Old Stumpstown* (Lebanon County Historical Society, Vol. 5, No. 5), recalled, "Another peregrinating entertainment that visited Lebanon County villages was a puppet show owned and operated by a certain man known as 'Old Lindsay.' He came to Fredericksburg in the 40's and 50's. His . . . puppets were Pennsylvania-German characters, and were named Mr. and Mrs. Wafflebach, or as expressed in the vernacular, 'der alt Wafflebach un' sei fraw die alt Wafflebachsy.' Lindsay was quite a ventriloquist, and the coarse and often vulgar jokes which he put in the mouths of his puppets were greatly enjoyed by the large crowds gathered under his canvas. His tent was pitched on the Pinegrove Road, a short distance north of the easternmost hotel, then kept by John Foesig, on the occasion of his last visit to Fredericksburg in 1857."

James H. Sharp continued Peter Hauntz, and became known by the name of the puppet. More will be said of him presently.

Nothing to refute the claim of priority of the "erstes deutsches Marionetten-Theater in Amerika" has turned up; it presented *Don Carlos* at Washington Hall, the Bowery and Hester Street, New York, on 26 October 1852 (New York *Staats-Zeitung* of that date). This was indubitably conducted altogether in German by a German puppeteer.

Don Carlos could hardly have been Schiller's drama, even in a tabloid version. It was more likely the puppet play, *Don Carlos, der Infanterist von Spanien, oder das [sic] kommt davon, wenn man seine Stiefmutter liebt,* published by the author, Silvius Landsberger, in Berlin, 1852. It had been played over a hundred times as a Christmas entertainment at Kellner's Hotel, Taubenstrasse, Berlin, and was full of political and topical allusions. Casper, in his droll dialect, conversed familiarly with Don Carlos; lines might have been changed here and there to make them suit New World events. The plot was derived incident for incident from Octave Feuillet's *Vie de Polichinelle* (Paris, 1846), a very popular children's story not without influence on the naughty *Max und Moritz* and *Pinocchio.* An English translation of Feuillet's story, *The Life and Adventures of Punchinello,* was published in New York in 1852, and one of Landsberger's puppet plays, *Punch's Merry Pranks*, was published shortly thereafter in London. If this were indeed the play that introduced the German puppet theatre to America, it is ironical that the author, after a life of ups and downs, died forgotten in New York in 1899 (H. S. Rehn, *Das Buch der Marionetten*, Berlin, [1905], p. 206).

In 1856, at 290 Broadway, New York, was exhibited a "Theater Mundi, oder die Welt im Kleinen" which, though it may have been a clockwork affair, was probably similar to the dioramas that were included on puppet bills.

By 1858 there were German newcomers far in the interior of the United States. On 7 August of that year, in Davenport, Iowa, where there was a colony of them, "Monsieur de Rathsckoff, late of Paris," played "some wonderful and highly amusing serio-comic pieces" in his hand-puppet theatre at Hoering and Hennie's People's Garden, Harrison Street between Second and Third (Joseph S. Schick, *The Early Theatre in Eastern Iowa*, New York, 1928, p. 230). If Rathsckoff was not indeed an international wanderer, he may have inferred that he was French, in a German beer garden, for the same reason that English showmen called their fantoccini Prussian.

For almost ten years following the close of the Civil War, an indefatigable German puppeteer, John Rach, was to be found performing in the beer gardens of New York. He changed his bill from day to day, playing a repertory of classic puppet pieces, adaptations, parodies, and what seem to be original dramas with local color and commentary. To keep up this pace he must have had a set of stock puppets and scenes; I believe that hand-puppets are indicated; he must have read his lines or improvised them. The pauses between lines—while a puppeteer consults his script or marshals a speech—would be filled by the cocking of a head, the frozen pose, the bits of frenetic activity, which hand-puppets can make very comic. I like to think that the audience talked to Casper and that he talked back; only a bored or self-conscious audience could have sat silently through his sallies. The plot would be merely a convenient framework on which to hang quips, repartee, and pieces of amusing business. Considering the informality and relaxed air of the places where Rach played, he must have been sufficiently in rapport with their frequenters to indulge in a considerable amount of give-and-take with them. Despite the variations in title of his plays, he must have used stock situations as well as characters over and over. But the titles of the pieces are interesting in themselves.

Advertisements for the first season of Casper plays at the Bowery Garten, 113 Bowery, to which 10¢ was the admission fee, began in the

New York *Staats-Zeitung* on Tuesday, 6 March 1866, but the shows may have been in progress for some time already, for the first offering, *Der Seeräuber von Tunis*, was noted as a repeat performance. The showman's name is not given, but since Rach was at the Bowery Garten in succeeding seasons and the repertory resembles his, it was undoubtedly he.

A Tunis pirate would then be a dim and romantic figure, with the realities of rapine along the north coast of Africa fading back to the War of 1812. This may have been just the fantastic encounter with pirates that forms part of *Vie de Polichinelle*, the model for *Don Carlos*. Although the Mexican scene had demanded serious consideration in 1848, *Max in Mexico* was probably a comic and not very topographical piece. *Casper als Einwanderer* must have caused sympathetic laughter in the immigrant audience. *Die Pfalzgräfin* was the classic puppet play of St. Genevieve. *Don Juan* was not the old puppet play to be published by Carl Engel at Oldenburg in 1875, but a version of Mozart's *Don Giovanni*, as later references make clear. *Er schlaft sehr gut, oder der verliebte Nachtwächter* gave Casper the role of night watchman which he had in Bonneschky's *Faust*. *Die Wette*, later given under alternative titles, may have been justified by timely allusions. *Die Mormone* was Americana. *Ein Unteroffizier Friedrich des Grossen* was based on a historic tale from the homeland. Was *Das Staats-Examen* the examination of an immigrant applying for citizenship? *Der Grossmutter Schnupfttabaksdose* has a low-comedy sound. *Der Fahnenkampf, oder drei Tagen aus dem Leben eines Vaterlands-Vertheidigers*, "Port Hudson, Ort der Handlung," showed the sort of banner contest, either athletic or musical, that German social societies held on a country picnic after a trip up the Hudson River by excursion steamer.

König Zohack von Persien, oder der Pantoffeln der Prinzessin has the air of an *Arabian Nights* tale. *Die lustige Gesellschaft* was "a farce with song and dance." *Die dicke Lotte und der geprügelte Amtmann* sounds like an opportunity for plenty of slapstick action. *Herr von Bismarkruh, oder wie es die Junker treiben* showed that interest in political events in Germany was still very active in this audience. *Die Entführung aus dem Serail* was given "with music by Mozart—and other great masters"! *König Wenzel von Böhmen* was concerned with Good King Wenceslas, known to English balladry. *Die Leichen-Rauber auf Greenwood Cemetery*, despite its macabre sound, was surely a farce, with Casper involved against his will in digging up skeletons. Scenes of New York life were later to become very popular on the big stage in such plays as Daly's *New York by Gaslight*, and they almost always showed the ragged edge.

Ein Mann mit einer schwarzen und einer weissen Frau, oder die Extreme begegnen sich was a subject—"a husband with a black wife and a white one"—which only puppets could treat in the United States, though this was a farce. Mozart's *Don Juan*, in a later performance, was done "with fireworks" for the exit to hell, doubtless the fireless kind previously encountered in this narrative. Was the surveyor of *Der Feldmesser* at work on some real-estate promotion scheme? *Ein Hundert Offiziere und ein Rekrut, oder er kam, sah, und siegte,* of course poked fun at the officer class in Prussia, which hardly stood high in the esteem of those who came to America rather than undergo unwilling military conscription. *Dies Bildniss ist bezauberend schön* has the ring of satire on the newly-rich's sudden love of art. Perhaps it was a variant of the charlatan portrait-painter situation in *Kasper als Porträtmaler*, a play produced in the Munich puppet theatre in 1858 but not yet published.

Eine diplomatische Heirath harked back to the old world; marriages of convenience were not common enough in America to be a subject for satire. *Ritter Kunerich von Drachenfels* was romantic German legend. *Schinderhannes, der grosse Räuberhauptmann* was a "Volksschauspiel in fünf Akten mit Feuerwerk," in short, a popular piece with blood and fire. There were as many robber chieftains in the fabric of early nineteenth-century melodrama as gangsters in the Hollywood movies of the 1920's—but here the tribe was laughed at. *Die Fahnenschlacht im Teutoburgerwalde*, "Ort der Handlung, Amerika, ¼ Meile von Richmond," was a sequel to the *Fahnenkampf*, doubtless with allusions to a Sunday junket still fresh in the memory of the audience.

The puppeteer who presented this widely varied repertory in a six-week period may now have made a tour among German communities in the hinterland; his last show at the Bowery Garten was on 14 April. Perhaps he played at summer gardens that did not advertise their attractions. John Rach drops from sight until 1867. He then reappears, his name displayed as director of the Casper Theatre in the Bowery Garten, for a five-month season which may be followed almost from day to day in the notice column of the New York *Staats-Zeitung*.

He was an industrious person to keep up this repertory, constantly adding new pieces, though some of them may have been largely improvised. He must have been a professional, giving full time to his puppets, and not an artisan or tradesman by day and a showman by night.

Along with farces and legends of the Old Country and parodies or adaptations of operas (Rach probably sang all the parts, with an outrageous falsetto for the soprano)—he did *Der Tannhäuser* when Wagner was still considered fair game—he presented timely pieces in which he could comment on political developments both in America and in Germany. *Das Sonntags-und-Mucker Gesetz in New York*, like many that were to follow, was directed against the blue laws that prevented a working man from enjoying his favorite recreations on his one free day in the week. "Frequent . . . are the accounts" in German newspapers in New York, wrote Fritz A. H. Leuchs in *The Early German Theatre in New York* (New York, 1928, p. 12), "of many a promising German picnic hopelessly spoilt by the operations of ordinances, so detestable to the German, which forbade the sale of beer and the staging of performances of various kinds on Sunday." *Der Sonntag in New York, oder schöne Seele finden sich zu Wasser wie beim Bier*, and *Ein New York Lumpaci, oder der Bier-Wein-und-Wasser Frage*, are examples of this kind of protest.

European events were mirrored in *Napoleon III und sein Werkzeuge, Conföderation und Kaiserthum*, and *Die Fahnenschlacht, oder das Ende der Conföderation und des Kaiserthums*. None of this could have been so solemn as it sounds. The American scene was reflected, also humorously, in *Die Ankunft in Amerika, oder der Patent-Artikel, Ein Müthiger ohne Courage, oder eine Amerikanische Generale-Flucht* (on 2 March Congress had passed an act forbidding the President of the United States to issue military orders or remove the general of the Army from command; was General Grant twitted on hiding behind the skirts of Congress?), *Das Maine Liquor Law*, and *Der erste Mai in New York, oder Kasper und sein Landlord*. The last was played on 20 April 1867, when, said the *Staats-Zeitung*, the puppet theatre was "in obern Saale," moved upstairs, perhaps, by something that had stopped performances for four days and that was to cause gaps in the schedule henceforth.

Rach moved to the National Assembly Rooms, 334-344 West 44 Street, on 20 May, where he played out the season to 30 May. Professor L. Gogler from Berlin had usurped the place of Rach at the Bowery Garten on 27 November of that year, when his Figuren-theater—which may have used string-puppets—played *Hunderttausend Thaler* for the second time. His season had begun somewhat earlier and lasted into February. But Rach was back on 1 October 1868, presenting his old repertory and a few new pieces until 30 November.

The wide range of his offerings speaks well of his resourcefulness as a puppeteer and the varied interests of his audience. In his two long seasons at the Bowery Garten he touched upon European and American politics, current events, and manners and morals; he gave perhaps a little of Wagner's music and quite a bit of Mozart's; his classic text included folklore, romantic drama, and melodrama. What entertainer could do such things in a New York night club of the 1940's? At the beginning of January 1869 he transferred his theatre to Union Hall, where Jefferson Davis and Robert E. Lee appeared as characters in *Der Fahnenkampf.*

Meanwhile, on 3 December, 1868, Professor Dessart's Zauber und Marionetten Theater had appeared at the Löwen Garten, 456 Pearl Street, New York, as the *Staats-Zeitung* recorded.

And Punch and Judy (its slapstick transcends languages) had invaded the German precincts of Central Park Garten on 15 December 1868, to remain for the Christmas season (again the *Staats-Zeitung*).

By 7 March 1869 Rach had flitted from Union Hall to Göring and Eckel's Harmonie Rooms, and on that date gave *Schinderhannes.* In July, if he played in town during the summer, he faced the competition of a Grosses Casperle-Theater at Louis Gross's Sommergarten, 254 William Street, which may have been identical with that conducted by Herr Julius at the Dritte Avenue Theater on 4 October. (The *Staats-Zeitung* is the source of all this.) Rach was back again at the Bowery Garten 4-14 January 1870.

On 11 February, Herr Julius began a run at the National Assembly Rooms, presenting *Kampf um Casper* and *Der lustige Barbier.* Then he migrated to the Harmony Rooms in Essex Street where on 20 March he played *Der lustige Rekrut,* on 3 April *Der Kampf um Casper* and *Der lustige Barbier,* and on 8 May *Bilder aus Amerika, oder der Reise von Syracuse,* a comedy in four acts.

A Casperletheater with an unnamed director on 24 March played at Frau Nanner's Garabaldi Halle the four-act drama of *Eheleiden und Freuden,* and on 27 March, *Die Anna-Liese.* At the Casino in east Houston Street another Casperletheater, Rach's it appears from the piece, presented *Der erste Mai in New York* on 8 April. Rach must also have played at the Dritte Avenue Theater 15 June—18 July 1870, for the repertory is his. On 29 October Casper appeared at the National Assembly Rooms in *Nur keine Rente,* which looks very much like another encounter with the landlord.

In 1871 John Rach was on the move from hall to hall, although his headquarters seem to have been at the Brooklyn Pavillon, 198-200 Court Street, Brooklyn. He played *Dr. Eisenbart* at the Concordia Rooms on Avenue A on 15 and 26 February, *Bilder aus Amerika, oder der Reise von Syracuse* (how did he happen to be doing Herr Julius' piece?) at the Brooklyn Pavillon on 13 April, and other pieces at the Germania Assembly Rooms and the National Assembly Rooms in May and June.

Though it was only a couple of blocks from my office, I found time to look at the site of the National Assembly Rooms only recently. In my endeavors to locate the landmarks of early puppetry in New York I have discovered few tangible links with the past; the city has swept almost all its eighteenth-century and a good part of its nineteenth-century buildings away. The National Assembly Rooms had disappeared. But where they had stood, on the south side of 44 Street a little east of Ninth Avenue, there was an obvious gap, now covered by one-story shops, between the brownstone tenement houses. Had this once been an airy new neighborhood, with clusters of trees in vacant lots and wildflowers growing in the clefts of the rock, as they had when it was farmland? Difficult as it was to visualize, here was an almost suburban pleasure spot, far uptown, perhaps a rallying place for Sunday excursionists on their way to the Weehawken ferry or back from a country jaunt in New Jersey.

For the benefit of Gustav Holbein Rach gave selections from several of his pieces at Walhalla on 28 January 1872. On 18 February he was in the upper hall of the Germania Assembly Rooms, playing *Grossfürst Alexis* (Russian atmosphere) and *Das Loch im New Yorker Stadtsäckel* (leave Casper to find the leak in the city treasury!); in March he there gave two performances of *Die Entführung*; and on 24 March he was at Harmony Hall, Essex Street. On 14 April he was giving "next to the last" performance of *Die Zauberflöte* at Union Hall, Williamsburg. Later in April he was back at the Harmony Rooms to play *Am Kreuz-Weg*, which sounds rather serious. On 1 May he revived, on the exact date, *Der erste Mai in New York*, but at the Brooklyn Pavillon. Perhaps it was his Casperletheater and Nebelbilder that were at D. Arnold's Mozart Halle, 134 Seventh Street, on 5 May. He was back at the Pavillon on 8 May with *Kunerich von Drachenfels*, and there on 2 June he took issue with *Der Sonntags-Gesetz in New York*.

It was probably Rach whose Casperletheater and Nebelbilder opened the new year on 1 January 1873 at Paul Falk's Tivoli. It was Rach who once more played in the upper room of the Bowery Garten in mid-January; the piece was *Bitzlibutzli*, which strikes the ear as a Swabian drama about the demon with the Mexican name in the puppet *Faust*.

On 2 February, since Herr Julius presented magic at Jefferson Hall, 253 Avenue A, it was undoubtedly he who animated the Casperletheater on the occasion. Rach's *Schinderhannes* swashbuckled at the National Assembly Rooms on 16 March. A new German puppeteer, or one new to New York, exhibited his show in the Thirteenth Ward House, Suffolk and Delancy streets, on the same day. Rach was at the Terrace Garden, 198-202 Court Street, Brooklyn (erstwhile the Pavillon), on 1 July with *Schulden und keine Hafen*, and on 24 July with his perennial *Seeräuber*.

Between his appearances a Punch and Judy edged in on 8-15 July; perhaps the patrons understood it, beyond the slapstick action, if its English was not too far corrupted by Cockney.

On Sunday, 20 July 1873, Rach, having supported the cause of entertainments on the Sabbath, had to work at Held's Hamilton Park, a Manhattan pleasure resort, and on 27 July he played *Der Seeräuber* there. His name thenceforth disappears from the papers, though it may have been his Casper who made a final appearance in his old haunts in the National Hall on 8 April 1877. The day for German puppet shows in the metropolis was passing. The younger generation was growing up without a knowledge of the language, as Italian and Greek scions were to do when they deserted the Orlando and Karagiozis shows of their fathers, and the old folks grew sensitive about admitting a fondness for such a reminder of the homeland. Punch was hired in the place of Casper in the beer gardens, and if German puppeteers did not learn the formula and tongue of his performance they found themselves without work.

At the Germania Assembly Rooms a Pariser Marionetten Truppe played on 4 April 1875; it may or may not have consisted of string-puppets, but it was certainly no more Parisian than a two-dollar Grand Street hat. It was reported, like most of the other German shows, in the *Staats-Zeitung* of its date of performance.

Though Punch alone survived in the beer gardens and musical-society halls, the names of the puppeteers often had a Germanic tone. At Eberle's Sänger Hall, East Williamsburgh, Punch and Judy rollicked on 4 April 1879 (Long Island *Star* of that date), their operator unnamed but their accent probably German. Eugene Blitz—a stage name, of course, but German—and his Punch were at Aberle's Tivoli 21-26 July 1879. Julius Hanson did Punch and magic at the National Theatre in the Bowery, 27 October—8 November 1879, and again 29 March—4 April 1880 (the playbills are at Harvard). Was he the Herr Julius of preceding years? Professor Lorento, illusionist and mimic, played Punch at the Volksgarten, 24-29 November 1879 (Harvard playbills). Then even the Germanic names in New York fade away. German puppetry had become submerged. Not until 1910, when Carl and Hans Schichtl came to the United States to show their transformation string-puppets in vaudeville, was there another identifiable German company—and even theirs, being in pantomime, did not indicate a language.

But there were other German puppets in the hinterland, sometimes belonging to elaborate shows. Such was the Weinkoetz troupe. It had become a local legend in Wisconsin when Madge Anderson mentioned it in her *Heroes of the Puppet Stage* (New York, 1923, p. 391). Harry Wintermute stated in his reminiscences (*Puppetry 1937*, p. 24) that he had heard of it at Hustisford, Wisconsin, in 1881; its headquarters were then in St. Nazianz; he saw the show in 1903 when it was presented by a father and his two sons. Felix J. Koch, in an article in the Milwaukee *Sentinel* Sunday Magazine of 8 October 1922, described it and called it "very nearly historic." Augustus Rapp, a widely traveled puppeteer, heard that it "worked among the Germans of Wisconsin and always drew large crowds. The people called it the Casper show."

Rozella Weinkoetz, a granddaughter of Peter John Weinkoetz, original proprietor of the show, told me its story. Weinkoetz came to the United States from Baden in 1865 or thereabouts; his father had had a puppet show in Germany. He brought with him three wooden puppets, a knowledge of puppet play production, and the scripts of several plays. At one time there were six play books in his possession, but these were lost somehow; he had, of course, committed the dramas to memory. They were *Don Juan, Der falscher Prinz, Die reiche Karoline, Der Prinz von Spanien, Dr. Faustus,* and *Genoveva,* all part of the popular puppet repertory in Germany. *Don Juan, Dr. Faustus,* and *Genoveva* were all to be published in Engel's editions starting in 1876.

Weinkoetz carved thirteen puppets of his own to add to the set. They were about four feet tall, weighed around eight pounds apiece, and were suspended by stout strings of fishline. The costumes of the leading personages, as they had survived in 1939, were of rich fabrics liberally trimmed with gilt braid, fringe, and spangles. The modeling of the faces and figures was bold; all the puppets had hair wigs and staring eyes. Felix Koch examined them (see his article cited above) and found that "clumsy hand-made hinges were used, and these were held in position by equally old-fashioned nails. Every so often, where one part or another was subjected to extra hard service in the course of the performance, hand-made bolts, of iron also, replaced hinges."

Weinkoetz constructed a portable stage and painted his own scenery. For music between the acts he had a hand organ from Germany, with a music roll of fifteen airs.

Going directly to Wisconsin upon his arrival, he found German-speaking communities where his performances were in demand. He traveled extensively among them but never far from home, presenting his classic repertory year after year. When he grew too old for this work, about 1900, he sold the show to his son, also named Peter John, who had of course grown up with it. The son and his wife put the puppets in repair, painted new scenery, and continued the annual tours, covering Wisconsin and making a trip into Minnesota every two or three years, usually during the summer.

The denouement of St. Genevieve *as played by the Weinkoetz family in Wisconsin. The in-training child plays a minor part (with the spear) while the seasoned child enacts the important role of Siegfried (pointing). The puppets are a huntsman, Casper (kicking), the villain Golo (kneeling), Genevieve, her child, and a deer. The painted forest backdrop with its vertical trees helps conceal the strings. After a photograph.*

Peter John's children, of whom there were ten living in 1940, were trained upon reaching the age of six to take their place among the puppets and act the leading parts. While their father spoke for all the characters in a variety of voices, they moved their heads and hands to indicate when the lines were theirs. There was no attempt to be stiff and puppet-like, but the restraint was such that human and wooden actors moved with pretty much the same stylization. The puppets and children were almost of a size, all were fitted out in the same wigs, beards, and heavy costumes, and audiences might well think the whole company puppets. After three years a child outgrew the costumes and was replaced by the next younger, who had been given minor parts for a few months.

Peter John Weinkoetz Senior had used his children in the same way, and when his son took over the show he knew the technique and the repertory through childhood familiarity. In performances so traditional as these the use of children could not have been an innovation. James Sharp used a little girl among his puppets in Pennsylvania. There was probably Old-World precedent for it. Since the puppets themselves were none too mobile, with their heavily hinged joints and unwieldy mode of operation, the children were used for such specialized business as changing clothes on stage, grasping weapons, or expiring in death tremors.

The puppeteer, wrote Felix Koch, "takes his position on a flight of three tall steps extending across the stage behind the scenes. What amounts practically to a board wall is put into place before him. The various cords—the fishlines—pass into the board, this preventing their tangling and snarling, of course; then up to a beam well above the man's head, and onto a second beam, rather straddling that first, very much like the walking beams on the river boats of half a century or so ago.

"The cords pass to the second beam; they continue through it and down to the puppets. They are joined and rejoined in such a way that an entire row of them—a chorus, possibly—may be set to dancing, walking, doing what is asked of them, at once. Or just one, two, any other grouping of the puppets, may be brought to do some of them this thing, some of them that, by manipulation of the strings."

This is not a very clear description. Perhaps tandem-strung groups were suspended from the walking-beam arrangement and held in position while others moved about freely. One of the operations that went with each scene change was platting, or laying out the characters in the order of their entrance on the stage.

The entertainment was known simply as the Casper show, after the comedian who appeared in every piece. When the movies became ubiquitous, business for the puppets declined. The audiences that had gathered in barns and dance halls to see the dry tears of St. Genevieve now preferred the glycerine of Hollywood. Young people no longer understood German or admitted, after 1917, that they did. In 1922 the Weinkoetz family deserted St. Nazianz for Elkhart Lake, Wisconsin, a resort place. There they kept a tavern, but they also put on performances for the summer visitors. These shows came to an end upon the death of Peter John the younger. The puppets were packed away but are still cherished, in the hope that they may again someday bask in the limelight, in the case in a museum of American puppetry.

James H. Sharp started on his travels in Pennsylvania in 1865, simultaneously with Weinkoetz in Wisconsin. He too used string-puppets and followed a tradition. His descent as a puppeteer came through Hugh Lindsay and the showman named Myers, who had invented or imported the character of Peter Hauntz and made it familiar in the German-settled regions. However, there were hearsay stories about how he had been initiated into puppetry, remembered by W. Howard Wolfe, whose father, Daniel Wolfe, had a blacksmith shop at Mill Hall, Clinton County, Pennsylvania, where Sharp stopped to have his puppets repaired. They too must have been put together with iron hinges and bolts. According to one story, while Sharp was in the Union Army during the Civil War (he seems to have been a sergeant in Company C, Fifty-second Regiment, Pennsylvania Volunteer Infantry, by the recollection of a correspondent of Henry W. Shoemaker's column in the Altoona *Tribune* of 1 December 1942), he befriended an Alsatian puppeteer whose puppets were being stolen for mascots by the soldiers, stopped the depredations, and was shown how to carve and work puppets by the grateful showman. Another version of the story has it that the puppeteer was a company mate in the Army.

Having seen action in some of the bloodiest engagements of the war and lost his left hand, he returned to his home in Salona and spent the rest of his life as a ventriloquist and puppet showman, being particularly well known in Centre, Clearfield, and Clinton counties, where he had a regular circuit of the schools to play, always a welcome interruption of lessons. He was a striking figure, tall and dark, not a little like Abraham Lincoln with his black beard; he wore the black broadcloth coat, tie, and silk hat of a circuit rider. He sold photographs of himself, as many stage people then did (unfortunately none has so far come my way), and sometimes endorsed them as season passes. On the back a Biblical verse was printed. Always somber in demeanor, as his shows were unexceptionable in content, he held his audiences by an air of mystery and even fearfulness.

His skill in ventriloquism added to the uncanniness of his presence. Once a heaping plate of hard-boiled eggs was placed on the breakfast table of a country hotel where he was staying. Immediately a succession of cheepings was heard. The guests drew back in horror as Sharp ate egg after egg despite the cries of the chicks in them, finishing the whole plate. At a school party on Epiphany at Cherry Run, Kolbe's Gap, where Sharp had done a puppet show, an old man, Sam Sherk, who had studied with Ole Bull and owned what was marked a Stradivarius, was to play his fiddle on the program. He sat in the front row nursing the precious instrument.

Sharp stepped to the front of the platform after his part of the entertainment and said, "Sam Sherk and I have been friends since boyhood. I respect his ability with that Strad, but I can do more with it than any man living."

There was a murmur in the crowd; nobody had ever heard Sharp perform on the violin. When silence fell, he pointed to the Strad and swept his arm slowly upward; as he did so, it rose out of the fiddler's grasp, floated upward, and brushed the garlands of greenery near the ceiling. The pointing finger moved a little up and down, the violin rose and dipped, and the sweet strains of a Christmas hymn sang from its unbowed strings. At another motion the Strad descended and came back gently into its owner's arms.

As a ventriloquial dummy, Sharp had a miniature of himself, complete to black beard and coat. This Peter Hauntz was somewhat more waggish than his original, however. As he sat on Sharp's knee his roving eye noted the pretty girls in the room, and he would say, "See that pippin in the next to last row, the one with the snapping dark eyes. And look at her nice red hat!" While Sharp remonstrated with the dummy for his boldness, the girl blushed in delight and the crowd snickered.

Sharp supplemented the puppet show not only with ventriloquism but with a variety of tricks. He would tell the audience that he had lost his sewing awl. Then he would call out, "Lou Schwarz, I believe you have it in your back pocket," or "Emmy Pumpel, what are you doing with my awl in your reticule!" and over their amazed protests, would find it where he had said it was. He could make what he called "lung music," a combination of vocalizing and whistling. He played on the comb, recited poetry, and sang favorite ballads in a powerful bass.

The farm folk were almost ready to believe that a man who did all this had puppets that came alive. There is a tale that some boys came upon his wagon stuck in a snowdrift at night; all the puppets were at the wheels trying to help him push; but the moment they were seen they hopped back into the wagon with a slam of the doors. "Peter Hauntz more than any other man of his time," it was said, "brought the animate and inanimate worlds closest together; with him it was only a hair's breadth dividing the living and the dead."

William O. Smith, in *Fifty Years of Rhyming* (Punxsutawney, 1932), has a verse of several stanzas chronicling a visit of Sharp to Cool Spring schoolhouse in 1869:

> I've seen a thousand plays and shows
>   Since I have grown to manhood's station,
> From dancing girls in dazzling hose
>   To Booth in Shakespeare's best creation.
> But never have I seen or heard—
>   Upon this statement I insist—
> A Thespian artist I preferred
>   To Sharp, the Great Ventriloquist.

Long years ago, in '69,
"When I was but a tender stripling"—
(This phrase I think is pretty fine;
I borrowed it from Rudyard Kipling)—
There came to Reynoldsville one day,
When folks were somewhat dull and moody,
A man who advertised to play
The thrilling drama, *Punch and Judy*.

❈   ❈   ❈

The wooden players large as life
Came forth and talked like human creatures,
And Mr. Punch and his good wife
Were certainly the leading features.
But presently a man came out
Who made the people roar with laughter.
He was as big and fat and stout
As Grover C. or General Shafter.

"My name is Peter Hauntz," said he,
In deep bass tones, and shook his fist,
Thus showing most conclusively
The skill of the ventriloquist.
"A lobster in the lobster pot,"
'Twas thus his favorite song began,
And then he told how much he thought
Of his old Mary Ann.

❈   ❈   ❈

Though I was then a little boy
In red-topped boots and homespun breeches,
I've never felt such perfect joy
Since Peter Hauntz quit making speeches.

When Sharp grew old and his beard turned white, little boys identified him with the Belsnickel, a sort of daemon quite different from St. Nicholas, who comes at holiday time to reward good children with gifts and to join in the festivities.

To the "plain people" of Pennsylvania the "Poppespel" was regarded with suspicion because it was so near witchcraft. There was a story going the rounds at the time of the vexed engagement of the Royal Marionettes in Lancaster that a farmer had invited the manager and his wife to a cornhusking to distract him from his worries. He gratefully accepted. When the farmer arrived with the wagon to pick the couple up, they were accompanied by thirteen small children, just the size of the marionettes, all eager for the outing (Altoona *Tribune*, 2 April 1943).

Sharp played upon the credulity of those who thought that the puppets came alive by using a real little girl in his shows, as the Weinkoetz family did. She was raven haired and beautiful and went by the name Herodia. Thanks to Sharp's talent for mystification, she has become legendary. The tale goes that the little girl was an orphan farmed out to foster parents who ill-used her. She was about ten when she went to Sharp's show secretly, hid in his wagon, and escaped with him. This was at Beech Creek in 1873. For the next four years she appeared with the puppets, then disappeared, either sent away to school as some think, or recovered by her foster parents as a less happy ending puts it. Eventually Herodia was married to a rich young man who had seen her in the show—which may not be fiction; such things do happen to girls on the stage. The legend forms the theme of Katherine Milhous' delightful story, *Herodia, the Beautiful Puppet* (New York, 1942). There is perhaps some basis for the story that Sharp was once arrested in Indiana County, Pennsylvania, for violating the child labor laws and cruelty to children; however, when his wagon was searched only puppets were found (Altoona *Tribune*, 17 June 1943). Whether the little girl was a runaway or Sharp's own daughter, who was also a striking brunette, no doubt she acted with the puppets.

Less is remembered of Sharp's plays than of his personal appearance. W. Howard Wolfe recalls *The Babes in the Woods*; it was so touchingly done that tears came into his eyes when he remembered it as an old man. The dead mother of the poor abandoned children descended from heaven to take them up with her. The part was played by a stock puppet, Julianne, who ordinarily was the consort of Peter Hauntz; she was thought to be almost real enough to be alive. What may have been this puppet came to light in 1945 in an attic in Lock Haven, Pennsylvania, and is now in the collection of Emma L. Thompson of Salona. It had been used as a doll by some little girl, for its face was badly battered and scuffed. Though Peter Hauntz had beaten Julianne, to keep up appearances the ravages were always repaired by a fresh coat of paint. The puppet is 22 inches tall. The head is 6¼ inches long, apparently of maple, gessoed and painted with black hair, bright lips and cheeks, and blue eyes. The figure is costumed in a lavender bonnet with a white frill, and a blue-and-white gingham dress. The present cotton-filled body is of blue chambray. The upper parts of the limbs are of black stocking, the lower of pine; the feet are missing. The base of the neck is bored with a hole ⅞ inch in diameter and 3¼ inches deep; a collar was once tacked to

The head of Julianne, wife of Peter Hauntz. Maple, gessoed and painted with pink cheeks, blue eyes, black hair. Original figure about 22 inches tall; head 6¼ inches. Found in an attic in Lock Haven, Pennsylvania, and now in the possession of Emma L. Thompson of Salona.

it. Julianne seems to have served at one time as a hand-puppet (*Puppetry 1946-1947*). *The Babes in the Wood,* to return to the play, was interlarded with songs, jokes, and dances, though it had its lachrymose moments.

Sharp also presented a dance number called La Scala Ballet (Altoona *Tribune,* 25 March 1940). In the 1870's Peter Hauntz became a puppet Garibaldi, and in 1898 a Colonel Teddy Roosevelt of the Rough Riders. It is likely that Sharp followed the classic English repertory of plays, some of them popular since the eighteenth century, with such changes and additions as current events suggested.

Born in Centre County on 29 March 1830, Sharp long survived the shocks he had received in the Civil War. At the beginning of his career as a puppet showman he traveled about alone in a covered market wagon, typical of the sort used in the region, which contained his equipment. Later, when his wife or daughter accompanied him to help with the engagement of halls (he would never play in tents and shunned fairs and carnivals), the distribution of handbills, and the selling of tickets, they sometimes used a carriage or sleigh in addition to the wagon. This was in 1880 and later. When his wife had died and his daughter married and settled down in Hublersburg—a granddaughter has been located near there—he found other relatives to help him, for he was in failing health. But year after year the boys whose fathers and grandfathers remembered him rushed home for pennies to see the show at the schoolhouse when the town crier rang his brass bell and announced, "Peter Hauntz has come to town! Peter Hauntz has come to town!"

While crossing a railroad siding in his covered wagon, so long familiar to the countryside, Sharp was killed by a backing switch-engine at Mill Hall, Pennsylvania, on 15 August 1908. He had been on his way home to Salona. His horse and wagon were destroyed, and presumably the puppets were reduced to splinters.

He used only string-puppets, most of them 30 to 36 inches tall. His stage was set up behind a curtain on the dais of a schoolroom or town hall and he took his position on a chair before it, his maimed arm evident, rolling his eyes, heaving his chest, and swishing his long beard to cow the children and reduce them to silence. They always feared him, but nothing could tear them from his shows. Though a great favorite in the Pennsylvania-German valleys, he always played in English. The children who could not understand the dialogue reveled in the brisk action.

Sharp followed an English tradition as well as a German. His repertory and language were English, but the construction of the puppets, the leading puppet character, and the introduction of a child actor among the puppets were German. German puppetry in America lasted about a century, counting from Myers, though it saw its greatest development in a fifty-year span which embraced hand-puppets and string-puppets, the old classic repertory and modern topical pieces.

XIII

Nineteenth-Century Spanish Puppets

1. In Mexico

As in English- and French-speaking America, so in Spanish America the increasing variety of amusements brought with the nineteenth century crowded the puppet theatre even from the back streets of the ordinary citizen. To be sure there were more puppets, as there was more of everything, but they were less apt to bid for attention. The established puppets of the eighteenth century which played month after month in places of their own gave way to itinerant puppets which sometimes shared the bill with other attractions. But in Mexico, where the first puppet show had followed the medieval pattern of belonging to a nobleman's retinue, the rate of evolution was unhurried, and elaborate string-puppet programs, sufficient in themselves as an evening's show, continued into the twentieth century when the only remaining puppets in the United States were ten-minute turns in vaudeville.

Until an exhaustive search of all theatrical records in Mexico has been made, there as elsewhere only scattered data of puppet shows will turn up. There is just a fragmentary chronicle so far. For instance, the first pieces to be played by puppets in the town of Palenque de Gallos, as mentioned by the historian Rangel and repeated by Rodolfo Usigli in *Mexico en al teatro* (Mexico, 1932, p. 75), were the play *El Pintor fingido* and the *sainete, Cafés y fondas*, in the year 1814. An 1830 street show in Mexico City, starting out from the Calle de Venero, where two of the eighteenth-century puppet theatres were located, drew children after it like the Pied Piper with its excitement and music as it went from stand to stand in the principal avenues. The troupe included the stock types of Juan Panadero, el Negrito, Don Folías, Nana Cota, and Juan Juanillo; the Negro was in the company at least as early as in Punch and Judy. This show is mentioned in the *Memorias* of Guillermo Prieto, who is quoted in Armando Maria y Campos, *Presencias de teatro* (Mexico, 1937, p. 221). The fame of the Calle de Venero as a puppet center was so great, even after the eighteenth century, that a political satire published in 1828 was called *Funcion estraordinaria de títeres*

FUNCION ESTRAORDINARIA

D E

TITERES MAGICOS

EN EL CALLEJON

DEL VINAGRE·

MEXICO: 1828.
Oficina de la testamentarìa de Ontiveros,
calle del Espìritu Santo nùm. 2.

Title page of a political satire punning on the name of the Calle de Venero, a street familiar for its puppet shows. Original page 5½ x 3¾ inches.

mágicos en el Callejon del Vinagre; there is an antithesis of meaning, as there is a similarity of sound, between Venero and Vinagre.

Before 1848 Juan de Colonia, a traveling showman who had played fairy-tale pieces and fantasies such as *El Cocodrilo, La Zorra,* and *El Hombre de Hueso,* devised *El policero,* filled it with political satire, and took it around the plazas of Mexico City to influence a municipal election (Arqueles Vela, *Introduccion . . . del teatro de muñecos Guiñol,* Mexico, 1935, p. 3). Guillermo Prieto wrote of "out of the way, barn-like barracks," in which a crowd of all sorts of people gathered nightly to be stirred by the patriotic offerings of the puppets. It would seem that Mexican puppets had greater political fervor than those in the United States.

Two playbills in my possession give a glimpse of the showman M. García, who on 10 and 21 June 1857, at the Teatro de la Esmeralda in Calle de Corchero No. 3, Mexico City, presented a "grand show of puppets and poetry," or, as the second bill has it, a "surprising and varied show of puppets, poetry, and song." This folder-type playbill, more elegant than the old banner-strip broadsides, is a good example of the fashionable typography of its period. The first program included six

Conquistadore and horse found in the church at San Ildefonso, New Mexico. Nineteenth century. The Indians of the pueblo remembered these puppets as part of a play once given in the church. After a woodcut by Gustave Baumann, frontispiece in Puppetry 1940.

variety numbers, the Cubans, the Jota Aragonesa (a dance), a cockmain, two acrobats, the ghosts in the graveyard (doubtless with come-apart dancing skeletons), and a Mexican fandango in the Barrio de la Palma; it concluded with a one-act play, the second part of *Casamiento de los Indios.* This show could not have lasted an hour unless the play were long drawn out.

The second program notes that the theatre is decorated and lighted abundantly, both inside and out; a military band plays in the lobby until the show begins. It all sounds very festive. The variety numbers on this occasion were the dancing of the Varsoviana, the Ferrolana by M. Carsinel and his wife, the cart of the Negro family, and a view of the Plaza Nacional on 16 September (Independence Day) with artificial fireworks and a grand illumination. Then followed a three-act comedy, *A Madrid me vuelvo*, and a singing piece which was not titled. These programs conformed to what Bragaldi offered in New York in 1837 and in London in 1852; it was to become the pattern for the Royal Marionettes.

Another playbill of mine, for the Patio del Nopalito, under the managership of Leandro Escalona, shows the variety program for 28 July 1861. Among acrobats and guitar players are sandwiched the puppets of José Maria Nava; they were also the last number on the bill. Admission to the show was half a real.

That puppets were still playing in barnlike buildings by 1865, and perhaps creating a nuisance in the capital city, is shown by a letter from the Emperor, dated at the Palace, 18 December of that year:

My dear Minister Esteva,
In reply to your letter of the 16th inst., telling of the extension asked for the fourth time by the puppet showmen, I state that I am entirely of your opinion.

TEATRO
DE LA ESMERALDA.

CALLE DE CORCHERO N. 3.

Gran funcion de Títeres y verso

PARA LA NOCHE DEL

Miércoles 10 de Junio de 1857.

La funcion que tengo el honor de presentar al ilustrado público, á quien deseo complacer, es una de las mas divertidas que se han puesto en escena en este Teatro, por lo que espero de su indulgencia, la recibirá con agrado.

PROGRAMA:

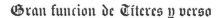

1.° Los tipos Cubanos.
2.° La Jota Aragonesa.
3.° Una bonita pelea de gallos.
4.° Los dos Acróbatas.
5.° Los Espéctros en el Campo-Santo.
6.° Un fandango mejicano en el

BARRIO DE LA PALMA.

Finalizando el todo de la funcion con la divertidísima pieza en un acto, titulada:

SEGUNDA PARTE DEL

CASAMIENTO

DE LOS INDIOS.

PAGAS.

Patio y palcos...... 2 rs. | Galería...... 1 rl.

M. García.

Tip. de V. Segura.

Playbill of the showman M. García for a performance in Mexico City, 10 June 1857. Half original size.

PATIO
DEL NOPALITO.

EMPRESA DE LEANDRO ESCALONA

Gran funcion de volatina, equilibrios, gimnásia, voladores columpios

Y MAROMA:

Domingo 28 de Julio de 1861.

COMENZARA A LA HORA DE COSTUMBRE.

La gratitud es un tesoro inestimable que hace latir el corazon del hombre; es el distintivo mas recomendable para alcanzarlo todo, porque penetra ante la sociedad, haciéndose lugar por su misma virtud. Yo, que no olvido jamas las muchas consideraciones que el indulgente público me ha prodigado, no encuentro aunque poseo esa gratitud, un lenguaje con que espresar mi reconocimiento. Al menos haré lo posible por agradarle, pues no llevo otro fin al presentarle este espetáculo, que he dispuesto bajo el siguiente

PROGRAMA.

1.° A la una de la tarde se dará el paseo de costumbre por toda la compañía.
2.° A las dos de la tarde se situará la música militar en la puerta del local á tocar bonitas y escogidas piezas.
3.° Saludo por toda la compañía.
4.° Eulogio Valdés dará principio á la funcion.
5.° Francisco Muñoz desempeñará dificiles equilibrios.
6.° José Maria Nava desempeñará los pasos de muñecos.
7.° Los intermedios quedan á cargo del recomendable gracioso

VALENTIN GONZALEZ.

El que se presentará con su guitarra á cantar bonitas piezas.

Concluyendo la funcion con unos graciosos pasos de

TITERES.
PAGAS.

Entrada general... medio real.

Venid aquí al Nopalito
que es bonita diversion,
tendrá mucha distraccion
el hombre y el jovencito;
bailará el jarabito
sonecitos y balona,
habrá columpios maroma,
todo esto por medio real
y con gusto os servirá
José Leandro de Escalona

Imp. de Sixto Casillas Rinconada de Sta Catarina Mr. núm 4

Playbill for a variety program with the puppets of José Maria Nava as the sixth number and the final one, 28 July 1861. Half original size.

The Emperor Maximilian sent a note on 18 December 1865 to evict a puppet company. Original sheet 8¼ x 10½ inches.

In consequence please give urgent terminating orders for the immediate removal of the barracks where that entertainment took place.

Cordially yours,
Maximilian

Was it the show to which someone objected, or was it the rickety building which constituted a public menace? Perhaps it was even more complicated, a case of a landlord objecting to the use to which his land had been put; the landlord may even have been the Church. In any event, if the puppet show were a popular one, Maximilian did no good for his reputation with the people by pre-emptory orders in the face of repeated pleas for extension of tenure. The document, in the hand of a secretary but with the Emperor's signature, is in my files.

TEATRO

DE LA ESMERALDA.

CALLE DE CORCHERO NUMERO 3.

*Sobresaliente y variada funcion, de Titeres
versa y canta.*

PARA LA NOCHE DEL

DOMINGO 21 DE JUNIO DE 1857.

———

*Program cover of the showman M. García for a performance in Mexico City, 21 June
1857. Original border 6¼ x 8¾.*

In 1869 F. Cabali, an Italian, in announcing his puppets at the Teatro Iturbide, Mexico City, as a new sort of spectacle in the country, was under the same misapprehension as Blancan in New York in 1808; European puppets in Mexico were then exactly 345 years new, counting from Cortés. The Autómates of Omarín played in the capital about 1872 and the Fantoches (a French derivative from fantoccini) of Gautier in 1888, at which time the títeres of Rinaldo Zane were in evidence. These shows are mentioned by Armando de Maria y Campos, *Presencias de teatro* (p. 222). The Bell family, which used both hand- and string-puppets, was active at this time.

About 1860 a man by the name of Margaraje had a playground in the San Lucas district of the town of Huamantla, Tlaxcala, where he amused the children with a small puppet theatre. He persuaded Leandro Rosete Aranda and his three brothers to operate it for him. All manipulated the puppets and their sisters costumed them and made the scenery. "These performances were given added interest," wrote Reuben M. Campos in *El Folklore literario de Mexico* (Mexico, 1929, pp. 211-216, 257-285), "by developing the dialogue of two or three characters into scenes such as festivals in which there were crowds and many speaking parts. The programs were rounded out by circus acts with a miniature ring, a funny loquacious clown, acrobats on the bars and rings, performers on the flying trapeze, tight-rope walkers, and equestrians who drove races, turned somersaults, and jumped through hoops. Then there were cockmains with a pit, handlers, fighting birds, judge, betters, umpire, singers, and musicians. The spectacle was remarkable for the realism of the cocks, which raised their neck feathers and fluttered their wings at each attack, the detailed representation of the death of the vanquished bird and the explosive jubilation of the victor, and the songs and music supplied by real musicians backstage. Bullfights were also done with all the detail of life; the illusion of seeing the real thing was perfect. The figures in the arena and the spectators in the balconies and boxes were all animated.

"The puppets were costumed very correctly. No one could consider them ridiculous. Candles were used for lighting the stage, or gas in the cities where it was available. Magic tricks and fireworks were neatly managed. A little bull that charged and kicked, along with other ingenious action, kept audiences delighted."

Having made a reputation in the provinces, the brothers came to the capital toward the end of 1880 and opened a season at the Teatro del Seminario. Maestro Altimirano wrote in *La Republica* of one of their scenes, "It is a beautiful and peaceful picture of village life in the mountains of Puebla, a religious idyll, a jewel of realism and charming sim-

SALON
DE LA
REFORMA.
NUMERO 3.
SITUADO EN LA PLAZA
DEL
Seminario.

FUEGOS ARTIFICIALES.

Magníficas y divertidas tandas de titeres para las
noches de la presente temporada.

Agradecida la empresa de la buena aceptacion que
ha recibido, han dispuesto poner para esta noche,
otros mas bonitos y divertidos pasos de Autómatas
y para ello cuenta con los mas inteligentes movilarios
y para la siguiente ha dispuesto: *para la noche de*
sábado 5 d'diciembre de 1880

GRAN CORRIDA DE TOROS

Tapada de Gallos.—Un feroz animal.—Paseo de
Santa Anita.—Baile del negro y la negra.—El Con-
vento y la Tentacion.

ENTRADA GENERAL Medio real

NOTA.—Se siguen preparando otros vonitos y divertidos ciseg-
los que se anunciarán pronto..

Playbill for a performance in Mexico
City on 6 November 1880. Half original
size.

Ranch characters; nineteenth-century puppets such as were used by the Rosete Aranda family. The cowboy to the right is dressed in leather with silver fringe. Average height 12 inches. From a photograph.

plicity. The scene shows a tiny village, a few rustic houses and ornamental trees at the left, an arcade and small village square at the back, the walls of another house at the right, and low green hills, gentle and smiling, in the distance. A well-to-do Indian, dressed in the fashion of the mountain people, in shirt and tobacco-brown leather trousers, awaits the coming of the figure of the Virgin of the Most Immaculate Conception, which is being brought by the curate, accompanied by a few of the faithful, from another village in solemn procession. Meanwhile he is decking with candles and flowers the altar he has prepared for the reception of the image, while his wife strews blossoms on the road along which the procession is to come. Finally it arrives, the acolytes bearing lighted candles and a tall cross, and the Virgin borne aloft on a platform, followed by the priest and a group of devotees. The Indian is beside himself with joy. He kneels, kisses the ground, helps to place the image on the altar, and courteously greets the priest and his acquaintances, inviting them to stop at his house for rest and refreshments. He then prays devoutly before the Virgin while his wife attends to the guests. He brings incense to the altar and lights the candles—a remarkable feat for a puppet.

"Meanwhile another Indian has arrived with an enormous mountain guitar. The orchestra plays a pleasant, melodious piece, 'The Little Bull of the Mountains of Puebla,' over and over. . . . The Indian finishes his devotions. Then comes the 'little bull' made of firecrackers, carried by another Indian. A group of dancing harvesters precedes him. The rear is brought up by a number of urchins scampering about and teasing the 'bull' by flourishing blankets and shouting at him. When the harvesters,

*Nineteenth-century Mexican clown. Col-
lection of Helen E. Reisdorf. From a
photograph.*

and the 'bull' too, have bowed before the altar, the Indian gathers his
guests and lights the 'bull' with a flaming brand. The miniature pyrotech-
nical marvel delights every child in the hall. The 'bull,' just as in a real
festival, runs about the square throwing off red, white, and blue sparks
and kicking among the youngsters, who run squealing and make as much
hubbub as in life. When the last firecracker has exploded the curtain
falls. This picture of Mexican folk custom is so naturally presented that
one forgets one is watching puppets; it seems rather that one is looking
on from a balcony at the simple, graceful fiesta in a tiny Indian mountain
village."

It would seem that these details were handled with the skill of a genre
painter. The Rosete Aranda family not only capitalized on the colorful
Mexican scene but drew such crowds that it was difficult to get into the
Teatro del Seminario.

After this engagement the family toured the country, playing not only
in theatres and halls but in bull rings. It adapted for the puppet stage all
sorts of native festivals, dances, and sports, and presented pantomimes
in the *Little Red Riding Hood* style, which had been popularized by the
Bell family. It gave versions of zarzuellas such as Macedo y Arbeau's
Manicomio de Cuerdos, ballets such as *The Crystal Palace*, and topical

pieces such as *The Comet of '88*; in short, it ran the gamut of all latter-half nineteenth-century puppet numbers, with emphasis upon the color of Mexico. Leandro Rosete Aranda died at the close of the century and his show was continued by his many sons.

The stock of puppets was divided among them, leaving a large number for each. The youngest son, who had become a shopkeeper in 1936, had about 350 articulated string-puppets and 750 unjointed ones as super-numeraries to dress the stage, 30 puppet animals, and a quantity of scenery, properties, packing boxes, and scripts of plays. Another son, who toured with a show of his own, 1910-1915, disposed of a lot of 30 puppets which I have seen. They are from 12 to 16 inches tall (on the small side for puppets to be seen by a sizable audience) and seem to have been made by various hands. They are carved of light, pithy wood, which does not allow good tongue-and-groove joints; the arms and legs are put together with cloth tubes. The faces are gesso covered and painted. The costumes, made of rags and scraps, do not bear close inspection but would be effective on the stage. They are operated by a minimum number of strings (supers sometimes having but one to the head) fastened to small wooden bar controllers. Among the characters are Indian types, a priest and acolytes, circus performers, a skeleton, a team of horses, a dog, and bull-ring frequenters, including a boy designed to lose his trousers when pursued by the bull.

It is said that Leandro Rosete Aranda once had over a thousand articulated figures and that his troupe of puppeteers had men, women, and children to the number of thirty. In 1936 there were still three small, separate companies going under the Rosete Aranda name, and at least one has continued to 1946. Donald Cordry saw one of the companies in the summer of 1932 in Mexico City; its program was very much like those of the Royal Marionettes in the nineteenth century. The harlequinade, Cordry reported (*Puppetry 1932*, p. 27), was *Aladdin and his Wonderful Lamp*. It had trick figures, a rainstorm of real water, fireworks, a chorus of twenty dancing girls which undulated in an Oriental dance in the throne-room scene, and an orchestra with twenty puppet Indian musicians. The stage was about ten feet wide, the floor raked up from the footlights to the backdrop like old opera-house stages, and there were four pairs of wings in painted perspective. Other visitors have sought out the Rosete Aranda shows, which sometimes play in tents, and grown enthusiastic about their adherence to the theatrical conventions of the past.

Walter Deaves, the American, having come into Mexico with a theatrical company which was stranded there, made an inadvertent tour to get out, showing his puppets in all sorts of halls and even in bull rings in 1877. This incident will be mentioned in the section devoted to his career.

For a season already running on 6 November 1880, announced by a playbill in my possession, an unnamed company played at the Salon de la Reforma, 3 Plaza del Seminario, Mexico City; it was evidently to be there for a while; a footnote said, "Other delights and diversions now in preparation will be announced shortly." The present delights were artificial fireworks, amusing puppet turns, a grand bullfight, a cockmain, a ferocious animal (kind not stated), the passing of Santa Anita, a dance of the Negro couple, and the convent and the temptation. All this local color has a Rosete Aranda look.

In 1880 was founded the Gallery of Juvenile Drama of Antonio Vanegas Arroyo, which purveyed penny booklets of plays "written especially for children or puppets." These 3 × 4-inch minuscules were notable for having covers with the typemetal-cut designs of Posada, the great popular print maker. Arroyo presently found competition from the similar plays of Ildefonso T. Orellana. These chapbooks now evoke nostalgic memories in the people who squandered their coppers on them when they were children. Armando de Maria y Campos has written warmly about them in an article translated in *Puppetry 1942-1943*, pp. 32-33.

"Every week," he wrote, "I had a premiere of a play by Orellana, with puppets sold by Orellana himself in his tiny shop, 'El Teatro,' at 50 Santa Teresa (later, without changing location, renumbered as 2 Santa Teresa, below 15 and 20 Guatemala Avenue). The Orellana business seemed to have a branch, or at least a stall, in the Portal de Mercaderes, for one of the opuscules which I have treasured from that time—one of my first theatre books—*La fotografía instantánea*, 'a diverting comedy in two parts,' shows this imprint: I. T. Orellana imp. Portal de Mercaderes 24. A notice in the inside . . . confirms this. The wording is delightful: 'Magic lanterns, perspectives, and chromotropes, fine selection. Decalcomanias especially for magic lanterns. Selection of parlor games. Scenery and plays for children. For rent, beautiful stage front and scenery, can be set up for home theatricals in three hours without marring ceilings, walls, or floor. Adapted for home presentation of dissolving views.' . . .

"Orellana's booklets lack illustrations. They are brief, generally 16 pages, by exception 24, and one—rare and wonderful—32. This is a 'dramatic fantasy, like the big drama,' so says the title-page, 'written especially for children or puppets,' entitled *Don Juan Tenorio*, 'the text of which, in verse, is quite different from that of Zorilla, respecting plot, action, and principal characters.' Ildefonso, not content with creating a new version of Don Juan, published an 'illusory drama' entitled *Don*

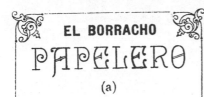

EL BORRACHO

PAPELERO

(a)

"EL COYOTE"

Juguete de Costumbres Populares

EN DOS ACTOS

Para Representarse con Titeres

Original de

ILDEFONSO T. ORELLANA

Av. Guatemala No 50. "EL TEATRO"

MEXICO

LAS CUATRO APARICIONES
de la Vírgen de Guadalupe

LEYENDA MELODRAMATICA EN VERSO
Y SIETE PARTES,

Escrito especialmente para Teatro
de NIÑOS o TITERES y original
de Ildefonso T. Orellana.

—FIGURAN:—

*Ntra. Sra. de Guadalupe -en apariciones-. Su
Illma, el Sr Obispo Zumarraga. Varios Familia-
res. Juan Diego, Juan Bernardino, su tio
Dos Sirvientes del Obispado, Un india,*

PROP. ASEGURADA CONFORME A LA LEY
—MEXICO—1918—

Para representarse por especulacion o reimpri-
mirse, se necesita permiso de su autor

I. T. Orellana, Imp, Sta. Teresa 50.

EL ALCALDE VIVIDOR.

ESCENAS POPULARES REPRESENTABLES
——POR TITERES O NIÑOS.——

por Agustin M. Orellana.
SEGUNDA PARTE.

AMORES

—DE—

D. QUITERIO

SEGUNDA EDICION,

PERSONAJES.
Casilda. Pascuala. D. Quiterio. Anton,
y un Topil de ronda,
La escena pasa en Xochimilco, años atrás

Prop, asegurada conforme á la Ley.
—MEXICO—1918.—

Orellana Imp.—2a. Sta. Teresa, bajos del 50·

D. JUAN
TENORIO
EN EL INFIERNO.

Dramita ilusorio, escrito por I. T. Orellana
para teatro de títeres ó niños.

El cual puede agregarse como conclusion final al dramita de D. JUAN
TENORIO, o representarse solo.

DIVIDIDO EN TRES CUADROS.

PROP. ASEGURADA CONFORME A LA LEY

—MEXICO—1924.—

Para representarse por especulacion o reimpri
mirse, se necesita permiso de su autor

I. T. Orellana, Imp, Sta. Teresa 50.

*Covers of four plays "for children or puppets" published by I. T. Orellana. Original
size.*

Four metal-cut covers by Posada for the Vanegas Arroyo juvenile drama. Original cuts about 3¼ x 5¼; covers 5½ x 3¾ inches.

Juan Tenorio en el Infierno, 'divided into three acts, which can be added as a conclusion to *Don Juan Tenorio* or played alone.' No doubt Orellana's most popular pieces were *Astucias de don Folías, El Borracho papelero* (*a*) *el coyote*, and the series of 'popular playable scenes' entitled *El Alcalde vividor*, taking place in Xochimilco or in the San Pablo region, published in six booklets. Orellana's tomes sold at five centavos.

"His only competitor was Antonio Vanegas Arroyo, publisher of popular literature, who had his printing shop at 40 Avenida de Guatemala, and the sales price for his works at No. 1 in the same street, when that part of town was called the Santa Teresa quarter. Arroyo's booklets achieved extraordinary popularity because of the sketches which they flaunted on their covers . . . by the outstanding draughtsman and masterful engraver, José Guadalupe Posada (1864-1916). It is supposed that Posada turned out thousands of cuts, and to facilitate his work the indefatigable illustrator of bull fights, ballads, stories of the saints, pastorals, broadsides, tales, riddles, etc., invented a method of engraving on zinc. [Engraving on type metal was traditional.] Almost all his engravings which were used as covers of the Galería del Teatro Infantil, published by Arroyo in the first fifteen years of this century, must be lost, because in the second editions printed by the Tipografia de la Testamentaría de A. Vanegas Arroyo, they are not reproduced. . . .

"In all the pieces typical Mexican folk characters figure, and all transpire in our city districts and squares, save, to be sure, the famous Tenorio. I shall mention a few titles and the reader familiar with the genius of Posada can imagine the types and scenes which the artist made for their covers: *Los Sustos del velador, Días pasados por agua, Los Celos del Negro con don Folías, La Casa de vecindad, Una Corrida de toros o el amor de Luisa, En la cocina, Los Gendarmes, Los Pulques mexicanos, Por besar a la gata, El Casamiento de indios*, and a delicious piece called *Juan Pico de Oro*."

While these literary pieces could have had little influence on the repertory of the professional puppeteer, they were no doubt in the vein of professional plays.

Toy puppets worked by a string or two could be bought in the market places of many towns until recently. On such holidays as Holy Week, Corpus Christi, and All Souls' Day, wrote Roberto Lago in *Mexican Folk Puppets* (Birmingham, Michigan, 1941), they could be found "in full array, ready to be taken home for a penny or two to the children for their toy stages, improvised from boxes or whatever is handy." But the deterioration of handicraft and the rise of prices has made many of these playthings disappear; some of them are now collector's pieces.

*Toy puppets, average height 6 inches, of
sun-baked clay, paper, and cloth. After
drawings by Fernando Ledesma.*

"What beautifully carved and colored wooden horses come from Ira-
puato!" continued Lago. "Strings pass down their supporting sticks to
move their heads, legs, and the arms of their riders. From Salamanca
come monkeys on a pole and Apache guitarists, liveliest of toys. The capital provides jumping-jack skeletons or caricatures of political personages
(appropriately pulled by strings) all cut from cardboard. Then there
are the delicate figures of Puebla, whose form is legion, and the sun-
baked clay puppets of Toluca and Metepec, crude but teeming with
earthy vigor. Whether made from clay, wood, rags, or corn-husks, these
creatures of fantasy, birds, animals, half-human monkeys, witches, demons,
and ghosts, have the quality of seeming alive. The native craftsman displays his genius in devising their articulation. His fertile invention, sense
of beauty, and aboriginal's unselfconscious skill, resolve every technical
and artistic problem. The Mexican puppet maker has his finger on the
pulse of life; with absolute freedom he transmits it to his puppets."

Though Spanish puppetry reached Mexico two centuries before English
came to the British colonies, by the eighteenth century it was following
a course parallel with English. It had fixed theatres and itinerant shows;
it had simple slapstick farces and elaborate bills with tricks and extravaganza. But in the programs of the Rosete Aranda family it emphasized
native material to a degree unknown in the United States. Elaborate
shows abounding in local color were given side by side with those of the
artistic revival in the 1930's, and the newer showmen profited by tradition
in using Mexican legend and characters.

2. In Peru

Though only scattered references to puppets in Peru may be given, it is evident that there was continuity between the work of Leonor Godomar and those who followed her. In 1828, for instance, there were puppets in a theatre in the Barbones quarter of Lima, as Manuel Moncloa y Covarrubias mentions in his *Diccionario teatral del Perú* (Lima, 1905). Sometime in the 1870's an Italian showman played in the country, for his performances inspired a native Peruvian to become a puppeteer. In the 1890's he was an old man, or so he seemed to José Galvez who, as a child, witnessed one of his shows at his grandmother's house in Lima. In *Puppets of Yore in Peru* (translated from *Turismo*, January 1938, in *Puppetry 1940*, p. 17) Galvez wrote, "Ño Valdivieso [Ño is something less than señor, applied to the colored, the poor, and the spiritless, according to Juan de Arona, *Diccionario de Peruanismos*, Peru 1938] was a solemn, tallish, raw-boned mulatto, humorous in an earthy way, with large, capable hands. . . . He was a craftsman, making his own puppets, devising the action, and creating his plays, which were the best part of his work.

"His characters became legendary: Mama Gerundia, Don Silvestre, Orejoncito, Perotito, Chocolatito, Misia Catia, Petit Garzon, the Faint-Hearted Soldier, and Big Carcancha and the Little Ghost which grew taller and taller in *The Haunted House* before the fascinated and frightened eyes of the youngsters. He invented the Padre del Sermon, full of precepts and Latin jargon, the Doctor with a huge syringe, the Angel which appeared at the opening of a performance, the grand bull fight, and the tempestuous dance finale. . . .

"When he began, the shows of the puppeteer were very modest. At first he presented his pieces to the accompaniment of guitar and *tirisuya* (native flute) in the courtyards and old houses of his neighborhood, but his fame spread quickly from one dinner table to another. He gave special birthday performances in aristocratic mansions. The children were tickled to death over a sort of Jabberwocky that Padre del Sermon recited.

"His puppets gave a running commentary on Peruvian manners and morals. In fact, they even got him into jail for some very pointed political allusions. His performances were given in the famous Salon Capella and were attended by people of all ages, who enjoyed the genuinely Creole witticisms of this illiterate genius. . . .

"Don Silvestre, with his big stovepipe hat, his faded Prince Albert, his light trousers, his alcoholic voice, his pompous manners, boastful babbling, and querulous mood, was copied from a local type. Many a

Don Silvestre has gone about, forever complaining, drinking, and prescribing for the ills of his country.

"Mama Gerundia, who was in her dotage, whispered, gossiped, and quarreled constantly with Don Silvestre; she was a scolding woman such as one met in the Lima of yesterday.

"Perotito was the lively half-breed, mischievous and timid by turn, slangy and vociferous. His voice was a masterpiece. Whoever heard the little squeak, going on at such a rate that it made one dizzy, never forgot it. Just as the commedia dell' arte types pointed up phases of human character, Perotito exemplified the fellow we saw everywhere, in politics, in society, and in print, hopping and squealing, always stirred up, never accomplishing anything."

Perhaps it is inevitable that the long-settled but isolated sections of America should develop puppet plays based upon local characteristics; subjected to little European influence from traveling shows, which generally go to population centers on the usual routes of travel, the local puppeteers and audiences tended to look inward upon themselves for dramatic material.

José Galvez in his article on Ño Valdivieso is ingenious in exploring the origin of terms; speculative etymology is dangerous; but I should like to quote it here. "In Spanish the word *títere*," he wrote, "is an old one; Covarrubias discusses it in his *Treasury of the Castilian Language* and supposes that it comes from the sound *ti ti* of the whistle which was once part of a puppet show; or that it comes from the Greek *tytizo* which, according to him, is the equivalent of 'warble' or 'gabble.' But with a bow to the great master, it seems to me (and I dare make no stronger assertion) that the word may well come from *tyttos,* meaning 'small,' or from *tityros,* meaning 'monkey' and also 'satirist' or 'comedian.' It may be added that *tityristes* means 'flute player' and thence perhaps comes the onomatopoeic and graceful word *titiritaina* which expresses a confused noise of flutes and includes noisy merriment. And since we are engaged in this wordy perambulation, I recall that portable box with movable figures which used to amuse us [theatrum mundi or peep-show] and which was called *titirimundi.* But, all else aside, it does seem evident that *títere* comes from the Hellenic *tityro.*"

Though Peru, like Mexico, developed its own puppet types, it was not cut off altogether from visiting companies, some of them perhaps from the United States. In a more complete listing of its puppet shows some of these would probably be discovered.

3. In the Argentine

In her study of *Florencio Sánchez and the Argentine Theatre* (New York, 1933, pp. 32-34), Ruth Richardson states that puppet shows flourished in all the towns of the Rio de la Plata, but especially in Montevideo, from 1800 onward. The puppets were carved, by the testimony of Vincente Rossi, *Teatro nacional Ríoplatense* (Cordoba, Argentina, 1910, p. 161), with a good penknife or *navaja* from a soft and pliable piece of wood such as the stem or sprout of the *agave* or century plant, which combines these qualities to a marked degree. The face of the puppet, a mask of papier mâché, was slipped on over the roughly shaped head.

These were the characters in the usual company: the Negro Francisco Pancho or Misericordia Campaña, who was the leading light and opened every performance; Pancha, his Negro wife, who closed the entertainment; Don Protasio, an old Creole schoolmaster with a Castilian lisp in his pronunciation; Teresito, an effeminate young man who designed women's clothes; a restaurant keeper from Genoa whose name was Pepín, Yucamín, or Gaitán—later in the century he might be from Naples; a Basque milkman, Martín; a Galician porter, Manuel, Baldomero, or Farruco, representative of the Spanish colonist; and a few who appeared only occasionally, including the Frenchman and the Englishman.

Rossi said that the newsboys of Montevideo gave puppet shows in stores where they were harbored by the shopkeeper as a means of attracting customers; they invented this international group of puppets; once it had crystallized they were reluctant to admit new characters, preferring to build their plays around the familiar, sharply defined ones that they knew. Those figures of authority, the Doctor and Priest, were absent— not, I am sure, because of youthful reverence, as Rossi thought, but because the boys just wanted to dodge them. In the 1890's the newsboy puppet theatre was at its peak of activity. There were puppets in Buenos Aires, but they came and went and were not so truly an expression of the people. Plays were written for the local puppet theatre by Martín Coronado some time before the Argentine playwright for the big theatre came into being.

The pattern of itinerant shows was much the same here as elsewhere in America.

4. In Chile and Other Places

An elaborate theatre for human actors was built in Valparaiso with capital founded upon the earnings of an Italian, Alexandri, from his puppet show. He came to Chile with his puppets about 1840 and was both saving and successful, wrote Jacques Arago in *Deux oceans* (Paris, 1854, Vol. 1, p. 175). During one of the wars between Chile and Bolivia he was able to lend money to Chile; it came back to him considerably increased. Wishing to benefit the country where he had made a fortune, he brought architects and painters from France, Spain, and Italy, and built the theatre as a civic monument.

Alberto Lano and his wife, on their way to California in 1849, played *Robinson Crusoe, Tom Thumb,* and *Damon and Pythias* in Havana, Cartago, San José, Limon, Cartagena, Bogotá, Guayaquil, and small settlements and ranches in Colombia and Ecuador. His son Oliver and his wife toured South America with a circus in 1887 and doubtless gave puppet shows.

When the puppets of southern Italy came to the Americas with the flood of Italian immigration in the 1890's, a showman called Don Bastian went to São Paolo, Brazil, in 1898; he moved to Buenos Aires in 1910. Agrippino Manteo, from Catania, Sicily, went to Buenos Aires in 1896, where he played until 1912; then he went to Mendoza and stayed until 1916; finally he came to New York, where his puppets were among the last of their kind. These Italian shows will be chronicled in a future chapter.

Much material must still be gathered before the story of puppets in nineteenth-century Latin America can take substantial form. But it appears, from these few instances, that they went almost everywhere and were a fixture in the life of the towns.

XIV

Nineteenth-Century Canadian Puppets

While the permanent puppet theatre in Quebec continued to entertain the families of that community, there were wandering puppeteers in French Canada. About 1830 two French-Canadian puppeteers visited St. Hughes, County Bagot, Quebec, to give a performance. Louis Richard of that town had occasion to help them; his nephew, as an old man in 1923, recalled the occasion in speaking to E.-Z. Massicotte, who wrote about it to me.

An English or Yankee puppeteer named Palmer played in large houses and barns in and around Montreal about 1850; he was something of a fixture in town, also giving magic and ventriloquial shows. His charge was 6 sous for children and 15 for adults. He was recalled by a senior officer in the Montreal Palais de Justice, who was quoted by Massicotte in his article, "Les marionnettes au Canada," in the *Bulletin des recherches historiques* (Vol. 28, Quebec, 1922, p. 338).

It will be recalled that McDonough and Earnshaw's Royal Marionettes played at the Theatre Royal, Victoria, British Columbia, 25-30 September 1876. Puppets did not, however, cross Canada as they did the United States; this isolated visit to the Northwest Coast was made by ship from California.

About the year 1883 there was a summer amusement place in the Encan Marleau (Marleau Auction Room), Rue Notre Dame west, opposite the Rue Dominion, Montreal. Among other features it had a merry-go-round and a puppet booth set up in a corner. The Punch and Judy show which occupied it was given in a mixture of French and English by Joseph Lemay from the United States, a thin, one-eyed quipster who had once played in minstrel shows. He made much of his characters of the Policeman and Gavroche, or "tough kid." After the show was over he would stick his head out under the curtain and sing, in the interests of the neighboring publican:

> Les Canadiens n'sont pas de fous,
> Partiront pas sans prendre un coup.

Which is to say that Canadians are not so foolish as to go away without having a drop to drink. The record of this is also to be found in Massicotte's article.

Again in this article it is mentioned that a resident of Kamouraska, a Quebec town south of the St. Lawrence, in 1885 saw a wandering showman who was following the lowlands along the river, tumbling and giving puppet shows. This would have been Oliver Lano, who was in Canada that season. The Lanos were all acrobats as well as puppeteers. In 1886-1887 Lano took his son David and an apprentice, Jenny, on another Canadian tour, presenting *Jack the Giant Killer*. David and Jenny spoke the lines in French which they had learned by rote without knowing what it meant. They played three weeks in Montreal in January 1887, visited Trois Rivières, and were sponsored by a brewery in Lachine to spread good will for its product.

About 1900 there was a remarkable manifestation of amateur puppetry among the people of French Canada. When traditional puppet shows have died out this is usually the result of an impressive professional show having been seen recently. But there are so few records for this region that the stimulus may have come either from a wandering company or a remembrance of Daddy Marseille's theatre. Perhaps the model was in itself amateur, the show of a vacationist who took his simple Polichinelle to all sorts of halls, stores, and even cheese factories, playing for a 10¢ admission fee. Those who brought along their own lamps to light the hall were admitted free, and because the audiences were thrifty, the auditorium was always well illuminated! This amateur is mentioned in Ernest Russell's "The Most Popular Play in the World" (*Outing Magazine*, January 1908, p. 473).

Whether it was the example of this showman or another, at Valleyfield, Beauharnois County, a local citizen, France Lebeuf, played a scene, probably based upon observation of the regional character, of two canny neighbors who tricked each other in fencing in land; another citizen, Leduc, played a scene of a shrewish, slugabed wife. At St. Eustache there was a farmer from Ireland named Jood (Joad?) who was a good fiddler and a puppeteer who did a scene of a blacksmith shoeing a horse. These amateurs had no stages. They merely placed two chairs at the end of a room and stretched a cloth between them as a masking piece. Then, squatting on the floor behind the cloth, they worked the puppets over the top of it. The puppets were crudely made of crossed sticks dressed up, perhaps in approximation of hand-puppets, though they amounted to rod-puppets. The scenery was rudimentary. But the performances, as Massicotte reported them, had tremendous verve. One admires these novices for their ingenuity in trying to reproduce the puppets they had seen, and for their native wit in dramatizing the life around them rather than copying the situations in a literary play. Had there been someone to show them a little more about puppet technique they would have had a good start for a long-lived folk theatre.

An offshoot of this activity may have been the show of Paul Galy and his partner, itinerant puppeteers, at Murray Bay College, Quebec, in 1905, the last of the performances of that era to be chronicled by Massicotte. When the archives of the St. Lawrence towns can be combed for evidence of puppet shows, it is probable that the names of other showmen, as well as the itineraries of those here mentioned, will be added to this meager record.

In such English-speaking parts of Canada as were not too remote from travel routes, many of the same companies that performed in the United States, the Lano and the Royal, for instance, along with later vaudeville manikins, could have been seen. But it was the French language shows that had the local color.

An interest in French puppets has always lingered in America, though the French companies that visited it were comparatively few. The New York *Post* of 4 July 1873 carried this story about one of the artistic Parisian troupes which was to influence the puppet revival in America fifty years later; and this was not the only story of French puppetry that would find a place in American newspapers:

"An entertainment which has been exceedingly popular in aristocratic circles in Paris during the past year, but which of course could not be exhibited in public, is described by the Paris correspondent of the London *News*. . . . Les Pupazzi of M. Lemercier de Neuville has won in private a 'succès fou.' The 'pupazzi' are simply dolls [hand-puppets], which represent with marvelous fidelity the outward appearance of the most prominent men of France. The faces, indeed, are finished with the most elaborate care, and the likenesses are so striking that anybody who once sees the 'pupazzi' has no difficulty, when he afterwards visits the 'assembly,' in immediately recognizing all the originals of the dolls at which he laughed so heartily. The peculiar gestures of all the speakers are imitated to perfection. . . . M. Lemercier de Neuville . . . models his puppets with his own hands, writes his own pieces, and plays all the parts, imitating the voices of all the persons represented."

XV

Vaudeville Manikins

1. Till's Royal Marionettes

Under the impetus of the success of Bullock's Royal Marionettes, a company which called itself the Royal Oriental Marionettes got to Philadelphia from England and opened in June 1874. Its property man, John Till, and his wife, Louisa (née Sanderson), one of the puppeteers, struck out for themselves when the company broke up. They were playing independently at Smith's Island, Philadelphia, in May 1875. They were no doubt a self-sufficient couple, he making the puppets and scenery, she devising the skits and action. Among the last flourishing scions of the Royal Marionettes, still playing in the 1890's, they were one of the first puppet acts in vaudeville, when the variety program came to be known by that name.

Vaudeville was not a new form of entertainment—music halls had presented a miscellany of jugglers and comedians—but an organization of that form. E. F. Albee states, in the *Encyclopedia Britannica* (14th ed., Vol. 23, p. 13), that it was originated by B. F. Keith at the Gaiety Museum, Boston, in 1883. That is, he codified the program: an opening dumb act of acrobats or whatever else would let a noisy audience get seated, a succession of singers, dancers, instrumentalists, then the climax, a stellar act which could be anything from a one-act drama to a monologue by a notorious figure just acquitted of murder, and finally something dull—a reel of movies was found to be just right—to clear the house for the next performance. The puppet act could lead the bill, not a flattering position, when it was reduced to pantomime; it could also take the stellar position. Because of its bulky equipment it always played in the full depth of the stage, whereas comedians and dancers could perform on the apron in front of the curtain. Vaudeville theatres were soon collected into chains under one management, so that a performer could be assured of a season's booking under a single contract. The older variety theatres could offer only a week's engagement. Puppets, under this arrangement, were more secure than they had ever been before, both in earning regular wages and in staying before the public.

It was not long before the Tills were playing quite steadily in variety theatres, mostly in and around New York. Their programs were capsule Royal Marionette bills, with a fairy-tale musical play and perhaps a couple of trick numbers worked into it, all for a ten- or fifteen-minute act. At first there were spoken lines; but because of the need for condensation, dialogue was cut to a minimum; eventually nothing but songs remained, and even they disappeared in some of the later vaudeville manikin companies.

For the fortnight beginning 1 April 1878, Till's Royal Wonders (a term that was applied to magic too) gave their version of *Little Red Riding Hood*, which was still recalled as a smash hit, at the New American Museum, 103 Bowery, New York (*Herald*, 1-13 April). For the week of 16 August they were across the street at the National Garten, 104 Bowery (Harvard playbill). Of course they had engagements between, perhaps in out-of-town places. The Royal Marionettes at Tony Pastor's for the week of 13 January 1879 were probably Till's (Harvard playbill), because starting 20 January Till's Royal Marionettes played *Beauty and the Beast* at G. B. Bunnell's Dime Museum, 430 Fulton Street, Brooklyn. On this occasion (Brooklyn *Daily Eagle*, 19-24 January) the Ebony-Headed Minstrels were an added attraction. The Bullock formula persisted.

The weeks that cannot be accounted for in Till's itinerary were spent out of town or at minor pleasure resorts that did not advertise; and there were times, in this pre-vaudeville era, when the puppets were at liberty. *Beauty and the Beast* was the play at Miner's Bowery Theatre 10-15 November 1879 (Harvard playbill). But at the Aquarium, 17-22 November, the Tills evidently gave a two-hour show, for performances were at 2 and 8 P.M. only. The billing read, "Till's Original Royal Marionette Troupe from St. James' Hall, London. The only troupe ever playing before the Queen and Royal Family of England. An entire automatic minstrel company performing pantomimes, plays, etc., like human beings" (New York *Times*, 16-22 November).

If the Tills had been with an English company that was honored by a royal visit, it could not have been Bullock's, or he would have mentioned the gracious recognition in his publicity. Whatever the puppets, they had probably been called Royal even before gaining the patronage of the Queen.

Till's troupe was at Tony Pastor's, 22-27 December 1879, with *Humpty Dumpty's Christmas*—a stock play refurbished for the holiday season (Harvard playbill). *Beauty and the Beast* reappeared at Hyde and Behman's Theatre, Brooklyn, 2-25 September 1880 (Brooklyn *Daily Eagle* for those dates). These theatres were revisited in 1881.

The company that played in Philadelphia at the Permanent Exhibition Building, 25 June—2 July, and at the Arch Street Opera House, 4-9 July 1881, as "the Original and Only Royal Marionettes," probably did not include the Tills. They had been announced to play in Philadelphia in August but had not appeared. "Original and Only" was a vain protest against the Tills and others who used the name Royal—all with as much right.

Blue Beard and *Humpty Dumpty* were played by the Tills at Hyde and Behman's, 13-18 March 1882 (Brooklyn *Daily Eagle* for those dates). In December, for a Christmas engagement at the Bowery Theatre, New York, their variety numbers were featured. Their old stand-by of *Beauty and the Beast* cropped up from time to time in later years, but they came more and more to use trick numbers as the exigencies of vaudeville crowded their condensed musical plays out.

I wish that I could say what became of the Tills and when their marionettes made a final appearance; these are facts for the future to reveal.

2. Middleton's Marionettes

In the summer of 1877 or 1878, Henry James Middleton, who had come to America with his family at the behest of one of the Royal Marionette troupes, died of sunstroke at Smith's Island. He was a short, bald man, and going hatless after a strenuous performance he may have been at the mercy of the unaccustomed American sun. His eldest son, Harry, had played for McDonough and Earnshaw on the West Coast in 1876, where he made some Chinese bell ringers, string-puppets, from actual Celestial models. Upon the death of his father a younger son, George William, took work outside the theatre to support his mother, but in the spring of 1883 he joined Harry in a marionette act styled the Middleton Brothers after that of their father and uncle in England. This information all comes from conversations and correspondence with George William.

The act became part of a combination show in Philadelphia. According to George's recollection it was at the National Theatre; but the nearest thing to such a show that was advertised in the papers was the Interocean Combination at the Broad Street Theatre, opening 9 April 1883; this did not mention the Middleton Brothers. Their show was managed by J. E. Sucket. With it they traveled across the continent to Livingston, Montana. There the party of ten was stranded. Five decided to continue to the West Coast; the Middletons and three others turned back East. They were to have opened at the Lyceum Theatre, Des Plaines Street, Chicago, on 15 October 1883. The theatre manager persuaded them to set up their stage on the preceding Friday and have everything ready for the Monday opening.

On Saturday the Lyceum was gutted by fire; there is an account of it in the Chicago *Tribune* of 13 October. The Middletons arrived on the scene to see firemen still playing water on the smoking ruins. Determined to salvage whatever might remain of their puppets, they asked if the box, a big one made of square-piano covers, from which the puppets had not yet been unpacked, were still in evidence. It was reported that no fragment of it remained. Ruefully the brothers were about to turn away when one of them spied something floating in the water underneath the board sidewalk in front of the theatre. Then, as now, Chicago street levels were raised a few feet above the sandy earth, leaving a cavity. Yes, it was the piano-cover box, borne out of the building on the stream from the fire hoses. It was hauled out and the puppets were found to be dry and safe.

A new stage was built and two drop curtains were painted by Salzman and Landis, Chicago's leading scene painters. The Middleton Brothers managed to open a few weeks later at the Olympic Theatre on the South Side. In mid-February 1884 they came to Detroit to play at Phil Milligan's Dime Museum, 9 Michigan Avenue, opposite the New Market (the Family Theatre), for a five-week run. As this house advertised "a grand stage exhibition hourly," specifying only the chief attractions, no billing for the Middletons can be found in the papers. The time of their engagement is marked, however, by the date 11 March 1884, engraved on the medals sent each of the brothers by "Phil Milligan and all attachés" of the museum in appreciation of the success of their run. Such medals were presented by managers to popular performers, and may be seen displayed on proud Thespian breasts in old photographs. George Middleton's is a bronze disc with silver figures of a clown and pantaloon. The medals arrived while they were playing their next engagement at the Grand Opera House, Pittsburgh. The brothers, still in shirtsleeves and wearing the carpenter's aprons which were a protection against the friction of the leaning rail, were called before the curtains to receive the award and were greeted with round after round of applause. After these memorable engagements they played in Baltimore and then once more at home in Philadelphia.

In an address at the first American Puppetry Conference in Detroit, 8 July 1936, George William Middleton said, "We used both three-foot and fourteen-inch marionettes, depending upon the hall in which we played. Our performances were much like those we had been doing when the whole family was together. They generally opened with a Negro minstrel first part, with nine characters; then came from twelve to fifteen olio specialties, including eight quadrille dancers and fairies. Then came a drama, chosen from our repertory of *The Miller and his Men, Othello, Beauty and the Beast, Colleen Bawn, The Sea of Ice, The Vampire's Bride, Babes in the Wood* [at six George had taken the part of the little boy, and his sister that of the little girl in this piece, as the Weinkoetz children and Herodia had played together with puppets], *Little Red Riding Hood, Cinderella, The Seven Clerks, Poll and her Partner Joe, Robin Rough Head, Dick Whittington and his Cat, Jack and the Beanstalk, Jack the Giant Killer, As You Like It,* and many others. Each drama was in three, four, or five scenes, and took about fifteen people to work; the backcloths were dropped one over the other for quick changes. After the play there followed fifteen or twenty pantomime tricks, and the performance closed with a grand transformation scene.

"My brother Harry was a splendid manipulator. . . . If our marionettes were not so artistic as many of yours today, I think that our manipulation was, upon the whole, much better. We did several shows a day, were in constant practice, and had no opportunity to grow rusty." This address is published in *Puppetry 1936* (pp. 12-13).

Harry died in 1884, and on 3 September of that year George married Sarah Jane Welsh of Cincinnati. Because George's mother was also a Sarah Jane, his wife was called Jenny. For a while George and his mother had done the puppet act together. Then Jenny was taught how to manipulate and the three worked together. During the summers of 1885, 1886, and 1887 Middleton's Royal Marionettes played from Decoration Day to Labor Day on Applegate's Pier, Atlantic City. In the winter they found engagements on the East Coast and in the Middle West. When the elder Mrs. Middleton decided to settle down in Philadelphia, George and Jenny carried on with the puppets, traveling five times across the continent. After 1891 George gave up puppetry for periods to undertake the management of theatres. He managed the Mozart Theatre in Elmira, New York, between 1906 and 1915. Thereafter the puppets were brought out to play on Redpath and Canadian Chautauqua circuits. They were a stage prologue to showings of the puppet movie *I Am Suzanne* in New York state theatres; they performed the puppet scene in the operetta *Naughty Marietta*. In 1932 they toured the East in a Model T Ford truck. In 1936 they were connected with Michigan WPA theatre units. The death of George in 1946 broke up the team and interrupted a record of some sixty years of puppet showmanship.

According to Jenny Middleton, George's mother was an excellent manipulator, particularly of dance numbers. When Jenny was learning to be a puppeteer, the puppet strings were of white linen, blacked with shoemaker's wax; the elder Mrs. Middleton called it "slang-stuff." The costumes were so made that they could be slipped off without unfastening the strings, to facilitate redressing. Jenny loved to make the bright costumes, and even prepared curtains of painted and beaded silk for transformation scenes. She recalled those that had birds of paradise, butterflies, and a sunburst which, successively revealed to music, had a gorgeous effect.

The Negro minstrel part of the Middleton show ended with a skeleton dance in a graveyard. A Rastus and Mandy duet was imitated from one of the blackface comedians, McIntyre and Heath. Three trunks contained the entire outfit on its vaudeville tours. The stage was mounted on rollers so that it could be whisked off to make way for the following act. The old harlequinade tricks of the clown stealing sausages from the butcher's stall and being pursued by a policeman were played almost to the end of the Middletons' career, always causing bursts of laughter. The controllers were single sticks, held horizontally, such as those used by most vaudeville performers. If a figure was so elaborately strung as to require more than one stick, one (such as that for walking) was held in one hand, the others in the other; all could be grasped in one fist when the puppet was held at rest.

In addition to string-puppets the Middletons presented shadow-figures, more about which will be said in the next chapter. Sometimes they would play a fortnight's engagement at a theatre, one week with puppets and the next with shadows. Or they would do both together, billed as the Middletons for the puppets and for the shadows as the Laroux or Imperial Shadowgraphs.

George and Jenny were an engaging old couple. Always considerate of each other, always courteous to visitors and associates, they seemed a perfect Darby and Joan. I remember my delightful chats with them as they sat in my studio, Jenny's hat abloom with flowers, her face sweetly smiling, George's face reflecting the flowers and the smile. Despite the adversity of conditions during their latter days, they managed to keep up their spirits. When playing at night clubs they stepped out from behind their stage, an unexpected elderly pair with snow-white hair, to enthusiastic applause. Little of the great tradition of Royal Marionette manipulation could be seen in their work, for their puppets had to be improvised out of odds and ends and they were not always in practice, but in their manner was something of the old grandeur.

3. Deaves' Marvelous Manikins

Walter Eugene Deaves had helped his father, Edwin Deaves, with occasional string-puppet plays, *Jack the Giant Killer*, *Jack and the Beanstalk*, and *Little Red Riding Hood*, at the old California or Bella Union theatres in San Francisco about 1864, according to the story passed on to his son, also named Edwin, from whom the following information has been obtained. Walter started so young that he had to stand on a box in order to reach over the leaning rail. Edwin the elder produced an occasional puppet play between his activities of managing theatres, designing scenery and effects, and acting, but he had been interested in puppets since childhood. It is therefore not surprising that his son had built a Punch and Judy to take about the streets of San Francisco in 1869 and worked as a puppeteer with McDonough and Earnshaw in 1874.

In 1875 he built a show of his own, giving the first performance for the German Club in San Francisco and later making a tour across California into Nevada. In 1876 he joined the *Black Crook* company in San Francisco as a technician and did a puppet specialty; with this he traveled to Mexico. When the troupe broke up (because so many of the girls had found rich Mexican husbands) Walter struck out for himself with his puppets, playing in all sorts of auditoriums as well as bull rings, often transporting his equipment by burro and seeing not a little of Mexico. In 1880 he returned to San Francisco. There in 1883 he married Mary Hanks, taught her how to operate marionettes, got her to costume some new figures, and sailed with her for Hawaii. In the Islands he presented an entertainment built around the puppet show, playing in the chief settlements and even in the palace of Queen Liliuokalani. The puppet numbers were *Cinderella*, a minstrel show, and an olio of variety in the Royal Marionette tradition.

From Hawaii they sailed to Seattle, played in the Puget Sound cities, and then made their way through California and Nevada before coming home. Walter took his younger brother, Harry, into the company in 1884 and revisited the Northwest Coast. On 22 and 23 September of that year the Deaves Brothers' Marionettes played at the Standard Theatre, Seattle, as is listed in the J. Willis Sayre record of bookings in the Seattle Public Library. Harry soon after returned to San Francisco, but Walter and his wife toured eastward through Utah, Colorado, Nebraska, Kansas, and the Middle West. Their daughter, Ada, was born in Cincinnati on 8 August 1885. They continued to play in the central states; in 1888 they appeared at Kohl and Middleton's Museum, Chicago.

At this time the increasing popularity of shadow-figures prompted

Walter to add a scene of them to his act. He devised a sailing vessel that could reverse its canvas and tack, and a battle between the *Monitor* and *Merrimac*. In May 1889 he and Harry showed a moving diorama at the Mount Morris Museum, New York City (*Odell*, vol. 14, p. 140). On 4 December 1889 the Deaves' son Edwin was born while they were playing an engagement at the Eden Musee, Lincoln, Nebraska. Their show is mentioned in the entertainment column of the Lincoln *State Journal* for 2, 4, and 6 December. In 1892, while the puppets were installed in a storeroom at Coffeyville, Kansas, the Dalton gang robbed a bank almost directly across the street.

For almost the entire duration of the Chicago Columbian Exposition in 1893, the Deaves played at the Vienna Café, a place of refreshment with a vaudeville entertainment. It will be recalled that David Lano was playing in a room outside one of the gates of this fair, and presently a French shadow-figure show which was also there will be recorded. The Middletons were at the Philadelphia fair in 1876. The appearance of puppets at more recent world's fairs is, therefore, in line with an established tradition.

In the final decade of the nineteenth century, elegantly presented or "polite" vaudeville found an audience that would pay regular theatre fees. It developed in the Eastern circuits managed by Keith and by Proctor, and Hammerstein's Victoria Theatre in New York, foremost of its houses, was the cynosure of all performers. The Deaves made themselves welcome in these circuits, though of course they played wherever opportunities opened.

In 1893 Edwin appeared, at the age of three, costumed as a policeman, to arrest a clown puppet in the act—another instance of a child appearing along with puppets—at Tony Pastor's Theatre on 14 Street, an auditorium in Tammany Hall. During the summers of 1895 and 1896, the Deaves manikins (a term applied to almost all marionettes at this time) appeared, next to Walter's diorama of the Chicago fair, in a specially built hall known as the Gilded Entrance, in Atlantic City. In the winter of 1896 the children were left with relatives in Boston, where they went to school, but they always rejoined their parents in the summer. Another Gilded Entrance was built for the Deaves Dual Show at Asbury Park, where Ada and Edwin helped the elder Deaves in the summers of 1897 and 1898.

In 1900 these manikins were again at Tony Pastor's, with the innovation of music played by two phonographs. As a child the writer heard Madam Jewell's manikins do a singing number with a recorded voice; in those days before electrical amplification, it was pretty thin and tinny, and

The Deaves stage had a proscenium with painted grand draperies and boxes in which sat applauding puppets; there was an orchestra of puppets in its orchestra pit. With everything about the framework in scale, there was nothing to dwarf the figures on the puppet stage. After a photograph in the possession of Perry Dilley.

much too quiet after the volume of the theatre orchestra. But Walter Deaves had a flair for innovation and was always devising new effects. He was the first puppeteer to model his act on the vaudeville form, abandoning the old Royal Marionette formula and making his variety numbers cohere within a miniature proscenium arch, flanked by boxes filled with hand-puppets that mimicked the vaudeville audience (sometimes at its rowdiest), and skirted with an orchestra of puppet musicians controlled by strings from below. This show-within-a-show was to become standard with all vaudeville manikin companies.

During the 1904 season, Deaves rented a studio in the old Arcade Building (now the Lincoln Square Arcade) on Broadway. This contained the studios of Garrett Becker and Sue Hastings, puppeteers of a later day, when it was gutted by fire in 1931. Here he built a production of *20,000 Leagues under the Sea,* based on the Jules Verne story, allowing a submarine scene with a diver and marine monsters behind a watery scrim curtain, and refurbished his old acts. During this period he played in clubs and private homes, among them several Fifth Avenue mansions.

In the summers of 1904, 1905, and 1906, he played in a specially built theatre at Midget City, Dreamland Park, Coney Island. In the winter he continued to present his vaudeville manikins.

In November 1907 he had reached Seattle on a tour across the country. The time seemed ripe for a trip around the world. He had his wife, the children, and two assistants with him. Besides he had a trunk of French motion-picture film and an Edison-Universal projector. Canceling his advance bookings in the East, he sailed for Japan. In 1908 he played in the larger Japanese and Chinese port cities, the Philippines, Vladivostock, French Indo-China, the Malay States, Siam, Java, Sumatra, the Celebes Islands, and British North Guinea and North Borneo. In 1909 he toured in Australia, Tasmania, and New Zealand. In 1910 he revisited Java and went on to Burma and the chief cities of India, going so far north as the Khyber Pass. Then he visited Kandy, the Seychelles Isles, and Zanzibar. He worked his way down the east coast of Africa during 1911 to the South African cities, thence moved north to Gibraltar, Malta, and Egypt. Still in 1911, he toured England, France, Germany, Austria, Italy, Spain, and Portugal. After a return engagement in England, he crossed to South America and played there. In 1912 he made an intensive tour of the cities of Central America and the West Indies. Entering at Key West, he came back to the United States after having been away for seven years. Once more he played across the continent, paused briefly in San Francisco, and was off again for Hawaii, Samoa, and the Fiji Islands. What a "grand tour" for his children! Seldom do youngsters see the world so extensively. The manikins were again in Australia, headed for another trip around the world, when war broke out in 1914. Finishing their engagements in New Zealand, they turned back home.

In 1915 they played for the summer in the amusement zone of the Panama-Pacific Exposition in San Francisco. Kept in the United States by the war, they continued to play in vaudeville and Chautauqua programs. Without a day of illness, Walter Deaves died suddenly on 9 January 1919. His ashes were scattered over the Pacific. The puppets were put away in storage.

Even the global wanderings of McDonough and Earnshaw's Royal Marionettes were put in the shade by those of the Deaves manikins. It is doubtful if any other company, European or American, has ever traveled so widely or been active for so many consecutive seasons on the international road. The achievement was due to the energy and resourcefulness of Walter Deaves, a figure who prided himself upon his physical resemblance to the dynamic Theodore Roosevelt. A photograph shows that he was thick-set in middle age, wore Roosevelt eyeglasses and a

The Deaves production of 20,000 Leagues under the Sea featured a fight between a diver and an octopus. Shark, diver, and octopus, with passing schools of fish were puppets; the rest of the undersea scene was painted. After a photograph in the possession of Perry Dilley.

bristling mustache, and had the alert cock of head of the President who was his contemporary.

The puppets remained in storage, almost forgotten, until they were stumbled upon by accident and acquired by Perry Dilley, San Francisco puppeteer, who has preserved them. He pieced together an account of their travels and listed their itinerary from playbills and contracts, which he found in the puppet boxes, for an article in *Puppetry 1933* (pp. 39-45). He also lent the puppets to be recorded in water colors by the California Art Project of the WPA. Over a dozen portraits of the Deaves manikins are now preserved in the Index of American Design archives at the National Gallery in Washington, D.C.

Perry Dilley's article describes some of the puppets. For the undersea ballet that came at the end of *20,000 Leagues under the Sea,* there were twelve coryphees, strung tandem four to a bar controller, in pink tights, their hands "snuggled in muffs in front of them." To place before the apron of the stage was a "ladies' orchestra." For the proscenium boxes were a florid old gentleman in a red velvet coat, his left hand grasping opera glasses, his right battered to a stump from his enthusiastic pounding on the edge of the box as the chorus kicked, and "two prim ladies whose behavior, one can tell from their faces, was the height of decorum; they undoubtedly whispered together about the vulgar person at the other end of the arch." Dilley wrote, "The company included a come-apart dancing skeleton, a donkey, shark, octopus, and red bull which served, as press clippings suggest, to 'toss the clown about on his horns like a rubber ball.' The gentleman partner of the cakewalk couple is a fine stepper and can, at the end of his turn, lift his silvered hat in a manner to invite instant and thunderous applause. There are 25 marionettes surviving, all of carved wood, averaging 26 inches tall, attached usually with seven strings of green fishline to a two-bar controller."

Humpty Dumpty was one of Deaves' skits which was sure to arouse laughter. Deriving from the harlequinade, it consisted of the hilarious adventures of Clown, Harlequin, and Pantaloon with bucking mules, exploding balloons, and the tempting display of a butcher shop. Independent of dialogue, it would be equally comprehensible in Bombay or Cairo, Yokohama or Johannesburg. With a program made up of such mute slapstick scenes, the manikins could girdle the globe.

The Deaves stage was compact and readily set up. Once it was unpacked and assembled, it could be got ready for a show in three minutes. It was mounted on rollers, and so were the lights which were carried with it, so that it might be whisked into the wings after a performance to make way for the following act. A cumbersome or immovable stage would have been impossible with the quick changes necessary in vaudeville.

Harry, Walter Deaves' younger brother, after his early partnership with him organized a manikin company of his own, also playing in vaudeville but not traveling so extensively as Walter. About 1919 he wrote to Helen Haiman Joseph, who quoted the letter in *A Book of Marionettes* (New York, 1920, p. 171), "I have on hand forty to fifty marionette figures, all in fine shape and dressed. I have been in the manikin business forty-five years, played all the large cities from coast to coast, over and over, always with big success; twenty-eight weeks in Chicago without a break with *Uncle Tom's Cabin*, a big hit." Edwin Deaves believed that this run of his uncle's travesty on the classic play—it had a Little Eva who towered above Uncle Tom—was in the mid-1890's.

The Deaves family, like David Lano and his parents, was all American born. Perhaps there were American professional puppeteers before them, though it is difficult to tell. The Lanos learned puppetry by transmission of technical knowledge from father to son; the Deaves brothers learned it partly this way, but in the case of Walter, also by apprenticeship to an English troupe. Yet, American as these showmen were, their shows were founded largely on Old World models. They did not turn to the American scene as did Latin American puppeteers to the Mexican or the Peruvian. Their art was international. Perhaps puppetry at its best is always so. Even today, though there are many individualists, there are no typically American, English, French, or German styles of puppetry.

4. Other Companies

In the last quarter of the nineteenth century, while there were American puppet companies, there was a constant succession of European visitors. On 5-10 August 1878, Sam Baylis presented his Royal French Marionettes at Harry Miner's New Theatre, in the Bowery near Broome Street, New York, a variety hall seating 1600, completely lighted by electricity; it had just opened on 1 July (a playbill for 5 August is in the Harvard Library). Baylis was an Englishman. George William Middleton told me that he later worked for him a while, and was roundly cursed by him when he fancied he saw a resemblance to his shadow-figure show in Middleton's. Why the Baylis marionettes were French is best known to the bill writer; they were Royal as a matter of course.

Henry Jerome's "celebrated marionettes" played at the Aquarium, Broadway at 35 Street, on 19-31 August 1878, according to the New York *Times* of those dates. Was Jerome the same showman who had been at Jones' Wood in 1859, his name Italianized to Jeronelli to give the show additional glamor?

Robert Heller, who had played Punch and Judy at the Brooklyn Academy of Music on 12 April 1877 (Odell, vol. 10, p. 326), appeared at the National Theatre, Washington, D.C., 4-17 November 1878, where Henry R. Evans remembers (as he wrote me) seeing his show, which included conjuring, second sight, piano playing, and "Heller's Original and Wonderful Band of Wood Minstrels, the most perfect set of block-heads in the world," which went through a typical Negro minstrel routine. While playing in Philadelphia on 26 November of that year he was taken ill, and died two days later.

Professor E. C. Taylor, who had played magic at the Denver Theatre in the summer of 1876, came back to Forrester's Opera House, Denver, Colorado, on 5-9 and again on 21-23 November 1878, with a variety show and a Royal Italian Marionette Troupe—whether Taylor's own or some-body else's I cannot say; there are no other traces of it near this time and place. To stimulate patronage, it was advertised that a hundred gifts would be distributed each night. These appearances are recorded in M. Schoberlin, *From Candles to Footlights* (Denver, 1941, p. 257), and Dean G. Nichols, *Pioneer Theatres of Denver* (unpublished thesis, University of Michigan, 1938, p. 570).

Professor Pharazyn—wonderful and exotic name!—a magician and ventriloquist, showed his "wonderful dancing marionettes," said the Philadelphia *Public Ledger* of the dates in question, at the New National Theatre, Tenth and Callowhill Streets, on 7-12 June 1880; at Ridgeway Park, formerly Smith's Island, 6 July—16 September 1881; and there again during the summer of 1882.

A company of Royal Marionettes, possibly those of Walter Deaves, played *Humpty Dumpty*, a pantomime, at Cheyenne, Wyoming, on 29 April 1884 (Cheyenne *Democratic Leader*, 30 April), to an unenthusiastic audience, I am sorry to say it was stated.

Many companies played in New York variety halls in this decade, as

From a drawing of one of his puppet numbers by Henry Wintermute. About 1935.

Odell records. Scott's Table Humorists (marionettes playing *Humpty Dumpty*) were at Bunnell's Museum, 5-10 February 1883. "A Lilliputian Combination of Automatic Actors and Actresses" was at Harry Hill's on Houston Street on 22 April that year. Davys and Blake's Royal Crystal Palace Marionettes were at Hyde & Behman's, Brooklyn, sometime between 9-23 September; when the troupe played at the London Theatre, 24-29 September, it was billed as making its first appearance in America; subsequently it filled engagements at Miner's Bowery and Eighth Avenue Theatres. Professor Goochison's Wooden-Headed Family of Marionettes appeared at Bunnell's Museum, 26 November—1 December 1883; the family may have been the marionettes that were there again after 17 October 1887. Fred Davys, having split with his partner Blake, continued to play regularly in 1885, 1886, and 1887. Harry Deaves was in evidence from November 1887 to February 1888 at Miner's Bowery and Hyde & Behman's in Brooklyn. The Tills were, however, the busiest of all; their engagements can be traced almost every week. Schwiegerling's Theatre Fantoches, which proclaimed that it had 106 marionettes when it appeared at Koster & Bial's on 23 Street on 19-24 March 1888, had a name that would place it as from Germany. On 18 April and thereafter that year it was at the Beethoven Männerchor Hall; the producer was then specifically called Professor P. Schwiegerling. Certain Imperial Marionettes (but whose?) played in the Curio Hall, Grand Museum, New York, 30 September—5 October 1889.

When I had a talk with Barry Gray in the sideshow tent of Barnum & Bailey's circus, with which he was playing Punch and Judy in 1927, he told me that he had bought a set of string-puppets from Walter Deaves in 1885, teamed with Harry H. Walker, and continued in the partnership for the next four years. They were at Doris's Eighth Avenue Museum, New York, 17-22 June 1889 (Odell, vol. 14, p. 133). In 1889 Gray got up an act by himself. The music for it was arranged by Warren Beebe, pianist at Drew's Museum, Cleveland. He started out by calling his actors "automets," but since nobody was sure what that meant, he reverted to the term "marionettes" until that was replaced by "manikins." He played in vaudeville until 1916; after that he was announcer and Punch man for Ringling-Barnum & Bailey.

Sometime before 1886, Professor Martin traveled in the Middle West with a variety show and trick marionettes, Harry Wintermute recalled (*Puppetry 1937*, p. 24). In his company were his wife, Clara, a grown daughter, and small twin sons, Denny and Danny. Each of his puppets was named for and imitated the performance of a well-known human player of the day. The program included a pole dance, Turkish ball tossing, a Highland fling, a plantation breakdown, a sailor's hornpipe, a grotesque dance by Scaramouch, various other dances, and the attempt of the clown Joe Grimaldi to ride his favorite mount, Spot.

Harry Wintermute, his wife wrote me, had played Punch and Judy in Wisconsin hall and tent shows in 1877 as a boy of eleven. He then joined Martin and they pooled their funds to buy a skeleton marionette from Judd, the New York puppet dealer. When he left Martin, Wintermute built himself a set of puppets similar to his former partner's. "For years my own troupe . . . was practically like this," he wrote in *Puppetry 1937*. "I added a few later, including the woman that turns into a balloon, which I never saw presented by anyone but myself. . . . I made several sets of marionettes; for a man, was handy with a needle, and sewed several wardrobes, horse trappings, show banners, etc., besides costuming the puppets. The last marionettes I made and used on the road I thought the poorest I ever made. I had an idea that larger figures than I had been accustomed to use (about 24-inch or less) would show off better, but I got them too large to handle well; besides, I did not get a good whittle on them. This was about twenty-five years ago. Twenty years ago I practically quit the road."

Wintermute settled down to farm life and died 25 May 1939. His puppets are still in the possession of his widow.

Professor Austin's Marionettes were at Pilling's Theatre, New York, 14-19 October 1889. What were Miaco's Marionettes, so Japanese sounding, which played at Worth's Family Museum, Sixth Avenue at 30 Street, New York, on 9-14 February 1891? Walker and Wood's Marionettes were at the Grand Museum 2-7 March that year; they had become Walker and Reedie's Royal Marionettes when they returned to the Grand on 25-30 May; Walker's partner in 1889 had been Barry Gray, a collaborator who stuck with him for a while. These scattered data are culled from Odell.

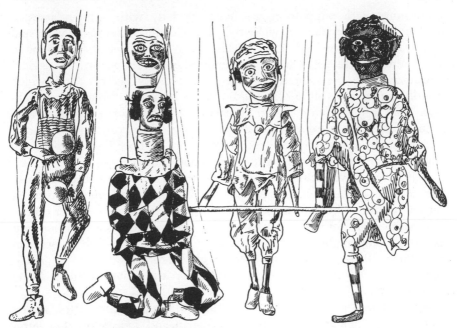

Trick marionettes, about 1900, obtained from Pinxy, Chicago, to whom they had been sold by an unknown showman. After Michigan Art and Craft Project, WPA, Index of American Design plates. Ball juggler by James McLellan. Two-headed clown (one flew off and the other sprouted) by Christ Makrenos. Pole tosser by David Ramage. Topsy by Dorothy Brennan.

Nicholas Nelson remembered that some of the outstanding vaudeville manikin acts at the beginning of the twentieth century were those of Belmont, Deaves, Faulkner, Jewell, Lamb, Mantell, and Middleton, in his *Looking Backward: Marionettes in Vaudeville* (*Puppetry 1935*, p. 13). Of course there were many puppet troupes on the variety stage; those that may not have been mentioned in these paragraphs are listed among the puppeteers at the back of this book.

Belmont was Nicholas Nelson's own stage name. He learned how to make string-puppets from Dave Lee, a showman he met in a museum in Minneapolis. His first figures, with which he started out in July 1899, were a mule, a skeleton, a contortionist, a juggler, and some blackface comedians. As he played in road shows he gradually replaced them with better-made puppets. He had three-foot figures for his tours throughout the United States, 1909-1923. He presented such pantomimes as *Down on the Plantation, The One-Ring Circus,* and *Red Lion Inn* (with a drunkard serving a meal in knockabout comedy). He had a miniature proscenium with puppets in the boxes: a lady with opera glasses, a gentleman who applauded violently, and a country bumpkin who spat water and rubbernecked with a telescoping neck. Nelson collaborated with James J. Hayes in writing a comprehensive book on the devices which used to be zealously guarded showmen's secrets, and which mystify audiences still, *Trick Marionettes* (1st ed., Birmingham, Michigan, 1935); they have made up at least a part of almost every American string-puppet show for the past two centuries. The trick about them is not so much in how they are constructed, but in how they are worked. They take deft manipulation and split-second timing.

Nelson, when vaudeville declined, revamped his shows to conform to the newer programs of the puppet revival, and has since played in schools, clubs, and department stores, as well as made puppets for others. He outfitted two of his sons with puppet troupes and started them out in theatre and night-club performances. The younger, Bobby Belmont (12 April 1920—13 February 1945), played a solo turn. The elder, Arthur Nelson, was helped by his wife; they are active as this is being written.

Walter Lamb played from 1902 to 1922. Mantell's Marionettes, at first called Royal, belonged to William Farleman and Len Ayres, the latter assuming Mantell as a stage name. Farleman had the idea to build a puppet act; Ayres was more interested in magic; but they formed a partnership to do puppets in 1903. Their first production consisted of a minstrel show and an olio of variety. It was built in the property room of the Central Theatre, Everett, Washington, Ayres told me. The partners had difficulty in finding bookings in their sparsely populated corner of the United States. After three years Farleman dropped out, Ayres cut down the show to vaudeville size, and managed to get contracts with such newly formed vaudeville circuits as those of Pantages, Sullivan, and Considine. While appearing in Elkhart, Indiana, in 1907, Mantell's Manikins were seen by Hi Henry and engaged by him for his minstrel show. The act was rebuilt on a more ample scale for this and toured the United States for a year. In 1909 Mantell played for the first time at Tony Pastor's in New York. He continued in vaudeville until 1910. Then he became a feature with J. Coburn's minstrel show in the South. In 1912 he played the Loew circuit and was booked by Richard Pitrot for a tour of Cuba, Central America, and Mexico. He returned to the United States in 1913 for another year with Loew. About 1920 the act, which had been billed as Mantell's Mechanical Midgets, or Marionette Hippodrome, was transformed into La Petite (*sic*) Cabaret and booked for a seven-year world tour by Keith and Orpheum, playing in Europe as well as the Far

A stage within a stage in Mantell's La Petite Cabaret; *variety numbers were played for an audience of hand-puppets seated at tables. The painted architectural setting helped fill the full stage in a vaudeville theatre without dwarfing the puppets. About 1925. After a photograph.*

East. In 1940 it was called the Puppet Revue, and taken out by Mr. and Mrs. Mantell only, as Mantell wrote, "when such occasions present themselves as to make it profitable."

For a 1925 engagement in San Antonio, Texas, La Petite Cabaret included a miniature orchestra (operated throughout the act by Julian Brack, a performer from another turn, to leave Mr. and Mrs. Mantell free for the rest of the manipulation), an announcer, Fatima the humorous oriental dancer, a page boy to change the placards for the puppet numbers (in imitation of the vaudeville custom—other puppet troupes had done this), puppet ladies in the left proscenium box and a rubbernecking husband and his shrewish wife in the right, a come-apart skeleton, a pianist, the Dixie Duo cakewalkers (the feminine dancer raising her parasol), a bullfight, a head-on airplane crash with planes piloted by Ben Turpin (film comedian) and Happy Hooligan (comic-strip character), and a finale of Russian dancers. Save for the last three numbers, all were traditional. The bullfight had been introduced at Mexico City in 1921, where audiences had resented it as too light an interpretation of the national sport, wrote Mary Carter, *Behind the Scenes with Clever Manikins* (San Antonio *Evening News*, 4 March 1925).

Stereotyped as the Mantell program was, it was excellent entertainment. R. Bruce Inverarity wrote of it in *Puppetry 1936* (p. 7), that it was "good vaudeville manikin stuff—moves like lightning—snap snap snap and the show's done. Tricks mostly, some automatic."

Jewell's Manikins came from England, playing in the United States for the first time at Tony Pastor's, New York, 1-14 August 1904, as Rex Faulkner, Mrs. Jewell's son-in-law, told me. Mae Jewell was a daughter of that Holden whose son Thomas was a puppeteer with McDonough and Earnshaw, and whose daughter Sarah Jane married Henry James Middleton. Mae married Jesse Jewell, who was a puppeteer with Thomas Holden when he played in Europe, and later organized a troupe of his own, which played in the Earl's Court Exposition Building, London, in 1897; it was mentioned by H. W. Whanslaw in *Everybody's Marionette Book* (London, 1935, p. 18). Jewell's Manikins appeared in vaudeville, museums, and circus sideshows. For their first ten years in America they were very active; thereafter there were rests of lengthening intervals, and in 1935 they gave their last performance.

While Mae and Jesse Jewell were playing in France, their daughter Lillian was born. She came to America with her parents. In 1911, when her mother had returned to Europe, she operated the Jewell's Manikin act for her, and met Rex Faulkner, who was playing on the same bill in a vaudeville theatre. An American, he had organized the Original American Newsboys' Quartette on 3 December 1899, and owned the act and sang bass in it. Faulkner and Lillian Jewell were married 7 October 1912. Mae Jewell, who was known as Madam Jewell, did not permit the use of her name in connection with the new manikin act prepared by her daughter, for fear of confusion between the two, and it therefore was styled Lillian Faulkner & Company, giving its first performance on 26 February 1913. Rex Faulkner continued to present his quartette while working in the manikin act, and booked both on the same programs. On 2 March 1914, at the Miles Theatre, Cleveland, Ohio, the Faulkners played a variety act ending with the playlet, *Play Ball*. It must have been shortly thereafter that I saw it at the Temple Theatre, Detroit. I remember a singing puppet with the faint and tinny voice of a phonograph, a page boy who changed the placards and scampered off so fast that he caused a burst of laughter at each dash, the puppet spectators in the proscenium boxes, and the playlet. In *Play Ball* a baseball batter stalled for time until a shower—real water falling from a perforated pipe in a curtain across the front of the stage—caused a halt to the game and a round of admiring applause.

The act was a popular one and continued until 1932, when the decrease of vaudeville drove it into stores, schools, clubs, and fairs. During the summer of 1939 it was at the Golden Gate Fair, San Francisco.

From Germany came the Schichtl Manikins, or Wonderettes, as they were sometimes called. The Schichtl family has furnished Central Europe with puppeteers since the middle of the eighteenth century. Carl Schichtl, born at Bamberg, near Munich, on 26 May 1870, came over with his oldest brother, Hans, as he told me (*The Work of Carl Schichtl, Puppetry 1935*, p. 14), and played a season starting in October 1910 with the Keith-Albee circuit. Hans Schichtl had left school in 1882 to devote himself to the invention of transformation string-puppets. He was shortly joined by his brother Julius, and then by Carl, in a puppet troupe. They worked together for a while and then drifted apart. Carl and Hans visited America for the second time in 1912, booked by the Keith-Albee-Orpheum circuit. Their act, altogether in pantomime, was made up of a number of the transformations in which they specialized.

In 1912 a popular metamorphosis scene, which was to be found also in the repertory of a cousin, Xaver Schichtl of Magdeburg, was introduced. A grinning Zulu leads out an ostrich; the bird squats and preens itself, refusing to move. When it finally rises, an egg which looks as big as its body is revealed. A little clown enters, inspects the egg with curiosity, and cocks his ear to its shell. The egg breaks and a long green dragon darts out to chase the clown round and round the stage. When blind and deaf Helen Keller was once on the same bill with the manikins, she expressed a great interest in them. She was allowed to run her fingers over each one as it was named and described to her. Two years later when she encountered them again she fondled them like old friends, felt the upcurled great toe of one, and exclaimed, "Why, here's the Zulu!"

Among the other numbers were a stiff gentleman who walked on, sprouted the wings and tail of an airplane, and rode off in it; a portly woman who turned into an automobile in which a dozen small puppets careened away; and the traditional lady-into-balloon which was the eighteenth-century equivalent of these vehicular changes. At one time a pistol shot accompanied each transformation, dazing the senses while the figure unfolded so that the change was almost undetected; but later the tricks were worked in silence, as the shots were not a little harrowing. As a child I jumped so hard that I failed to enjoy the act.

After Hans left, Carl married Lilly Keene, whom he had met while playing at the Alhambra Theatre, London; she was a member of the corps de ballet. She assisted him as a puppeteer and her brother helped backstage in handing on and hanging the puppets, and acted as contact agent. After vaudeville gave way to movies, the Schichtls appeared in the stage shows that preceded feature films in big theatres. For one such in 1931, a painted curtain of a Mother Goose cottage rolled up to disclose

The trick marionettes of Nicholas Nelson as exhibited at Marshall Field's store, Chicago, summer 1933. After a photograph by Sarra Harra.

their stage. Mrs. Schichtl and her brother, immaculately clad in evening dress, came out to acknowledge the applause after the show, while Carl, in comfortable apron and shirtsleeves, remained hidden to put away the puppets. He was a small, deft, smiling man, with pink skin, blue eyes, and gray hair close cropped and upstanding; he was fond of his cigar, his joke—and most likely of his beer. Mrs. Schichtl, dark and pretty, made a good stage appearance.

I think that it was another branch of the Schichtl family, perhaps one of the cousins, who presented the most striking puppets I have ever seen before Remo Bufano's giant inventions. They played at the Hippodrome Theatre, New York—my windows now look over the parking lot where it stood—in the season of 1913 or 1914. Upon a dark stage, to mysterious music, danced half a dozen six-foot figures, one of them an owl that flapped its wings, composed of electric lights on open frameworks; they were, for all their bright illumination, eerie as ghosts. I imagine that they stayed in America only for the Hippodrome engagement; they required its vast stage for proper effectiveness.

After a sensationally successful season in London, The Teatro dei Piccoli of Rome, managed by Vittorio Podrecca, opened at the Frolic New Amsterdam Theatre (a roof-garden auditorium), New York, in September 1923. Podrecca had developed the traditional Italian operatic puppet program by commissioning Respighi and other contemporary composers to write fairy-tale operettas for him. In Rome he had played to a music-loving artistic audience. For his international tours he had to do more variety numbers than operettas; his puppeteers, selected from families devoted to the work for generation after generation, were very skilled at tricks and dancing. I regret to say that César Cui's *Puss in Boots* left the Frolic audience yawning, while it showed its preference for Salome, a jazz-dancing blackamoor, a rope dancer, and a lively scene of Fortunello (Happy Hooligan) with a lot of little Fortunellos popping out of pumpkins. This engagement was short and unhappy. Podrecca returned to New York in December 1932, heralded by fanfares of publicity. Gerald Goode, hired as press agent, turned out such nonsense as, "There simply does not happen to be any tradition of marionettes in this country." Hence the Teatro dei Piccoli was a novelty!

Goode, continuing in this vein, wrote, "The normal conception of a marionette theatre is that of an amusing little venture on an extremely small scale conducted by two or three bright and energetic people with a lot of leisure on their hands. . . . They give one or two Sunday afternoon performances or they appear for the week of Christmas, and that is the last heard of them until the next Noel rolls around. Now this is not for a second to disparage our local puppeteers."

Whether because of the puffery, or because times were more auspicious, the Teatro dei Piccoli played in a Broadway theatre for several weeks on this visit. The newspaper critics were all enthusiastic—all but Brooks Atkinson of the *Times*, who said that his column was "not qualified to give Sr. Podrecca the cosmic accolade." The Piccoli are included in this section because they offered a typical vaudeville manikin program upon this tour, trimming down their material to a ten-minute act for the stage show of big movie houses in other American cities. They worked across the continent, lent some of their puppets for a scene in the film, *I Am Suzanne*, which featured the work of the Yale Puppeteers, and then departed for South America. During succeeding years they divided their time between there and Europe, but did not return to the United States. During World War II they continued in South America.

Another Italian company, that of the Enrico Salici family of Mantua, worked its way up through South America and Mexico to arrive in the United States in the season of 1934-1935, where it played in movie houses. The troupe consisted of Enrico and his wife Ada, their sons Adolpho, Edgardo, and Gino, their daughter Benilde, a singer, and their granddaughters, children of a daughter who remained in Italy, Emma and Rina Ferrari. A sketch of the history of the Salici marionettes appeared in *Puppetry 1935* (pp. 15-17). This large troupe presented a thirty-minute variety program: a song and dance by five pink-and-blue girls in hoop skirts, a concert pianist, soprano, and flautist—with two vociferous little clowns to move the piano on the stage and off, three couples in a song and dance (the boys bringing out gilt chairs and sitting on them during the routine), a strolling gentleman who smoked a cheroot, Mistinguette in sequins and ostrich plumes, and an exciting bicycle race as a finale. Like the Piccoli, the Salici marionettes had a repertory of operettas which it was obliged to drop in America. Its act was further truncated during the succeeding years as it was allowed fewer minutes on a bill and

Neapolitan number, Salici Marionettes, about 1934. The best in traditional north Italian puppetry.

the sons went off. It spent its time altogether in the Americas thence-forth, and was still playing there in 1947.

Puppets were of course to be found in Latin-American variety shows, though specific dates and places have not been given. A European or American company, which must have passed through Peru, played *Los Sobrinos del Capitan Grant* at the Teatro Municipal, La Paz, Bolivia, in 1914 or 1915, as my friend Victor A. Lemaitre remembers. It was a musical piece; there may have been other numbers on the program.

Compared with the Royal Marionettes—their two-hour shows of Negro minstrels, variety, and harlequinade, their heavy advertising, and their companies of twenty people—most of the vaudeville manikin acts were small and unimpressive. Compared with the witty plays of Powell, the motley program of the Royal Marionettes seems a retrogression, and the repetitious, silent manikins seem almost decadent. However, the manikins amused their audiences, which often could not find or afford the legitimate drama, and mirrored their taste.

If manikin subject matter was negligible, the technique was remark-able. By it was held the attention of a rough-mannered and impatient public. Having passed through a period of creative intensity in the eight-eenth century, puppetry came into one of technical elaboration. Spurred by the demands of vaudeville, it developed speed, dexterity of manipula-tion, and sure-fire effect. But when the perfected motion picture took over technical elaboration, there was nothing for the puppet to do but to seek a new period of creative intensity.

XVI

Latter-Day Shadow-Figures

After the fading of the vogue for shadow-figure plays at the beginning of the nineteenth century, there is little evidence of them in professional entertainment until the 1880's. Such isolated examples of their use as that of Oliver Lano's buffalo-hide shadow-figures in 1851 suggest that they were merely a quickly made substitute for three-dimensional puppets. But with the adoption of the electric light there was a resurgence of all kinds of projected-light entertainments, and shadow-figures held sway. But this very resurgence hastened the arrival of the motion picture, which literally monopolized the limelight.

To illuminate a shadow-figure screen large enough to be seen in a capacious theatre, the light source had to be powerful. Neither patent kerosene lamp, acetylene torch, nor gas jet would light a screen properly. But the limelight, throwing an intense white light when a cylinder of lime was heated by an oxyhydrogen flame, gave way to the carbon arc light with the coming of electric current, and that to the incandescent lamp, so that better and better light sources were available. Progress from shadow-figure to movie is marked as much by improvement in light as by any other factor.

The tradition of shadow-figures had been kept alive in home shows. Because the figures were easy to cut from cardboard, they were described in many books on the domestic handicrafts, and the generations of boys who came after Séraphin were all familiar with the kind of show he had presented.

Mason and Titus were the first exhibitors of the shadowgraph in the new era. They played at Miner's Bowery Theatre 4-9 December 1881, at his Eighth Avenue 12-17 December, and again at the Bowery 30 January —4 February and the Eighth Avenue 6-11 February 1882. In 1883 Mason had a partner named Otto, and in 1884 Frank Titus had one named Fanny Knight. In 1885 the Braham Brothers, Abe and Lew, and Mel Reed took to shadowgraphs. Ralph Terry presented them in 1887, Rogers and Owens in 1889, and Howe the same year. Odell lists these performances.

Requiring less bulky equipment than puppets, shadow-figures traveled to the remotest theatres. The Lincoln, Nebraska, *State Journal* of 4

December 1889, announcing the program at the Theatorium of the Eden Musee, said, "Deves [Walter Deaves] and wife, who have sent the visitors away roaring with laughter at the funny marionettes, will remain another week and introduce their shadowgraphs."

When shadow-figure plays were first given by the religious communities at Ephrata and Snow Hill, Pennsylvania, is not known, but they gave morality and Old Testament Biblical pieces for their own edification. Traces of the shadow screens, or "shadow bilts," could still be seen in the assembly houses of these "cloisters" about 1900, reported Henry W. Shoemaker in his column in the Altoona *Tribune* of 4 February 1943; but in the subsequent alteration of the buildings they were removed. There is a tradition that these shows were open to all. Only the gypsies, who had a dread of entering the hall, perhaps because the shadows looked like witchcraft to them, would not come when they were invited. Here were shadow-figure plays in the direct tradition of Lanthorn Leatherhead's Biblical pieces, whether they stemmed from older antecedents or from the revival of the 1880's.

The Grand Museum, New York, Odell chronicles, saw Barton's shadowgraphs 20-25 April 1891, Harry Sparrow's 4-9 May, and James Bradley's 25-30 May. They must have been an expected feature at that hall of entertainment. The number of shadow showmen would suggest that the ease of getting up a number was too great for the good of the craft. Anybody could hack shapes out of cardboard, hold them against a screen in a ray of light, and move them back and forth. Repletion may have done as much to kill the shadow-figure as did the movies.

While Sam Baylis, the showman of the Royal French Marionettes, was playing at the Gilmore Theatre, Eighth and Walnut streets, Philadelphia, George Middleton helped him, as he told me, with his shadow-figures, acquiring a knowledge of them which he was later to apply to his own shows. Middleton's shadow-figures, which probably followed in the pattern of Baylis' program, included a tight-rope walker, a Highland fling dancer (supported by a horizontal rod from Middleton's belt; the operator himself danced to give the figure its motion, while controlling its limbs with wires held in his hands), a hurdle race, a wooden-legged man butted by a goat, an old woman from whose basket an elephant stole things, and a stag hunt. The stag, wandering in the forest, licked its knee and its back with delicate, natural motions, and browsed in the foliage. A hunter stole up behind a tree, took aim, and shot. The stag started, trembled, sank down, and died to the strains of "Hearts and Flowers." This was a scene that never failed to bring tears to the eyes of an audience.

Then there were a scissors grinder who drove an old horse and cart and sang at his work, and an aquatic panorama that was the century-old *Duck Hunt*. Ducks and swans swim past; a hunter rows out in a boat in which sits his dog; birds fly overhead; the hunter aims and shoots; a bird falls and the dog swims out to retrieve it; he comes back and the hunter rows away; then a rear-wheeler tug paddles on, puffing smoke and towing a sailboat with canvas furled; the ship is cast loose, raises sail, and moves off.

Walter Deaves, his son Edwin wrote me, managed the tacking of a shadow-figure ship like this. The sails were made up of series of telescoping strips; little by little they were drawn in and bellied out on the opposite side.

Middleton's aquatic scene continued with a fight between a Chinese junk and a clipper ship, the engagement between the *Cumberland* and *Merrimac* (shots clip off the masts of the *Cumberland*, and it splits and sinks in a glow of red fire), and then the historic duel between the *Monitor* and the *Merrimac*, in which the *Merrimac* sinks and the *Monitor* hoists the flag of the United States as a finale. The colors of the flag, a translucent part, were visible on the screen. The rest of the scene was, of course, in black silhouette. Walter Deaves and many others presented the fight of the *Monitor* and *Merrimac*, a naval battle that remained as long in popular memory as that of the *Constitution* and *Guerrière*, which had been re-enacted often on earlier shadow screens. Such spectacular naval battles were just the right thing for vaudeville.

Middleton's human figures were from 12 to 18 inches tall, and his ships of course much larger. To keep the cardboard flat and rigid they were fastened to flat sticks on the side away from the screen. Some of the big pieces could be folded for ease in packing. Cords and wires were used to operate the moving parts.

The emergence of the motion picture caused the disappearance of the shadow-figure, which was so much like it in effect, from the variety stage. The puppet, still a much more live thing than the film, was driven from some of its popular haunts by the movie, though in the first years of movie showing it very often shared the bill in the same tent or theatre, but in the end it refused to be routed, and still survives, oblivious of competition. Edison began his investigations toward the motion picture in the fall of 1887, his work on the electric light well under way. He showed his peep-show kinetoscope commercially in April 1894. Latham's panoptikon was shown in April 1895 and Lumière's cinématographe in December of that year. Paul's projector came into use in February 1896. Edison's Vitascope, substantially the movie of today, was first seen at Koster & Bial's vaudeville theatre on 34 Street, New York, on 23 April 1896; a tablet on Macy's store commemorates the fact. Silhouette duck hunts were to seem pretty tame after ocean surf or locomotives flung themselves at the audience from the movie screen.

Were it not that the hurly-burly of the world's fair drowned out the faint music of a French shadow-figure show at the Columbian Exposition in Chicago in 1893, America might have witnessed shadows of a new artistic order when Léon-Charles Marot presented his Théâtre des Ombres Parisiennes amidst that welter of attractions. His entertainment was the kind of show that had started at the Chat Noir cabaret, a meeting place of Montmartre artists, in 1887, and spread to other night resorts in Paris. Paul Jeanne's history, *Les Théâtres d'ombres à Montmartre* (Paris, 1937), tells of the remarkable scope of these shows.

To a musical accompaniment and the singing or telling of a story, shadow-figures designed and cut by outstanding artists of the day moved across a screen. While they were opaque, colored lights cast upon the front and back of the screen in varying intensities relieved them of blackness, and even suggested planes of distance in a Japanese-woodcut sort of way. At least, this is how Ernest Maindron says it was done, in *Marionnettes et guignols* (Paris, 1900, p. 339).

The repertory in Chicago included *L'Eléphant* by Henry Somm, a piece dating from 1886 before public shows were given at the Chat Noir; *La Potiche* by the same author, 1887, a chinoiserie; *Coeur inflammable*, also his; *La Conquête de la lune* by Michel Utrillo; and *Le Virtuose* and *Une Page d'amour*, both by Steinlein. The devisers of these scenarios also designed the figures. This information is to be found in *Théâtre des ombres Parisiennes*, Programme général des représentations données à l'Exposition de Chicago, Paris, Léon Vanier, 1893.

I have been unable to find any comment on these Chicago performances, though Americans of artistic inclination made a point of going to the Chat Noir in Paris. Claude Bragdon the architect, for instance, did so and described his visit in *More Lives than One* (New York, 1938, p. 48). Richard Harding Davis wrote of the cabaret in *About Paris* (New York, 1895, p. 74), "Three times a week there is a performance in the theatre upstairs, at which poets of the neighborhood recite their own verses, and some clever individual tells a story, with a stereopticon and a cast of cardboard actors for accessories. These latter little plays are very clever and well arranged, and as nearly proper as a Frenchman with such a temptation to be otherwise could be expected to make them. It is a most informal gathering, more like a performance in a private house than a theatre, and the most curious thing about it is the character of the audience, which, instead of being bohemian and artistic, is composed chiefly of worthy bourgeoisie and young men and young women properly chaperoned by the parents of each. . . . The lights are put out and a tiny curtain is run up, showing a square hole in the proscenium covered with a curtain of white linen. On this are thrown the shadows of the pasteboard figures, who do the most remarkable things with a naturalness which might well shame some living actors."

Comparatively few could have seen the show at the Chicago fair, if indeed its engagement may not have proved abortive. Had these shadows played in a more favorable time and place, they might have had some influence in America, and even marked the dawn of the revival of puppetry as an artistic medium. As it was, shadow-figures and puppets remained a popular rather than a sophisticated art for another quarter century.

It might be noted here that the early twentieth-century films of Georges Méliès, French pioneer of the fantastic scenario, often had effects cognate with puppetry. He was fond of monsters and animated scenery moved by strings and rods. For a painting that came alive he used a flat jumping jack. He even had a double-exposure scene of a Guignol booth, the showman inside expostulating with the puppets that had climbed out (actors diminished to puppet size). The latter two episodes were pictured in stills in *Puppetry 1940* (p. 64). The Méliès films were shown in America.

While the Chinese brought their puppets to America, there is no record of a shadow show played by Chinese there. A very close approximation of their performances, using actual Chinese shadow-figures and presenting Chinese plays in English versions, has been seen since 1931, when Pauline Benton, an American, started her Red Gate Shadow Players.

Greek Karagiozis plays came to America, however, at the beginning of this century with the influx of Greek immigrants. They used translucent colored shadow-figures derived from China by way of India, Persia, and Turkey. Like their Chinese ancestors, the Greek figures were made of painted parchment, or latterly of such substitutes as painted celluloid or even opaque fiberboard. As in the Chinese plays the action was interspersed by songs, generally set to Turkish or Near Eastern tunes. It was a curious experience for me, in the 1930's, to step from a dingy Detroit or Chicago street into a Greek coffee house, full of workmen sitting with their small cups of Turkish coffee or glasses of anisette, rapt in the nasal singing and bright images on a screen.

Though other Karagiozis showmen may have arrived earlier, Harry Patrinos is the first I have been able to find. He told me that he gave shows in Chicago in 1906. He came from Patras, Greece. Active in and about Chicago until 1912, he went back to Greece for a few years, then returned to resume his performances, giving shows in coffee houses wherever there were Greek colonies in the United States. His repertory included such pieces about the struggle for Greek independence as *The Flag of '21, The Sufferings of the Greeks during Turkish Oppression,* and *The Enemy of the Christians,* as well as such comedies as *The Wedding of Karagiozis* and folklore drama such as *The Lost City,* full of the sorcery of the enchantress Gilda.

Karagiozis, the central comic character of all these plays, is ribald, cunning, and bellicose. He has been compared with Punch, though they have only the slapstick in common. Often accompanied by an obtuse crony who serves as a feeder for his jokes, Karagiozis makes himself at home in any sort of a play, interrupting even the romantic and serious with his sallies. Playing for an all-male audience, he is outspoken about his sexual exploits; his Turkish progenitor wore a huge phallus in the manner of the players in ancient Greek farce. When an American lady intrudes in a coffee house, innocently bent upon studying the shadow-figures, the dialogue, even though in Greek, tempers itself to her chaste ears. Occasionally, out of courtesy to American visitors, a whole scene is played in outrageous broken English, and the hoariest of jokes are interlarded, all to the intense delight of the Greeks and the wonderment of the Americans.

Harry Tsouleas, inspired by the shadow-figures of Antonios Mollas in Athens, made his own set and turned showman at the age of seventeen. He came to the United States in 1915 and settled in Detroit. In the winter he played in one of the Monroe Street coffee houses (I saw him in at least three); in the summer he went to a suburban coffee house or sold soda water and ice cream. His repertory was inexhaustible, for he improvised upon events from Greek history, current events, and popular narratives. He did an entire evening's show himself, with intervals of rest to take up a collection, speaking the lines for all the characters; a boy assisted in handing him the figures and putting them away.

Most of his figures were made of sheet celluloid, stained with electric-lamp dip in variegated colors. They were simply jointed, some at the waist only, others at the shoulder and knee as well. A figure was controlled by a stick or two at right angles to it, attached to small angle irons bolted to the figure for solid support. One arm of Karagiozis was jointed in half a dozen places to make it preternaturally flexible. A row of soldiers with joints at the knees only marched as a unit at the end of a

Shadow figure of a Greek soldier cut from fiberboard by Harry Tsouleas, Detroit, about 1935. From a photograph.

single stick. Fiberboard figures were chopped out with a hammer and chisel, having an openwork pattern like Chinese shadows; the slits were sometimes covered with colored tissue paper.

Fights—of which there were many, with Karagiozis always emerging victor—were expressed with terrific din. Shuffling and stamping backstage by the showman and his assistants, the loud whack of a rolled newspaper, the blowing of a whistle or beating of a drum, to say nothing of hoarse yells, accompanied each fracas. And the more nearly the ceiling was lifted, the better the audience liked it!

Two other Karagiozis showmen, William Ballamos and John Katsas, played *Alexander the Great and the Dragon* in a coffee house for the assembled puppeteers at the third American Puppetry Conference in Chicago, June 1938. The exciting scene in which the saurian is annihilated and Alexander shouts, "Tek det, you snek!" has become proverbial among those who witnessed it.

Like other puppets that catered to foreign-language audiences, the Greek shadow-figures are fast losing ground as a younger generation grows up in ignorance of their parents' tongue; it will be only a matter of time before the last of them disappears.

XVII

Paladins from South Italy

When large numbers of Italians from Naples, Calabria, and Sicily arrived in the United States in the last decade of the nineteenth century, they brought with them their charactcristic form of puppet theatre. Their puppet playhouses were improvised in lofts, outbuildings, and vacant stores in the crowded sections of American cities where they settled. A visitor to Naples or Palermo might sometimes have ventured so far astray from the Baedecker sights as to discover the popular theatres where puppets enacted the legends of Charlemagne and his knights, but little was known of them in the New World. When an explorative journalist or searcher-out of the quaint came upon one of these playhouses in Brooklyn or the lower east side of New York, it was with as much of a thrill as if he had found a lost culture.

The puppets were generally large and heavy, sheathed in armor beaten out of copper or light steel, adorned with plumes and velvet cloaks, and worked, as were eighteenth-century puppets, with a rod to the top of the head; an auxiliary rod went to the sword arm, a cord to the shield arm, and others where they might be necessary. Some of the puppets weighed as much as the youths who manipulated them. To swing them into combat was no small feat of strength. Naturally it would have been out of the question to support them by strings, even if this had been desired.

American visitors to the Paladin playhouses found the exploits of Orlando against the Saracens, which made up the chief part of their repertory, colorful and strange. They did not happen to connect them with that remote period when the Normans ruled Sicily and left their own legends in that crossroads of many peoples. Indeed, the same legends were until recently enacted in Flanders by similar rod-puppets, their lore being of common origin in the Middle Ages.

Isabel Emerson, writing of Sicilian marionettes (*Contemporary Review*, March, 1930, p. 372), observed, "wherever we go in Sicily: Palermo, Catania, Syracuse, Taormina, Trapani, even at Enna in the heart of the island, we may . . . spend an enthralling evening watching the unfolding of the old, yet ever new, story of Orlando and the Paladins . . . repre-

South Italian marionettes hung from a beam; the weight of their armor and large wood bodies is considerable. Each figure is controlled by two iron rods with subsidiary strings. After a drawing by Arthur I. Keller of dramatis personae in a Spring Street theatre near the Bowery. From Century Magazine, *March 1902, p. 677.*

sented by wooden puppets." But by 1930 these plays were already obsolescent in the United States, for the children and grandchildren of the immigrants who loved them no longer understood Italian or cared for drama that made such demands on the romantic imagination. The theatre of the Manteo family in New York, though revived through the interest of American audiences and puppeteers in the later '30's, had already gone through several seasons of enforced inactivity, and was the last of its kind to be in operation. The Italian-language puppet theatre became extinct even more quickly than the German.

The first showman of the Paladins to come to America was Antonio Parisi from Messina. He considered himself their introducer in the United States (Victor Rousseau, "A Puppet Play which Lasts Two Months," *Harper's Weekly*, 3 October 1908, p. 15) and no evidence has arisen to refute it. He went to Boston, opening a theatre there about 1888. The name Antonio Parisi is not found in a Boston city directory until 1892; its bearer was then listed as a carpenter living at 212 North Street; in 1894 he was at 216 North Street, in 1895 at 177 North Street, and in 1898-1899 at 121 Richmond Street. He was probably a carpenter by trade, devoting his evenings to the sideline of puppetry, for the pennies to be collected from a workman audience would have afforded a precarious existence. North Street was in the heart of the Italian quarter of Boston, and if the theatre was not somewhere on the premises at these addresses, it must have been near. Nunzio, Parisi's eldest son, and two others born in America, helped work the puppets. Their mother collected admission fees.

In 1889 the theatre of Carlo Comardo from Palermo flourished at 25 Union Street, South Brooklyn, New York. Its proprietor thought that it and the one in Boston were the only two of their kind in America. (Stewart Culin wrote of it in "An Italian Marionette Theatre in Brooklyn, N. Y.," Philadelphia *Public Ledger*, 19 April 1890.) The shows began at 7 P.M., the auditorium held about 100, the stage was estimated at 6 feet square and the puppets 2 feet tall, the dialogue was spoken by two male and two female voices, and there was a company of over 100 puppets. The plays were based upon episodes in the Orlando cycle, and the audience, as was usual in Italy, consisted of men and boys only.

Comardo's handbill, translated into English, ran thus. "In the present history are described the sufferings of France in the time of Charlemagne, and the strange adventures which the Paladins had to undergo. Fighting with the Infidels and for the sake of love, they were never defeated. It should also be mentioned how many treasons Ganelon of Mayence hatched against Charlemagne and his court, corresponding secretly with

An excited audience watches the duel of Paladins in a typical playhouse. "The dingy little theatre had once been a stable. Pietro had turned the loft into a gallery, with tiers of benches receding high into the gloom. He had cut off the stall-room with a wooden proscenium. Upon it twisted a mastodon of a vine, the like of which no botanist ever beheld. The toy curtain bore, upon its forty-eight square feet of canvas, a representation of a Roman triumph that would have insured Pietro's admission into any Academy with a sense of humor." Pietro and the theatre were fictional but real. After a drawing by W. Glackens in Scribner's *Magazine, August 1899, p. 173.*

Young Nunzio, son of Antonio Parisi, at the workbench. The control rod is pushed through a hole in the wooden head and hooked into an eye on the torso. After a drawing by Helen Wood in Harper's Weekly, *3 October 1908, p. 15.*

the Saracens to overthrow his greatness and that of his forces. Nor should it be concealed that Malagigi brought his magic power to bear for the good of the invincible Charlemagne. Rather it will be heard how, according to the story, he commanded that all be felled for the safety of the men of Chiaramonte and of Montalbano." There was a postscript that seats were reserved for ladies, but evidently they did not avail themselves of this convenience.

How long this puppet theatre was in operation cannot be determined. A. E. Sumner, who visited it later ("The Smallest Theatre in the World," *Frank Leslie's Illustrated Newspaper,* 25 October 1890, p. 199), gave details at variance with Stewart Culin's. The theatre was at 35 Union Street, was run by Camaldo (perhaps a garbled spelling), seated between 46 and 60, and had a stage 6 by 3 feet. Perhaps the showman had moved in the meanwhile into a smaller place. The theatre had been duly licensed by the mayor; admission was 5¢. The Boston playhouse, it was reported by this rival, seated 300 and the admission was 10¢—perhaps an exaggerated rumor.

The 1890 location of the Brooklyn theatre was in a sort of store. "The block is surrounded by a high board fence," wrote Sumner, "the exterior of which is broken by a blacksmith's and carpenter's shop. Between these is a modest show-window. Regarded with relation to the surroundings, this window might be called a 'crown-setting' upon the otherwise flat surface of the fence. The casual passer-by would not give a second glance at the unattractive little store, but above the entrance door there is a very garishly colored, yet artistically drawn sign board."

About 1900 Wilbur Macey Stone visited this theatre, or another one in the same region of Union Street, not far from the Hamilton Ferry. He described his visit in *Puppetry 1938* (p. 23). "A short walk and we came to a rather dark alley, halfway down which a solitary gas lamp over a doorway shone out. Thither we went and found a buxom Italian woman seated at the receipt of custom. 'How much?' we asked. 'Fiva cents.' We gave up our two nickels and in we went.

"It was an old barn with rough plank seats, and, above the cow stalls, a hayloft utilized as a balcony for the ladies. Here were seated several young Italian women, one of them nursing her baby. The main floor was well filled with an expectant audience of men young and old. Many of the younger were dressed in the advanced fashion then prevailing; among the older were stevedores in overalls. One of the latter, after a hard day's work, was stretched full length, asleep.

"Some accommodating young men shoved along and made room for us, their smiling faces welcoming the strangers from over the water.

"Presently the curtain creaked up and we saw a small stage with a backdrop of a forest scene. Clank clank; clank clank: a figure emerged from either wing, paused, each facing the other, and a conversation began in Italian. The master of the show, a tall, well-built fellow, spoke from one wing, first for one, then for the other, modulating his voice to give a difference. The marionettes, about four feet tall and weighing over fifty pounds each, were supported by rods from the top of their heads. A semblance of walking was attained when the whole figure rocked from its rod and the legs swung of their own weight. While the movements were a bit jerky, the appearance of life was convincing.

"After a brief colloquy there enters a lady in regal gown. She is greeted and replies in a feminine voice with an underlying rumble, for the master's wife speaks for her, repeating the speeches after him from the wing opposite. The plot thickens. Fighting men in armor enter, Christians on one side, Saracens on the other. Much boasting talk from both sides; the regal lady screams and retires. The warriors fall to and belabor each other with clatter of metal on metal and resounding thuds on wooden heads. Reinforcements for each side appear. Soon the stage is a shambles, with splintered corpses piling high.

"The audience, tense with excitement, applauds vociferously. Down goes the curtain. The first act is over. Peace reigns, the dust settles, the

Backstage in Antonio Parisi's theatre, in a rear building reached by a passageway between tenement houses at 418 East 11 Street. Mama and Papa Parisi read the lines while their three sons manipulate. Gas jets light the stage. After a drawing by Helen Wood in Harper's Weekly, *3 October 1908, p. 16.*

placid soda-pop boy circulates. We buy one of his quart bottles for five cents, each takes a swig, and pass it on to our next neighbor; that's the last we see of it; it vanishes down the line. But good fellowship has been established. In good English our neighbor tells us the plot."

Each act has a similar battle and massacre. After the show Stone went backstage to interview Papa Pietro, the puppet master, and was introduced to his beaming wife and the sweating puppeteers. They were delighted to show the puppets and explain their operation, as were later Italian puppeteers when the truly interested sought them out at the conclusion of a performance.

The New York *Tribune* of 20 October 1895 reported the findings of another writer who went to see the marionettes in Brooklyn—perhaps still others investigated this transpontine drama; their accounts will continue to turn up.

About 1900 another such puppet theatre ran in the Italian quarter of Chicago. It was mentioned in an article, "Teaching History by Puppets," in the *Kindergarten Primary Magazine*, December 1908 (p. 91). Behind a billiard parlor, it occupied a small room with a gallery under the ceiling for children. A hat was passed for the collection of the 10¢ fee. Music was

CHILDREN'S MATINEE	EVENING PERFORMANCE

THE

Sicilian Marionettes

OF

ROSARIO SAVASTA

OF

MESSINA

will perform some thrilling legendary deeds of arms of the young Rinaldo, a Paladin of Charlemagne, who kills TWO LIONS and a GIANT in defense of his mother Beatrice.

Dancing by Pulcinelli

Mysterious Sleight of Hand Tricks

BY

A PEERLESS PRESTIDIGITATOR

Italian Confections and Popcorn will be for sale

HISTORICAL NOTE

These marionettes bear no relation to the ordinary Punch and Judy show sometimes seen in the streets of European cities. The figures employed are made and dressed with much care to represent Crusaders, Saracens, and Knights and Ladies of the time of Charlemagne. They produce the effect of life-size figures and some of them even show change of facial expression.

The origin of this form of theatre dates back many centuries, and the performances to be given in Brattle Hall will be exact counterparts of those given for the last three hundred years in Sicily, where these theatres are still popular.

The pantomime of the marionettes is so dramatically effective that even without the dialogue the action of the play is at all times clear; in addition, however, there will be suitable explanation in English.

THE

Sicilian Marionettes

OF

ROSARIO SAVASTA

OF

MESSINA

will perform more legendary deeds of arms of the Paladins of Charlemagne.

There will also be

Dancing by Pulcinelli

AND

A Tarantella

NATIVE GREEK DANCES

AN ITALIAN CAFE

will be open from 9.30 P.M. to 11 P.M.

Ices and Italian dishes will be served, and tables may be engaged in advance by applying to the Social Union, Telephone, Cambridge 1206-4.

Flower Girls and Fruit Venders

NEAPOLITAN SINGERS

DANCING IN BRATTLE HALL TILL 1 A.M.

TICKETS

Children's Matinee (No reserved seats) { Adults, 75 cents / Children, 50 cents

Evening Performance (Reserved seats) $1.50 and $1.00

Tickets may be secured on written application to Mr. Lawrence G. Brooks, 8 Francis Ave., Cambridge, enclosing check for the number of tickets desired, or may be purchased at Amee's Book Store, Harvard Square.

Program of an Italian Fiesta to benefit the Cambridge, Massachusetts, Social Union, Thursday, 15 April 1909, performances at 3 and 8 P.M., in Brattle Hall. Original in the Harvard College Library theatre collection.

supplied by a grind organ, the puppets were 30 to 36 inches tall, and all the lines were recited by one man.

From about 1896 to 1912 Agrippino Manteo ran such a theatre in Buenos Aires. He had promised his father, Michael Manteo of Catania, to continue in his footsteps. Michael had gone to work in 1846 in a Sicilian theatre where small puppets were used; when he started on his own he made 5-foot ones. These Agrippino inherited, and he added to his father's stock. He played in Mendoza from 1912 to 1916. Then he returned to Italy to fight in World War I. Coming back to America at its close, he settled in New York, learned the trade of electrician, sent to South America for his family, and opened a theatre on Mulberry Street sometime after 1920, a theatre that was to prove to be the last survivor of its kind in the United States. All this was told me by Agrippino's son Ritz, who wrote of "Papa Manteo's Marionettes" in *Puppetry 1937* (p. 8).

A Buenos Aires contemporary of Manteo was Vito Cantone, from Catania also, who played from 1900 to 1910, I was told by Alfredo Hermitte, enthusiast of Argentine puppet history.

But perhaps the most successful of the Paladin puppeteers in Buenos Aires was Don Bastian, from Terranova. With his wife Doña Carolina, he went to São Paolo, Brazil, in 1898, setting up his theatre there. Thence he came to Buenos Aires in 1910, found an old movie house in La Boca, the Italian quarter bordering the River Plata, and established his San Carlino theatre in it. When this was torn down he removed to a new location which was not so successful. World War I forced him to close his doors. After the war he reopened under happier circumstances and continued to play until 1937, when illness put an end to his regular performances. Since then he has played sporadically.

His puppets were carved for him by various sculptors, among them Antonio Merlino, Aquiles Taormina, and Camilo Udine. The armor was particularly well wrought, with the effect of gold chasing on silver. He had over 200 30-inch puppets and 100 48-inch ones, a galaxy of kings, princesses, knights, centaurs, legendary monsters, and devils. At the top of the hooked iron supporting rod was a cylindrical wooden grip. Alfredo Dolver wrote an illustrated feature article about him in a Buenos Aires newspaper of which I do not have the date. A flood of the Plata inundated La Boca and caused considerable damage to Don Bastian's puppets in 1940; a benefit puppet performance was given him by the younger generation of Argentine puppeteers.

In New York, starting about 1901, a theatre was operated by Mariano on Spring Street a little westward of the Bowery. He used 3-foot puppets. Admission ranged from 5¢ to 15¢. Here Clayton Hamilton "used to be a welcome guest," wrote Frank Weitenkampf in *Manhattan Kaleidoscope* (New York, 1947, p. 226), ". . . and served on more than one occasion as a puppeteer. Mariano's eldest daughter, Isabella, read the women's lines until the Society for the Prevention of Cruelty to Children put a stop to it, in its zeal to keep children from working in the theatre. Then Mariano himself did the women's parts in falsetto. Dr. Weitenkampf can remember the haunting tones of a queen as she cried to her son, "Oh, mio figlio, fuggiamo, fuggiamo!"— "Oh, my son, let us flee!" Two younger children, Rafael, eleven, and Helena, nine, acted as ushers and assistants. About 1905 the company moved to California. Francis H. Nichols wrote of this theatre in *Century Magazine* (March 1902, p. 677), and Arthur H. Gleason in *Collier's Weekly* (23 October 1909, p. 26).

In 1907 there was a theatre up a flight of stairs on Elizabeth or Mulberry Street, north of Spring. The 15¢ fee was collected as one went out.

This is mentioned by Elizabeth Irwin in *Craftsman* (September 1907, p. 667).

Antonio Parisi moved from Boston to New York about 1896. For a time his playhouse was at 258 Elizabeth Street. When Dr. Weitenkampf visited it in 1904, he had difficulty in finding it because no one would direct him, fearful that he might be an investigator of the crime that had just come to light when a murdered man was found in a barrel in front of the grocery store almost directly across the street from it. By 1908 Parisi had his theatre in an outhouse behind 418 East 11 Street, according to Victor Rousseau in the *Harper's Weekly* article already cited. In that year, said Rousseau, there were five Paladin theatres in New York and still others in Brooklyn. Parisi was long remembered as a dean of puppeteers, though I cannot say just when he ceased to perform regularly.

Educators saw that Italian children, attending puppet shows, learned the Charlemagne legends better than from a book, and school authorities became interested in the process. The Drama Committee of the People's Institute, now allied with Cooper Union, wished to have Parisi's theatre located somewhere near Washington Square in 1908 so that it might be made more available to the school children of lower Manhattan. This is reported in *Kindergarten Primary Magazine* (December 1908, p. 91). Unfortunately nothing came of the project.

About 1895 the family of Achille Greco went from Palermo to Rio de Janeiro to try its fortune with puppets there; after five years Greco's eldest son, Gaetano, was left in charge and the others returned to Sicily. In 1911 Gaetano was still operating the Rio theatre, while his brothers had one in Rome in 1934 (*Puppetry 1934*, p. 36 and Henry Festing Jones, *Castellinaria*, London, 1911, p. 93).

The theatre of Salvatore Lo Cascio was on East 107 Street, New York, about 1906, and at 111 Street and First Avenue, up one flight, in 1909. The gaslit stage was 20 feet wide, the 4-foot puppets numbered 125, a two-hour show was given nightly, and there were two on Sundays. Maria Grasso, of the noted actor and puppeteer family, read the women's parts. There were five puppeteers. For the more exciting scenes ragtime music was pounded out on a piano. One puppet could smoke a cigar and puff real smoke. In addition to the Charlemagne legends a Passion Play was given (Arthur H. Gleason, *Collier's Weekly*, 23 October 1909, p. 16). For a benefit at Harvard College, Cambridge, on 15 April 1909, the Paladins of Rosario Savasta from Messina performed *The Adventures of Rinaldo*. Giannino Savasta (aged six) appeared in the finale with two puppets to make a rescue. The playbill of the performance is in the Harvard Library.

Controlling the Paladins. The puppeteers stand on a wooden scaffolding or bridge, each gripping the two rods of a puppet. Various gaits and body movements are imparted through the head rod; the arm rod directs the sword arm and helps turn the puppet. The scenery is on rolled drop curtains. Note the trap door in the stage for apparitions and disappearances. After a drawing by Arthur I. Keller in Century Magazine, *March 1902, p. 680.*

Before 1910 a Paladin theatre, probably that of Mariano, was in the Italian settlement in San Francisco. The auditorium was "frescoed as to ceiling and white tiled as to walls," wrote Lucy B. Jerome in *New England Magazine* (February 1910, p. 745). Shows began at 8 o'clock at night and admission was 10¢. A playbill inscribed on brown paper outlined the action for the day. For instance, "Tonight: Ruggiero, overcome by a terrible storm, is separated from Claudiana," etc. Music was supplied by a piano. There were about three dozen 30-inch puppets.

In 1913 Joseffi Caldo's Tripoli Theatre, on East 112 Street near Second Avenue, New York, was thought to be the last surviving one of its kind. The Marionette Society was organized to preserve it, but this failed to survive its formative enthusiasm. Caldo, according to his business card, was by day "lathing contractor and plasterer boards." His puppets were about 2 feet tall, and not so well made as some of the Paladin type ("The Old Puppet Show Is to Be Restored to Favor," New York *Times*, Magazine Section, 4 May 1913, p. 5).

In 1916 Joseph Scionte and his brother John operated a Paladin theatre at 2125 Woodward Avenue, Cleveland, Ohio, which was described in the Cleveland *Plain Dealer* of 2 April that year.

Early in March 1917, Remo Bufano, then a boy (he was to grow up to be a leading puppeteer of the artistic revival), assisted by Tony Sisti, made puppets in the traditional Paladin style, to the best of his ability, and gave a couple of performances at Richmond Hill House ("Marion-

ettes March Once More," New York *Evening Sun,* 9 March 1917,
p. 10). It is significant to see how the new puppetry sprang from the
old order.

From 1918 to 1924 Pasquale Provenzano conducted a theatre at 84
Mulberry Street (Margaret Sperry, New York *Tribune,* Magazine Section, 27 January 1924, p. 5), and by 1927 the Manteo family was en-
sconced at No. 109. It is possible that the Paladins could have survived
without artificial stimulus if severe immigration measures had not been
adopted both by the United States and Italy at this time. Now even
the Manteo puppets, hung away in a damp cellar, are succumbing to
decay and rust. Perhaps something will bring them out to be refurbished
once more. It is cordially hoped so.

The Paladin playhouses were social institutions, bringing together the
same audience night after night. While the action followed recurrent
patterns, the episodes differed and suspense was maintained, as in film
or radio serials of a later day. The Spring Street showman of 1901 told
his interviewer that he had a book of *The Seven Paladins*; familiarizing
himself with a chapter each day, he put it into action on the boards. The
story of Orlando played by the Manteos had 394 episodes, so that it
could last thirteen months of nightly performances. "Hardly any traces
remain of the octaves in which these knightly adventures were originally
recited," wrote Paolo Milano in "L'Opera dei pupi in Sicily," *Puppetry
1934,* (p. 41). "The *puparo* (puppeteer) speaks prose in Sicilian dialect,
unless the presence in the audience of some person of importance in-
duces him to italianize his eloquence."

Because the characters appear again and again, a stock set of puppets
served for the entire cycle, though this was necessarily large if one
figure were reserved for each hero. The faces, simply characterized or
even alike, gave little clue to identification; habitués knew the knights
and ladies by their costumes, particularly by the crests on their helmets
and the bearings on their shields. The armor was rich with repoussé,
bosses, bands, and heraldic devices. The velvet fabrics were encrusted
with spangles, embroidery, braid, and fringe. The high-waisted, long-
legged Paladins wore kilts gorgeously ornamented. Their ladies wore
ample gowns and streaming wigs of real hair. In America there were
few characters who were not noble; hence most of the costumes were
costly in effect. In Sicily there were characters of low degree who spoke
peasant dialects; because they were local they may have been omitted
in America where audiences included Italians of widely scattered origin.
Frank Sabatello LaRosa described such Sicilian comedians in "Vertichio
and Nofrio," *Puppetry 1931* (p. 52).

Combat in the theatre of Joseph Scionte, 2125 Woodland Avenue, Cleveland, Ohio. After a photograph reproduced in the Cleveland Plain Dealer, 2 April 1916.

"The theatre was a genuine social center," Elizabeth Irwin wrote in the article cited. "To the Sicilians the show was as serious and moving as any tragedy on the Broadway stage. As for the artists who made the marionettes sing, recite, and dance, they had inherited their metier and were upholding family and racial traditions.

"There is real pathos in the dying of these puppet shows through the competition of motion pictures and the drift of the Italian population. . . . The economic changes that are going on in city life due to congestion are sweeping art and public amusement along with them. The fact that this is a natural condition does not make it a good condition, nor does it mean that it is going to be a lasting condition." But the Paladins have disappeared.

For a few hours at night the exhausted and homesick Italian could forget himself in puppet adventures. As one of the children of the Spring Street showman explained to Francis Nichols, in talking about *The Forest of Pain*, "We sometimes have sorrows all around us, and sadness. We have a kind of lost feeling. That is *The Forest of Pain*." Elizabeth Irwin observed, "The tired laborer forgets . . . that the country is America where sweatshops and tenement houses bound his horizon. To him it is the age of chivalry; he basks in eternal sunshine, he smells ever-blooming flowers, he is again in the land of his dreams, of his youth, of all his romance, under the sea-blue skies of his beloved Italy."

Because they were a curiosity and good copy for journalists, the Paladins drew sightseers from uptown. However, the strange language and monotonous action failed to gain them a wide following, and even puppet enthusiasts were unable to save them. The only place where the Paladins may henceforth be found may be museum cases. Their blank countenances cannot tell the frenzy of action that pulverized the boards, the excitement of the audience that shook the rafters, and the heartache that they deadened.

XVIII

The Toy Theatre

To the pleasures of puppetry many a grownup can add the pleasures of recollection. He can recall his own toy theatre when he was a child, and with it an aura of childhood happiness and security. Puppets are thus fun for what they have been and for what they are. This is a strong force in the perpetuation of the puppet theatre from generation to generation.

Children have played with puppets at least as long as there has been a puppet theatre. The play is different than with dolls. It takes place on a formal stage, no matter how simply improvised, and follows the conventions of the theatre. The little jointed clay figures exhumed from the graves of children in ancient Greece and Italy may not have been puppets. But the jousting knights, worked with cords by boys in the Middle Ages, were indeed puppets of a sort, the table top representing the field of chivalry. When settlers in the New World still faced too many sources of excitement to want the thrill of the theatre, children in England had toy puppets. Sir Thomas Browne of *Religio Medici* wrote to his daughter-in-law from Norwich on 13 February 1682, "Your Tommy [his grandson] grows a stout fellow. . . . He is in great expectation of a tumbler you must send him for his puppet show; a Punch he has and his wife, and a straw king and queen, and ladies of honor, and all things but a tumbler, which this town cannot afford: it is a wooden fellow that turns his heels over his head." (*Works* of Sir Thomas Browne, London, 1931, vol. 6, p. 244.) Tommy was then nine.

In France Polichinelle was a favored children's toy in the eighteenth and nineteenth centuries. Perhaps some rich American child was brought a Polichinelle by a traveling parent or relative; however, no record of it has come to light.

John Lothrop Motley the historian, said Van Wyck Brooks in *The Flowering of New England* (New York, 1936, p. 334), derived the love of costume and dramatic effect which "appeared in his writings from first to last" from the miniature theatres he had made and played with as a boy. This was in the early nineteenth century. What sort of theatres had they been?

CHINESE SHOW OF ARTIFICIAL FIREWORKS.

The Chinese showman, by an ingenious arrangement of punched pictures, transparencies, and revolving wheels, imitates brilliant stars, cones, jets, and cascades of fire so cleverly, that his exhibition rivals a display of real fireworks. The Chinese show is not difficult to construct, and may be exhibited, like the gallanty show, in a doorway leading from one apartment to another.

Have a frame made some three or four feet square, and twelve or fourteen inches deep, and let there be a ledge or groove along the bottom in front, and a corresponding one, also in front, at the top, sufficiently wide to slide a picture in. Two wires are to be placed across this frame, each having a loop in its middle, for the purpose of bearing an axle or spindle, which may be made of stout wire. On the front end of this spindle, a wheel, of about two feet in diameter made of a thin hoop, and six or eight wire spokes, must be fastened, and the other end should have a handle securely fixed on it. The wire wheel must be placed as close to the front as the sliding groove will allow. Next have as many straining frames prepared, like those made for pictures, as you intend to have subjects, and stretch upon them either calico or parchment, or paper, and paint them on both sides with oil paint, or else with lamp-black mixed with water and size. When thoroughly dry, you must proceed to sketch out upon them the different designs you wish to exhibit, taking care, if they are intended to appear in motion, that the centres of the pieces correspond with the centre of the wire wheel, and then punch an innumerable quantity of holes, of various sizes, to the shapes of the

Pages from The Boy's Own Treasury of Sports and Pastimes, *London and New York, 1866. Whereas the fireworks section had appeared in the fourth American edition of the book, published by Clark, Austin & Co. of New York in 1850, the model theatre one was new; in Edmund Routledge's* Every Boy's Book, *1868, which lifted this material, it was stated that the "papers on . . . shows . . . appear now for the first time."*

Were they small Punch and Judies? Were they shadow-figures? Or were they the cut-out cardboard stages that had already become a little old-fashioned when Robert Louis Stevenson wrote his essay on them, *A Penny Plain, Twopence Coloured,* in the 1880's?

CHINESE SHOW OF FIREWORKS.   197

figures: of course having the largest holes and greatest quantity nearest the centres, from whence the sparks are supposed to jet, and if a few narrow slits are intermingled with the holes, radiating from, and close to the centres of the pieces, much will be gained in their effect. As much is added to the beauty of this species of exhibition by producing the appearance of various coloured fires, it is as well to paste over the backs of the designs, when punched out, a piece of tissue paper, colouring it according to the nature of the display you intend, either with Prussian blue, carmine, gamboge, a purple composed with carmine and Prussian blue, or a green made with gamboge and Prussian blue, &c. Indeed, any transparent colour, or combination of colours, may be used for the purpose of adding richness and variety to the figures; and if you wish them to be extremely brilliant, either varnish the paper after colouring it, or mix varnish with the colours at first.

As the mere objects themselves, in a quiescent state, possess little interest, the means of producing motion next demand our attention. It being necessary to employ three different motions, three hoops must be procured of a size sufficient to fit tightly upon the hoop of the wire wheel, and upon three pieces of blackened paper, of the same kind as that employed on the object frames, the dimensions of the hoops should be sketched. For the first species of motion, that by which a quivering, glittering light is imitated, a wheel of twelve radii or spokes must be drawn upon one of the pieces of paper, as in the annexed figure, and the intervening white spaces cut out with a penknife.

For the second species, producing the effect of fire flowing from a centre, in one uniform motion, the wheel must have a great number of radii-flowing in regular curved lines from the centre, as delineated in the illustration, and the white spaces carefully cut out.

For the third motion wheel, the direction of the radii must be varied: an inner series flowing from the centre in one course, whilst an outer series should proceed in exactly the reverse way, as in this figure, and the white spaces cut out.

After the figures of the motion wheels are properly drawn and cut on the pieces of paper, they should be pasted upon the hoops prepared for them, and they are then ready for use. The first kind of

K K

Punch was of course familiar in New England and elsewhere in the United States in the early nineteenth century, and together with Judy he was known in their classic play after 1828. Children's books introduced Punch where he may not have been seen in person. There were Philadelphia editions of *Pug's Visit to Mr. Punch* in 1810, 1815, and 1821. The American editions of *Punch and Judy* from 1828 onward may have been given to children. A chapbook with the tale in verse, *The Serio Comic*

493 CHINESE SHOW OF FIREWORKS.

wheel is adapted for anything requiring a wavering light; the second is exceedingly well calculated for brilliant stars, the sparks from which are to appear as if they were radiating from the centre to the circumference. The third is intended for such pyrotechnic figures and stars as have jets of fire playing from points away from the centre of the piece, as well as those immediately from it; of this kind are the three annexed marginal figures, and the different directions in which the fire will seem to be ejected, particularly if variously coloured fires are imitated, will produce an animated and interesting scene.

A shower of fire requires but little art to imitate it; have a roller fastened at the top of the box, close to the front, and another at the bottom, likewise close to the front, and let there be handles affixed to them; upon these rollers wind a very long coil of blackened paper, profusely punched with holes of various dimensions; and when by moving the lower roller the paper is pulled down and wound upon it, a shower of brilliant sparks will seem to be falling. By reversing the movement of the paper by turning the upper roller, the sparks will then appear to be moving upwards, and if an object frame with a figure like a fountain is put before it, the effect of a fountain of fire will be very neatly displayed.

If a cone or globe is intended to appear in motion, figures of the annexed shape must be drawn and cut out.

When showing these objects, three or four lamps or candles should be placed along the sides of the frame, and care must be taken that the wheels are not turned too quick, else a haziness will be produced, instead of the tremulous, varying light necessary for the proper display of the pieces.

The cheap paraffin lamps, which give a steady brilliant white light, are admirably adapted for illuminating the pyrotechnic figures of the Chinese show, and one of them may advantageously be used for exhibiting the shadows of the Wonderful Crocodile and his friends.

Story of Punch and Judy, (8 pp. 5¾ × 4½ inches), was published about 1840 by Turner & Fisher of Philadelphia and New York and Fisher of Boston in a joint imprint. There were innumerable English chapbooks that may have been imported for American sale, most of them undated but belonging to the period of 1835-1850: *Punch and Judy, a Comical Tale,* London, E. Wallis (8 leaves and cover, 5⅛ × 7⅞); *The Histories of Punch and Judy and Jenny Wren,* London, Darton & Son (8 pp. and covers,

Other and more complicated designs than those we have given will doubtless present themselves to the minds of our young readers, and we trust that the really pretty effects which can be obtained in these artificial fireworks will tempt them to lay aside the use of the perhaps more lively, but certainly dangerous, real ones.

To possess a model stage with a complete set of characters and scenes, is doubtless the aim of many a lad into whose hands this book will fall. A few practical hints upon getting up a stage will not, therefore, be out of place in this section, which treats of juvenile shows.

Having decided on the play you intend to represent, you may purchase the characters, which are sold in sheets at almost all the smaller toy-shops, and at many booksellers. After painting the sheets in water-colours, they are to be stuck on cardboard with paste or gum, and when dry you must carefully cut out each character with a sharp penknife. In painting the same characters in different attitudes, be careful to make use of the same colours, as nothing can be more absurd than to make a figure change the colour of its coat, every time it kneels, sits, or draws its sword. When all the characters have been prepared, the scenes, side-wings, and drop-pieces may be purchased; these you must paint in their natural colours, and then paste upon cardboard.

The stage may be bought ready-made, but you may save the expense and earn the praises of your companions by constructing it yourself. The frame-work of the stage is not unlike a four-post bedstead, and may be easily formed by gluing a few straight pieces of deal together; the stage itself must be made of a square piece of board, planed very smooth on its upper surface. Slips of wood must

3¾₁₆ × 4½); *Punch's Nursery Hymes* (*sic*), London, W. S. Johnson (8 leaves and covers, 4 × 4½); *The History of Punch and Judy*, Finsbury, A. Park (8 leaves and covers, 5¼ × 7⅛); *Punch's Pleasantries*, London, D. Martin (48 pp. and cover, 4⅜ × 7); *The Serio-Comic Drama of Punch and Judy*, Spitalfields, H. Paul (8 pp., 4½ × 7½); and *Punch and Judy*, Gibb's Good Child's Picture Library, no place (8 pp. and cover, 3½ × 6½). There were broadsides such as *The Downfall of Punch*, London, Pitt's Whole-sale Toy Warehouse (7⅜ × 9¾, printed in two columns). From 1850 onward there were colored lithographic books with cut-out moving figures of the puppets in such series as Darton's Moveable Books or

500   THE MODEL STAGE.

be glued on the stage, and corresponding slips on the upper framework, so as to form grooves for holding the scenery. The *proscenium*,
or frontispiece of the stage, shown in our heading, is sold as a scene;
it should be painted with bright colours, and pasted on very stiff
card-board. A tin lamp, with five or six burners, is to be let into
the front part of the stage. The curtain may be formed of any dark-
green stuff, and may be wound on a roller placed behind the upper
part of the proscenium: besides the curtain there should be a painted
scene or *act drop*, to let down between the acts of a drama. During
an exhibition, lamps or candles are to be placed on each side of the
stage to illuminate the scenes.

To move the characters and work the scenery two operators are
required, and each should have the entire management of one side of
the stage. The play should be read by a third person, who should
endeavour to distinguish the different parts by different tones of
voice. A little tin foot, soldered to the end of an iron wire, is the
contrivance by which each character is supported in an upright position and moved on and off the stage. When a character has to strike
a new attitude while on the stage, the two figures required to exhibit
the change of posture may be stuck in two slits made in a square rod
of deal, as shown in the annexed cut, and by turning the rod, one

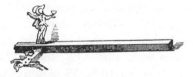

figure will be made to take the place of the other; this plan is much
better than the ordinary one of pulling one figure off the stage and
pushing another on in its place.

When you exhibit your theatre you must hang drapery all round
it, so as to completely screen yourself and your assistants from the
spectators. In a house where there are two rooms with folding
doors opening from one to the other, the theatre may be placed on a
high table in the doorway between the apartments. In a single
room a large clothes-horse may be covered with curtains and used as
a screen.

In conclusion, we recommend you to study the play you intend to
represent very carefully, so as to get all the parts tolerably perfect,
and to persuade your assistants to follow your example; we have
seen so much confusion arise from the neglect of this important point
that we cannot insist upon it too strongly.

A. N. Myers & Company's Magic Picture Books. Various novelty toy
books on Punch and Judy have continued to appear even in recent years.

But until sets of Punch and Judy puppets were made in quantity for
sale in the 1870's there were none to be found in the toy shops. Such
as there were would have had to be homemade. Now America was a
busy land. Children were expected to perform household tasks and
farm chores; their elders, even the very old, worked from dawn until late
candlelight; only an occasional superannuated or bedridden person would
have had time to build a puppet theatre for a child, and children had
insufficient spare time or inclination to make anything elaborate for

themselves. It would seem that young John Motley did not have carved puppets if he were a typical American boy of his period.

He could more easily have had shadow-figures. They did not consume so many hours in the making. The tradition of Séraphin lingered in how-to-do-it books. There are directions for preparing ombres chinoises in the *Manuel complet des sorciers* of Julia de Fontenelle (Paris, 1831, pp. 174-175). An anonymous book of shadow-figure plays, *Le Petit théâtre des ombres chinoises* (Paris, 1825), came to the assistance of the juvenile showman. A few of these little books in French may have found their way into cultivated American households. Toy cut-out sheets of shadow-figures published in Germany and France may have been imported after 1865. Such were *Quelle nützlicher Beschäftigungen zum Vergnügen der Jugend* by C. W. Döring, New Series I, Carlsruhe, 1852 (bound sheets with miniature prosceniums, transparencies, shadow-figures, and other theatrical things to cut and color) and a box of ready-cut figures, its cover the shadow screen in translucent paper, sold by Lion of 210 Rue St. Martin, Paris, about 1870. Penny sheets of shadow-figures were imported from England also, but they seem to have been nosed out by the competition of cheaper Continental wares. *The Wonders of Optics* by F. Marion, translated by Charles W. Quin (London, 1868), contained a chapter on making Chinese shadows (pp. 200-205). *What Shall We Do Tonight?* by Leger D. Mayne (New York, 1873), included a chapter on shadow-figures and a play for them (pp. 246-255). An undated booklet, perhaps from the 1890's, *Shadow Entertainments and How to Work Them*, by A. Patterson, appeared in London. *The American Boy's Handy Book* by D. C. Beard, (New York, 1882), had a chapter on making shadow-figures (called a puppet show) and a play (pp. 323-344). A child need not have been at a loss to know how shadows were operated.

But shadow-figures were for a darkened room or night time when young children were supposed to be in bed. They lacked the color that children love. Perhaps John Motley had no shadow-figures but gained his taste for costume and dramatic effect from the miniature cardboard stage.

Whether it was a cardboard theatre or a shadow-figure screen has not been specified in the story, but it is related, on the authority of Henry W. Shoemaker in his column in the Altoona *Tribune* of 6 May 1943, that in 1864 Mrs. L. L. Deming, who was a hostess and entertainer to the Tenth Michigan Regiment during the Civil War—a sort of USO all by herself—found an unused puppet theatre in the country house, "Tall Trees," at Bentley Creek, Pennsylvania (near Elmira, New York), a theatre which it is said had been obtained from Séraphin, and

POLICHINEL.

After a French cut-out of a jumping-jack Punch. The original 7 inches wide and colored.

with it put on performances to entertain the Southern officers who were detained there as prisoners of war. Of no avail to search in the attic of "Tall Trees" to see what kind of a theatre it might have been! The old mansion burned to the ground in the 1870's.

But it was certainly a cardboard theatre which Tad Lincoln, the President's youngest son, had fitted up in the White House in Washington at this time. Francis B. Carpenter, an artist who was painting a portrait of Lincoln and his cabinet, under the date of 26 April 1864, tells about it in his *Six Months at the White House* (New York, 1866, p. 91). "Some photographers came up to the White House to make some stereoscopic studies for me of the President's office. They requested a dark closet in which to develop the pictures, and without a thought that I was infringing upon anybody's rights, I took them to an unoccupied room of which Tad had taken possession a few days before and, with the aid of a couple of servants, had fitted up a miniature theatre, with stage, curtains, orchestra, stalls, parquette, and all." Tad was angry at the intrusion. He had locked up the room and taken the key. The photographers could get at their chemicals only when his father talked to him and got him to surrender the key.

With "penny plain, twopence coloured" sheets available at stationers' and toy shops, any boy could now get his miniature stage in pre-fabricated form. He would not have to build and paint everything himself, as did Hans Christian Andersen at Odense, Denmark, in 1816, or Johann Wolfgang von Goethe at Frankfurt, Germany, half a century earlier. He would have at least the proscenium front printed in color ready for mounting on board, as did Charles Lutwidge Dodgson (later to become Lewis Carroll) at the rectory at Croft, Yorkshire, England, in the 1840's. In fact, many a boy who grew up to be famous managed a miniature theatre: Edmond Rostand, Henrik Ibsen, Jean-Jacques Rousseau, H. G. Wells, Robert Louis Stevenson, Claude Lovat Fraser, and others, as their biographers have mentioned.

If there were no shop with the cut-out sheets in the neighborhood (they were a great lure if hung up in the window), they might be obtained by mail. An advertisement in *Theatrical and Musical News*, London, 2 April 1864, offered, "The Little Showman. How to make Punch's show, with all the characters beautifully colored, post free for eight stamps; a marionette show, seven stamps; a model circus, seven stamps; a galanty show, eight stamps. H. G. Clarke & Company, 252 Strand." An advertisement in *Youth's Companion*, New York, in the mid-1870's said, "Miniature theatricals for young people. Complete play consisting of 16 sheets of characters, scenes, side wings, &c., with dialogue and full directions for performing. Price 50¢, beautifully colored or

Paper players might have been found in the parlor in America as well as in France, where they were delineated after a colored lithograph of Gangel & P. Didion, Metz, about 1850. Note the toy Polichinelle on the floor.

German toy booth and puppets, about 1910. These calico-covered wooden stages ranged in size from 18 inches wide upward. The puppets had paper-pulp heads and hands, wooden legs, and costumes of paper muslin and other cheap materials. Nevertheless, because of the high import tax on toys, they were rather expensive in America. After a photograph made by the Toledo Museum of Art.

mounted on card, $1. Sent post free by the publishers, Scott & Company, 146 Fulton Street, New York, or can be had by all booksellers and toy dealers." In George Munro's *Girls and Boys of America* for 9 September 1876 there was an announcement, *"The Red Skeleton, or the Dead Avenger* . . . paper containing play 5¢; . . . 16 colored plates 10¢. Sold separately, or paper and plates together 15¢. . . . The stage, scenery, musicians, actors, and accessories are easily cut out and mounted on cardboard, and then moved on to the stage by means of grooves in the floor. The dialogue may be read by anyone standing behind the curtain."

Mark Salom's shop at 333 Washington Street, Boston, carried toy theatres in the 1860's. W. A. H. wrote a letter to the Boston *Transcript* of 3 July 1931 in which he said he remembered a Boston toy shop that carried miniature theatres in three sizes, with sheets and characters and scenery in a 5 x 3½-inch and a 10 x 12-inch size. The dramatis personae of these late nineteenth century sheets were drawn from photographs of the actors of the day in *Hamlet, Romeo and Juliet,* and other pieces of the classic repertory.

Sheets of figures printed from wood engravings, Selz's American Boys' Theatre, were published by Scott & Son of Fulton Street, New York, in the 1880's. The repertory included *The Miller and his Men, Sir Launcelot and Guinevere, The Pirates of the Florida Keys, Red-Headed Jack, the Terror of London, The Boy Sailor or the Pirate's Doom*, and a panto-mime, *The Fiend of the Rocky Mountains*. Each play had sixteen sheets of characters and scenery; the price was 25¢ plain, 50¢ colored. The firm also sold stages and settings, footlights (oil and gas), slides to put the figures in, and other supplies. I am indebted to Mr. Malcolm Horley, through Mr. Gerald Morice of England, for this information.

More children knew the circus than the theatre; for them there was a cut-out toy published by Brown, Taggard & Chase of 29 Cornhill, Boston, between 1850 and 1860; it was contained in a green-paper-covered card-board box, 6½×9¾×¾ inches, with the label *American National Circus*, I am told by Herbert H. Hosmer, Jr., who has one that was treasured in his family. The cut-out sheets were probably designed and printed by the Boston lithographic firm of Samuel W. and John G. Chandler, for proofs of some of the circus animals were found together with proofs of Chan-dler paper dolls. This is the wording of the 5¾×7¼ inch descriptive sheet in the box:

THE GREAT AMERICAN CIRCUS

We have the pleasure of being able to present our little friends with this new divertisement [*sic*] for the season.

First, there is an Elephant, not quite so large as life, but just as handsome, dressed in splendid trappings. His rider, I am sorry to say, cannot mount him-self, so you must help him. He will stick fast enough, if put on right. Be sure and examine all the figures on the back side, and there is no danger of mistake.

Mr. Summerset you will find on the box-cover, taking a ride for his health, standing on his head! But he can stand on his feet just as well.

Mrs. Summerset is airing herself on the opposite corner. She does not attempt any of the eccentricities of Mr. S., but is content with standing on her feet. She is also furnished with an extra dress, and hat ornamented with feathers.

Jeremiah Clown, Esq., rides the pony, wearing his pointed cap. Sometimes, when a warlike fit comes over him, he puts on a helmet and short sword and mounts the elephant; but his courage is not of the kind that would lead him into danger.

Last and least, we have Master Cupid. He is quite a smart rider for a young beginner, and bids fair to do as well as the best of them in the course of time.

"The figures are all attractive and gay in color," writes Mr. Hosmer, "and full of dash and style. I am missing a horse or two and Jeremiah Clown and part of a costume or two as well as an arm and leg here and there. I hope some day to find a complete set somewhere." He has written an article on his great uncle Chandler's printed sheets in *Antiques* (July 1947).

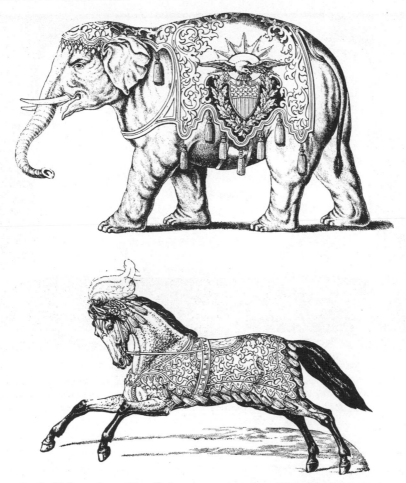

Horse and elephant from Chandler's cut-out American National Circus. By courtesy of Herbert H. Hosmer, Jr.

Paper theatres were published in the 1890's by McLoughlin Brothers, New York. They showed Joseph Jefferson as Rip Van Winkle and George L. Fox as Humpty Dumpty; Thomas Nast made some of the drawings. These were colored and were meant to be shown as transparencies within a frame depicting proscenium boxes filled with a fashionable audience. There was a panorama in the form of a roll with *Rip Van Winkle* and the afterpiece of *Yankee Doodle*. In the 1920's there was considerable activity in publishing shadow-figure and model stages, either in cut-out books or in boxes with die-stamped cardboard sheets ready to be assembled. E. Raymond Ellis made a large collection of these toys which he bequeathed to the Harvard Library Theatre Collection.

Proscenium for a paper stage in the Art Supplement of the Boston Sunday Globe, *15 March 1896. On the wings were directions for use and the note, "This theatre is to be used in exhibiting the Boston* Sunday Globe's *series of historic tableaux, five in number, one tableaux [sic] each Sunday until completed, and it should be carefully preserved." Collection of Herbert H. Hosmer, Jr.*

In the winter of 1869 Henry Ridgely Evans and a playmate, two young boys, gave cardboard theatre performances in the stable behind the house of Henry's grandfather on E Street between Sixth and Seventh streets, Washington N.W., D.C. This was like the showmanship of many another American boy. "The stable was full of eager children," wrote Evans in *From Puppetry to Prestidigitation* (*The Linking Ring*, September 1934, p. 574). "The entertainment was cleverly gotten up, with miniature stage, curtain, and scenery, and the youthful showmen exhibited much dexterity in manipulating the puppets. The play presented was *Sinbad the Sailor*." The figures were made of painted cardboard, Dr. Evans wrote me, mounted on small blocks of wood. From the blocks ran stiff wires which enabled the operators to push and pull them to and fro from the wings of the miniature stage.

Yes, it was probably a cardboard theatre which young Motley used as a testing ground for histrionics.

About 1902 toy theatres, perennially delightful to boys as dolls' houses are to girls, were to be found in many homes, to judge from the references in the diary of a young Philadelphian written at that time (*Diary of a Twelve-Year-Old*, by Benjamin Musser, Caldwell, Idaho, 1932, p. 47). In his own spelling: "Nov. 19. . . . I found in Fred's closet a little theatre which he and I made a year ago and which I loved. He said it could be his and mine together, and we will often have plays in it for Julia and her friends. Gee but we'll have fun! Today I've been writing a play to be acted in it. The play is woven around the French revolution, dealing with Louis XVI, Marie Antoinette, Cardinal Roan, etc. It is very tragic, especially the last act. The theatre is about 2 ft. each way, the stage I mean, and has arrangements for the curtains and is slick. . . . Norris also has a theatre, not a big homemade one like ours but one of those flimsy ones you buy at Swartzes, still it isn't bad. He is writing a play for his, and he wants me to draw the actors for in it. I said I would. . . .

"Saturday 21. Our first play will be next Saturday and will be called *The Guillotine*, dealing with Marie Antoinette, Louis XVI, etc. It is very exciting and terribly tragic, I made it just as tragic as I could so the audience (Julia) would be fearfully moved and cry maybe. The prison scene is horrible, where they stick Princess Lamable's head through the bars and tear the dauphin from his mothers arms. And I made the priest who says, 'son of Saint Louis, assend to heaven.' Fred says I'm a royalist, and I said he bets his life I am at least regarding France, and Fred said then I ought not to let my own feelings show in things I write. Well but whose feelings ought to show, that's what writers are for."

In Latin America, French and German cut-out theatre sheets were sold. Until comparatively recently a little shop in Mexico City had a stock of Images d'Epinal, including theatrical characters, left over from the era of Maximilian. The juvenile drama of Orellana and Arroyo, Mexican publishers, has already been described.

If I may quote from my *Repertory of Marionette Plays* (New York, 1929, p. 22) I can add my own experience with a paper theatre to the record. "It came complete in a folio, held together like a magazine with wire pins, ready to be cut out and set up. I remember there was no name to it, not even the designer's initials; I looked closely. On the last day in February 1914 . . . I went visiting in Flatbush with my parents. Flatbush was then very suburban, full of open lots and trees. The children of our hostess took me for a walk, its objective a stationer's shop where something fine and cheap was to be seen. The bargain excited me too when I examined it. . . . Ten cents got me the folio; no theatre before or since gave such value.

"I have the impression that the sheets were large, no less than 12×15 inches. The cardboard cover of the folder, when cut out and pasted, made a decorated frame for the front of the stage. One sheet, mounted on brown paper to give it backbone, made the gold-roped, red velvet grand drapery to mask backstage activity. Other sheets had wings with trees and half-timbered houses, and backdrops with perspective scenes, to make settings of a wood or street. The characters, in bright and dashing costumes, I supposed were for something Shakespearean; they bore a resemblance to the illustrations in my Lamb's *Tales*. Underfoot there was no lettering to give a clue of who they were supposed to be. To this day I am no wiser about them.

"After the red curtain had been pulled up (to reappear in the air above the proscenium frame) and the wood scene stood revealed with figures in arrested motion, I gazed my fill—there was no point in shifting the characters about dramatically, or in inventing speeches, for that would have spoiled the illusion for me. Then down came the curtain, and presently it lifted to show the street. My labors as scene-shifter did not deprive me of surprise as a spectator out front to behold the new revelation. How I'd lie on my belly peering into the bright miniature scene, no diminished theatre, but a whole real world!"

When I was a boy, German miniature stages, both for hand-puppets and for cardboard actors, were sold in all big toy stores. I remember them in Woodward and Lothrop's in Washington, D.C., in 1912, and in F. A. O. Schwarz's in New York in 1913. In the shop of the latter (then at its old location in lower Fifth Avenue) the stages were ranged in diminishing size, safely out of reach, atop some display cases. The smallest model stage then cost about $10; the largest was $50 or more; they were expensive toys, their fronts and scenery, I distinctly remember, very ugly in design. A small Punch and Judy booth with sides that folded flat and a black muslin backdrop, together with four hand-puppets with papier-mâché heads, cost $6. Cheaply made as this set was, it could not be duplicated in 1947 for three times that price. I still have mine, a little the worse for wear, but almost old enough by now to be classed as an antique.

Children from 1870 onward were given ready-made toy theatres, which they generally added to with their own handiwork. Clarence Day and his brothers had a Punch and Judy booth in their playroom in New York about 1880, as he tells in "No Movies Then" (*The New Yorker*, 31 October 1936, p. 22).

But there were directions for constructing one's own Punch show in the books of Frank Bellew, Edmund Routledge, O. B. Hubbard, Pro-

Box top of a theatre toy, about 1890, after a chromolithograph by Milton Bradley & Co., Springfield, Massachusetts. Collection of Herbert H. Hosmer, Jr.

fessor Hoffmann, and Leger D. Mayne, to name the principal ones. So, with sheets to cut out for model stages, and directions for making hand-, string- (these were in Routledge), and shadow-puppets, children could have whatever they wanted if they but made it.

America was a rural country until the beginning of the twentieth century. Perhaps only one in three children had ever seen a theatre. Toy theatres were therefore unrelated to the experience of all but certain city youngsters. Today, with movies the only form of theatre known to nine-tenths of the population, a model stage would be so exotic that most children would take it for a fantastic invention; thus few are to be found as toys. But puppets are known, through the work of traveling companies and magazine articles, in the remotest hamlet. That children should create their own puppet shows in the pattern of those they have seen is to be expected. Many a school child's production is as ambitious as that of the professional troupe he has encountered; and young amateur puppeteers are constantly reinforcing the band of professionals.

XIX

The Dawn of the Puppetry Revival

Puppet shows had been manifestations of folk art. In repertory and technique they were largely traditional, transmitted by example from showman to showman, from generation to generation. No puppet playwright, no puppet maker depended upon academic training for his skill, or approached his work with that regard for fine points which marks sophisticated art. Puppetry was carried on to gain a livelihood.

Toward the end of the nineteenth century emerged the phenomenon of the amateur Punch and Judy man, who gave shows for the fun of it. However, when children put on their own performances, it was always for a home audience, never for show in public. Such amateurs as John Difenderfer and Ernest Russell cut in upon the field where professional Punch men had earned their bread; it is no wonder that the old-timers became doubly zealous of their technical secrets and deaf to the questioning of journalists about them in the face of this unfair competition.

But by 1915 American amateurs were thinking seriously of the aesthetic and educative possibilities of puppetry. By 1920 they had brought about a revival of puppetry as an artistic medium and explored new applications for it. Thenceforward professional puppeteers, recruited from the ranks of amateurs, took on a new character. So forceful was the movement that the existence of an older order was almost completely forgotten. Some thought that puppets were an original invention, if not of Tony Sarg, at least of some European contemporary.

That puppetry could be the expression of an artist had been abundantly demonstrated in private or semiprivate performances in France in the nineteenth century, and in public shows in Germany in the early twentieth century. Whatever inspiration Americans had for puppet art was derived from Europe. But they discovered the possibilities and applications of the medium for themselves.

Along with its traveling puppet troupes which played at fairs and in theatres, with its established local companies in Amiens, Lille, and Roubaix, with its Guignol in Lyons and its lesser Guignols in Paris, France in the nineteenth century had a number of puppet performances staged by artistic amateurs, studio performances they might be called, which were well publicized by the writers included in the audience. Maurice Sand, who started out with a couple of hand-puppets carved from firewood and dressed in rags, which he operated behind the back of a chair, was a pupil of the painter Delacroix. He had a talent for drawing and writing. His puppets, first at Nohant and then at Paris, became an obsessing hobby. He made portrait puppets of his friends and of the celebrities of the day. He wrote plays in parody of the latest hits and peppered them with topical allusions. It was a privilege to be invited to see his Théâtre des Amis. George Sand, his mother, described it in her *Dernières pages*. The plays were collected and published in 1890. Everyone had heard about these puppets, though comparatively few had seen them.

Louis Emile Duranty, one of the incumbents of the Tuileries Gardens, published his repertory in a handsome volume in 1863. Lemercier de Neuville, devising shows to amuse a group of writer and artist friends in 1862, became a professional, showed his Pupazzi (they were hand-puppets) in Paris and Monte Carlo, published his satiric pieces, played solo, and became the prototype of the puppeteer who did everything in the designing, making, and production of a show. The Chat Noir shadow-figures were produced by successful artists and writers. But perhaps the most renowned puppets were those of the Petit Théâtre, managed by Henri Signoret, which gave performances of Cervantes, Aristophanes, Shakespeare, Hroswitha, and Maurice Bouchor to specially composed music with stately rod-puppets. Anatole France was warm in their praise. This theatre played from 1888 to 1892 and its original dramas were published.

The effect of Goethe's encomiums was to turn the attention of German writers, scholars, and artists to puppetry. The texts of folk plays were collected and published. The local folk theatres at Aachen, Cologne, and Dresden were encouraged. Joseph Schmid, an artistic young man in Munich, approached Franz von Pocci, who was known for his children's stories, to write plays for him. From the collaboration of these two as puppeteer and playwright, Munich's civic puppet theatre sprang. Schmid was just an amateur at the outset of his career in 1858. By 1900 he had so endeared himself to the people of Munich that they built him a special building for his theatre (still in use by his successor) and called him Papa Schmid.

Inspired by Schmid's example and using string-puppets of his scale, Paul Brann organized the Munich Artists' Puppet Theatre in 1910, producing plays of literary quality with beautifully designed and executed puppets and scenery commissioned from Munich artists. In 1911 Ivo Puhonny, artist and illustrator, began to give puppet performances in Baden-Baden. In 1912 Anton Aicher, also following in Schmid's footsteps, set up a puppet theatre in Salzburg. A group of enthusiasts in St. Gall, Switzerland, were indebted to Schmid in the shows they had inaugurated in 1904. All of these theatres, playing on announced schedules, publicized in the illustrated papers, presented themselves to the eye of the American tourist.

The start of the artistic revival in England was more obscure. In the winter of 1908 J. A. Fuller Maitland, editor of Grove's *Dictionary of Music*, chanced upon a folk puppet maker who provided him with a few string-puppets and explained the rudiments of working them. Using these as models, Fuller Maitland and his friends converted small artist's lay-figures into puppets. They recalled that Maeterlinck had designated some of his early pieces as plays for puppets and worked on a production of his *Interior*. This made an impression on its small private audiences. George Bernard Shaw was invited (but didn't arrive) and the *Illustrated London News* reported it in its number for 6 March 1909.

Dora Nussey translated the old German puppet play of *Doctor Faust*, found a small string-puppet as a model, and produced it before a private audience of adults at Clifford's Inn Hall, London, on 7 March 1910. Margaret Bulley borrowed one of these puppets and put together her own experimental production of the same play for the Sandon Studios Club in Liverpool shortly thereafter. In 1912 the Camera Club in London woke up to the fact that Clunn Lewis had a charming old folk show and engaged him to play at one of its meetings. Early in 1914 Arthur and Walter Wilkinson, who were painting in Italy, fitted out a gay puppet wagon with which to travel through the countryside; toy Italian puppets with a wire from the head for manipulation had so charmed them that they carved and costumed puppets of their own. William Simmonds, sculptor, caught the puppet fever from them when they began to give public performances in England at the end of World War I. Tony Sarg, a young illustrator, gave a few private studio performances in 1914 (Bernard Shaw was able to come this time) of trick acts modeled upon the Holden Marionettes which he had studied in the London music halls. No one would, of course, have been able to see these faint stirrings unless he had made a special point of it.

In Italy too (seedbed of art) Gordon Craig had experimented with puppets from 1907 onward, working toward new concepts for their use. In 1912 Vittorio Podrecca, a writer and secretary of the Royal Musical Academy of St. Cecilia in Rome, gathered a group of young artists and musicians and founded the Teatro dei Piccoli. Its first productions were of operettas such as Respighi's *Sleeping Beauty* or they were explorative of new forms. Gordon Craig saw a Futurist ballet staged by Depero in May 1917. "A *huge* figure," he wrote in *The Marionnette* (Florence, 1918, p. 126), "as high as the stage, enters with much unintentional creaking of the joints, all kneel down but him, and out of his cabinet belly (he is a she, it seems), in which two doors spring ajar, comes a tiny figure, which dances about inside before emerging, then hops out. The big figure is remarkable in that it lacks one forearm and is painted a nice red like a garden chair."

Also in 1917 Craig had seen a studio performance in Rome by an artist he concealed under the initial V. "V's astonishing work is that he has made a marionette which is also a mere block of wood," wrote Craig of this Cubist sketch in *The Marionnette* (p. 116), "and yet which dances, not like a marionette or a block of wood, but like Caliban and like Ariel."

Podrecca's programs tended more and more to conform to popular time-tried material when he visited Milan in 1915 and toured north Italy in 1919. By the time he first got to South America in 1922 his program was almost indistinguishable from the old Royal Marionettes pattern.

The artistic revival came about as much through books as through stimulating performances by skilled old-timers and experimental new-

COMEDIES AND LEGENDS
FOR MARIONETTES

A Theatre for Boys and Girls

BY

GEORGIANA GODDARD KING

ILLUSTRATED BY ANNA R. GILES

Title page of the first collection of puppet plays in English, containing three commedia dell'arte comedies, two legends of saints' lives, and two fairy-tale pantomimes, intended for home performance. Original page 5½ × 7¾ inches.

New York
THE MACMILLAN COMPANY
LONDON: MACMILLAN & CO., LTD.
1904
All rights reserved

comers. Anyone who grew excited about puppetry wanted to find out more about it. The old-timers were not communicative. So the novice went to the library. He was surprised to find that there was so little in print on the subject, and most of that not in English. He found John Payne Collier's introduction to *Punch and Judy*, Charles Magnin's history, a few notes in E. K. Chambers' *The Medieval Stage* (Oxford, 1903), and Ernest Maindron's *Marionnettes et guignols* (Paris, about 1900) with information about the French developments after Magnin—studio performances, Thomas Holden, Dicksonn, John Hewelt, and the Petit Théâtre. If he read Italian, the searcher got hold of P. C. Ferrigni (Yorick), *La storia dei burattini* (Florence, 1884), with a chapter on Italian puppetry that supplemented Magnin. Or if he delved into German he got Hermann Siegfried Rehm, *Das Buch der Marionetten* (Berlin, about 1905) with its new material on German puppetry.

He read about shadow-figures in the various booklets and articles of Georg Jacob which were to be collected in his *Geschichte des Schattentheaters* (Hanover, 1925), or in *Feu Séraphin: Histoire de ce spectacle* (Lyons, 1875).

There were also a great many scattered magazine articles that he could track down if he had plenty of time. But there was no really up-to-date history until the appearance of Helen Haiman Joseph's *A Book of Marionettes* (New York, 1920).

In general literature there were passages written by people who were evidently fond of puppets. *Wilhelm Meisters Lehrjahre* (Berlin, 1795), depicting a theatre-mad young man who was evidently Goethe himself, had a puppet theatre; its first six chapters are filled with the bright wonder of it. Goldoni's *Memoirs* tell how the future playwright produced Martelli's *The Sneeze of Hercules* in a completely equipped puppet theatre which he found in a palazzo on the Brenta that he visited with his father in the mid-eighteenth century. George Sand wrote at length about her son's theatre. Charles Dickens made a sympathetic and humorous report of an Italian puppet show at Genoa in his *Pictures from Italy*. Théophile Gautier described a Karagheuz show in *Constantinople*.

William Hazlett observed, in *Leading English Comic Writers*, "The drollery and wit of a piece of wood is doubly droll. Punch is not merry in himself, but 'he is the cause of heartfelt mirth in other men.'" Anatole France wrote charming reviews of the Petit Théâtre performances in *Le Temps*, later collected in *On Life and Letters*, Series 2 and 3. Arthur Symons included *An Apology for Puppets* in *Plays, Acting and Music* (London, 1903). Something of France and Symons went into Gordon Craig's concept of the Ubermarionette.

The reader inevitably came to Heinrich von Kleist's philosophical dialogue, *The Puppet Theatre*, first published in the *Berliner Abendblätter* about 1810 and reprinted in his *Works*, Berlin (Part 5, Vol. 9). Kleist observed that the movement of the string-puppet is either centrifugal or pendular. The puppeteer's hands are to its movement as numerals are to logarithms or the asymptote to the parabola. The motion is so direct in cause and effect that it might be wholly mechanical. Whether or not one agrees with this (no puppeteer would do so), it is a soundly mechanical, not an emotional approach. Kleist stipulated that these qualities are necessary in the puppet: symmetry, mobility, lightness—all as with the human dancer, but in a higher degree; and a natural disposition of the centers of gravity. In the experiments of W. A. Dwiggins in the 1930's a neatly counterbalanced figure was developed (*Marionette in Motion*, Birmingham, Michigan, 1939). Kleist considered it an affectation for the motor force to be elsewhere than at a center of gravity; he pointed to the puppet which moved its limbs like pendula (at any rate the toy puppet with a wire to its head). Isadora Duncan's rationalization of her dancing was that all movement started at the solar plexus. Another puppet advantage, said Kleist, was its lack of weight. Being light it had little inertia. It grazed the ground as a momentary contact. And he concluded on a mystical note: grace is purest when most unconscious or most conscious, as in puppet or deity; hence the puppet, by mechanical imagery, coincides with the god as when lines intersecting at infinity recurve in reverse.

The reader was even more apt to encounter Gordon Craig's writings on the puppet in *The Mask*. Craig was visionary and belligerent. When he was a child his toys were chosen by his mother, Ellen Terry, with a taste formed by George Frederick Watts, Walter Crane, E. W. Godwin the historical revivalist, and Whistler the iconoclast. He was given only the bright, naïve, handmade wooden things known as Nuremburg toys. Penny plain, twopence colored sheets were probably considered passable. He would not have grown up to like naturalistic puppets.

When he went to work in Florence in 1907, he was joined for a few months by Michael Carmichael Carr, an American, who watched his experiments with puppets and later made a few Cubist puppets himself. When Craig's school of the theatre was opened in 1913, his students made numbers of puppets, and he set up a wood-carving room at the Arena Goldoni where trial marionettes were to be made by Italian workmen. He had begun to collect old puppets casually; in 1934, when he was preparing to leave Italy, he wrote me that he had packed some 150 puppets in boxes.

With this background his essay, *The Actor and the Ubermarionette*, dated at Florence, March 1907, is clear. It was published in *The Mask*, Vol. 1, and then in *On the Art of the Theatre* (London and Chicago, 1911, p. 54). When it appeared everyone wondered how literally it was to be taken; actors who took it altogether literally were up in arms against it; those who cared for puppets wanted to take it literally, but were on guard against doing so. It was based, of course, on the parallel of Nietzsche's superman. Nietzsche had died in 1900; Shaw's *Man and Superman* had been published in 1903; the "super" idea was still new, unjaded by application to highways, movies, and markets.

This is a brief of the article: Acting is not an art, for art is not accidental; the actor, swayed by emotions, is an imperfect instrument. Hence a new form of acting must be devised of gestures that are fresh and significant, which indicate rather than imitate in the manner of actors. Realistic acting is not even as accurate as photography. The strong appeal of the actor's personality overpowers any attempt at representation. If realistic scenery is to be used, it calls for realistic acting. Therefore the actor must go, and in his place the inanimate figure, the Ubermarionette, will hold sway. The marionette is not evolved from a doll or toy but from the sacred image. It has the majesty of godhead, the mystery of spirit force, the marvel of divinity come to life from stone. "The marionette appears to me to be the last echo of some noble and beautiful art of a past civilization. But as with all art that has passed into fat and vulgar hands, the puppet has become a reproach. All puppets are now but low comedians.

"They imitate the comedians of the larger and fuller blooded stage. They enter only to fall on their back. They drink only to reel, and make love only to raise a laugh. They have forgotten the counsel of their mother the Sphynx."

This was the document that heralded the dawn of the puppet revival.

In 1915 Craig reaffirmed his beliefs (*The Mask*, Vol. 7, p. 104), looking back to his earlier essay. "I was at that time overwhelmed by a conviction that the marionette, even though but distantly related to the idol, held something vital to the development of the theatre; I felt that it was one of the few things which counted in all the discoveries in the land of the stage." In a letter to me he wrote (24 September 1933), "Puppetry is a true art—the true art of the theatre-in-little—theatricals having got their deserts and become a false kind of photography enlarged." And in another (1 January 1936), "I can only like the primitive expressionless puppets—and cannot force myself to endure the 'artistic' ones. They defeat the whole purpose of the existence of true puppets." This attitude would seem at first glance quixotic—denial of what one prophesied—but the artistic revival has not always improved upon the older order of puppetry.

Lest it be thought that Craig's writings on the puppet were all theoretical, it should be said that, at a time when little information on technique was available in English, he published *A Game of Marionettes* (*The Mask*, Vol. 5, pp. 145 ff.), telling how to write a play, build a stage, make string-puppets, and operate them. "Don't get it into your head," he cautioned, "that they want to be jiggled up and down; they don't appreciate much movement." He pointed out that if a fixed stage is to represent a palace, the puppets should be 6 inches tall, as against 12 if the same stage is to be a cottage. "Man is always greater or smaller; *things* don't change." In *The Chapbook*, No. 20 (London, 1921), he gave exercises for practicing puppet manipulation and added, "The wood is much, the wires, the stage, the whole technique very much—but far more important is who it is that is holding the puppet. For it is he who knows how to let it move and how to let it speak—and so he it is who counts most. Consider his task—how admirable it is."

Not only *The Mask* but *The Marionnette* contained much information for the reader. This little monthly, which lasted only a year in 1918, had puppet plays, translations from the French, German, and Italian, and Craig's own wood-engraved designs.

In 1920 Mrs. Joseph summed up Craig's experiments in *A Book of Marionettes*. "With the marionette used as a sort of symbol," she wrote, Craig has conducted "research into the very heart of dramatic verities. . . . Before inventing the action of a puppet, Craig would study, for days or weeks, watching various people make the movement, and expressing the emotion he desired to portray. Then he would extract from these observations the general and essential qualities of this particular gesture; all else, due to the peculiarities of individuals, he left out as irrelevant for the stage. Hence when Craig's puppet moves, it moves simply, significantly, and—one more essential—surely. For nothing is left to chance."

For the American who had recourse to books, there was, then, a good deal of historical and critical material to be found. For the one who traveled abroad, there were artistic performances to be seen. All this had built up a considerable reservoir of stimulus on the eve of World War I.

In the spring of 1913 William Patten, a New York editor and educator, who had seen puppets in France and Italy and read extensively, planned a society to restore puppetry to a stronger position in American life. He wanted puppet shows in the schools and playgrounds, in the theatres and art galleries. He was quoted in "The Old Puppet Show Is to Be Restored" (New York *Times*, 4 May 1913) as saying, "Our children may in the future learn their geography lessons and their United States history not from dry textbooks, but from an adapted Guignol family; Cubists and Post-Impressionists will be forgotten in the rage for marionette exhibitions; we shall see the plays of Maeterlinck produced as their author intended them, by marionettes." All this came to pass.

Patten continued, "Founders of the marionette society believe that puppets have a use which nothing else can take place of in the education of children and grown people, and that the marionette can be used as one means of bringing imagination and local color back to the stage. At the present day we are flooded with actualistic and realistic drama. Moving picture shows which take the place of all imaginative effort are viewed by eight or nine million people every day. Not only can anybody make marionettes and dance them, write plays for them, and recite the dialogue, but every child actually does so in playing with dolls."

Sanguine Mr. Patten! Hasty amateurs took him at his word, presented their maiden efforts to a paying public, and did tremendous disservice to the whole cause.

Patten expatiated, "A large amount of capital is not needed. A boy's club can create a marionette theatre for itself. The classes in our kindergartens through making and operating marionettes and composing the play to be performed can get a unified teaching along manual and imaginative lines, which will include a study of elocution, history, composition, and rhythm.

"On the educational side the marionette attains its highest value as a means of expression. The marionette can be anything or anybody. . . . It can play high tragedy or low burlesque. The value of the marionette as a cartoon should not be overlooked. . . . In the State of Wisconsin . . . school buildings are used as social centers for purposes of recreation. In all such buildings marionette shows could easily be given. . . .

"Judging from the enthusiastic reception given to the society's plans by many of our best-known educators, teachers, settlement workers, authors, artists, actors, and theatrical managers, success seems assured for the marionette movement."

A charter member of the society, John Collier of the People's Institute, wanted the Paladin shows to be given for all school children in New York, at least those in its tenement districts. "This is one of the activities," he said in the same *Times* article, "around which you can center the home life of the alien. We are always looking for something that will bring aliens together; give them a common interest through which they may be reached.

"Amusement is the most direct route. Marionette shows would organize the alien element of New York City as baseball has organized China. The Y.M.C.A. let baseball loose all over China, and the team work that has resulted has made for civilization." This would have been an unfortunate argument twenty years later! "The foreigner here feels alien in most of our recreation places; he prefers his own coffee house and his own conventions. . . .

"Our entire tendency is toward symbolism, the foundation principle of the puppet show. . . . Consider the recent art exhibition at the Armory, and remember the extreme symbolism, the tendency away from photographic realism, of Matisse and Picabia. . . .

"Marionettes will seem to many people crude and ludicrous, adapted only to the amusement of children, but that is because they have always been the affair of peasant folk and are in this country wholly undeveloped to suit our present-day civilization.

"The educational possibilities of the marionette appeal very strongly to me. . . . Think what it would mean to have school children witness the wanderings of Ulysses and the French and Indian War in operation! Witnessing would be half the advantage of the plan. The child would do all the work connected with the presentation of any fact or scene."

Though many famous people lent their names to the marionette society, it petered out and came to naught. Its ideals were by now in the air, however. Elnora Whitman Curtis cautiously wrote in *The Dramatic Instinct in Education* (Boston, 1914, p. 194), "There is a very general tendency in this country to adapt for school use everything that is of recognized educational value. The puppet play, it is true, could be brought to school. While we would scarcely advocate its introduction as mere entertainment, doubtless some subjects could be vivified and made more interesting by means of marionettes. For the large number of children who never get beyond the grades, the deepening of the impressions in literature and history would be of special value, as also for older children the training in writing dialogues and declaiming, and the practice in fashioning puppets, costumes, scenery, and properties, and in acting as operator and showman. But better yet, put little puppet theatres into settlement and playground, into boys' club and social center, into the small park or recreation place. . . . Finally create a marionette theatre run on high and artistic principles . . . and make it in the end a civic institution."

Many of these visions have now materialized for the puppet theatre, and have even in a degree received civic sanction and support.

Before 1914 there was an isolated example of the use of puppetry in teaching at Earlham College, Richmond, Indiana, where Arthur M.

Charles, it was reported in *Drama League Monthly* (December, 1916, p. 223), presented *Dr. Faustus* and certain Hans Sachs plays with hand-puppets to illustrate a course in the Faustus story for the German department. His example and that of the Chicago Little Theatre puppets, the first of the new artistic order in America, prompted the Richmond, Indiana, Drama League to present, in the winter of 1915, *Hansel and Gretel* with the Humperdinck music, *Dornröschen,* and other pieces as a variation of the storytelling hour at the public library. Some eighteen performances in all were given, with great success. One eight-year-old "hardened vaudeville and movie devotee" was overheard telling a companion that the puppets were "the best show I've seen in years."

And so puppetry entered an era of approval from educators. Tony Sarg and those who branched from his companies were soon to make the whole United States aware of puppetry. By 1925 only the hindmost schools were not using puppets, or not intending to use them, as an educative tool.

The stage was set for the artistic puppet production.

XX

Contemporary Puppets

1. The Artistic Revival

It was the suggestion of one of the patrons of the Chicago Little Theatre, Mrs. Seymour Edgerton, that puppet plays be given along with the regular performances by human actors; she wanted them inaugurated for her own children and those of Chicagoans in general, having known them in Germany and Italy. She made it possible for Ellen Van Volkenburg, wife of Maurice Browne, the director of the Little Theatre, to go to Europe to see for herself what was being done there. After watching many puppets that were dull and traditional, performing variety acts or plays not interesting to children, she came upon three sisters in Sölln, a suburb of Munich, who presented dramatizations of fairy tales and old German legends that they wrote themselves. Their productions, given in the family dining room, had a delicate fantasy that made an immediate appeal to her. Marie Janssen was the leader of the family group; she was still giving performances in Herrsching in 1946. Some of her puppets were bodiless, a mere film of veiling with head and hands; Titania, in the Chicago production of *A Midsummer Night's Dream*, was to follow this misty pattern.

Ellen Van Volkenburg could not persuade the Janssens to give up one of their puppets for a model, and had to be content with the purchase of four puppets made by Papa Schmid. These showed jointing and stringing. When she got back to Chicago she had a young English sculptor, Katherine Wheeler, carve puppets to suit her needs. They were in the Schmid scale, only about a foot high, but with sharp little planes where the tool sliced the wood, to catch the light and make the features clear at a distance. The Little Theatre seated about 100; it was in a studio in the Fine Arts Building on Michigan Boulevard, a building replete with artistic activities. In it was the bookstore of that Browne (not Maurice) who had published Gordon Craig's *On the Art of the Theatre* in its first American edition; the store was designed by Frank Lloyd Wright. Thus the Little Theatre was a more practical auditorium for puppets than for live actors, and the foot-tall figures could be seen readily from the back of the house.

331

Girl puppeteers of the Chicago Little Theatre. The proscenium opening was about 4×5 feet, the puppets averaged a foot high. After a photograph reproduced in Theatre Magazine, *September 1916, p. 152.*

The first play decided upon was *The Deluded Dragon*, written by Ellen Van Volkenburg on a theme in a book of Japanese legends by Fiona McLeod. Special lyrics and piano music were composed. But in performance the piano seemed too heavy for the puppets. A celestaphone played in Tony Sarg's production of *The Rose and the Ring*, which she later directed, seemed much better.

When rehearsals of *The Deluded Dragon* started, it was found that the operators had difficulty learning their lines while manipulating. The director then established a routine which she always followed thereafter. Mrs. John Martin, who was one of her company in Chicago, wrote (*Puppetry 1944-1945*, p. 5) that "she rehearsed them on their own two feet like any ordinary actors. Thus they could establish in themselves the characterizations and feeling for movement which later they poured down the strings, bringing the puppets to life in a truly dramatic and kinesthetic sense.

"As for the word 'operator'—they did not know what to call the manipulator-actor back in that day. Nelly hit on the word 'puppeteer,' feeling a little sheepish, she said, 'because it sounded so put on. But,' she continued, 'I thought if you could say "muleteer" you could say "puppeteer."' Hm, well—!

"Anyway, here was born a word which has since come into use sufficiently accepted and universal to be included in the latest edition of Webster's Dictionary.

"When they had their production all ready they presented it to Maurice Browne, who had the last word to say about any production appearing in the Chicago Little Theatre. Nelly laughed as she repeated what he had said, 'That's the worst thing I've ever seen and I shall never allow it to go on in this theatre.'

"They all went home and cried. After Nelly had dried her eyes, she

Pig and pepper scene from Alice in Wonderland, *Chicago Little Theatre, 1917. After a photograph reproduced in* Joseph, A Book of Marionettes. *The unity of scenery and puppet grouping is evidence of a new artistic approach.*

made a decision, which, as I see it, influenced the whole course of puppet history. She decided to work again and *make* it a good production, instead of giving up then and there as she was tempted to do.

" 'What did he object to?' I asked her.

" 'I think it was too much movement. Everything wiggled all the time.' We then decided to make it a positive rule that no puppet should move on the stage except the one speaking. When a puppet was about to speak, it would raise its right arm with an accent, thus calling attention to itself."

The dramatic presentation was the main thing; mechanics came afterward. In the early days the puppeteers each had a pin in case the strings got tangled, and a scissors was kept handy on the bridge in case of a desperate muddle. The puppets were beautifully carved but sketchily put together. One of the dragon's heads floated away from its body in the middle of a scene. Little brass hinges were tried for joints; these were too stiff. Fishline embedded in slits cut into the arms and legs was tried; this broke. When Carroll French came to the theatre, he made joints of cloth or of linked screw eyes. These were more satisfactory.

"When I first saw Tony Sarg, shortly after he came to the United States and before I left the Little Theatre," continued Mrs. Martin, "he was using the airplane-type controller just as he did right along afterwards." This was a development of the horizontal bars used by operators of trick marionettes. Mrs. Martin took the idea back to Chicago and Mr. French adapted it on a smaller scale for some of the *Alice* puppets. Mrs. Martin did not, however, like it as well as the vertical controllers, in the Papa Schmid style, which had been used at first. There had also been a wire to the middle of the head at first, then a wire to each side of the head, and finally two pieces of fishline, more difficult to manage than the wires. "All sorts of colors and string were tried, but black was settled upon as least likely to reflect light; for other strings than those to the head, tailor's linen thread was used, as fishline was expensive. It tangled badly—hence the pin.

Scene at the court of Theseus from A Midsummer Night's Dream, *Chicago Little Theatre. Actual draped curtains and plastic set pieces instead of painted scenery. After a photograph reproduced in* Theatre Magazine, *September 1916.*

"However they were constructed, Nelly came to the conclusion that for dramatic purposes each puppet should have only one or two characteristic movements. This emphasized character and reduced wriggling confusion in the stage picture. Nelly never handled puppets herself (except in one dreadful emergency), hence she brushed aside all mechanical difficulties, and would sweetly call from 'out front' for anything impossible just so it produced the dramatic effect she wanted. There were grumblings and groans from the concealed bridge, but that sweet and terribly cheery voice was insistent. And so it was done!"

The Deluded Dragon, together with *Columbine,* by Reginald Arkell, was produced in 1915. *The Little Mermaid,* after Andersen, *Jack and the Beanstalk,* and *A Midsummer Night's Dream* were done in 1916. *The Frog Prince, Little Red Riding Hood,* and *Alice in Wonderland* were the 1917 productions. The Little Theatre was then obliged to close—blame it upon the war.

In the meanwhile Tony Sarg, having come to New York and found work as a magazine illustrator, gave shows for friends in his studio in the Flatiron Building at Broadway and Fifth Avenue. In 1915-1916 he revived his London sketch, *A Night in Delhi,* and added a musical turn, *The Singing Lesson.* In one of his audiences Winthrop Ames, the theatrical producer, happened to be present. It had been a hope of his to bring the Munich Artists' Marionette Theatre to America. Since the war had

Scene from The Little Mermaid, *Chicago Little Theatre production. After a photograph reproduced in* Theatre Magazine, *September 1916, p. 153.*

put a stop to the project, he asked Sarg whether he wouldn't like to put on a professional show. Sarg was delighted to. Ames furnished the capital.

The first floor of an old brownstone house on Thompson Street, in the district where Paladin puppets were familiar, was rented for a workshop. Sarg made designs and hired assistants to execute them. For one of the pieces *The Three Wishes* by Pocci, from Papa Schmid's repertory, was chosen. Two more playlets were written especially to exploit trick marionettes. Mrs. Hamilton Williamson, the playwright, said to Anne Stoddard ("The Renaissance of the Puppet Play," *Century Magazine*, June 1918, p. 176), "When Mr. Sarg first told me that he wanted a snake-charmer, a juggler, an oriental dancer, an elephant, and a donkey in one play, I thought I couldn't possibly get them together; but, you see, I did." The Oriental fantasy that accommodated them was called *A Stolen Beauty and the Great Jewel*. Then, for magic, a ghost, a come-apart skeleton, and a boy who sprouted to a surprising height, *The Green Suit* was devised. Everybody pitched in to sew and build, but Lilian Owen and Persis Kay made most of the properties. To supplement the kitchen furnishings for *The Three Wishes*, a miniature bird cage, pots, pans, baskets, and plates from Sarg's collection were requisitioned. The puppets were a little crude and unfinished compared with the properties, but they had style.

For the Pocci play the curtain rose on "a sunny knoll with a glimpse of red roofs in the valley below; bright butterflies flutter above the grass; a saucy molly cottontail bobs across the hillside. The personages of the play are four: a blue-smocked wood-chopper, his wife in mob-cap and panniers, the neighborhood gossip, a little man with a round paunch, and

Scene from The Shadowy Waters *at the Cleveland Play House. Ten-inch puppets gave the small stage an effect of vast space. After a photograph reproduced in* Joseph, A Book of Marionettes.

a fairy such as children dream of. A frisking woolly dog is perhaps the most engaging actor in the cast. This little play . . . is the most interesting of the three pieces presented, from the point of view of the critic of legitimate drama," wrote Anne Stoddard. The bill was presented for a short season at the Neighborhood Playhouse, New York, in November 1917. All the puppeteers were young women. They wore Rembrandt caps over their bobbed hair, and smocks, trousers, or pajamas, which set a tradition for picturesque work garb for puppet operators; it lasted many years.

For his second public presentation Sarg chose *The Rose and the Ring*, dramatized from Thackeray by Hettie Louise Mick, one of the Chicago Little Theatre puppeteers. (She became Mrs. John Martin just before she finished this piece of writing.) Ellen Van Volkenburg came from the West to direct the production, giving it the benefit of her puppet play experience and sure dramatic sense. Lilian Owen worked on the puppets and scenery. Charles Searle, who had helped with the shows in the Flatiron Building, built properties. Winthrop Parkhurst composed the music and played it at the performances. There were eleven a week, at the Punch and Judy Theatre, in April and May 1919. Afterward there were engagements in Detroit and Cleveland. On a 1920 tour the show got to Brattle Hall, Boston, playing on 11 March (playbill at Harvard).

There was a considerable degree of finish in the staging, I believe (I am told that I saw one of the New York performances, but for the life of me I can't recall anything but the second production of *The Rose and the Ring* with larger puppets a few seasons later), though a program

THE SHADOWY WATERS
BY WILLIAM B YEATS

Scene: The Deck of an Ancient Ship

Persons of the Play:
Forgael
Aibric
Sailors
Dectora

Readers:
Harry Mereine, Ralph Silver,
John L. Black, Ray W. Irvin,
Martha Jaeger

Manipulators:
Julia Flory, Emma Horwitz,
Blanche Nicola, Marion Morris,
Helen Joseph

Given under the direction of
Helen Joseph.
Settings and costumes designed by
John L. Black and executed
by Group members.
Incidental music
by Phillip Krumesc

THE SOVL OF CHOPIN
BY ALBERT GEHRING

Adapted from Liszt's "Life of Chopin".
Dedicated to Wilson G. Smith

Scene: Chopin's Study

Persons:
Chopin, Liszt, the Countess Potocka,
Chopin's Sister, Priest and Acolytes

Reader:
Karl Germain

Manipulators:
Betty Long, William J. Luck,
Elsa Weitz, Florence Cunnea

Given under the direction of
Virda Stewart.
Piano accompaniment by Pauline Weitz.
Settings and costumes designed by
Carl Broemel and executed
by Group members.
Cherubini's "Ave Maria" sung by
Mrs. Thomas J. Mizer.

*Program designed by John L. Black for two plays at the Cleveland Play House,
15 March, 1918. Original in the possession of Helen Haiman Joseph.*

note prepared the audience for backstage mishaps: "These strings are not always as well behaved as royal strings should be; they sometimes twist round each other. Should so dire a thing as a tangle occur, and a marionette consequently wind his right leg around his left ear, the curtain will drop a moment to hide his marionette spasm, and rise again an instant later when all is once more fair!" The showman of the older order would have blushed at the admission of such a possibility; to him strings just *couldn't* tangle during a show. And it must be said that most of the showmen of the newer order are no longer so easily defeated by mere strings.

There was certainly finish in the action and in the dramatic use of voices. The play was well suited to puppets and well written. The test was in its popularity. The first puppets, inadequately made, were replaced with a new set; the play outlasted its accoutrement. Compared with the shows of the older school, Sarg's was superior in so many ways that it threw the fading tradition completely into shadow. It set up an ideal for American puppetry: a good play, as a rule based on a familiar tale, with all production details carefully worked out and integrated. Puppets, scenery, lights, properties, and even the printed program, exhibited artistry.

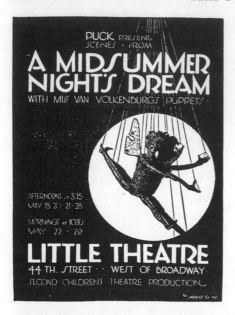

*Poster for a New York appearance of the
Chicago Little Theatre puppets, 1920.
Original 9¾ x 12¾ inches.*

After his first public production, Sarg no longer took time to act as a puppeteer. His work was limited to designing and supervision. But no matter who carried out the production details, the impress of his personality was evident. His bent for gaiety and humor, his love of odd effects, animals, and the marvelous, found just the right combination with Ellen Van Volkenburg's power to achieve dramatic intensity. Even after the collaboration, Sarg's shows retained something of this intensity. At times it was weakened by emphasis upon the merely bizarre. But Sarg's productions, in their earlier years, were almost always good entertainment. They made an impression wherever they were seen. They set people's fingers itching to make puppets for themselves.

From among those who worked with him, either as students, puppet makers, or puppeteers, came scores who branched out for themselves in puppetry. His influence was strong on many professional puppeteers who had merely seen his shows. He trained for careers of their own such producers as Lilian Owen (Thompson), Wilson (Bobby) Fulton, Rachel Sewall, Jean Gros, Helen Lyvers, Sue Hastings (who studied with him but was never a puppeteer in a company of his), Richard Odlin, Harold Hestwood, Bil Baird, Margaret Skewis (Rose), Herbert M. Dawley, Rufus Rose, and David Pritchard. Many of his puppeteers went to work for other companies, while some who had started out on their own—Donald Cordry, for instance—or who had had experience with other companies, gravitated to him.

JONY SARG'S MARIONETTES

These uncanny little wooden-headed actors, direct from three seasons on Broadway, present the quaintest, most novel and artistic entertainment imaginable. Operated by more than four hundred invisible strings, they dance, sing, play the piano, smoke, play ball, ride prancing chargers and do a host of other things—just like real people. Lovely miniature stage sets with elaborate lighting and scenic effects and specially arranged music add to the charm of the performance.

IN

RIP VAN WINKLE
by WASHINGTON IRVING

Poster for Sarg's Rip Van Winkle, *first produced in 1921 and revived in 1929. Original 28 x 40 inches.*

Everyone who knew Sarg was won by his boyish smile, his pleasantly modulated voice (with more than a trace of English accent), his ability to be gracious, and his indomitable enthusiasm. Because his name cropped up everywhere it was felt that he must be the most successful of artists. But he was sometimes in financial quicksands; he made money hand over fist on one project and lost it on the next. It is doubtful whether his puppet company was ever his most profitable enterprise, though it was his most publicized, but at any rate, it paid for itself and yielded him thousands of dollars' worth of newspaper lineage.

On the morning of his sixtieth birthday, 21 April 1940 (according to *Who's Who* he should have been only fifty-eight), he was presented with a portfolio containing greetings from many American puppeteers, including some of those who had been in his companies. He dropped his work and, as he turned over the sheets and recognized the names, tears filled his eyes. Only occasionally can a man look back upon his accomplishments at sixty and see the extent of his influence. On 7 March 1942 Tony Sarg was dead. His estate was involved in bankruptcy. What puppets he still had (his last company manager had been obliged to keep the material of his road show in lieu of back salary) were sold off precipitously. Some of them were purchased by Cedric Head for his collection.

Sarg's Professor Herkimer, a comic pi-anist in the old vaudeville tradition, used for studio parties. After a photograph reproduced in Current Opinion, *July 1916, p. 29.*

But because old puppets had always been remade into new ones (save for a few of the *Alice in Wonderland* set, with heads carved of wood after the Tenniel illustrations) there were few left. Sarg's work must be remembered chiefly through memories of his shows, his *Rip Van Winkle* with Charles Searle's moving characterization of the title role, his swash-buckling *Treasure Island,* his *Alice* with Elsie Devorak, the very personi-fication of Lewis Carroll's little girl, appearing in person where she grew big and managing the Alice puppet in other scenes, his competent 1931-1932 *Rose and the Ring,* and his *Mikado* with Denise Dooley working three puppets and singing the "Three Little Maids" trio all by herself—because she was the only girl puppeteer.

There were, of course, other forces in the revival of puppetry besides the work of Sarg. Raymond O'Neil, director of the Cleveland Play House, an adherent to the beliefs of Gordon Craig, suggested that puppets be part of the activity of that theatre when it was still a nebulously or-ganized amateur group. Accordingly a shadow-figure play, *Seven at a Blow,* was given in 1915. *The Death of Tintagiles* by Maeterlinck was produced with 10-inch stuffed cloth string-puppets in 1917. This was followed by *Shadowy Waters* by William Butler Yeats and *The Death*

Prince Bulbo in bed. Sarg's Rose and the Ring. *The furniture and properties were perhaps more meticulously made than the puppets. After a photograph reproduced in* Literary Digest, *17 May 1919.*

Scene from A Night in Delhi *as given at studio parties in the Flatiron Building, New York, by Tony Sarg in 1916. After a photograph.*

of Chopin, a pantomime to Chopin music, both with puppets of the same type. Helen Haiman Joseph was the director. So small were the puppets that facial features and movements were simplified to a minimum. In such dramas of inaction the slightest gesture was telling. This work, seen by but a few, had its effects in firing Helen Haiman Joseph to write the first modern English history of puppets (which in turn made many other enthusiasts) and to organize a company of her own. For many years it used hand-puppets as skillfully as any troupe in the eastern United States, both for children's performances in schools and for advertising. The Play House shows also had their influence on the Cleveland schools (Winifred Mills, a teacher, and Louise Dunn, a museum director of education, wrote the first comprehensive American book on puppet making, *Marionettes, Masks and Shadows*, New York, 1927) and at the Cleveland Museum of Art, which included puppetry in their programs.

Sarg's studio at 54 West 9 Street, New York, drawn from life with due playfulness. Here Sarg, assisted by Charles Searle, gave his summer course in puppet making for the first time in 1922.

In 1914 Remo Bufano, a youngster with vivid impressions of Paladin puppets, had put on his own version of *Orlando Furioso* in Richmond Hill House, New York. Growing up, he became a professional puppeteer and played pieces by Alfred Kreymborg, Edna St. Vincent Millay, Schnitzler, and other Greenwich Village dramatists of the time. In fact, Kreymborg got from Bufano the two puppets that Mrs. Kreymborg manipulated as the author read his own *Lima Beans* (included in his *Plays for Puppets*); this was done on a coast-to-coast tour in 1920. Jack Tworkov, one of the partners of the Mojacot Spiel, a Yiddish puppet troupe that traveled in Europe as well as the United States, gained his skill with hand-puppets while working with Bufano. A. Spolidoro, long a right-hand man of Bufano's, was later a partner of the Suzari Marionettes and director of puppet shows for the New York City Department of Parks, taking a stage built onto a truck from park to park so that thousands of children could see plays in their own neighborhoods.

I recall vividly what an expert hand-puppet showman Bufano himself was when he gave a performance of a later version of his *Orlando* for a special Theatre Guild matinee about 1923; the vigor with which the dragon was slain, and the slow death of that creature (named Amoroso),

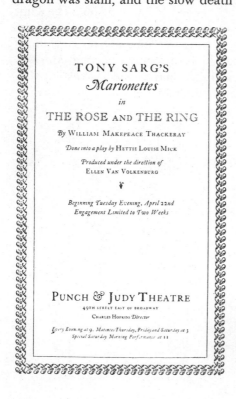

Cover of the program for a New York run in 1919. Typographically and textually it is delightful. Original in the Harvard College Library theatre collection.

Cover of the prospectus for a course in puppet making. Original 5¾ x 9 inches.

to the last convulsion of the tip of its tail, held the sophisticated audience spellbound.

Because Bufano seldom traveled outside New York City he was never so well known as Sarg. But the range of his work was far wider; he was always attempting the experimental. In the construction of his puppets he did not care too much for polish; the figures were dashed off, designed for an effect, and seldom used long enough to warrant painstaking craftsmanship. He was called in for the special puppets needed in such plays as Rostand's *Last Night of Don Juan*; he made puppets for the Walrus and the Carpenter scene in *Alice in Wonderland* for Eva LeGallienne's Civic Repertory Theatre production in 1935 and its Art Repertory Theatre revival in 1946. He made life-sized puppets of Don Quixote, Sancho Panza, and Pedro's Boy to use with puppet-sized puppets in a 1924 production of Manuel de Falla's *El Retablo de Maese Pedro* at Town Hall. He made 10-foot puppets, controlled with strings from above and rods from below, for a production of Stravinsky's oratorio, *Oedipus King*, in 1931. He made 12-foot puppets, operated on a 30-foot turntable stage, for the production, *From Sorcery to Science*, in the Hall of Pharmacy at the New York World's Fair in 1939, and he did a 35-foot telescoping clown for *Jumbo* in 1935.

He produced Em Jo Basshe's *Fantasy in Flutes*, using marionettes representing algebraic symbols, together with actors, in a studio performance in 1926. He did *Pinocchio* with a mixture of puppet and human actors at Richmond Hill House in 1927. He presented seasons of puppet plays at the Provincetown Playhouse in 1928 and later years. He played at the Thimble Theatre, perhaps New York's smallest playhouse, at Fifth Avenue and Eighth Street, and at the Galerie Au Sacre du Printemps in

Bufano's 35-foot telescoping clown never stood beside John Carter Ford's 31-foot figure, made in 1932 for a San Francisco Bohemian Club play and worked from a crow's nest 75 feet up in a redwood tree (it was destroyed immediately after the performance and the clown was made in 1935), but if it had they would have looked like this, towering over a 6-foot man. From photographs.

Paris. He went to Europe on another occasion to study puppets on a Guggenheim fellowship. He has written a book on puppet making, *Be a Puppet Showman* (New York, 1933), and a book of excellent puppet plays, *Magic Strings* (New York, 1939). He was director of New York's huge WPA puppet project for at least half of its stormy existence. Always ably assisted by his wife, Florence Koehler, he has engaged indefatigably in all sorts of puppet activities.

Perry Dilley, who began to work with puppets in San Francisco in 1919, and who has used hand-puppets almost exclusively (he made a set of string-puppets for Ellen Van Volkenburg's 1924 revival of her production of *A Midsummer Night's Dream*), made his influence felt in the revival on the West Coast. His productions were a yearly event at the University of California, and his studio on Montgomery Street was the gathering place for puppeteers from far and wide. His puppets had a stylized realism; he tended to choose fantastic plays; and he has played for audiences of adults as often as children.

Mathurin Dondo, a professor of French, did three plays in French at Smith College, Northampton, Massachusetts, in connection with his teaching in 1918; coming to Columbia College, he devised and patented rod-puppets that ran on bars across the stage. With them he directed, using students for puppeteers, two medieval French farces in English versions of his own: *Two Blind Men and a Donkey* and *The Wash Tub*. One day I was crossing South Court; a friend hailed me and asked, "Want to be in a puppet show?" Without an instant's hesitation I said, "Sure. Where?" "In the attic of Philosophy Hall." We climbed to that appropriate eyrie for puppets (Brander Matthews' theatrical collection, including some French hand-puppets he had bought in Paris in 1867, was housed there)

Remo Bufano with two of his ordinary-size hand-puppets and a ten-foot string-puppet, made of molded paper over a wooden framework and controlled by three bars (here on the floor). After a photograph.

and I was assigned the role of one of the blind men. That is how I happened to make my debut as a puppeteer; a performance was given in Earl Hall on 16 May 1922.

At this time Mrs. Dondo opened a shop for the sale of puppets, puppet stages, and equipment at 145 West 45th Street in midtown New York. It was an excellent idea, but there was not sufficient patronage to support it. Dondo went to the University of California a year or so later and packed his puppets away. But his work was not without effect. When I built the first puppet production of my own six years later, I chose to do a Nativity play with rod-puppets. I used a much simpler sort than Dondo's. Mine had two discs on their supporting rod by which they could be fixed in position on one of the wooden bars across the stage; but they could also move freely between the bars. There were three manipulating rods to their head and arms—umbrella ribs, a discovery that others have found usable too.

There was another college group of puppeteers in 1922, founded by G. Fletcher Clark at the University of California before Dondo's arrival. *The Singing Master* and Marlowe's *Faustus* were produced with hand-puppets inspired by Perry Dilley's.

In 1935 the English translation of Nina Efimova's *Adventures of a Russian Puppet Theatre* appeared (Birmingham, Michigan). In it were described the hand-and-rod puppets which the author had invented. Marjorie Batchelder produced Edgar Caper's *St. George and the Dragon*

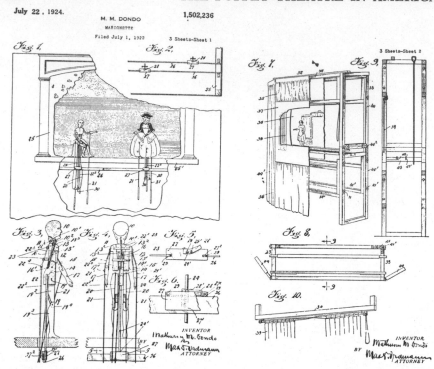

Plates from Mathurin Dondo's patent for a rod-puppet to be moved on bars parallel with the proscenium of the stage, filed 1 July 1922.

with rod-puppets in January, and a piece from Perry Dilley's repertory, *Columbine's Birthday* by Grace Stearns, with hand-and-rod puppets in May 1936; both plays were shown at the First American Puppetry Conference in Detroit in July that year, when Miss Batchelder also gave a talk on rod-puppets (the text is to be found in *Puppetry 1936*, p. 36). Though there had been a few sporadic uses of rods for puppet manipulation before this, in addition to my production of *Noël* which was revived every year at holiday time until 1934, the rod-puppet began to receive attention only after Miss Batchelder's enthusiastic advocacy of it. Roy Patton designed and made rod-puppets for the Tatterman Marionettes' *Ferdinand* in 1939. Ernest Wolff used rod-puppets moving in slots in the stage, as had David Dodd for private performances in 1929, to interpret opera recordings in the Gas Industries Building at the New York World's Fair in 1939; this type was used in the Kungsholm Restaurant operas in Chicago.

Miss Batchelder concentrated on the rod-puppet. She gave an impres-

Linoleum-cut poster for a performance by Columbia College students with Dondo's rod-puppets, 1922. This was the author's first public puppet performance—and linoleum-cut poster. Original 11 x 22 inches.

sive performance of Maeterlinck's *The Death of Tintagiles*, with the puppet booth in the form of a medieval castle and the acting areas on its ramparts, towers, and ramps, in 1937. Her students at Ohio State University conducted studies and experiments with the type. She wrote her doctoral thesis on their history and technique in 1942 (published as *Rod-Puppets and the Human Theatre*, Columbus, 1947). A further study, in collaboration with Vivian Michael, *Hand-and-Rod Puppets*, also was published at Columbus in 1947. Rod-puppets have been found suitable for restrained or exaggerated action; they can have all the form and articulation of string-puppets without requiring a stage with a bridge or a high ceiling on that account; they can be handled more easily by children than either hand- or string-puppets. The trend toward greater and greater use of the type is evident.

String-puppets have won the greatest number of followers, not because there is anything to recommend the type above all others, but because they were most often seen to advantage in the productions of Tony Sarg and Ellen Van Volkenburg and the school that they founded. Hand-puppets were skillfully handled by Remo Bufano, Helen Haiman Joseph, Perry Dilley, and others whose work was not so widely seen; there was no strong movement, however, that made the use of the hand-puppet conspicuous. Rod-puppets have stirred up interest for their novelty and adaptability. Both hand-puppets and rod-puppets require less of a stage

Aug. 17, 1943.   E. T. WOLFF ET AL   2,327,234
                        PUPPET SHOW
              Filed Nov. 22, 1942   5 Sheets-Sheet 2

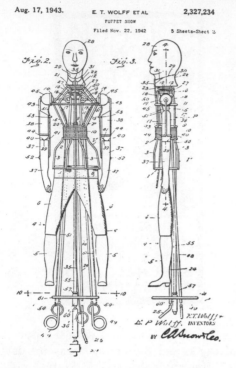

Puppeteers operating the Wolff puppets from below the stage. After a photograph.

Plate from a patent granted Esther T. and Ernest Wolff for a rod-puppet to work in slots in a stage. The wire cage of the body is filled with the wires which govern the movements. Puppets of this type have been used largely for performances of operas, wherein the gestures are stylized and limited.

than string-puppets, which is a distinct advantage. During travel restrictions in World War II many puppeteers changed to them because they could be shown over a simple screen, as string-puppet acts discarded their stage altogether. The shadow-figure has been used occasionally by others, but only in the Chinese programs of Pauline Benton has it been consistently put forward. It remains for someone to use it in such a way that it will catch the fancy of numbers of performers.

In the United States, it has been seen, the revival of puppetry as an inventive art was due to the work of a handful of pioneers and to the appearance of a dozen stimulating books. The ensuing growth of puppet activity may be attributed to many factors which will be mentioned presently.

In Canada a trickle of visiting companies as well as the books of the 1920's set the stage for the revival. In 1923 the first production of the new era was seen at Hamilton, Ontario, when Rosalynde F. Osborne (Stern) staged *Punch and Judy of Long Ago* with hand-puppets, hoping to bridge the gap between the Punch shows familiar to most British Canadians and the newer puppetry in this play by Mary Stewart. Miss Osborne had worked with Lilian Owen, in whose show she puppeteered

Rod-puppets of bird characters by Marjorie Batchelder for Danny Duck's Dizzy Day. *Umbrella ribs make excellent control rods, having an eye at one end for attaching and being painted black.*
After a photograph.

at Gloucester, Massachusetts. She later gave many lectures on puppet history and technique, wrote a puppet page in *Curtain Call*, a Canadian theatre magazine, produced Aristophanes' *Clouds* with string-puppets at McMaster University, and organized the first Canadian puppet conference at Hamilton in May 1939. In 1925 Dave Keogh of Toronto began to work with string-puppets. Thereafter there were many companies. That of Muriel Heddle, who had been a partner of Keogh, toured not only in Canada but in the United States. Because of the size of the country and the distances between its cities, touring in Canada is difficult; it may be for that reason that Canadian puppetry has grown slowly.

In Mexico in 1929 Bernardo Ortiz de Montellano, Julio Castellanos, and Louis Bunin (the last an American), under the patronage of the Department of Fine Arts, set up a theatre in the Escuela del Estudiante Indigena, dramatizing Mexican folk tales and using simply made string-puppets. Puppet work continued under government support in later years as an educative tool. In 1929 Montellano founded the artistic Teatro del Peri-

Bronze and silver dancers by Rosalynde Osborne Stern.

Greta and Jack, hand-puppets by Alfredo Hermitte of Buenos Aires. After a photograph by Saderman.

Traveling cart and Maese Trotamundos and Devil of Javier Villafañe.

quillo, which performed in the parks and playgrounds of Mexico City. Regular hand-puppet troupes have been maintained by the Ministry of Education since 1932. The Teatro Rin-Rin, at first directed by Germán Cueto, was taken over in 1934 by Roberto Lago, renamed the Teatro Nahual, and operated by him thereafter. It was active in such campaigns as that against illiteracy.

In Argentina in 1935 Javier Villafañe, a young government employee, persuaded his superior that he was not needed particularly at his desk, but that he would be much more useful if he took a puppet show out to perform poetic pieces for school children. The superior kept him on a salary while he set out from Buenos Aires, with Juan Pedro Ramos as a partner, in a horse-drawn wagon for a year's tour among the towns and villages of the country. Wherever he went his hand-puppet theatre, La Andariega, was enthusiastically received; the school children answered its stimulus by starting puppet shows of their own. The next year he made another tour, this time taking Liber Fridman the painter along. They canoed on the rivers of Paraguay and Uruguay with their pack of puppet equipment. Upon their return Fridman built a show of his own. And so have many of Villafañe's subsequent helpers. Mauricio Lasansky the print maker helped him establish puppet theatres in the schools of the province of Córdoba. The Council of Education of that province has put puppet making in the curriculum of the elementary schools.

Later tours took Villafañe to Chile and Brazil. He stayed at each school where he performed long enough to get a puppet group started. As a

American puppeteers travel with their equipment in small motor trucks. Here are the Yale Puppeteers in their itinerant days, about 1930, posing in velveteen trousers and satin blouses before their Ford. After a photograph.

result the countries of southern South America teem with young puppeteers. He has published *Títeres de la Andariega* (Buenos Aires, 1936), *Teatro de títeres* (a book of plays, Buenos Aires, 1943), and *Los Niños y los títeres* (Buenos Aires, 1944), as well as newspaper and magazine articles on puppetry, sharing the pen name Alfredo Dolver with Dr. Alfredo Hermitte, an amateur and enthusiast who accompanied him on a short tour and gave performances of his own in the capital. Because of his activity the hand-puppet has come into its own; the Italian Paladins, though known to these newer puppeteers, have not converted them to string-puppets.

In Peru, Amadeo de la Torre, sculptor and caricaturist, was giving performances in 1937; there were two other puppeteers who gave shows for children in private homes; but there is no puppet movement of any importance.

Thus the revival has spread pretty widely through the Americas, and may be expected to produce a continuing growth of interest in puppetry.

2. The Traveling Show

Puppets have always needed less baggage than any other kind of show with as much scenic effect. They have therefore reached remote corners before the bigger theatre could get there—sometimes corners the bigger theatre never reached at all. Much of the modern excitement with puppets has been stimulated by traveling shows. School children from coast to coast in the United States have seen puppets, either one of the important companies that crosses the continent, a local company, or some little show of their own. That generation which was in school in the 1920's grew up knowing about puppets. It is doubtful if many adults in their thirties and forties can admit not having seen them. All this may be credited to the peregrinating troupe.

When Tony Sarg produced his first professional show he contemplated a New York run but not a trip on the road. He had chosen all young women as puppeteers. Who was to do the heavy work of tearing down and re-erecting the stage, lifting the puppet trunks, and loading the outfit

A double-bridge stage used by Tony Sarg's company for tours of Alice in Wonderland, The Mikado, *and other plays.*

on a truck? Stagehands or teamsters could do it, of course, but their
services were expensive. It may have been hoped that a metropolitan run
would pay the production costs of a show. This hope was forlorn. If a
show were well staged, it would be bound to cost money; if the money
were to be recovered and a profit made, since no city had a large enough
audience to keep a play running long, other cities would have to be
visited. It was found that there were well-paying dates for one or two
performances in each of the larger cities. But one-night stands were not
feasible when the jumps between them were long. So the traveling show
eventually found that if it went to its audiences, playing in the schools,
it could do several performances in each city, and one or two in the
smallest towns. These shows brought little; the children paid only a
nickel or a dime; but there were enough of them to keep an energetic
company busy all the school year.

    After a few explorative shows in Detroit, Cleveland, and Boston, Sarg
got into the routine of touring widely every season. Ernest Briggs, a
concert booker, handled the details of getting the engagements. Charles

Lilian Owen's Marionettes

Announcement, Lilian Owen's Marionettes.

Searle went out with the show as company manager in the earlier years. There were six or seven in the company at first; the fee for a performance was $500. This was all whittled down, by 1930, to a company of three or four and a fee of $100, or less if two performances were given in the same auditorium.

The offshoots of Sarg's troupes were generally too new and unknown to command fees such as his; the shows of his puppeteers who formed companies of their own were generally less ambitious in scale than his, were able to underbid him, but played in smaller places; thus they were not strongly competitive. After finding a scattering of engagements in New York and Massachusetts in 1924, Bobby Fulton confined his activities to the New Jersey region, touring extensively in the suburban communities of the state; he still did solo shows in 1947. Rachel Sewall joined forces with Lilian Owen for a while, then made independent tours in Ohio and Michigan for a few seasons starting in 1923. Jean Gros did a puppet version of *I Pagliacci* in Pittsburgh in 1922, then made annual tours of the Middle West and West with large productions such as *Babes in Toyland* with Victor Herbert music, Shakespeare's *A Midsummer Night's Dream*, and Maeterlinck's *The Blue Bird*. Lilian Owen and her husband William Thompson made the puppets for some of these productions, so they were very much in the Sarg manner. Sue Hastings' initial piece was a travesty of *Uncle Tom's Cabin* (Harry Deaves had done one in Chicago a half-century before) after she had studied in a

Musicians by Lilian Owen Thompson for Jean Gros' production, The Magical Land
of Oz.

class of Sarg's in 1923. Her performances consisted of variety bills of
short pieces which she presented in the New York region; later she sent
out companies both on tours and for holiday-season engagements at department stores throughout the country. Harold and Robert Hestwood,
whose puppets were beautifully designed and made, did a bird pantomime, *The Gawpy Ballet,* in California in 1928; later they joined Jean
Gros on a transcontinental tour. Rufus Rose and Margaret Skewis, who
met while playing in a Sarg company, married and began with a tour of
New England with *Dick Whittington* in 1931. Later they were to play
in wide tours.

Ellen Galpin produced shows for the Los Angeles Playground Department in 1922. In 1925 she toured in Alaska, even making an Eskimo version of the Cinderella story with the help of Eskimo women and carrying
it in a pack on her back for 1500 miles over the snow to the nearest white
settlement. In 1928 she played in Hawaii. William Duncan and Edward
Mabley, Detroit boys, met at an exhibition of model stages in which
each had an entry. They joined to found the Tatterman Marionettes,
gave their first production, *The King of the Golden River,* in the Detroit
schools in 1923, toured more and more widely, and soon were playing
from coast to coast. One of the most alert of the younger companies, their
productions showed more care, artistry, and business sense than Sarg's,
and were obviously better than his in all details but design in the early
1930's. After that they added excellent designers too, and reached the
peak of their career with an imaginative large-scale production of Ibsen's
Peer Gynt in 1937. This unfortunately had a short tour, but it visited
half a dozen cities where the incidental music by Grieg was played by
local symphony orchestras.

Fannie Goldsmith Engle and George W. Kegg played up and down
the West Coast with *Cinderella* in 1923 and *The Nightingale* in 1927.

The flight, from the Stevens' Nativity.

Anne Hardy and George New seen back-stage in their Puppet Caravan.

Characters from Rufus Rose's Noah's Ark.

Anthony and Cleopatra, from the Stevens production.

Puppets from Rufus Rose's Pinocchio.　*Blowing up the clown's balloon with a bicycle pump on the bridge is hot work; Rufus Rose and assistant. After a snapshot, 1941.*

Harry Burnett and Forman Brown began as The Puppeteers of the University of Michigan, barnstorming with Ann Arbor as a base in 1923. Going to Yale University for the theatre courses, they became The Puppeteers of Yale University for summer tours of New England. Richard Brandon made the third member of the triumvirate at Yale. Soon the title was shortened to The Yale Puppeteers. After tours back and forth across the continent (they were the first to drop front masking—really to lighten baggage—attention was directed to the puppets by spotlighting them and keeping puppeteers in the dark) and valiant attempts to set up permanent theatres in Los Angeles and New York, their efforts at last were rewarded in the Turnabout Theatre in Los Angeles.

With the 1930's came still other new companies, the Stevens Marionettes, Basil Milovsoroff's Folk Tale Marionettes, the Proctor Puppets, the Domino Marionettes (a summer lark of college students), Bernard Paul, Robert and Edith Williams, the Kingsland Marionettes, C. Ray Smith, Franc Still, and others listed in the next chapter, which toured more or less extensively. So long as panel-delivery trucks and station wagons (the favorite vehicles for transporting puppeteers and puppet equipment in one load) could be had and fuel was abundant, puppets followed all the highroads and byways of the United States. But with the incidence of wartime shortages this activity was curtailed. Many puppeteers went into the armed forces or war work. Those who continued as puppeteers were forced to simplify their equipment, perhaps to travel by train. This brought about the stageless floorshow, which was a reversion to old vaudeville turns, done, however, with the puppeteer as a feature of the act, and sometimes with no setting or platform at all.

After the war traveling began once more. It will probably continue in a country with few communities large enough to support permanent puppet theatres. Thus will puppetry perpetuate itself: shows will come as a novelty and a delight to those who have never seen one before, and stimulate them to create puppets of their own.

3. The Fixed Playhouse

Numerous as are the advantages of taking a puppet show to its audience, there are certainly as many in staying in a fixed spot and getting the audience to come to it. A permanent auditorium may be chosen with proper sight lines, acoustics, and lighting facilities; those who have played in school and other auditoriums throughout America can testify that almost all of them lack the fundamentals of comfort in these items. They seem to have been designed by architects, and approved by school boards and civic bodies, who have never seen a theatre or heard of its functions. In a permanent theatre the stage may be large and solid; it doesn't have to be torn down and hauled away after each performance. The lighting equipment may be more than a bare minimum. The puppets can hang undisturbed, without the wear and tear of packing. Rehearsals

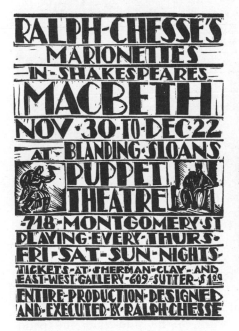
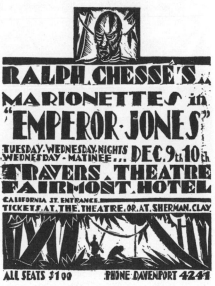

Linoleum-cut playbills by Ralph Chessé for his productions in San Francisco.

View backstage at the Yale Puppeteers' Teatro Torito, Los Angeles, from a wood-engraving by Gustave Baumann, 1931. Original 7 x 8 inches.

may be held in the same hall where the show is to be seen, so that they can approximate an actual performance in voice intensity, lighting strength, and other details. But with a fixed playhouse in most cities the show must be changed frequently in order to keep audiences coming; there must be repertory; the time the puppeteers save in packing and traveling must be put into building and practicing new things. Puppeteers would rather have this stimulating work, to be sure, than the plain physical labor of tearing down and setting up.

Paul Walton, of the team of Walton and
O'Rourke, draws a crowd by working a
puppet outside the theatre at 21 Olvera
Street, Los Angeles, training ground for
many puppeteers, in 1938.

Blanding Sloan's studio theatre at 2625
Polk Street, San Francisco, about 1930.
From a linoleum cut by Blanding Sloan.

Such a fixed theatre as that of Papa Schmid in Munich, or of one in an
artist's studio, has always been the ideal toward which puppeteers of the
revival aspired. Sarg made no preparations for travel at first. Bufano
played in his studio or in a theatre throughout a season. Ellen Van Volken-
burg's puppets were sheltered under the roof of the Chicago Little
Theatre. Edith Flack Ackley gave studio shows from 1923 onward. Bland-
ing Sloan made a theatre out of an old warehouse at 718 Montgomery
Street, not far from Perry Dilley's studio, in San Francisco, in 1928
("Reminiscence of the Blanding Sloan Puppet Theatre," by R. Bruce
Inverarity, *Puppetry 1930*, p. 33). In it Ralph Chessé first staged his
Hamlet. Later he set up his own theatre at 566 Merchant Street and other
San Francisco addresses. The Yale Puppeteers had their Teatro Torito in
Los Angeles. Olvera Street in that city had puppet theatres in at least two
locations, occupied by half a dozen companies. From these companies
stemmed a dozen other companies or solo puppeteers. Catherine
Reighard's Puppet Players had a studio for regular performances in 1931.
Meyer Levin gave seasons of plays in the Relic House, Chicago, in 1926
and 1927; this remarkable building had walls made of the rubble, molten
glass, and charred remains of the Chicago fire of 1871. Helen Smiley
fitted up a handsome little theatre in an old Philadelphia stable in the
1930's. I myself managed to stay in one location at least for a season at a
time; my last Detroit seasons were in a little auditorium in the Artisan
Guild, which occupied the disused administration building of the old

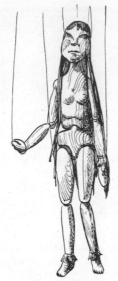

Eve, from Blanding Sloan's production of Heavenly Discourse *by* Charles Erskine Scott Wood.

Announcement from Catherine Reighard's studio theatre, New York.

Ford factory in Highland Park; previously I had been in an art museum, a hotel lobby, the ballroom of a mansion fallen to a boarding house, and a little theatre made out of a night club. Romain Proctor's theatre in Springfield, Illinois, was a refurbished movie house. The puppets holed into almost anything with four walls. Of course there were many studio, school, club, and home puppet theatres in established quarters.

The inestimable value of a fixed playhouse is to enable people to find it when they want to see a show. The question is always being asked, "Where can I see a good puppet show?" Even those who know of them can seldom answer; puppets play one night in a parish house, the next afternoon in a suburban school, and the following week they are a hundred miles away. The somewhat rudimentary variety shows to be found in department stores for a month before Christmas are often the only ones that puppet seekers discover. Many potential puppet fans never get to see a show unless they visit Europe—or Los Angeles, where the Turnabout Theatre has been running nightly for many years.

"A House for Puppet Drama" (*Puppetry 1931*, p. 77) was a visionary project, still unrealized, of a specially built structure to seat 150; it had ample work and stage space, an exhibit hall, and a library, with ground coverage of less than 50 feet square. "This little house," I wrote, "pre-

Scene from Brother Jeromy *as drawn from the production in his studio theatre by W. A. Dwiggins, Hingham Center, Massachusetts, about 1940. By courtesy of G. Gehman and Millard D. Taylor, who printed the play at their private press in Stoneham, Massachusetts, in 1944.*

supposes some moving spirit—an artist who can make and produce fine puppet shows with a minimum of outside assistance—and an artist who is eloquent enough to fire his group with ardor. It will necessarily be small; money profit will not be its aim." Such a small theatre would have to receive civic support. It might be connected with a school or college. It might even be maintained by a club; club buildings have been erected by groups with even more specialized interests.

The tendency of puppeteers is to build studios in their homes, where small audiences can be accommodated upon occasion. W. A. Dwiggins of Hingham Center, Massachusetts, has an admirable studio with his puppet stage in it. The living room of my parents' house in Birmingham, Michigan, held my stage and an audience of eighty; the ceiling height was calculated for string-puppet operation. Rufus Rose has a studio home in Waterford, Connecticut, where he played host to a national gathering of puppeteers on the occasion of a conference of the Puppeteers of America in 1946. Basil Milovsoroff also has a studio in his home at Thetford Center, Vermont. Olga and Martin Stevens give regular seasons of per-

Made over from a disused neighborhood movie theatre (too small for today's super-cinemas), Romain Proctor's puppet theatre in Springfield, Illinois, was very agreeably housed. About 1935. After a photograph.

formances in their home studio at Middlebury, Indiana. It is notable that none of these studios is in a city.

A city puppet theatre, operated as a regular place of amusement, would have to conform to building codes and observe fire precautions; it would probably be subject to union electricians, musicians, and stage-hands. Obviously its cost of operation would be prohibitive. It could, however, get along under the guise of a club; it could be attached to a restaurant. When somebody really wants a city puppet theatre, he will have the ingenuity to overcome all these obstacles to get it.

4. In Education

The theory that it was desirable for children to learn through seeing puppet shows with historical or literary content, or even to gain manual skills through building them, was expressed by educators just before the artistic revival of puppetry. The dawn of the revival may have given even a progressive teacher misgivings, for the shows performed for special audiences, sometimes in studios and sometimes in little theatres, had little of the verve of the Paladin theatre (puppeteers were too concerned with their strings to develop a brisk tempo); they chose avant-garde plays and décor; in short, they would have bored children. It was only after the revival was in full swing that the theory became practice. And then it was forced upon the schools because children had an irresistible urge to re-create the lively doings of the puppets they had just seen in their assembly hall, or teachers themselves had fallen in love with puppetry.

Elnora Whitman's study, *The Dramatic Instinct in Education* (Boston, 1914), conceded that the puppet play "could be brought to school." She would "scarcely advocate its introduction as mere entertainment." She felt that some subjects might, however, "be vivified and made more interesting" on the puppet stage. For older children, producing a puppet

Suzette and Paul Gauguin, characters by Cherry Barr Jerry for Van Gogh and Gauguin, *Grand Rapids Art Museum, 1936.*

play would afford training in the use of words, voices, and hands. She even hoped that puppet theatres "run on high and artistic principles" might become part of playgrounds, boys' clubs, parks, and recreation places as a civic institution. She had a prophetic sense. All this has come to pass.

It had been a custom for small traveling shows such as that of Peter Hauntz in Pennsylvania to visit schools. Punch and Judy men found them a haven when cold weather set in. I fear that these shows were all "mere entertainment," though some of them had dramatic themes drawn from the Bible or folklore which were consonant with what the pupil was expected to read. No one had any notion that these shows were more than a surcease from the tedium of lessons. It is remarkable that teachers who saw how raptly the children watched them did not perceive that the showman's educative techniques were better than their own.

A few teachers, notably Arthur M. Charles at Earlham College who gave German puppet plays to illustrate his course in the Faustus story, had the courage to introduce puppetry before 1914; in this case, puppets were so mingled with the subject taught, because of Goethe and his interest in them, that no dean or supervisor could have objected. For an elementary grade teacher to have taken class time to show a puppet play of Columbus or *The Legend of Sleepy Hollow* would then have been to risk discharge.

It was easier for puppets to penetrate education under the pretext of keeping the children off the streets. Settlement houses encouraged them, as has been noted from the boyhood activity of Remo Bufano, for recreation. Boys' clubs took them up. At the Madison Square Boys' Club,

Marionettes of sponge rubber for Shen of the Sea, *made by children in the Saturday morning design class at the Metropolitan Museum of Art, New York. After a photograph reproduced in* School Arts, *October 1936, p. 120.*

because of the direction of Albert B. Hines, puppet shows started as early as 1926. Sue Hastings, Otto Kunze, and others have been the coaches.

But where puppetry was introduced by an enthusiast, the warmth of its reception assured its remaining year after year. Certain elementary and secondary schools, thanks to the efforts of teachers who continued to encourage the use of puppets, have seen puppet shows, both those of the students and of visiting professional companies, for over two decades. Many schools and colleges have offered courses in puppet making, which have trained teachers to use puppetry, since the early 1930's. When Emma Pettey conducted a survey, "Puppetry in American Schools and Colleges" (*Puppeteers of American Pamphlets* No. 3, Columbus, 1941), she found thirty-five institutions that offered accredited courses; many had been doing so for ten years or more. Among them were the Chicago Art Institute, Columbia University Teachers College, Hunter College of the City of New York, New York University School of Education, Ohio State University College of Education, the University of Washington, and Wayne University College of Education. There were many other colleges that had nonaccredited puppet workshops as an extracurricular activity. The greatest number of these courses were given in art departments; some appeared in education, English, language, and speech departments.

Miss Pettey reported, "Puppetry is faring better in the hands of the colleges than in those of elementary institutions. In the colleges it is treated as a subject to be studied not only for itself but as an enrichment of other . . . courses. . . . In schools the puppet serves the arts rather than the arts the puppet, as in the professional show. The teacher thinks of it

Nativity play by children at Dr. Gabriel Carrasco school, Rosario, Argentina.

not so much as puppetry as visual education, or costume, or therapy, or social science. Therefore showmanship may easily become secondary in college puppetry, or even take third place, since the development of the student, regardless of whether his participation adds to or detracts from the show, must come first; and next must come the demands of the subject which the puppet is serving. Yet the fact is indisputable that if we turn to drama in any form, puppet or stage, we cannot ignore its prime force, which is expert showmanship."

Marjorie Batchelder observed, in "Puppetry, its Place in Education" (*Puppeteers of America Pamphlet* No. 9, Columbus, 1944), that while a versatile person may present a one-man puppet show, the various departments of an entire school may collaborate upon one in a socialized program of wider scope than that of the human actor theatre. The art department, for instance, may conduct historical research and design and make scenery, costumes, puppets, posters, and playbills; the wood-working shop may build the stage, scenery, and puppet bodies; the electrical workshop may plan and install the lighting and sound effects; the mechanical drawing department may make the working drawings; the English department may prepare the script of the play; history, geography, and literature may find themes; dramatics may direct; music may provide the musical background; physical education may devise dance routines and exercises to improve the puppeteer's co-ordination; business may take over ticket selling, publicity, and bookkeeping; printing may produce posters and handbills; and photography may make a record of all the activities.

In the elementary school, Miss Batchelder suggested, "Puppets can be used for improvisation and spontaneous conversations, for rhythmic musical interpretations, and general creative experience in art and dramatics." In the junior and senior high school they can dramatize themes drawn from the subjects studied. "Students of this age level are interested in puppet history, the technical phases of puppetry. They demand well constructed and expressive puppets." In colleges and universities puppetry offers "unlimited opportunity for creative and experi-

The adoration scene from The Second Shepherd's Play *of the Townley Cycle, produced by New York University students under the direction of Catherine Reighard.*

mental work," and of course trains the teacher who is to use puppets. Museums and libraries find puppet shows an excellent tool in their educational programs because of the appeal of puppets to children. But they have adult appeal too. While they have not entered the field of adult education formally, their presence in many Junior League entertainments, presented by adults for children, amounts to a training of the grown up.

So widespread has been puppet activity in the schools that it is impossible to cite here more than a few examples to indicate its extent. In Cleveland, where the professional companies of the Tatterman Marionettes, Helen Haiman Joseph, Franc Still, and others played yearly for many seasons, almost every school had a troupe of its own. These troupes were brought in turn to the Museum of Art, where a stage to the dimensions of which the productions had been built was available; there one school could show its puppets to children from all over the city. The project of getting productions built in uniform scale was carried out by Louise Dunn of the Museum of Art and Winifred Mills, who taught in a junior high school. The community puppet theatre tradition has continued in Cain Park, Cleveland Heights, under the direction of Mrs. Joseph.

The Tatterman Marionettes also visited most of the Detroit schools; Wayne University in Detroit offered a puppet course; a survey made in 1937 showed that one out of every three Detroit schools had an active, continuing program of puppetry. These cities were unusual in the degree of their devotion to puppets, but Seattle, San Francisco, Dallas, Denver, Cincinnati, and the suburban communities around Boston, Philadelphia, and New York, have all had the same stimuli from professional companies and burst out with innumerable school puppet troupes. The puppet companies that traveled throughout Mexico under the auspices of the Ministry of Education, chief among them the Teatro Nahual directed by Roberto Lago and Lola Cueto, have been the model for many school theatres, as has been the Teatro Andariega of Javier Villafañe in Argentina and its neighboring countries.

The puppeteer, a linoleum-cut poster for a theatre exhibition, Mexico City, 1936, by Gabriel Fernando Ledesma. Original 13½ x 16½ inches.

The collective experience of New York City has been put into *Puppetry in the Curriculum,* a manual issued by the Board of Education of the City of New York (1947-1948 Series, No. 1). Truda T. Weil assembled many reports from laboratory classes where puppets were used by pupils and from the committee members engaged in the study. That such a 171-page handbook could be prepared in a school system so large, complexly organized, and variegated in background, indicates how well established puppetry in education has become.

Many specific school shows are listed in the next chapter; these are the merest sampling of all that have been done by pupils in connection with their studies.

5. In Recreation

While the American tendency to capitalize upon anything that grows to be impressive has operated even in puppet shows started for fun in home or studio, there have been many who resisted the urgings of their friends to turn professional, and who continued to give private performances with puppets worthy of wider audiences. The shows of W. A. Dwiggins in Hingham Center, Massachusetts, have always been given by invitation only. Dwiggins devised the puppets and plays and his neighbors helped him with the string pulling. The shows of Gustave Baumann in Santa Fe, another artist in the graphic field, were family affairs at the Christmas season for many years; so were those of K. M. Ballantyne in Baldwin, New York. All were of skilled caliber, all were by practicing artists. Fred

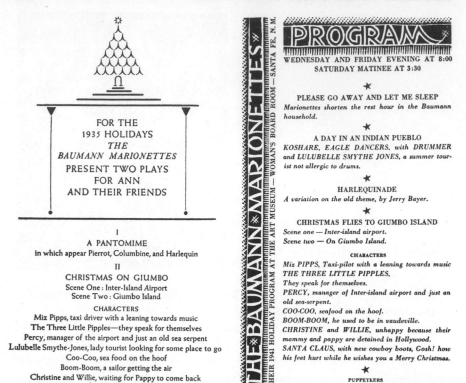

FOR THE
1935 HOLIDAYS
THE
BAUMANN MARIONETTES
PRESENT TWO PLAYS
FOR ANN
AND THEIR FRIENDS

I
A PANTOMIME
in which appear Pierrot, Columbine, and Harlequin

II
CHRISTMAS ON GIUMBO
Scene One : Inter-Island Airport
Scene Two : Giumbo Island

CHARACTERS
Miz Pipps, taxi driver with a leaning towards music
The Three Little Pipples—they speak for themselves
Percy, manager of the airport and just an old sea serpent
Lulubelle Smythe-Jones, lady tourist looking for some place to go
Coo-Coo, sea food on the hoof
Boom-Boom, a sailor getting the air
Christine and Willie, waiting for Pappy to come back
from Epthiopthia
Santa Claus

PLAYS MARIONETTES AND STAGING by the Baumanns
LYRICS by E. Dana Johnson
MUSIC—Xylophone, bassdrum, and orthophonics
by Margaret Jo Fiske; with Muriel West at the organ
PUPPETEERS—Virginia Hunter, Spencer Barefoot, Jane Baumann
SANTA FE, NEW MEXICO

WOMAN'S BOARD ROOM — SANTA FE, N. M.

THE BAUMANN MARIONETTES
PRESENT THEIR 1941 HOLIDAY PROGRAM AT THE ART MUSEUM

PROGRAM

WEDNESDAY AND FRIDAY EVENING AT 8:00
SATURDAY MATINEE AT 3:30

★

PLEASE GO AWAY AND LET ME SLEEP
Marionettes shorten the rest hour in the Baumann household.

★

A DAY IN AN INDIAN PUEBLO
KOSHARE, EAGLE DANCERS, with DRUMMER
and LULUBELLE SMYTHE JONES, *a summer tourist not allergic to drums.*

★

HARLEQUINADE
A variation on the old theme, by Jerry Bayer.

★

CHRISTMAS FLIES TO GIUMBO ISLAND
Scene one — Inter-island airport.
Scene two — On Giumbo Island.

CHARACTERS
Miz PIPPS, Taxi-pilot with a leaning towards music
THE THREE LITTLE PIPPLES,
They speak for themselves.
PERCY, *manager of Inter-island airport and just an old sea-serpent.*
COO-COO, *seafood on the hoof.*
BOOM-BOOM, *he used to be in vaudeville.*
CHRISTINE *and* WILLIE, *unhappy because their mammy and pappy are detained in Hollywood.*
SANTA CLAUS, *with new cowboy boots, Gosh! how his feet hurt while he wishes you a Merry Christmas.*

★

PUPPETEERS
PAUL BRINEGAR — BETTY WILEY — CAROLINE KELLY
JANE BAUMANN   —   ASSISTED BY BEN HILLS
PLAYS MARIONETTES AND STAGING
BY THE BAUMANNS

Playbills for two productions of Gustave Baumann, Santa Fe, 1935 and 1941.

Dana Marsh, the father of Reginald Marsh, a painter also, made caricature rod-puppets of movie actors for a film, but they were seen chiefly in his studio in New York. Fritz Kredel the illustrator has made puppets for home showing in the same city.

The vast majority of home shows have been given by people who, though not artists, were handy in making things and getting up performances. Almost always children were an excuse for the shows. Sometimes the parents started the activity, sometimes the children; frequently both generations worked together in the construction and presentation. Because they are private, these shows are seldom heard of outside the domestic or neighborhood circle. Occasionally a newspaper will get wind

Hand-puppets of the Catalan type, with a shoulder block into which the operator's three center fingers fit, and arms worked by the thumb and little finger inserted through the puppet's elbows, though puppet-sized, suggest giants alongside a smaller puppet, in Jean Ballantyne's production of The Brave Little Tailor.

of them—the tendency to capitalize!—and they will be written up as if they were as important as the best professional show of the season. By the frequency of such pieces of publicity may be guessed the proliferation of these shows.

America also tends to organize recreation in such public places as parks, playgrounds, and settlement houses. Puppetry is one of the supervised activities in them. The Los Angeles Playground Department sponsored the performances of Ellen Galpin so early as 1922. Many cities have followed suit. Some have leaders who show children how to build their own shows, some offer professional shows ready made. In New York, where they are taken about from park to park by a truck that opens to become a stage, they have been under the direction of A. Spolidoro in recent seasons.

During the years of the WPA, 1934-1941, thousands of puppet shows were given free to the public by workers trained as puppeteers while on relief rolls. At one time there were more WPA puppeteers in New York City alone than there had previously been in the entire United States. Some of the shows were done by the Theatre Project, others by the Recreation Project; a few puppets were even made by art projects to

A scene from an Easter play, The Three Marys at the Tomb, *produced by Marjorie Phillips DeVertier for the Cranbrook Sunday School, Bloomfield Hills, Michigan.*

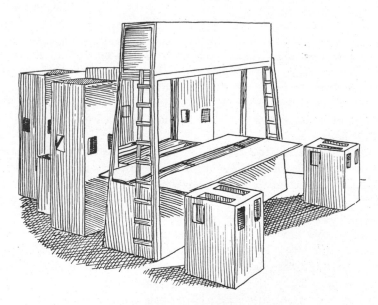

Unrealized project for a production of Capek's R U R *with light towers, pylons, and bridge units to be assembled in various combinations, designed for string-, hand-, and rod-puppets by the WPA Federal Theatre puppet project of New York under the supervision of Remo Bufano, 1936.*

The Life of Stephen Foster *presented by singing Negro puppeteers of the Buffalo Historical Marionettes of the WPA, 1937.*

A hand-puppet performance by children given out of doors in a park under the auspices of the San Francisco Recreation Commission.

turn over to workers on community-chest campaigns. Unfortunately the existence of all these projects was so brief or so vexed by problems extraneous to puppetry that little survived from them. I wonder what became of all the hundreds of puppets they made? And few of the puppeteers they trained went on in this work. Had some of the productions that were planned come to maturity, they would have been milestones in American puppetry.

With the entrance of the American nations into World War II, all activity came to be marshaled toward the war effort. Recreational activities such as puppet shows, it was found, had a distinct place in it. They sustained morale. At one extreme they carried inspiriting messages or belittled the enemy; at the other they merely took one's mind from one's worries by presenting something pleasant or amusing. Some puppets aided in selling government bonds or in publicizing the scrap-collection drive; others made war-weary citizens or bored soldiers relax long enough

Herb Scheffel made Miss Trellis Divine as a pin-up puppet, sending her photograph to men in service during World War II.

Rod-puppet clown by Roy Patton, made
to entertain displaced children in Spain
at the time of the civil war, 1937. After
a photograph by Harry Patton.

to be able to face their jobs again. In the armed forces puppets were sometimes sponsored directly by military authority, through its recreational branch; sometimes they were shown by outside agencies such as the Red Cross or USO; sometimes they were improvised by soldiers or sailors for their own fun. They helped to while away the tedium in many a camp, transport, or overseas outpost.

Wounded service men made puppet shows in hospitals. A good show would bolster spirits for a large group that saw it, or provide muscular exercise, relearning of co-ordination, and pastime for those who made it. Thus recreation and therapy were afforded at once. The American urge to see values in everything, to capitalize on every activity, has lifted puppetry into significance even when it aimed at nothing but a little fun.

6. Subsidized Troupes

America has never seen the point of allocating public funds to public recreation such as the theatre, though tax-supported theatres are the rule on the Continent in Europe. Even during the WPA, the intention was not to support art but to afford livelihood for the jobless. Thus we have never had a truly civic puppet theatre such as Papa Schmid's in Munich. But there have been a few examples of noncommercial puppet theatres in America that have served to indicate what important things might be done by a troupe without the responsibility of money-making.

The puppets at the Chicago Little Theatre, important in their repercussions, were a by-product, and so in a sense were supported by the

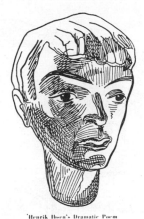

'Henrik Ibsen's Dramatic Poem

PEER GYNT

as presented by
THE TATTERMAN MARIONETTES

Cover of souvenir booklet of the Tatter-
man Marionettes Peer Gynt.

Little Theatre itself. Catherine Reighard obtained a small money grant for her Puppet Players in New York in 1930. This served to enable her to experiment with Cubist scenes, abstract movement, and puppets made of unusual materials; but there was an insufficient sum to insure a continuing program. Remo Bufano was the only puppeteer to travel abroad on a Guggenheim fellowship; this presumably gave his work stimulus. But most puppet producers have had to supply their own capital. Sometimes they put earnings from advertising shows into productions of higher caliber or elaboration than they could have attempted otherwise. The Tatterman Marionettes' *Peer Gynt*, one of the largest-scale achievements of the puppet revival in America, was underwritten by profits from less significant work.

It has not been difficult, however, for troupes to gain support from agencies that wished to sell services or products, promote public relations, or disseminate information through puppet shows. Numbers of these have eluded the records because they were lightly regarded by the puppeteers or not publicized on purpose.

The advertising show seldom attempts the direct sale of a product. Through a playlet or lively interlude it may point out the advantages of possessing the product, or show in humorous terms the disadvantages of not possessing it. For instance, the drawbacks of the horse and buggy may be inferred in a Gay Nineties scene, while the merits of the automobile may be set forth in a modern one. But the chief value of an advertising show is to attract attention and create good will. Such shows are

Truck that toured the United States in 1938, presenting scenes from the film Marie Antoinette, *with puppet portraits of its players, to advertise the picture. From a photograph.*

often to be found at fairs, expositions, and conventions, and in department stores (sometimes in a show window), shops, and even schools.

The Tatterman Marionettes built a diving girl of aluminum and had her plunge repeatedly into a tank of real water to advertise a bathing suit. When the puppet was shown in a department-store window on 42 Street, New York, so large a crowd gathered to watch it that traffic was interrupted. The same thing happened in other places when Edith Flack Ackley made puppets that applied a well-known brand of make-up to their faces at miniature dressing tables. The Chicago World's Fair of 1934 had many advertising shows (that of 1933 had but one). Bil Baird operated two, alternating at fifteen-minute intervals; the Tatterman Marionettes, the Pasadena Puppeteers, and Meyer Levin had them. The voices and music for these shows were generally recorded, but even with amplification were apt to be drowned out by the din of surrounding exhibits. Some of the audience areas were air-conditioned and provided with comfortable seats, a lure for footsore visitors. The New York and San Francisco world's fairs of 1939 had even more advertising shows. In New York, Remo Bufano made puppets twice as large as life to appear on a turntable stage with a 30-foot diameter; Sue Hastings had a revue; and the Tatterman Marionettes two shows, one a chronicle and the other a musical comedy.

When children are to be reached, puppet shows are an especially effectual medium. Sometimes the puppets are invited into the schools when the message they carry is approved by educators. The Oxford University Press of New York, emulating a Soviet Russian technique, dramatized some of its children's stories and presented the plays as a means of increasing the circulation of the books. The Animal Rescue League of Boston taught school children kindness to animals. Dairymen's councils in many states carried on a campaign for children to drink milk through showing puppet plays in which wan little boys became supermen through consuming the proper quantities of lactic liquid. The Good Teeth Council of Chicago, starting with a small educational show at the world's fair in 1933, continued its efforts to instruct children in the care of their teeth until it was sending out as many as eight troupes, each giving fifteen performances a week during the school year in schools throughout the United States. All these shows were offered free of charge, their expenses being paid for by the sponsoring agencies.

To reach everybody in the family for the maintenance of public relations, public utilities, the makers of household appliances, and the distributors of food have resorted to the use of puppets. Sometimes the puppet characters who act as announcers are animated trade marks or identification figures. Sometimes the puppet shows are tied in with a large advertising campaign in the magazines. More and more they are being broadcast by television. They are more individual, more attention-getting than the ubiquitous film, and can be modified to suit local conditions and special audiences so long as they are not "canned"—that is, have recorded dialogue and a standardized pattern.

The best results have been obtained from the medium when the show is made up of nine parts of entertainment and only one of instruction, when it is done under conditions where everybody can see and hear, when the message is not too solemnly or insistently delivered, and when it is a "live" presentation, the puppeteers varying the lines and action to the temper of the audience and so drawing its vocal response. It is not a small matter to pay for a specially built show and the services of puppeteers, but the expense compares very favorably in result with other forms of advertising.

A dramatization of a Maya legend with puppets derived from Maya bas-relief figures, by Tulane University, New Orleans.

7. In Therapy

The behavior problems of children are difficult to analyze when the child is too young to volunteer necessary information. The therapist is able to find out what he wants to know by performing a scene with puppets. The child identifies himself with a character and his responses to the typical situations in the puppet action are accurate clues to his maladjustment. The show might be a modification of the familiar old Punch and Judy; there is an older child as well as the baby. The older child may carry the baby to the window and say, "Shall I chuck my little brother out?" If the spectator concedes that it's an excellent idea, as he may in an unself-conscious crow, it is clear that he has resentment against his own young brother for having displaced him in his parents' affection. This is only one of a number of such test situations.

An older child may be given a set of simple puppets (preferably hand-puppets or rod-puppets which he can work without trouble) with which to enact a play of his own. The therapist watching what he does, and understanding the genesis of fantasy, has an insight into his behavior patterns.

Grownups in a group who might be too shy to express themselves in words can be made to get out their thoughts, all on an impersonal level, through a similar dramatization with simple puppets. A parent group being guided in its attitudes to children might, for instance, elect two of its members to improvise a mother-child scene. It is easy enough for one of this pair to play a naughty child. The other may lecture it or spank it, as he really is disposed to do. But when the leader points out that this may not be the thing to do, he is absolved from the blame of knowing no better—it was all play acting.

Puppet plays for the psychoanalysis of children have been a regular part of the technique at Bellevue Hospital, New York, since about 1935, when Dr. Loretta Bender, Senior Psychiatrist in Charge, assisted by Aldolf Woltmann, puppeteer, began using them. A report of their work appeared in *The American Journal of Orthopsychiatry* (1936, pp. 341-354) and other articles have subsequently been published.

In operating string-puppets an airplane-type controller may be held in each hand, but the action so produced is broad rather than specialized. Crossed-stick controllers, held horizontally, were popularized by Tony Sarg, but have given way to paddle and other simpler forms. After photographs of Catherine Stuberg's puppeteers, 1938.

A puppeteer using his own hands and a puppet head atop his own formed this gesticulating "Sandy" of J. Arthur MacLean, Toledo, 1942.

Puppetry can hasten the recovery of those convalescing from illness or injury. To see a good show distracts them, takes them from brooding on their condition, and may actually whet anticipation and interest to the extent that there is a fresh impulse to get better. To devise a puppet show gives the patient not only something to think about but something to do. If he has received injury he may train a disused body to its former activity by the use of tools that require exercise and co-ordination. He may regain strength through the mild activities of handicraft work. Best of all, he may be brought to confidence in his future usefulness through presenting a show for his fellow-patients.

A variety of stages which may be improvised from hospital equipment, designed by Ben Yano, a puppeteer who spent a long time with a fractured leg in the United States Army's Camp Luna, New Mexico, is shown in Marjorie Batchelder's *Puppet Theatre Handbook* (New York, 1947, pp. 118-123), which started out as an Army manual for the use of wounded soldiers.

What has been learned about puppets for occupational therapy in St. Louis by Susan Barnes, in Philadelphia by Emma Warfield, in Ypsilanti by Sarah Brown, and in other places by others, has been summed up in "Puppets in O. T.," by Susan Barnes and Marjorie Batchelder (*Puppeteers of America Pamphlet* No. 7, Columbus, 1944). There is a considerable body of information about the phases of puppetry that may be applied to specific therapeutic uses.

8. New Applications

One of the most popular of American radio characters since the early 1930's has been a puppet, Charlie McCarthy. Ventriloquists have used such puppets as instruments of their art for at least a century and a half; they were usually subordinate to the marvel of voice throwing, so that it is difficult to say when they were first used in America; they were merely one of the pieces of ventriloquial apparatus among talking heads and spirits in boxes. A bright boy character, seated on the knee of the operator, who controlled its movements by strings in the inside of its body,

Group of ventriloquial zanies by the brothers George and Glenn McElroy of Harrison, Ohio. Manner of controlling wink, opening jaw, and other facial movements by cords inside body; a dummy by Frank Marshall of Chicago, who made the first Charlie McCarthy. After photographs.

was a natural mouthpiece for humorous dialogue. A bright Irish boy, like Charlie, conforms to a stage type of the 1870's. Edgar Bergen bought a standard ventriloquial dummy from Frank Marshall in Chicago, gave him sophistication by a monocle and tails, and made him more alive than many a human clown by the uninhibited wit and briskness of response with which he endowed him. Charlie McCarthy satisfies that urge in us to say what we please regardless of consequence, and so we love him for doing what we dare not do. His commonplace immobile face need not be seen for his repartee to be appreciated; the mystification of ventriloquism has little to do with his effectiveness; hence his great popularity on the air waves.

As a foil to Charley, to point up his sparkle, Edgar Bergen devised a dullard, a country-bumpkin character, Mortimer Snerd, got Wolo to draw the sketches for his face and Virginia Austin to model it, and invested him with a deep drawl and immoderately slow reactions. Mortimer too is a stock character from the stage, but Bergen has made him a living personality.

If the effect of puppets is largely lost on radio, it is intensified by television. Richard V. Trusdell's puppet variety bill was presented by the WGXF studio in Chicago in 1930. At that time the area that could be

Burr Tillstrom with his puppet "Kukla" before a television camera in Chicago, 1939.

scanned with clarity by the television eye was a small one, and the fact that puppets were small allowed them to appear in a group when actors could not. Mme Pinxy broadcast Punch and Judy over station W9XAO, in connection with WIBO, Chicago, in 1931. In 1934 Nicholas Nelson's marionettes were televised in Chicago and their images projected on a screen 11 feet square, a sight that has not been duplicated in 1948. Puppeteers have had high hopes of making a place for themselves in television, and while puppets are more and more used in skits, scenes, and commercial announcements, the uncertain development of this application has left them waiting at the door.

At the beginning of movies all sorts of experimental subjects were filmed. The Film Department of the Library of Congress has on deposit a paper print of an Edison film of 1897, *Dancing Chinamen,* which records the stock vaudeville act of string-puppet Celestials. The productions of the Frenchman George Méliès, widely shown in America, had all sorts of effects: cardboard monsters worked by strings, animated pictures, and so on, which were applications of puppetry to the human scale. In October 1916 the Gaumont Company of America announced a short film of a marionette baseball game, in all probability Lillian Faulkner's. Thenceforth many films were made from puppets not intended for the camera, with the result that crudities, sway, strings, and other incidentals were too prominent. It was thought by some that all puppet films were failures.

Tony Sarg, assisted by his staff, made a series of humorous short sketches, *Tony Sarg's Almanac,* in 1921, with shadow-figures placed horizontally over back-lighted translucent scenery and filmed by stop-motion: that is, the figures were photographed, moved a little, photographed again, and so given the effect of continuous movement when the panels were shown in rapid succession. Stop-motion was an early movie trick, but it calls for very exacting manipulation when applied to puppets.

Still from a film made with stop-motion figures by Louis Bunin to show in the Petroleum Building of the 1939 New York world's fair.

Louis and Maury Bunin made a color puppet film by this process, shown by Petroleum Products at the New York World's Fair in 1939, and the films of George Pal and others were made for regular distribution a few years later.

But properly finished puppets with strings, lighted so that the strings are nearly invisible, can be very successful, as was demonstrated by Bil Baird's films made for release in Latin America through the Co-ordinator of Inter-American Affairs. These were educational, presenting in a humorous way the benefits of truck gardening and dairy farming. Baird has since made even smoother color films of puppets for the public relations of the Bell Telephone Company.

Puppet films for advertising are a variant of puppets for advertising, and have been made both with string-puppets and stop-motion. While they can be shown to vast audiences, they do not have the effectiveness of impact of the "live" show.

Caricature of Sinclair Lewis by Louis Bunin, about 1930. After a photograph.

Tandem-strung chorus of girls by Russell Patterson for the 1937 film, Artists and Models.

Puppets have been posed in scenes to be photographed as illustrations for advertisements. Tony Sarg made a series of burlesqued scenes from Shakespeare for cigarettes. This is a novelty that has a limited usefulness and may easily grow tiresome. Stop-motion figures for illustrations are practicable to show setting-up exercises, dances, and other bodily motion, but effect no saving over the use of live models, for they are expensive to build well.

Huge animated figures which are a sort of puppet are carried in advertising parades on Thanksgiving, such as that presented yearly by Macy's in New York (the Tony Sarg balloons, wobbling in the wind, were as lively as his puppets). In a parade for a store in Dayton, Ohio, Roy and Harry Patton made more-than-life-sized puppets worked from below with rods. Mardi Gras and other parades in Philadelphia, Mobile, New Orleans, and elsewhere, use an occasional animated figure on a float. These are the least common denominator of puppetry if they are puppets at all.

Ballerina by Paul Walton and Michael O'Rourke, about 1935. After a photograph.

Making the puppet film, Jerry Pulls the Strings, *an advertising piece staged by Rufus Rose, 1938. While considerable studio space was required, it was but a fraction of what a film with human actors would have demanded. The camera is lower right. After a photograph.*

9. Entertainers with Puppets

Before World War II there was a trend to travel light. Puppeteers, tired of lugging heavy and cumbersome stages, got rid of all the equipment they could. About 1935 the Yale Puppeteers dispensed with their masking draperies for road engagements, using a platform with a backdrop and emphasizing the puppets with spotlights. Soon after, Bob Bromley was playing in night clubs without a vestige of a stage. His puppets were hung on a rack; he selected them and went through each turn with a light on the puppet on the same level with him. While the puppeteer worked in darkness he was as shadowy as ever, but he was very much in the open as he came out and bowed. He therefore had to "make an appearance" himself and dressed for the occasion like any entertainer.

In an article, "Floor Showmanship," in *Puppetry 1942-1943* (Detroit, p. 24), it is stated, "Whether or not the audience likes the looks of the puppeteer influences the reception of the puppets." This form of show

Floor-show entertainers, like Frank Paris with his caricature of Carmen Miranda, appear together with their puppets, but their dark costumes and the concentration of light on the puppets hide them almost as completely as if they were behind a screen. After a photograph.

became widespread during the war. Many puppeteers who had previously presented full-length dramatic pieces turned to variety programs without stages. Many new puppeteers took up the style. Usually supported by an orchestra, dancing and acrobatic numbers were most effective and dialogue was unnecessary. Most of the performers worked solo. They operated the four or five puppets of their act in ten or twelve minutes and were done. Much simpler than the cumbersome old shows! And they had the satisfaction of feeling that the applause was as much for them as persons as for their skill with the puppets.

But night-club business declined in the tapering-off of spending after the war. Puppet acts were not so much in demand. Some puppeteers went back to more elaborate shows which they could present in schools, while others disappeared. But the simplification of equipment has continued. Front draperies are seldom carried. The puppeteers are hidden by darkness instead. Scenery is reduced to a minimum of painted backdrops, set-pieces and properties are eliminated wherever possible. Whereas there could be a company of four or six puppeteers at the beginning of the revival, nowadays there is seldom more than a pair. The lighter baggage can be handled by two; two can travel comfortably in the front of a station wagon or panel delivery truck; two can share a room; the return is greater when only two share the fee.

The traveling puppet show is the most usual in America; it will probably continue to travel light and carry few hands. Because the personalities of the puppeteers are more easily discerned when there are only a

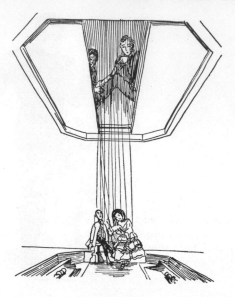

The puppeteers worked in a tower hung from the ceiling for Tony Sarg's floor show at the Bal Tabarin night club of the Hotel Sherman, Chicago, about 1928.

couple of them, because their faces are seen when the puppets are not in evidence, they will tend to become entertainers in their own right. They will be prominent as they make announcements and say a word of explanation between scenes. They will, in fact, like Peter Hauntz, be characters in their own shows.

10. Exhibitions and Organization

At the beginning of the revival of puppetry, puppeteers seldom knew each other save as business rivals. The old mistrust and secretiveness of an ancient "craft and mystery" clung to puppetry. But the new generation was eager to learn, to make friends with other puppeteers and to exchange information; it had broken with tradition—it was even unaware of tradition—and had no transmitted lore of techniques. One puppeteer made the effort to seek out another; letters passed back and forth; there was a professional feeling that puppetry should be advanced.

In the spring of 1932 Helen A. Smiley organized a representative exhibition of puppets at Temple University in Philadelphia, showing the work of fifty puppet makers from the United States and Canada. So strong was the domination of the string-operated type that only one group of hand-puppets was included. During the summer of 1933 a selec-

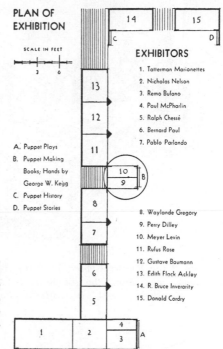

PLAN OF
EXHIBITION

SCALE IN FEET

3   6

A. Puppet Plays
B. Puppet Making
  Books; Hands by
  George W. Kegg
C. Puppet History
D. Puppet Stories

EXHIBITORS

1. Tatterman Marionettes
2. Nicholas Nelson
3. Remo Bufano
4. Paul McPharlin
5. Ralph Chessé
6. Bernard Paul
7. Pablo Parlando

8. Waylande Gregory
9. Perry Dilley
10. Meyer Levin
11. Rufus Rose
12. Gustave Baumann
13. Edith Flack Ackley
14. R. Bruce Inverarity
15. Donald Cordry

Exhibitors at Marshall Field's store, Chicago, 1933. From the catalogue, which illustrated each of the scenes set up as if in actual performance. There was also a book list. This exhibition was seen by thousands of visitors during the summer of the Chicago world's fair.

tive showing of puppets which I gathered and set up was to be found at Marshall Field's in Chicago. To quote from *Puppetry 1933* (p. 7), "In a series of stages, with backgrounds and lighting suggesting the actual performances, were displayed groups of puppets and marionettes by the Tatterman company of Cleveland, Nelson of Chicago, Ackley, Bufano, Gregory, and Levin of New York, McPharlin of Detroit, Chessé and Dilley of San Francisco, Paul of Baltimore, Rose of New London, Baumann of Santa Fe, Inverarity of Vancouver, and Cordry of Minneapolis. . . . The two marionettes by Waylande de Santis Gregory, a nymph and silenus, well-jointed nudes, one of stoneware and the other of terra cotta, were notably successful experiments. Thousands of visitors from all over the country saw the exhibit, and many for the first time learned the extent of the puppet movement."

Other exhibitions followed. Puppeteers were getting to know each other; the public learned that Tony Sarg was not the only puppeteer.

In the spring of 1913 a Marionette Society was founded in New York by a group of literary and theatrical people who deplored the disappearing Paladin puppets of Mulberry Street and believed that puppets could be used in schools and social centers (New York *Times*, 4 May 1913).

Visitors at the Puppet Center, 78 Fifth Avenue, New York, where model puppets and stages were shown by the Recreational Puppetry Project of the WPA, 1937. After a photograph.

An exhibition, "Puppets Old and New," at the Philadelphia Museum of Art, April-May 1939. Note the tall Robert Edmund Jones-Remo Bufano string-and-rod-puppet from Stravinsky's Oedipus Rex *against the wall. From a photograph.*

Ten-foot puppets controlled from above by cords and below by rods, designed by Robert Edmund Jones for Stravinsky's Oedipus Rex *and executed by Remo Bufano, 1931. After photographs by Maurice Goldberg.*

This Society was as short lived as Gordon Craig's Society of the Marion-ette, which he had endeavored to establish in Florence in 1912 (*The Mask*, vol. 5, p. 144). In June 1929 William Herrschaft wistfully wrote me, "It would be good someday to call a conference of all interested in marionettes." When I published *Puppetry 1930* it announced the estab-lishment of the Marionette Fellowship of America on 15 October of that year. This proved an abortive organization; its head disappeared and nothing was done about it. In March 1932 a festival of performances by the Tatterman Marionettes, Remo Bufano, and Meyer Levin, organized by the last, was held at the New School for Social Research in New York. A group consisting of Edith Flack Ackley, Remo Bufano, the Kingsland Marionettes, Agreppino Manteo, the Puppet Players Studio (Catherine Reighard), the Red Gate Shadow Players (Pauline Benton), Tony Sarg, and Val Smith banded together that same spring for lecture demonstra-tions. The time grew more and more ripe for a real organization.

In 1936 the organization of the first national puppet conference was thrust upon me. The chamber of commerce of a Michigan town had offered to underwrite it, backed out at the last minute, and left the expectant puppeteers high and dry. I had no choice but to try to make something of the contretemps, so I transferred the scene of the event to Detroit and managed to hold a meeting. Everybody seemed to value and enjoy it despite broiling July weather. There were an exhibition, a series of technical talks, a dinner, and performances by several troupes. The world premiere of Gertrude Stein's *Identity, or I am I* gave éclat; it was produced by Don Vestal of Chicago. A detailed account of this confer-ence is contained in my *Puppets in America* (Birmingham, Michigan, 1936). We sat about, wilted by the heat, and said we ought to get an organization started, but put off the actual work until we met for another national conference, this one managed by Martin and Olga Stevens in 1937 at Cincinnati.

There the Puppeteers of America was founded. Its purpose was to provide a meeting ground and information center for all interested in

Pauline Benton's Red Gate Shadow Players with authentic Chinese shadow figures and English versions of Chinese Plays.

puppetry, and so to further the cause of puppetry. The society took over the management of the yearly conference, which was thenceforth held in cities where a member or group of members could arrange details locally, to be interrupted only in the war years. The yearbook, *Puppetry*, which I had established, became the official organ of the society, and its own publication after the war. To supplement it, a bimonthly news letter, *The Grapevine Telegraph*, was also issued. Book lists and technical pamphlets as well have been published from time to time. Among the officers of the Puppeteers of America have been advisors on technical matters, on puppetry in education and recreation, and on professional co-operation. Because professional puppeteers in some cases carry over the lone-wolf attitude of the showmen of an earlier period, and because they

Marionette Fellowship	SATURDAY 2:30 P.M.	ADULT 55 CENTS
ARTISAN GUILD Woodward Avenue near Manchester		

Ticket for the Marionette Fellowship of Detroit, 1935.

Linoleum-cut poster for the Detroit Marionette Fellowship production of the old German Dr. Faust, 1935. By Paul Mc-Pharlin. Original 10 x 15 inches.

have never had a strong enough economic menace to force them together for mutual protection, they have tended to ignore this provision for their welfare. The society has flourished, possesses a membership throughout the United States and in Canada and Latin America, and has encouraged the establishment of local puppet societies in cities such as Philadelphia, Chicago, Detroit, St. Louis, Minneapolis, and St. Paul.

Local puppet groups, transitory by their very nature, had preceded the foundation of the national society. About 1930 the teachers' colleges of New Jersey, all interested in puppetry, held joint conferences and contests. In 1934 and 1935 Michigan puppet conferences were housed at Wayne University in Detroit; the Marionette Fellowship there, which I directed, had been a focus for puppeteers in the area since 1931. This was also true of other quasi-civic companies with studio theatres in San Francisco, Los Angeles, Cleveland, Baltimore, Philadelphia, and Boston. The Junior Leagues of many cities maintained puppet troupes as part of their program to establish children's theatres, and so provided a nucleus for puppetry in their communities. The colleges that offered courses in puppetry were also centers. This scattered activity is now stabilized and given continuity through the Puppeteers of America, with which local groups may become affiliated.

11. The Printed Word

Many who had never seen a puppet show or managed to get backstage to peep at how one was worked, were warmed to the idea of puppetry by enthusiastic accounts which they read. This explains why shows cropped up in the unlikeliest remote places, almost as if by spontaneous com-

Setting by Piney Kanakis for the Decatur Marionette Guild's production of the often-played Gooseberry Mandarin *by Grace Dorcas Ruthenburg.*

bustion. There were the Victorian books on magic and boys' pastimes, already mentioned, which had sections on making puppet or shadow shows; these had a widespread influence. I doubt whether Georgiana Goddard King's *Comedies and Legends for Marionettes* (New York, 1904) got around very much; it was an excellent book of plays with a preliminary note on making a simple home theatre with puppets of the Italian toy variety, worked by a wire to the head and a string to each arm. "Long ago," wrote Mrs. King, "when people gave me toy theatres in which the actors were paper dolls, or mere silhouettes for shadow comedies, I always threw away the accompanying printed plays because I found them dull and silly. The plays I made up in their stead were much like those in this volume."

And these substitutes had a pleasant literary flavor while remaining quite playable. There were comedies such as *Columbine's Marriage* and *The Magic Hat*, legends of *St. Francis* and *St. Dorothy*, and pantomimes of *Snowflake and the Dwarfs* and *Mother Hubbard and her Dog*. But one stimulating book was not enough to start the revival. It took the writings of Gordon Craig, the articles in illustrated magazines such as *Deutsche Kunst und Dekoration*, and newspaper stories of what was happening in Europe to wake up Americans to the possibilities of puppetry.

Helen Haiman Joseph's *A Book of Marionettes* was a harbinger of the revival. It first appeared in New York, 1920, and came out in a revised edition in 1929. This illuminating history, with its note on puppet making, encouraged many an isolated would-be puppeteer to build a show. F. J. McIsaac's *The Tony Sarg Marionette Book* (New York, 1921), told how

Bandleader from Santaland *of the De-catur Marionette Guild. Puppet designed by Martha McCown.*

Sarg had managed some of his tricks and went about staging a production; it contained two short plays and intensified the excitement created by his shows.

In 1922 Mary Stewart's collection of puppet plays for children, *The Land of Punch and Judy*, was published in New York. Madge Anderson's *The Heroes of the Puppet Stage* (New York, 1923) was a combination of romanticized stories with a check list of articles about puppets in magazines. H. W. Whanslaw's *Everybody's Theatre*, on model theatre making, was done in London, 1924. Georg Jacob's history of the shadow-figure, which had appeared in various preliminary versions, was published in German at Hanover in 1925. *Notes and News* of the British Model Theatre Guild began to be issued in London in 1926 and was seen by some Americans. The German puppet magazine, *Das Puppentheater*, had started at Leipzig in 1923. Paul Jeanne's *Bibliographie des marionnettes* appeared in Paris, 1926. Walter Wilkinson's first book about adventuring with a puppet theatre, *The Peep Show*, came out in London in 1927 and was afterward reprinted in New York. In the same year Winifred H. Mills and Louise M. Dunn launched *Marionettes, Masks and Shadows* (New York), containing very helpful directions for choosing a play, building a production, training puppeteers, and performing; it had excellent illustrations.

Emma Pettey's *The Puppet as an Elementary Project* (Fort Worth, 1925) dealt with an educational application. *School Arts* (December 1922, p. 202) and other magazines reported other facets of puppetry as an educational tool. Catherine Reighard's *Plays for People and Puppets* (New York, 1928) included some of the pieces she had written for the Tatterman Marionettes. A centennial edition of the Cruikshank-Collier *Punch and Judy* was brought out this year in London.

Though these puppets are but 10 inches high, to give an effect of the soaring space of a cathedral on an ordinary puppet stage, their costumes, made of jersey, hang in folds of the proper proportion. From Jean and Wesley Wiksell's Medieval Legend.

Sis Goose and Br'er Fox *of the Rag Bag Alley Puppets.*

Chicken, dragon, and witch from Don Cordry and Virginia Upson's The Tale of a Tomcat.

Jonah and the Whale by Joseph Bushé.

A scene from the Berkeley Marionettes' Toby Tyler.

Drawing by Jero Magon of Scene 2 of his production of Eugene O'Neill's The Emperor Jones.

In 1929 the flood of puppet books reached high water. Among them were Edith Flack Ackley's *Marionettes: Easy to Make, Fun to Use*, Maude Owens Walters' *Puppet Shows for Home and School*, *The Show Book* of Remo Bufano, Hilary D. C. Pepler's *Plays for Puppets*, and my own anthology, *A Repertory of Marionette Plays*, all published in New York save Pepler's, which he himself printed and issued at Ditchling, Sussex. Thereafter, puppet books appeared so frequently that there was no longer much novelty about them. They were noted year by year, and so were the magazine articles about puppetry, in my yearbook, *Puppetry*. From this yearbook I got into publishing books on technique, plays, and histories as well, eventually having a list of some four dozen titles, comprising the Puppetry Imprints, all issued from Birmingham, Michigan. I trust that this is something of a record for specialized publishing.

An assiduous collector may now find hundreds of books about puppets in the European languages, with a few in the Oriental ones, to say nothing of thousands of magazine articles. Some of the latter have valuable data not to be found elsewhere, but most of them are superficial, fragmentary, and inaccurate. Nevertheless, they serve to stir up interest, and the more of them there are (it is a classic tenet of publicity) the more interest will be created. Anyone who needs a selective list of useful puppet books may turn to the one compiled and annotated by Marjorie H. Batchelder for the Puppeteers of America (revised edition, Columbus, 1947). The section on books about puppets in her *Puppet Theatre Handbook* is supplemented by lists of books about the theatre and sources for puppet play themes, altogether the most valuable that I know.

Card of a Punch showman, about 1920.

A proscenium with boxes for hand-puppets and a stage for string-puppets devised by Mary P. Johnson of Tacoma, Washington.

12. The Future

The development of any art in America depends upon its vitality and its environmental fortunes. Puppetry had grown with remarkable vigor, holding its own against movies, motor cars, sports, and the many other recreational activities in which people might indulge, withstanding the economic privations of a depression, only to find itself facing extinction in World War II. This serious menace it lived through. Whether it can continue to take such buffetings will be determined by its strength.

Strength is built by nourishment and challenge. Puppetry need not lack for nourishment so long as it dwells amid plenty and attracts artists who can bring it to more and more perceptive fulfillment. As for challenge, that it should always have. It must be on the defensive because it is small, special, and a little esoteric. It must fight its way as no obvious art need do.

The conditions of theatregoing are changing fast. The living actor survives only in a bare hundred playhouses in half a dozen big cities and in their pallid counterparts in the amateur or summer theatre. These playhouses are apt to be so expensive, old-fashioned, and uncomfortable that the majority of the public goes to the movies. But the movies and their home outlet, the television screen, are mechanical, mass-produced, impersonal entertainment; they fail to set up rapport with the audience, adapt themselves to its local temperament and taste, or have the timbre of life. The puppet theatre might well establish itself in this breach. Less ponderous, costly, and immovable than the legitimate theatre, more supple than the movies, it has enviable advantages.

The history of the puppet theatre, until its revival as an independent art, was a course of imitation of the larger theatre. It took over Punch when he was nearly played out on the stage. It presented medieval moralities far into the Renaissance. It celebrated naval engagements and sieges until they had become legendary. It perpetuated dances and vaudeville turns when they were hoary. This made it a minor and reflective branch of the theatre.

But it has been learned that moving figures under human control may transcend human actors. They can be shaped to play any role. They can be as realistic, as expressionistic, as fantastic as an artist can make them. They can present many of the classics of the stage, in full antiquarian accoutrement, for the benefit of students and the cultivated. They can do experimental drama, ballet, and spectacle. They can please the special audience. They can fit into the classroom or the living room. Their potentialities are as vast as they themselves may be small.

If the art continues vital, if it is allowed to live, the puppeteer in America can look back upon this history as a mere opening chapter.

Set of nineteenth-century Punch and Judy puppets from the collection of the late Wilbur Macey Stone. After photographs.

XXI

A List of Puppeteers, 1524-1948

Showmen whose activities have already been considered are briefly identified in this chapter, and reference is made to the pages where further information about them may be found. The list of puppeteers not considered in the text has been compiled from questionnaires, production records in *Puppetry* and *A Repertory of Marionette Plays*, as well as miscellaneous sources. Incomplete as it is, this biographical index suggests the types of plays presented, the distribution of showmen, and the duration of their puppet activities.

ABBOTT, BESS   Highland Park, Mich., High School Marionettes. In 1933 this group from her art classes presented *Snow White*.

ACKLEY, EDITH FLACK   (Pp. 359, 374, 385, 387, 393). 1923–1935, plays and variety, New York and vicinity. Specialized in cloth marionettes, the method of making which is described in *Marionettes, Easy to Make! Fun to Use!* New York, 1929.

ADAMS, BARBARA T.   The Show Box, Massachusetts School of Art, Boston. 1931, *Snow White;* variety. 1932, *The Frost King*. 1933, *The Man Who Married a Dumb Wife* (after Anatole France).

ADAMS, DALE   Made puppets as fashion models for New York firms, c. 1936.

ADAMSON, DOROTHY   The Adamson Marionette Theatre, St. Paul, Minn. Beginning 1935 presented children's shows based on fairy tales and adult productions such as O'Neill's *The Emperor Jones, The Story of Queen Esther* from the Bible, *The Passing of the Third Floor Back,* Wagner's *The Ring*.

AGNICH, ANGELINE   Director, Eveleth, Minn., Junior High School Puppet Club. 1933, *Tom Sawyer* and clown interlude. 1935, *Chinese Fantasy* and other plays.

AGUILAR, MARÍA PETRA   (P. 73). Proprietor of a theatre in Mexico City, 1783–1786.

AGUILAR, RAUL UGHETTI   A showman of Italian extraction who played c. 1944 in the Colombian Andes. His Nuevo Teatro Pinocchio had a stage mounted on a truck with loud-speakers. Many people in the villages had never seen any theatrical performance. The company played pieces such as *The Judge, The Somnambulist, The Sick Child, The Mother-in-Law, The Bill Collector, The Statue,* and skits containing advertising for their sponsors.

AHRENS, HENRY W.   Ozone Park, N. Y. Beginning 1941 produced with school group a condensation of Wagner's *Ring* operas with marionettes, Bible stories with hand-puppets, Mozart's *Magic Flute, Punch and Judy* with a perambulating theatre.

AIKEN, VIVIAN   Los Angeles, Cal. 1919, Kreymborg's *Lima Beans*.

AIRMET, ELLIOTT   Salt Lake City, Utah. Toured Northwest c. 1945 with variety show later called *Hallucinations on Strings*.

ALBRIGHT, CHARLES W., and HARDIE, H.   Pittsburgh, Pa. 1925, *Punch and Judy* in modern dress. 1926, *Uncle Tom's Cabin* and variety.

ALCANTRA, FRANCISCO JAVIER   (Pp. 70, 71). Mexico City, 1785.

ALEŠ PUPPET THEATRE   See Griffin, Zaidee.

ALEXANDRI, MONSIEUR   (Pp. 257, 258). An adventurous Italian who, arriving in Chile c. 1840, penniless but with a small puppet show, built up a substantial fortune. Wishing to repay the country which had brought him wealth, he built a handsome theatre for human actors and bestowed it on Valparaiso.

ALEXIS (P. 98). Promised shows in Salle St. Phillippe, New Orleans, 1828.

ALLEN, HARRY *Punch and Judy* at Doris's Museum, Harlem, N. Y., at intervals during January and February, 1890. Odell, vol. 14, p. 411. Played at Rollins College, Winter Park, Fla., 1946.

AMADOR, GRACIELA Mexico City. One of the group which started the educational puppetry movement in Mexico in 1932. She became director of the state-sponsored theatre El Periquillo in 1935. This theatre was closed in 1939, but she continued her work in the Women's University through courses in puppetry for teachers, 1946.

ANDERSON, CATHERINE Abington, Mass. School productions with children, c. 1932.

ANDERSON, DOUG and GAYLE New York. First played 1936 with Michael Marionettes, Columbus, Ohio, in *The Three Wishes* and variety. 1941, advertising show at Ohio State Fair with hand-and-rod-puppets. 1941-1945, variety for Army shows. 1946-1948, puppet variety with magic and chalk sketches for children's parties in the New York area. 1947-1948, *The Adventures of Puncho the Puppet*.

ANDRESS, CHARLES Performed magic and *Punch and Judy* in the 1870's, in halls in the winter, with circuses in the summer. With Carnival of Novelties c. 1875. In the 1890's, manager of side show for Ringling Brothers circus, playing *Punch*.

ANDREW, SILOMA H., and PENDLETON, MARY S. Hamburg Puppet Guild, Hamburg, N. Y. Beginning 1936 produced children's plays; interested in educational values of puppetry; taught summer courses in Chautauqua and Buffalo; won Ivory Soap Buick car in 1939 and with it spread puppet work over a wide territory; authors of *Dancing Dolls,* a book of plays published by Samuel French; manufacturers of "Puppet Paks," ready-to-assemble marionettes for school and home use.

ANDREWS, E. 1866, *Punch and Judy*, Williamsburgh, N. Y.

ANONYMOUS

1524. Puppeteer and magician with Cortés.

Before 1708. Bridgetown, Barbados.

30 December 1742. Punch and Joan at the Coach and Horses, Philadelphia.

25 July–27 November 1749. Punch's Company of Comedians, next to the Sign of the Dolphin, New York.

2 April 1767. Mr. Punch and his Merry Family at the Sign of the Orange Tree, New York.

1771. Spanish hand-puppet show, Place d'Armes, New Orleans.

17 March–13 June 1785; 3–7 July 1790. Italian and Chinese shades at the Theatre, Southwark, Philadelphia.

21, 27 January 1790. Chinese shades at 14 William Street, New York.

11 February 1792. Large Italian shades at the Theatre, Northern Liberties, Philadelphia.

19 May, 21 June 1796. Italian and Chinese shades, Ricketts' Amphitheatre, New York.

11 March 1799. Ombres chinoises and Prussian fantoccini, Mr. Grant's, 242 Water Street, New York.

Before 1814. Puppet show at Melville Island prison, Halifax, N. S.

8 January–13 February 1829. Italian fantoccini and *Punch and Judy* at Chatham Museum, New York.

1814. *El Pintor fingido* and *Cafes y fondas* at Palenque de Gallos, Mexico.

1830. A company with Mexican types, Calle de Venero, Mexico City.

1830. Two French-Canadian puppeteers at St. Hughes, County Bagot, Quebec.

24 December 1835–1 January 1836. Fantoccini at Peale's Museum, New York.

18 March–15 April 1836. Mechanical Theatre of Arts, *Mother Goose* at Colon's Hall, New York.

1–6 July 1838; 26 February–4 May 1839. Italian fantoccini at Peale's Museum, New York.

30 March–4 April 1840. Italian fantoccini at the American Museum, New York.

21 July 1840. Italian fantoccini at Vauxhall Gardens, New York.

22 December 1841. Italian fantoccini at the American Museum, New York.

23 February–5 March 1846. "Les Fantocinis Italiennes, or Life Moving Figures," at the Chestnut Street Museum, Philadelphia—Philadelphia *Public Ledger,* above dates.

26 October 1852. "Erstes deutsches Marionetten-Theater in Amerika," Washington Hall, New York.

August 1853. Portsmouth Plaza, San Francisco. Chinese puppet show.

1856. "Theater Mundi, oder die Welt im Kleinen," 290 Broadway, New York.

29 June 1857. Adams' Pacific Museum, San Francisco, marionette show.

7–18 November 1857. Pacific Museum, San Francisco. *The Children in the Woods* and *The Sea Fight between the Constitution and the Guerriere.*

24, 27 March 1869. Casperletheater at Garabaldi Hall, New York.

16 March 1873. Casperletheater at Thirteenth Ward House, New York.

4 April 1875. Pariser Marionetten Truppe at Germania Assembly Rooms, New York.

6–7 November 1880. Fireworks and puppet turns at the Salon de la Reforma, No. 3 Plaza del Seminario, Mexico City.

22 April 1883. "Lilliputian Combination of Automatic Actors and Actresses." Harry Hill's, Houston Street, New York. Odell, vol. 12, p. 138.

After 17 October 1887. Bunnell's Old London Museum, 728 Broadway. "Advertising . . . marionettes." Odell, vol. 13, p. 538, from the New York *Herald.*

30 September–5 October 1889. Imperial Marionettes at Curio Hall, Grand Museum, New York.

1900. French amateur hand-puppet shows in country around Quebec.

1900. Sicilian puppet theatre, Chicago.

1900 or shortly after. A set of string-puppets, obtained third hand through Mme Pinxy of Chicago, and now in the collection of the author, was probably used in vaudeville performances. The puppets have been recorded by the Michigan Art and Crafts Project of the WPA for the Index of American Design: Juggler, Clown, Two-headed pop-out figure, Topsy, Pole-tosser, listed under MSCL. and numbered 16, 17, 18, 24, 27, respectively.

1907. Sicilian puppets on Elizabeth or Mulberry Street, New York.

ANONYMOUS PUNCH AND JUDY

1850. Sandy Bar, San Francisco.

18 July 1859. Jones Wood, New York.

19–24 December 1861. Canterbury Hall, New York.

1867. On Boston Common.

4 February 1867. Staten Island, New York.

15 December 1868. Central Park Garten, New York.

1868. Harry Hill's dance hall on Houston Street, New York.

1870. At Harry Hill's, New York—Matthew Hale Smith, *Sunshine and Shadow in New York,* quoted in *Puppetry* 1935, vol. 6, p. 13.

1870 or soon after. Grand Circus Park, Detroit.

8–15 July 1873. Terrace Garden, New York.

14–19 July 1873. Hooley's Theatre, Brooklyn—Brooklyn *Daily Eagle,* those dates.

1875 or thereabouts. On Jefferson Avenue near Meldrum, Detroit.

9–15 August 1875. Metropolitan Theatre, New York. Odell, vol. 10, p. 84.

17–25 August 1876. Tony Pastor's Theatre, New York. Odell, vol. 10, p. 88.

June 1877. Association Hall, Staten Island, New York.

April 1879. Sänger Hall, East Williamsburgh, New York.

22–26 April 1880. Aquarium, New York. *New York Times,* those dates.

7 May 1881. First Baptist Church, Noble Street, Brooklyn. Odell, vol. 11, p. 423.

c. 1911. Wonderland Museum, Detroit.

ANTES, HERBERT East St. Louis, Mo. Toured summer 1942; built new floor show.

ARANA A Peruvian showman who played c. 1940 in Lima, using old character types such as Mama Gerundia and Don Silverio.

ARMSTRONG, W. B. and RUTH G.   Ames Marionettes, Ames, Ia. Beginning c. 1932 played *Bremen Musicians*, Dickens' *Christmas Carol*, *Undersea Ballet*. At Iowa State Fair, Des Moines, 1934, *The Fairy Tale that Came True*, and 1935, *Marionette Circus*.

ARNOLD, M. LOUISE   Redlands, Cal. 1921–1923, *Sleeping Beauty*, *The Man Who Tried to Please Everybody*, *Pierrot and Columbine*, *Krazy Kat and Ignatz Mouse* (after Harriman).

ART-JON MARIONETTES   Pella, Ia. 1942–1943, fairy tales with 30-inch marionettes.

ASH AVENUE MARIONETTE CLUB   Jefferson, Iowa, High School. 1931, fairy scene from *A Midsummer Night's Dream*, *The Magic Whistle*, and other plays.

ATKINSON, MRS. H.   Carman, Manitoba, Canada. 1946–1947, *The Puppet Who Wouldn't Take His Medicine*, Christmas play and fairy tales.

ATKINSON, LOTTIE A.   Portage la Prairie, Canada. Began 1935; repertory of 7 plays and 35 marionettes in 1938. A giant turns into a lion at the drop of a controller!

AUDET, ANDRÉ, and PELLETIER, JACQUES   Les Grandes Marionettes, Montreal, Canada. This theatre, founded c. 1935, played sporadically for French-Canadian audiences until 1941, possibly later.

AUGUR, MUNRO   Monro Marionettes, Teatro Torito, Los Angeles, Cal. 1931, 170 performances of *Pageant of the Founding of Los Angeles*, with 55 marionettes. *Hollywood Revue*, same year.

AUSTIN, VIRGINIA (Mrs. George Curtis)   (P. 378). New York. After the 1933 earthquake in Los Angeles which forced her to close a tearoom she ran on Olvera Street, she joined the Olvera Street Marionettes of C. Ray Smith and Bob Bromley. This company was doing a Jimmy and Mary Jane series at Bullock's department store with a new show each week. While touring later with the Smith company, Miss Austin discovered a market for a low-priced toy puppet. Returning to Los Angeles, she hired an old storeroom in Chinatown where she designed and built the first clown, which she named Clippo after a puppet in the Smith company. Bullock's was the first to stock Clippo, other Los Angeles stores following. One day Edgar Bergen came to the studio with sketches made by Wolo for a new ventriloquial dummy. Miss Austin then modeled and cast the head of Mortimer Snerd. Finding that she could not produce enough Clippos to fill the large order from Marshall Field's in Chicago, she made a contract with the Effanbee Doll Company, which made Clippo and other Austin marionettes for eight years, while she promoted them. In 1938 she began theatre work at the Village Barn where she performed with Clippo and her other marionettes for four months. An agent took over her act, and soon she was in big-time vaudeville. She met George Curtis who aided her in perfecting her act. Later they were married. She played in the principal theatres and night clubs throughout the country, making a number of coast-to-coast tours. A featured number was a large Clippo which worked a smaller Clippo, this one in turn working a tiny clown. During World War II the Curtises took over the manufacture of Clippo, and expanded the line of toy marionettes to include stages, scripts, and the Clippo Club, to which all children who own a Clippo puppet may belong.

AUSTIN, Professor   (P. 276). Marionettes at Pilling's (National) Theatre, New York, 14–19 October 1889. Odell, vol. 14, p. 377.

AYALA, SISKA   Worked with puppets in the movies and originated ideas for some of George Pal's Puppetoons.

AYRES, ELIZABETH   Toronto, Canada. c. 1937, fairy tales and *The Man Who Married a Dumb Wife*.

AZELLA, PAUL   Early twentieth-century Punch and Judy man.

AYRES (MANTELL), LEN   (Pp. 277, 278, 279). With Farleman, Everett, Wash. Royal Manikins, 1903–1906. Independently, 1907–1927, vaudeville and minstrel shows, touring the world.

BADGER, PATRICIA   Beverly Hills, Cal. 1934, amateur show. 1942–1948, professional shows, including *Sorcerer's Apprentice*, *Why the Chimes Rang*, *Circus*.

BAEDER, WILHELMINA West Seattle High School Puppet Club. 1934, *Dirty Hank Triumphant* with marionettes and jigging puppets.

BAGALIO, ALFREDO S. (P. 77). Buenos Aires, Argentina. Uses puppets in teaching. Author of *El Teatro de Títeres en la Escuela*, Editorial Kapelusz y Cia, Buenos Aires, 1944.

BAIRD, BIL (Pp. 338, 374, 380). New York. First show September 1922; worked five years with Tony Sarg. Commercial productions include: shows at Chicago World's Fair, 1933, 1934, for A. & P. Carnival, Swift and Company; road shows for De Soto and Shell Oil, 1937, 1939, 1940; Atlantic Refining Company shows, 1938, 1947, 1948; Philadelphia *Bulletin* shows, 1939, 1940, 1941; show at New York World's Fair, 1939, 1940, for Swift and Company; United States Steel Show, 1940; New York *Times* Fashion Show, 1947. With his wife Cora, Baird has appeared at frequent intervals since 1936 in New York night clubs—the French Casino, Ruban Bleu, Cotillion Room of Hotel Pierre, Persian Room of Plaza Hotel. Special productions for Radio City Music Hall include a dragon, 1936; Christmas show, 1940; Melodrama, 1941; and Bullfight with hand-puppets, 1945. With hand-puppets Bil and Cora Baird appeared in the stage productions of Orson Welles' *Dr. Faustus*, 1937, and a revival of *Liliom*, 1938. With marionettes they worked in the *Ziegfeld Follies*, December 1942–September 1944, and *Nellie Bly*, 1945–1946. From 1942 to date they have taken vaudeville engagements between productions. They have also produced (script, puppets, music, photography) two motion pictures, *Gardening Is Fun*, 1943, and *A Boy and His Cow*, 1944, for the Office of the Co-ordinator of Inter-American Affairs; also *Party Lines*, 1946, for the American Telephone and Telegraph Company. Baird marionettes were used in the motion picture, *The Wee Cooper of Fife*, 1945.

BAKER, BOB Hollywood, Cal. Did shows in Chinatown's "Rice Bowl," 1945; has large puppet manufactory; does store-window decorations; worked with Pal Puppetoons. Built elaborate circus, 1947.

BAKER, EVERETT B. Bay View, Wis. 1924–1934, *Gulliver's Travels, Wizard of Oz, Tom Sawyer, Pinocchio*, and variety in Florida, New England, and Wisconsin.

BAKER, FRANK San Francisco, Cal. Punch and Judy man, magician, and clown who played in San Francisco, 1931 to c. 1936.

BAKER, GEORGE Philadelphia. From c. 1940 produced variety shows and collaborated with John Hall in his production of *The Sleeping Beauty*.

BAKER, LILLIAN Quincy, Ill. 1942, taught children in day nursery to make hand-puppets, marionettes, and shadows.

BALFOUR, W., and BEVIER, E. Balvier Marionettes, Battle Creek, Mich. 1934, *Hansel and Gretel* with Humperdinck music.

BALLAMOS, WILLIAM (P. 291). Partner of John Katsas. Greek shadow-figure shows, Chicago, c. 1935, and possibly earlier; active in 1942.

BALLANTYNE, JEAN (Pp. 367, 369). Baldwin, Long Island, N. Y. Between 1932 and 1939 the Ballantyne family (Jean, Kenneth, Mary, and Robert) produced a series of fairy-tale plays including *The Snow Queen, The Brave Little Tailor*, and *The Old Woman and Her Pig*, using all types of puppets. Experiments in scenic effects and lighting included the use of movable silhouettes in backgrounds and distorted figures done with spotlights and stencils.

BALLINGER, BERTHA Director, Puppet Club, Shaw Junior High School, Philadelphia. 1931, produced a series of hand-puppet plays in French: *Le poisson d'or, Le corbeau et le renard, Le déjeuner de Napoleon*, as well as *Ali Baba, Tweedledum and Tweedledee*.

BANNISTER, VIRGINIA Attic Marionette Theatre, Des Moines, Ia. 1931, *Pinocchio* with 12-inch marionettes.

BARBEAU, MASTER (Pp. 80, 82, 83, 84). Stepson of Daddy Marseille, played in Quebec early 19th century.

BARKER, ENOLA At Blanding Sloan Marionette Theatre, San Francisco, 1928, *Ten Nights in a Barroom*. 1930, performed with Javanese puppets, San Francisco.

BARNES, GRACE   Seattle, Wash. c. 1925, *Peter Rabbit* and circus.

BARNES, SUSAN   (P. 377). St. Louis, Mo. Had many years' experience in the use of puppets at the Occupational Therapy Workshop, St. Louis. Two shows a year were given, in which 30 to 40 patients participated, each being assigned a function which had the greatest therapeutic value for him. 1942, *Pinafore* was adapted by patients. 1943, *The Constant Tin Soldier* was produced with shadows. During the war used puppets in rehabilitation work in a number of Army hospitals. 1938, theory and laboratory work in puppetry for Washington University School of Occupational Therapy.

BARNSDALL JUNIOR PUPPETEERS   See Shull, Margaret.

BARTON   (P. 286). Shadowgraphs at the Grand Museum, New York, 20–25 April, 1891.

BASEMENT MARIONETTES   See Mohler, Ruth Ann.

BASSETT, MERCEDES C. and PHIL D.   The Quixie Marionettes, Boston, Mass. 1935, *The Little Clock Maker*. 1938, Phil and Chic Bassett performed *The Blind Bishop's Goose* at a Vermont summer camp.

BASTIAN, DON   (Pp. 258, 299). San Carlino Sicilian Marionettes. 1898, played São Paolo. 1910, Buenos Aires. Newspaper article in *La Vanguardia*, 1939, by Alfredo Dolver (pseudonym of Hermitte and Villafañe), describes the San Carlino theatre.

BATCHELDER, MARJORIE (Mrs. Paul McPharlin)   (Pp. 345–347, 349, 365, 377, 393). Columbus, O. First performance 7 May 1931 *Rumpelstiltskin* (from Scott-Gatty operetta) with students at Florida State College for Women. 1932, Flastacowo Puppeteers organized and played *Doctor Faust, The Gooseberry Mandarin,* and Christmas plays. 1933, Dunsany's *Fame and the Poet,* Van der Veer's *St. Cyprian and the Devil, The Wolf at the Door, Weather.* 1933–1934, built marionette production of Aristophanes' *The Birds* for M.A. degree at Ohio State University. Gave puppet demonstrations at Ohio State Fair, 1934, 1935, and a series of short plays with students. 1936, began rod-puppet experiments with *St. George and the Dragon, Columbine's Birthday,* and a group of Christmas plays including Ruthenburg's *The Miracle of the Virgin of Guadaloupe.* 1937, rod-puppet production of Maeterlinck's *The Death of Tintagiles.* 1938, revived previous productions and added *Father Christmas,* a mummer's play. 1939, used large plastic wood rod-puppets in *Danny Duck's Dizzy Day* by Martin Stevens, built for the Seventh World Poultry Congress; class productions at Ohio State of *Mr. Fish and Mrs. Bones,* by Gordon Craig, and other plays. 1940 was a year off duty to prepare for Ph.D. exams; degree received June 1942. That year and the next, various propaganda plays and class productions relating to the war effort were built and shadow-figures of colored Vinylite were used for a circus. In collaboration with the Romance Language Department, Villafañe's *La Calle de los Fantasmas* was produced in Spanish and in English. 1946, hand-, rod-, and hand-and-rod-puppets were used in a children's play, *Baba Yaga,* by Peg Blickle, produced for the Columbus Community Theatre. 1947, *Baba Yaga* revived, and short children's plays for parties. Under the name, Marjorie Batchelder's Puppet Players, most of the above productions were given professionally in and around Ohio. Books include: *The Puppet Theatre Handbook,* Harper and Brothers, New York City, 1947; *Rod-Puppets and the Human Theatre,* The Ohio State University Press, Columbus, 1947; *Hand-and-Rod-Puppets* (with Vivian Michael), College of Education, Ohio State University, Columbus, 1947.

BATES, BEVERLEY   Richmond, Va. Worked with Caroline Lutz at Westhampton College, University of Richmond, giving shows in her English courses. 1937, *Thunder Witch.* 1940, *The Night Before Christmas.* 1944, Negro songs and dances at the American Red Cross headquarters, London. 1946, *Stringing Along.* 1947, *T. B. Daze,* in connection with occupational therapy work for which she is taking hospital clinical training.

BAUMANN, GUSTAVE   (Pp. 358, 367, 368, 385). Santa Fe Puppet Wranglers, Santa Fe, N. Mex. 1933, *The Birthday of the Infanta, The Golden Dragon Mind, No*

You Don't!, Is It Not Monstrous? Baumann specializes in Indian ceremonial scenes and dances which he has derived from close study of the Southwest Indians. 1942–1943, *Please Go Away and Let Me Sleep, Harlequinade,* and *Christmas Flies to Giumbo Island.*

BAYLIS, SAM (Pp. 273, 274, 286). Presented his Royal French Marionettes at Miner's Bowery Theatre, New York, 5–10 August 1878. Later gave shadow-figure shows.

BEACH, CURTIS The Strolling Puppeteers. 1931–1935, toured New England with plays and dances including: *Jack and the Beanstalk, A Night in a Garden, Dance of Skeletons, Box and Cox, Rip Van Winkle, The El'phant's Child, The Piper Takes a Wife.*

BEAUX ARTS MARIONETTES See Woodhouse, Henry W.

BECK, E., and brother (P. 128). Acrobats from London, England, in fall of 1865 came to America. In spring 1866, played *Punch and Judy* in streets of Brooklyn. 1866–1869, Boston Common.

BECKER, GARRETT (P. 270). Manager for Jean Gros, then assistant manager for Tony Sarg until November 1928. Founded the International Marionette Laboratory, New York, in 1929, and built *The Mummy* (after Edgar Allan Poe); *The Golem.* In January 1931, the Laboratory, as well as Sue Hastings' studio, was destroyed by fire.

BEER, ELOISE Miami Beach, Fla. Studied under Sue Hastings at the University of Miami then took over the day classes in puppetry there. 1947, *Orlando Furioso* with hand-puppets, *The Prince and the Mermaid.* 1948, *Punch and Judy,* with hand-puppets.

BELL FAMILY (Pp. 245, 248). Played in Mexico with string-puppets in 19th century.

BELLENFANT Punch and Judy showman, played as a prologue to a Tony Sarg show in 1922, and was active long before—"Tony Sarg's Puppeteers," *Puppetry 1932,* p. 33.

BELMONT, BOBBY (P. 278). Chicago, Ill. Robert Nelson, b. 1920, son of Nicholas Nelson, played theatres and hotel floor shows until his death in 1945.

BELMONT'S MANIKINS See Nelson, Edward "Nicholas."

BELOFF, ANGELINA Mexico City. 1938, was sent to Europe by the Ministry of Education to study puppets in order to improve the work of its theatres. Upon her return she designed puppets and settings for them.

BENNER, LARRY *Punch and Judy* and ventriloquism with Beatty-Wallace Circus, 1943 season.

BENNETT, BUD Used puppets in his work with Junior Chamber of Commerce, St. Paul, and Boy Scout troops in Ohio. Lectures on puppetry at regional conferences of Boy Scout leaders.

BENNINGTON HIGH SCHOOL MARIONETTE THEATRE Bennington, Vt. 1930, Mourguet's *The Coq Brothers.* 1931, Chekhov's *The Marriage Proposal* and *The Boor, Three Heads in a Well, Dear Little Wife.*

BENTON, PAULINE (Pp. 289, 348, 387, 388). Red Gate Shadow Puppets until 1937, then Red Gate Players, New York. Studied manipulation with a Chinese shadow showman, and has collected Chinese shadow-figures with which she has presented shows, c. 1931 to date, throughout the United States. Music, scripts, puppets, and scenery are authentic, with a minimum of adaptation to Western audiences. Repertory includes: *The Land of Shadow Puppets, The Legend of the White Snake, How Shadow Puppets Came to Be, The Chinese Nightingale, The Foolish Toad, How the Elephant Got Its Trunk, The Magic Garden, The Cowherd and the Weaving Maid, The Spider and the Dragon, The Drum Dance, Festival in Peiping, The Fox Spirit, The Temple of the Golden Mountain, The Feast of the Long Life Peaches.* For the 1937 season, the Chinese dancer King Lan Chew acted as mistress of ceremonies. During the Golden Gate Exposition in San Francisco, 1940, the Red Gate Players performed in Old Chinatown.

BERDAN, GEORGE Detroit, Mich. 1933–1934, *Punch and Judy* and *The Forty-Niners*. 1935, his company was named The Blockhead Puppets and added *Casper in the Haunted Mill* to its repertory. 1935, directed *Ali Baba and the Forty Thieves* at the Utley Branch Public Library Puppet Workshop. 1936, directed Dathan Class of the Scovel Presbyterian Church in shadow-figure production, *The Story of Joseph*, produced *Hansel and Gretel*, variety, with the Studio Puppets of the Parkman Library, and *Puppet Potpourri* with the Utley Library group, using several types of puppets.

BERG, HARRIET Detroit, Mich. 1946, *Byrano de Cyranac*, whose adventures with his nose were inspired by, but are quite different from, those of the famous Cyrano.

BERGEN, EDGAR (Pp. 140, 378). Ventriloquist, began c. 1923. Created the character of Charlie McCarthy c. 1930; later introduced Mortimer Snerd.

BERKE, MIRIAM LEVIN Detroit, Mich. 1934–1935, hand-puppet productions at the Jewish Community Center, *Epaminondas, The Golden Ball, The Three Wishes, Mr. Sunny and Mr. Rainy*.

BERKELEY MARIONETTES See Lowe, Florence.

BERNARDO, MANE Argentina. Director of a puppet theatre, Títeres de Cachiporra, which was shown at the International Puppet Exposition Theatre Museum, Buenos Aires, 1943.

BEST, WARREN Chicago, Ill. String-puppet shows, grand opera with rod-puppets, telecasts over WBKB and W9XKB, 1946–1947.

BETHUNE, GEORGE Ann Arbor, Mich. Marionette productions of *A Christmas Carol*, 1936, *A Chinese Fantasy*, 1937, and *The Knave of Hearts*, 1938. Worked with the Grand Rapids Art Gallery Puppeteers.

BIEHLER, MARY Austinburg, O. 1935, with high school students produced *Le cousin moutardier* and *Lima Beans*.

BILINSKY, B. MARYA St. Louis, Mo. 1932, *Aladdin and His Wonderful Lamp*.

BIRKHEAD, FLORENCE VAN ECK St. Louis, Mo. For the Pevely Dairy, *Marionettes in the News*, 1937.

BISHOP, MARION Ridgewood and Roselle, N. J. Performed with 3-foot marionettes in a tent in Children's World, New York World's Fair, 1939. During summer of 1940 played at Hamid's Million Dollar Pier, Temple Theatre, Atlantic City. 1942, gave performances in Jersey schools of *Ali Baba and the Forty Thieves* and *The Magic Cloak of Oz*.

BIXBY, MEREDITH Meredith Marionettes, Ferndale, Mich 1932–1934, *Dr. Faust*. 1934–1935, a commercial show for Norge Refrigerator Co. 1935–1936, *Ali Baba*, with Norge show continued. 1936–1937, *Treasure Island*. 1937–1938, *Treasure Island* with one troupe; *Dr. Faust* and *The Little Humpbacked Horse* with a second. 1938–1939, *The Little Bear and the Wizard* (from Russian folklore). 1939–1940, *Aladdin*. 1940 and 1946, *The Magic Stalk and the Circus*. 1946–1947, *Aladdin*. 1947–1948, *The Little Humpbacked Horse*, completely rebuilt. These shows are played to school children in midwestern and eastern states.

BLACK, ALAN Palo Alto, Cal. 1942–1943, Christmas pantomime with hand-puppets.

BLAINE, ELEANOR G. Attic Puppets, Winnetka, Ill. 1923, *Snow White and the Seven Dwarfs*. 1924, *Dr. Doolittle*. 1925, *A Christmas Carol*. 1927, *The Three Princesses in the Blue Mountain*. These plays were performed in Chicago and Winnetka. See also Winnetka Attic Puppets.

BLANCAN, PETER (Pp. 91–93, 245). "Pitoresque and Mechanique Theatre," Columbian Museum, Boston, 26 September 1808; Broadway, opposite the Hospital, New York, 27 December 1808. Fantoccini and Chinese shades.

BLASE, PANSY Princeton, Ind., High School. 1933, *Rhythm and Color Revue* with marionettes, by students.

BLATT, WILLIAM MOSHER Brookline, Mass. 1932, 1933, *The Story of the Second Kalendar* (from Arabian Nights), *The Square Triangle*, a modern farce, *My Lady's Tongue* (from *Much Ado About Nothing*), *The Lost Charm*, and 8 other one-act plays with marionettes.

BLICKLE, PEG   Columbus, O. 1934, variety. 1936–1937, in Grand Rapids, Mich., with Cherry Jerry, George Bethune, and Millicent McElwee: *The Frog Prince, My Lady's Juggler*. 1938–1940, in Racine, Wis.: *Beauty and the Beast, Aladdin, The Mermaid's Secret*, variety, assisted by Hilda Greenquist, Helen Fancher Marshman. 1946–1947, wrote *Baba Yaga* for Marjorie Batchelder and worked with her on children's shows. 1947–1948, continued children's programs with Ohio State University students.

BLITZ, EUGENE   (Pp. 125, 128, 229). At Grand Central Variety Theatre, Philadelphia, 8–20 December, and again in Christmas week, 1874—Philadelphia *Public Ledger* for these dates. At Tivoli Hall, New York, 21–26 July 1879. In 1857 "Signior Blitz," magician, gave two shows in New Brunswick, N. J.—"The First Century of the New Brunswick Stage," by Oral Summers, *Journal of Rutgers University Library*, vol. 5, No. 1, p. 32.

BLOCKHEAD PUPPETS   See Berdan, George.

BLUM, MAX   San Rafael, Cal. 1946, a young puppeteer who began making marionettes when eight years old.

BOECK, ORVILLE   Friendly House Marionette Club, Davenport, Ia. 1936, *The Mysterious Hindu* with 22-inch trick marionettes; *Spanish Bull Fight*. 1937, *Circus Days* with 30 marionettes. 1938, previous shows with variety. 1939, with Mississippi Marionettes produced *Christmas Varieties, Under the Stars, The Big Circus, Oriental Varieties*.

BOTTINI, PATRICK   San Rafael, Cal. A young man, without the use of his legs, began making small cardboard figures and costuming them while flat on his back with both legs broken and his left arm in a cast. A teacher showed him how to make puppet clowns. When, after five years, he was able to sit in a wheel chair, he began to give shows. His friends operated the figures and he directed. All his performances were benefits for the Red Cross, children in China, and other worthy causes. His productions include: *Petroushka* (Stravinsky), *Madama Butterfly* (Puccini), *Hansel and Gretel*. His 1948 show was the Bottini Marionette Revue with dances, circus acts, and a pink-and-blue ballet.

BOTTINIER, NED   String-puppet showman, early 20th century.

BOYD, ALFRED   Grand Forks, N. D. 1921, *Red Riding Hood*. 1922, *Snow White*, and *A Pirate Play*. 1924, *Two Blind Men and a Donkey*, by Dondo. 1925, *The Wash Tub*, by Dondo. 1927, *The Pie and the Tart*, by Dondo, and *University Burlesque*.

BOYD, SHEILA   Pulcinella Puppet Players, Victoria, B. C. 1938, *Rumpelstiltskin* and variety.

BRADLEY, JAMES   (P. 286). Shadowgraphs at Grand Museum, New York, 25–30 May 1891. Odell, vol. 14, p. 682.

BRAGALDI   With Palmo, presented a season of marionettes in ballet and English-style pantomimes at the Apollo Theatre, New York, 4 December 1837–4 February 1838.

BRAHAM BROTHERS   (P. 285). Shadowgraphs at Miner's Eighth Avenue Theatre, New York, February and April 1885; spring 1886, National Theatre, and fall 1887, Tony Pastor's. Odell, vol. 12, p. 535; vol. 13, pp. 91, 92, 510.

BRAITHEWAITE, SHIRLEY   Mayfair Marionettes, Cleveland, O. 1933, *Jack and the Beanstalk*.

BRAND, LOUISE   Milwaukee, Wis. 1926, *Know-Naught, the Witch of Ignorance*, a health play for children, presented by the Wisconsin Anti-Tuberculosis League.

BRANDON, RICHARD   See Yale Puppeteers.

BRAUN, PAUL   d. 4 August 1940. Baltimore, Md. 1929, *Monkey Business*, a marionette revue. 1930, *Ching Ling Fei* and *The Three Wishes* (American style). 1931, *Little David* (from *The Green Pastures* of Marc Connelly), and *The Three Wishes* (German style). 1932, *George Washington Revue, The Tar Baby, The Archaeologists*, and *Decameron Nights* (with marionettes and shadows). 1937, worked on an experimental film. 1939, had a permanent theatre in a Baltimore store.

BREDT, DOUGLAS   Wonderland Marionettes, Mason City, Ia. A young puppeteer who heard *Traviata* on the radio and determined to build puppets to enact opera. By

1943 he had prepared small shows of *Traviata, Faust, Carmen, Madama Butter-fly*, and built productions of *Aladdin, Bluebeard, Cinderella, The Prince Without a Tongue, Star of the East*, and *Stick and Strings Revue*.

BREON, JOHN   Rockford, Ill. 1939, *Alice in Wonderland* and *The Dragon Znee Zee*.

BRICKELL, RICHARD   (Pp. 42, 43, 44, 46). Partner of Richard Mosely in presenting string-puppets in New York, 7 September 1747, and possibly in Philadelphia, 30 December 1742.

BRIDGE, PEGGY   Bridget Puppets, Roosevelt School, Hackensack, N. J. 1932, *Mr. Punch's Magic Shop*. 1933, *How the Elephant Got His Trunk* and *The Elephant's Child*, with hand-puppets.

BRIGGS, WINIFRED G.   Governor George Clinton School, Poughkeepsie, N. Y. 1941, *Rumpelstiltskin* and *Western Knight*, a musical comedy by Ruth M. Shafer, played with marionettes and hand-puppets.

BROCKWAY, ALTHEA   1934, *The Easter Story* and *The Christmas Story*, with marionettes.

BROMLEY, BOB   (P. 382). New York. c. 1930, worked with the Yale Puppeteers in the Teatro Torito, Los Angeles. 1932, *Pup-Pup-a-Dup*. 1933, *Jimmy's Adventures at the Circus, Puppet Gaieties of 1933*. With C. Ray Smith's Olvera Puppeteers, Los Angeles, c. 1936, started floor-show act, and has played it constantly to date. 1939, England and Germany. 1941, Bob Bromley's Personality Puppets in variety programs. 1943, toured with Ray Kinney and his orchestra in *A Salute to Hawaii*. 1944, toured South America. 1946-1947, toured America and England and while in the latter country made a color film, *Cinderella*, with his marionettes.

BROWN, CHARLES E.   d. 11 February 1947. A solo performer, started out with six trunks full of equipment for a string-puppet show in the Middle West in 1883, and discarded them soon after for two suitcases in which he carried only Punch and Judy and ventriloquial figures, remaining active until the 1930's.

BROWN, FORMAN   See Yale Puppeteers.

BROWN, SARAH   (P. 377). State Hospital, Ypsilanti, Mich. c. 1936 used puppets in occupational therapy.

BROWNCROFT PUPPETS   School 46, Rochester, N. Y. 1935, *Ali Baba*.

BRUNCLIK, MILOS   Argentina. Director of a Czech puppet theatre in Buenos Aires. At International Puppet Exposition, Theatre Museum, Buenos Aires, 1943, showed regional characters and devils, dragons, magicians, and witches.

BUCK HILL MARIONETTES   See Pugliesi, Constance.

BUCKNELL, BRUCE   1942-1943, used 39-inch marionettes in floor show while stationed with the Army in Oregon and California; 1944-1945 while stationed in the Aleutians.

BUEHLER, ANNE   Pasadena, Cal. 1935, *Cinderella*, variety, and *Vaudeville of the Fairies*, with 18-inch marionettes.

BUFANO, REMO   (Pp. 1, 282, 301, 342, 345, 347, 359, 363, 370, 373, 374, 385, 386, 387, 393). New York. 12 November 1894-17 June 1948. After seeing a Sicilian marionette show, built his own version of the *Orlando Furioso* legends which he presented in Italian to the neighborhood children, 1914. Next year he did the scenes in English, and added in following years *Pagliacci, The Doctor in Spite of Himself* (after Molière), *Bluebeard, Hansel and Gretel, Red Riding Hood*, and *Snow Drop*. In March 1917, gave a Paladin play at Richmond Hill House, so bridging from the old traditional to the new artistic period. 1918, *Orlando Furioso* revived, with *Uncle Sam, the Devil, or the Kaiser* performed at the Thimble Theatre. 1920, built a curtain raiser for *Wake Up, Jonathan* and did *Lima Beans* at the Provincetown Playhouse, New York. 1922, *Orlando Furioso in Fantastic Fricassee*, and *Two Slatterns and a King*, by Edna St. Vincent Millay. 1923, *The Tinderbox* (in Baltimore, Md.) and *Gallant Cassian*, by Arthur Schnitzler. Manuel de Falla's operetta *El retablo de Maese Pedro* was presented in Town Hall, December 1925. String-puppets were built for *The Knife in the Wall*, by Frances Lightner, at the Selwyn Theatre, and hand-puppets for Rostand's *The Last Night of Don Juan* at the Greenwich Village Theatre, with Augustin Duncan as one of the puppeteers.

In 1926 a studio theatre was opened at 51 West 12 Street with this repertory: *The Tragedy of Mr. Punch, Jack and the Beanstalk, The Three Bears, Mother Goose Review, The Giant of the Enchanted Voice, The Old Man of the Mountain, The Frog Prince, Fantasy in Flutes and Figures.* Directed *The Oracle Drum*, by Julian Freedman, in Paris. 1927, *Rumpelstiltskin*, and *Pinocchio*, with actors and marionettes. In 1928 presented at the Provincetown Playhouse, New York: *Cinderella, Julius Caesar's Circus, The Big Fight, The Fisherman and His Wife. El Retablo de Maese Pedro* revived at Jolson Theatre in same year. 1929, *The Tinderbox* and *The Fox and the Grapes.* 1930, *In Shushan, the Capitol* (Syracuse, N. Y.), and *A Midsummer Night's Dream.* 1931, built a group of 10-foot figures from the designs of Robert Edmund Jones, worked by rods and strings, for Stravinsky's *Oedipus Rex*, sponsored by the League of Composers and performed at the Grand Opera House, Philadelphia, with Leopold Stokowsky leading the Philadelphia Orchestra. Later presented at the Metropolitan Opero House, New York. 1932, revived several previous productions, and added *The Little King* (after O. Soglow) and *In 1492.* For Le Gallienne's production of *Alice in Wonderland*, 1933, built 7-foot marionettes of the Walrus and the Carpenter. 1934–1935, directed, with Grace Wilder, WPA puppet work in New York. By March 1935, over 1000 performances had been given to audiences totaling nearly 182,000. Forty-seven workers were employed and 47 productions presented, 19 of which were built in the WPA workshop. Plays included: *Treasure Island, Babar, Oliver Twist, Great Mikko.* 1935, built a 35-foot marionette for Billy Rose's production of *Jumbo* at the Hippodrome. 1939, *Revue* with *Esquire* characters. 1940, *Esquire* Christmas Fair. In 1942, built masks of Mammoth and Dinosaur and played part of the latter in Thornton Wilder's *The Skin of Our Teeth.* 1944, built television shows for later presentation. 1945, worked in Hollywood on a puppet sequence for the film, *Yolanda and the Thief*, produced by MGM. 1946, shows for children's parties. 1947, built marionettes and masks for American Repertory Theatre production of *Alice in Wonderland.* 1948, experimented with puppet films for television using a combination marionette and stop motion technique. Returning from the West Coast, where he had been appearing in a commercial television broadcast, he was killed in a plane crash. Publications: *Be a Puppet Showman*, The Century Company, New York, 1933; *Magic Strings*, The Macmillan Company, New York, 1939.

BULLOCK, WILLIAM JOHN (Pp. 156–184, 186, 188, 190, 191, 193, 199, 262, 263). Proprietor of the Royal Marionettes. He sent his first company to America under the agents McDonough and Earnshaw, who had been associated in October 1871, as managers of the St. James Theatre, New York—Odell, vol. 9, p. 194. The company sailed to America in Guion & Co.'s U. S. Mail Steamship *Nevada*—Playbill for Horticultural Hall, Boston, May 1874, in Harvard College Library Theatre Collection. This company followed the itinerary below: New York, Robinson Hall, 8 September–1 November 1873; Brooklyn, Athenaeum, 4–15 November; Newark, Kimball's Opera House, 24 November–12 December; Philadelphia, Concert Hall, 15 December 1873–10 January 1874; Washington, Willard's Hall, 12–30 January; Baltimore, Maryland Institute, 3–14 February; Harrisburg, 16–28 February (McDonough and Earnshaw were jockeyed out of their connection by McLaren, Bullock's agent, on 23 February. At the end of the Harrisburg run, the best members of the company joined McDonough and Earnshaw for a new troupe, leaving McLaren to continue the tour as best he could): Reading, Mishler's Academy of Music, 5–7, 12–14 March; Baltimore, Maryland Institute, 26 March–11 April; Pittsburgh, Academy of Music, 13 April–2 May; Chicago, Kingsbury Music Hall, 13–30 May; St. Louis, De Bar's Opera House, 8–13 June. Meanwhile, to thwart McDonough and Earnshaw, Bullock sent over a second company, which also arrived on the S. S. *Nevada.* It played this itinerary: Brooklyn, Hooley's Opera House, 6–11 April 1874; Boston, Horticultural Hall, 16 April–16 May (one of the later playbills for this engagement, preserved in the Harvard College Library Theatre Collection, states that the scene for the opening minstrel-show numbers was aboard the *Nevada*); Hartford, Allyn Hall, 18–23 May; New York, Robinson Hall, 6–13 June.

BULOW, VIRGINIA   Junior High School, Poplar Bluff, Mo. 1938, *Snow White and the Seven Dwarfs.*

BUNIN, HOPE and MAURY   New York. Hand-puppets in floor shows. 1946–1947, played in a musical comedy in London, and made a six months' tour of England.

BUNIN, LOUIS   (Pp. 349, 380). New York. 1929, with Bernardo Ortiz de Montellano and Julio Castellanos in Mexico City founded a marionette theatre under the patronage of the Department of Fine Arts and performed *The Hairy Ape*, by O'Neill, *The Astute Rabbit, The Well of the Saints*, by John M. Synge. 1933, *The Ball of the Mannequins*, a comedy by Bruno Jasienski, at the New School for Social Research, New York. 1939, stop-motion movie in the Petroleum Building, New York World's Fair. 1940, *The Three Wishes*. 1946, puppet sequence in Ziegfeld Follies. 1947, puppet film in color of *Alice in Wonderland*, photographed in Paris.

BURHAUS, HOPE   Burlington, Ia. 1932, Scenes from *Alice in Wonderland.*

BURNETT, HARRY   See Yale Puppeteers.

BURNS, LORENE BYRNES   Sioux Falls, S. D. 1934–1935, produced with 5- and 6-inch marionettes: *Little Boy Blue, Alice in Wonderland, Baby Moses, The Little Red Measles, Mistress Mary's Mysteries, The Good Samaritan, Hickety Pickety Pie, Moon Princess, The Christmas Gift*. Performances given in churches, day nurseries, and libraries.

BURNS, ROBIN (Miss)   Sioux Falls, S. D. 1934, *The Little Red Hen Show* with 5-inch marionettes.

BURROUGHS MARIONETTE THEATRE   See Shirley, Lenna L.

BUSHÉ, JOSEPH M.   (P. 392). Omaha, Neb. In 1621 one of his ancestors in Strasbourg gave a show with a moving doll. The tradition of showmanship was carried on by other members of the family. His grandfather performed in American vaudeville and circuses. Bushé began working puppets at the age of eight; 1912–1914, assisted Max and Al Klass, Punch showmen. c. 1933, took up puppets as a means of livelihood. 1935, gave nearly 200 performances (some in Mexico) of a minstrel and variety show and taught puppetry through the Omaha Recreation Department. 1936, over 400 performances of an advertising show for the Commercial Shirt Corporation of New York. 1942, circus with marionettes and rod-puppets. 1948, continues performances in night clubs, side shows of circuses, and for commercial sponsors.

BUSHONG, MARGARET   Bushong Marionettes, Lawrence, Kan. Inspired by Edith Flack Ackley's book on marionettes, she and her sisters became interested in giving shows. 1933, *The Enchanted Princess*. 1934, *The Three Wishes, The Foam Maiden*. 1935, *Puss-in-Boots*. 1936, variety. 1937, *Pinafore*. 1938, *Hansel and Gretel, Arachne's Web*. 1939, *Daniel Boone, Kentucky Settler; Christopher Columbus*. 1940, *A Midsummer Night's Dream*. 1944, *The Brewing of Brains*. 1945, *Grandmother's Red Boots*. 1947, program of dancers and musicians. Has taught classes in marionette making at Lawrence Summer Art Studio, Lawrence Junior High School, Lawrence Recreation Center, and Cheley Camps, Estes Park, Colorado. Has built marionettes for other puppeteers.

BUTLER, HORACIO   Argentina. 1934, with company called La Sirena, presented children's show in Diapasón. Assisted by Silvina Ocampo and Alberto Morera.

BUTLER, MURRAY   Cleveland, O. 1925, *Punchinello.*

BUXTON, ROGER K.   Buxie's Marionettes, Watertown, Mass. A family group which played: *The Bell Tavern*, a drama of Old Salem, 1921. *Hansel and Gretel*, 1922. *The Three Wishes*, 1923. *The Night Before Christmas*, 1924. *Nini-Nini-Nott* and *Childe Rowland*, from Old English tales, 1925. *Fatima*, 1927. *The Piper of Roussilon*, 1928. *Safety at High Noon*, 1931.

CABALI, F.   (P. 245). Showed Italian marionettes at the Teatro Iturbide, Mexico City, 1869.

CAIN PARK THEATRE Cleveland, O. See Joseph, Helen H.

CALDERON, PASQUAL (Pp. 74–76, 78). Granted a license to perform puppets in Lima, Peru, 1786.

CALDO, JOSEFFI (P. 301). Proprietor of a Sicilian puppet theatre, the Tripoli, in East 112 Street, New York, 1913.

CAMPBELL, GERALDINE and CHESTER Grand Rapids, Mich. 1942, *The Golden Beetle* with marionettes and shadows.

CAMPBELL, PROFESSOR *Punch and Judy* at the Gaiety Museum, New York, at intervals from September 1890 to June 1891. Odell, Vol. 14, pp. 682–686.

CAMP KIWANIS South Hanson, Mass. Summer 1938, *Any Child, The Bridge, The Feast of Lanterns, The Dragon with the Thirteen Tails, The Fancy Flower Thief, Midsummer Eve, Kiwanee Magic, Camp Memories, Tinkle Bell, Aunt Grumpie.*

CAMP TALCOTT MARIONETTE GROUP Huguenot, Orange County, N. J. 1936, *Robinson Crusoe* and *Hiawatha and the Great Pearl Feather.*

CANDLER, "DOC" December 1943, *Punch and Judy* in Toyland of Farmer's Supply Company, Lancaster, Pa.

CANTERBURY MARIONETTES See Stolp, James.

CANTONE, VITO (P. 299) Puppet showman from Cantania, Sicily, who played in Argentina between 1900 and 1910.

CANTOS, JOSEF IGNACIO (Pp. 75, 76). Granted a license to perform puppets in Lima, Peru, 1786.

CARL and MINOKA Los Angeles, Cal. Played a puppet act on the USO circuit, c. 1945.

CARLSON, MYRTLE 1945, took over Virginia Upson's production of *Dame Wiggins* and presented it in Minneapolis schools.

CARNEVALE, CARMEN R. Los Angeles, Cal. Punch and Judy showman, still active in 1948.

CARR, MICHAEL CARMICHAEL (P. 325). (d. 1928.) Worked with Gordon Craig in Florence, c. 1914. In 1919 worked with Ben Hecht on an unproduced play. Carr specialized in abstract puppets.

CARROLL and DIETRICH and their marionettes played their *Fun Parade* on USO White Circuit, Unit 72, 1942.

CARSON "Automatic figures" at the Star Museum, Eighth Avenue, New York, 21–26 October 1889. Odell, vol. 14, p. 404.

CASADY, RICHARD R. Oklahoma City, Okla. 1929, *The Sleeping Beauty.* 1930, *Hansel and Gretel* and *The Coq Brothers* (Mourguet). 1932, *Every Dog Has His Day* (Dondo). 1933, *Casper Among the Savages* (Pocci), *Harry, Unemployed.* 1934, revival *Caspar* and variety. 1937, *Portraits by Punch* and *Punch and Judy.* 1940, *The Black King* and *The Green Nose* (both by Perry Dilley). 1941, revivals of previous shows.

CASCIO, SALVATORE Sicilian showman playing in New York c. 1920.

CASTLE MARIONETTES Dubuque, Ia. 1934, *The Three Wishes, Belinda and the Dragon, A Minuet, The Flying Carpet, Zolan and his Violin, Melodrama, A Nativity Tableau.* Around 150 performances given 1934–1935.

CENTRAL PARK PLAYERS Louisville, Ky. See Noonan, Tommy.

CENTRAL PUPPETEERS See Magon, Jero.

CHAMPLIN, E. E. Seward, Neb. 1921, *Jack and the Beanstalk.*

CHAPMAN, MERCEDES Chicago, Ill. 1929, *The Three Wishes.* 1930, *The First Christmas Tree,* at Northwestern University Settlement House.

CHARLES, ARTHUR M. (Pp. 330, 363). Instructor at Earlham College, Richmond, Ind., who used hand-puppets to illustrate his Faustus course before 1914.

CHEATLE, ESTHER Cheatle Marionettes, Chicago, Ill. Played variety in the Chicago area for several years c. 1944–1945.

CHEEK'S MARIONETTES North Division High School, Milwaukee, Wis. 1933, variety.

CHESSÉ, RALPH (Pp. 357, 359, 385). San Francisco, Cal. First show 10 May 1928, *Hamlet,* at Blanding Sloan Puppet Theatre. *Emperor Jones* and *Macbeth* also produced the same year. 1929, *Don Juan.* 1931, *Romeo and Juliet.* 1932, *The Miser,* Molière, and *Noël,* Bouchor. 1933, *The Mikado, Pinafore, Uncle Tom's Cabin, The Merchant of Venice.* 1934, *Alice in Wonderland, Dr. Jekyll and Mr. Hyde, Mistress of the Inn,* Goldoni. In 1936 directed the WPA production of Meyer Levin's dramatization of *The Crock of Gold* and produced *Hansel and Gretel.* 1939, *Snow White* for the Federal Theatre. 1940, *Pinocchio* for Golden Gate Exposition (a Federal Theatre project). 1945, variety for window display and *Night Before Christmas* for City of Paris Department Store. 1947, *Soliloquies and Scenes.* Chessé's special contribution to puppetry was adult productions of drama comparable to those of the human theatre.

CHICAGO MARIONETTE GUILD 1940, *A Midsummer Night's Dream* produced by a group of Chicago puppeteers including John and Viola Annal, Esther Cheatle, George and Lucile Cole, Henrietta and Rose Dekker, Ed Fricke, Lavinia Haigue, Esther Hixson, Agnes and Ida Mae Hoffmann, Edward Merrington, James and Mrs. John Stolp, Helene Thurston.

CHICAGO PARK DISTRICT MARIONETTES See Vestal, Don.

CHICAGO PUPPET PLAYERS See Tillstrom, Burr and Follmer, Frank.

CHISOLM, MARY B., and STEWART, MARY c. 1920, produced plays by Mary Stewart published in her book, *The Land of Punch and Judy.*

CHRAMER, FREDRIK Chicago, Ill. Opened 23 February 1942 at the Kungsholm Restaurant with *La Traviata* done with rod-puppets, and lavish scenery and costumes to recorded music. Until the restaurant burned in 1947, productions of many operas were given its patrons. 1948, theatre being rebuilt.

CHRIST, MAYME High School, Clear Lake, Ia. 1936, *Happy Landing.* 1939, *Sleeping Beauty* and *Adventures of the Peppermint Boy.*

CHRISTINE, JOHN ELLWOOD See Ellwood and Ripel.

CLAREMONT, N. H., MARIONETTES 1933, *Red Riding Hood* and variety: *The Mouse Trap; Holly Goblin's Christmas Eve* and other plays.

CLARK, G. FLETCHER (P. 345). 1922, founded puppet club, University of California, which produced *The Singing Master* (from the French), and an adaptation of Marlowe's *Faust.* 1923, *The Bird Feng.* 1926, devoted his time increasingly to sculpture.

CLARK, MARIE Middletown, O. 1944, presented a marionette dancer with her piano recital. The same year she did *Noah's Ark* with shadows and variety. She gives occasional talks on puppetry.

CLEARY, MRS. VINCENT Margot's Marionettes, Montreal, Canada. Started 1934 with a packing box stage; later developed a larger theatre and played in department stores.

CLEVELAND, WILLIAM H., JR. Playbox Puppets. 1941, *The Rusher Rushed, Monkeyshines,* a pantomime, *Punch and Judy* (at Tulsa, Okla.), *Pensive Puppets,* by Efimora (at Milton, Mass.).

COBB, ALICE Pine Mountain Settlement School, Harlan County, Ky. 1934, variety with ballads and folk dances.

COBB, OTIS 1931, *Red Riding Hood and the Wolf* and *Cinderella* (with hand puppets and a flat rod-puppet).

CODMAN, RICHARD (Pp. 132, 156). Liverpool, England, Punch and Judy man, who made two trips to America sometime after 1879.

COHEN, MILDRED Harrisburg, Pa. 1933, *Snow White* at Jewish Community Center.

COHEN, THEODORE Mad Hatter Marionettes, Edmonton, Canada. First production 1934. Staged 7 plays and scenes with 50 marionettes.

COLBY, ELINOR Claremont, N. H. Between 1933 and 1936 produced plays and variety including *On a Cannibal Island, Harvest Moon, With the Help of Pierrette.*

COLE, GEORGE L. Chicago, Ill. 1936, *The Singing Lesson* and *Sleeping Beauty.* 1937, *Jack and the Beanstalk.* 1938, *Cinderella* with marionettes and jigging puppets, *The Fate of a Pearl Necklace,* with rod-puppets (assisted by John Annal). 1939, circus. 1942, revival *Beauty and the Beast.* 1944, *Thumbelina.* 1946, under the name of Cole Marionettes, produced *The King of the Golden River* and *The Tinderbox.*

COLEMAN, FAY ROSS   Milledgeville, Ill. Began 1932 with *The Three Wishes* and *Three Little Pigs*. 1933, *The Sire de Maletroit's Door*. 1934, *Pierre Pathelin*. Worked with Victor Charles Puppeteers, 1940–1941. Did variety in Army shows 1941–1942. Upon discharge from the Army in 1945 married Barbara Foxwell and with her gave floor shows while attending the University of Wisconsin. 1948, working with the Cole Marionettes in *The King of the Golden River*.

COLLIE, BENNADETTA   In October 1937 at Dallas, Tex., organized a puppet group with the Recreation Project of the WPA and produced *Punch and Judy, Under Western Skies, Klowns in Minstrelsy, Thanksgiving, Witches' Pranks, Choir Christmas Carols, Wishing for the Moon, Seasons Ballet, Nebucadnezzah* and divertissements.

COLLINS, ETHEL D. W.   Abington, Pa. 1936, *The Flowering Staff* and *The Shield of Roland* produced with Negro school children. 1938, directed Friends' Guild Marionettes at University of Pennsylvania in *Poor Penguins* and *Punch and Judy*. 1939, *Detour*, produced at the Solebury School, New Hope, Pa.

COLTA, CHARLES J. and MIMI   Harrisburg, Pa. Bought a "living marionette" show from Peppito the Clown who was with a Schubert Unit, *World of Pleasure*. First used the act, season 1927–1928. 1929, did *Punch and Judy* and magic in *Artists' Revels*. Now doing combined magic and puppet act, mostly in night clubs, within 50-mile radius of Harrisburg.

COMARDO (CAMALDO), CARLO   (Pp. 294, 297) Sicilian puppeteer in Union Street, Brooklyn, 1889–1890.

COMMUNITY FEDERAL ART CENTRE   Sioux City, Ia. 1938, *Hansel and Gretel, Rumpelstiltskin, The Dragon Znee Zee.*

CONANT, H. WESTON   Pratt Institute, Brooklyn, N. Y. 1931, *Doctor Faust*, with caricatures of the faculty for Mephisto's apparitions.

CONLON, ALFRED SANFORD   Punch and Judy showman with Ringling Brothers, early 20th century.

CONNELL, HAROLD W.   Milwaukee, Wis. 1919, began with hand-puppets, later used string-puppets for private shows. 1929, *The Dancing Lesson*. 1933, *The Tom Thumb Theatre Variety* with 40 marionettes.

CONWAY, JOHN   Toronto, Canada. Began marionette making at the age of eight. At fifteen had a company of three which played fairy tales and variety in schools, clubs, hospitals. 1937, changed to hand-puppets for *Punch and Judy, Three Wishes*, and *Tweedledum and Tweedledee*. 1939, joined Muriel Heddle's Royal Canadian Puppet Ballet as operator. Produced shows with children at summer camps, settlement houses, and boys' clubs. 1947, made a walking-flying umbrella for an infernal character in James Bridie's *Mr. Balfry*, produced by the New Play Society.

COOK, NADINE   Library of Hawaii, Honolulu. 1937, *Variety*. 1938, *Weather* and *Red Riding Hood*.

COOLIDGE, WALT   1941, floor-show act, *Strings on Parade*. Played in 1944 under name Renee and Calvert. Coolidge plays mostly movie dates in New England and Eastern states.

COOMBS, JACK   d. 1939. New York. 1929, *The Wicked Wang-Pah, Snow White*, and *Revue*.

CORDRY, DONALD   (Pp. 249, 338, 385, 392). Minneapolis, Minn. 1931, *The Bootlegger's Baby* and *The Tale of a Tom Cat*, with hand-puppets. 1933–1934, *The Three Bears*. Designed marionettes for Tony Sarg's production of *The Mikado*. 1937, while living in a small mountain village in Mexico, made two marionettes, one a devil, which led the Indians to believe he was a sorcerer. He and his wife were forced to leave the village. Still in Mexico, they are now engaged in craft work.

CORLEY, CATHERINE   Chicago, Ill. 1934, *Columbine and Harlequin*, *Knaves Will Be Knaves* (from a 16th-century French comedy), *Our Lady's Juggler*, *Romance of Dixie Belle*.

CORNISH PUPPETS   Cornish School, Seattle, Wash. 1933, *Peter Rabbit*, *Goldilocks* and variety. 1935, *The Prince and the Dragons* and *The Wizard of Oz*.

CORRIN, MR. and MRS R. L.   Chicago, Ill. From 1935 have presented *Punch and Judy* in the Chicago area, having made a special study of the subject and collected books on it. They have given television shows. A "mellerdramer" was built in 1936, but discarded in favor of Punch. A shadow-figure production of *Rumpelstiltskin* was ready for presentation, 1948.

CORRINGTON, HELEN   Corrington Marionettes, Elmhurst, Ill. Began 1935, built *Romeo and Juliet*, *Lady of the Portrait*, *The Magic Bracelet*, *Katinka and the Fingerkins*, *Adventures of Tony Bear*. Gave puppet performances Los Angeles, 1948.

COSSETTINI, LETICIA and OLGA   Argentina. Sisters active in educational work. The latter, director of the Gabriel Carrasco school in Rosario, is the author of a book, *El Niño y su Expresión*. Leticia has presented a wide variety of plays, selections from ballads, folk tales, romances, and poems, and *El Retablo de Maese Pedro*.

COTTAGE MARIONETTES   Organized as a family hobby in 1935, this company traveled in Ontario, c. 1937, with a good-sized repertory and 65 marionettes.

COVINGTON, RUTH   Covington Puppeteers. Aberdeen, S. D. School and club shows in this region: *Jack and the Beanstalk*, *Punch and Judy*, *Three Billy Goats Gruff* (with shadows), and variety, c. 1940.

COX, WALTER S.   Falmouth, Va. 1946–1947, *Vaudeville on Strings*.

CRAIG, JUANITA   Skinner Junior High School, Denver, Colo. 1931, *The Three Wishes*.

CRAIL, HELEN L.   Long Beach, Cal. Worked with Walsworth Puppeteers since 1938. Has produced independently: Vaudeville and circus acts, 1946. 1947, *The Three Wishes*, *Three Kings*, a Christmas pageant, *Lady Artist and Fuller Brush Man*, and *The Three Bears* with fist-puppets for a children's summer project.

CRAYTOR, HALLIE L.   1930, *Marionetting from the Classroom to Albania*, presented at the County Fair, Berea, Ohio.

CRIST, ABAGAIL P.   Delaware, O. 1935, *When the Toys Awake*.

CROSS, CHRIS.   Ventriloquist (with cowboy dummy) and puppeteer. Played movie-vaudeville circuits in 1940's.

CROTHERS, J. FRANCES   Salem, O. Began puppet work 1941. Was director of puppetry at Cain Park Children's Theatre, Cleveland Heights, summer 1942, and designed the present Alma Puppet Theatre, which was built by the park architect, a permanent brick structure with three stages. Recent work largely with handicapped children; found puppetry valuable in overcoming speech defects as well as for spastic and polio cases. Now working on master's degree in speech at Northwestern University. Has written about 40 scripts including those for the following productions: 1942, *The Wizard of Oz*, 1943, *Nursery Rhymes*, 1944, *Beauty and the Beast*, 1945, *Dorothy and Toto*, *Ali Baba*, *Tom Sawyer*, and *Snow White*. In 1946, *Comic Minstrel Show*, *Rip Van Winkle*, *Blondie and Dagwood* produced with children afflicted with polio. In 1947, organized the Salem Guild of Puppeteers with about 50 members. Working (1948) on a life of Christ to be presented under the title, *Behold the King*.

CRUMB, SARAH F.   Shoemaker Junior High School, Philadelphia, Pa. 1933, *Little One-Eye, Two-Eye and Three-Eye*. 1935, *Two Blind Men and a Donkey* and *The Scarecrow*.

CUETO, GERMÁN   (P. 350). 1932–1934 directed the Teatro Rin-Rin in Mexico City.

CUETO, LOLA   (P. 366). Mexico City. In the home of Lola and Germán Cueto met the group which established the puppetry movement in Mexico in 1932. Germán directed a company until 1934 when it was taken over by Roberto Lago. Lola became designer and puppeteer for this troupe, El Nahual, c. 1935, and worked with it during the following years. In 1946 she set up her own hand-puppet theatre, El Chapulin. She is an artist noted for her prints. A portfolio of 50 of her aquatints, *Títeres populaires mexicanos,* was published in a limited edition in 1947.

CUEVAS, FRANCISCA PULIDO   b. 1861. A strolling puppeteer who goes about the public squares and markets of Mexico City, playing for pennies to amuse passers-by. She uses puppets of Death and the Devil (male and female), arranged in a couple which hang by thin chains from either end of a stick. With one hand she makes them dance on a little wooden floor, while with the other she holds a harmonica. She dresses in the traditional garb of the country folk of Queretaro. Lola Cueto has made a portrait print of her.

CUNNINGHAM, HALLIE   (Mrs. Chester Patingale.) Frank B. Willis High School, Delaware, O. From 1936 has produced shows with high school students. *Punch and Judy, The Three Bears, Hansel and Gretel,* variety were done with hand-puppets. Has experimented with finger-puppets and stylized hand-and-rod-puppets.

CURTIN MARIONETTE THEATRE   Curtin Junior High School, Williamsport, Pa. 1936, *A Russian Pipe Dream, The Frog Prince,* and *Laetitia.*

CUSHINGS, EILEEN and WILFRED   1946, toured with USO in the Caribbean, presenting *The Picadilly Revue.*

CUTLER, YOSL   New York. In 1925 established with Zuny Maud and Jack Tworkov the Modicots, a Yiddish puppet theatre. Produced *Purimspiel,* from the Bible story of Esther; also a sketch, *What Ails You?* Wrote *The Tin Bride, The Pepper Merchant,* adapted *The Dybuk.* 1927, closed the theatre and toured America and Europe with his puppets. 1933, parted from Maud and devoted himself to plays dealing with the economic struggle. 1934, The Workers' Laboratory presented his puppets at Irving Plaza in *Punch Goes Red.* Hand-puppets were his medium. Died 11 June 1935 as the result of an automobile accident.

DAGMER, AND COMPANY   A Punch and Judy act advertised as "A Wooden-Headed Family" which played c. 1945.

DAISEY, JOHN   (Pp. 132, 138). *Punch and Judy* at Central Park Garten, New York, 19 May 1877. Odell, vol. 10, p. 297. Associated with Collins. Played for many years thereafter in and around New York.

DALE, CLIFFORD   Long Beach, Cal. Built a miniature show of *Hansel and Gretel* in Honolulu which was about to open when, on 7 December 1941, a bomb went through the roof of the auditorium. 1948, has garage with a large stage in which a neighborhood show is being built.

DALLAS, WEAVER   (P. 392). 1927, presented with hand-puppets at the University of Georgia, Athens, a series of plays in Negro dialect: *Br'er Wolf an' de Little Rabs, In Mistah Man's Gyard'n, Ghostes, Helpin' de Lawd, Followin' de Fashion, De Courtin' Couple, De Basket Trap.* With the troupe named The Rag Bag Alley Puppets, Kathryn and Weaver Dallas presented in 1930: *Conjurin' Witches, De Wonderful Tar Baby, 'Skeeters and Sweethearts.* 1931, *Duck Duck Goes to the Fair* at Kresge's Department Store, Newark, N. J., *Adventures of Muggsy and Buggsy Bear,* Stanford University, Palo Alto, Cal., *How the Little Pig's House Caught on Fire.* 1932, *The Little Black Boy and the Ferocious Pirate, Jan and Marta, Hansel and Gretel, De Little Rabbits' Christmas Dinner, Christmas Gif'.* Various eastern tours were made in 1932 and 1933. In 1935, played at the White House, Washington, *De Courtin' Couple, Br'er Wolf an' de Little Rabbits, Ghostes.*

DANN, HARRY   Circus clown who, dressed as a snake charmer, manipulated a large kelly-green hand-puppet snake in one of his walk-arounds, 1941–1945.

DAVIES, E. D.   (P. 132). Ventriloquist and Punch and Judy showman, playing in halls, c. 1865. A portrait of him with two ventriloquial figures is reproduced in Odell, vol. 9, op. p. 112.

DAVIS, ALEX   (P. 190). Ventriloquist and string-puppet showman, played at the Grand Central Theatre, Philadelphia, 21 September–3 October 1874, and the Arch Street Opera House, 19–31 October 1874.

DAVY and BLAKE   (P. 275). Royal Crystal Palace Marionettes, London Theatre, New York, 24–29 September 1883. Subsequently played under the name of Davys's Royal

Marionettes and others until 1887. Odell, vol. 12, pp. 317, 125, 331, 333, 372, 373; vol. 13, pp. 87, 101, 102, 110, 104, 106, 374.

DAWLEY, HERBERT M. (P. 338) Dawley's Marionettes, New York. 1931, *Captain Kidd* and variety. 1932, *The Legend of Sleepy Hollow*. Worked on *The Legend of the Willow Tree* and other Sarg productions.

DAWN, CARL and FAITH In 1942 were playing floor-show variety in the East.

DAY, CLARENCE (P. 319). As a boy in the 1880's had a toy paper theatre and a Punch and Judy show—"No Movies Then," and "Father and Mr. Punch," *The New Yorker,* 31 October and 7 March 1936, pp. 22–24 and 25–26.

DEAN, MARY Manchester-by-the-Sea, Mass. Among the productions built in her Lantern Lane Workshop were: a Nativity play presented annually at the Old Gothic Church, Salem, Mass., 1932–1938; *Betsy Bunnie,* hand-puppet play with all-animal cast, and *Jack and the Beanstalk,* given at the Second New England Puppetry Conference.

DEAVES, EDWIN (Pp. 185, 192, 269). (1809–c. 1890). Introduced a marionette specialty into a minstrel show about 1838. Gave occasional marionette shows in San Francisco in the 1860's.

DEAVES, EDWIN (P. 269). (4 December 1889–26 August 1941). Appeared among the puppets of his father's show in vaudeville, 1893. Helped his father, Walter Eugene, 1907–1915.

DEAVES, HARRY (Pp. 268, 273, 276, 353). (c. 1860–1927). In partnership with his brother Walter Eugene in the Northwest, 1884. During 1887 and 1888 played in New York and Brooklyn. Odell, vol. 13, pp. 520, 521, 571. Coast-to-coast tours from 1890's to about 1918.

DEAVES, WALTER EUGENE (Pp. 135, 185, 186, 188, 189, 200, 249, 268–273, 274, 275, 277, 286, 287, 353). (1854–1919). Married Mary Hanks (b. 1858). Helped his father with marionettes about 1864 in San Francisco. 1869, had a Punch and Judy show. 1874, toured the West Coast with McDonough and Earnshaw. 1875, did private shows for clubs, and toured California and Nevada. 1876, to Mexico. 1883, to Hawaii and the Northwest. 1884, in partnership with his brother Harry. 1893, at Chicago Fair. 1893–1906, in East. 1908–1914, round-the-world tours. 1915, San Francisco fair. In the archives of the Index of American Design in Washington, D. C. are the following drawings of Deaves' puppets, listed under Northern California, Miscellaneous: Mrs. Shelby, 320; Negro Bride, 311; Octopus, 122 (used in *20,000 Leagues Under the Sea*); Puppet with Opera Glasses, 305 (one of the figures which sat in a proscenium box); Shark, 123 (used in *20,000 Leagues Under the Sea*); Uncle Tom, 316; Backdrop for *20,000 Leagues Under the Sea,* 324; Simon Legree, Liza, Bull, Cake Walker, Clown in semi-formal dress. This list has been furnished through the kindness of Joseph Allen, State Supervisor, Northern California Art Project.

DECATUR, ILL. MARIONETTE GUILD See New, George.

DE COLONIA, JUAN (P. 240). Played fairy tales and political pieces in Mexico City before 1848.

DE CREVECOEUR, JEANNE Montreal, Canada. 1935, *Beauty and the Beast.*

DE ESTA Played marionettes c. 1890.

DE HEIJÓ, HORTENSIA S. Organized a children's puppet theatre in the Normal Institute of Montevideo, Uruguay, c. 1940.

DEKKER, ROSE 20 October 1937, performed *The Three Wishes* at Marshall Field Puppet Exhibit (Chicago, 16–23 October 1937).

DE LA CANAL, LOLITA ALVA Mexico City. Became director of "El Comino," one of three state-supported puppet theatres established in 1935.

DE LA CANAL, RAMÓN ALVA Mexico City. 1941, became director of the puppet theatre "El Comino" which his sister, Lolita Alva, directed from 1935. He was one of the original group which began educational puppetry work, but was commissioned to paint murals and so did no puppets for some years.

DE LA TORRE, AMADEO (P. 351). A Peruvian sculptor and caricaturist who is a successor to Ño Valdivieso, in that he creates everything in his show. During 1937–1938 he played at La Pascana a program of dances, songs, and *genre* scenes such as *Lima after Dark* and merry-making in the Malambo district of Lima.

DE MARCHAND, ELSA CARAFFÍ Established a children's puppet theatre in the Malvin School, Montevideo, Uruguay, c. 1942.

DE MONTELLANO, BERNARDO ORTIZ (P. 349). Mexico City. 1929, with Louis Bunin and Julio Castellanos, sponsored by the National Department of Fine Arts, founded a puppet theatre in the Native Student House of the Escuela del Estudiante and produced *The Astute Rabbit* and *The Rural School Combats Alcoholism*. 1930, when Bunin returned to the United States, work continued with Juan Guerrero as collaborator. *El Sombreron* was produced by alumni of the school; *Viva la revolución* was inspired by Orozco's frescoes. El Teatro del Periquillo, directed by de Montellano, gave hand-puppet shows in the parks and playgrounds of the city, 1929, and Periquillo is still a favorite character.

DENISON, HELEN LEE St. Paul, Minn. First performed 1923, with a single marionette. 1926, 1929, *Blue Beard, St. George and the Dragon, Marionette Circus* (with a live kitten used in a lion tamer act). 1930, *Nativity* with Christmas Carols (shadows and hand-puppets). 1932–1940, produced Japanese fairy tales with hand-puppets carved by country folk in the Japanese Alps. 1924–1940, *Punch and Judy*. Three summers as puppetry counselor, Camp Bryn Afon, Roosevelt, Wisconsin. Collected puppets, plays, and books in a trip around the world. Has lectured at the University of Minnesota and taught puppetry classes at the Summit School for Girls.

DE NOYER, MR. and MRS. ALFRED LORING Rockport, Mass. Summers 1937–1939, gave hand-puppet shows based on fairy tales and familiar children's stories. Played for parties and gave Christmas shows in winter.

DEODATA, MARY Order of St. Francis. Alvernia High School, Chicago. 1928, *Jack and the Beanstalk*. 1929, *Snow White and the Seven Dwarfs*.

DE SAMORA, JUAN (P. 7). 1569, petitioned for permission to present three puppet shows in Tezcuco, Mexico.

DE RATHSCKOFF, Monsieur Performed with hand-puppets at the Peoples' Garden, Davenport, Ia., in 1858.

DESMOND AND DESMOND (P. 207). English performers who had a humanette act in their American tour c. 1887.

DESSART, Professor Performed with string-puppets at Löwen Garten, New York, 1868.

DE STERN, ANA BIRÓ and EMILIO Argentina. In Chaco organized a theatre, *Los Títeres de Doña Ana*, among pupils of the primary schools, c. 1942.

DETROIT COLLEGE OF EDUCATION PUPPETRY CLASS, WAYNE UNIVERSITY See Markle, Ella.

DETROIT FEDERAL THEATRE See Lano, David.

DE VERE, CHESTER Had manikins in early 20th century.

DEWEY, ETHELYN A. High School, Albia, Ia. 1936, *Hansel and Gretel*.

DICKINSON, DON Dicken's Royal Puppets, Fargo, N. D. 1938, *Where the Sunsets Come From* (hand-puppets), *Tale of a Whale, Raggedy Ann and Andy* (marionettes). 1942, Talks on puppet history with various types of puppets, in Los Angeles.

DIFENDERFER, JOHN (Pp. 149, 153, 154, 320). (16 February 1866–6 February 1933). Born at Redford, and dying at Three Rivers, Mich., this amateur Punch-and-Judy showman first became interested in puppets when he saw a drunken Punch man play in Toledo about 1888. He gave his shows for the amusement of children in and about Three Rivers. To the usual Punch and Judy scenes he added a Negro dance and a realistic chicken fight. This information was obtained from his daughter. His set of puppets was recorded by the Michigan Art and Crafts Project for the Index of American Design, listed under Miscellaneous: Snap-Dragon, 14; Pirate, 15; Punch, 19; Judy and Baby, 20; Devil, 21; Chinaman, 22; Beadle, 23; Policeman, 33.

DILLEY, PERRY (Pp. 192, 193, 194, 197, 198, 272, 344, 345, 346, 347, 385). San Francisco, Cal. Began with hand-puppets (which became his specialty) in 1919, playing California universities, theatres, and clubs. Presented a group of plays by the French showman Duranty which included: *Adventures of a Chimneysweep, A Hungry Man, Pierrot and the Pastrycook.* 1922, *Dr. Glyserobobolus* (Duranty), *The Green Nose.* 1923, *A Merry Death*, done first with abstract ovoid-headed puppets, later with more realtistic ones. 1924, built marionettes for second Ellen Van Volkenburg production of *A Midsummer Night's Dream.* During the 1924–1925 season, was director of puppetry at the Cleveland Playhouse and produced *Red Riding Hood and the Wolf, A Barrel o' Trouble, Snow White and the Seven Dwarfs, Mysterious Playthings* (Maurice Sand). 1926, *Boiled Celery* (from the Japanese). 1927, *The Three Wishes, The Dragon Who Couldn't Say Please* (Grace Stearns). 1928, *Columbine's Birthday* (Stearns). 1929, *The Bricklayer's Dilemma* (for the Community Chest campaign), *Guignol Goes A-Fishing* (Lemercier de Neuville), *The Emperor's New Clothes*, at the University of California, Berkeley. With Ralph Geddis, conducted a puppetry class at Mills College and produced *The Birthday of the Infanta* and *Concerning Florizel.* 1930, *The Tinker and the Teakettle* (a Japanese fable), and *Pierrot's Wedding.* With puppet class at Mills College: *Seven Blue Devils, Cinderella, Dr. Faust.* 1931, *Booby Hans, Alice in Wonderland*, revivals of previous plays. 1932, *The Tub, The King of the Golden River, A Slight Misconception.* During 1932 a total of 165 performances of plays in repertory was given. 1933–1934 season, from 8 September onward, performances were given every Friday and Saturday in the Studio-Theatre, San Francisco. Revivals of previous works were presented together with these new ones: *The Enchanted Canary, Strawberry Shortcake, The Ox and the Ass.* 1935, *Cinderella* revived. 1936, *The Bean Boy.* 1941, revivals and *Box and Cox.* Summer 1942, *Red Riding Hood, The Fisherman and the Genii.*

DIXON's (CHET) MARIONETTES Summer 1947 played variety at Long Beach Hotel, Rockport, Mass.

DOBBINS, EMELINE Columbia, S. C. 1946–1947, director of puppets for State Parks division, presented *Day Camping is Fun* at State Fair.

DODD, DAVID HASELTINE (P. 346). South Newbury, Vt. 1929, *Through the Looking Glass* with rod-puppets moved through slots in stage.

DOHM, DOROTHY G. Ellensburg, Wash. 1938, *Christmas Judgment* and *If You Don't Weaken.*

DOMINO MARIONETTES See Ransom, Charles.

DONALDSON, SAM Pixie Puppets, Wichita School, Milwaukee, Ore. 1934, with 16-inch marionettes, performed *Jack and the Beanstalk, The Fox and the Crane, Epaminondas, The Three Wishes, The Reason, Little Black Sambo*, circus, and variety.

DONDO, MATHURIN (Pp. 344, 345, 346). 1918, *L'Oncle d'Amerique, Après la guerre, Pathelin* at Smith College, Northampton, Mass. 1922, directed Columbia Marionette Players of Columbia College, New York, in *Two Blind Men and a Donkey* and *The Wash Tub.* Developed and patented a rod-puppet which could be operated on bars across the stage. Interested in the possibilities of puppets as dramatic actors.

DONNER, MRS. E. R. Portland, Ore. 1940, *Goldilocks* and variety.

DON RODRIQUEZ A Mexican family playing a tent show in the southwestern United States, c. 1935. Included with the tumbling, singing, dancing, music, and comedy was a string-puppet show featuring Emanuel, the bull fighter, a boaster who successfully piled up his adversaries in a heap but was himself carried off by a vampire bat—described by Jo Bushé in *Puppetry 1942–43*, p. 22.

DORLAND, RETTA MAE O.B.U., Shawnee, Okla. 1932, *Dust of the Road* with marionettes.

DOUGLAS, CHRISTINE   Inkster, Mich. Occupational therapist who uses puppets with her patients at the Wayne County General Hospital and Infirmary at Eloise, Mich. Began 1942 with *Hansel and Gretel*. 1943, *Every Dog Has His Day*. 1944, *The Scarecrow Who Wished for the Moon*. 1947, *Horton Hatches the Egg*. Now working with hand-puppets which can be taken into the wards.

DOWNING   A marionette showman and his family who traveled in Michigan during the summer of 1935 with a two-truck outfit. They also exhibited a hermaphrodite hog.

DOWNINGTON, PA., HIGH SCHOOL FRENCH CLUB   1940, *Ali Baba et les 40 voleurs* with hand-puppets.

DRAKE, FLORENCE   Palm Beach, Fla. 1929, variety. 1933, *Alice in Wonderland*, at Laguna Beach, Cal.

DRAKOULALOS, BILL   Greek shadow-figure showman, toured out of Chicago, 1926, and possibly before.

DRYSDALE, GRACE   From c. 1938 toured the United States with hand-puppet floor show. 1942–1943 toured with USO. 1944, injured in a plane wreck at Lisbon, Portugal, but recovered and continued with her work.

DUERKOB, MANFRED and DOROTHY   St. Louis, Mo. From 1935, interested in puppet theatres with elaborate electrical and scenic effects. Presented *Hiawatha* and in 1947 gave television shows over KSO-TV.

DUGGAN, DOROTHY   Fredericksburg, Va. 1935, *The Highwayman* (after Alfred Noyes). 1936, *East of the Sun and West of the Moon*, produced in art class at State Teachers College.

DUMILIEU   (P. 100). 1830, shadow-figures at Summer Pavilion, Nashville.

DUNBAR PUPPET PLAYERS   School 133, Baltimore, Md. 1933, *Jack and the Beanstalk*, *Little Red Riding Hood* (also produced in 1934).

DUNCAN, WILLIAM   See Tatterman Marionettes.

DUNN, LOUISE M.   See Mills, Winifred H.

DWIGGINS, W. A.   (Pp. 325, 361, 367). Hingham Centre, Mass. 1933, in a studio theatre, 0.5 Irving Street, assisted by neighbors, "under the Püterschein Authority," produced *The Blind Beggarman* (revived in 1934). 1945, mechanistic puppets and script for *Millennium I*, published by Alfred A. Knopf, New York. 1939, author of *Marionette in Motion*, Puppetry Imprints, Birmingham, Mich. His counter-balanced marionettes have had an influence on many producers.

EARNSHAW, HARTLEY A.   Partner of McDonough, John E., *q.v.*

EASTERBROOK, HARRY   Brantford, Ontario, Canada. Worked with puppets between 1930–1938. Discontinued activities because of World War II.

EATON, FRANCES E.   Director, Harrisburg, Pa., Community Theatre Marionettes. 1933–1934, *Cannibal Gold*, *A Nice Young Man*, *Further Adventures of Puss in Boots*, and other plays.

ECKERSON, OLIVE   Glendale, Cal. 1932, *Commedia*.

EDLO PLAYERS   See Finney, Edith.

EDMONDS, EDITH   Glencoe, Ill. 1934–1937, presented hand-puppet shows in churches and schools. *Slithers Made King*, *Little Black Sambo*, *Peter Rabbit*, *Lord Cyrus Hecklenose*, *A Rag Doll in Love*, *Sleeping Beauty*.

EDMUNDSON, CAROLYN   Glen Rock Junior High School, N. J. With Winifred White-house, presented *Merchant of Venice* with *Danse Macabre* as a curtain raiser.

EGE, HELENA GREGG   Wilkinsburg, Pa. 1931, *Cinderella*. 1932, *Little Black Sambo* and *Dame Drudgery Dreams*.

ELLWOOD and RIPEL   (Mr. and Mrs. John Ellwood Christine). Philadelphia, Pa. 1935, *Punch and Judy*. 1936, Gus the Imp, a marionette which gave a complete magic show, was awarded a silver cup at the International Brotherhood of Magicians Convention in Batavia, N. Y.

EMERSON   Marionettes, about 1890.

ENGLE, FANNIE GOLDSMITH   (P. 354). Kegg and Goldsmith's Marionettes presented,

1923, an elaborate production of *Cinderella* at the Players' Club, San Francisco. In 1927, the Goldsmith Engle Marionettes gave *The Nightingale* (after Andersen) at Riverside, Cal. 1932, variety, Gimbel Brothers, New York.

ENGLE MARIONETTES See Laurence, Gilbert.

ENTRIKIN, PAUL and HELEN Entrikin Marionette Company, Baton Rogue, La. 1945, first made puppets in Sunday school class, later produced show for daughter. 1946–1947, *The Princess in the Moon*, based on an Aztec legend, presented for school children under sponsorship of the Parish and Municipal Recreation Commission.

EP-WEP PUPPETEERS Franklinville, N. Y. 1934, *Poor Ol' Robinson Crusoe, Beauty and the Beast.*

ERWIN, MARGIE DeWitt, Ia. A young puppeteer who became interested in puppets in 1942 when given two of Virginia Austin's toy puppets. Presented *Hansel and Gretel, Cinderella,* and the Christmas story, for which she wrote scripts and built all puppets and scenery. Gave benefit shows for the DeWitt band uniform fund and the soldiers' smoke fund.

ESPINAL, CARLOS Mexico City. In August 1940 a pavilion featuring "Los Títeres de Rosete Aranda," sponsored by a newspaper, was opened in Mexico City under the direction of Espinal, who used the name of the famous 19th-century puppet family for his troupe, which had an elaborate outfit consisting of trucks, amplifiers, and lighting equipment. The repertory included circus, magic, dances, topical and regional numbers, as well as *The Marvelous Spring, or the Fountain of Youth, The Benediction of the Saint.* The latter was done in the Indian folk style of the Sierra de Puebla, with *danzantes,* fireworks, and processions. One thousand puppets comprised the actors. 1941, the shows continued in their *carpa* or tent (sometimes in cinema houses on Sunday). In 1943, Gilbert Laurence saw a variety show, and next day *Rey de Reyes,* a Passion Play in 12 scenes, which he praised highly. See Rosete Aranda for notes on the earlier company.

ESTRADA, JOSÉ (Pp. 71, 72). Mexico City showman, 1786.

ETHONETTES, THE See Page, Elizabeth.

EVANS, HENRY RIDGELY (P. 316). As a boy gave toy theatre shows, winter 1869, in the stable of a house on E Street, N.W., between Sixth and Seventh streets, Washington, D. C.

EVANSTON, ILL., FRENCH CLUB 1932, Guignol play.

EVELETH, MINN., JUNIOR HIGH SCHOOL PUPPET CLUB See Agnich, Angeline.

EWING, LOUISE See Finney, Edith.

FAIRY TALE MARIONETTES See McKay, Paula F.

FALCONI, Signor (P. 62). Exhibited Chinese shades, Punchinello, and diorama at the Assembly Room, William Street, New York, 1795.

FARLEMAN (P. 278). With Len Ayres, Everett, Wash., 1903–1906.

FAULKNER, REX (Pp. 277, 280, 379). Married Lillian Jewell, with whom he presented Lillian Faulkner & Co. in vaudeville from 1913 onward.

FAUST, JOHNNY (Faustman, John C.) Ripon, Wis. 1932, *The Haunted House, Jack and the Beanstalk.* 1933, variety, *The Gold Bug* (after Poe), and other plays. 1935, variety, *Little Red Riding Hood.* 1936, his company was called Pixie Marionettes and revived the program of preceding year. 1940, worked with Bil Baird, New York World's Fair, then two seasons with Sue Hastings. 1942–43, gave 1200 performances of variety on tour. 1946 to date, continued floor show tours with 50 marionette (26 inches high) and 25 routines.

FAUZIO 1929, *The Duchess Liberated* and *St. George and the Dragon* at Hull House, Chicago.

FENWAY PUPPETS Boston, Mass. 1933, *Little Black Sambo, Jack and the Beanstalk,* variety.

FERGUSON, DR. H. W. Toothland Puppet Show, presented by the Newark, N. J., Academy of Medicine at Century of Progress Exposition, Chicago, 1934.

FERNANDEZ, PUNCHO (CHARLES)   Learned Punch and Judy operating and carving from his father. Began career in home town of Chelsea, Mass., 1900. Played at New England Puppetry Institute, Boston, November 1938, with his 50-year-old puppets. Still active 1940.

FERNANDO, JOSEPH, and FAIR, CECIL   Chicago, Ill. Active 1948 with a night club routine.

FERREE, M. E.   Woodlynne, N. J. 1936, *Rip Van Winkle*.

FERRIS, HARRY   1934, gave over 500 performances of *Punch and Judy* in Children's Theatre on the Enchanted Island, Century of Progress Exposition, Chicago.

FETTERER, HARRY   1934, presented over 600 performances of *Punch and Judy* in Merrie England, A Century of Progress Exposition, Chicago. Same show at New York World's Fair, 1939.

FETZER, HENRIETTA   From c. 1927–1929 presented plays in Chicago South Park playgrounds: *Jack and the Beanstalk, Robinson Crusoe, The Casting of the Great Bells, The Stolen Prince, The Cow-Herd and the Weaving Maid,* and *The Wicked Wang-Pah Meets the Dragon,* the last four being adapted from Chinese folk tales.

FICKLEN, BESSIE ALEXANDER   (P. 144). First as a child and later to amuse her children and grandchildren, Mrs. Ficklen made hand-puppets for many home shows. *Punch and Judy, Br' Rabbit and Br' Fox, Somebody Nothing,* and many short turns and ballads were included in her repertory. Author of *A Handbook of Fist-Puppets,* Frederick A. Stokes, New York, 1935. (10 Dec. 1861–3 Mar. 1945).

FIFIELD, ANNE   Pierre, S. D. 1936, *The Singing Lesson.* 1939, *Adventures in the Cabbage Patch* and *The Peppermint Boy.* Also made marionettes and masks for sale, lectured on puppet history, and gave demonstrations of puppet making.

FINNEY, EDITH   Edlo Players, St. Louis, Mo. With Louise Ewing presented childrens' hand-puppet shows from 1937 to date, including: *Li'l Napoleon and the Squinch Owl, Li'l Napoleon and the Scarecrow, Humpty Dumpty, Jackie Rabbit and the Last Carrot, Bald-Headed Pixie, Clowns and Jack-in-the-Box, New Three Bears.*

FITZGERALD, FELICIA   Winnipeg, Canada. 1938, *Punch and Judy.*

FLINCH, BOB   (Flinchbaugh). York, Pa. 1935, *Jack and the Beanstalk, Salmagundi,* ballyhoo for Standard Oil Company of Pennsylvania at York County Fair (100 performances). 1939, variety with marionettes.

FLOSSO, AL   Punch man, with Al Barnes circus 1919 to the present, but began earlier.

FOELEY, CORA VIRGINIA   1930–1935, produced children's shows in the schools of Wellesley, Mass., and vicinity. 1939, gave *Hansel and Gretel* with the puppets of the Animal Rescue League as part of the program of the New England Puppetry Institute, Boston.

FOGLE, GEORGE   Chicago, Ill. Made many experimental puppets which he displayed at the Puppetry Festival in St. Louis, 1941. Presented *The Wizard of Oz* at Marshall Field's. Served with the Army in the Pacific area, and was killed in China in 1944.

FOLEY, ELIZABETH P.   Petoskey, Mich. 1942, *The Three Wishes* and *Christmas Piece.*

FOLLMER, FRANK and FINK, LUCILLE   Chicago, Ill. 1934, *The Great Zenith,* with marionettes. 1937, worked with Burr Tillstrom as the Chicago Puppet Players and presented *Kukla, Gus, and Oscar* at Wisconsin State Fair, West Allis, and *The Prince and the Maiden,* a pantomime fantasy at Marshall Field Puppet Exhibition. 1938, at Chicago Puppetry Festival, *Island Legend* with finger-puppets and a soldier drill impromptu with hand-puppets. As supervisor of the Southern Illinois Puppet Center, directed groups in various cities in plays, revues, carnivals, mostly with hand-puppets. 1944, produced a Christmas shadow play with Richard Scammon while stationed in the Pacific area.

FOLTZ, WILLARD   1942, showed a perambulating puppet booth and gave a condensed version of Punch and Judy at the Midwestern Puppeteers Festival, Springfield, Ill., 11–12 July 1942.

FORBES, JOHN DOUGLAS   1930, *The Seven Ages of College,* University of California, Berkeley.

FORBUSH, GLADYS   *The Stubborn Cow,* presented with shadows at the New England Puppetry Institute, Boston, November 1939.

FORD, JOHN CARTER   (P. 344). Oakland and nearby California cities. 1927, *The Jester Who Sat on the Throne* (hand-puppets). 1928, *The Enchanted Horse.* 1929, *Briar Rose, Iolanthe, The Silver Lute* (paper puppets worked by rods) given in Ralph Chessé's Marionette Playhouse, San Francisco. 1930, *Bellerophon and the Chimera* (from a Greek myth, with hand-puppets, marionettes, and shadows), *The Three Wishes, Pirates of Penzance, Cinderella, The Aftermath, The Princess of Cheesemania* (hand-puppets and shadows). 1931, *Uncle Tom's Cabin, The Fairy that Bounced* (marionettes). 1933, built a 31-foot marionette for the Grove Play of the San Francisco Bohemian Club. Weighing over 300 pounds, it was controlled from a crow's-nest 75 feet up in a redwood tree, had a loudspeaker in its head, rolled its eyes, opened its mouth, and walked around the tree.

FOREMAN, JANE   1930-1933, gave performances in Detroit schools of *The King's Cobbler, Rumpelstiltskin, Nutcracker Suite, Jacquenetta and the Queen's Gown, The Interdependence of Nations, Toy Shop Review.*

FORREST, STELLA B.   1932, presented plays with 15-inch marionettes at a hospital, Fitchburg, Mass. 1934-1935, showed Christmas and Easter plays in New London, Conn., churches.

FOWLER, HARRY   Chicago, Ill. Became interested in puppets while doing a practice teaching project in puppetry at the John Herron Art School, Indianapolis, Ind. 1931, *The Three Wishes, The Gooseberry Mandarin.* 1932, *Danse Macabre, Br'er Rabbit and the Tar Baby.* 1933, *Jack and the Beanstalk, Pinocchio.* 1934, *Little Black Sambo, Hansel and Gretel.* 1935, *The Great Bell of Peking, The Wonderful Teakettle, The Painted Pig, Poppy Seed Cakes, Through the Looking Glass, Sokar and the Crocodile.* In 1936, joined the staff of the Good Teeth Council for Children, Inc., and puppeteered in dental health shows played with hand-puppets in elementary schools from coast to coast. Later became designer and director of the shows, and in 1948, art director.

FOX, MRS. ALICE   Cooperstown, N. Y. 1929, with two artist friends, made marionettes for *Spanish Interlude, The King's Breakfast,* and *Clever Babbett,* which were presented in a barn theatre. 1945-1947, made hand-puppets for *The Willow Tree* and *The Empty Rice Bowl.* These figures are loaned to high school groups; Mrs. Fox directs rehearsals. During the war *Round the World with a Red Cross Nurse* had 40 performances. 1946-1947, worked with children in a museum producing original shows for benefits. Plays included *The Stolen Jewels* and *Make-Believe Land.* 1948, wrote in Spanish and produced *Navidad en Mejico* for Spanish classes in San Diego, Cal., schools.

FOX, FRANCES   1924, introduced puppetry in playground programs of Houston, Texas. Later gave lectures and demonstrations. 1931, worked in own studio and with the Recreation Department.

FRANELLI PUPPET PLAYERS   Alta Lorna Playground, Los Angeles and nearby towns. 1930-1934, children's plays and variety.

FRANK, KATHRO   Placer Union High School. 1944, *The Green Nose.* 1945, *The Three Little Pigs.* 1946, *Rumpelstiltskin* and *Jack, the Beanstalker.* 1948, *Pinocchio.*

FRANKLIN   West Orange, N. J., 1940, *Musical Marionettes* presented by six members of this family.

FREDERICK, JOHN   Director of a group of young puppeteers in Paterson, N. J., who presented *The Enchanted King* and specialties, 1942.

FRENCH, CARROLL   (P. 333). Summer 1921 French and his wife, Loretto Clarke, toured Long Island, N. Y. with a puppet show and camping equipment fitted into a wagon drawn by a horse. On the animal's blinder were three initials, RLS, and this became his name. The show was an informal affair, given at beach houses, clubs, or busy street intersections, and consisted of short turns and dances, with Peter Pantry as manager. He also circulated among the audience after the show to collect coins. Fall 1921, *A Puppet's Petticoat* was performed in the mid-west; during the Christmas season shows were given in the Chicago Little Theatre where the

Frenches had worked earlier with Ellen Van Volkenburg. The string-puppets for this play were of mahogany, with the costumes carved into the wood. The following summer, RLS and the wagon were again taken on a tour as far as Narragansett Pier, Rhode Island, by way of Long Island Sound shore.

FRENCH, MRS. H. E.   Grand Forks, N. D. Her first puppets were made to amuse her children. Later, when her daughter Mary Margaret was in college, she helped the members of Zeta Phi Eta to put on shows for a children's theatre project in 1932. From that time until her death, 29 September 1945, she was an ardent puppeteer, working with various groups of students at the University of North Dakota and presenting plays for children. Among her productions were: 1931, *Abraham and Isaac* (a 14th-century mystery play). Later: *De Courtin' Couple, Pinocchio,* Christmas plays—*Beasts in the Stable Yard, Toys in the Pack, Christmas for the Giant, Punch and Judy,* variety.

FRENCH, MARY MARGARET   Grand Forks, N. D. Worked with her brother and mother on home shows, later had a small floor variety show which she used while attending college.

FRIDMAN, LIBER   Argentine painter who toured with Javier Villafañe in 1936, and built a show of his own upon their return to Buenos Aires.

FRIEDMAN, SIDNEY   Stellar Marionettes, Philadelphia. 1938, *Minstrel Show, Epaminondas* (with humanettes). 1940, *Trial by Jury.*

FRIENDLY HOUSE MARIONETTE CLUB   See Boeck, Orville W.

FRIENDS' GUILD MARIONETTES   See Collins, Ethel D. W.

FRY, NELLIE E.   St. Paul, Minn. Began 1933 with puppets purchased from Ruth Shrank; made novelty numbers and trick marionettes for variety. Worked with Dorothy Adamson, giving shows in schools. 1948, gave shows with Irene Odegaard.

FULGHAM, MARY H.   1932, *Adventures of Betty* at High School, Franklin, Tex.

FULLER (BUELL R. and JOHN W.) MARIONETTES   East Lynn High School, Mass. 1933, *The Frog Prince, The Ming Fong Pepper Tree, The Musicians of Bremen, Aladdin.* 1934, *Dawn on the Desert, Soup from a Nail,* variety. 1939, *Death of Ase* from *Peer Gynt* and Circus presented at the New England Puppetry Institute.

FULTON, WILSON (BOBBY)   (Pp. 338, 353). Worked with Tony Sarg and other puppeteers, then, 1924, independently in New York and the Cape Playhouse, Dennis, Mass. 1933, *Pirates' Gold, Country Gardens* (with Percy Grainger's music), *The China Plate* (from the willow pattern legend). 1942, turned to adult plays with *The Bishop's Candlesticks* from *Les Miserables.* 1948, continued to give children's programs.

FUTOR, MILDRED   Oklahoma City, Okla. 1940, *Little Black Sambo, The Peppermint Boy, The Three Wishes, Bluebeard,* (all with hand-puppets). 1942, *My Day* (a colored minstrel wedding), *Bluebeard,* and Minstrel Show (last two with child puppeteers).

GAINES, EARL   1931, *The Anointing of David,* Itasca, Ill., public school.

GALLAVOTTI, SIGNOR   (P. 112). At the Adelphi Theatre, Dupont Street near Clay, San Francisco, presented Italian marionettes in an "elegent comedy," 19–26 November 1855. The *Daily Alta California* of 21 November 1855 said, "The exhibition is a peculiar one in California and cannot fail to interest and please the curious." On 24 November there was a 2 P.M. matinee for ladies and children. The readers for these performances were local people, D. C. Anderson, William Barry, and Mrs. J. B. Booth—McCabe's MS *Journal* at the Sutro Public Library, vol. 1, p. 62.

GALPIN, ELLEN   (Pp. 354, 369). 1922–1924, presented children's plays for the Los Angeles Playground Department. 1925–1926, *Hansel and Gretel* and *The Juggler of Our Lady* in Juneau, Alaska, and more children's plays in Los Angeles, including *Noon Time Moon,* an Eskimo version of *Cinderella.* In 1928, revived *Hansel and Gretel* in Honolulu, Hawaii. 1930–1931, continued shows in the Bird Cage Theatre, Los Angeles, and went on a nine months' tour.

GALY, PAUL   (P. 261). French puppeteer, performed with an assistant at Murray Bay College, Quebec, in 1905.

GARAVAGLIA, FLORENCIO and AÏDA   Buenos Aires, Argentina. Directors of the Teatro de la Cruz del Sud. 1944, made a tour of Bolivia, Peru, Ecuador, and other South American republics. Under the sponsorship of the Ministry of Education of these countries they gave performances for children, conducted classes for teachers, and lectured on the history of puppetry and its educational uses. Señor Garavaglia is also a painter, and his wife, who holds a doctor's degree, is a student of law.

GARCÍA, M.   (Pp. 240, 241, 242, 244). Variety, *Barrio de la Palma*, and *Casamiento de los Indios*, Mexico City, 10 June and 16 September 1857.

GARCIA, SIGNOR   (P. 108). Exhibited fantoccini at Elysian Fields, Hoboken, N. J., 1844.

GARDINER, GEORGE R.   Hagerstown, Md. 1938, *Snow White and the Dwarfs*, with marionettes at the Y.M.C.A.

GARDINER, PETER   (Pp. 48, 49, 50, 51). Strong man and puppeteer, played at the Theatre, Williamsburg, Va., in 1769 and 1772.

GARDNER and BREWER   (Pp. 134, 135, 146). Punch and Judy men at Tammany Hall, New York, 1869.

GARDNER, EDITH   1940, *Nativity Play* with 16-inch marionettes at Central Presbyterian Sunday School, Hamilton, Canada. 1941, *Hansel and Gretel* as an opera, assisted by members of the Duet Club.

GARDNER, MARGARET   Chicago. c. 1940, used puppets in art classes, and taught puppetry to groups of the National Coöperative Association, and to alumni of Northwestern University in their August Institute. These recreation leaders met one summer in Steamboat Springs, Colo., and produced a play in which Sleeping Giant Mountain came to life.

GARRICK PUPPETEERS   See Lachlan, Jean.

GARRISON, GERALDINE   Neodesha, Kan. 1934, *Jack and the Beanstalk*, 1937, *The Little Lame Prince* with marionettes. 1938–1939, revival *Jack and the Beanstalk*.

CAUTHIER   (P. 245). Presented fantoches in Mexico, 1888.

GAYE MARIONETTES   See Harding, Blanche and Roland.

GAYLE, WALTER   Drewry's Bluff, Va. 1939, *Hansel and Gretel*.

GEDDIS, RALPH, and MARTIN, FRANCOIS   (Pp. 87, 130). While in high school in San Francisco helped in Ellen Van Volkenburg's production of *A Midsummer Night's Dream*, c. 1924. Played hand-puppets for many years. Bought an old mill at Russell's Mills in which to live and a country church for a puppet theatre. Combined forces with Jean Gros, 1932. Conducted a repertory theatre on Beacon Hill, Boston, c. 1934, and taught puppetry. Have made mechanical displays for Macy's and played Punch and *Alice in Wonderland* in a Boston department store. Summer 1943, revived Punch and Judy shows on Boston Common. 1948, working in Santa Barbara, Cal.

GEHRIS, WALTER   Summer 1936, Palisades Amusement Park, N. J., with marionettes and shadows in variety.

GENRICH, ELIZABETH   Castelar Evening High School, Los Angeles. 1929, *The Three Wishes* with hand-puppets.

GERARD, BILL and BETTE   The Three Bee Puppeteers, San Diego, Cal. 1945 to date have played a school circuit in California consisting of one hundred and fifty schools. Repertory: *Jack and the Beanstalk*, *Jack the Giant Killer*, *The Three Wishes*, *Rumpelstiltskin*, Circus and Mexican Variety. Summer 1948, played for ten county fairs.

GIBBES, JOSEPH   (Pp. 48, 50). Gave puppet plays at the house of John Moore, Boston, 1768.

GIBSON, DAVID   Detroit, Mich. Produced Elizabethan plays with puppets while a student of the University of Michigan. 1945, variety in Italy while stationed there with the Army. 1948, experimental work in marionette ballet.

GILBERT AND BENNET SCHOOL MARIONETTE CLUB   See O'Neill, Iva.

GILES, VERNA   Glens Falls, N. Y. 1938, *Hansel and Gretel* and variety.

GILMORE, SPENCE   Denver, Colo. December 1925–July 1928, performed every other Saturday at the Women's Press Club, repertory including: *The Dark Forest, The Land of the Man in the Moon, Pierrette, The Three Wishes, Master Pierre Patelin,* variety. 1946, *The Dark Forest* and variety. 1947, *Birthday Wishes.* 1947–1948, *How the Chipmunk Got His Stripes* (with hand-puppets).

GLADMORE, JOHNNY   1946–1947, *Punch and Judy* in eastern N. J. theatres.

GLASS, THEODORE T.   Opened 1927, with a newly carved set of Punch and Judy figures and twenty-one blisters. This set replaced a battered set with composition heads used for several years before in side shows and carnivals in an act along with ventriloquism and magic. Played in many states, especially in New England; still performing in 1940.

GLEASON, DOROTHY   Puppetown Players, Cincinnati, O. 1935, *Susie Sees Santa.* 1936, *Darktown Doin's* (both shows with marionettes). 1938, built a variety show presented with hand-puppets which is still making the rounds. Two years taught a puppetry class for children at the Cincinnati Art Museum. Summer 1945, taught puppetry at Fenimore Riding Camps. 1946–1947, at Noyes Junior Camp. The Rhythm Puppets Summer Theatre was developed at the latter camp, and presented *Ching Foo and the Emperor, Lambie Pie, Adventures of an Irish Potato,* and *The Three Wishes.*

GLEN ROCK PUPPETEERS   Herb Scheffel and William Schuring, N. J. and New England. 1933, *Jack and the Beanstalk.* 1934, *The Snow Queen.* 1935, variety, including *Rosamund Ballet, Rapunzel, The Wishing Fairy.* 1936, revivals of previous shows, *Alice in Wonderland.* 1937, *Mr. Nutcracker* (with 56 marionettes and Tchaikowsky music), *Strings and Shavings.* 1938, *Stringtime,* including *Ping; Weather; Hans von Bulow's Last Puppet.* 1939, variety and *The Yellow Claw* (after Sax Rohmer). 1941, *A Midsummer Night's Dream.*

GLOVER, DOROTHY H.   Akron, O. 1933, *Alice in Wonderland.* 1934, *The Circus.*

GODOMAR, LEONOR   (Pp. 7, 74, 255). Introduced puppets into Peru at the end of the 16th century.

GOGLER, L.   Presented German puppet plays at the Bowery Garten, New York, from November 1867 to February 1868.

GOLDEN STATE MARIONETTES   See Kegg, George.

GOLDNER, DOROTHY T. and ORVILLE, C.   See Nawn, Tom.

GOLDSMITH, LEWIS   Goldsmith Marionettes, New Brunswick, N. J. 1935, *King of the Golden River, Judas Maccabeus.* 1936, *Mordecai Laughs Last, Moses and His People, Hansel and Gretel,* variety.

GONOTY   (P. 62). Showed Punch, Chinese shades, and artificial fireworks at a room in Courtlandt Street, New York, in November 1795, and at Martling's Long Room, 87 Nassau Street, in January 1796.

GOOCHISON, Professor   (P. 275). "Wooden-Headed Family of Marionettes" at Bunnel's Museum, Brooklyn, N. Y., 26 November–1 December 1883.

GORDON, MRS. E. S.   1934, *The Legend of Sleepy Hollow* with marionettes.

GRABOWSKI, LENORE   1931, *Bluebeard* and other fairy tales at North Woods Camp, Douglas Lake, Mich., and in Detroit schools. 1932, at the same camp, *The King of the Golden River.*

GRAHAM, MILDRED   Clayton, Mo. 1941, made first puppet in an occupational therapy workshop while recuperating from pneumonia. 1946, completed string-puppets for the Music Box Theatre, an hour performance including a play, *Lotus Cloud,* two short scenes, and a circus. This show is still playing, 1948, with Ruth Quinn as partner.

GRAY   (Pp. 101–2, 146). From London. Fantoccini at Peale's Museum, New York, 1832.

GRAY, DR. ARTHUR D.   Washburn College Marionettes, Topeka, Kan. Taught puppetry and produced shows in night school in addition to his medical work. 1933, *Snow White, Ali Baba.* 1934, *The Coppersmith of Bagdad, Jack and the Beanstalk.*

1935, *Washburn Marionette Orpheum.* 1939, *Ali Baba and His Swing Band.* In some of the above productions Earl Seigfred assisted with the direction.

GRAY, BARRY (Pp. 275, 276). Had Harry H. Walker as partner, 1885–1889; thenceforth played independently in vaudeville and with the circus. Marionettes at Doris's Eighth Avenue Museum, New York, 17–22 June 1889, Odell, vol. 14, p. 133. In 1894 with the Ringling Brothers side show. Still active 1940.

GRAY, HELEN Manual Puppeteers, Manual Training High School, Brooklyn, N. Y. 1934, *Rumpelstiltskin* and variety. 1936, *Amateur Hour.*

GRECO, ACHILLE (P. 300). With his family, gave Paladin performances in Rio de Janiero, 1895–1900, when they returned to Sicily.

GRECO, GAETANO Son of Achille. Had a theatre in Rio de Janiero, 1900–1911 and possibly later.

GREEN AND LUND PUPPETRY See Lund, Adrianne.

GREEN, ELIZABETH c. 1942, introduced puppetry as craft work into a Negro art center in St. Louis.

GREEN, NATHALIE SMITH Wickenburg, Ariz. 1932, *Babuska,* a Christmas play, and *Doctor Faust.* After graduating from Briarcliff Junior College, continued art training in England where she organized the Bushey Marionettes and produced *Gentle Gertrude, The Tinder Box,* and *The Jealousy of Le Barbouille* (translated from Molière), 1932–1934. Taught puppetry in various camps during war years. 1946, special puppetry teacher with the Playschool Association of New York City; presented *Alice in Wonderland* and other plays. 1946–1947, continued building and performing hand-puppet plays.

GREEN, RAY and BRYAN, ARTHUR San Francisco, Cal. *Perronik the Fool,* musical play after George Moore.

GREENE, ROBERT A. Geneseo, N. Y. First show 1916, *Lima Beans.* Other marionette productions: 1920, *The Wishing Ring.* 1922, *The Man Who Married a Dumb Wife.* 1920–1932, *Ali Baba.* 1948, making plans for a new playhouse and series of plays.

GREENWICH PUPPETEERS See Schuring, William.

GRESHAM, EDGAR 1940, *Oklahoma, a Story of the "Run,"* presented in Oklahoma City.

GRIFFIN, ZAIDEE The Aleš Puppet Theatre, Webster Branch, New York Public Library. 1924, 1929, presented Czech puppet plays for children.

GRIMALDI See Rinaldi.

GROS, JEAN (Pp. 338, 353, 354). 1922, *I Pagliacci* (after Leoncavallo). 1923, *Babes in Toyland, The Blue Bird* (Maeterlinck), *The Magical Land of Oz,* a series of Uncle Wiggley plays, and other productions. 1931–1932, *Huckleberry Finn, Mickey Mouse the Champion,* and other plays. 1933, about 2500 performances of *Orphan Annie at the Circus* with 36-inch marionettes on the Enchanted Island, Century of Progress Exposition, Chicago. 1934, continued tours. 1945, director of Caravan Players at the Civic Center, Pittsburgh, a repertory company and dramatic school which included puppetry.

GUERRERO BROTHERS Mexico City. In 1940 made a few appearances in the circus and popular theatres; also worked for Espinal's Rosete Aranda group.

GUIRIGAY PUPPET COMPANY Argentina. Formed by Spanish refugees under the direction of Mejuto and Cotes, gave performances in the Casa del Teatro, Buenos Aires, c. 1941.

GUTIERREZ, MANUEL B. Peru. A folk-artist who played in the plaza during the 1940 festival of St. James, patron of the village of Pallasca. There was no speaking, only a voicelike whistle made from a leaf. The play concerned a shepherdess, a potter, and a village mayor, with a pastoral setting. There was musical accompaniment by the *caja* and flutes peculiar to the region.

HAINES, ELIZABETH Philadelphia. 1932, *Aucassin and Nicolette, The Nativity, Sleeping Beauty.*

HALL, JOHN   Philadelphia. c. 1940 built marionettes for variety and *The Sleeping Beauty*.

HALL, KATE C.   Atlanta, Ga. 1933–1935, presented plays with marionettes and hand-puppets including: *The Moon for a Prince, The Disconsolate Dragon, The Library Imp at Hallowe'en*, sketches about the composing of *Old Kentucky Home, The Dragon to the Rescue*.

HALLANGER, ISABEL   Chicago. c. 1940, used puppets as an avocation, producing variety and short plays.

HAMDEN, CONN., HIGH SCHOOL MARIONETTE WORKSHOP   1936, *A Christmas Rose*, circus, and other plays.

HAMM, MRS. C. S.   Chillicothe, O. With puppets constructed by Gene Cadden, produced variety and *Rumpelstiltskin*, c. 1940.

HAMMOND, ZEY   West Clarksville, N. Y. 1941, *The Enchanted Princess*. 1942, *Pageant of Champlain Spring*.

HANCOCK, MATTHEW   Inherited Peter Hauntz show from Prof. King in 1884 after having played it on road with him. In 1895, the act was Hancock Brothers' Mystic Show, with ventriloquism. Retired c. 1930.

HANLEY, ETHEL   Muscatine, Ia. 1936–1945, toured with variety, revues, and fairy tale plays for children.

HANNA, JOHN BASTICK   Fort Worth, Tex. *Marionette Follies of 1934*. 1935, *Jack and the Beanstalk, The Disappointed Dragon*. The *1937 Sketchbook* with marionettes and shadows on a triple revolving stage.

HAN(N)INGTON   (Pp. 97, 103, 108, 109). 1837, fantoccini at Peale's Museum, New York. 1845, Theatre of Arts and diorama there. 1850, diorama and fantoccini at Washington Hall, New York.

HANSLEY   "The man with the talking hand." He performed the Victorian parlor trick of forming a loose-jawed face of his hand, and also had puppets; a one-man show, c. 1900—Letter of Augustus Rapp, 14 January 1940.

HANSON, JULIUS   (P. 229). Played *Punch and Judy* at the National Garten, New York, 13 April 1879—Odell, vol. 10, p. 663. At the National Theatre, New York, 27 October–8 November 1879 and 29 March–4 April 1880.

HANSWURST'S MARIONETTES   See Suhrs, Susan.

HARDING, BLANCHE and ROLAND   Gaye Marionettes, Dickinson, N. D. 1933, *Aladdin and the Wonderful Lamp*. 1934, *Rapunzel*. 1935, *Lady Loses Her Hoop*. 1937, *The Enchanted Princess*. 1938, *Jack and the Beanstalk*. 1939, *Cindrella, Wander Wits and the Dragon*. 1941, *Teddy Roosevelt in the Badlands* (with marionettes and shadows).

HARGRAVE, ANNA and MARTHA   Martana Marionettes, Aurora, Ill., and Long Beach, Cal. Their grandfather owned a small circus, their father was a showman. Anna did commercial art and taught handicrafts, Martha was interested in writing. Puppetry combined all these interests, inherited and acquired. First show 7 March 1942, *Alice in Wonderland*, followed by circus. 1944, *Revue on Strings*. 1946–1948, Second *Revue on Strings*. During war presented shows in hospitals.

HARMS, DONALD   Young puppeteer of Peoria, Ill., who carves wooden puppets and has produced marionette plays, 1947–1948.

HARRIS, CORNELIA CLARK   In and about Mill Valley, Cal., 1931, *The Last of the Leprechauns, Just an Old Spanish Custom*, and other plays. 1932, with Portia Hawley at the Puppet Workshop, Berkeley: *The Sea Green-Blue*.

HARRIS, GENEVIEVE H.   Douglas High School, Baltimore, Md. 1935, *Jack and the Beanstalk* and *Recital* with 9-inch marionettes.

HARRIS, JOE   High School, Otwell, Ind. 1937, *And the Christmas Chimes Rang Again*.

HARRISBURG (PA.) COMMUNITY THEATRE MARIONETTES   See Eaton, Frances.

HARTO, JAMES   Punch and Judy man of the early 20th century.

HARVEL   Vaudeville manikins, remembered in 1928 by Mr. Carmody of Radio-Keith-Orpheum.

HASKELL INSTITUTE MARIONETTES   See Malm, Sibyl.

HASKINS, INEZ CLARE Butte, Mont. Produced shows annually from 1931–1938, working with the Marionette Club of the High School and privately. Plays include: *The Staff and the Fiddle* (after Howard Pyle), *Mummers' Legend of St. George, The Storming of Torquilstone* (after Scott's *Ivanhoe*), *The Rose and the Ring, Boiled Celery, The Cap That Fits* (Austin Dobson), *Pedro and the Beautiful Donkey*, and *The Three Bears*, presented by Junior League members.

HASTINGS, SUE (Pp. 270, 338, 353, 364, 374). New York. 1924, began puppet work in play writing course at Columbia University with a travesty of *Uncle Tom's Cabin*. Also studied with Tony Sarg. Produced many short plays including: *The Gooseberry Mandarin* and *The Pancake Princess* by Grace Dorcas Ruthenburg, *The Yellow Dwarf, Pies and Pirates, Sleeping Beauty, A Trip to the Moon, Puppet Follies* with a wide variety of plays and special numbers. 1926, played at the Washington Stables, Sesquicentennial Exposition, Philadelphia. By 1930, five companies were on tour playing a repertory of 12 plays and 25 revue acts, with 500 puppets and 11 stages. 1931–1932, *Puss in Boots, Dora, the Beautiful Dairymaid* (a melodrama), *How the Elephant Got Its Trunk, Little Black Sambo, Peter Rabbit*. Series of plays were presented for Columbia University, Brooklyn Institute of Arts and Sciences, RKO vaudeville, Bermuda Steamship Lines, and other organizations. 1933, *The Three Little Pigs* and *The Magic Ring*, and variety presented on RKO circuit. 1934, program of *Peter Rabbit* and *Little Black Sambo* played in Children's Theatre on the Enchanted Island, Century of Progress Exposition, Chicago. 1935, toured England and Scotland in summer, presented *At Home Abroad* in autumn. 1936, 11 companies were on tour, with another at the Texas Centennial Exposition. 1939–1940, played variety with portrait puppets for Standard Brands, Inc., at the New York World's Fair. 1941, Thanksgiving to Christmas, had a show in Gimbel's window, New York. 1942–43, plays for USO and for recruiting women for industry (*Mrs. Bumble Sees the Light*, for Westinghouse Electric), Saturday afternoon programs for children in New York and Brooklyn, Belles and Beaux of Gay Nineties for Gimbel's windows. 1944, entrusting the work to a company manager, from October through November gave Saturday shows with variety and *Wizard of Oz* at 48 Street Cinema, New York. 1945, *Alice in Wonderland, The Pig and the Pepper, The Princess and the Hobgoblins, Peter Rabbit*. 1946–1947, played school, college, and church engagements in addition to advertising shows: *The Happy Ending* for *Mademoiselle* magazine's bridal consultants convention and *He Done Her Wrong* for Barbour-Abelson Company, manufacturers of boys clothing. Has taught puppetry at the University of Miami, 1943–1948.

HATCHER, ALTHEA Pompton Plains, N. J. 1939, played *Hansel and Gretel* in libraries, schools, churches, and community centers in New Jersey.

HAUKANE and LONYA 1944, used novelty dancing puppets for floor shows.

HAWLEY, PORTIA Oakland, Cal., and vicinity. 1929, *The Lost Circus* (with rod- and hand-puppets) and *Under the Sea Green-Blue*. 1930, *The Dragon of Lantern Land* (with hand-puppets).

HAYES, JAMES J. (Pp. 98, 101, 102, 278). Morningside Marionettes, Morningside College, Sioux City, Ia. and Oklahoma City University. 1927, original version of *Punch and Judy* (later published by Puppetry Imprints). 1928, *Jack and the Beanstalk*. 1929, two short farces. Began performances in Oklahoma City, 1932, with *Punch and Judy*. 1933–1936, played *Bluebeard, Variety, Punch and Judy* in Oklahoma City schools. Organized WPA puppeteers, and assisted the Junior League Puppeteers launch their puppet program. 1948, did occasional one-man shows.

HAYNEN, IRMA Glens Falls, N. Y. Amateur puppeteer presenting marionette variety for clubs, parties, schools, 1947–1948 and several years preceding.

HAYWARD, ROGER Beroju Puppet Theatre, Pasadena, Cal. 1933–1934, played variety and a few plays such as *The Sorcerer's Apprentice* and *Punch and Judy*.

HAYWARD, TOM 1931, 40 performances of *Jack and the Beanstalk* in Milwaukee, Wis.

HEAD, CEDRIC and MABEL (Pp. 339, 356, 387). Kingsland Marionettes, Boonton, N. J. 1930, began repertory for sales promotions and played in stores of 27 towns during this year and 1931. 1935, opened summer school of puppetry at Lake Dunmore, Vt., which continued until World War II. From his large collection of historic puppets (including many of the late Tony Sarg's), Head selects actors for such plays as *Robin Hood, Humpty Dumpty, Marco Polo,* and variety, with which he tours in the East and South.

HEATH, LESLIE   Leselli Marionettes. 1942, had half-hour variety show as a regular feature at the San Diego Army-Navy YMCA, a USO center. This company tours with programs of variety and plays.

HECHT, ETHEL, and HOFENMANN, MRS. E.   Bancroft School, Montreal, Canada. 1942, *Cries of London* produced by children of the school.

HEDDLE, MURIEL   (P. 349). Toronto, Canada. From c. 1933–1938, worked with Dave and Violet Keogh, first under name of Kay's Marionettes, later Kay-Heddle Marionettes (see Keogh). 1940–1941, played variety and various ballet-pantomines such as Debussy's *La Mer* with her own company.

HEDGES, HAZELLE   Hazelle's Marionettes, Kansas City, Mo. From 1933–1939, possibly later, presented string-puppet shows for and with children, for stores, clubs, and for advertising. Programs consisted of variety, well-known fairy tales, and such plays as *Old King Joel and His Bag of Gold, Children Should Be Seen, Not Hurt, Why Live with Folly?, Marionette Amateur Hour, Alice at the Art Fair, Nurse's Dilemma, Mrs. Brown Goes into Action* (for Cook Paint and Varnish Company). From c. 1936 to date has manufactured toy marionettes which are stocked by department stores.

HEININGER, ROBERT M.   Puppeteers Club, Munhall, Pa., Neighborhood House. 1933, *The Red Shoes, Rip Van Winkle.*

HELLER, ROBERT   (Pp. 132, 274). d. 28 November 1878. *Punch and Judy* at the Academy of Music, Brooklyn, 12 April 1877—Odell, vol. 10, p. 326. Minstrel show with puppets, Washington, D. C., 4–17 November 1878.

HENDERSON   Punch and Judy man of the late 19th century, mentioned by Ernest Russell, "The Most Popular Play in the World," *Outing Magazine,* January 1908, p. 473.

HENDRICKS, STEVE   Originated a puppet act in the East, now carried on by his son— letter of Nicholas Nelson, 21 October 1939.

HENNING, FRANCES   From 1931–1938, worked with a school puppet club presenting original scenes, variety, and well-known stories such as *Dick Whittington's Cat, Snow White and the Seven Dwarfs.*

HENRY   (P. 123). Punch and Judy at Chatham Museum, New York, December 1828 and January–April 1829.

HERBERTT, STANLEY   A dancer in the Ballet Theatre Company, 1947, he and his sister, assisted by neighbor children, formed a puppet company which produced folk and fairy tale plays: *King of Schnorrers, The Rose and the Ring.*

HERMITTE, ALFREDO   (Pp. 350, 351). Argentina. Leader of a group of professional people who, c. 1940, became interested in the puppet theatre and produced plays which were taken on a tour of the provinces. With Javier Villafañe, published during 1939 a series of articles about puppets and puppet showmen in the newspaper *La Vanguardia.* 1941, with his company, *Títeres de la Tolderia,* presented: *The Prodigious Woman Shoemaker, The Knight of the Fiery Hand, Tirulé the Magician, The Little Tin Soldier, Pied Piper of Hamelin* (with music), *Hansel and Gretel.*

HERNANDEZ, JUSEPE   (Pp. 7, 74). 1597, in Lima, Peru, offered the Castle of Marvels, possibly a puppet show.

HERRSCHAFT, WILLIAM   (P. 387). Marionette Theatre Workshop, Hartford, Conn. 1929, *The Cow Died of . . . , Olga the Russian Spy, Troll Scene* from *Peer Gynt, The Arkansas Bear.* Later experimented with larger-than-life-size rod-puppets for *Jack the Giant Killer* and other plays.

HESS, CONSTANCE   Musinette Productions, Inc., New York. 1938, for the shut-in children of St. Vincent's Hospital, presented *The Barber of Seville* with 14-inch marionettes. The action was synchronized with the Metropolitan Opera broadcast.

Later a color film was made of the show. Studio performances of scenes from other operas were presented in the same year, as well as *Sunday Night Concert*, with portrait puppets of Metropolitan Opera stars.

HESTWOOD, HAROLD and ROBERT   (Pp. 338, 354). 1928, *The Gawpy Ballet*, a fantasy with stylized birds and beasts presented in Carmel, Cal., and later in the Little Theatre, New York. Reproduced by Movietone. 1932, *Mickey and Minnie in the Olympic Games*, Bullock's Store, Los Angeles.

HIGGINS, FRANK L.   Vaudeville manikin show, played with son, dating from early 20th century, called Old Si's Show. The proscenium an opening in a curtain painted like the side of a brick building. A puppet audience, including a man who pounds on the floor with his cane, and a lady pianist with a flexible neck, sat in a row at the bottom of the opening. There were variety numbers of Old Si, who could apply his handkerchief to his nose, a skeleton, a clown and horse, a Chinese pole dancer, a "wench with a big bustle," and a lady-into-balloon—letter from Frank L. Higgins, 13 November 1939.

HIGHLAND PARK, MICH., HIGH SCHOOL MARIONETTES   See Abbott, Bess.

HILDEBRAND, Sisters   Monterey, Cal. Played at the Golden Bough, and for parties in Carmel valley, 1948.

HILL, PAT   1944, had a puppet act in Ed Wynn's USO unit. 1947, played RKO vaudeville circuit.

HILL, RUTH (Mrs. Francis Poppenburg)   Chicago, Ill. 1941–1947, toured with floor-show act. Has played for Chicago YWCA, for USO Camp Shows, Monte Carlo, Reynosa, Mexico, and various hotels and theatres. Mother and father assist with construction of the 26-inch marionettes.

HILL, VIOLETTE   Puppet Club, Farragut School, Joliet, Ill. 1942, Variety, *The Enchanted Tree, Pyramus and Thisbe* with hand-puppets.

HINES, ALBERT   (P. 364). Beginning c. 1926, used puppets in his recreational work at the Madison Square Boys' Club, of which he is director. Variety and plays such as *The Wizard of Oz, They Ain't No Ghosts*, and *A Christmas Carol* have been produced.

HOFFMANN, AGNES   Chicago, Ill. A retired teacher who began making puppets c. 1940, taught puppetry at the YWCA, and has been performing variety and plays ever since.

HOFFMAN, LOLA B.   Hurdy-Gurdy Studio, Brooklyn Avenue School, Los Angeles, Cal. 1927–1931, presented puppet plays based on familiar children's stories.

HOHENSTINE, JOANN (Mrs. Stuart Cox, Newark, O.)   While a student at Ohio State University wrote, built, and presented *Private Wilbur, Spy Catcher*, with hand-and-rod-puppets, 1943. Subsequently produced other plays and gave talks and demonstrations of puppets.

HOLLINGSHEAD-LOVE, KERMIT   1932, *The World to Come*, at St. Luke's, Metuchen, N. J.

HOLLIS, R. W.   Tanglestring Marionettes, Hollywood. 1936, *Christmas Fantasy* with 20-inch marionettes.

HOLLYWOOD MARIONETTE THEATRE   1933, *Puppets on Parade* presented by Joseph Finley and Gordon Graves.

HOLLYWOOD PLAYERS   See Nawn, Tom.

HOLMES, ANNA M.   The Attic Theatre, Seattle, Wash. 1930–1931, played well-known stories such as *Rumpelstiltskin*. 1933, as Shadowlawn Lodge Puppet Theatre, played variety, *The Russian General, There Was an Old Woman*. 1934, *Bad Times at the Punches'*.

HOLMES, KATHLEEN (Mrs. Walter Smith)   From c. 1940 has conducted puppet classes with Mexican children in San Antonio, Tex., public schools.

HOLT, HENRY   Dancing master and diorama showman, New York, 1739.

HOSMER, HERBERT, JR.   (Pp. 314, 320). The Toy Cupboard Theatre, South Lancaster, Mass. The Toy Cupboard, a little country toy shop, opened in the summer of 1940. Next summer, puppets were added to the attractions, and performances were given twice a week on the permanent stage built for both puppets and marionettes. A new play was staged each week, dramatized from Perrault, Andersen, *Winnie the Pooh*, Aesop's *Fables*, and the Thornton Burgess tales. Appropriate sweets were served during intermissions—ginger-cookie men when *Hansel and Gretel* was performed, sugar-cookie pigs for *The Three Little Pigs*. During the 1944 season, performances on Thursday evening were given, with Chinese lanterns strung through the shrubbery and over the terrace where punch and cookies were served by candlelight. At present Hosmer is devoting his entire time to the production of puppet plays, research on toys, and writing.

HOUDIN, ROBERT   (P. 189). Marionettes with Dr. Haskell in the Northwest, 1874.

HOUDINI, HARRY   (Pp. 133, 212). Was engaged to play *Punch and Judy*, among other things, with the John and M. H. Walsh circus in the spring of 1895—Harold Kellock, *Houdini, His Life Story*, New York, 1928, p. 72.

HOUGHMASTER, JOHN   Schenectady, N. Y. 1929, joined Helen Haiman Joseph's company in Cleveland; became manager and partner c. 1932. Puppeteered with the touring troupe until 1938, then devoted his time to planning, building, and managing. 1942, the company was disbanded, when most of its members went into the armed services or essential industry.

HOULIHAN, MILDRED   Angell School, Boston, Mass. 1936–1938, presented variety and fairy tales with 18-inch marionettes.

HOULUSKAS, ANTON   A Czech puppeteer who came to America c. 1912 and began presenting shows c. 1920, with his wife, son, and two daughters. Plays were drawn from Czech folklore; puppets were operated from above by a rod and strings. Performances were given to Czech audiences in Minnesota, the Dakotas, Iowa, and Nebraska.

HOWE   (P. 285). Shadowgraphs at Pilling's (National) Theatre, New York, 7–12 October 1889. Odell, vol. 14, p. 377.

HOYT, G. W.   (Pp. 89, 123). Punch and Judy show at Haworth's Institute, Brooklyn, in 1838.

HOYT, HAZEL   The Panel Playhouse Puppets, New York. 1927, *Phillida and Her Bear, St. George and the Dragon, The Sleeping Beauty, Torquil MacFerron*.

HOYT, RICHARD   (Pp. 87, 88, 89, 90, 91, 116, 123). Gave a hand-puppet show at Russell's Mills, Dartmouth, Mass., c. 1800.

HUBBARD, JACK   Wichita, Kan. 1933, *Amos in Hades* and *Continental Varieties* with 13-inch marionettes.

HUBBARD, O. B.   Punch and Judy man, published a text of the play at Lawrence, Mass., 1874.

HUBIN, FRANK B.   Atlantic City, N. J. Played Punch and sold whistles (earning $10 to $20 a week from the 5c whistles) c. 1887. 1889, played at Golden Gate Park, San Francisco, to crowds of 65,000 and sold 2,500 whistles: the city paid $15 for the day's work. During the Klondike boom worked at Dawson City, staked a claim but let it lapse. Played Punch on steamboats from the Missouri to the Ohio rivers, setting up his booth on shore when the boat stopped to take on wood. Also played in department stores, museums, and circuses.

HUNT, GALE   Spokane, Wash. 1929, *The Toymaker's Dream*. 1930, *The Lost Prince*. 1931, *Celebrities*.

HUNTZINGER, JOHN H.   John Paul Jones High School, Philadelphia. 1930, variety and *The Three Wishes*.

HURD, GEORGE N.   Detroit, Mich. 1914–1920, produced plays and operas with 5-inch figures moved across a cardboard stage on a ribbon parallel to the footlights. This toy theatre was complete with lights and scenery.

HURDY GURDY MARIONETTES, THE   See Stout, Mary Frances.

HUSEN, ELLY   1942, lecture, demonstration, and skit *How Ladies Aid*, at the Morristown, N. J., Art Association.

HUTCHINGS, CHIQUITA   1943, used small marionettes termed "humanettes" for floor show at Club Stevadora, Detroit.

HYKES, ADELAIDE   Ardmore, Pa. c. 1940, gave performances for children's parties and churches.

HYMAN, SPAFF   Magician and puppeteer of the late 19th century, taught Edward Ross how to play Punch and Judy—Katherine Scarborough, "He Has Pulled the Strings for 43 Years," Baltimore *Sun*, 3 March 1940, Section 1, p. 2.

INVERARITY, R. BRUCE   (Pp. 8, 13, 279, 359, 385). Made his first puppet in 1927 and in 1929 produced *Pulpit* with marionettes and shadows at Blanding Sloan Puppet Theatre, San Francisco. 1932, *Adventures of Captain Catfish Pete* in Vancouver and the Northwest. 1934, became director of University of Washington Puppeteers, Seattle, produced variety, *Cinderella, Robinson Crusoe,* and other plays.

IRVING, GEORGE H.   (Pp. 132, 146, 149, 151, 152). (8 October 1858–1936). Born in Rochester, N. H., Irving joined a circus at an early age, and was engaged with the Sparks, John Robinson, Lee's London, Forepaugh, Welch, Hargraves, Andrew Downie, Walter Main, and other circuses, in later years as side-show manager, when he played *Punch and Judy.* He obtained his puppets from a well-known Punch man (whose name was not recalled by his widow), and though they went through cyclone, fire, and wreck, they have survived. Known as "Punch" Irving, he spent his last years in Haverhill, Mass. His set of puppets has been recorded by the Michigan Art and Crafts Project for the Index of American Design under Miscellaneous: Sambo, 43; Devil, 48; Punch, 58A; Punch's head, 58B; Judy, 59; Horse, 62; Policeman, 63; Figure in plum-colored velvet, 64; Boxing Clown, 65; Ghost, 66; Baby, 67; Boxer in blue coat, 70; Properties—stick, gibbet, and coffin, 71; Chinaman, 72.

JACK-A-GREEN COMPANY   1932, *Hansel and Gretel*, Fullerton Hall, Art Institute of Chicago.

JACKLEY, JANICE   1933, *Peter Pan* and variety with 15-inch marionettes.

JAFFE, PHIL   Jaffetto Puppets, Beverly Hills, Cal. 1948, marionette plays in his backyard theatre as well as in private homes for children's parties.

JAMES, LEN   Canadian Punch and Judy showman, active 1948.

JAN HUS HOUSE MARIONETTES   See Raym, Mrs. Max.

JANNUZI, GAIL   Detroit, Mich. 1942, *Hansel and Gretel*. 1947, *St. George and the Dragon.*

JENNINGS, DOROTHY L.   Providence, R. I. 1936, variety, with marionettes, handpuppets, and shadows in a store toy department. 1938, *Mr. Pickle's Grocery Store.*

JEROME, HENRY   (P. 274). Marionettes at the Aquarium, New York, 1874.

JERONELLE   (Pp. 113, 126, 275). (Jerome Italianized?) Italian fantoccini at Jones Wood, New York, 1859.

JESTER, G. W.   Appeared at Fox's American Theatre, Philadelphia, 31 October 1870, as a "talking hand" entertainer, like Handsley and Morley—Philadelphia *Public Ledger*, 31 October 1870.

JEWELL, JAMES   Detroit, Mich. 1930, with 68 Marionettes presented: *The Selfish Giant, The Happy Prince* (after Wilde), *Circus Days,* and *Jack and the Beanstalk.*

JEWELL, MAE   (Pp. 269, 277, 280). Vaudeville manikins, 1904–1935.

JOHN, MRS. ROBERT   Waukegan, Ill. 1936, *The Adventures of Jack, Punch and Judy, The Scarecrow Who Wished for the Moon.*

JOHNSON, ALMA   Helena, Mont. 1934, *On the Range,* variety, *Jack and the Beanstalk, Robinson Crusoe.*

JOHNSON, EDWARD   Highland Park, Mich. Presented first show c. 1928. In 1938 began experimenting with the idea of a one-man string-puppet show and produced *The Three Wishes* during the 1939–1940 season. 1940–1941, *Jack and the Beanstalk,* a more elaborate production. 1941–1942, *The Enchanted Island,* an original play based on folk tale material. After more than three years overseas in the Army, revived this play for the 1946–1947 season. While in the Philippines studied lore and legends of the people, made sketches of them and of scenery. This material was utilized in the 1947–1948 production, *Wonder Mountain*.

JOHNSON, ELIZABETH CLARK Lincoln School, Corona, Cal. 1941, *Princess Lemon Pie's Intrigue*. 1942, *The Nativity* and *The Three Bears* (with hand-puppets).

JOHNSON, LLOYD Sioux City, Ia. 1928, *Hallowe'en Night, The Three Wishes*, variety.

JOHNSON, MARJORIE PRISCILLA New Haven, Conn. 1936, *Jack and the Beanstalk, King of the Golden River*.

JOHNSON, MARTHA CAROLINE Camp Nahanawa, Maryland, Tenn. 1935, *Shirley Temple's Arrival at Nahanawa, Further Adventures of Shirley, Jack and the Beanstalk, Cinderella*.

JOHNSON, MARY P. (P. 394). 1931–1934, presented fairy tales, excerpts from children's classics, and variety in schools and clubs of Tacoma, Washington and vicinity. Plays included: *Columbine and Her Playfellows* (from a 16th-century pantomime), *The Golden-Haired Princess, The Wolf at the Door, The Amazing Adventures of Pinocchio, The Littlest Shepherd*.

JOHNSTON, LORA Waterloo, Ia. From 1932 to date has presented plays and variety with marionettes and hand-puppets for churches, schools, lodges, and theatres.

JOHNSTONE, RALPH, and HARRIS, PALMER 1932, *Doctor Faust* with marionettes in Cicero, Ill.

JOLLY CAPER'S MARIONETTES. See Adams, Barbara.

JONES, DORIS GOODRICH Waco, Tex. Began puppet work summer 1934 with the Hamburg Puppeteers at Chautauqua, N. Y. Has written her own short plays, mostly around Texas characters. 1936, *Peter Rabbit the Magician* and *Patsy and the Cake*. 1938, *Twinkletoes the Elf*. 1939, *Sally Practices*. 1940, *Elizabeth Ney, Sculptress*. 1941, *Asthma's Adventure, Jimmy Scarecrow*, and other one-act plays. 1942–1943, Texas scenes. 1947, *Jimmy Scarecrow's Vocation*. 1948, *Zephyr, the Mustang Pony*.

JONES, RAYMOND R. Washington State College, Pullman, Wash. Began 1929 with *Jack and the Beanstalk*. 1930, *Punch and Judy*. 1940–1948, floor shows with string-puppets. 1948, *Little Red Riding Hood* (at College) with hand- and-rod-puppets.

JONES, VICTOR CHARLES The Victor Charles Marionettes. Began 1938 with *Snow White* and *Hansel and Gretel*. 1939–1940, *Tom Sawyer*. 1940–1941, *A Christmas Carol* and revivals of previous productions. The following season tours were continued but no new shows were built. Company disbanded during war; Jones continued with a one-man floor-show act, and was with Belita's ice show for a time.

JONLIN MARIONETTES See Keogh, John.

JOOD (Joad?) (P. 260). Amateur puppeteer at St. Eustache, Quebec, early 20th century.

JORDAN, MARGARET 1925–1926, produced familiar fairy tales as school projects in Battle Creek, Iowa, and Rockwell City, Iowa. 1928, *Ichabod Crane* and 1929, *In the Morning*, both in Rockwell City.

JOSEPH, HELEN HAIMAN (Pp. 3, 273, 324, 327, 333, 337, 341, 347, 366, 390). Cleveland, O. Began puppet work 1915 at the Cleveland Playhouse with a shadow play, *Seven at a Blow*, followed, in 1916, by Yeats' *Shadowy Waters* and, in 1917, Maeterlinck's *The Death of Tintagiles, The Death of Chopin*, a pantomime, *Hansel and Gretel, Snow White and Rose Red, Aladdin, Beauty and the Beast, Red Riding Hood, The Black Spot* (from Stevenson's *Treasure Island*). After working with the Playhouse group, lived abroad for three years, writing, studying, and visiting puppet theatres. Upon return, formed a professional company (c. 1925), which played a repertory of well-known stories adapted for puppets, many with original lyrics and music: *A Midsummer Night's Dream, King John and the Abbot of Canterbury, Puss in Boots, Jack and the Beanstalk, Little One-Eye, Two-Eye, and Three Eye, Pandora and Epimetheus, Punch and Judy, The Coat of Many Colors, The Golden Fleece, Robin Hood and His Merry Men, The Life and Death of Doctor Faustus, Adventures of Pinocchio, Ali Baba and the Forty Thieves, Joseph and His Brethren* (with shadows). 1929, John Houghmaster joined the company, becoming manager and partner c. 1932. 1931, the company played repertory of children's plays, while Mrs. Joseph was in Europe. 1932, returned to direct company in *Beauty and the*

Beast and older productions. Each year extensive tours were made, and in 1935 a troupe was in the Education Building at the San Diego Exposition. Around 1936 began building commercial advertising shows, and in 1938 the children's fairy story shows were discontinued. By 1942 there were nine companies playing in all parts of the country. In this year operations were suspended because of World War II. Mrs. Joseph became interested in the children's programs at the Cain Park Theatre in the summer of 1945, and produced *Pinocchio* there. In 1946, five shows were presented in the eight-week season. These included *Snow White, Bug in a Rug* (by George Latshaw), *Uppity Puppets* (by Bill Ryan), *Hansel and Gretel*, variety. 1947, *Puss in Boots* and *Tom Sawyer* were added to the repertory. In addition to the shows presented, children's classes in puppetry have been conducted each summer. Mrs. Joseph has written articles about puppets for *Theatre Arts Monthly*, and other magazines and the *Encyclopaedia Britannica*. She has published plays and stories, and her *A Book of Marionettes* (first edition Huebsch, New York, 1920, second edition, Viking Press, New York, 1929), is a standard history.

JOWERS, LUCIE GILES   Worcester, Mass., Art Museum. 1927, *The Snow Queen*. 1928, *Don Quixote*. 1929, *Jack and the Beanstalk*.

JOY, K. E.   1938, *Pleasure Before Business, Dipsy Doodle Demo, Esky Barks—and Buys*.

JULIO, EL DOCTOR   See Hernandez, Jusepe.

JULIUS, Herr   (Pp. 227, 228, 229). German puppeteer, appeared in New York at the National Assembly Rooms, 11 February 1869, the Harmony Rooms, 20 March–5 May 1869, and at Jefferson Hall, 2 February 1873.

JUNIOR FINE ARTS CLUB OF PANHANDLE, TEX. 1933, *Cinderella*. 1934, *Rumpelstiltskin*.

JUNIOR GREENHILLS PLAYERS   Council Crest, Ore. 1933, *The Three Bears*.

JUNIOR LEAGUE   For the past 20 years, Junior Leagues throughout the country have built and presented puppet shows as part of their children's theatre programs. The Leagues not only endeavor to do good shows themselves, but also sponsor professional companies in order to develop greater appreciation of puppetry in the community. In 1938 a five-day national conference was held in Dayton, Ohio, at which there was a puppet exhibit, demonstrations, and criticisms of several League performances, all designed to improve the quality of puppetry. Under the direction of Jean Starr Wiksell, institutes have been held by various groups, and she has been available as a consultant. (Pp. 366, 389).

The following list indicates the types of plays produced, and the uses to which puppets have been put.

Ashville, N. C. For several years c. 1940 puppets were used to advertise children's plays at the local theatre.

Atlanta, Ga. 1940, variety, *The Three Wishes*; assisted Girl Scouts in their puppet work.

Birmingham, Ala. 1944, *Goldilocks and the Three Bears*. 1945, *The Three Little Pigs*. 1946, *Little Black Mingo*. 1947, *Peter Rabbit, Blondie Presents*.

Boise, Idaho. 1929, *The Three Bears, Jack the Giant Killer* (with shadows). 1933, *Treasure Island* (with shadows).

Bridgeport, Conn. 1933, *The Gooseberry Mandarin, Aladdin, Wizard of Oz*. 1940, demonstrated puppet construction and manipulation in public school art and dramatic groups and used puppets in occupational therapy for children.

Boston, Mass. 1929, *Robin Hood in Sherwood*. 1944–1945, sponsored Suzari Marionettes in *Pinocchio*.

Buffalo, N. Y. 1928, *The Three Bears, Hansel and Gretel, Peter Rabbit, Little Black Sambo*.

Butte, Mont. 1937, *Pedro and the Beautiful Donkey*. 1940, programs in school auditoriums. 1944–1945, *Seven at a Blow*. 1947, show for Community Chest.

Brooklyn, N. Y. 1944–1945, *Jack and the Beanstalk*.

Cedar Rapids, Ia. 1944–1945, sponsored Tatterman Marionettes in *The Legend of the Lightning*.

Dayton, Ohio. 1932, *Peter Rabbit, Little Black Sambo, The Three Bears, The Three Little Pigs, The Night Before Christmas.* 1933, *Little Red Riding Hood.* 1934, *Ali Baba, The Lost Hammer, The First Noël, Puss in Boots.*

Charleston, S. C. 1940, *The Princess and the Riddle, Layovers to Catch Meddlers, The Princess and the Swineherd.* Regular free presentations of these plays at the Museum; pay performances at Dock Street Theatre to finance the others.

Charlotte, N. C. c. 1940, *Uncle Remus* and fairy tale plays.

Chattanooga, Tenn. 1928, *Snow White and the Dwarfs.* 1929, *Jack and the Beanstalk, Little Red Riding Hood, Hansel and Gretel.* 1940, eight performances to large audiences of children in poorer sections of the city.

Columbia, S. C. 1939, *Rumpelstiltskin,* under cooperative arrangement with Town Theatre.

Columbus, Ga. 1940, *Old Lady Cross Patch, The Yellow Dwarf, The Tinder Box.* These shows were played in other Georgia towns, including Palm Springs for the poliomyelitis patients there.

Elmira, N. Y. 1940, worked with marionettes.

Flint, Mich. 1939–1940, performed hand-puppet plays in schools.

Great Falls, Mont. 1945, *Katinka and the Jewel Tree.* 1946, *The Three Boxes.* 1947, *Arkansas Bear, Red Feather's Counter Attack.* 1948, *Rumpelstiltskin.*

Greensboro, N. C. 1929, *Little Red Riding Hood, Snow White and the Seven Dwarfs.*

Hartford, Conn. 1946, *Rabbit Hill.* 1947, *Nestor, the Talking Horse* (with hand-puppets).

Honolulu, T. H. 1940, The Pahauoli Puppet Players with a group of 77 hand-puppets presented fairy tales adapted to both oriental and occidental children, and used marionettes in the occupational therapy department of Queen's Hospital.

Indianapolis, Ind. c. 1940, *Marco Polo, The Painted Pig, Don Quixote,* all played in public schools.

Jacksonville, Fla. 1944–1945, *The Stolen Tulip.*

Kansas City, Mo. 1944–1945, *Pinafore, The Christmas Clock.*

Knoxville, Tenn. 1933, *Snow White.*

Lancaster, Pa. 1928, variety, *Jack and the Beanstalk.* 1932–1933, *Snow White and the Seven Dwarfs.*

Louisville, Ky. 1938–1939, played *The Night Before Christmas* and *Goldilocks* in each ward of the crippled children's hospital.

Mobile, Ala. 1940, cooperative work with organizations and individuals in building hand-puppet shows for schools and hospitals.

Montgomery, Ala. 1933, *Jay Bird's Dream, Peter Rabbit, Snow White, The Sugar Plum Tree, The Night Before Christmas.* 1947–1948, *Hansel and Gretel, Three Little Pigs.*

New York City. 1944–1945, *The Three Wishes, Punch and Judy.*

New Haven, Conn. 1940, hand-puppet performances of *Henry and the Tiger, Beauty and the Beast* for children in hospital.

New Orleans, La. 1940, *Little Black Sambo, Jack and the Beanstalk* performed at libraries, children's homes, private parties, and homes for the aged.

Norfolk, Va. c. 1940, *Red Riding Hood, Hansel and Gretel, Three Little Kittens, Santa Claus Skit* with hand-puppets for underprivileged children.

Oklahoma City, Okla. 1944–1945, *Jack and the Beanstalk.* 1946–1947, *Rumpelstiltskin.*

Omaha, Neb. 1928, *The Three Bears, Jack and the Beanstalk, The Town Musicians of Bremen, Red Riding Hood.* 1930, *Pinocchio.* 1931, revivals. 1932, *Alice in Wonderland.* 1933, *Toyland Circus.*

Pasadena, Cal. 1938–1940, marionette performances at children's agencies; gave course in hand-puppets to Boys and Girls Aid Society.

Philadelphia, Pa. 1940, a few paid performances in members' homes to finance free shows in settlement houses and day nurseries.

Pittsburgh, Pa. 1929, *Bobby Jones, His Voyage.*

Plainfield, N. J. 1933, *Jack and the Beanstalk, Hansel and Gretel, Cinderella, At the Baree.*

Portland, Ore. 1928, *Jack and the Beanstalk, Cinderella, The Three Bears.* 1929, revivals. 1933, *Hiawatha.*

Poughkeepsie, N. Y. 1929, *The Three Bears.*

Providence, R. I. 1940, free performances in hospitals and orphanages financed by a few paid performances.

Raleigh, N. C. 1940, *Little Black Sambo, Punch and Judy, Red Riding Hood, The Story Book Christmas.* 1944–1945, *The Great Lie, Aladdin.*

Richmond, Va. 1947–1948, collaborated with Westhampton College, University of Richmond, in the production of a group of plays.

St. Louis, Mo. 1926, *Jack and the Beanstalk, The Three Wishes, Hansel and Gretel, Red Riding Hood, One-Eye, Two-Eye, Three-Eye, Cinderella, Bluebeard.*

St. Petersburg, Fla. 1944–1945, *Jack and the Beanstalk, Three Little Pigs, Little Black Sambo.*

Shreveport, La. 1935–1940, gave marionette shows, including *Two Unhappy Ghosts,* in schools and library.

Stamford, Conn. 1940, *The Cat and the Goldfish* presented in public schools, and a Community Chest play in a store window.

Texarkana, Ark. 1930, *Jack and the Beanstalk.* 1933, *Snow White.* 1934, *The Three Pigs.* 1935, short skits. 1936, *Hansel and Gretel.* 1938, *The Three Wishes.* 1947, *Hansel and Gretel.*

Toledo, Ohio. 1940, taught marionette construction to children's classes which produced *Snow White and the Seven Dwarfs, Cinderella.*

Trenton, N. J. 1933, *Peak's Punch and Judy.* 1940 and previous years, gave marionette performances in public schools.

Washington, D. C. 1936, *Further Adventures of Goldilocks, Aladdin, Red Riding Hood.* 1938–1939, performances under auspices of child welfare agencies. 1947–1948, television performances of variety and circus acts, *Princess Dalia and the Jewel, The Adventures of Jim, Julie, and Willie Butts the Goat.*

Wichita, Kans. 1936, *Rip Van Winkle.* 1937, *Aladdin and His Wonderful Lamp.* 1938–1939, *Jack and the Beanstalk.* 1940, *Hansel and Gretel.* 1941, *Rumpelstiltskin.* 1942, *The Arkansas Bear.* 1943–1944, *The Magic Jam Pot.* 1945–1946, *Sleeping Beauty.* 1947, *Rumpelstiltskin, The Three Little Pigs.*

JUNIOR PLAYERS   See Marie Anthony, Sister.

JUPENLAZ, MATILDA D.   Mansfield, Pa., kindergarten. 1929, *The Poppy Seed Cakes* and *The White Goat,* after stories by Marjorie Clark.

KALB, DOROTHY B.   Wilson Normal School, Washington, D. C. 1924–1927, presented eleven children's puppet plays.

KALTENBACK, PAUL   Detroit, Mich. c. 1924, *Jack and the Beanstalk* and variety.

KAMMERER, DAVID EAMES   Clayton, Mo. 1934–1936, *Second Shepherds' Play* (from Towneley Cycle), *Hansel and Gretel, The Three Wishes, Mr. Shortall and Dr. Charlatan* (an 18th-century skit).

KATSAS, JOHN   (P. 292). Partner of William Ballamos, Creek shadow-figure showman in Chicago, 1935, and possibly earlier.

KAUFMAN, JACK M.   Alcatraz Island, Cal. 1930, *Every Dog Has His Day.*

KEEN, JANE   Watertown, S. D. 1936–1939, dramatized children's stories, *Major Bowes' Amateurs, The Business and Professional Women's Club Emblem,* variety.

KEGG, GEORGE   (P. 354). Golden State Marionettes, San Francisco. 1928, *The Moo Cow's Party,* a show advertising Golden Gate Milk Products Company.

KEIFFER, FRED and GRACE   Produced shows in and around Cincinnati, Ohio. 1941, *Jack and the Beanstalk.*

KELLBERG, MARJORIE   Morton, Pa. Became interested in puppets while painting at the Art Institute, Chicago, 1940, produced *The Rubaiyat of Omar Khayyam* (30 verses) with hand-puppets, hand- and rod-puppets, paper-, and rod-puppets. 1945–1947, *Bell of the Farm, The Milky Way, Sawbuck Nose His Oats* produced for Bell Telephone Company and presented at 14 fairs in Pennsylvania, Maryland, and Delaware. Also gave talks about puppets to high school students, and taught puppetry.

KEOGH, DAVE and VIOLET   (P. 349). Kay's Marionettes, Toronto, Canada. Began c. 1925; by 1933 had a company of four people performing *Aladdin,* Circus, and variety. 1934–1935, the Keoghs alone presented *Jack and the Beanstalk, Westminster's Cavalcade of Kings, Magic Carpet,* revue, and minstrels. 1936, formed the Kay-Heddle Marionettes with Muriel Heddle and sent out three companies (one working in French) with *Hansel and Gretel* and variety. 1937, *Nutcracker Suite* accompanied by the Toronto Symphony, variety at Toronto Exhibition, *Terry Hudson Gets His Man* for Hudson Motor Company at the National Motor Show, *Mother Goose Suite* (Ravel), *Nutcracker Suite, Hansel and Gretel* (Humperdinck); played *Danse Macabre* and *Nutcracker* with Toronto Symphony. 1938, to the above musical interpretations were added *Mosquito Dance* and a special preview of Moussorgsky's *Pictures at an Exhibition* for Eugene Ormandy. Other productions were: *He Ain't Done Right by Our Nell, Chemistry Marches On,* for Canadian Industries at the National Exhibition, *Northern Highlights,* for Northern Electric Company, national dances for Handicrafts Association of Canada. 1939, continued shows, and performed dances at New York Puppetry Festival.

KILLORAN, JOHN   Miniature Playhouse, New York. 1939, *Trial by Jury* with 13-inch marionettes.

KINDIG, WALLACE   Peru, Ind. 1935, hand-puppet productions of *Little Red Riding Hood* and *Punch and Judy.*

KINDSCHY, ROBERT   Centralia, Wash. 1933–1937, *The Witches' Visit, The Three Wishes, The Magician and the Dragon,* variety.

KING, MONSIER L.   d. 1887. Apprenticed as a boy to Prof. Lile, from whom he inherited Peter Hauntz and his family, c. 1840. Used these puppets with magic during a stage career of 65 years, and in 1879 gave them to Matt Hancock. Had a small museum in Cincinnati with objects which he collected, and another near the wharves in San Francisco, which burned in 1872. Traveled in Europe, playing before royalty—from a 1938 letter from Matt Hancock to Mme. Pinxy.

KINGCOB MARIONETTES   See Osborne, Rosalynde.

KINGSLAND MARIONETTES   See Head, Cedric and Mabel.

KIRCHNER, BILLY   Chicago. 1939, at age of thirteen gave school shows which were written and built by himself. His interest started at the age of nine when he was given a cardboard theatre.

KLINE, EDITH L. B.   Sponsor, Sultzberger Junior High School Marionette Club, Philadelphia. 1931, *Rip Van Winkle.* 1932, *The Three Wishes, Treasure Island, A Christmas Carol.* 1933, *Casper Among the Savages.* 1935, *Dr. Faust.* 1936, *Aladdin.*

KRAFT, ADELAIDE   Puppet Club, Church of the Unity, St. Louis, Mo. 1932, *The Life of David, the Shepherd Lad* (with hand-puppets), *The Finding of Moses in the Bulrushes* (with marionettes).

KRAMER, CLORINDA P. DE GUDINO   Argentina. Director of a children's puppet theatre, Adriana, in a Santa Fe school.

KRAMER, STAN   In 1940's presented a puppet floor show in clubs and theatres.

KRAUS, EVELYN, and GOUTHIER, OLGA   Public School, New Orleans, La. 1936, *Cinderella* with 18-inch marionettes.

KREDEL, FRITZ   (P. 368). New York. An illustrator who made puppets for home shows.

KREYMBORG, ALFRED and DOROTHY   (P. 342). 1920, *Lima Beans,* by A. K., which has been frequently performed by other puppeteers. Toured with the Merry-Andrews and Mushroom Theatre to California and back. Performed *Jack's House,*

Lame Minuet, and *Monday* at Wheeler Hall, Berkeley, Cal. 1926, made a second tour with a booth designed by Herman Rosse. Author of *Plays for Puppets*. Harcourt Brace, New York, 1923.

KRITSCHIL, BERTHA K.   1940, *Rumpelstiltskin*, with children of Jay Cooke Junior High School, Philadelphia.

KROFFT, SID   Bronx, N. Y. 1948, and several years preceding, performed floor and theatre shows in the metropolitan area.

KUNGSHOLM RESTAURANT   See Chramer, Fredrik.

KUNZE, OTTO   (P. 364). Brooklyn, N. Y. As a child participated in family puppet shows. 1911, *Don Fernando, Prince of Spain* presented in a Chirstmas play at the Royal Opera House, Dresden. At that time was a member of the Royal Opera Orchestra. Took part in performances of the marionette theatre of the Royal Court conductor, Adolph Hagen's, opera productions. Pietro de Gorni, of the orchestra, and Leonardo Fanti, costume designer for the opera, performed Italian light opera with marionettes made in Italy. Coming to America, Kunze began puppet performances in November 1932 with *Dr. Faust*, presented at the Roerich Museum, New York. *Hakeem the Wise One* and *The Hollow Tooth* were produced the same year, assisted by Caroline Sutherland, whom he later married. 1934, *The Smithy in the Rocky Mountains*. 1935, *The Magic Box*, *The Ghost of Pike's Peak Inn*, *The Trip Around the World* (with an open-proscenium stage having several playing levels). These were all hand-puppet plays, although *Hakeem* was also done with marionettes. 1938, gave *The Brave Little Tailor* at the Puppetry Festival. 1940, played *The Magic Box* at the New England Puppetry Insitute, Boston. 1944, built marionettes and scenes for window displays in McCreery's department store, New York, celebrating its 100th anniversary. 1946–1947, advertising shows: scenes from *Don Pasquale*. 1948, *The Frog Prince*.

KURTIS MARIONETTES   1937, variety, featuring *Mae West at the Pearly Gates*, at Marshall Field Puppet Exhibit. 1942, *Their Little People's Revue*, at Hotel Nicollet, Minneapolis, Minn.

LACARSE, ESTHER M.   1932, *The Three Bears* and *Cinderella* (with 12-inch rod-puppets).

LACHLAN, JEAN   Garrick Puppeteers, Brooklyn, N. Y. 1928, *Medusa*.

LAGO, ROBERTO   (Pp. 253–4, 350, 366). Director, Teatro El Nahual, Mexico City. In 1932, Lago was one of a group of people who organized and built children's puppet shows which were performed in the schools. 1933, he produced *El Gigante Melchor* for the directors of the Ministry of Education, who saw the possibilities of using puppets in educational work. By 1935, three companies, sponsored by the Ministry, were operating: El Nahual, directed by Lago, with Lola Cueto, Francisca Chávez and Guillermo López; El Periquillo, directed by Graciela Amador, with Manuel Carrillo, Fausto Contreras, and Carlos Sánchez; El Comino, directed by Lolita Alva de la Canal, with María de los Angeles de la Canal, Alfonso Contreras, and Cárlos Andrade. From 1935 to date, El Nahual has produced a wide variety of plays, songs, and dances based on folklore, propaganda shows, and plays by foreign authors. Among the productions were *The Cherry Tree*, based on the life of George Washington, *Three Blind Mice*, *The Olives* (Lope de Rueda), *The Nahual* (a pantomime), *The War with Ventripond*, *The First Distiller* (after Tolstoy), *Ya Vieno Gorgonio Esparza* (based on a *corrido*, or popular romantic ballad), *Don Juan Tenorio*, *The Trip to the Moon*, *The War of the Cakes*. In November 1944, Lago and Cueto made a two months' tour of the United States, and played a number of engagements, showing dances, songs, and a few scenes from the Nahual repertory. In March 1945, the Ministry of Education launched its campaign to stamp out illiteracy in Mexico. Lago's group built a special show mounted on a truck, which was taken to parks and public squares in Mexico City and villages in the provinces. Early in 1946, a tour through Oaxaca was made, and the puppets played to more than 10,000 people. A special celebration was given in the village of Soledad de Etla, for it was the first to become 100% literate. Besides building new shows and presenting them, Lago's group is active in the teaching of puppetry, in preparing exhibits at the Palace of Fine Arts, and in writing articles and books about puppets. It made a tour of South America in 1947.

LAMB, WALTER (Pp. 277, 278). Vaudeville manikins, 1902–1922.

LAMOND, ROBERT and JOYCE Long Beach, Cal. Robert began puppet making as a youngster. c. 1944 started new variety show featuring a Philippine scene.

LANGPAAP, FRANCES K. San Francisco. Has performed for children in hospitals, schools, and Camp Fire groups with new shows annually, 1931–1939. Plays include fairy tales, variety, *King of the Cats, On Pixie Hill, The Blue Rose, Rip Van Winkle*.

LANO, ALBERTO (Pp. 25, 100, 201, 202, 203, 204, 205, 206, 209, 211, 212, 214, 258, 261). (c. 1810–c. 1895). 1825, came to America. 1830, with Thayer circus. 1849, toured Havana, Central America, and South America. 1856, with Dan Rice circus. 1850–1851, to California and Alberta, Canada. 1858, to West. 1884–1886, in South. 1890, to West and Alaska. 1894 at fairs.

LANO, DAVID (Pp. 13, 98, 201–220, 260, 269, 273). (b. 1874). 1884, apprenticed to Alberto Lano, his grandfather. 1887, with his father in Canada and the United States. On 7 November 1887, at age of 13, began working independently in circuses. 1889–1893, at St. Louis, gave studio performances. 1893, in Chicago at dime museums and in a store room. 1894–1898, in South and Midwest with medicine shows, fairs, and independent tent shows. 1938, directed Children's Marionette Unit of the Detroit Federal .Theatre. 1942, did floor shows with a five-piece WPA Music Project orchestra, and hand-puppet shows on war and safety themes under the Michigan Recreation Project. 1945, playing with the Clyde Beatty circus, Lano celebrated the 120th consecutive season of the Lano family puppets. 1948, still active with circuses. Among the plays (mostly with hand-puppets) produced during Lano's long career are: *Why the Sea Is Salt, The Life of Lincoln, The Emperor's Daughter, Little Red Shoes, Why the Chimes Rang, Doctor Faustus, Ali Baba and the Forty Thieves, The Moon Princess*. Has also done various short plays with shadows, and many trick numbers, some with puppets used by his father and grandfather. The following Lano puppets have been recorded by the Michigan Art and Crafts Project of the WPA for the Index of American Design. They are listed under Miscellaneous, with their respective numbers and the designation h.p. (hand-puppet) or s.p. (string-puppet). Dog Toby (h.p., 3); Punch (h.p., 4); Negro (h.p., 5); Devil (h.p., 6); Baby (h.p., 7); Goliath (s.p., 8); Blind Man (h.p., 9); Man Friday (s.p., 10); Judy (h.p., 11); Skeleton (s.p., 12); Indian (h.p., 13); Chinese Juggler (s.p., 49A); Head detail of same, (49B); Profile detail of same, (49C); Turbaned character for *David and Goliath* (s.p., 50); Cannibal (s.p., 51); Missionary (s.p., 52); Juggler (s.p., 54); Lady-into-Balloon (s.p., 57); Painter (s.p., 60); Tight-rope Walker (s.p., 61); Second Cannibal (s.p., 68); Pop-out five-headed figure (s.p., 69A); Heads detail of same (69B); Fan Dancer (s.p., 90); Lady (s.p., 98); King Saul (s.p., 103); Policeman (h.p., 164); Captain in *Sinbad* (s.p., 165); Ahab, Sinbad's father (s.p., 166); Skeleton (h.p., 167); Scaramouch (h.p., 170); Jester (s.p., 171); Barnacle Bill (h.p., 172); Pretty Poll (h.p., 174); Sally, the Innkeeper's Daughter (h.p., 175).

LANO, OLIVER (Pp. 112, 202, 204, 205, 208, 212, 214, 258, 260, 285). (1832–1902). With his parents' show until 1857, then on his own, in circuses, in Civil War army camps. 1885–1887, in Canada. 1887, in South America. 1894–1895, at fairs and dime museums.

LA PRELLE, GERTRUDE PORTER Galena Park, Tex. 1946, used puppets in the teaching of music.

LARKIN, OLIVER Boston, Mass., and neighboring cities. 1922, *Androcles and the Lion* (G. B. Shaw). 1923, *Pantaloon* (J. M. Barrie). 1927, *The Birthday of the Infanta* (after Wilde).

LARSEN, GEORGE (PINXY)   Chicago, Ill. *Punch and Judy* showman for many years. Built ventriloquial dummies, trick marionettes, and Punch puppets to order.

LASANSKY, MAURICIO   (P. 350). Argentina. 1940, directed a school for child puppeteers in Cordoba; later had a similar one at La Sirena school in Rosario.

LA TOURE   Marionettes, early 20th century.

LATSHAW, GEORGE   Summer 1947, Cain Park Theatre, Cleveland Heights, O. *Bug in a Rug.* 1947–1948 season, operated Martin Stevens' school assembly show, *This Funny World.*

LATTO, EVELYN   Whittier School, Waukegan, Ill. 1941, *Silly Andy* with small marionettes and *The Golden Pears* with hand-puppets.

LAURENCE, GILBERT   Engle Marionettes, Brooklyn, N. Y. 1938, *Hansel and Gretel, Snow White and the Seven Dwarfs*, variety. 1940, *Puppet Varieties of 1940*, Grolier Society, Philadelphia. 1942, *Schnozzle Goes to Town*, television station W2XWV, New York.

LEBEUF, FRANCE   (P. 260). Amateur puppeteer at Valleyfield, Beauharnois County, Quebec, in early 20th century.

LEDUC   (P. 260). Amateur puppeteer at Valleyfield, Beauharnois County, Quebec, in early 20th century.

LEE, DAVE   (P. 277). Marionettes in a Minneapolis dime museum, 1899.

LEE, HELEN MORRIS   1930, with child puppeteers at Camp Bryn Afon, Roosevelt, Wis., marionette Circus.

LEE, MILES   A member of the Royal Air Force stationed in Canada, c. 1942–1943, produced *Puppet Parade* and entertained Air Force units in Canada. Played at Stage Door Canteen, New York. With J. C. Rodber and Bill Calvert produced *The Proposal* (Chekhov).

LEE, YVONNE R.   Cincinnati, O. c. 1942–1943, *Cinderella.* Worked with a WPA adult education project and did *Le visite d'Isidore* with a French class. With Jewish Center class gave *The Fall of Haman.* Conducted classes at the Catholic Club and the Art Museum.

LEIDY, RUSSEL and SNYDER, WILTON   Little Rock, Ark. High School. 1929, ·*The Three Wishes, Punch and Judy.* 1930, *The Wishing Fairy, Little Red Riding Hood.* 1931, *Dick Whittington and His Cat.*

LEMAY, JOSEPH   (P. 259). *Punch and Judy* at Montreal, 1883.

LE MESSURIER, BILLY   Hickory Grove School, Pontiac, Mich. 1937, *Rip Van Winkle.*

LE MONIER, JOSEPH   (P. 98). Trick marionettes and diorama at Washington Hall, New York, 11 July–2 August 1826.

LENHER, MRS. SAMUEL   The Market Players, Wilmington, Del. Director of a group of five women who have produced two hand-puppet shows each year, beginning 1945. Favorite children's stories used. 1948 productions, *Peter and the Wolf* and *The Reluctant Dragon*, with string-puppets.

LENOIR'S ROYAL MARIONETTES   An English troupe which toured with Haganbeck-Wallace circus sideshow, 1899–1900. Numbers included a walk-around with all characters singing, songs and dances, a short: *Ten Nights in a Barroom*, comedy numbers, such as the singing of "Oh father, dear father—" which was interrupted by a shower of tin cans on the puppet's head—From a conversation of Ed Moore, a musician with the circus, with Franc Still, 1942.

LEONARD, MELANIE ELIZABETH   Gave shows in a garden at Sandwich, Cape Cod, Mass. c. 1927.

LEROY BROTHERS   1944–1945, floor show act. 1946–1947, featured a 48-inch marionette xylophone player.

LESELLI MARIONETTES   See Heath, Leslie.

LES GRANDES MARIONETTES   See Audet, André.

LEVIN, MEYER   (Pp. 359, 374, 385, 387). Relic House Marionettes, Chicago, Ill. Beginning c. 1926, played such adult shows as: *From Morn to Midnight* (Kaiser), *Abraham and Isaac, Affairs of Anatol* (Schnitzler), *The Bow-Legged Leaf, Dr. Faust, Maitre Pierre Patelin, The Crock of Gold* (after James Stephens). 1927, *Alice in Wonderland, Jack and the Beanstalk.* 1931, with Louis Bunin produced

The Hairy Ape (O'Neill), and presented it at the New School for Social Research, New York. 1932, revived *The Crock of Gold* and added *Esther,* done with shadows. 1934, *Buster Brown,* in General Exhibits Bldg., A Century of Progress Exposition, Chicago.

LEVY, MERVIN 1932, *Commonwealth Hereafter* with hand-puppets in Mena, Ark.

LEWIS, MARGARET ESTHER Merbav Marionettes, Santa Barbara, Cal. 1930, *Queen Balkis* (after Kipling) and *The Fire Quest.* 1931, *Star Lovers* (the last two from Japanese legends).

LIL(?L)E, Prof. Used Peter Hauntz for 50 years to c. 1840, then gave his puppets to Monsieur L. King—Letter from Matt Hancock to Mme. Pinxy, 1938.

LINCOLN, "TAD" (P. 311). Amateur showman, who had a completely equipped miniature theatre in the White House in 1864.

LINDERGREEN, HAROLD F. Boston, Mass. *The Young King* (after Wilde) with marionettes, hand-puppets, jigging puppets, *The Gooseberry Mandarin,* variety. 1930, *The Pot of Marigolds, Nature Study* (a satire on worm and bird), *Il Gabinetto.* 1931, *Aladdin and His Wonderful Lamp.* 1933, *Hermann Joseph,* variety.

LINDHOLM, CEDRIC M. 1933, *Aladdin and the Wonderful Lamp* with 5-inch paper puppets worked from the wings of a Danish paper theatre. Presented in Music building, University of Minnesota, Minn. Had marionette and magic acts.

LINDSAY, HUGH (Pp. 97, 106, 110, 221, 222, 232). Began to use "Old Hons" and other Pennsylvania German characters, 1828, learning puppetry from Myers, for whom he worked as a helper. Still playing in 1857.

LITTLE GREEN HOUSE MARIONETTES See Parlin, Florence.

LITTLE PLAYERS See Smiley, Helen A.

LITTLE ROCK, ARK., HIGH SCHOOL PUPPET CLUB 1929, *Jack and the Beanstalk* with 18-inch marionettes.

LITTLE THEATRE MARIONETTES See Rankin, Dorothy Louise.

LITTLE THEATRE OF THE MARIONETTES Lakewood, O. 1932, *Sadko.* 1933, *Hansel and Gretel, Don Quixote, Anguetil et Selimonde,* all with 8-inch marionettes.

LO CASCIO, SALVATORE (P. 300). Sicilian puppet theatre in East 107, and later, 111 Street, New York, 1906–1909. Maria Grasso, assistant for reading female parts.

LOGRENIA, Professor (P. 132). *Punch and Judy* at Volksgarten, New York, 1879.

LOHMAN, BOB Indianapolis, Ind. 1935, *A Christmas Carol.*

LONGFIELD, ROBERT (ANDRÉ VERN) Minneapolis, Minn. Gave amateur shows, beginning 1924, with *Mr. Pipe's Revue.* 1927, added *Goldilocks and the Three Bears.* 1932, *The Elves and the Shoemaker, Florabelle the Cow.* 1935, *Mae West Revue, Christmas Revue.* 1936, *Television Revue* and a stage show. Began professional work 1939, with *Florabelle's Revue* which he played until 1941. Joined the Army 1942 and entertained in hospitals, service clubs, Army theatres. Spent nearly a year with the Army show, *Ten Minute Break,* which played, among other places, in the Municipal Opera House, Oran, Africa. From 1941–1948, presented *Puppets by André* with 36-inch marionettes in the Army, night clubs, and theatres from coast to coast.

LONGSTAFF, GRACE Puck's Players, Children's Library, New Toronto, Canada. 1942–1943, *The Reluctant Dragon, The King's Breakfast, Carnival of Animals.*

LOOMIS, GEORGE Mt. Vernon, O., High School. Worked in a production of *Pinocchio,* 1933; later did puppet work at Ohio State University. 1941, *Thief of Bagdad.* 1947, *Ali Baba and the Forty Thieves.* 1948, *Black Magic.*

LORD, DE FOREST DODGE Sante Fe., N. Mex. 1933, *Rumpelstiltskin.* 1934, *Old Juan Mora's Burro,* played at the Fiesta.

LORENTO, Professor *Punch and Judy* at Volksgarten, New York, 1879.

LORETTS, THE "World's greatest shadowists," at Vallamont Park, near Williamsport, Pa., 3–9 August 1896—Playbill in miscellaneous scrapbook, Sanders Collection, University of Michigan Library.

LOUISVILLE CHILDREN'S THEATRE GUILD See Ruthenburg, Grace D.

LOVITTS, JEROME   Began working with puppets when five years old and presented first show 1940. Since 1947 has worked professionally with marionette acts.

LOWE, FLORENCE   (P. 392). The Berkeley Marionettes, Scotch Plains, N. J. With this company were Bruce Williams, Paul Worth, Herbert Black, and Arthur Zwerling. A large touring show was built annually, beginning with *The Rhyme for Orange*, 1932. This was followed by: 1933, *Pinocchio*. 1934, *Jack and the Beanstalk*. 1935, *The Prince and the Pauper*. 1936, *Tom Sawyer*. 1937, *Toby Tyler with the Circus*. 1938, *Hans Brinker*. 1939, *Johnny Appleseed*. 1940, *The Mysterious Island*. 1943, *The Magic Salt Shaker*. Since this time revivals of previous plays have taken place, notably *Toby Tyler* in 1945.

LOWERY, BERT   *Punch and Judy*, early 20th century.

LUBIN, FRED and JEROME   (P. 183). Original Imperial Marionettes played week ending 9 May 1874 at the Colosseum, New York, under management of P. T. Barnum. Two shows daily, 3:30 and 9:00 P.M. in the Lectorium—from the Playbill.

LUDGATE, JANE STEARNS   State Teachers College, Edinboro, Pa. 1928, *The Sleeping Beauty, A Modern Aladdin, Pierrot and Pierrette*. 1929, *The Knave of Hearts, The Gooseberry Mandarin*, variety. 1930, *The Tempest*.

LUFT, JOHN and JAMES   Wernersville, Pa. Puppets were a hobby in the Luft family. The brothers gave their first important show, *Strawberry Corners*, in 1935 with marionettes. 1936, *The Hex of Willow Valley* proved too real a dallying with witchcraft for local Pennsylvania audiences and was therefore abandoned. 1937, *A Modern Fairy Tale*. 1938, *Down on the Farm* and *Drink More Milk*. 1939, *Ye Old Punch and Judy*. By this time puppetry was a full-time business. 1940, *The Nutcracker*, based on Tchaikowsky's music and Hoffmann's story, *The History of Krakatuk*, with 16 scenes, 70 marionettes, 5 operators, and a double-bridge stage. During the war both brothers served in the armed forces. Resumed work in 1946: *The Life of Santa Claus, The Cat and the Fiddle, A Historical Pageant*. 1947, half-hour show for a local bakery. Besides puppet shows, the Luft Studio constructs animated displays with figures from 10 inches to 4 feet high for local and national advertisers.

LUITJENS, HELEN   Emerson Junior High School, Los Angeles, Cal. Variety produced by eighth grade students.

LUND, ADRIANNE   Berkeley, Cal. First show 1938. 1946, *Snittle's Sleigh Ride, Hansel and Gretel*. 1947, Advertising show. Worked with Bette Green under name of Green and Lund Puppetry until autumn 1947, when the former wanted to travel farther afield.

LUTZ, CAROLINE   University of Richmond, Va., Marionette Repertory Theatre. After seeing Tony Sarg's *The Rose and the Ring* and supervising a puppet theme in sophomore English (1930), became interested in the dramatic possibilities of the puppet theatre. 1931, used hand-puppets for *Hansel and Gretel*. 1932, string-puppets for *Alice in Wonderland*. 1933, *The Jester* (Lady Gregory). 1934, *The Magic Sea Shell*. 1935, five original one-act plays. These productions were given in connection with English classes; for many of them Beverley Bates acted as laboratory assistant. In 1936, Richard Scammon became technical director and held this position until called to the Army c. 1942. During these years experiments were made with all types of puppets and a variety of plays such as: 1936–1937, *Stringing the University of Richmond*. 1937–1938, *The Nativity* (with rod-puppets). 1938–1939, *The Women Have Their Way* (with marionettes) and scenes from American life. 1939–1940, *Stringing the Stars*, (with all types of puppets) and *Peter and the Wolf* (with colored plastic shadows). 1940–1941, *The Taming of the Mew, Negro Sermons in Verse, Indian War Dance*. A large collection of puppets (belonging to Miss Lutz) is housed at the University and is used for lecture-recitals on puppet history and for exhibits on campus and in the city. For the annual May Day celebration, a Punch and Judy show has become traditional. 1947–1948, the University worked with the Junior League in the presentation of a group of puppet plays.

LYMAN, MR. and MRS. PERCY Gary, Ind. 1938, *Elder Brother and the Buzzard,* an Indian legend played at the Chicago Puppetry Festival.

LYONS, MILTON P. Played *Punch and Judy* as well as a Lyonese Guignol in Philadelphia, late 19th century. Cited by Ernest Russell, "The Most Popular Play in the World," *Outing Magazine,* January 1908, p. 473.

LYVERS, HELEN (P. 338). With Tony Sarg for four seasons. c. 1928, *Master Peter Patelin* and variety at South End House, Boston. 1930, Jack-in-the-Box Marionettes opened in Boston.

MABLEY, TED See Tatterman Marionettes.

MACDONALD, ABEL Mexican puppeteer who in 1928 and earlier played variety with humorous dialogue in small movie theatres in Mexican colony of Santa Barbara and valley cities of California. Used 30-inch marionettes including acrobats and come-apart skeletons on bicycles.

MACDUFF, MRS. GRACE GIBSON Burlingame, Cal. 1934, *The Three Wishes* and *Punch and Judy.*

MACGILL, BESS Elementary School, Palatka, Fla. 1932, *George Washington* with 18-inch marionettes.

MACKAY, GILBERT S. 1923–1929, operated The California Theatre, later The Lilliputian Playhouse, in his home in Oakland. Plays: *Around the World, A Trip to Australia, New Zealand and the South Seas,* variety, *The Original Ziegfeld Sillies Revue, Little Red Riding Hood.*

MACLEAN, J. ARTHUR, and BLAIR, DOROTHY (P. 377). Museum of Art, Toledo, and Lakeside, O. 1929, *Ono-no-Komachi and the Philosophy of Oriental Art.* 1935, *The Arts of the Orient* (with shadows), *Fantasie Cherubique* (with flat rod-operated board puppets), *The Melon Thief* (with hand-puppets). 1937, *The Merry Widow Spider* (with hand-puppets), a nature study play presented by members of the Toledo Naturalists Association. 1939, *The Craft Club Meets.*

MACK, CHARLES "London" *Punch and Judy* at the Cincinnati Zoo for many seasons, still active 1937. Mack, an American, it may be noted, has never visited London. One amusing point in his show: at the mention of the Kentucky Derby, Punch's horse, Hector, trots round and round, envisioning himself a racer. Played also with Ringling Brothers-Barnum and Bailey circus.

MACKEY, MR. and MRS. WARREN B. The Mackey Marionettes, Yokima, Wash. 1935, *Pierre Pathelin* with 18-inch marionettes.

MAD HATTER MARIONETTES See Cohen, Theodore.

MADCAP MARIONETTES See Stewart, Doris.

MAELZEL (Pp. 97–8, 100, 101, 106). Exhibited an antomaton chess player, mechanical figures, and a show, *The Conflagration of Moscow,* 1826–1842.

MAGINNIS (Pp. 86, 90, 91, 100). Fantoccini at Rickett's Circus, New York, 11 June 1799, and possibly at the Water Street Theatre, 11 March 1799; also at Mechanics' Hall, New York, 26 April 1804.

MAGON, JERO (P. 393). Marionette Guild of New York. Began work in theatre of Fannie Goldsmith Engle at Provincetown, Mass. 1931, built *The Porcelain God* (after Lafcadio Hearn's *Chinese Ghosts*), using a sliding wagon stage for scene changes. 29 April 1933, premiere of *The Emperor Jones,* done on a revolving stage, with marionettes and flat rod-puppets designed by Ben Yano. 1935, *Puppet Parade,* a satirical revue with hand-puppets. 1937, *Puppet Follies of 1937.* At the Chamber Music Hall, Carnegie Hall, *Marco Millions* had its premiere in 1938. Marionettes and shadows with reversible scenery were used. 1939, *Arabian Nights, The Search for Health.* 1940, *Somebody-Nothing,* with hand-puppets. 1946, *Punch and Judy.* 1948, *The Man Who Married a Dumb Wife,* hand- and rod-puppets.

MAHON (P. 61). A singer who offered a miscellaneous program including fantoccini and shadows at Kingston, Jamaica, 1790.

MALIKOWSKI, HELEN C. Waukegan, Ill. 1936, *Red Riding Hood,* variety, Circus.

MALLORY, MARY LU Merrie Guilders, Oak Grove, Ore. 1931–1934, *The Troll King, A Pot of Marigolds, A Medicine Show, The Workshop Journey, A Range Courtship,*

The Gooseberry· Mandarin, A Toyshop Frolic, The Walrus and the Carpenter, Desert Necromancy.

MALM, SIBYL   Haskell Institute Marionettes, Lawrence, Kan. 1935, *Scarface* (after an Indian legend). 1936, Indian legends and ceremonies. Occasional tours were made. In 1937 the marionettes played in Detroit, Oberlin, Washington, D. C., and other cities.

MANLEY and BREWER   (Pp. 134, 146). Punch and Judy at Tammany Hall, New York, 1869.

MANLEY, LOUIS   Long Beach, Cal. Punch and Judy showman who played every Saturday 1935–1948 with the Jack-Rabbit Racer on the Pike at Long Beach.

MANN, LLOYD   Ex-ballet dancer, played a floor show puppet act, 1944.

MANTELL   See Ayres, Len.

MANTEO, AGRIPPINO   (Pp. 258, 293, 298, 299, 387). Sicilian puppets. At Mendoza, 1912–1916. At 109 Mulberry Street, New York, c. 1920–1936, assisted by his wife Catherine, his daughter Aida, and his sons Miguel, Leo, Ritz and Johnny, presented romances of chivalry in *Charlemagno, Guido Santo, Orlando Furioso*. The 394 episodes of the last play took thirteen months to play. 1939, played episodes from *Orlando* at the New York Puppetry Festival, and performed for a time in a permanent theatre in Brooklyn.

MANTOR, MARJORIE   Las Vegas, N. Mex. 1934, *Rip Van Winkle*.

MANUAL PUPPETEERS   See Gray, Helen.

MANVERS   (P. 132). Punch and Judy man from England, New York c. 1866— *Puppetry 1935*, p. 80.

MARCH, BENJAMIN   1917 and later, *Punch and Judy*, Bohemian Settlement, Chicago.

MARDIN, JEAN I.   A Massachusetts teacher who worked from 1928 to c. 1940 with groups of children, many of them at settlement houses and schools for the blind. Her productions were largely of well-loved children's stories. In 1932 she did *The Secret Garden, The Romancers* (Rostand), and *Legend of the Alhambra*.

MARGARAJE   (P. 245). Operated a puppet theatre in his playground in Huamantla, Tlaxcala, Mexico, c. 1860.

MARGO   Vaudeville manikins, early 20th century

MARGOT'S MARIONETTES   See Cleary, Mrs. Vincent.

MARIANO   (Pp. 299, 301). Sicilian puppet theatre in Spring Street, New York, c. 1905, and later in California.

MARIE ANTHONY, SISTER   St. Mary's Academy, Denver, Colo., and Loretto Heights College. For over ten years has been interested in the use of puppetry in education, and has produced many shows with and for children. Author of a booklet, *Marionettes Teach Them* (Miles and Dryer Printing Co., Denver, Colo., 1939) which describes simple methods of puppet making.

MARIONETTE GUILD OF NEW YORK   See Magon, Jero.

MARIONETTE GUILD OF PLAINFIELD, N. J.   See Williams, Bruce.

MARIONETTE PLAYERS, THE   See New, George.

MARIONETTE TROUPE   Regina, Sask., Canada. This company grew out of a marionette circle organized c. 1931 in the Metropolitan Church. By 1938, it had about 95 marionettes, 18 to 22 inches high, a repertory of seven plays and variety, and 12 puppeteers.

MARIONETTE WORKSHOP, THE   See Snyder, Don.

MARION'S MARIONETTES   See Parris, Marion, and Myers, Marion.

MARKS, KILBOURN   Until c. 1942 made puppets, especially animal figures. Worked for Sarg, Hastings, and Lowe companies. Was one of Sarg's operators at the Texas Exposition, 1936.

MARLETTE, BOB   Vaudeville manikins, beginning in 1912, listed in *Vaudeville Yearbook*, 1915.

MAROT, LÉON CHARLES   (Pp. 288–289). Théâtre des ombres Parisiennes at Chicago fair, 1893.

MARQUETTE, HAL, and RENÉE   Marquette Marionettes, Toronto, Canada, 1946, *Big Top Topics* and television shows with marionettes. 1947, ballet excerpts (with

marionettes) and *Peter Rabbit* (with shadows). Commercial productions include
over 180 performances as operators for the Dick Haymes Show, sponsored by
Electric Auto Lite Company, and *Tired Tilly* with shadows for the Premier Vacuum
Company.

MARSEILLE, DADDY   See Natte, Jean.

MARSH, FRED DANA   (P. 367). Built seven caricature puppets of movie actors,
operated by rods from below plus one string. Filmed by Pathé as a feature in *A
Master of Murals.*

MARSH, HAL S.   The Riverbank Players, Cazadaro, Cal. 1933, *Sultan's Charity, Punch
and Judy, Frankie and Johnnie, Road to Mandalay, Toot and Tiot.*

MARTIN BROTHERS   1942, played act in vaudeville and night clubs with portraits of
movie stars. 1943, toured with USO White Circuit, Unit 83, *Bubbling Over.* Since
the war, have made extensive tours with floor show.

MARTIN, GEORGE ANDRÉ   A Frenchman who, c. 1936, showed finger-puppets in
American night clubs and theatres.

MARTIN, Prof.   (P. 276). Marionette showman before 1886.

MARY ANN'S PUPPETEERS   1943, played at Ocean Pier, Wildwood, N. J., in the
Kiddies' Theatre.

MARY CLAUDE, SISTER   Nulato, Alaska. With two other Sisters of St. Ann who taught
and did social work, produced c. 1936 a Christmas program for the Indians. Limited
by lack of experience and materials, they nevertheless made the show great fun
for the audience. At this time, Sister Mary Claude had been in Alaska for nineteen
years with only one trip back to the States.

MARYLAND INSTITUTE PUPPETEERS   See Paul, Bernard.

MASON, FRANK and JEAN   Mason Marionettes, Pittsburgh, Pa. First show, inspired
by Sarg and Bufano publications, given 1933. 1936–1937, *Rumpelstiltskin, Santa
Claus, Jr., Queen Esther, Rapunzel, Melodrama,* and performances for the Y.M.C.A.
Community Fund. 1939, *The Enchanted Nutcracker, Punch and Judy, Treasure
Island,* commercial shows for Atlantic Refining Company and Pittsburgh Auto
Show: nearly 500 performances of *Variety Tent Show,* Conneaut Lake, Pa. 1940,
Babes in Toyland, Superman Helps Santa at Frank and Seder Store. 1941, *Siegfried,*
show for United Jewish Fund. 1947, *Treasure Island.* Also Christmas shows given
annually with hand-puppets.

MASON and TITUS   (P. 285). Shadow-figure showmen, New York, 1881–1882. Otto
was Mason's partner, 1883–1884. (Odell, vol. 12, pp. 327, 333, 373.)

MATHEWS   (Pp. 116–118, 123). *Punch and Judy,* New York, September, 1828.

MATTSON, JULIA   Grand Forks, N. D. 1943, at summer camp in Tulsa, Okla., made
200 rag doll puppets.

MAUD, ZUNI   See Cutler, Yosl.

MAYCOURT CLUB   See Sipherd, Clara.

MAYFAIR MARIONETTES   See Braithewaite, Shirley.

McBETH, EDITH   Merry Mac Marionettes, Des Moines, Iowa. 1946–1947, *Proof for
Santa, Merry Mac Medley, Puppet Propaganda.*

McCADDEN, MARGARET COLE   Parlor Puppet Guild, Memphis, Tenn. Worked with
puppets for small audiences in Memphis and Babson Park, Fla.; *Old Mother Goose*
was produced at the latter place. In 1947 the Guild expanded its activities, taking
part in the Cotton Carnival. Marionettes were used in a fashion show and a puppet
entertainment for children was given at the Zoo. Puppets were included in Pan-
American Day celebrations, while a sixth grade class directed by Lois Laman
presented *America the Melting Pot* for Pan-American Day. Earl Montgomery and
Agnes Haage are Guild members.

McCARTNEY, FRANCINE   Junior High School, Aberdeen, Wash. 1931, *The Magic
Harp* and *Fantasia* with 15-inch marionettes.

McCLELLAND, CURTIS   Kensington, Ohio. In 1930, finding himself without a job, made
a set of puppets for *Punch and Judy* and gave his first show. Up to 1937 had
presented over 2000 shows in town halls, schools, churches, and clubs. One holiday-

time played Santa Claus and a puppet show in a department store for 25 days. 1936, played 100 days in front of the Old Globe Theatre at the Great Lakes Exposition, Cleveland, O.

McCONKEY, MILTON Moraga, Wash. 1936, *The Bluebird Princess*. 1937, *The Prince and the Dwarfs*.

McCORD, BETTY, and HAWXHURST, WINIFRED 1937, did *Punch and Judy* at the Marshall Field puppet exhibit.

McCORMACK's MARIONETTES With Edward Fossett and Sons circus in Ireland, summer 1942.

McCORMICK, LORETTA Girard College, Philadelphia. 1936, *Hansel and Gretel*.

McCOWN, MARTHA ROSE Urbana, Ill. 1932, *Punch and Judy*. 1933, *Jack and the Beanstalk*. 1934, *Cinderella, Little Mr. Picklenose, Make Believe*.

McDONALD, EDITH and RUTH Paterson, N. J. 1942, toured with *Rumpelstiltskin* and comedy skits.

McDONOUGH, JOHN E. (Pp. 156, 157, 163, 166–189, 191–199, 259, 264, 268, 271). Partner of Hartley A. Earnshaw in the management of the Royal Marionettes, at first for Bullock, later independently, 1873–1876. The independent company followed this itinerary: 21 March–25 April 1874, Philadelphia, Concert Hall. 18 May–13 June, Cincinnati, Robinson's Opera House. 7 July–8 August, San Francisco, Platt's Hall. 10–15 August, Vallejo and Napa? 17–22 August, Oakland, Brayton Hall. 24–29 August, San Jose, Opera House. 31 August–5 September, Stockton, Mozart Hall. 14–19 September, Grass Valley. 21–26 September, Virginia City, Piper's Opera House. 28 September–1 October, Carson City, Theatre. 5–12 October, Salt Lake City, Theatre. 5, 8 December, Honolulu, Royal Hawaiian Theatre. 8 May–7 July 1875, Sydney, School of Arts. 13 July–28 August, Melbourne, St. George's Hall. 30 August–11 September, Geelong, Mechanics Institute. 13–29 September, Ballarat, Mechanics Institute. 30 September–2 October, Castlemaine, Theatre Royal. 4–16 October, Bendigo, St. James' Hall. 18 October–11 November, Melbourne, St. George's Hall. 15 November–13 December, Adelaide, White's Rooms. 1876, 26–30 December, Hobart (Tasmania), Town Hall, and 31 December–14 January, Theatre Royal. 17–24 January, Launceston (Tasmania), Theatre Royal. 9–27 May, Auckland (New Zealand), City Hall. At the last theatre there also played Webb's Royal Marionettes with J. Smith's Combined Troupe, 4–18 March. Returning to the United States, the Royal Marionettes played: 17 July–5 August 1876, San Francisco, McGuire's Opera House. 21–26 August, San Jose, Vallejo?; Oakland, Dietz Hall. 11–16 September, Stockton, Theatre. 25–30 September, 2 October, Victoria Theatre Royal. 4–6 October, Seattle, Yesler's Hall. 9–14 October, Salem, Reed's Opera House. 16–27 October, Portland, New Market Theatre. 30 October–2 December, Philadelphia, Concert Hall. From 1877 to 1880 McDonough was an actor on the larger stage in New York, playing in *Secret Service* and *M'liss*—Odell, vol. 10, p. 408; vol. 11, pp. 49, 389.

McFADDEN, G. ANDREW 1932, *A Matter-of-Fact Fairy Tale* at the Leland Powers School, Boston, Mass.

McGAUGH, GENEVA Peabody School, Fort Smith, Ark. 1935, *The Wishing Fairy*, with 10-year-old children as puppeteers.

McKAY, PAULA F. Fairy Tale Marionettes. From 1931–1933 produced shows with children: *The Princess Who Hid Her Shoes, The Enchanted Princess, Fishing, The Three Bears, The Fortune Teller, Little Black Sambo, Epaminondas and His Mammy*.

McLAREN, JOSEPH DIXON (Pp. 156, 167–179, 181, 182, 183). Manager for Bullock, 1873–1874.

McMARTHY, MAX, and WYNNYK, BERYL Corvallis and Philomath, Ore. 1929, *Beauty and the Beast* and *The Golden Bird*.

McNAIR, A Humberside Collegiate School, Toronto, Canada. Produced plays related to school projects c. 1938–1942.

McNEIL, LAURENCE Butte, Mont. 1938–1940, *St. George and the Dragon, Holy Bread*.

McPharlin, Paul (Pp. 4, 317–318, 344, 345, 346, 359, 360, 361, 385, 387, 388, 389, 393). 1913, toy Punch and Judy theatre. 1916, model theatres. 1922, participated in M. Dondo's rod-puppet production of *Two Blind Men and a Donkey* at Columbia College. In 1928 organized the Marionette Fellowship of Evanston, Ill., and presented *The Taming of the Shrew*. 1929, *Noël, or the Mystery of the Nativity* (Maurice Bouchor), *The Tragedy of Tragedies, or the Life and Death of Tom Thumb the Great* (Henry Fielding), *The Chinese Nightingale* (after Andersen), *The Drum Dance* (with Chinese shadows), *Mr. and Mrs. H. Abroad,* a comedy of hats (with shadows). Moved to Detroit the same year and organized the Marionette Fellowship of Detroit, reviving *Noël* and *The Tragedy of Tragedies*. 1930, the Fellowship presented three ballets: *Les Petits riens* (Mozart music), *Tower with Terraces* (music, Franz Freund), *Krazy Kat* (music by John Alden Carpenter). There were revivals of past productions and hand-puppets were used for *Pensive Puppets;* the puppet show in *The Last Night of Don Juan* (E. Rostand), *The Coq Brothers* (after Mourguet). *The Barn at Bethlehem* was played with rod-puppets, *Pink Plush* with marionettes. In 1931, there were revivals, variety (including *The Coming of Spring,* a ballet, and *The Gooseberry Mandarin*), *St. George and the Dragon*. New productions in 1932 were: *The Vixen's Spell* (from the Chinese, done with shadows), *Esther* (a shadow play by Meyer Levin), *Bastien and Bastienne*. In 1933, directed *Eastern Market* with hand-puppets in his puppetry class at Teachers College, Detroit. 1934, the same course, now within Wayne University, presented *Sir Gammer Vans*. The Fellowship added *Lincoln and the Pig, Doctor Faust,* and *Cannibal Island* (adapted from Pocci). In 1935, revivals of previous shows were presented. 1936, an advertising show for Old English Floor Wax was played with Catalan-type hand-puppets, *Dr. Faust* was revived, and *Punch's Circus* (with hand-puppets and rod-puppets) was added. In 1940, while director of the Michigan Art and Crafts Project of the WPA, wrote and designed *That's The Way to Do It* with hand-puppets for the Detroit Community Fund. While in the Army, 1941, used a marionette, G.I. Joe, for entertainment in camp shows and safety instruction at Keesler Field, Miss. Beginning in 1929 with *A Repertory of Marionette Plays* (Viking Press, New York), McPharlin has written, edited, and published as Puppetry Imprints many books, including *Adventures of a Russian Puppet Theatre* by Nina Efimova, 1935, *Trick Marionettes* by Nicholas Nelson and James J. Hayes, 1935, *Chinese Shadow-Figure Plays and Their Making* by Benjamin March, 1939, *Marionette in Motion* by W. A. Dwiggins, 1939, and *Puppetry, A Yearbook of Puppets and Marionettes,* from 1930 to date. (22 Dec. 1903–28 Sept. 1948).

McSpadden, C. B. Santa Fe, N. Mex. Began puppet making in 1936 with carved wood caricatures. From 1941 has sponsored a puppet club in the Harrington Junior High School which produces variety shows for schools and civic organizations.

Mead, Alice 1928, *Bluebeard*. 1930, *Doctor Faust,* both at Berkshire Summer School of Art, Monterey, Mass. 1931, *Pierre Pathelin*.

Meader, Daniel (Pp. 192, 193, 194, 196, 197, 198, 200). Played with McDonough and Earnshaw on the West Coast, 1876, and independently, 1882–1898. The California WPA Art Project made water-colors of some of Meader's figures, which are now preserved in the archives of the Index of American Design, Washington, D. C. They are classified under Miscellaneous with their respective numbers: Chinese Minstrel, 131; Clown, 352; Clown "on the Tear," 297; Devil, 326; Drunken Clown on Stilts, 298; Minstrel End Man, 299; Mother Goose, 353; Negro Bell Hop, 325; Negro Cotton Picker, 121; Negro Minstrel, 92; Negro Minstrel head, 310; Punch, 91; Wood Chopper head, 321; Biddy; Harlequin; Tight Rope Walker, and Turk.

Meader, Deborah St. Paul, Minn. c. 1928, *Hansel and Gretel*. 1931, *Beauty and the Beast, The Rabbit Who Wanted Red Wings,* also worked with Sunday School groups from third grade to high school, building puppets and dramatizing Bible stories. Experimented with the making and use of shadow-puppets in schools.

Medhurst, Dorothy 1937, produced *Pinocchio* with rod-puppets made by children's class at the Art Gallery, Toronto, Canada. *Gulliver* was presented by another children's class in Aurora.

MEJUTO, ANDRÉS, and CORTÉS, F.   Directors of Teatro el Guirigay, with Spanish refugee puppeteers, which gave performances in the Casa del Teatro, Buenos Aires, playing the works of native and foreign writers. c. 1940 also played in Montevideo and other cities of Uruguay.

MENDEZ, LUZ VIEYRE   Argentina. Founded the Teatro de Títeres Perico for the Friend of Education kindergarten in Parana; plays by Villafañe, pantomimes to music (*The Little White Donkey*), ànd Negro spirituals. Later transferred to the Normal School at Córdoba where she continued her puppet work.

MENDHAM, NELLY   Kirkwood, Mo. 1934, *The Holy Night,* given as part of a Christmas pageant at the University of Idaho, Pocatello. 1942–1943, variety. 1946, *St. George and the Dragon, Going Up or Going Down?* (at St. Louis Public Library), *Punch and Judy.*

MERCER   (P. 132). Punch and Judy man, Wood's Museum, Philadelphia, 3–16 November 1879—Philadelphia *Public Ledger,* 3–16 November 1879.

MERCIER, Sieur   (Pp. 53, 54). Perspective theatre and fantoccini at the Theatre, Southwark, Philadelphia, 12 May 1773.

MEREDITH MARIONETTES   See Bixby, Meredith.

MERINGTON, EDWIN   1937, Variety presented by the Wandering Puppeteers, a group of fourteen-year-olds, at the Marshall Field Puppet Exhibition.

MERRIE GUILDERS   See Mallory, Mary Lu.

MERRY MAC MARIONETTES   See McBeth, Edith.

MERRY MANIKINS   James Bisset, Margaret Davis, and Ruth Keith. Andover, Mass. 1937, *The China Pig, The Three Trees, Red Riding Hood,* variety, all with hand-puppets.

METAYER, Monsieur   "Famous ventriloquist, with nine speaking automata," at Temperance Hall, Philadelphia, 9 December 1847—Philadelphia *Public Ledger,* that date.

MEYER, CAROLINE   St. Louis, Mo. Teacher who used puppetry in school work. Gave demonstration of simple puppets at Puppet Guild of St. Louis exhibit at the Art Gallery, 1942. At Maryln School produced *Swinging on a Star* with shadows to illustrate a song.

MEYER, ROSALIND   Punchinello Puppets, Milwaukee, Wis. 1933–1936, played hand-puppet repertory of: *Punch and Judy, Blue Beard, How the Little Devil Fell into the Holy Water, The Three Wishes, The Three Little Pigs, Mickey and Minnie Mouse's Christmas, Dr. Faust, Mickey Mouse's Birthday, Mickey Mouse at Art School, Hansel and Gretel, Cinderella,* variety.

M G M   1938, Marionette Moviettes presented scenes on a truck-stage which toured the country advertising the film *Marie Antoinette.*

MIACO   (P. 276). Marionettes at Worth's Family Museum, Sixth Avenue and 30 Street, New York, 9–14 February 1891. (Odell, vol. 14, p. 675.)

MICHAEL, VIVIAN   (P. 347). Ashville, Ohio. Became interested in puppets through an article by Tony Sarg in the *Ladies Home Journal* and a performance of his *Rip Van Winkle.* Studied at the Sarg puppet school, then in 1929 built marionettes for her own *Jack and the Beanstalk* and *Hansel and Gretel.* Most of the following productions have been a part of Mrs. Michael's work in the art department of Everett Junior High School, Columbus, O.: 1930, *Puppets in Toy Town.* 1931, Circus. 1932, Variety, 1933, *Treasure Island.* 1934, *Carnival.* 1935, *Legend of the Willow Plate* with hand-puppets. 1936, *The Three Wishes.* 1937, *Carolina Folk Tales.* Summer 1941, *Joe Finds Out About College,* produced with hand- and rod-puppets for the College of Education, Ohio State University, at the Ohio State Fair. In 1943, marionettes were replaced in school shows by hand- and rod-puppets which have been used in *Rip Van Winkle,* 1943, 1948. 1944, *Legend of Sleepy Hollow.* 1945, *Aladdin.* Mrs. Michael is co-author with Marjorie Batchelder of *Hand-and-Rod-Puppets, A New Adventure in the Art of Puppetry,* College of Education, Ohio State University, Columbus, 1947.

MICHEL, STELLA   Scullin School Puppet Club, St. Louis, Mo. Club organized 1938 with seventh and eighth grade pupils. Hand-puppet plays produced: *Punch and*

Judy, Rip Van Winkle, Christmas plays. The group performed for the school, the Patrons' Association, and in 1942 and 1944 gave demonstrations at the Art Museum during the Autumn Puppet Exhibit.

MICK, HETTIE LOUISE (Mrs. John Martin) (Pp. 332–334, 336). Began puppet work with Ellen Van Volkenburg; played with Tony Sarg; constructed marionettes and wrote plays and about puppet technique.

MIDDLETON, MRS. GEORGE EDWARD Cincinnati, O. 1939, presented marionette *Novelty Acts,* Spokane, Wash. 1942, *School Comedy* in Atlanta, Ga. Summer 1947, taught puppetry in Girl Scout Camp.

MIDDLETON, GEORGE WILLIAM (Pp. 158, 163, 184, 192, 200, 219, 264–267, 269, 274, 277, 286, 287). (1865–16 October 1946). In 1883, as the Middleton Brothers, with Harry. In 1884–1887, with his mother Sarah Jane Holden Middleton, and his wife. Thereafter with his wife only. Marionettes and shadow-figures. Among an incomplete collection of programs of the Middleton appearances are: 20–22 Jan. 1896, Weeks Theatre, Corry, Pa., 22 Aug.–4 Sept. 1898, Columbia Garden, Atlantic City, N. J., 12–18 Sept. 1898, Museum, Ninth and Arch, Philadelphia. 7–13 Nov. 1898, Strouder & Smith's Wonderland, Ft. Wayne, Ind., 28 Nov.–3 Dec. 1898, Howard Athenaeum, Boston. 31 Dec. 1900–5 Jan. 1901, Olympic Theatre, Chicago. 14–20 Jan. 1901, Columbia Theatre, St. Louis, billed as "Fantoccini or Funny Manikins." 9–15 Apr. 1903 or 1904, National Theatre, Kansas City, Mo. 4–10 June 1905, Lake Michigan Park Theatre, Muskegon, Mich. beginning 3 Sept. 1906: bookings through the Western Vaudeville Managers' Association, Chicago.

MIDDLETON, HENRY JAMES (HARRY) (Pp. 184, 196, 198, 199, 200, 264, 266, 270). (1858–1884). 1876, played on the West Coast with McDonough and Earnshaw. 1883, toured to West and back.

MIDDLETON, HENRY JAMES (Pp. 178, 184, 191, 192, 264). (c. 1840–1877). With his wife, Sarah Jane Holden, c. 1845–c. 1910, came to America with Bullock or the Royal Oriental Marionettes, 1874. 1876, played at the Philadelphia Centennial.

MIHLEIS, ALICE State Normal School, Newark, N. J. In the early 1930's helped found the Marionette Guild which helped teachers in the state to plan and execute puppet productions.

MILLARD, LYN Towertown Marionettes, School, Midlothian, Ill. 1934, *Three Little Pigs, Hansel and Gretel* (Toy department, Marshall Field and Co., Chicago), and *Perry, Percy, Peter, and Boom-Boom.*

MILLS, LOUISE Philadelphia. Started 1936, using marionettes in school work: *Sir Walter Raleigh and Queen Elizabeth;* play about cotton, another about silk; orchestra, singer, and dancers used for teaching music.

MILLS, WINIFRED H. and DUNN, LOUISE (Pp. 341, 366, 391). Fairmount Junior High School, Cleveland, O., and the Cleveland Museum of Art did experimental puppet work with children. Productions included: 1921, *The Childhood of David Copperfield.* 1922, *Sigurd the Volsung.* 1923, *The Knave of Hearts* and *Men of Iron.* 1924, *Adventures of Alice.* 1925, *Petroushka* (with Stravinsky music) and *Arjuno,* a Javanese hero play. In 1929 the Fairmount students initiated the new art museum marionette stage. 1930, shadow-figures were used for *Tom, the Watet Baby* and *The Carnival of Animals.* As a result of their educational work, Mills and Dunn published *Marionettes, Masks and Shadows,* Doubleday Doran and Co., Garden City, New York, 1928 and *Shadow Plays and How to Produce Them,* same publishers, 1939.

MILNE, ISABEL From 1931–1940, played children's story dramatizations in the schools of Detroit and vicinity, with occasional advertising shows in stores. Productions included: *Jack and the Beanstalk, Peter Rabbit, Hansel and Gretel, Master Peter Patelin, Monkey Business, A Morning in Our Clinic* (at Hudson's department store), *Happy Heart, The Tinder Box, Rumpelstiltskin, Aladdin, Hidden Treasure, The Wonderful Bottle.*

MILOVSOROFF, BASIL and GEORGIA (Pp. 356, 361). Thetford Center, Vt. 1934, *Two Blind Beggars.* 1935, *Ivan the Fool, The Peasant and the Stupid Imp.* 1936,

The Little Humpbacked Horse. 1937, *Tsar Saltan.* 1938, *The Hut on Chicken's Legs.* 1939, *The Rabbit and the Fox.* 1940, *Grandma and Her Little Gray Goat,* with rod-and-string puppets, and *The Golden Fish,* with hand-puppets. 1945, *The Crow and the Fox.* 1947, *The Fox and the Rabbit,* both with rod-and-string puppets. Many of the above plays are drawn from Russian folk tales and reflect Russian decorative style and color in the costumes, settings, and finely carved puppets.

MISSISSIPPI MARIONETTES See Boeck, Orville.

MITCOFF, ELENA d. 20 April 1943. Petroushka Puppets, Detroit, Mich. Born in Novgorod, Russia, came to America before World War I. Attended Wayne University and University of Chicago; lived in many sections of the United States; made trips to Europe. From 1932–1937, maintained a hand-puppet theatre in Detroit, playing regularly on Saturday mornings at the Woman's City Club and filling engagements elsewhere. Among her plays were: *The Bride of Jack Frost, The Sick Petroushka, The Dutiful Bear, Petroushka, the Bugaboo of the Bourgeoisie, The Green Nose, The Maid was in the Garden, Christopher Columbus, The Tinderbox, Rapunzel, The Bear* (Chekhov), *The Real Princess, The Bride of Jack Frost, The Knock-Out, The Finder of Lost Things, First Christmas Presents,* and many favorite children's plays. Her dramatization of Boccaccio's *Ninth Novel of the Seventh Day* was played at the First American Puppetry Conference, Detroit, 1936. Among her writings are the version of the classic Petroushka play in *A Repertory of Marionette Plays* and the translation of Efimova's *Adventures of a Russian Puppet Theatre,* Puppetry imprints, Birmingham, Michigan, 1936.

MITTON, MILDRED Minneapolis, Minn. Studied with Irene Odegaard under the Adult Education Program, Sept. 1937–June 1939. 1938, produced a variety show. Has entertained with marionettes since this time in hospitals, parks, schools, and clubs. 1947, taught puppet making to a group of ten boys convalescing from poliomyelitis.

MOBET'S PUPPETS Chicago, Ill. 1930, *Rumpelstiltskin, Little Black Sambo, Snow White and the Seven Dwarfs,* all with hand-puppets.

MODJACOT PUPPET PLAYERS See Cutler, Yosl.

MOHLER, RUTH ANN Director, Basement Marionettes, John Muir School, Whittier, Cal. 1931, *Good-for-Nothing Ganiche,* a Basque tale adapted from Frances Carpenter.

MOLARSKY, OSMOND Saw a demonstration one summer by Lilian Owens, and began at age of twelve to make his own puppets. From 1929 to 1932 presented 250 performances of *Puppet Gaieties* with 18-inch marionettes in New Jersey and Pennsylvania.

MONRO MARIONETTES See Augur, Munro.

MONTAGU, HARRY 11–26 May 1879, his "marionnettes americaines" played at the Théâtre de la Renaissance, Brussels, Belgium.

MONTAGUE, DUKE 1937, over 200 performances of *Hollywood Dollies* with marionettes.

MONTANO, Signor (P. 108). Fantoccini at Peale's Museum, New York, 1845.

MONTGOMERY, JEAN Attic Playhouse, Antioch College, Yellow Springs, O. 1926, *The Marriage Proposal* (Chekhov). 1927, *The Three Wishes.* 1928, *The Boor* (Chekhov).

MONTIVEDO, Signor (P. 108). "Grand mechanical exhibition of nine performers" at Peale's Museum, New York, 1844.

MONTOYA Y GADENA, FRANCISCA TOMASA (P. 71). Proprietor of puppet show, Mexico City, 1786.

MOORE, JESSIE Charlotte, Mich. c. 1930, *The Wizard of Oz* with marionettes and jigging puppets.

MOREAU (P. 93). French puppets in Detroit, 22 January 1811.

MORENO, MIGUEL NAVA Mexico City. His string-puppet company has played since 1935; programs consist of variety numbers and sketches of Mexican life in the

Rosete-Aranda tradition. In August 1946, presented in Pachuca a new play, *The Treasure at the Bottom of the Sea.*

MORERA, ALBERTO   See Butler, Horacio. 1934, had an exhibit of his theatre, La Nave, a stage on a cart, at the International Exposition of Puppets, Theatre Museum, Buenos Aires.

MORLEY, Professor   (P. 132). "The original man with the talking hand," at Tony Pastor's Theatre, New York, 17 October 1871. On 24 October of the same year he also showed *Punch and Judy*—Odell, vol. 9, p. 78.

MORNINGSIDE MARIONETTES   Olin Doane and Maynard Heacox. Beginning 15 June 1929, toured from Sioux City, Ia., to Pennsylvania with *Jack and the Beanstalk,* variety, *Punch and Judy.* Fall of same year performed *Blue Beard, Snow White, Red Riding Hood, Punch and Judy of the Past, The Night before Christmas.* 1930, *Rumpelstiltskin.* Philadelphia, 1932, *The Legend of the Rainbow, The Doctor in Spite of Himself.*

MOSELY, RICHARD   (Pp. 42, 43). Partner of Richard Brickell, New York, 1747, and possibly in Philadelphia, 1742.

MOTLEY, JOHN LOTHROP   (Pp. 305, 310, 316). "Motley's love of costume and dramatic effect—he had made and played with miniature theatres also—appeared in his writings from first to last."—Van Wyck Brooks, *The Flowering of New England,* (New York, 1936), p. 334. As Motley was born in 1814, he would have had his toy theatre c. 1824.

MOWREY, MARGARET   1932, *The Three Wishes* and *The Singing Lesson.*

MULLER, CATHERINE   Peter Pan Puppeteers, Kenilworth, Ill. 1930, *Box and Cox* with small marionettes, *The Fairy Riddle, The Bluebird* (Maeterlinck), *The Witch and the Good Fairy.* Also built an advertising show for a paint company and traveled with it from Des Moines. 1931, scenes from *Hansel and Gretel.* 1934, *Christmas Fairy.* 1936, *Fourth of July Revue* with marionettes, jigging puppets, finger puppets.

MULLER, EDWARD   Institute of Art, Flint, Mich. 1933, *Rumpelstiltskin* and *Long Nose.*

MUNGER, JOHN   Young puppeteer of Cleveland, O., who began presenting puppet shows c. 1941 with puppets made by his grandmother, Mrs. Virginia Couper. 1946, played *Hansel and Gretel* and *The Wishing Fairy.* Conducted class in puppet making at the Fairview Summer Day Camp.

MURDOCH, SAMUEL   (P. 128). (1838–1896). Assisted the Beck Brothers in *Punch and Judy,* c. 1866, later set up his own show and played for many years inside the west gate of Boston Commons. Mentioned by Ernest Russell, *Outing Magazine,* 1908, p. 473.

MUSHROOM THEATRE   See Kreymborg, Alfred and Dorothy.

MUSINETTE PRODUCTIONS, INC.   See Hess, Constance.

MUSSER, BENJAMIN   (P. 317). A twelve-year-old Philadelphia boy who with a friend had a toy theatre c. 1902.

MYERS   (Pp. 97, 222, 232, 238). Pennsylvania showman, before 1828, the master of Hugh Lindsay.

MYERS, GALENE   Excelsior, Minn. Through the Midget Hand-Puppet Theatre of the Excelsior public schools, which was built in 1934 and operated until 1943, elementary school children were given an opportunity for creative work in puppetry. 1937–1938, a musical play *In and Out* was done by the fifth grade. *Red Riding Hood, Hansel and Gretel,* scenes based on the exploits of Paul Bunyan, and variety numbers such as an animal orchestra were also presented. 1943–1948, at the Grant School, Redondo Beach, Cal., Western pioneer scenes were given.

MYERS, MARION   Marion's Marionettes, Wilmington, Del. 1 December 1934, presented her first professional show. Every Christmas season since 1934 has played at Sear's Toyland. Floor show act has played in theatres and clubs in Delaware and Pennsylvania.

NARANJO, BEN   An Indian puppeteer who graduated from the Cheyenne Mountain High School, Colorado Springs, and the Haskell Institute, Lawrence, Kan. While at the latter school he worked with Sibyl Malm and built Chief Sunburn. Before entering the army in World War II he was a commercial artist and professional bronc rider.

NATTE, JEAN (Pp. 29, 79–83, 260). (c. 1730–1803). Called Daddy Marseille, showman in Quebec, c. 1775 onward.

NAVA, JOSÉ MARIA (Pp. 241, 242). Mexico, 28 July 1861.

NAWN, TOM 1926, at Hillsdale, N. J.: *Rip Van Winkle, Snow White, The Barnstormers, Punch and Judy.* 1929, organized the Hollywood Players with Dorothy T. and Orville Charles Goldner and presented *The Three Little Pigs, The Tongue-Cut Sparrow.*

NAY, JOSEPH Amateur Punch showman of Chicago who died in 1928.

NAYLOR, MARJORIE Bellville, Canada. 1937, *The Princess and the Swineherd* produced by a class of teen-age girls. 1939, *Mammy's Magic Washing Day* for puppetry conference at Hamilton.

NELSON, ARTHUR (P. 278). Chicago, Ill. Son of Edward "Nicholas" Nelson, plays floor-show act in hotels and theatres, touring from coast to coast. 1939, played in England. 1942–1944, *Stringin' Along.* (d. 22 Oct. 1948).

NELSON, EDWARD "NICHOLAS" (Pp. 98, 101, 102, 277–278, 283, 379, 385). Chicago, Ill. Has worked continuously with marionettes since 1899. With his wife, toured the vaudeville circuits, 1909–1923, as Belmont's Manikins. All six of their children worked in the act at various times. Arthur and Robert had acts of their own; the latter died 1945. A daughter, Lorraine, is playing her own marionette act in the Chicago area, 1948. Among the vaudeville numbers were the pantomimes *Down on the Plantation, The One-Ring Circus, Red Lion Inn, Krazy Kat Theatre.* Plays included: *Rip Van Winkle, Puss in Boots,* and other children's classics; *The Night Before Christmas, Punch and Judy.* In 1932, two companies were on tour—The Nelson Marionettes and The Marionette Players—giving children's shows in schools and department stores. 1938, played in the Wiebolt Stores in Chicago and other sections of the country: *Cinnamon Bear, Looney Tunes, Mickey Mouse Circus, Popeye Show.* 1943, built a show for the Palmer House which ran 12 weeks; also made rod-puppets for the Kungsholm Puppet Opera—"all wire work and a lot of soldering," as Nelson expressed it. 1946–1948, special productions for clubs and national conventions and advertising shows; new puppets for Kungsholm to replace those destroyed by fire in 1947.

NELSON, NICK Olvera Puppeteers. 1934, *Adventures of Jimmy and Mary Jane in Seedland* and *Adventures of Ann Apple in Storybookland* for Bullock's Store, Los Angeles. *Puppet Passions of 1934* at Balboa Beach. 1946, continued shows for stores, and also played for the Red Cross.

NELSON, ROBERT See Bobby Belmont.

NEW, GEORGE (P. 355). 1933, *The Hangman's Dream, The Silver Ball, December Night.* 1934, *The Three Wishes, In the Sultan's Palace,* variety. 1935, with the Marionette Players of the Hermann, Mo., High School: *Marionette Follies, Rip Van Winkle,* variety. 1936, over 200 performances of *Intimate Revue.* 1937, as director of the Decatur, Ill., Marionette Guild, produced *Santa's Circus, Little Red Riding Hood, Sunshine and Showers, Santa's Toyland Revue, The Nativity.* 1938, the Guild gave daily performances from Thanksgiving to Christmas week of *Noël* sponsored by the city. In 1938, with a permanent staff under the Illinois Recreation Project of the WPA, New directed plays in a number of Illinois towns. Among the productions were: *Three Sketches with Alcibiades, The King's Toothache, Darby and Joan, The Glittering Gate* (Lord Dunsany), *The Princess of Xanadu, Cinderella, Rip Van Winkle,* one hundred performances given by children. 1940, as director of Puppet Caravan, presented *Legend of Noah* with hand-puppets. Also built 36-inch marionettes for the fairies in the Children's Theatre of Evanston, Ill., production of *A Midsummer Night's Dream.*

NEW YORK PUBLIC LIBRARY 1939, *Perez and Martina,* directed by Pura Belpre, presented by children of the 115 Street Branch at the New York Puppetry Festival.

On the same occasion the Washington Heights Branch gave *Rapunzel* and the Tremont Branch *Hanicka and the Waterman*, a Czech fairy tale.

NEWMAN, JEANNE MARJORIE   1928, *The King of the Golden River* and *The Stonish Giant* at Cleveland, O., playgrounds. 1932, *Toyland Revue*. 1935, *Stringing 'Em All* at Shaker Heights High School. 1936, *Adam and Eve*, variety, *Samson and Delilah*. 1938, *The Princess and the Painter Lad*. All shows with 14-inch marionettes.

NIXON, DAVID   New Orleans, La. 1938, presented *Venus and the Faun* at Cisterine, Taormina, Sicily. 1943, remodelled an old warehouse in the Vieux Carré, New Orleans, and held an exhibition of his paintings, with a marionette act as an added attraction. Later presented variety, including a live cat which is put through its paces by a puppet lion tamer. 1946, presented a circus in his theatre. Nixon, a violinist by profession, gave recitals in Europe, conducted a jazz band in Berlin (1925), and founded the International Vivaldi Society (1935).

NOBBE, MARTHA JOHNSON   Memphis, Tenn. 1936, *Brooksie Saves the Day, Castles in the Air, Santa Claus Comes to Town*.

NOONAN, TOMMY   Central Park Players, Louisville, Ky. This group of young dramatic players and puppeteers was founded in 1927, with Tommy Noonan, then 12 years old, as director of puppets. By 1935, 1200 puppet shows had been given in churches, clubs, and schools. In addition to the usual well-known fairy tales, the group produced *Harlequin Breaks a Heart String* (Grace Dorcas Ruthenburg), *The Happy Prince, Why the Chimes Rang*, and *The Clown Revue* (which had over 600 performances in 1935).

NORBERT, NAT   Brooklyn, N. Y. 1942, gave hand-puppet variety at the American Puppet Pageant sponsored by the American Hobby Federation at Sach's Auditorium. 1945, used puppet and magic act as promotional stunt for Hearn's department store, New York.

NORMA   and her family of puppets. Appeared 1944, as one number in *Fun on the Fourth*, a children's show at Macy's, New York.

OBERWAGER, JEROME   1944–1945, used puppets in psychiatric treatment of soldiers at Aberdeen Proving Ground, Md.

O'BRIEN, LIVIA F.   Lawrence, Kan. 1931, with members of the local branch of the American Association of University Women, produced a series of children's plays including: *The Peppermint Boy, Through the Back of His Head, A Gift for Mother*, and *The Prince and the Stable Boy* by Ernestine Songer, *Peter Rabbit Decides to Change His Name, Alice in Wonderland, The Moon Looks On*.

OCAMPO, SILVINA   See Butler, Horacio.

O'CONNELL, HAROLD   River Forest, Ill. A young puppeteer who produced *Hansel and Gretel*, 1945.

ODEGAARD, IRENE   Taught puppetry in the Minneapolis, Minn., schools, and in 1948 joined Nellie Fry in the presentation of shows.

O'DELL MARIONETTES   See Sexton, Mildred B.

ODLIN, RICHARD   (P. 338). 1918–1919, with Ellen Van Volkenburg's Chicago Little Theatre Marionettes. 1925, built *The Willow Plate* for Tony Sarg and puppeteered for him five seasons at the Bal Taborin, Hotel Sherman, Chicago; worked caricature puppet of Fred Stone in *Stepping Stones* prologue; toured with Sarg's *Ali Baba*. Then assisted Sue Hastings. Summer 1928, taught puppetry, Cornish School, Seattle, Wash., producing: *The King's Breakfast, Peter Rabbit*, and variety. Summer 1929, *Hynd Horn* (puppets by John Martin) and Debussy impressions; fall, revived *A Midsummer Night's Dream* in London for Maurice Browne, Van Volkenburg production with Perry Dilley puppets. Has done portrait puppets of well-known actresses.

OEHRLE, MARIE L.   High School, Salem, N. J. 1933, *Little Red Riding Hood* and *Hansel and Gretel* with small marionettes.

OGILVIE, MARY A. H. Oakville, Ont., Canada. c. 1938, worked with puppets in Girl Guide groups.

OLIVER MARIONETTES See Sutch, Marian Adams.

OLNEY, MARY High School, Waverly, N. Y. 1936, *Cinderella*.

OLVERA PUPPETEERS See Bromley, Bob.

OLVERA STREET PUPPET THEATRE See Walton, Paul.

OMAN, LESTER and DOROTHY 1938, began marionette work in St. Charles, Ill. Sept. 1940, opened at Paramount Theatre, New York. Taught at Seton Institute, Sante Fe, N. Mex. and played at the La Fonda Hotel there. Toured the South and Southwest.

OMARÍN (P. 245). Puppeteer in Mexico, c. 1872.

ONE HUNDRED THREE PUPPETEERS See Pugliese, Constance.

O'NEILL, IVA Gilbert and Bennet School Marionette Club, Norwalk, Conn. 1933, *Jack and the Beanstalk*.

ORCUTT, DAVID Yellow Springs, O. Designer and manufacturer of Shadowcraft puppets. 1947–1948, *Hansel and Gretel* with black plastic shadow figures. 1948, *Ma and Pa on the Ferry Boat*.

ORONO, ME., PUPPETEERS 1933, *The Taming of the Shrew*.

O'ROURKE, MICHAEL See Walton, Paul.

OTT, CAROLINE East Boston, Mass. 1936–1938, produced dramatizations of fairy tales; variety, *Punch and Judy, Why the Chimes Rang, Rip Van Winkle, The Prince and the Dragon, Somebody-Nothing*.

ORÚS, MAGDELENA LAGUNA Buenos Aires, Argentina. Director of the Títeres de la Mojarrita, a school puppet theatre in which Mexican and Argentine stories and legends dramatized, c. 1944.

OSBORNE, ROSALYNDE R. (Mrs. Clem Stern) (Pp. 348, 349). Hamilton, Ont. Studied with Lilian Owen at Gloucester, Mass. Produced, as King Cob Puppets, plays and variety with hand-puppets and marionettes in Canada. 1923, *The Land of Punch and Judy*. 1929, *The Gift of the Fairies*. 1931, variety. 1935, held exhibition of puppets from her collection at the Toronto Art Gallery and gave performances. 1937, made puppet films and sent them to Scotland to raise funds for the Girl Guides and Women's Rural Institutes. 1938, *The Clouds* by Aristophanes at McMaster and Toronto Universities. 1940, gave shows "to buy socks for soldiers and make them laugh while wearing them." 1942–1943, *La Grand Main* by Duranty, played with hand-puppets for the French colony at Camp Ouareau, Quebec. 1948, occasional lectures and demonstrations.

OSCAR 1945, played in New Orleans at Pete Herman's.

OSGOOD, MILDRED M. Muncie, Ind., and New York. 1944, *A Modern Fairy Story* with 10-inch marionettes. Experimented with stringpuppets made from tubes of organdie and other transparent materials for airy effects. 1946–1947, *A Christmas Dream, Vaudeville, The Weather Man* at St. John's Parish House, New York. Has worked experimentally with puppets for television.

OSTRANDER, BOB Marionette maker who, among other things, designed Lily May and Jim for the U.S. Rubber Company, c. 1940.

OWEN, LILIAN (Mrs. William Thompson) (Pp. 335, 336, 338, 348, 353, 354). Played with Tony Sarg. 1920, *Hynd Horn*. 1921, portrait puppets of actors for prologue to *Greenwich Village Follies, A Christmas Carol, Cyrano de Bergerac*. 1924 and later made puppets for Jean Gros.

OWENS, JOE Schenectady, N. Y. With his wife, daughter, and son, has produced plays and variety in northern New York, and television shows for WRGB, c. 1944–1948.

OWENS, LLOYD Canadian puppeteer who played *The Missing Million, The Frozen North, Pickling Pickering, The Beautiful Queen Esther, The Adventures of Billy-Boy*, 1933–1934.

OWENS, Mr. and Mrs. A company touring Canada, 1935.

OWINGS, IRENE Central School, Chico, Cal. 1935–1937, plays presented with child puppeteers.

OXFORD MARIONETTES 1929, *A Fairy to Stay* with marionettes by Remo Bufano. Shows for advertising children's books published by the Oxford University Press.

PAGE, ELIZABETH S., and RUTLER, GEORGE W. A. The Ethonettes Club, Evanston, Ill. High School. 1928, *Rip Van Winkle*. 1929, *A Connecticut Yankee in King Arthur's Court*. 1930, *Treasure Island*. 1931, *The Gooseberry Mandarin*. 1932, *The Tragical Comedy of Dr. Faust*.

PAL, GEORGE (P. 380). 1939, arrived from Europe with "animated puppets" for films. Has produced shorts with puppet figures animated by stop motion. 10 December 1941, premiere of *Rhythm in the Ranks* at Paramount Theatre. New York,

PALL MALL MARIONETTES See Rice, Virginia.

PALMER (P. 259). Puppet shows in Montreal, c. 1850.

PALMER, RUBY M. Santa Barbara, Cal., Marionettes. 1924–1928, produced fairy tales; variety, plays including: *The Way to Happiness, Adelai, The Miraculous Window, The Coming of St. Nicholas, The Last Dream of Don Juan, A Legend of Monterey, A Desert Minstrel, Mr. Abbott's Nightmare*.

PALMER, WINTHROP BUSHNELL Fairfield, Conn., and vicinity. 1927–1928, *Maitre Pierre Patelin, Old Put and Tom, Tom and the Tailor, Jack and the Beanstalk, The Cat That Walked by Himself* (after Kipling).

PAMEO PUPPETEERS Kitchener, Canada. A children's group which began in the early 1930's and continued to work together as they grew up. In 1938 they produced *Rapunzel, Amanda and the Ghosts, The Three Wishes*. Some of the members teach at camps.

PANEL PLAYHOUSE PUPPETS See Hoyt, Hazel.

PAPPAS, GEORGE c. 1940, worked with puppets at Central High School, Paterson, N. J., and had basement puppet theatre in which he and Jack Fredericks presented a show a month. One of these was an original play, *The Enchanted King*.

PARIS, FRANK (P. 383). New York. Having read a magazine article by Tony Sarg, built a variety show (1928) and thus began his career with puppets. 1931, *The Lost Ruby*. 1932, *Bimba the Pirate*. 1937 to date, *Stars on Strings*, a night club variety show with which Paris has toured the country from coast to coast. 1947–1948, *Toby of the Circus*, a play for children. 27 December 1947 began a series of weekly television shows for N.B.C., *The Adventures of Toby*, a kind of marionette "soap opera."

PARISI, ANTONIO (Pp. 293, 295, 297, 300). Sicilian puppet theatre in Boston 1888–1895, thereafter in New York until about 1914.

PARKER, WOODY Shawnee, Kan. 1937, *Greedy Old King Michael* and *Folies d'amour*.

PARKIN, FLORENCE W., and PATTEE, GLADYS 1933, *Third Center Medical* (A Patient's Day in the Hospital), *Dance of the Dwarfs* at Mayo Clinic, Rochester, Minn. 1934, *Cinderella* and variety at St. Mary's Hospital.

PARRIS, MARION Marion's Marionettes, Seminole, Okla. 1933, *Goin' Bugs*.

PARSONS PUPPETEERS See Welty, Susan F.

PASADENA PUPPETEERS See Smith, Lydia Sutton.

PASEK, CEPHA Sioux City Art Center. 1939, *Uncle Tom's Cabin* and *Creatures of Impulse*.

PAT PENDING'S PUPPETS See Rosecrans, Carol.

PATRICK, FLORENCE 1945, *December Night* with Junior High School students in Augusta, Mont.

PATRIDGE, WILLIAM (Pp. 50, 53, 58). Puppets at the Sign of Lord John Murray, New York, 1770.

PATRINOS, HARRY (P. 290). Greek shadow-figure showman, Chicago, 1906–1912; American tours thereafter.

PATTEN, MRS. MARC Bloomfield Hills, Mich. 1946–1947, hand-puppet shows for recreation and education at Christ Church, Cranbrook.

PATTERSON, Prof. and Mrs. D. H.   University campus, West Lafayette, Ind. 1933–1934, *Red Riding Hood* and *Jack and the Beanstalk*. 1935, a group of plays in French, *Hansel and Gretel*, variety, *Little Black Sambo, Babouschka*. 1936, *Le Voyage dans le sabot blanc, Land of Nod, Romance of the Willow Plate*.

PATTERSON, FRANCES H.   Dayton, O. c. 1930–1942, used puppetry as part of art room activities. Sixth grade children built and produced: *Le Petit Chaperon Rouge* (in French), *The Legend of the Willow Plate* (presented for the Junior League Puppetry Conference, Dayton, 1938), *The Magic Gold* (an original play), and *Humpty Dumpty and Alice*. Summer, 1935, studied with Tony Sarg. 1937, attended puppet theatre conference, Paris.

PATTERSON, OSCAR   1937, lectures and demonstrations with marionettes and hand-puppets.

PATTERSON, PAT   Worked with puppets while at the University of Kentucky. After serving in the Army, built 30-inch marionettes for a variety act c. 1945, which he played on the West Coast.

PATTERSON, RUSSELL   (Pp. 134, 381). 1934, showed his Personettes at the French Casino, New York. 1935, played aboard S. S. *Monarch of Bermuda*. Used puppets for sophisticated displays, movies scenes, as in *Artists and Models*, and floor shows. 1944, made shadow box miniatures for the W. R. Darling Company, Los Angeles, manufacturer of sportswear and playclothes.

PATTISON, EVELYN   1931–1933, played well-known fairy tales, children's stories, and variety in Tacoma, Wash., and Carmel, Cal.

PATTON, ROY E.   (Pp. 346, 353, 372, 381). Roy Elbert Marionettes, Dayton, O. 1931, *The Firebird* and variety. 1932, *The Wishing Bird, The Intruder* (by Maeterlinck), *Robinson Crusoe, Hollywood Stars Revue*. 1933, *Robinson Crusoe* and variety. c. 1934, *Hansel and Gretel*. From 1934–1940, Patton, assisted by his brother Harry and his mother, designed costumes and built figures for the annual Thanksgiving Day parade sponsored by the Rik-Kumler Company, Dayton. Some of the figures were articulated and manipulated by rods and strings. The Patton Brothers also worked in the Tatterman Marionette studios, where Roy designed and carved heads for the puppets in many Tatterman productions.

PAUL, BERNARD   (Pp. 356, 385). Paul's Puppets, Linthicum Heights, Md. From 1929, when *The Gooseberry Mandarin* was produced, have toured in the eastern and midwestern states, presented shows in department stores, and appeared in advertising shows. The *Undersea Fantasy*, built in 1929, is still a favorite. 1930, *The Elephant's Child*. 1931, *Snow White* (television W3xk), *Three Bears, Cinderella*. 1932, *Ali Baba, A Midsummer Night's Dream* (built fairies for the Vagabond Theatre production). 1933, *Christmas Dream, The Fiery Dragon* (performed at the White House, 2 April 1934). 1935, *The Brave Little Tailor*. 1935, Christmas Pantomime. 1941, *The Tinder Box*. Commercial enterprises include: window display for Janitrol, 1935, 1937, 1938; window Christmas scenes (1936) and coronation of King George (1937) with partly articulated figures for Hoch Kohn & Co.; appliance advertising show at Baltimore Home Exposition, 1938; variety at Timonium Fair, 1938. Classes in puppetry at the Maryland Institute have produced among other plays, *The Princess' Birthday* and *In an Oriental Garden* (1933), *Rip Van Winkle* (1937).

PAXTON, PHOEBE   The Attic Theatre, Greenville, Miss. From 1928–1932, presented plays with many types of puppets. In addition to favorite fairy tales there were: *Ali Baba and the Forty Thieves, Aladdin and His Wonderful Lamp, Faust, Advice from a Caterpillar, The Wooden Horse* (with shadows), *Our First Flag*.

PEASE, KENT   Worked with a group in high school, then at college in Springfield, Mass. *A Tale of Two Cities* was produced 1938, but the group disbanded at beginning of World War II.

PEASLEY, HARRIET   Cheshire, Conn., and Winter Park, Fla. 1938, *The Elephant's Child, The Butterfly That Stamped, Jack and the Beanstalk*. During World War II, christened her puppet troupe the Merrie English Puppets, and gave many hand-puppet shows for British War Relief. Many hundreds of toy puppet clowns (Peekaboos) for British children in bombed cities. Her puppets were a part of *31 on Parade*, a show at Rockefeller Plaza sponsored by the New York War Fund.

PEEK, JOSEPH P. The Saroff Marionettes, Springfield, Mo. 1929–1936, presented children's performances of fairy tales, *Punch and Judy, Ali Baba, Uncle Eph's Return, A Marriage Proposal, A Concert of Dancing.*

PEEPSHOW PLAYHOUSE See Wallace, Alfred.

PEGASUS PUPPETEERS George School, Bucks County, Pa. 1935, *Jack and the Beanstalk, The Old Man of the Mountain, The Jolly Little Elves,* variety, scene from *A Midsummer Night's Dream.*

PENNY, LAURA San Luis Obispo, Cal., High School Puppet Club. 1933, *The Legend of Sleepy Hollow* with 18-inch marionettes.

PENROD, MABEL A. Friends School, Wilmington, Del. 1926, *The Ancient Mariner.* 1927, *Drake* (after poem by Alfred Noyes). 1928, *The Boatman of Mytilene.* 1929, *Columbus's First Westward Voyage.*

PEPPY PUPPETEERS See Shelly, Miss.

PERCY, BETTY Rochester, N. Y. 1946–1947, played floor-show act in northern New York State. Later worked with Frank Paris in *Toby of the Circus.*

PETER PAN PUPPETEERS See Muller, Catherine.

PETER PAN PUPPETEERS High School, Waterville, N. Y. 1935–1936, *Plum Preserved, Venetian Carnival, The Three Bears, Alice in Wonderland, While the Sandman Sleeps, The Snappy Dragon.*

PETERSON, BYRON 1940, *Boys and Gulls,* a commercial show for the Petroleum interests at the Golden Gate Exposition, San Francisco. Marionettes, hand-puppets, and mechanical figures were used.

PETROUSHKA PUPPETS See Mitcoff, Elena.

PETTEY, EMMA (Pp. 364, 391). Dallas, Tex. 1922, learned puppet making from Hettie Louise Mick at a Drama League Institute. 1923, produced *The Three Wishes,* 1924–1926, *Jack and the Beanstalk, Goldilocks, Red Riding Hood,* and *Circus.* 1928, at the Dallas Little Theatre: *Snow White, Aladdin, Lima Beans, Pyramus and Thisbe.* Also, *Hansel and Gretel, Rumpelstiltskin* in other towns. 1930–1931, *Mother Goose,* variety, and folk plays at Dallas Little Theatre. 1932, scenes with Mexican music and dances, oriental scenes, variety. 1933, traveling road show. 1934, *Esther, St. Patrick Festival, Musicians of Bremen, Persephone, The Nativity.* 1935, *Christmas Pudding* and revivals of earlier plays. 1936, revivals and *How Humpty Dumpty Was Mended, Miss Muffet Tries a New Plan, Goldilocks Turns the Tables.* 1937, *The Magic Woods, Magic Pills, Judas Maccabeus,* revivals and Christmas plays. 1938, *April Follies, Goats in the Rye Field, The Wishing Well, The Goats and the Troll, Mother Goose Parade, Medicine Show, Puppet Follies, Christmas Revue.* 1939, *Puppet Valentine Party, Marionette Carnival.* 1940, floor shows for clubs, churches, and parties with variety and short plays. 1945, with puppet club at junior high school, worked out the *Nutcracker Suite* as a mural; words written to the *Waltz of the Flowers* were used as a recurring theme. During her career as a teacher, Miss Pettey has carried on many experiments with puppetry for children. Her book, *The Puppet as an Elementary Project* (Pioneer Publishing Co., Fort Worth, Tex., 1925) was one of the first to deal with educational puppetry.

PETTEYS, THE 1946, played a floor show marionette act at Leon and Eddie's, New York.

PETTIT, LOUISE Worked with marionette variety in the early 1940's, and later with her husband, Kent More.

PHARAZYN, PROFESSOR (Pp. 191, 274). Philadelphia magician and marionette showman, 1880–1882.

PHILLIPS, B. MAUDE In 1933 with children at St. Anthony in Labrador produced *Peter Rabbit* and *Little Red Riding Hood.* Upon return to Boston played over 200 shows in schools. Worked with the Animal Rescue League.

PHILLIPS, MARJORIE D. K. (Mrs. Tom Devertier) (P. 370). Birmingham, Mich. 1934–1935, *December Night, Three Women at the Tomb, Jack the Promoter, Little Red Riding Hood, The Birthday Party.*

PICKENS, HELEN JEAN   Marshalltown, Ia. 1941 produced *Faust* with 12-inch marionettes.

PIDGEON, JOHN (P. 132). Royal Punch and Judy, Miner's Theatre, New York, 2–7 February 1880 and 8–13 May 1882. Odell, vol. 11, pp. 136, 565. 14–19 January 1889 in Curio Hall, Grand Street Museum, New York. Odell, vol. 14, p. 134.

PIED PIPER PUPPETS   Los Angeles, Cal. 1931, *The Piper's Fair* with marionettes.

PINAFORE PLAYERS   See Witt, Eleanor.

PINE MOUNTAIN SETTLEMENT SCHOOL   See Cobb, Alice.

PINXY, MADAME (Mrs. George Larsen) (Pp. 140, 277, 379). Chicago, Ill. Played *Punch and Judy* since she was a child. Worked in circuses and night clubs, and was a popular entertainer until her death in January 1948.

PITT, ISABEL   c. 1928, variety and scenes from *Winnie the Pooh* at Stamford, Conn.

PIXIE PUPPETS   See Donaldson, Sam.

PLACE, HARVEY   Pontiac, Mich. Played in schools and clubs. 1929, *Ivanhoe* and variety. 1930, 1931, variety, *Punch and Judy. Bugville Follies of 1932* and of *1933.* 1938, *Snow White.* 1939, *How Mr. Rabbit Got Long Ears, The King of the Golden River.*

PLACE, VIVIKA   San Francisco, Cal. During 1937 and 1938 as director of a group of N.Y.A. workers, produced *Mr. Gulliver in Oz, The Magic Teakettle, The Three Wishes, The Envious Neighbor, Frontier Days, Pilgrim Puppets, Mitsima and the Jumping Totem, Little Brother, George Washington Tableaux, Patrick O'Lalley and the Leprechauns, The Deeds of Mani, The Adventures of Mr. Coyote, The Pranks of Tyl Eulenspiegel, The Golden Parrot, The Two Pierrots* (Edmond Rostand), *The Venetian Night* (Alfred de Musset). Many of the above were adaptations by Etha Wulff. Beginning 11 September 1937 and continuing about a year, the group played every two weeks at the M. H. De Young Memorial Museum, Golden Gate Park.

PODRECCA, VITTORIO (Pp. 282–283, 322, 323). Teatro dei Piccoli. In September 1923 this company from Rome, Italy, played at the Frolic New Amsterdam Theatre, New York, a program of variety and *Puss in Boots,* and an operatta after Perrault. Following this engagement a Latin American tour was made, and the company returned to Europe. In December 1932, returned to New York for another engagement and toured the United States. 1933, lent some old puppets for scenes in the film, *I Am Suzanne,* with puppet sequences by the Yale Puppeteers. 1934, toured Argentine and South America, with several return bookings. Still active in 1944.

POLISH CLUB   University of Wisconsin, Madison. 1942, *Pan Twardowski.*

POLLOCK, EDITH   Sioux City, Ia. 1935, *The Three Wishes, Tom Tit Tot,* variety.

POPKIN'S MARIONETTES   See Whempner, Verna Huber.

PORCARO, VINCENT   Became interested in puppets while in junior high school and produced shows with friends. In college, c. 1940, presented *Cinderella,* a Japanese Noh play, *Alice in Wonderland.*

PORTILLO, FRANK   Washington, D. C. 1935, as a clown in the Hagenbeck-Wallace Circus, used a portrait marionette in the clown walk-around. Entertained with ventriloquism and puppets in and around Washington. 1936, worked with WPA projects, playing *Punch and Judy.*

POSE, RICHARD E.   Buenos Aires, Argentina. c. 1945 used puppets for teaching English in the Belgrado Day School.

POSTIGO, AUGUSTO   A puppeteer who was giving shows for private birthday parties in Lima, Peru, c. 1940.

POTEAUGHT, BEN   1924, worked with Jean Gros as The Kilsolving Marionettes in *Robin Hood.*

POWERS, NELSON   Training School, Presque Isle, Me. 1938, *Hansel and Gretel* with 18-inch marionettes.

POYNTER, P. KINGSLEY   Port Washington, N. Y. and vicinity. 1932, *The Hunchback, The Witches' Tale.* 1933, *Aladdin. Marionette Gaieties of 1934, Jack and the Beanstalk, Sleeping Beauty and the Dragon.*

PRENTICE, GEORGE   1934, played *Punch and Judy* in vaudeville. 1935, went to England for two years. 1938, toured the United States. 1939, went abroad for three years. 1941, volunteered for USO service and entertained troops until August 1945. Traveled twice across the United States playing in Army camps. Performed in South America and the Carribean area; in Europe, Africa, the Persian Gulf, South Pacific, and the India, China, and Burma theatres of war. In 1944 played at Central Park Mall, New York, with other acts from the *Foxhole Circuit Cavalcade,* to an audience of 50,000. 1946–1947, toured eastern United States. 1948, continued engagements.

PRESTON, HAROLD   Preston Puppets, New York. 1941, *Sinbad the Sailor* with hand-puppets.

PREVOSTI, CARLOS   A painter who organized a children's puppet theatre in Las Piedras school in Montevideo, c. 1940.

PRICE, JOE ALLEN   Decatur, Ala. 1945, *Punch and Judy.*

PRITCHARD, DAVID   (P. 338). With Denise Dooley, gave a few performances of Sarg's *Robin Hood* as his own production, in and about Flint, Mich., c. 1940.

PROCTOR, EDITH M.   J. B. Stetson Junior High School, Philadelphia. 1935, *Sleeping Beauty.* 1942–1943, variety.

PROCTOR, HESTER   Developed an active puppet program at San Francisco playgrounds, 1933–1936. At one time there were thirteen puppet groups made up of children 8–12 years of age. During the summers many performances were given from a trailer in the form of an Italian puppet booth, which was transported from place to place. Among the productions given were: *Green Nose, Jack and the Beanstalk, Little Black Sambo, Hansel and Gretel, The Peppermint Boy, Bluebeard.*

PROCTOR PUPPETS   (Pp. 356, 360, 363). Romain and Ellen Proctor, Springfield, Ill. At first a family activity with their three children, the work was developed professionally by the Proctors, who have been playing children's shows, advertising, and promotional programs from 1929 to date. First shows included: *The Three Bears, Little Black Sambo, Jonah and the Whale, Cinderella, Punch and Judy* with 35 hand-puppets. 1931, with 47 marionettes, performed *Hansel and Gretel,* variety, *Humpty Dumpty, The Three Pigs.* Also taught children's classes in puppetry under sponsorship of the Springfield Art Association. 1935, remodelled a movie house into a puppet theatre, built two productions for it, and had a financially successful season. 1939, revived *The Three Pigs* and played it over 300 times; added *Adventures of Sambo and his Hound Dog* to repertory. c. 1940, *Did She Fall or Was She Pushed?* a melodrama. 1941, health shows for state fairs in Iowa, Illinois, and Indiana. Revived former productions for general programs. 1943, discontinued tours because of war, but played occasional dates. 1944, *A Panorama of Puppets,* a demonstration. Conducted Puppet Institute at the Peoples' Art Center, St. Louis. Played Thanksgiving to Christmas at Scrugg, Vandervoort & Barney store, St. Louis. 1946, health shows at state fairs. 1946 to date, Midwest tours with revivals of previous shows.

PROVENZANO, PASQUALE   (P. 302). Sicilian puppet theatre at 84 Mulberry Street, New York, 1918–1924.

PUGLIESI, CONSTANCE M.   The 103 Puppeteers, Public School 103, New York. 1934, *Rumpelstiltskin, A Christmas Toy Parade.* 1935, as director of the Buck Hill Marionettes, Buck Hill Falls, Pa., presented: *Comedy Concert, At the Pocono Mountains Horse Show, Major Bowwow's Miniachoor Amachoor Hour, Ali Baba and the Forty Thieves, Author! Author!, The Cap with Silver Bells, In the Patio, Epaminondas and his Mammy, Strings.*

PUNCHINELLO PUPPETS   See Meyer, Rosalind.

PUPPET BOX THEATRE, THE   See Shepard, Dick.

PUPPET GUILD OF ST. LOUIS   1946, at the Art Museum: *Round Her Neck She Wore a Yellow Ribbon* (a bib-puppet novelty), *Jackie and the Magic Carrot* (with hand-puppets), *Christopher Cricket* (with shadows), *Danny in Numberland* (with marionettes).

PUPPET PLAYERS STUDIO   See Reighard, Catherine.

PUPPET SHOW, THE   See Dallas, Weaver.

PUPPET SHOW CLUB   Stetson Junior High School, Philadelphia. 1933, *The Enchanted Princess*.

PUPPET STUDIO, THE   See Rich, Brenda Kittredge.

PUPPET WORKSHOP   See Harris, Cornelia Clark.

PUPPETEERS CLUB   See Heininger, Robert.

PÜTERSCHEIN AUTHORITY, THE   See Dwiggins, W. A.

QUARTERMAN, LEONORA   Savannah, Ga. Produced her own adaptations of: 1932, *Peter Gray* (a ballad) and *Rumpelstiltskin,* both with hand-puppets. 1935, *Alice in Wonderland,* with marionettes. 1936, scenes from *The Mikado,* with marionettes, *The Knits Win,* an advertising show. 1938, *In a Balcony,* by Robert Browning, *Aladdin* (at the Dock Street Theatre, Charleston, S. C.). 1939, *Why the Sea is Salt; Rose of the Alhambra,* after Irving.

QUINN, RUTH   See Graham, Mildred.

QUIXIE MARIONETTES   See Bassett, Mercedes C.

RACH, JOHN   (Pp. 128, 223–228). German Casper showman in halls and beer gardens, New York, from before 6 March 1866 to 8 April 1877. The 1866 repertory at the Bowery Garten included, 6 March, *Der Seeräuber von Tunis* ("another performance" of this), 7, *Max in Mexico,* 8, *Kasper als Einwanderer;* 10, *Die Pfalzgräfin* ("Grosses dramatisches Tugendspiel in drei Akten"); 12, *Don Juan;* 13, *Er schlaft sehr gut, oder der verliebte Nachwächter,* also *Die Wette;* 14, *Der Mormone,* also *Ein Unteroffizier Friedrich des Grossen;* 15, *Das Staats-Examen,* also *Der Grossmutter Schnupftabaksdose;* 16, *Der Fahnenkampf, oder drei Tagen aus dem Leben eines Vaterlands-Vertheidigers;* 17, *König Zohack von Persien, oder der Pantoffeln der Prinzessin;* 19, the above repeated by request; 20, *Die lustige Gesellschaft;* 21, *Die dicke Lotte und der geprügelte Amtmann;* 23, *Herr von Bismarkruh, oder wie es dei Junker treiben;* 24, *Die Entführung aus dem Serail;* 26, *König Wenzel von Böhmen;* 27, *Max in Mexico;* 28, *Die Leichen-Räuber auf Greenwood Cemetery, Gemalde von New York bei Nacht;* 29, *Ein Mann mit einer schwarzen und einer weissen Frau, oder die Extreme begegnen sich;* 30, *König Wenzel;* 31, Mozart's *Don Juan;* 2 April, Easter Monday, the above repeated; 3, *Der Feldmesser;* 4, *Ein Hundert Offiziers und ein Rekrut, oder Er kam, sah, und siegte;* 5 *Don Juan;* 6 *Dies Bildniss ist bezauberend schön;* 7, *Eine diplomatische Heirath;* 9, *Ritter Kunerich von Drachenfels;* 10, *Schinderhannes, der grosse Räuberhauptmann;* 11, the same; 12, *Max in Mexico;* 13, *Die Fahnenschlacht im Teutoburgerwalde;* 14, *König Wenzel von Böhmen und seine Scharfrichter.* In 1867, played a five-month season at the Bowery Garten, with the following repertory: 5 January, *Der Granzwächter, oder Zündnabel und Pickelhaube;* 7, the same; 8, *Der gute Geist, Lumpaci Vagabundus der Zweite;* 10, *Don Juan;* 11, the same; 12, *Das Offizier-Examen,* also *Das Sonntags-und-Mucker Gesetz in New York;* 15, *Die Entführung aus dem Serail;* 18, *Eine Nachtwächtersgeschichte,* also *Sachsenhausen ist ein Staat für sich;* 19, *Der Tannhäuser;* 22, *Friedrich von Bleierne, oder der Klostergang;* 23, *Ich bin ein Preusse;* 24, *Kasper als Löffelgiesser;* 26, *Schinderhannes;* 28 the same; 29, *Der Fahnenkampf;* 30, the same; 31, *Der Ehescheidungsprocess;* 1 February, *Der deutsche Mucker in New York;* 2, the same; 4, *Don Juan;* 5, the same; 6, *Graf Dietrich von Schnabelinskie und sein Bedienter, Hannsgurgel;* 7, the same; 8, *Der Krondiamant und der Kampf um die alte Schachtel;* 9, the same; 11, *Der Sonntag in New York, oder schöne Seele finden sich zu Wasser wie beim Bier;*

12, the same; 13, *König Wenzel von Böhmen und sein Scharfrichter*; 14, the same; 15, *Der Professor und der Knödelfresser;* 16, *Der Seeräuber von Algier;* 19, *Dr. Rhabarb, oder der Bierstudent;* 20, *Napoleon III und sein Werkzeuge;* 21, the same; 22, *Ein New York Lumpaci, oder der Bier-Wein-und-Wasser Frage;* 23, *Kunerich von Drachenfels;* 26, *Die Entführung aus dem Serail;* 27, the same; 28, *Die Ankunft in Amerika, oder der Patent-Artikel;* 1 March, *Die dicke Lotte und der geprügelte Amtmann;* 2, *Don Juan;* 4, *Die Bartholomäusnacht, oder Pariser Bluthochzeit;* 5, the same; 6, *Der Tausendsappermenter;* 7, *Die Werbezeit in America;* 8, *Ein Müthiger ohne Courage, oder eine Amerikanische Generals-Flucht;* 9, *Der gute Geist Lumpaci Vagabundus der Zweite;* 11, *Der schwarze Gesandte;* 12, the same; 13, *B[r]unhilde von Radenshorst;* 14, the same; 15, *Conföderation und Kaiserthum;* 16, the same; 18, *Die Zauberflöte;* 19, the same; 20, *Vogel von Falkenstein in Frankfurt;* 21 and 22, the same; 23, *Schinderhannes;* 25, the same; 26, *Kasper als Hieronymus Jobs der Zweite,* also *Ein Unteroffizier vom alten Fritz;* 27, the same; 28, *Das Maine Liquor-Law, oder Strenge Herren regieren nicht lange;* 30, *Die Bartholomäus-Nacht;* 1 April, the same; 2, *Der Granzwächter;* 3, the same; 4, *Herr Gickas und Frau Gackes;* 5, *Die Wette,* also *Der langbeinige Hannes;* 6, *Die Entführung aus dem Serail;* 8, *Kunerich von Drachenfels;* 9, *Der Eisenbarth;* 10, *Don Juan;* 11, *Der Ritter ohne Furcht und Tadel;* 12, *Dietrich von Schwabelinskie* (*sic: Schnabelinskie* before); 15, *Der Kalif Haroun al Raschid;* 20, *Der erste Mai in New York, oder Kasper und sein Landlord;* 23, *Der König von Dahomei;* 27, *Hanus* [sic] *von Storchenstein, der Stammvater des Hauses Hohenzollern;* 2 May, *Lumpaci Vagabundus der Zweite in Amerika;* 4, *Die Fahnen-schlacht, oder das Ende der Conföderation und des Kaiserthums.* The season was concluded at the National Assembly Rooms, 334-344 West 44 Street: 20 May, *Der Seeräuber von Tunis;* 22, *Die Ankunft in Amerika;* 23, the same; 24, *Ein alter Corporal;* 27, *Don Juan;* 28, *Die Wette, oder ein Mann mit zwei Weiber;* 30, *Die Schnupstabacksdose.* 1868 Rach played again at the Bowery Garten: 1–3 October, *Auch eine Schützen Gesellschaft;* 5–8, *Conföderation und Kaiserthum;* 9–10, *Der Seeräuber von Tunis;* 12–14, *Der Vetter aus Brasilien;* 15, *Der Pfalzgraf vom Rhein;* 19–21, *Das Sonntags-Gesetz in New York;* 22, 24, *Der Granzwächter;* 27, 28, *Der schwarze Gesandte, oder die Pantoffeln der Princessin;* 29, 31, *Die Verwickelungen;* 2–4 November, *Wette und Geldklemme;* 5–7, *Kunerich von Drachenfels;* 9–11, *Hansdampf in allen Cassen;* 13, *Don Juan;* 16, *König Wenzel von Böhmen;* 19, *Die Leichenräuber;* 24, 25, *Dr. Eisenbart;* 26, 28, *Die Zauberflöte;* 30, *Die Entführung aus dem Serail.* January 1869, Rach moved to Union Hall and presented *Der Fahnen-kampf;* on 7 March he had moved to Goring and Eckel's Harmonie Rooms and gave *Schinderhannes.* At the Bowery Garten in 1870 the following were presented: 4–5 January, *Der Eremit;* 6–7, *Dr. Eisenbart;* 8, *Die Entführung aus dem Serail;* 11, 12, *Der Werbezeit in Amerika;* 14, *Lange Hannas Geschichten.* 8 April, a Casperletheater, probably Rach's, played *Der erste Mai in New York* in East Houston Street. A summer run at the Dritte Avenue Theater was probably Rach's: 15, 16 June, *Hans Belhoin in New York, oder Dr. Eisenbart der Zweite;* 30, *New Yorker Nebelbilder, oder das Schnüffel Committee;* 4 July, *Die Zauberflöte;* 6, *Das Staats-Examen,* also *Landesschutz und Landesvermessung;* 18, *Don Juan.* In 1871, he moved from hall to hall, with headquarters at the Brooklyn Pavillon, 198-200 Court Street. The following performances were at this hall unless otherwise noted: 15 February, *Dr. Eisenbart;* 26, the same (at Concordia Rooms, Avenue A); 1 March, *Napoleon auf Wilhelmshöhe;* 5, *Schinderhannes* (at Concordia Rooms); 8, *Die Zauberflöte;* 15, *Hansdampf in allen Gassen;* 22, *König Theodorus von Abyssinien;* 30, *Wette und Geldflamme;* 8 April, *Don Juan,* also *Kasper als Leporello;* 13, *Bilder aus Amerika, oder der Reise von Syracuse;* 19, *Der schwarze Gesandte;* 26, *Dr. Eisenbart;* 7, 21 May, same (at Germania Assembly Rooms); 5 June, *Mit dem Teufel in kein Spatz zu machen;* 24, *Schinderhannes;* 25, the same (National Assembly Rooms); 30, the same (Brooklyn Pavillon). On 28 January 1872 Rach gave selections from *Die*

Räuber, Das Grab auf der Haide, Humoristische Studien, and *Dr. Eisenbart* for benefit of Gustav Holbein at Walhalla; 18 February, *Grossfürst Alexis* and *Das Loch im New Yorker Stadtsäckel* at Germania Assembly Rooms; at same place in March two performances of *Die Entführung;* 24 March, Harmony Hall, Essex Street; 14 April, *Die Zauberflöte,* Union Hall, Williamsburgh; later in April at Harmony Rooms in *Am Kreuz-Weg;* 1 May, *Der erste Mai in New York* at the Brooklyn Pavillon; perhaps played at D. Arnold's Mozart Halle, 134 Seventh Street, 5 May; on 8 May at the Pavillon with *Kunerich von Drachenfels;* 2 June, *Der Sonntags-Gesetz in New York.* Probably it was Rach who played 1 January 1873 at Paul Falk's Tivoli; in mid-January played *Bitzlibutzli* at the Bowery Garten; 16 March, *Schinderhannes* at National Assembly Rooms; 1 July at Terrace Garden, 198-202 Court Street Brooklyn, *Schulden und keine Hafen;* 24, *Der Seeräuber.* On 20 July, 1873, was working at Held's Hamilton Park; 27, played *Der Seeräuber* there. After this his name disappears, though it may have been his Casper which played in the National Hall on 8 April 1877.

RAG BAG ALLEY PUPPETS   See Dallas, Weaver and Kathryn.

RAINES, LESTER   Las Vegas, N. Mex. 1934, *The Miller and His Men, The Daughter of the Regiment,* both with Webb and Pollock paper puppets and toy theatre. 1936, *Don Quixote, The Silver Palace, Paul Clifford, Uncle Tom's Cabin,* with flat paper puppets. 1940, at University of Alabama, *Bremen Town Musicians* and *Rip Van Winkle,* with hand-puppets.

RAMÍREZ, GILBERTO   Mexico City. Director of the Teatro de Don Ferruco, which was founded, September 1943, by the Municipal Department of the Federal District of Mexico City. In its early days it specialized in civil defense and anti-fascist propaganda. 1944, one of its productions, *The Witch Goat,* by the Mexican poet Gomez, was witnessed by Gilbert Laurence who reported that the puppets were well made and the manipulation skilful. Several shows a week were given at the Teatro del Pueblo, with other shows in the schools. The programs were free, as they were part of the city's cultural activities for underprivileged neighborhoods. Two men and two women assisted Ramírez.

RANKIN, DOROTHY LOUISE   Little Theatre Marionettes, Peabody, Mass. Built a show to amuse children at daughter's birthday party, 1945. Next year produced *Review.* 1947, *Hansel and Gretel, Fantasy* (a variety show with a cast of 40 puppets), *Why the Chimes Rang.* 1948, further performances of above productions.

RANSOM, CHARLES and SACKETT, ERNEST   (P. 356). The Domino Marionettes, Massachusetts and other parts of New England. In the decade from 1924–1934, presented repertory of unusual plays. New productions were built each year, and old ones revived. 1924, *Julius Caesar* with hand-puppets. 1927, *The Grand Cham's Diamond* and *The Adventures of Cellador.* 1929, *The Student from Paradise* (after Hans Sachs), *Love and Sausages.* These plays were all produced at Tufts College, Mass. 1930, *Saved from Saucepans* (adapted from Bedollière's *La Mère Michel et son chat*) and revivals. 1931, *The King of the Black Isles,* with marionettes. Ransom, with the Pie-Powder Puppets, produced: *The Jewel and the Toad-Man, Catherine Parr, Xanthippe's Box, Upon My Word, The Old-Fashioned Dragon.* 1932, with the Domino Marionettes, presented: *Three Billy Goats Gruff, The Grand Duke's Candlestick, St. George and the Dragon, The Frogs* (after Aristophanes), *Popoff and Dropoff, Pan and the Charmer.* 1933, *Aladdin Lamps the Lamp, Aladdin* (nonmusical version), *The Fourth Day, an Astronomical Frolic* (at Harvard Observatory). 1934, *St. George and the Dragon.* Produced at camps with boys as puppeteers: *Pinocchio in America, Theft at the Bull Fight.*

RAPP, AUGUSTUS   (P. 230). Having been with a road show in Kansas which used a small set of 28-inch marionettes, in 1902 he made a set for his own magic and variety show, starting to use it at a small town near Toledo, O. His first puppets were carved of wood; later ones had heads of papier maché, which he learned to handle from association with Carl E. Akeley, African explorer and taxidermist. His puppet proscenium was painted to represent a circus tent, and he performed various tricks and circus numbers with 18-inch figures. Occasionally worked with Nicholas Nelson, 1920–1930. Still active 1940. Has performed *Punch and Judy* in his variety show, with which he played one-week stands in small towns, changing his bill nightly. 1948, made puppet heads for sale.—Letters from Rapp, 1939 and 1940. An account of *Punch and Judy* written by him appeared in *Linking Ring*, August 1945.

RATHSCKOFF (Pp. 126, 223). "Late of Paris," played in Davenport, Ia., 7 August 1858.

RAYM, MRS. MAX At Jan Hus House, New York, dramatized folk tales and incidents in Czech life which were played in Czech.

REBER, MRS. LLOYD Columbus, O. c. 1940, gave traditional Christmas show each year for her young daughter and a group of her friends.

RED GATE SHADOW PUPPETS. RED GATE PLAYERS See Benton, Pauline.

REDMOND London Marionettes. "Wooden figures are made to sing, dance, play musical instruments, etc., in fact, a perfect facsimile of a genuine minstrel performance," at the New Park Theatre, Brooklyn, 25–30 December 1876.—Brooklyn *Daily Eagle* for those dates.

REED, MARGARET, and McCARTER, FRANCES Crestline, O. 1947, an adaptation of *The Christmas Story* with hand-puppets. Amateurs at the outset of their puppet work.

REED, MEL (P. 285). Shadowgraphs, 14–19 December 1885, at the National Theatre, New York. (Odell, vol. 13, p. 89.)

REEMTSMA, MRS. H. J. A family group which produced plays in Oklahoma, Ohio, and New Mexico. 1933, *Happy House, Red Riding Hood, The Tiger, the Brahman and the Jackal*. 1934, revivals of previous shows, plus *Honorable Mother*. 1935, *The Tongue-Cut Sparrow, Peter Rabbit, Good Luck Beans, Epaminondas and His Mammy*. 1936, same repertory as preceding year. 1937, *Punch and Judy* and revivals.

REEVES, CHARLENE Grand Junction, Colo. 1938, *Jack and the Beanstalk* with high school students.

REGO, MARÍA DEL CARMEN SÁNCHEZ Buenos Aires, Argentina. Teacher of puppetry in the schools; author of *El Espiritu Creador del Niño y un teatro de títeres en la escuela primaria* (Libreria y Editorial "La Facultad," Buenos Aires, 1943), an account of her school theatre from 1939–1942.

REID, THEODATE N., and KENT, SARAH S. Rome, N. Y. 1923–1924, *Jack and the Beanstalk, Red Riding Hood, Snow White, The Miraculous Pitcher*. 1925, *Treasure Island*. 1928, *Two Slatterns and a King, The Birthday of the Infanta*. 1929, *The King's Breakfast*—repeated in 1930.

REICHARD, CATHERINE (Pp. 359, 360, 366, 373, 387, 391). New York. 1930, established a company, The Puppet Players, which had its own studio in 1931. Later had a puppet workshop in connection with her work in English at New York University. 1941 produced *The Second Sheperd's Play* from the Towneley Cycle. 1944, *Puppet Voters*, for the New York League of Women Voters.

REISDORF, HELEN E. (P. 248). Detroit, Mich. Puppeteer at intervals between 1922–1937 with Rachel Sewell, Paul McPharlin, and Elena Mitcoff. Bibliographer of puppetry, taught at libraries and Y.W.C.A., arranged puppet exhibitions at Hudson's store, disseminated general puppet information by telephone and letter, and collected antique and foreign puppets.

RELIC HOUSE MARIONETTES See Levin, Meyer.

RENÉE and CALVERT See Coolidge, Walt.

RETTIG, RICHARD Indianapolis, Ind. 1944, *Rip Van Winkle*.

RICE, DAN (Pp. 106, 112, 201). Engaged with a traveling puppet show near Reading, Pa., 1840.

RICE, MRS. P. E. With Mrs. E. E. Williams and Mrs. P. J. Leaper, presented *The Frog Prince* and variety at Naugatuck, Conn., 1929.

RICE, Professor (P. 188). "Wooden minstrels," Honolulu, 1874. Mind reading and marionettes, 20, 22 December 1875, Yesler's Hall, Seattle.—*Complete Bookings* at all Seattle Playhouses, by J. Willis Sayre, in Seattle Public Library.

RICE, VIRGINIA   Pall Mall Marionettes, Chicago and Midwest. 1934, *Pied Piper of Hamelin, Jack and the Beanstalk, Bilking's Collapsed*. 1936, *Peter Rabbit, Sleeping Beauty*, revivals of previous plays.

RICH, BRENDA KITTREDGE   The Puppet Studio, Port Washington, N. Y. 1935, *Winnie the Pooh*.

RICHARDSON, DOUG. C.   1938 had a puppet night club in Los Angeles, working the hand-puppet act alone. c. 1940 started with small marionettes in night clubs: featured Doogan, the drunk, in a character study of inebriation. Perry Dilley made him a group of 36-inch marionettes, including an Uncle Tom after Meader's famous puppet. 1947, Richardson toured Japan with the USO.

RICHARDSON, ESTHER   Joliet, Ill. 1932, *The Mikado*.

RICHARDSON, KENNETH   Mt. Lebanon, Pa. 1934, *The Story of Joseph*.

RINALDI   (Pp. 108, 123). 4–6 September 1843, "mechanical figures" at the American Museum, New York, 23–27 October 1843, marionettes at Peale's Museum. 25–30 December 1843, *Punch and Judy* at the same place.

RINGLING, AL.   c. 1885, marionettes in *Little Red Riding Hood* played in halls. c. 1887, *Babes in the Wood*, at which time Ringling was associated with one Brown— "Reminiscences of Harry Wintermute," *Puppetry 1937*, p. 24.

RIVADAVIA, COMODORO   Argentina. Director of the theatre, Títeres de la Velata in Patagonia, c. 1943.

RIVOLI, BENEDICT   Played *Uncle Tom's Cabin* with marionettes about 1867.—Helen Haiman Joseph, *A Book of Marionettes* (New York, 1920), p. 214.

ROBB, KATHRYN   A professor of English at Marygrove College, Detroit, began using puppets c. 1935 as an extra-curricular activity to dramatize the lives of the saints and present the teachings of the Catholic Church. Primary stress was laid upon good theatre and the special quality of puppets to present material objectively so that the plays may teach, move, and entertain.

ROBBINS, MRS. R. B.   Seattle, Wash. Having worked with young people for fifteen years in camps, Sunday school, and scout troops, began puppetry in 1946 when her daughter bought three Hazelle puppets. Books were read, a stage built, more puppets were discovered among the Girl Scouts (who did not know how to use them). Interest grew, and soon shows were being given for parties, children's homes, libraries, Scout troops. Productions include: *Mother Goose Guessing Game, A Valentine for Miss Muffet*, circus. With her Sunday school class Mrs. Robbins has presented *Why Be A Christian?* and *Jesus in Jerusalem*.

ROBERTO   c. 1940 played night clubs on the West Coast with Mexican characters made for him by Perry Dilley.

ROBINSON, M. LOUISE   Joseph Sears School, Kenilworth, Ill. 1930, *Cox and Box*.

RODBER, JOHN D.   RAF Depot, Moncton, N. B. 1942, while stationed in Canada, produced *St. George and the Dragon, Punch and Judy*.

RODGERS, G. W.   (P. 132). From London; played *Punch and Judy* at Colosseum, Philadelphia, in 1877. Also, on 29 November–26 December 1880 played Punch at the New Museum, Brooklyn.—Brooklyn *Daily Eagle*, those dates.

ROGERS and OWENS   (P. 285). Shadowgraph of *The Monitor and the Merrimac* at the Grand Street Museum, New York, 8–13 April 1889. Perhaps one of the partners was G. W. Rodgers.

ROSE, RUFUS   (Pp. 338, 353, 354, 355, 356, 361, 382, 385). Rufus Rose Marionettes, Waterford, Conn. At Antioch College, Yellow Springs, O., participated in his first marionette show, 1924. In 1928, joined Tony Sarg's company. 1931, married Margaret Skewis, who also had been puppeteering with Sarg, and formed their own company, first producing *Dick Whittington and His Cat*. Until 1942, the company toured the United States from coast to coast, with a new production each year as follows: 1932, *Hansel and Gretel*. 1933, played at the A & P Carnival, Century of Progress Exposition, Chicago. 1934–1935, *Ali Baba and the Forty Thieves*. 1935–1936, *Pinocchio, Scrooge, The Tinder Box, The Dutch Marionettes*. 1937, *Jerry Pulls the Strings*, a movie depicting the story of coffee made for the American

Can Company, which had thousands of showings throughout the country. 1937–1938, *Snow White and Three of the Seven Dwarfs* (by Martin Stevens), *Treasure Island,* and *The Tempest.* 1938–1939, revivals of previous shows. 1941, *The Mouse in Noah's Ark* (by Martin Stevens), *Rip Van Winkle.* The last countrywide tour, 15 September 1941–1 May 1942, covered 26,400 miles and 157 towns with 300 performances. From 1932 to date, 30 different variety acts have been developed and have formed a part of all the Rose programs. The winsome clown, Togo, has become a trade mark of the company. In 1942, construction began on a permanent theatre in Waterford, Conn., and it is now home, studio, and auditorium. The Roses were hosts to the Puppeteers of America, who held their annual festival in Waterford, 1946. Today the Rufus Rose Marionettes is a family organization, with two sons, James and Rufus, Jr., actively participating in all the shows. Performances are given in the studio-theatre, which draws patrons from a 50-mile radius. For out-of-town engagements, a one-man show, Rufus Rose and His Marionettes, is presented. *A Christmas Carol,* 1947–1948, was the first of a projected series of shows built especially for a permanent theatre.

ROSECRANS, CAROL (Mrs. Wood)   Detroit. 1930–1932, presented hand-puppet plays including: *Scarecrow, Why the Cow Jumped, A Pirate Story of Treasure, The Jolly Sign Posts, Genghis Khan, The Three Little Pigs, Weather,* and plays for the Detroit Dairy and Food Council. 1943, introduced a puppet theatre called Panamecos into Brazil. During 1944, this theatre traveled throughout the country, showing scenes of American home life and history. It also assisted in teaching health to Brazilian children. The tour was sponsored by the Department of Education of the State of Rio, which adopted a statewide plan for the use of puppetry in the schools.

ROSENHEIM, MR. and MRS. RICHARD   Milwaukee, Wis. Refugees who fled from Czechoslovakia and came to America in 1943. Mr. Rosenheim was formerly a theatrical producer in Germany, and a guest lecturer at the Masaryk Institute in Prague, from which he graduated. His wife designed stage settings, costumes, and puppets. Upon coming to Milwaukee she enrolled in English classes at Lapham Park social center. They built a small marionette theatre and presented a show as a token of thanks for help received at the center. The following year they played at hospitals for soldiers and children, at the center, and elsewhere.

ROSETE ARANDA, LEANDRO and three brothers   (Pp. 245–249, 250, 254). About 1860 operated puppets for Margaraje at Huamantla, Tlaxcala, Mexico. 1880, opened a season at the Teatro del Seminario, Mexico City. See Espinal, Carlos, for notes on a revival of this company name.

ROSS, BETTY   1916, with Ellen Van Volkenburg's Chicago Little Theatre Marionettes. 1919, *The Tents of the Arabs* (Dunsany). 1920, *But They Didn't.*

ROSS (ROSELLA), EDWARD   Learned operation and got set of puppets for Punch and Judy from a magician and showman, Spaff Hyman. In April 1897, gave his first Punch show at Pat Harris' Dime Museum, East Baltimore Street, Baltimore. In 1911, after an accident which prevented him from continuing as an acrobat, he devoted himself exclusively to Punch and Judy, playing at private parties in Washington before distinguished people, including Mrs. Nicholas Longworth and Mrs. Theodore Roosevelt, Jr. During the summers of 1913 and 1914 he played on Young's Million Dollar Pier, Atlantic City.—Katherine Scarborough, "He Has Pulled the Strings for 43 Years," Baltimore *Sun,* 3 March 1940, section 1, p. 2.

ROSTETTER, ALICE   Washington Irving High School, New York. 1927, *Ferdinand and Miranda* (from *The Tempest*). 1928, *The Queen's Dignity.* 1929, *St. George and the Dragon.*

ROWLSON MARIONETTES   Presented variety at the spring festival of the Puppet Guild of St. Louis, 1942.

ROY ELBERT MARIONETTES   See Patton, Roy.

RUSSELL, ERNEST   (Pp. 146, 149, 180, 260, 320). Amateur Punch and Judy man, flourished before 1908, playing in kindergartens, among other places. "The Most Popular Play in the World."—*Outing Magazine,* January 1908, p. 473.

RUSSELL, T. J.   El Paso, Tex. 1924, *Hazards of the Desert, Wonders of the Deep, The Enchanted Bowl, Aladdin's Lamp.* 1925, *Jack and the Beanstalk.*

RUST, MILDRED   Washington, D.C. During the 1930's was manager of a professional marionette company, and also assisted the Junior League with its productions.

RUTHENBURG, GRACE DORCAS   Louisville Children's Theatre. 1930, *Little Hannibal, The Moon for a Stocking* (G.D.R.), *The Cherry Blossom Tree.* 1931, *The Mad Hatter's Tea Party, Rumpelstiltskin, The Miracle of the Virgin of Guadaloupe* (G.D.R.). The last was presented in a theatre made from a garage. Also played in 1931: *Pinocchio Arise* (G.D.R.) and *The Elephant's Child.* Among the Ruthenburg publications are many puppet plays, of which the most famous is *The Gooseberry Mandarin,* and *How to Produce Puppet Plays* (with Sue Hastings) Harper & Brothers, New York, 1940.

RYAN, BILL   Used puppets in variety programs while in the Army, c. 1942. Worked, summer 1946, at Cain Park, Cleveland Heights, O., where his variety show was expanded and presented as *Uppity Puppets.*

RYAN, LILLIAN, and PELTON, DORIS   Wilmington, Del. 1943, presented *Hansel and Gretel, Little Black Sambo,* to entertain children at library.

SAAL, ALFRED, JR.   A young puppeteer who did variety in Toledo, O., and vicinity, 1947. Sometimes worked with his father.

SAAL, ALFRED P.   Toledo, O. A professional magician who worked shadows he got from Theo Bamberg, a Hollander, in 1913.

SABIN'S PERSONETTES   Wire-controlled marionettes in floor show with stock acts, played in Paterson, N. J., December 1944.

SACKETT, ERNEST   See Ransom, Charles.

SAGINAW MARIONETTE PLAYERS   See Zubler, Susan.

SAHLIN, DON   Stratford, Conn. A young puppeteer who began working with puppets c. 1942. 1945, produced *Hansel and Gretel.* 1948, puppeteer with Stevens' show, *This Funny World,* playing on school assembly programs.

ST. GERMAIN, TERESA   New London, Conn. Uses puppets in her teaching. 1946, presented *Jack and the Beanstalk* at the Puppetry Festival, Waterford, Conn.

ST. PAUL'S CHURCH   Philadelphia. 1938, *Advent at the Inn.*

SALICI MARIONETTES   (Pp. 283, 284). Enrico Salici is the third generation of a line of Italian puppet showmen. His grandfather began about 1845 in northern Italy. His father Ferdinando carried on the work, and so did his sons. Enrico attended Ferrara University, built eight stages and 48 marionettes. Then he went to Australia where he played in a waxworks museum in Melbourne. Returning to Italy he married Ada Feri. In 1934, the Salici Marionettes came to the United States after having toured around the world. The company consisted of Enrico and Ada; their sons Adolpho, Edgardo, and Gino; their daughter Benilde; and their granddaughters, Emma and Rina Ferrari. They played a 30-minute variety program for vaudeville and cinema houses, although their repertory included plays and operettas. With various changes in the company, but with little in the program, the Salicis are still playing. 1940, they were at the Golden Gate Exposition, San Francisco, where they performed on Treasure Island. 1945, three of the younger Salicis (the sixth generation) were doing a 12-minute routine consisting of a jazz band, can-can dancer, a hand-balancing team, two boisterous stage hands, an eccentric pianist, and a quartet. At the end, the masking drapery is lifted to show the operators at work.

SANDERS, DOROTHEA K.   Little Theatre, New Haven, Conn. 1928, *Rumpelstiltskin, Hansel and Gretel, Pipes and the Dryad, St. George and the Dragon.* 1929, *The Bad Little Lucky Girl, The Princess and the Elf,* variety.

SANDERSON, ANNE   New York. 1940, *Beauty and the Beast,* with marionettes. Studied with Tony Sarg.

SANDERSON, JOHN (Pp. 184, 199). Puppeteer who came to America in 1874, either with Bullock or with the Royal Oriental Marionettes. There were Sanderson Marionettes, perhaps his, remembered in 1928 by Mr. Carmody of RKO.

SANFORD, ALEXANDRA Produced shows in various branches of the New York Public Library as a variation from the library story hours. In 1936, ten or twelve of the branches made use of puppets in this way. Twelve different countries have been represented in characteristic puppet plays by story-tellers in different branches of the Library—Czech, Russian, Chinese, Italian, Hungarian, and so on.

SAN FRANCISCO RECREATION DEPARTMENT 1936, *Nutcracker Suite* presented with marionettes as part of the WPA Federal Music Project.

SAN LUIS OBISPO, CAL., HIGH SCHOOL PUPPET CLUB See Penny, Laura.

SANZ, C. MONEO Títeres del Triángulo, Buenos Aires, Argentina. With Gregorio Verdi and José J. Vaccaro, founded this theatre in 1942 and began puppet performances in April 1943. In December 1943 the Argentine Education League sponsored a puppet exhibit which Sanz and his associates set up in the National Postal Savings Bank. During his first year over 70 performances were given in Buenos Aires and other towns and cities, mostly sponsored by the League. Plays for both children and adults were given, some with themes drawn from legend and folklore, others adapted from the classics, native and foreign, with dances and musical interpretations for variety. In spite of a promising beginning, this theatre did not long survive.

SARG, TONY (Pp. 320, 322, 332, 333, 334–341, 342, 343, 347, 351, 352, 353, 354, 358, 379, 381, 384, 385, 387, 390, 391). (21 April 1880–7 March 1942.) New York. Began giving puppet shows in his studio in the Old Curiosity Shop, London, then came to New York and during the 1915–1916 season gave performances of *A Night in Delhi, The Singing Lesson,* and *Jack and the Beanstalk* in his studio in the Flatiron Building. 1917, *The Three Wishes,* from Pocci, *The Green Suit, The Stolen Beauty and the Great Jewel* by Hamilton Williamson. 1919–1920, *The Rose and the Ring,* after Thackeray by Hettie Louise Mick. 1921, *Rip Van Winkle,* after Boucicault by George Mitchell, *Olla Podrida.* 1922, *Don Quixote,* after Cervantes by Anne Stoddard. 1923, *Treasure Island,* after Stevenson, *The Rose and the Ring* revived. 1924, *The Chinese Willow Plate Story,* a translucent shadow play by Hamilton Williamson. 1925, *Treasure Island* revived, variety for the Bal Taborin, Hotel Sherman, Chicago. 1926–1927, *Ali Baba,* by Knowles Entriken. 1928, *Adventures of Christopher Columbus,* after Irving by Anne Stoddard. 1929–1930, *Rip Van Winkle* revived. 1930–1931, *Alice in Wonderland,* by A. C. M. Azoy. 1931–1932, revivals of *The Rose and the Ring* and *Rip Van Winkle.* 1932, *Sinbad the Sailor,* by Charles E. Searle. Summer 1933, Children's Theatre, Enchanted Island, A Century of Progress, Chicago, excerpt from *Alice in Wonderland* and variety for A. & P. Carnival; autumn, *Uncle Remus Stories.* 1934, *Faust, the Wicked Magician,* adapted from the old puppet play by Staz Azoy. 1935, *A Connecticut Yankee in King Arthur's Court,* by Staz Azoy. Summer 1936, repertory including *Alice In Wonderland, Connecticut Yankee, The Mikado* at the Texas Centennial, Dallas, variety at Palisades Amusement Park, N. J. 1936–1937, *The Mikado,* summer repertory in Globe Theatre, Great Lakes Exposition, Cleveland, autumn, *Robinson Crusoe.* 1938, *Treasure Island,* also episodes from earlier plays. 1939, *Robin Hood* and revival of *Treasure Island.* From 1940 until his death, Sarg gave many lectures and demonstrations (which he had also given at intervals earlier in his career), using trick figures such as Greedy Gus, formed by his fist. In his studio was a collection of puppets, including a set of Spanish marionettes, some of which were remade for his production of *Christopher Columbus.*

SAROFF MARIONETTES See Peek, Joseph.

SASSEVILLE (Pp. 84, 85). Proprietor of the Quebec puppet theatre until its end in 1837.

SAVASTA, ROSARIO (Pp. 298, 300). A puppeteer from Messina who performed *The Adventures of Rinaldo* for a benefit at Harvard College, 15 April 1909.

SAZONOVA, JULIA   Having produced puppet plays in St. Petersburg, Russia, in 1916, and in Paris in 1924–1926, touring Holland in 1925, she created a new puppet theatre at the Putney School in Vermont and gave performances during the winter of 1944.

SCAMMON, RICHARD   Jackson, Mich. 1929, variety. 1931, *The Adventures of Bobbie and Mary in Mother Goose Land, Hansel and Gretel*. Continued to make puppets and produce shows until 1936, when he became co-director of the Richmond Marionette Repertory Theatre. See Lutz, Caroline. While in service during World War II, he presented a Christmas shadow show with Frank Follmer in the Pacific area, 1943.

SCARLET, JOHN, MARIONETTES   See Vestal, Don.

SCHEFFEL, HERB   (P. 371). New York. See Glen Rock Puppeteers for work with that company. 1939, *Big Top Variety* with Barnumesque skit, *One Born Every Minute*, Rudolf Brothers Circus Headquarters, Newark, N. J., and *A String Tonic*, revue with marionettes and hand-puppets. 1940, *Chips Off the Old Block*, revue at Schrafft's 57th St. 1941, *Tomfoolery, The Small Timers*. 1942–1947, occasional performances of variety.

SCHEIER, MARY   University of New Hampshire. 1944, taught a puppet course for occupational therapy students.

SCHICHTL, CARL   (Pp. 98, 229, 281, 282). Played, together with his elder brother Hans, in vaudeville, 1910 and 1912. Married Lilly Keene in London c. 1916, and with her was still playing in 1937.

SCHIEDLER, JOHN   (P. 204). Punch and Judy man at the Ninth and Arch Street Museum, Philadelphia, in 1887.

SCHIMPFF, MARY FRANCES   Bloomington, Ill. 1940 to date, has been presenting marionette vaudeville acts.

SCHIRLE, JOHN   1944–1945, variety with USO shows in camps in the southern United States.

SCHMIDT   Showed transparencies at the American Museum, New York, 3–9 January 1837.

SCHMITTS, CHARLES and HAZEL   South Bend, Ind., Center Township School. 1942, *Rip Van Winkle*.

SCHOLA PICTORUM   Schola Theatre, Boston, Mass. 1939–1940, produced *French Vaudeville, King of the Golden River, Punch and Judy, Ten Girls to Marry, Love Will Find a Way, The Holy Night, Mother Goose Fantasy, Puss in Boots, Hansel and Gretel, Legend of the Bell.*

SCHURING, WILLIAM   New York. See Glen Rock Puppeteers for work with that company, 1933–1941. Summer 1941, worked with Marion Bishop's company on the Million Dollar Pier; later enlisted in Army. 1947, worked six months with Suzari Marionettes. 1948, organized own company, The Pied Piper Puppeteers, in Greenwich Village.

SCHWENTKER, MRS. O. H.   Rapid City, S. D. 1929, *The Adventures of Alice*.

SCHWIEGERLING, Professor P.   (P. 275). Marionettes variously known as Theatre Fantoches, Schwiegerling's Marionettes, and Fantoches Marionetten, in New York March–April 1888 and thereafter. (Odell, vol. 13, pp. 490, 536.)

SCIONTE, JOSEPH   (Pp. 301, 303). Traveling showman of Sicilian puppets, played in Cleveland in 1918.

SCOTT   (P. 275). Marionettes called "Table Humorists" in *Humpty Dumpty*, 5–10 February 1883, Brooklyn, N. Y. (Odell vol. 12, p. 180.)

SCOTT, WALTER G. and LE   The Scott Marionettes. Did a mechanical show at the City of Paris, San Francisco. Played in a movie theatre in Alameda c. 1933: in the foyer of the Golden Bough in Carmel-by-the-Sea one season. After Walter's death, the show was carried on by Le and their son Hilton; still active 1948. Repertory included *Goldilocks, Six Who Pass While the Lentils Boil, Aladdin, King Midas*, and *None Too Easy*.

SCRUTTON, MAUD E.   Petaluma, Cal. With hand-puppets presented shows, especially for domestic celebrations, written by herself. 1935, *The Revolt of the Elf.* 1936, *The Dream Maker, How the Puppet Saved the Dinner, The Woodland Rivals.* 1937, *Punch and His Shadow, Santa and the Salesman.* 1938, *In Sherwood Forest, Viva Brings Home the Bacon* (for Thanksgiving), *The Youth's Dream* and *The Magic Chest* (for Christmas). 1939, *The Rabbits' Quarrel* (for Easter), *The Three Wishes, Pensive Puppets.* 1940, *Paul Bunyan, Almost a Bullfighter.* 1941, *Death Wants His Job, Almost a Potboiler.* 1942, *The Rainbow, Punch and the Spy.*

SEEGER, PETER 1944, show at Camp Sibert.

SEIFERT, F. A. Daggett, Mich. 1935, Circus, *One-Eye, Two-Eye, and Three-Eye,* variety, *Oriental Sketch.*

SEIGFRED, EARL C. See Gray, Arthur D.

SELCH, GRANT W. Winfield, N. Y. 1937, *No Other Gods* (after Pearl Buck), Japanese Noh Play. 1938, *The Emperor's Nightingale.* 1942, *Macbeth, Baker's Dozen* (after Saki).

SELKIN, MARGARET Oklahoma City. 1944, *Circus is Coming to Town,* with child puppeteers.

SELLERS, SALLIE Cincinnati, O. 1937, *Hansel and Gretel, The Night Before Christmas.* 1938, *Christmas Show.* 1939, *Easter Parade Variety, Hansel and Gretel.* 1948, taught puppetry and stage design at Western College, Oxford, O.

SELLERS, THOMAS Ft. Wayne, Ind. 1938–1940, musical interpretations: *Danse Macabre* with marionettes and shadows, *Dance of the Hours, Gaieté Parisienne, La Valse,* three finger-puppet ballets presented at Ball State College, Muncie, Ind.

SEMON, ZERA As part of a gift show, had string-puppets about 1889.

SÉRAPHIN THEATRE (Pp. 63, 64, 65, 66, 100, 113, 114–115, 285, 310, 324). Played at Stuyvesant Institute, New York, 19 June–5 July 1865.

SERAPHINE, NICOLA (Pp. 139, 140). Punch and Judy in New York c. 1905, later opened a movie house on Third Avenue between 84 and 85 streets. In movie house at 49 Street and First Avenue he had the picture screen to the right, the Punch and Judy stage to the left.

SEVERAL MARIONETTES See Severance, Julia.

SEVERANCE, JULIA G., and ALLEN, PERMELIA The Several Marionettes. Oberlin, O. 1932, *Weather, The Dream Fairy of the Spider.* 1933, *Jack and the Beanstalk, The Fountain of Youth.* 1934, *The Straw Ox.* From 1933–1936, when all the equipment was destroyed by fire resulting from an auto accident, the Several* Marionettes played in Ohio, Florida, and points between. 1940, moved to California, but puppets were not rebuilt. Miss Allen died in 1946; Miss Severance resided in San Diego, 1948.

SEWALL, RACHEL (Pp. 338, 353). Worked with Tony Sarg, then Lilian Owen. Beginning 1923 with Puppets Intimes in Urbana, O., produced: *The Workhouse Ward* (Lady Gregory), two scenes from *Antigone* (Sophocles), balcony scene from *Romeo and Juliet, George Washington and the Cherry Tree, The Peasant and the Bear, The Bailiff's Daughter of Islington,* a ballad, and variety. Active till c. 1924.

SEXTON, MILDRED B., and RANDOLPH, HESTER S. O'Dell Marionettes, Macomb, Ill. 1934, performances in churches and schools of variety, *Alice's Adventures in Wonderland, Jack and the Beanstalk, Rip Van Winkle.*

SEYMOUR, KATHERINE 1943, *Punch and Judy* at Metropolitan Museum and clubs in New York.

SHANAFELT, MARJORIE Nebraska State Museum, Lincoln. 1936, *Little Black Sambo, Musicians of Bremen.* 1937, *Jack and the Beanstalk, The Gooseberry Mandarin, Community Chest Puppets,* variety, *One-Eye, Two-Eyes, and Three-Eyes.* 1938, *St. George and the Dragon, Hansel and Gretel, On With the Show.* 1939, *Stephen Foster's Music, Puppeteerishly Yours, The Fairy Wish.* 1940, *The Music Lesson, The Little Humpbacked Horse.* 1941, revivals of past productions. 1942, *Let Us Have Fun, Sleeping Beauty, Dick Whittington and His Cat.* 1942–1945, many talks, demonstrations, and shows at the Lincoln Air Base. For the USO during

1944–1945 gave five complete programs in rotation. 1947, *The Nightclubbers.* Originally inspired by a passing vaudeville act, Miss Shanafelt has regarded puppets as a creative activity, building them and writing for them as a painter paints pictures.

SHARON, ANN   Chester, Pa. Studied with Frank Paris, played floor-show act at Glass Hat, New York, 1943. 1944–1945, with USO show in Iran and other areas. 1946–1947, floor shows throughout United States. Sister of Catherine Westfield.

SHARP, JAMES H.   (Pp. 222, 231, 232–238). (Peter Hauntz, 29 March 1830–15 August 1908). Puppeteer and ventriloquist in rural Pennsylvania, 1865 to the time of his death.

SHAW, ALMA   Vagabond Puppeteers, Oklahoma Federal Theatre. 1938, *Beauty and the Beast,* variety; *Swing Low, Treasure Island, Joseph, Rumpelstiltskin.* Three companies played at this time, each with a play or two and variety numbers.

SHELDON, HARDY   Played *Punch and Judy* at Hooley's Opera House, Brooklyn, 14–19 July 1873.—Brooklyn *Daily Eagle,* 14 July 1873. Sheldon's Royal Marionettes at Allen's Dime Museum, Brooklyn, 20 December 1880–14 January 1881.—Brooklyn *Daily Eagle,* those dates. The January advertisements drop Sheldon's name.

SHELLEY, MISS   Peppy Puppeteers, Kitchener, Ont., Canada. 1941, director of a group of child puppeteers which paid for its stage equipment and raised funds for war charities through its performances.

SHEPARD, DICK   The Puppet Box Theatre, John Hay School, Seattle, Wash. 1934, *The Tin Wedding,* and *Yes, Tomorrow,* both plays by Esther Shepard.

SHEPARD, LUCILLE   John Adams Junior High School, Santa Monica, Cal. 1931, *Aladdin,* and *The Little Mermaid.*

SHIRLE, JOHN   1945, played with a USO unit.

SHIRLEY, MR. and MRS. JOHN   1947, presented a puppet show in the elementary schools of Minneapolis and St. Paul, Minn., under sponsorship of the Better Breakfasts movement.

SHIRLEY, LENNA LANDES   Burroughs School Marionette Theatre, Detroit. 1930, *Six Who Pass While the Lentils Boil.*

SHOW BOX, THE   See Adams, Barbara.

SHULL, MARGARET   Director, Barnsdall Junior Puppeteers, Barnsdall Center, Los Angeles. 1932, produced a series of plays based on fairy tales, *Uncle Tom's Cabin,* and *Weather.*

SIBER, MAX   La Salle, Ill. c. 1939, variety for organizations in the vicinity.

SILLAS, HARRY   1930, Karaghuez showman playing in Greek coffee house, Monroe Street, Detroit.

SILVER, MARY S., and COOPER, MARY F.   1932–1938, first in Omaha, then in Long Beach, Cal., played favorite children's stories such as *Pied Piper of Hamelin, The Tin Woodman, Rumpelstiltskin.*

SILVERS, MAURICE   (1841–1928.) Punch and Judy man with circuses in the United States; in and about Chicago, where he died.

SIMONIAN, ROY   Fresno, Cal. 1925, *Sleeping Beauty.* 1926, *The Three Wishes, Jack and the Beanstalk.* 1928, *Adventures of Pinocchio.* 1929, *The Gooseberry Mandarin.*

SIMPSON, CARL and FAITH   During 1940's played floor-show act throughout the United States.

SINGLETON   Punch and Judy man, late 19th century, mentioned by Ernest Russell, *Outing Magazine,* January 1908.

SIOUX CITY ART CENTRE   See Pasek, Cepha.

SIPHERD, CLARA   1931–1933, clown acts and circus revue, *Pirate and the Chest, Little Black Sambo, Mary and Her Lamb.* 1933–1934, as director of the Maycourt Club, London, Ont., produced *The Three Bears, Mickey Mouse Capers, Rumpelstiltskin, Clown Revue.*

SIX PUPPETEERS, THE   Community Playhouse, Ventura, Cal. 1932, *The Cow Next Door.*

SKARDA, ELSA Chicago puppeteer who did variety numbers, 1944.

SKEWIS, MARGARET See Rose, Rufus.

SKINNER, DOROTHY State Teachers College, Edinboro, Pa. 1931, *Puss in Boots.*

SLOAN, BLANDING (Pp. 359, 360). San Francisco. 1919, made papier-mâché puppets for Mrs. Fiske's production of *Jonathan Decides*; worked also with Michael Carmichael Carr and Remo Bufano. 1924, for City of Paris department store, San Francisco, built a series of six stages for Santa Claus fantasy. 1928–c. 1931, operated the Blanding Sloan Puppet Theatre, first in Polk Street, later in Montgomery Street. Worked with Ralph Chessé on *Emperor Jones* and *Hamlet*, with Enola Barker on *Ten Nights in a Barroom*, produced *Heavenly Discourse* (Erskine Scott Wood), did scenery and lights for Smith-Barclay production of *Anna Christie*, with R. Bruce Inverarity presented *Sky Girl.* During this same period had a studio in the Hollywood School for Girls at La Brea. 1931, at 53 Olvera Street, Los Angeles, played *Heavenly Discourse, Emperor Jones, Rastus Plays Pirate, Limpy Ad.* A short film, designed by Willy Pogany and B. S., was also made. 1933, worked on plans for a restaurant with puppets on Ivar Street, Hollywood, but the project did not materialize. 1935, state supervisor of a puppet project under the Federal Theatre Project, and worked on a production of *Genesis* after the Bible, with music and chorus, but it was not performed. 1946, with Wah Chang, formed the East-West Film Company to produce 16-millimeter three-dimensional animations in color and sound. 1947, completed *Ways of Peace*, a stop-motion puppet movie.

SLOAN, ISOBEL Regina, Sask., Canada. Summer 1942, taught a puppet class at Regina College, University of Saskatchewan; also a class of 45 children at Regina Civic Handicraft Center.

SMILEY, HELEN A. (Pp. 359, 384). Little Players, Philadelphia. 1927, *Sleeping Beauty*—out of this production grew the Little Players. 1928, *One Good Turn, Jimbo and His Dog.* 1939, *The Shoemaker and the Elves, The Nativity.* Had a handsome playhouse remodelled from an old carriage house at 1925 Delancey Place.

SMITH, CHARLES ELLIS and LYDIA SUTTON Toto's Marionettes, Pasadena, Cal. 1931, *The Night Before Christmas.* 1932, *With Peggy in Holland, The Enchanted Scarecrow, Frolic of the Freaks.* See also Smith, Lydia Sutton.

SMITH, C. RAY (P. 356). 1936, countrywide tour with *Tom Sawyer.* 1937, *The Pied Piper of Hamelin.* 1938, a floor show which toured the night clubs. 1939, a one-man show in South America. 1942, appeared with his "almost human dolls" with the Circo Continental at the Teatro Arbeu, Mexico City. See Bromley, Bob, for reference to his work at the Olvera Street Theatre.

SMITH, HEISEL Philadelphia, 1937, *She Stoops to Conquer.* 1938, *Peter Rabbit, All the King's Coats* (a musical comedy), *A Bed of Hay* (with rod-puppets).

SMITH, HENRY MORE (Pp. 94–96). While in prison at Kingston, New Brunswick in 1815, made a set of ten puppets from straw, dressed them in material torn from his own clothes, and gave performances with them. In 1817, again in jail in New Haven, he made another set of puppets, carving them from the timbers of his cell.

SMITH, HOWARD W., JR. c. 1928, *Sham, The Dyspeptic Ogre, Hard-Boiled Hampton*, Washington, D. C. 1929, with Barry Mulligan, Jr., produced *The Tinder Box, Beauty and the Beast, The Marionettes' Reunion*, variety, *So This Is Love.*

SMITH, LYDIA SUTTON (P. 374). Pasadena Players. 1934, *What A Night*, a marionette show in the Electric Building, Century of Progress Exposition, Chicago, and *All You Could Wish For*, in Home Planning Building. Each of these shows played nearly 6000 performances.

SMITH, MARTHA E. Vineyard Marionettes, Martha's Vineyard, Mass. 1936, *The Sheriff's Shoes, Peter, Peggy and the Prince, Christmas Carol, Night Before Christmas.* 1937, *Rip Van Winkle, Jack and the Beanstalk, Columbine's Birthday, Hansel and Gretel.*

SMITH, VERNON Recreation Department, Albany, Cal. 1935, *The Gay Nineties*; played at the San Diego exposition as the Theatre Guignol. 1936, directed a NYA group in Berkeley in *Red Riding Hood*.

SMYTH, ELEANORE M. St. Denis School, Merwood Park, Pa. 1936, *Hansel and Gretel*.

SMYTH, FELIX JOSEPH Philadelphia. 1922, was given a toy Punch and Judy outfit for Christmas, and magazine articles by Mathurin Dondo and Tony Sarg started his experiments with puppets. 1935, joined the marionette group of the Philadelphia Hobby League and taught puppetry there. Productions include: *The Tinder Box, The Three Wishes, Christmas Fantasy*, and variety. During the war used puppets for camp entertainment while in service.

SNYDER, DON The Marionette Workshop, Greensburg, Pa. 1935, *Master Pierre Patelin*.

SONGER, ERNESTINE Fort Worth, Tex. 1931, *Peter Rabbit, Alice in Wonderland, The Peppermint Boy, The Owl and the Pussy Cat* (after Lear, with music). 1931–1932, played a seven-month season of hand-puppet shows for children at the Fort Worth Little Theatre: *The Gooseberry Mandarin, A Gift for Mother, Hansel and Gretel, The King's Shirt, The Whiffinpoof Makes a Suggestion, When George Washington Was Young, Red Riding Hood, The Prince's Birthday Present, The Gingerbread Boy, Snow White and the Dwarfs, Through the Looking Glass*. In the autumn of 1932, went to Lawrence, Kan., to establish a puppet theatre, but after a few performances became ill and died 4 July 1933. Her last days were enlivened by a robin that battled with its reflection in a windowpane of her home in Kansas City, and so became a newspaper celebrity.

SONTAG, ART St. Louis, Mo. A young puppeteer who made puppets in school. Edited the Junior page of the Puppeteers of America *Grapevine Telegraph*, 1944.

SOUTH MILLS COLLEGE CLUB PUPPETEERS 1936, *Hansel and Gretel, Jack and the Beanstalk, The Three Wishes, Santa Sends a Scout*.

SOUTHERN ILLINOIS PUPPET CENTER See Follmer, Frank.

SPANN, MENO Northwestern University, Evanston, Ill. Became interested in puppetry through seeing shows in Germany, and Rufus Rose's performances in the United States. January 1941, produced *Dr. Faust* with hand-puppets and rod-puppets while at the University of Iowa. Since then continued to produce the play. After the war took up puppets again as a hobby and teaching device. 22 January 1948, gave a benefit performance to aid European students, the price of admission being a thirty-cent notebook. Other performances are planned to raise money for food packages to be sent to Europe.

SPARROW, HARRY (P. 286). Shadowgraphs at the Grand Museum, New York, 4–9 May 1891.

SPOERL, DOROTHY T. Played in Boston and New England towns. 1932, *Frankie and Johnnie, Cyrano de Bergerac, Abraham and Isaac*. 1933, *Peter Rabbit*. 1935, lecture on puppet history illustrated with short plays done with marionettes, hand-puppets, shadows. 1937, *Odin at Mirmir's Well*, and Act I, scene 3, from *Die Walküre*. These plays were acted with 12-inch marionettes.

SPOLIDORO, ASCANIO (Pp. 342, 369). New York. During 1920's worked with Remo Bufano and afterwards with other puppet companies. c. 1944, active with the New York WPA Puppet Project. 1946–1948, built and presented shows for the City Park Department, playing in recreation centers and parks.

SPOONER, WILLIAM River Forest, Ill. 1927, *The Three Wishes*, variety. 1928, *The Comical Tragedy of Dr. Faust*, variety.

SQUIRES, RUTH 1929, *Snow White and the Seven Dwarfs, Frankie and Johnny*. 1930, *The Elves and the Shoemaker, Hansel and Gretel*.

STAHL, GRACE New York. Used puppets while a teacher in the city schools. 1939, directed *Flight*, a shadow play presented at the Puppetry Festival by the Puppet Guild of Haaren High School Aviation Annex. 1944, professional engagements in the city with the San Souci Marionettes: *Peter and the Wolf, Manhattan Echoes*.

STATE HOSPITAL   Norfolk, Neb. 1938, *De Courtin' Couple*, presented by the occupational therapy department.

STEINMETZ, LEE   1934, *The Frog Prince* in Pleasant Ridge, O. *Epaminondas* in Kennedy Heights, O., *Why the Chimes Rang.*

STELLAR MARIONETTES   See Friedman, Sidney.

STEPHENS   Punch and Judy man, late 19th century, mentioned by Ernest Russell, *Outing Magazine*, January 1908.

STEVENS, MARTIN and OLGA   (Pp. 355, 356, 361, 387). Middlebury, Ind. Stevens says of their beginnings with puppets, "Piccoli inspired us, Sylvia Meredith encouraged us, and hunger compelled us." First show 19 September 1934, Cincinnati, O.—variety, including *The Big Good Wolf*, balcony scene from *Romeo and Juliet*, *Schnozzle and Zasu; The Haunted Castle*. 1935, built *The Passion Play* and *The Nativity*, both of which are still being played annually. In that year also continued performances of variety, built *Knowing Your Onions* for the Community Chest, and *Alice and Humpty Dumpty, The Photograph Gallery, The Revenge of Truth*. 1936, worked with Rufus Rose on tour with *Snow White* and *Treasure Island* (both scripts by Martin Stevens). 1937, *Joan of Arc* (by Clem D. Easly). 1938–1939, countrywide tours with *Joan*, the *Passion*, and *Nativity*. 1940, built studio-home-theatre (named The Mousetrap) at Middlebury, Ind. Same year, built and performed *Cleopatra*. During the war, gave a few performances at The Mousetrap, notably a summer season in 1942. In 1946, for the Coöperative League of America, produced *The Goolibah Tree*, adapted from the book by Joe Gunterman and Bill Darr, with hand-puppets designed after Darr's illustrations and a special unmasked stage with several playing levels. This production was taken on a Midwestern and California tour. A string-puppet variety show, *This Funny World*, was built the same year and sent out for school assembly programs under the management of Dick Myers. 1947, *The Taming of the Shrew*, with hand-puppets in a specially modified version by M.S., and *Macbeth*. For the latter, an all-aluminum unmasked stage was built; the principal characters were made as rod-puppets, the apparitions as colored plastic shadows, designed and executed by Marjorie Batchelder. A sound-color film of *The Goolibah Tree* was made. Stevens has written puppet scripts for Rufus Rose, Ray Newton, Cherry Jerry, Marjorie Batchelder, Blanche and Roland Harding, and in 1948 was writing a show for a peace organization. With the exception of some of their early shows and *This Funny World*, the Stevens' work has been with puppet drama for adult audiences; they are among the few who have devoted their major efforts to this end.

STEWART, DORIS and WOLL, NAOMI   The Madcap Marionettes, Reno, Nev., and Birmingham, Mich. 1932, *The Sorcerer's Apprentice, The Lady and the Lawyer, The Three Wishes, Why Boy Blue Was Blue.*

STILL, FRANC   (Pp. 356, 366). Cleveland, O. c. 1933, built a marionette circus with which he has toured in the United States for many years. In 1934, *Miss Minerva and William Green Hill*; at Christmas played his circus at the White House. 1941, *The Magic Nutcracker, A Night in a Club*. 1944–1945, toured again with the circus.

STOLP, JAMES   Canterbury Marionettes, Kenosha, Wis. 1936, *Hansel and Gretel*. 1937, *Rip Van Winkle*. 1938, *The Wishing Well.*

STONE, DON and WIFE   Worked with Bob Hestwood at Monico's, San Francisco, c. 1942, and later played night clubs and vaudeville circuits.

STOUT, MARY FRANCES   The Hurdy Gurdy Marionettes, Los Angeles. c. 1930, variety, *Red Riding Hood, The Pied Piper, Alice in Wonderland, The Elephant's Child.*

STRING PULLER'S PLAYHOUSE   First Congregational Church, Madison, Wis. 1933–1934, *Jack and the Beanstalk*, with 10-inch marionettes.

STROLLING PUPPET PLAYERS   See Vrooman, Elizabeth.

STROUT, MRS. ALAN   Lubbock, Tex. 1941 to date, has presented Christmas shows for a department store, for churches and schools, and for private parties. Uses various types of puppets.

STURY, ALFRED   Chicago, Ill. 1925, *Sleeping Beauty, The Legend of the Evening Star*. 1926, *Hansel and Gretel, Snow White and the Seven Dwarfs, Puss in Boots* (with marionettes by Nicholas Nelson), *The Tragedy of Dr. Faust, The Legend of Hallowe'en*. 1927, *The Tragedy of Punchinello, Rumpelstiltskin, Ali Baba and the Forty Thieves*. 1928, *Cinderella, The Birthday of the Infanta, And A Little Child Shall Lead Them*.

SUHRS, SUSAN H.   Hanswurst's Marionettes, Quincy, Ill. 1931, *The Wizard of Oz, Sleeping Beauty, The Magic Ring*.

SUIB, LEONARD W.   Yonkers, N. Y. Put on shows in high school and made small marionettes for stage models while studying stage design at Pratt Institute. Had a home puppet playhouse. 1934, *The Princess and the Goblins*. 1936, *Babes In Toyland*. 1937, *The Silver Web*. 1938, *Gnome Gnobodies*. 1939, *The Great American Circus*. 1941, *Our American Heritage*. 1942, toured New York and New Jersey with *America—Land of Democracy*, selling war bonds. 1945, *David and Goliath*. 1946, *Goblin Christmas*. In 1947, *Hansel and Gretel* was given by Suib with his wife Arlene. 1948, *Peer Gynt and the Trolls*.

SUNDERLAND, ETHEL   Her company was founded in 1930, played in and around Winnipeg, Canada, and by 1938 had 60 marionettes and a repertory of 10 plays.

SUTCH, MARION ADAMS   Oliver Marionettes, Oliver High School, Pittsburgh, Pa. 1928, *Snow White and the Dwarfs*. 1929, *The Little Lame Prince*. 1930, *The Wanderings of Aeneas*. 1933, *The Moor's Legacy*.

SUTHERLAND, ALLENE and FRANCILDA   Salt Lake City, Utah. 1932, *The Day Before Christmas, The Fatal Circus*. 1933, *Crossbones Buried Treasure, The Fatal Circus*. 1935, *Fairyland, The Magic Key*.

SUZARI MARIONETTES   See Zaconick, Dorothy.

SWANSON, HAZEL S., and PAPEZ, MRS. JAMES W.   Cayuga Heights School, Ithaca, N. Y. 1936, *Snow White*.

SWEENEY, JACOB   High School, Florence, Ariz. 1935, *Red Riding Hood*, variety.

SWEIGERLING   Came from Europe, played in vaudeville, early 20th century.

SWINEFORD, MERLE (Mrs. Paul Dilley)   Columbus, O. Taught puppet class of 300 children ranging in age from 6 to 18 years at Chautauqua, N. Y., c. 1940.

SYMPSON, MARTHE   Played in various cities, New York to San Francisco. 1923, *Aladdin and the Lamp*. 1924, *The Sea Child*. 1926, *Beauty and the Beast*. 1927, a group of French songs and *Bab Ballads*. 1928, went to Hawaii, playing in Maui and Honolulu: *Kafoozlum, Cinderella, Sleeping Beauty, Little Black Sambo, The Christmas Truants, 'Twas the Night Before Christmas, The Silly Jelly Fish* (after a Japanese fairy tale), *Tittymouse and Tattymouse, Captain Bing the Pirate King, Moneybags the Miser* (from the French), *Rumpelstiltskin*.

TANGLESTRING MARIONETTES   See Hollis, R. W.

TATTERMAN MARIONETTES   (Pp. 354, 366, 373, 374, 385, 387, 391). William Duncan and Edward Mabley organized this company in Detroit in 1922 as an outgrowth of their interest in the theatre during their high school days. In 1923 *The King of the Golden River* was produced. 1924, *Androcles and the Lion, The Melon Thief, The Three Wishes*, Circus, variety, all with marionettes. With shadows: *The Three Billy Goats Gruff, Puss in Boots*. 1925, *The Fisherman and the Genii, The King of the Golden River, Hey Diddle Diddle* (a Mother Goose Fantasy). At this time for about four years, the Tatterman plays were written by Catherine Reighard. 1926, *Jack and the Beanstalk, Master Pierre Patelin*. 1927, *Rumpelstiltskin, Picaninny Dancers*, variety. 1928, *The King of the Golden River* and *The Marriage Proposal*, both with hand-puppets, and later in the season with string-puppets, *Aladdin and the Wonderful Lamp*. 1929, over 250 performances of *Pan Pipes and Donkey's Ears*, and revivals of seven former plays. In 1930 a studio was opened in Cleveland, Ohio, which remained headquarters until 1938. 1930 productions: *The*

Glowing Bird (this and many subsequent plays were written by Mabley), *Stringing Broadway*, a puppet revue with music by George Cottle. 1931, *The Legend of Lightning, Something for a Song*, and revivals of both 1930 productions. 1932, two new versions of *Stringing Broadway*, new script by Mabley for *The King of the Golden River*. Summer 1933, *The Wife Wins*, a motion picture made for the Kroger Food Foundation. 1933 road shows: *Dick Whittington, Toyland Follies*, and revivals. 1934, tours with the usual repertory. Built *From Cave to Kelvinator* (later titled *The World on a String*) which played nearly 1300 performances in a special theatre at the Century of Progress Exposition, Chicago, 1934. During the 1934–1935 season *Aladdin, Dick Whittington*, and *The Glowing Bird* were sent on tour. Besides *The World on a String*, which chalked up nearly 1500 performances in its countrywide tour, other commercials were produced: *Summer Sports Fashion Show, The Glo-Coat Marionette Show*, the *Jantzen Diving Girl*, an aluminum marionette which performed in a tank of water in store windows. Three units of this act were sent out, and a total of 2460 performances was given. From 1936, the commercial enterprises of the company were handled under the name of Duncan-Mabley, Inc., while the theatrical productions continued as The Tatterman Marionettes. In the former were: continued performances of the Glo-Coat show, *Santa Claus Workshop, Fibber McGee and Molly, Jantzen Diving Girl, Jantzen Style Revue* (two units), *Formfit Marionette Style Revue*, four units which played a total of more than 8000 performances, *Firestone Puts the Farm on Rubber*, over 2000 performances at the Great Lakes Exposition, Cleveland, O. While the Kelvinator show had 30 marionettes and many scenes, most of these commercial shows were done by one operator with just a few characters. Theatrical productions in 1936 included revivals, *Pi-Pa-Ki, or The Song of the Lute* (adapted from a Chinese play translated by Mrs. C. H. Prescott), *The Taming of the Shrew, Jason and the Golden Fleece* (two units, known at the Wesleyan and the Globe, were sent out). 1937, an elaborate production of *Peer Gynt*, designed by Terence Von Duren, with puppets made by Roy and Harry Patton and Carl Saleske (Ryan), was built and sent on a brief tour. With a stage large enough for human actors, a double bridge of tubular steel capable of supporting eight operators, 44 marionettes, and 11 scenes, this was the most ambitious puppet production in the annals of American puppetry. 1938, three previous plays were revived, and *She Stoops to Conquer* built. 1938–1939, *Ferdinand*, done with rod-puppets for a store window at Higbee's, Cleveland, and later shown in Boston and Detroit. 1938, the Tatterman studio was moved to Suffern, N. Y., and a group of commercials built for the 1939 New York World's Fair: *Writer's Cramp* for the A. B. Dick Company, *Cavalcade of Chemistry* for DuPont, *Mrs. Cinderella* for General Electric, *Bus Bondage* (with hand- and rod-puppets) for Willys-Overland. *The Wizard of Oz* was also built. 1940, a show for General Electric at the New York World's Fair. In 1941, the Duncan-Mabley company was disbanded; Mabley remained in New York, and Duncan moved to Oxford, O., where he became director of the Leonard Theatre at Western College. With his wife Ruth, he gives some puppet shows, adapted from the large repertory of the Tatterman Marionettes. 1 Nov. 1947, *The Glowing Bird* had its 1200th performance and the Tatterman Marionettes their 25th anniversary. 1948, *The Magic Water*, a sequel to *The Glowing Bird*.

TÄUBER, HARRY Vancouver, Canada. 1932, *The Witch Doctor, Petroushka* (with Stravinsky music).

TAYLOR, AZELLA Oakland, Cal. Studied puppetry at the University of Washington. In 1940, under the name of the Washington Puppeteers, with Miss Manhenberg as partner, sailed to Hawaii and played *Hansel and Gretel* (with additions) to schools and clubs.

TAYLOR, Professor E. C. (Pp. 196, 274). Marionettes, together with a magic and aerial suspension act at Yesler's Hall, Seattle, Wash., 9–10 April 1876. Royal Italian Marionettes at Forrester's Opera House, Denver, 1878.

TEFFT, AL   Springfield, Ill. 1940, *Bertha the Sewing Machine Girl* and variety, for schools, churches, and clubs in the vicinity.

TELEGRAPH HILL MARIONETTE PLAYERS   See Van Orden, Edith.

TERRANOVA, BASTIAN and CAROLINA   Sicilian puppeteers who emigrated to São Paolo, Brazil, 1898, where they started a puppet theatre in the Bratz quarter. In 1910, moved to Buenos Aires where they were still playing in 1941. When the Plata river overflowed and caused the Terranovas considerable loss, a benefit performance was given for them, 10 March 1941, by Javier Villafañe and Alfredo Hermitte.

TERRY, RALPH   (P. 285). An actor who used shadowgraphs at Tony Pastor's, New York, 31 January–5 February 1887; 26 September–1 October 1887 at F. F. Proctor's (Novelty) Theatre. (Odell, vol. 13, pp. 311, 588.)

TESCHAU, WALTER E.   Shorewood High School, Milwaukee, Wis. 1930, *The Ancient Mariner, A Visit from Caesar.*

THOMPSON, STANLEY   High School, Renton, Wash. 1934, *The Clown Circus.* 1935, *Parade of Nations.*

THORNTON, GENE   Atlanta, Ga. 1937, *Cinderella, The Witches' Box of Magic.*

THURSTON, HELENE   (Mrs. Mason)   Chicago, Ill. 1934, variety. 1936, *Major Bowes' Amateur Hour.* 1937, *Marionette Minstrel Show, Too Much Candy, Three Billy Goats Gruff.* 1938, *Canadian Legion Review.* In 1942 and thereafter till c. 1946, toured with a floor-show act.

TILL, JOHN and LOUISA (SANDERSON)   (Pp. 184, 190, 191, 199, 200, 262–264, 275). Came to America in 1874 with Bullock or the Royal Oriental Marionettes. They played a "reengagement" at Smith's Island summer resort, Philadelphia, in 1875, and were active in variety theatres, 1878–1891, principally in Brooklyn and New York. Odell lists many of their engagements from October 1882 to March 1891 in Vols. 12–14 of his *Annals.*

TILLSTROM, BURR   (P. 379). Chicago, Ill. In 1936 made a portrait puppet of Tamara Toumanova for *Balletomania,* a dance by Nathan Krevitsky in which the portrait of Tamara comes to life. 1937, began work with finger-puppets. With Frank Follmer and Lucile Fink, formed The Chicago Puppet Players and produced *The Prince and the Maiden, a Fantasy in Pantomime,* with finger-puppets, which was performed at the Marshall Field Puppet Exhibit in October. The same year, played *Kukla, Gus, and Oscar* with hand-puppets at the Wisconsin State Fair, West Allis. In 1941, began performances in the toy department of Marshall Field's, which developed into a permanent marionette theatre for children's entertainment. By 1946 there had been 146 shows and 1000 performances. In addition, 400 performances with hand-puppets for commercial display and promotional purposes were given. From 1943 on, Tillstrom played regularly at the Great Lakes Naval Station Hospital, featuring Kukla. As Kukla the Patriotic Puppet this favorite character was active during the war selling war bonds. October 1947, began a daily television show, the *RCA Junior Jamboree,* over station WBKB, Chicago, with Kukla as emcee. Tillstrom's shows for children at Field's were built around toy puppets stocked in the toy department, such as Virginia Austin's Clippo, with other characters built as needed. His most characteristic work was with hand-puppets, which he handled with great dramatic sensitivity.

TIRRELL, AUDREY NORDIN   Petaluma, Cal., Junior High School. 1932, *Hope,* a Christmas play. 1935, *Musical Variety.*

TÍTERES DE LOS SIETE   Argentina. A group of young painters who formed a puppet group, c. 1942, which traveled in the interior of the country, often playing at art show openings.

TITUS, FRANK, and KNIGHT, FANNY   Shadowgraphs at Tony Pastor's Theatre, New York, 31 March–5 April 1884. (Odell vol. 12, p. 304.)

TOBEREN, CHARLES   University of Kansas. Class in high school art methods presented John Ise's *Sod and Stubble,* 1938. 1939, *Peter Pan.*

TOBIE, CHARLOTTE Greenwich, Conn. c. 1942, created the Rainbow Theatre for rod-puppets in her home and produced *George Washington, Nightmare Near the Delaware, or Cap't Tobie's Dream.*

TOTO'S MARIONETTES See Smith, Charles Ellis.

TRAPPAN, RUTH Orange, N. J. In summer of 1933, opened The Puppet Barn at Campgaw, N. J., as a theatre and workship. Played there two summers: *The Butterfly That Stamped,* variety, *Rapunzel, The Tar Baby, A Bit of Shavianimation, Juke's Jungle, La Influenza.* In the following winters played in the metropolitan area. In summers, 1935–1938, in hotels and camps in Pennsylvania and New England. 1935, *Millions of Cats* (after Wanda Gag), *The Sophomore Symphony,* and *A Medieval Triptych* were presented. 1936, *Mary and the Lamb Seek Justice.* 1937, *Step-Mother Goose, Waiting for the Boat,* variety. Directed school shows for 14 years. 1948, supervised art and encouraged school puppetry of all types from kindergarten through high school.

TREE, ROSE New Hope, Pa. 1947, *Peter Rabbit, Mother Goose, Sleeping Beauty,* with marionettes.

TRENT, TOMMY 1942, played floor-show act in vaudeville. 1943–1944, with hand-puppets played the Blue Circuit of the USO. 1946 to date, on tour coast to coast.

TRESSEL, GEORGE and MARY ANN Chicago, Ill. 1946–1947, *The Mystery of Missin' Gulch,* with marionettes and hand-puppets, *Fiends in Need, A Christmas Carol.*

TRIGGS, DUDLEY Uncle Sam Puppeteers, School, Pasadena, Cal. 1934, *The First 400 Years,* with 45 marionettes, 18 inches high.

TRUE, VIRGINIA University of Colorado, Boulder. 1935, *Jack and the Beanstalk, Hansel and Gretel, An Oriental Sketch.*

TRUJILLO, ESTELITA A member of the Women's Auxiliary Corps who gave many puppet performances in the United States and overseas during World War II.

TRUSDELL, RICHARD V., JR. (P. 378). Evanston, Ill. c. 1927, *Gareth and Lynette, Ivanhoe, Androcles and the Lion, The Birthday of the Infanta.* 1929, *Lima Beans,* variety. 1930, *Hansel and Gretel,* variety at Television studio WGXF, Chicago *Daily News.*

TSOULEAS, HARRY (P. 290–291). Greek shadow-figure showman in Detroit c. 1930 and possibly earlier.

TULANE UNIVERSITY 1939, *Maya Indian Legend.*

TWORKOV, JACK (P. 342). 1923, worked with Remo Bufano. c. 1925, Mojacot Spiel Yiddish Marionette Theatre, New York: *What Ails You?* and other secular pieces; *King Ahasuerus* and other Biblical pieces.

TYSON, J. H. Punch showman, early 20th century.

UNCLE SAM PUPPETEERS See Triggs, Dudley.

UNIVERSITY OF RICHMOND, VA., MARIONETTE REPERTORY THEATRE See Lutz, Caroline.

UNIVERSITY OF WASHINGTON PUPPETEERS Seattle. The Puppetry Department was organized 1934 by Glenn Hughes, director of the School of Drama, aided by R. Bruce Inverarity, who directed the puppet shows. Audiences were created through Parent Teacher associations. Teachers were helped in puppet production, puppet clubs througout the state were formed, and puppets were used in speech clinic work. As far as possible, students wrote the scripts, constructed the sets and characters, and composed special music. Productions included: *Cinderella, Robinson Crusoe, Captain Catfish Pete,* variety (Inverarity, director). 1937, *Aladdin, The Sleeping Beauty, Peter Rabbit, We Dine at the Colonel's* by Maurice Sand (Irene Phillips, director). 1939–1940, under direction of Alanson Davis, developed program of two hand-puppet and one or two marionette shows per year, presented in schools and clubs, with an average of three performances per week: *Hansel and Gretel, Pinocchio.* 1941–1942, 86 performances given to audiences totalling over 15,000. 1942, Catherine Mills directed while Davis was in the Army. Productions 1941–1943 included: *The Princess and the Goblins, Beauty and the*

Beast, Aladdin, Rumpelstiltskin, Pinocchio, Alice in Wonderland, Robin Hood, Ali Baba, Rip Van Winkle, Jack and the Beanstalk, The Snow Queen.

UPSON, VIRGINIA (Mrs. Houghtelling) (P. 392). Minneapolis, Minn. 1930, *Pinocchio.* 1931, *Rip Van Winkle, Red Riding Hood.* 1935, *The Nose,* Christmas program in Power's store window, Minneapolis. 1936, *Bricklebrit* and *The Water Babies* played in schools. 1940, *The Rose and the Ring,* and Travelwise window display. 1940, Style review of period and modern bridal costumes, *Dame Wiggins of Lee and Her Seven Marvelous Cats,* and Car-loan show for window display. 1941–1942, *Sonny Elephant, Paul Bunyan and the Giant Cornstalk* and *Poison Turnips.* 1943, *Paul Bunyan and his Big Blue Ox.*

UTLEY BRANCH PUBLIC LIBRARY PUPPET WORKSHOP   See Berdan, George.

VAGABOND PUPPETEERS   See Shaw, Alma.

VALDIVIESO, NŌ (P. 255–256). String-puppet showman in Lima, Peru, c. 1880–1900.

VALENCIN, Señor (P. 101). Showed fantoccini and a diorama at the New York Museum, 1830.

VANDERGOULD, CHARLES W.   See Albright, Charles W.

VANECK, FLORENCE M.   St. Louis, Mo. 1934–1935, over 350 performances of *Mother Goose's Surprise Party,* with hand-puppets and rod-puppets.

VAN ORDEN, EDITH   Telegraph Hill Marionette Players, San Francisco. 1932, *The Silver Thread* (Constance D'Arcy MacKay). 1933, *Heart of Oak* (Rose Netzborg Kerr). 1935, *The Moon for a Prince.*

VAN TINE, MARGARET   Rock Island, Ill. 1940, *Punch and Judy* and *Little Ghost* with hand-puppets.

VAN VOLKENBURG, ELLEN (Pp. 331–334, 336, 338, 347, 359). At the Chicago Little Theatre, 1915, produced *The Deluded Dragon.* Other experimental plays, such as *Columbine* and *Jack and the Beanstalk,* followed. In 1916, *A Midsummer Night's Dream* was presented, and marked a new era in artistic puppetry. 1917, *The Frog Prince, Little Red Riding Hood, Alice in Wonderland.* 1919, staged *The Rose and the Ring* for Tony Sarg. 1924, revived *A Midsummer Night's Dream* in California, with new figures by Perry Dilley. Later worked at the Cornish School, Seattle, Wash. producing *Peter Rabbit.* The second *Dream* production was revived in London, 1929.

VAN WINKLE MARIONETTES   Grand Prairie, Tex. c. 1945, played in schools of the area.

VAREY, J. E.   Moncton, N. B., Canada. A member of the Glyn Puppets, Blackburn, England, worked with Miles Lee and John Rodber on puppet shows while stationed at the R.A.F. Depot, c. 1942.

VAVRINECK, ELAINE   Des Plaines, Ill. Since 1939, has gven occasional shows with string-puppets while in school and college. After graduation, June 1948, planned puppetry as an avocation.

VERNENGO, MARISA SERRANO   Director of the puppet theatre Ki Ki Ri Ki, Buenos Aires, Argentina.

VER VALIN   *Punch and Judy* and marionettes, early 20th century.

VESTAL, DON (P. 387). In Pasadena had a company called the John Scarlet Marionettes, 1933–1934, which played: *Rancho, The Back Page, King of the Golden River.* In the Children's Theatre at Marshall Field's, Chicago, played *The Near-Sighted Hippogriff,* 1934. 1936, with the Chicago Park District Marionettes, produced: *Hansel and Gretel, Pirates, Scenes from Shakespeare, Further Adventures of Goldilocks, WPA Burlesque, McSnozzle at the Beach, Your Guess Is as Good as Mine, Every Cat Has Its Day, Punch and Judy, Three Moods of Chopin, Chicago Park Revue* (with finger-puppets, hand-puppets, marionettes). At the first American Puppetry Conference, Detroit, 1936, presented premiere of *Identity,* written for his puppets by Gertrude Stein, with special music by Owen Haynes.

VILLAFAÑE, JAVIER (Pp. 350, 351, 366). Buenos Aires, Argentina. In 1935, with the poet Juan Pedro Ramos, made a tour in a horse-drawn cart with his theatre, La Andariega. They played hand-puppet scenes, dances, songs for school children. This was followed by other tours. Aided by Mauricio Lasansky and others, he set up a string-puppet theatre, called El Gallo Pinto, in the Zoological Garden of Buenos Aires. c. 1940, traveled widely in Uruguay, where he played in 48 schools to 10,000 children. 1941, as similar tour to Paraguay. 1943, organized an international exposition of puppets in the Theatre Museum, Buenos Aires. Twenty theatres were represented. Under Villafañe's direction, a series of classes in puppetry for teachers was held, in which over 1200 received instruction. Special programs for children were given by eight companies. Not only did Villafañe give shows to the children, but he taught them how to make puppets and present their own shows; as a result, there were in 1944 about 500 puppet theatres in Argentina conducted by children in the schools. In the summer of 1944, Villafañe gave a course in puppet making at the University of Chile, then toured in the interior of the country. In order to encourage creative expression, he encouraged children to paint or draw their impressions after a puppet show. From the thousands of sketches which they made, Villafañe selected typical ones and published them in a book, *El Gallo pinto* (1944), a selection of favorite pieces from his repertory, and in *Libro de cuentos y leyendas* (1945). Both volumes were published by the National University of La Plata. His other books: *El Figon del palillero* (in collaboration with Juan Pedro Ramos, Agotado, 1934), *Coplas, poemas y canciones* (Ed. El Bibliófilo, Premio Municipal de Poesía, 1938), *Títeres de la Andariega* (plays from his repertory, Francisco A. Colombo, 1936), *Teatro de títeres* (more plays, Titirimundo, 1943), *Los Niños y los títeres* (Colección Titirimundo, El Ateneo, 1944).

VINALDI   See Rinaldi.

VIOLA, W. N.   Senior High School, Pontiac, Mich. From c. 1925 has used puppetry in his drama department. Various types of puppets were made, and plays presented before classes. Productions included: *Punch and Judy, Two Cooks and a Lady, Little Red Riding Hood, All's Well That Ends Well, Mountain Love, Dogs in Blankets, Revenge, Now for a Bath, Popeye the Sailor, Three's a Crowd, Mystifying Rose, Big Broadcast, Try Again, Old Mother Hubbard, Youth in the Moonlight, A Peek Under the Big Top, The Duel, Does Baby Know Best?, Court Alibis, A Change from the Cannibal Isles, Snow White and the Seven Dwarfs, Holy Goblin's Christmas Eve, St. George and the Dragon, Pierre Pathelin.* Three chapters in his book, *Creative Dramatics for Secondary Education,* are devoted to puppetry. Directed puppet plays at Playhouse, Cape Cod, Mass.

VITALI, DOMINIQUE   (Pp. 96–97, 185). Fantoccini and diorama at Washington Hall, New York, 1819.

VITO, Signor   (P. 109). Fantoccini at the American Museum, New York, 1847.

VON PILAT, VERA   1927–1928, produced hand-puppet shows in the San Francisco art gallery which became the Blanding Sloan Puppet Theatre in 1929. Moved later in this season to Filbert Street, where string-puppet shows were added. Among the plays performed on Thursdays and Saturdays were: *A Nativity Play* (from the Provençal), *Good King Wenceslaus, Booby Hans, The Frog Prince, Punch and Judy, Ali Baba and the Forty Thieves, Aladdin and the Wonderful Lamp, The Sorcerer's Apprentice, The Wooing of Clementina, A Bull Fight in Seville, The Sheperdess, The Green Bird.*

VROOMAN, ELIZABETH   Strolling Puppet Players, Vancouver, Canada. c. 1935, made extensive Canadian tours from headquarters in Vancouver.

WACKSMAN, RUTH   See Zaconick, Dorothy.

WADDINGTON, HELEN   1934, *Br'er Rabbit* stories, variety.

WADSWORTH, LOUIS and LUCILLE   Milford, O. 1935, *A Little Comedy of Macabre,* based on the life of Edgar Allen Poe.

WAITE, EMILY E.   New Haven, Conn. 1935, *Mad Tea Party*, variety, *Tweedledum and Tweedledee*. 1936, *Hansel and Gretel, Epaminondas*. c. 1940, taught puppetry, gave talks and demonstrations.

WALKER, HARRY H.   (P. 276). Marionette showman, partner of Barry Gray, 1885–1889. Joined Reedy, c. 1890.

WALKER and REEDIE   (P. 277). Royal marionettes at Grand Museum, New York, 25–30 May 1891. (Odell, vol. 14, p. 682.)

WALKER and WOOD   (P. 276). Marionettes at Grand Museum, New York, 2–7 March 1891. (Odell, vol. 14, p. 680.)

WALLACE, ALFRED   Peepshow Playhouse, New York. Around 1932, produced puppet plays with children as part of the craft program for a New York City Community Center. 1936, *Me and God, Make Believe* (both by Harold Preston; Irwin Schapiro worked on the former, and Morris Singer wrote the music). 1938, *Adventures of Sinbad the Sailor* (an operetta), *Talk of the Town* (a musical revue for adults by Preston and Wallace). 1939, *Talk of the Town* continued, *Sinbad Makes More Friends*. For night club work an act called *Alfred Wallace and His Dancing Puppets* was organized. 1939–1940, *Make Believe, Esau Gets the Soup*. 1940, *A Show Within a Show*, which played over 1600 performances between 1940 and 1943. 1944, toured spring and summer, then went overseas in the fall with a USO unit for six months, playing in England, France, Luxembourg, Germany, and Belgium. 1947, *Johnny Gremlin's Varieties, Goober's Party*. 1948, *Kitty Kat*. The above productions have all been done with hand-puppets and rod-puppets.

WALSWORTH, BERTHA   Walsworth Puppeteers, Long Beach, Cal. In 1935 a small group of amateurs, all otherwise employed, began variety performances which were being given up to 1948, for schools, libraries, hospitals. The personnel changed from time to time, but among the most constant were: Kenith Ross, Mrs. Crail, Alice Ingle. Over 150 puppets are used by this troupe.

WALTER, EUGENE F.   Willoughby Theatre, Mobile, Ala. From 1935 to 1941 the Willoughby Theatre played in southern Alabama. 1935, *Hansel and Gretel, The Clown in the Hat*. 1936, *Little Red Riding Hood*. 1937, *The Jitterbug Grandma, Sleeping Beauty*, and *Tom-Tit-Tot*. 1938, *The Taming of the Shrew, The Child that Cried for the Moon*. In addition to the marionettes which were used for the above plays, performances of *Punch and Judy* were occasionally given with a set of old German hand-puppets.

WALTON, PAUL, and O'ROURKE, MICKEY   (Pp. 359, 381). Of their beginnings in puppetry O'Rourke says, "Our first show was in a huge bottle advertising beer at a fair. Columbia pictures picked us up from there and we made enough to open the Olvera Street Puppet Theatre." This was in 1935. Until 1939, when the theatre was abandoned, productions included: *The Demi-Tasse Revue*, which had nearly 750 performances in 1935, *Shim Sham Revue, The Sketch Pad Revue* (with board puppets, marionettes, hand-puppets, shadows), *Wrongs of Spring, Television She Are Here*, a burlesque. From 1939 to date, Walton and O'Rourke have been on tour, taking their floor-show acts to theatres and clubs throughout the country. They had a scene in *Sons o'Fun* at the Winter Garden, New York, which ran for over a year, 1942–1943. Concurrently they played at the Rainbow Room, featuring the Love Bugs, Susie and Butch, who capered on tables, made saucy remarks, and passed out favors to the ladies. Late in 1943, left *Sons o'Fun* and joined Ed Wynn's vaudeville show, *Big Time*, which closed after one week. September 1944, left with a USO unit to entertain service men overseas in Germany, England, France. After returning to America in 1945, continued their coast-to-coast tours.

WALTON, "PUNCH"   (P. 132). Played at National Garten, New York, 8 August 1878, and 4 March and 3 April 1879, on the last occasion being billed together with his wife. (Odell, vol. 10, pp. 468, 663.)

WARFIELD, EMMA   (P. 377). Philadelphia. 1935, studied puppetry at Moore Institute. 1938, *The Eagle and the Cat, Good King Wenceslaus, Ballet of Purim Goodies* (all with shadows). 1939, *The Painter and the Princess, Cinderella, The Tiger and the Brahmin, The Spider and the Fly, The Quizzical Olifant.* 1940, *The Willow Tree.* 1943, shadow show for the U.S. Forestry Bureau Christmas party. 1945, conducted puppet class for the Junto, adult education school. Taught puppetry at the Philadelphia School of Occupational Therapy. Has given lectures and demonstrations, and been active in puppet organizations.

WARNDELL MARIONETTES   See Williams, Brinley.

WASHBURN COLLEGE MARIONETTES   See Gray, Dr. Arthur D.

WASSER, ARTHUR   Grant High School, Portland, Ore. 1938, *Man in White.*

WEBBER, THEODORE LYMAN   (P. 133). (1840–1932). Born at Prescott, Mass. About 1873 acquired a set of Punch and Judy puppets from McClure, a ventriloquist, with which he traveled in circuses. After his retirement from the road, he kept up the show for local entertainment in and about Walnut Hill, Orange, Mass., where he died. This information is from his daughter, Mrs. Amber Webster of Walnut Hill, who gave it to Lewis N. Wiggins, owner of the set, who wrote that the puppets are well carved and costumed in old homespun materials. They were, in 1948, on display in Mr. Wiggins' Hotel at Northampton, Mass., and illustrated in a booklet issued by the Wiggins Old Tavern.

WEBER, BILL   Chicago, Ill. A young puppeteer who began puppetry c. 1945. In 1947, gave 36 performances in schools, churches, lodges, orphanages, etc., of *Bill's Weberettes,* a puppet variety show.

WEBER, HENRY   Punch and Judy showman of Detroit who played during the 1930's and 1940's.

WEBSTER, ORPHA M.   Miami University, Oxford, O. c. 1940, worked with elementary and college students who produced: *The Soldier and the Demons, The Tumbler of Notre Dame, Gabriel and the Hour Book, Punch and Judy, The Ant and the Grasshopper, The Painted Pig,* using various types of puppets.

WEIL, GRACE F.   Hackensack, N. J. c. 1938, began experimenting with marionettes and music. With a group of children ranging in age from 6 to 16, produced *Hansel and Gretel,* with recorded dialogue and musical selections. Next year (1939) *The Rheingold* was produced, using a simple translation and spoken dialogue instead of vocal music for most of the story, but with certain scenes played to music. This show, built first as a home entertainment, was later taken on a short tour and seen by many children. Then came *The Valkyrie,* 1940, which was equally popular.

WEINKOETZ, PETER JOHN   (Pp. 229–232, 236, 267). German string-puppet showman from Baden, who played in Wisconsin and Minnesota, c. 1865–1900.

WEINKOETZ, PETER JOHN, the younger   (Pp. 229–232, 236, 267). German shows in Wisconsin and Minnesota, c. 1900–1922.

WELISCH, WALTER T.   Welisch Puppet Theatre for Children, San Francisco. 1928, *The Three Bears.* 1929, *Jack and the Beanstalk, Little Red Riding Hood and the Wolf.*

WELLS, GEORGE   Yonkers, N. Y. 1936, *Pirates of the Black Falcon.*

WELTY, SUSAN FULTON   The Parsons Puppeteers, Parsons College, Fairfield, Ia. 1933, *The Friendly Lion, Beauty and the Beast, Jack and the Beanstalk.*

WENTWORTH, W. NORRIS   Madison, Wis. 1933, *Punch and Judy.*

WENZELL   Late 19th-century Punch and Judy man, mentioned by Ernest Russell, *Outing Magazine,* January 1908.

WERNICKE, ENRIQUE   Argentina. A writer who showed his puppet theatre, Los Cuatros Vientos, at the International Puppet Exposition, Buenos Aires, Theatre Museum, 1943.

WESTFIELD, CATHERINE   Chester, Pa. 1934, studied in summer class with Tony Sarg. 1934–1937, played annual Christmas show at the Boston Store, Wilkes-Barre: *Christmas at Mickey and Minnie's House, Santa's Surprise, Joe Palooka's Amateur Hour, Santa's Workshop.* 1936–1937, two seasons with C. Ray Smith on his coast-to-coast tours. 1937, taught puppetry at Camp Chattooga, Athens, Ga. and produced *Sleeping Beauty* and variety. 1938, at the same camp produced *Snow White and the Seven Dwarfs.* 1938, opened with floor-show act. During World War II played for the USO and went overseas with Unit 64 of the Red Circuit. Since returning, has been playing night clubs and theatres in the eastern United States with her floor-show act. Sister of Ann Sharon.

WEST SEATTLE HIGH SCHOOL PUPPET CLUB   See Baeder, Wilhelmina.

WHEAT, GLADYS M.   Began puppet work in 1922. c. 1927, produced *The Antimacassar* with marionettes and child actors at Columbia, Mo.

WHEELER, DELL HINSHAW   Duluth, Minn. 1935, *Trial by Jury*. 1936–1937, Circus. 1938, scenes from *Elizabeth and Essex,* performed at the Chicago Puppet Festival. 1939, *Háry János Suite,* played at the St. Paul Puppet Festival, and with the Duluth Symphony Orchestra.

WHEELER, RICHARD   Evanston, Ill. 1930, *Spree, Rambles in Rhythm*. 1931, *King Arthur's Socks, Black-Out,* a revue, all with 6-inch marionettes.

WHEELOCK, DORIS MANNING   Hyannis, Neb. 1937, *Snow White, Amateur Hour, Jack and the Beanstalk*. 1940, *Red Riding Hood, Esther*.

WHEMPNER, VERNA HUBER   Popkin's Marionettes, Fargo, N. D. This troupe started as an entertainment for a son, who with his chum and mother built puppet shows. Schools and clubs demanded performances, so more members of the family were enlisted and the troupe toured North Dakota. 1927, *The Rubies of Omar Khayyam* (150 performances); *Red Riding Hood, Jack and the Beanstalk, Tummyache, The Frog Prince*. 1928, over 300 additional performances of *The Rubies of Omar Khayyam, Hansel and Gretel, Puss in Boots, Gandhi the Fakir, Circus Echoes, Ole and Lena, Red Riding Hood*. 1930–1932, performances continued, with company of 50 puppets.

WHITE, GUS   *Punch and Judy* at Doris's Eighth Avenue Museum, New York, at intervals during February, March, and June 1890. (Odell, vol. 14, pp. 393-5.)

WHITE, T.   (P. 107). Fantoccini at Colonnade Garden, New York, 1841.

WHITEHOUSE, WINIFRED   See Edmundson, Carolyn.

WHITEMIRE, LAURA G.   Roosevelt High School, Seattle, Wash. 1926–1927, *Aladdin's Wife, There Was an Old Woman, The Four Princesses, The Knave of Hearts, The Slave with Two Faces, Six Who Pass While the Lentils Boil, The Three Wishes, The Birthday of the Infanta*.

WIDMER, MRS. S. W.   The Don-Jack Dolls, La Grange, Ill. 1921, began shows with hand-puppets and shadows: *The Cat and the Mouse, The Tar Baby*.

WIEGAND, PAUL SAYRE   In high school built a miniature stage and equipped it with puppets, but other interests intruded and the work was abandoned. In the winter of 1941–1942, a new start was made with experiments in construction and operation, with a production of *Aladdin* in mind. War came, he joined Ethel Hanley's company to finish out the season of *Pinocchio,* then entered the service.

WIKSELL, JEAN STARR and WESLEY   (P. 392). Columbia, Mo. With their combined art and dramatic training, turned to puppetry and presented their first show, December 1932. 1933, *Jack and the Beanstalk*. 1935, *Birthday of the Infanta*. 1936, *The Fakir*. 1937, *The Three Wishes, Medieval Legend,* a Christmas pantomime repeated annually since 1937. 1939, *Ozark Tale,* color motion picture *Construction of Marionettes and Hand-Puppets*. 1937 to date, Mrs. Wiksell has been puppetry consultant for the Association of Junior League of America, holding institutes, training leagues in puppetry, advising groups working with puppets.

WILDER, GRACE   New York. 1934, working with Remo Bufano, organized seven puppet units to play in parks, playgrounds, hospitals, under sponsorship of the Works Division of the Department of Public Welfare. See Bufano for further details.

WILKINSON, WALTER   (Pp. 322, 391). English hand-puppet showman who brought The Peep Show to the United States in 1937, playing at the second American Puppetry Festival, Cincinnati, O., and in various sections of the country. After a year's visit, returned to England and recorded his impressions in *Puppets Through America* (Geoffrey Bles, London). In 1939, he and his wife, Winifred, returned to America, where they remained until late summer, 1946. The shows given during their sojourns had a strong influence on the development of hand-puppets in

America, for they demonstrated the dramatic force of this type. Before his American visit, Wilkinson took many walking tours with his puppet show through Britain and wrote a series of books which sensitively interpret provincial life as he saw it.

WILLIAMS BRINLEY A. The Warndell Marionettes, East Cleveland, O. 1942, *Ali Baba and the 40 Thieves*. Work interrupted by the war, production resumed 1946, with *Ali Baba*.

WILLIAMS, BRUCE Marionette Guild of Plainfield, N. J. During the 1940–1941 season with Paul Worth and Herbert Black produced: *The King of the Golden River, Huckleberry Finn, The Count of Monte Cristo, The Prince and the Pauper, The Nurnburg Stove, Aladdin and His Wonderful Lamp*, and *The Magic Carpet*. With Ronald Hotson added to the company, produced 1942–1943: *The Boy Knight of Reims, Tom Sawyer*, with revivals of *The Nurnburg Stove* and *The Prince and the Pauper*. The activities of this company were suspended during the war.

WILLIAMS, LEMUEL St. Paul, Minn. From 1940 to date, has presented puppet programs such as *Marlem's Revue* (with 50 marionettes) and the *Starlight Revue*, 1946–1947. Especially interested in the mechanics of puppetry, he has made many developments in construction. For Dell Wheeler's *Háry János Suite*, he built a model of a medieval town clock for the Viennese Clock scene.

WILLIAMS, MARY (Mrs. Lemuel) St. Paul, Minn. From 1943 to date, has given performances of *Punch and Judy* with hand-puppets, and variety with marionettes. A series of shows in 1948 was sponsored by the Junior League of St. Paul.

WILLIAMS, ROBERT and EDITH (P. 356). Seattle, Wash., and vicinity. 1929, *The Glittering Gate* (Lord Dunsany), *Alice in Wonderland, The Lonely Princess of Yang*. 1930, *Clarence Clarewick among the Indians, The Miser's Avaricious Daughter, Hansel and Gretel, Romeo and Juliet*. 1931, spring and summer at the Seattle Repertory Playhouse. 1946, still active.

WILLIAMS, REV. WILLIAM JOHN Cleveland, O. 1932–1933, reinstituted the medieval custom of using marionettes in the church to enact Bible stories. The plays were given at regular Sunday evening services, and included the stories of: *Cain and Abel, James of Galilee, The Good Samaritan, Queen Esther, Elijah*.

WILMOTT, GARY, JR. Valley Stream, Long Island, N. Y. A young puppeteer with a puppet theatre in his home in which he performed variety and plays. He first used Virginia Austin's stock marionettes but in 1948 built some of his own. Produced *The Three Wishes* and *Boiled in Oil*, 1946.

WILSON, HARRY LEON, JR. Carmel, Cal., and Portland, Ore. 1927, The *Curse of Money*, a farce. 1928, *Crime in the Far East, Once Upon a Time, Foolish Father, The Juggler of Notre Dame, Farmer Grigg's Boggart, Clever Peter*, variety (the last in Portland). 1929, *The Untamed Shrew*, at the Portland Art Museum.

WILSON, MRS. HELEN M. Riverside, Ill. c. 1940, produced plays in home and school, including *The Nativity* with shadows.

WINDERECKER, SAM Early 20th-century Punch and Judy man.

WIN LOVE MARIONETTES See Winlow, Anna.

WINLOW, ANNA C. Win Love Marionettes, Los Angeles. 1922, *Father Frost*. 1923, *The Tinder Box, The Real Princess*. 1925, *The Princess and the Pea, Long Broad and Strong-Sight* (from the Czech), *The Silver Cobweb* (from a Czech puppet play). 1934, in Sacramento, played 50 performances with hand-puppets in a repertory of plays including: *Red Riding Hood, Beauty and the Beast, The Three Wishes, The Princess and the Pea, Hoh Lee and the Dwarfs, Cruel Frederick, Father Frost, Tom Thumb, Ghosts*.

WINNETKA ATTIC PUPPETS 1932, *Barnacle Bill and the Mermaids*. 1936, *Ba-bar the Elephant*. See also Blaine, Eleanor G.

WINSOR MARIONETTES A company which played in northern New Jersey, c. 1941, a group of short plays and a variety show called *Puppet Town*.

WINTERMUTE, HARRY (Pp. 230, 275, 276). d. 25 May 1938). *Punch and Judy* and marionettes in tent shows, 1877–1917. Joined Professor Martin in 1886.

WINTERS, CHARLES New York. 1928–1929, *Princess Dulcinea, The Magic Powder, The Adventures of Felix*.

WITT, ELINOR, and ORTEGEL, ADELAIDE   Pinafore Players, Wilmette, Ill. Used puppets for Saturday morning programs at the Wilmette Library, 1946.

WITTELSHOFER, ALLAN   St. Louis, Mo. Presented first show in 1938, another in 1941. 1943, *Castle of Blainwick, Lands of Enchantment.* 1948, taught a class of children to make hand-puppets and give shows.

WITTY MARIONETTES   Francis Withopf Junior High School, Great Neck, Long Island, N. Y. 1939, *"218" Variety, Robinson Crusoe.*

WOLFF, ALBERT   Montreal, Canada. 1945, *Bastien and Bastienne* for the Mozart Festival of Montreal.

WOLFF, ERNEST and MRS. ESTHER   (Pp. 346, 348). Ernest Wolff's Puppet Opera Company, Chicago. Mrs. Wolff traveled extensively in Europe with her two sons Ernest and Leonard. At twelve, Ernest had seen and become fascinated with the color of Continental opera. He built a puppet opera company in the basement of his Chicago home, aided by his mother, whose experience as a couturiere enabled her to costume the puppets with proper lavishness. She helped devise the patented rod mechanism by which the figures are controlled. 1930, produced *Carmen, Madame Butterfly, Aida.* 1935, *La Boheme, Die Walküre, Salome.* 1939, *Rigoletto, Aida, Faust, Pagliacci.* These operas were played at the New York World's Fair in the summer of 1939 as the Victor Puppet Opera Company, and subsequently toured until December 1941, when Ernest enlisted in the Navy. Before leaving he installed the opera in the Kungsholm Restaurant, Chicago, and Mrs. Wolff added a number of new operas, with improved rod-puppets. The management of the Kungsholm opera was later turned over to others. When Ernest returned from overseas, a new group of operas was built, and the present company formed, playing first as the Tivoli Grand Opera Company. The 1947 repertory included: *Aida, Traviata, Faust, Carmen.*

WOLL, NAOMI   See Stewart, Doris.

WOLO   (P. 378). San Francisco. Born in Germany, came to America as an exchange student in agricultural engineering, although he wanted to be an artist. He soon left agriculture and worked at all sorts of jobs, one of which was drawing caricatures in night clubs. He went to San Francisco as a front-page cartoonist; later ran a column which he illustrated. The president of William Morrow, Publisher, happened to see an exhibit of his animal pictures, and gave him a job illustrating children's books. He designed Mortimer Snerd for Edgar Bergen. c. 1941 he began making hand-puppets to use in talks about his books, which he gave in schools and libraries. Finding them effective, he built a booth and more characters, most of them from his own stories. By 1946 he had developed an hour-and-a-half show, handled by a booker, which played for child audiences in stores, clubs, and schools.

WOLTMAN, ADOLF G.   (P. 376). New York. First became interested in puppets c. 1931 when his step-daughter was ill and he made a couple of potato-head puppets to entertain her. They cheered her so much that her recovery was hastened. Around 1935 he began using puppets in the psychiatric work with children at Bellevue Hospital. He found simple hand-puppet shows useful in studying behavior problems. Until he entered the Army in 1942, this was a regular part of his work. After the war he continued his work at Bellevue, and incorporated his experiments in the use of puppets in his practice of psychotherapy.

WONDERLAND MARIONETTES   See Bredt, Douglas.

WOOD, EVELYN   Baltimore, Md., and vicinity. 1930, *Jack and the Beanstalk, Skullface, Lollipop Capers, Puppet Follies.* 1931, *The Feather Princess, Rag Bag Alley Revue, Hansel and Gretel, Peter Rabbit.* During the summer of 1931, presented repertory selected from the above plays at Stonecrest Summer Camp near Denver, Colo. Also produced: *The Mermaid and the Star, Puss in Boots,* both in Baltimore. 1937, *Aladdin, Rumpelstiltskin, Spring Marts.* 1939–1941, toured with children's fashion show in many department stores: eight life-size marionettes were used to display children's clothing. 1948, *Lollypop's Circus, Rumpelstiltskin, Epaminondas, The Three Wishes, Peter Rabbit.*

WOOD, MRS. HELEN E.   Holland, Mich. An amateur who began in 1942 and gave occasional children's shows.

WOODHOUSE, BERTHA O.   Cincinnati, O. For several years before 1940 worked with children and produced: *Snow White and Rose Red, One Eye, Two Eyes, and Three Eyes,* and religious plays.

WOODHOUSE, HENRY W.   Beaux Arts Marionettes, Jersey City, N. J. 1937, *Christmas Fantasy.* 1938, *The Dwarf Prince.*

WOOLLEY, DE GRAFFENRIED   During the 1930's was a professional puppeteer, produced a puppet movie. 1947–1948, technical director of the Junior League television productions.

WRAY and WIFE   Early 20th-century showman. c. 1920 played in San Francisco; had stage with elaborate proscenium and boxes occupied by comic characters.

WYMAN   (Pp. 190, 199). Marionette "seances," Philadelphia, 1875, 1876.

WYNN, ED   1932, a *Punch and Judy* skit in *The Laugh Parade.*

YALE PUPPETEERS   (Pp. 283, 351, 356, 358, 359, 382). Forman Brown, Harry Burnett, Richard Brandon. Began 1923 as the Puppeteers of the University of Michigan, touring the Middle West and New England. While studying at Yale they acquired the title by which they have since been known. Productions up to 1928 include: *Weather, On the Road to Bombay, The Lavender Elephant* (all by Forman Brown), *The Five-Foot Shelf* (Ernestine Songer), *The Three Wishes* (Ruthenburg), *Bluebeard* (designed by Norman Bel Geddes), *The Gooseberry Mandarin, The Poetic Whale* (both by Ruthenburg), *Pyramus and Thisbe* (from *A Midsummer Night's Dream*). In 1927, opened a small theatre, the Club Guignol, in Hollywood. 1928, Brown wrote incidental music for *Bluebeard* and *Hansel and Gretel.* 1929, The *Princess of the Hibiscus, The Poet Keeps His Head, Puss in Boots* (music by Brown, text by Burnett). 1930–1933, played in the Teatro Torito, Olvera Street, Hollywood. During the first season gave 300 performances of *My Man Friday,* the first of the musical comedies produced by this company, in which music, satire, and action were combined to form a sophisticated adult entertainment. The Haydn Trio, which was retained from the elaborate orchestra built for *Bluebeard,* opened each performance, and is still used as a curtain raiser. *Belittling Hollywood, Uncle Tom's Hebb'n,* and *Bearding Bluebeard* (Ruthenburg) were added to the repertory. 1931, two new musical comedies, *Mister Noah* and *Caesar Julius,* were built. In 1932, the company had a brief season in New York, then returned to Hollywood (1933) to do a puppet sequence in the film, *I Am Suzanne.* At the Cosmopolitan Club, New York, 1936–1938 played a short season of repertory, beginning with *Mister Noah.* During 1937, Sunday matinees were presented at the Barbizon-Plaza Hotel, New York, followed by a series of cross-country tours. On 10 July 1941, opened the Turnabout Theatre in Los Angeles, in which live actors (including Elsa Lanchester) performed on a stage at one end of the theatre, and the puppets on another at the other end. The audience was seated on street-car seats, reversed during intermission. With older pieces, *Tom and Jerry* figured in the puppet repertory; special numbers were written by Forman Brown for the human actors.

YANKEE MARIONETTE GUILD   Friendly House, Davenport, Ia. 1934, variety, with marionettes and hand-puppets.

YANO, BEN   (P. 377). New York. 1936, *Wise Men of Chelmen* (from Jewish folklore). 1933, worked with Jero Magon as designer for *Emperor Jones.* While hospitalized at Camp Luna, N. Mex., c. 1944, presented a show with soldier patients and designed stages improvised from hospital equipment.

YARRICK, JOSEPH   Cambridge, Mass. 1931, *Punch and Judy* for Neighborhood House fete. c. 1937, played *Punch and Judy* two years on liners for the Dollar Steamship Company.

YORE, BARBARA   St. Louis, Mo. From c. 1944 has supervised a puppet club in the Scullin School, which has produced *Looking Up, The Fox and the Shadow,* and many other plays and variety numbers.

York, Helen Clute Maywood Players Puppet Group, Maywood, Ill. A group of adults recruited from the Little Theatre began in the summer 1947 to present shows for children in the Maywood parks. The first plays were: *Amanda and the Ghost, Little Red Riding Hood,* and *The Giraffe.* Additional performances were given as benefits for church, library, school groups, and finally, out-of-town dates were played. A class of 35 children made puppets and presented *Snow White and the Seven Dwarfs.* 1948, the group had ten plays in its repertory and 53 puppets.

Yost, Maurice Meadville, Pa., High School. 1931, *Felix in the Inferno, Tom O'Shanter.* 1932, *Puppets on Parade.*

Yost, Thomas W. Exhibitions of magic, ventriloquism, and marionettes at the Main Centennial Building, Philadelphia, 4 July 1881.—Philadelphia *Public Ledger,* that date.

Young, S. D. Ogden, Utah. 1930, *Peter Pan* with 12-inch marionettes.

Zabita, Giovanni Played in a Cleveland church, 1933, possibly earlier.

Zaconick, Dorothy (P. 342). Director, The Suzari Marionettes, New York. With Ruth Wacksman, organized the company, c. 1935, and gradually built up an active business in the metropolitan area. 1942, played *Buffalo Bill* and *Peter and the Wolf.* 1943, *Pinocchio.* For the 1943 Yuletide season the group appeared in *Christmas Puppet Parade* for the eighth consecutive puppet season at the World Theatre with a repertory of five plays and several performances daily. In 1945, appeared in the Children's Easter Carnival at the Barbizon-Plaza Concert hall. During the 1945 Christmas season, seven companies played in various department stores in New York and elsewhere. 1946, played *Pinocchio, Rumpelstiltskin,* and *Nobody's Boy* in the New York area. 1947, an eight-week summer tour through New England.

Zane, Rinaldo (P. 245). Marionettes in Mexico, late 19th century.

Zarrilli, Humberto Worked with Fernando Amado, 1938, and gave puppet performances in Montevideo.

Zeidelman, Claire Philadelphia. Working with junior high school students, found that they outgrew costumes (and sometimes their voices changed) between the beginning of a play and its final presentation, so turned to puppets. She found the students less shy, than in regular stage plays, and their voices could be used to better advantage. Began 1937. 1940, produced *The Clockmaker of Genf.* 1942, *Shop Windows, Little Red Riding Hood.* 1945, *Fight On, China!* 1946, *In A Persian Market.* 1947, *The Willow Plate.* 1948, *A Russian Melody, Mexican Fiesta.*

Zubler, Susan Saginaw Marionette Players, South School, Saginaw, Mich. 1935, *Epaminondas and His Mammy, The Peppermint Boy, The Reward.* 1936, *Bluebeard Here and Hereafter, The Wishing Fairy, Rus and Gus Make a Fuss, Jerry Sees the Gorilla, Punch and Judy.* 1938, *Brownie the Boaster, The Other Side of the Wall.* 1939, *Monkey Business.* 1941, *Rumpelstiltskin.*

Zwickey, Fern Detroit, Mich. Instructor in puppetry, Wayne University College of Education. 1948 her students presented *Byrano De Cyranac* with hand-puppets, *Hansel and Gretel* with shadow-figures, and original Christmas plays.

Zygowicz, Julia Chicago, Ill. 1946, *Little Lost Angel.*

SUPPLEMENT

PUPPETS IN AMERICA SINCE 1948

by Marjorie Batchelder McPharlin

Contents of Supplement (since 1948)

Introduction

In this supplement to Paul McPharlin's book, *The Puppet Theatre in America*, I have tried to fill in the work of the two decades since it was originally published with enough detail to bring up to date, however incompletely, the information in "A List of Puppeteers: 1524–1948" with which his book concludes (Pp. 396–483). The first such list was included in McPharlin's *A Repertory of Marionette Plays* (1929) and thereafter, beginning in 1930, the annual work of producers was recorded in *Puppetry: A Yearbook of Puppets and Marionettes*, which he edited, with a selection of photographs and articles from America and around the world. These, with the lists of producers, constituted an overview of international puppetry. It was from both these sources that "A List of Puppeteers" was compiled. The last volume of *Puppetry* appeared in 1947. Since that time there has been no mechanism for recording the activities of American puppeteers, and I have had to base the material in this supplement on reports sent by puppeteers, notes from the *Puppetry Journal*, and other sources. It is incomplete for several reasons: systematic records do not exist, accurate addresses are often not available, and it has not been possible, in eight months, to compile the sort of record found in "A List of Puppeteers", which Paul McPharlin spent twenty years in assembling. In addition, some people did not respond to requests for information, and there are doubtless many who should have been included but whose activities did not come to my attention.

My association with Paul McPharlin began with the publication of the first issue of *Puppetry*, a couple of years after my first participation in a puppet show. Having moved from Tallahassee, Florida, to Columbus, Ohio, I found it easy to dash up to Detroit to see his latest productions. In those days, puppeteers avidly sought out each other's shows, a custom made easier by the annual puppet festivals which began in 1936. I was teaching art at Ohio State University and experimenting with puppets, aided by a group of University students. My production of *Columbine's Birthday* by Grace Stearns at the 1936 Festival introduced the hand-and-rod puppet, a type invented by Nina Efimova in Russia, and now used throughout Eastern Europe and other parts of the world. On the same program I presented *St. George and the Dragon* with rod-puppets, then virtually unknown to American audiences. In subsequent years, I produced shows at intervals, wrote many articles for *Puppetry*, received a Ph.D. degree for my work on the history and technique of rod-puppets, wrote *The Puppet Theatre Handbook* for the Army Special Services, and worked with Virginia Lee Comer on a creative approach to puppet and playmaking which was published as *Puppets and Plays*. Since 1958, when I went to Bucharest for the First International Festival of Puppet Theatres, my interest in the international puppet theatre has been greatly stimulated, and I have been fortunate in observing puppetry in most of the important centers around the world.

In this supplement I have described the careers of some puppeteers more or less in detail, depending on the material at hand, and the insight their activities might give to an understanding of the total picture of puppet activity. The work of other people, a large group, indeed, has been mentioned to illustrate certain aspects of puppet theatre which I felt should be elaborated upon, and thus to supplement Chapter XX on Contemporary Puppets (Pp. 331–395). For instance, the various roles of the puppet have been treated fully enough in my Chapter I, so that the nature of these activities might be plain. In subsequent chapters, this same plan has been followed, and I have tried to describe typical work in the various areas of puppetry, as well as to note unusual developments. Thus, the work of individual puppeteers is described in connection with what seemed to be their most important contribution, yet their names may recur elsewhere because of their varied activities. I have *not* attempted to estimate the incidence of puppet shows in any category, nor to evaluate them, nor to indicate which are professional and which are amateur productions. The reader can make his own deductions.

This record deals largely with puppetry in the United States and Canada. Some references to puppet activities in Latin America are included, but to do justice to them would require a whole book, for which the material is not presently at hand.

The diversified pattern of puppetry established in previous years has continued. Puppets entertain and educate; they advertise; they ease physical and mental ills; they give personal satisfaction as an avocation; they sometimes provide a living. They are seen in museum exhibits and often wind up in collections; they perform in theatres and dozens of other places; they whet intellectual curiosity, and provide subjects for research.

Who are the people who engage in all this activity? Some are professionals who travel, perform on television, or in permanent locations; some are amateurs who work alone or in groups to provide entertainment for children in schools, hospitals, or recreation centers; some, a great many, in fact, are teachers who find puppets useful in many ways; some are people who, being interested in the pictorial or performing arts, strive to gain recognition for the puppet theatre as a unique theatrical form. Because puppetry combines well with other activities, we have puppeteers who are also real estate agents, airplane pilots, actors or actresses, theatre directors or technologists, artists, writers, college professors, or foreign service officers who have gone to their posts with a few puppets tucked into their luggage. A large number of people who were active in puppetry before 1948 still are, but there is a long list of those who have passed on. Others have come onto the scene and distinguished themselves in recent years. Some are known mostly for activity in one field, but most puppeteers turn their hand to whatever comes up, be it television, film, shows for children or performances with orchestras; for teaching, advertising, propaganda, or protest.

More than fifteen years ago, J. Frances Crothers, a Connecticut teacher of art and puppetry, set out to make a bibliography of writings about the puppet theatre. Now the six-volume work, *The Puppeteer's Library Guide: The Bibliographic Index to the Literature of the World Puppet Theatre,* is almost complete, and publication is near. Foreign as well as American authors are included; articles, books, and research papers of the past and present, covering every phase of puppetry, are listed. This monumental work is the most extensive piece of research in puppetry to be done in America during the past two decades. When published, it will be a major reference book in the field of puppetry. I am glad to refer readers of this supplement to the Crothers bibliography.

Without the *Puppetry Journal,* it would have been impossible to write this record, and without the interest of A. S. Burack, Editor of PLAYS, INC., it could not have been published, nor *The Puppet Theatre in America* reprinted. I am grateful to both the magazine and the man.

M. B. McP.

Santa Fe, New Mexico
March 1968

I

The Role of the Puppet

In America, the puppet has many roles, but they are all based upon its capacity as an entertainer. Sometimes this is forgotten by those who use puppets as educational tools or advertising tricks, but it is the puppet's talent to delight, to amuse, to ridicule, and to hold up a mirror to mankind which makes it effective in its various roles.

Most American puppeteers produce shows for children, for in this part of the world, people generally regard puppetry as children's entertainment or as a device to teach them, although adults may sometimes be reached. Whether any given show is weighted toward teaching or entertainment depends upon the producer, but it is generally agreed that, whatever the purpose of the show, the element of entertainment must be present, or children will not look or listen.

Almost every kind of program possible to produce with puppets is used for children: variety, plays based upon childhood story classics, original plays, musical extravaganzas. Even musical works performed by symphony orchestras and interpreted by puppets are usually given for children, with the fervid hope of the puppeteer that adults may also be interested. They often are. More will be said about kinds of programs in Chapter II. Here we will discuss some of the many ways in which the puppet in its traditional role as entertainer is being used for education, therapy, advertising, and as a means for developing creativity.

Puppets in education

Puppets are used as teaching aids in many fields: in health and language programs, civic activities, religious education, and such government programs as Head Start and the Peace Corps.

For example, the Children's Museum in Detroit sends out to schools sets of simple puppets with which children make up their own stories about good health habits. Burr Tillstrom's Kukla demonstrates proper tooth care in an illustrated article in *Better Living*, and in a brochure published by the American Dental Health Association. In a film produced for the Auxiliary of the Pennsylvania State Dental Society, a dental health expert and a puppet dog, Happy, are featured. Sally Sellers Hayes produced *Sonny's Lucky Dream* in 1964 for the Auxiliary of the Cincinnati Dental Society, and trained two teams of women to operate the marionettes. Each year the show is booked for the primary grades by the Board of Education.

The Chicago Good Teeth Council for Children subsidized puppet shows for educating children in dental health from 1933 to 1950. At first these were the "animated vegetable" type of show, but more dramatic forms of presentation were soon introduced in the *Little Jack Shows*. Most of the puppeteers were college graduates with speech or drama majors, and their training in the Chicago workshop insured performances of professional caliber. Harry Fowler and his wife Cleo, Catherine McAndrews, and Rhea G. Sikes were in charge of the program. Fowler later became Educational Director of the Cereal Institute in Chicago, a position he still holds. In 1953 he produced *Bill's Better Breakfast Puppet Show* for presentation in the New York City public schools, and it was later filmed.

Ted and Jean Mason specialize in shows which promote civic activities such as Red Feather, Palestine Appeals, the Humane Society, or which have a message for children, such as traffic safety. A well-equipped trailer is their mobile theatre, in which they perform for children throughout Pittsburgh.

From 1933 on, the Animal Rescue League of Boston has presented about 500 shows annually to more than 350 schools. Through well-known stories such as *Peter Rabbit* and *The Three Pigs*, desirable attitudes are introduced for the care of animals, for kindness to them and for the responsibility of people to beasts and birds. These shows often inspire children to make their own puppets and plays. In Waco, Texas, Doris Goodrich Jones has worked with the Humane Society for twelve years. She makes puppets for a new play each year and presents it eighty-four times in the schools, on a stage consisting of a large covered box hung around her neck. Roberta Mack's marionette, Smokey the Bear, sponsored by the United State Forestry and Conservation Department, has been a favorite with California children for many years and has taught them the dangers of fire to forest and animals.

Puppets are used in various language programs. John McInnes of Toronto encountered a "nonreader" at the Columbia University Reading Clinic. With the aid of puppets he was able to excite interest in reading (directions for making figures), word-building (names of materials) and creative writing (the play). Theresa Casey, Methuen, Massachusetts, designed "jiffy puppets" for children to make and use in remedial reading. On television, Bil Baird has used puppets to teach beginning French, and Katherine Parkman, to teach Spanish. Mollie Falkenstein promotes their use in language teaching with hand-puppets performing live in an attractive booth. Margaret Bennington conducted an experimental project in 1960 for the New York Board of Education, in which the use of puppets in the language arts program from kindergarten through the eighth grade was explored and the results evaluated.

Among many American Indians, English is a second language and this poses problems in their education. A program to help teachers is supported by the New Mexico State Department of Education, which sponsored a two-month experiment in the use of puppets. I conducted the program in Cuba, New Mexico, where the school has a predominance of Navajo children and many Spanish-American children. Simple puppets were made and used in plays based on various language difficulties. The Navajos are very shy, and there was not enough time to make much progress in their fluency. Since only one of the four teachers involved really had an understanding of the possibilities of using puppets, the project ended with the school year.

Puppets are widely used in religious education. For example, in January 1951, CBS Television presented a series of four color films, *Lamp Unto My Feet*. Mabel and Les Beaton built the puppets and the elaborate sets placed on rolling stages. They were assisted by Dave and Denny Pritchard, with special music scored by Morris Mamorsky and scripts by Nina Millen. Charles Schwcp directed and Peter Elgar was the producer. All the work was under the supervision of Everett C. Parker, Director of the Protestant Radio Commission in New York City. The meticulous attention to authentic details of costumes, properties and settings, and the excellent production facilities made these plays powerful interpretations of *The Good Samaritan, The Ten Talents, The Lost Sheep* and *The Prodigal Son*.

Reverend William Jacoby and his wife Rose were among the most active promoters of puppets in religious plays, which they wrote and performed from 1936 on. Puppets and scenes were as realistic as possible to convey the traditional image of Biblical times and places. Reverend Jacoby was first appointed Consultant in Religious Education for the Puppeteers of America in 1954, a post which he held until his death in 1965, after which Mrs. Jacoby served for several years. In various articles published in the *Puppetry Journal*, in his letters to correspondents, and in special sessions at puppet festivals, Reverend Jacoby did a great deal to point out the advantages of puppets. He wrote down guiding principles for their use in a number of published pamphlets.

Puppet projects have also become a part of Sunday school programs, where children make puppets, write plays and present them. Shows are often presented by adult puppeteers for various church functions, such as bazaars, Sunday school parties or Christmas celebrations. Frances Meharg produced *Mirij Calling*, a show to raise funds for a medical school in India, sponsored by the Presbyterian Mission Board, New York. Doris Goodrich Jones has given many Bible stories with puppets in Waco, and the Duvalls, Bill and Marion, have a considerable repertory of religious plays, including *The Pilgrim's Progress*.

When puppets perform in church, they are continuing a tradition which began in the Middle Ages. No one who has seen Martin and Olga Stevens perform their puppets in *The Nativity, The Passion Play,* or *Joan of Arc* can doubt the dramatic impact which puppets can give to these stories, nor their suitability for participation in religious services. Today, the trend is increasing. Elizabeth and Fletcher Vondersmith, of McLean, Virginia, perform an annual show during Lent in a dozen churches in the Washington area, under the sponsorship of the Drama Cycle of the Episcopal Church. The Vondersmith theatre was purchased from a military family who got it in Vienna after World War II from a refugee family in need of money to come to America. With the theatre came sixteen marionettes (probably Czechoslovakian) about ten inches tall, and seven sets of interchangeable scenery in eighteenth-century style. For their church presentations, the Vondersmiths have done *Dr. Faust* and *Jeremiah*, with *Jonah* in preparation for 1968.

In 1958, when Bishop Nelson M. Burroughs, of the Episcopal Diocese of Ohio, sent an invitation to Sunday schools for a children's pilgrimage to the Cathedral, about 200 were expected. More than 1,700 showed up. They came in busloads, and were treated to a talk about the building, and a demonstration of how stained glass windows are made. Wilbur, Little Monk and Lady-in-Waiting, puppets manipulated by George Latshaw, were there to assist. They asked leading questions of the architect, Travis Walsh, and of Margaret Kennedy, who designs and makes windows. There was also a demonstration of organ making, and for a finale an impressive service in which a massed choir of children joined. The program was repeated the following year.

Elaine Miller, of Manhattan, Kansas, conducted a creative project with a group of nine- to twelve-year-old children. For several months they met once a week, experimented with different types of simple puppets and used them in short plays. All this was directed toward a Christmas program. Many stories were discussed; the children liked especially those about animals, so several of them were woven together—the American Indian tale of the deer who knelt in respect for the Child; the robin whose breast turned red as he fanned the embers of the fire in the manger, and a Mexican account of Pablo and his donkey. A narrator told the stories, the puppets provided the action, which was augmented by music, and the performance ended with a Nativity scene.

The B. Gay Puppets presented *David and the Spider* and *The Rabbit Who Wanted Red Wings* for a children's Christmas service in New York, and this company also has a repertory of plays for Jewish audiences, such as *The Ten Commandments, Solomon and the Serpent, The Purim Story, Noah's Folks,* and others. In Los Angeles, Betsy Brown has produced many religious plays, some based on the lives of St. Nicholas, St. Patrick and St. Jerome, others on tales of faith such as *Noah's Ark, The Magi and the Star* and *The Wedding Feast at Cana.*

Walter Webb, a native of California, became dissatisfied with his life and found fulfillment in an unusual way. Inspired by the interest of a group of children watching a puppet show in a park, and by the drama of the life of Christ, he built a puppet show on this theme and made a stage in a truck. After three years of preparation, he began travels which took him to many places in many states, where he played free of charge to children, mostly in poor areas. Sometimes churches or other groups hired him, and the fees paid gas and grocery bills.

With the inauguration of government programs such as Head Start, puppets have found yet another outlet for their activities.

In the summers of 1965 and 1966, the B. Gay Puppets played to Head Start groups throughout the New York City-New Jersey area. A forty-five minute program which could be adjusted to a given audience proved successful. Since the children had never experienced theatre in any form, Ann Cohen welcomed them and gave a few pointers on how to listen and enjoy the show. Then came two short plays, *Johann and the Black Sheep* and *The Rabbit Who Wanted Red Wings.* The first expressed the idea that it is not necessary to be big to be successful, and the second that it is wiser to be one's self than to try to imitate others. Bea Geller then had the children stand up and stretch, and with attention re-established, she showed different puppets and how they worked, and introduced a little African boy puppet who showed off his jungle friends. They performed to music, and a few notes about their lives were given.

Other puppeteers in the New York-Pennsylvania area who have enriched the lives of underprivileged children with their programs are Larry Berthelson, Frank Paris, Bernice Silver, the Puppet Associates (Carol Fijan, Director) and the Wonderland Puppet Theatre (Nancy Schmale and Alice Swann). There are many more.

During the summer of 1966, a group of thirty teen-agers took part in a Self Help Against Poverty program in Long Island City, New York. Under the direction of Lea and Gia Wallace, they built puppets and a mobile puppet theatre which performed for Head Start groups and patients in hospitals. The next year Lea Wallace had a similar program at Carver House, where she led more than fifty children through the whole process of making puppets, operating them and inventing stories for them. Attendance was fluid, but by the fifth week a core of twelve to twenty children who had stuck with the project remained. They gave sixteen shows in three weeks, bearing up like real troupers in the hot weather. Different construction methods were used for the various segments of the program, including some three- to four-foot rod-puppets with heads made of shopping bags or styrofoam wig bases. The program consisted of a Prologue, a Commedia dell'Arte-style mime, and a scene, *In the Office of the Housing Authority*, with animated cardboard buildings and such characters as Mr. Housing, Mr. Authority and Miss Puppeteer. *Peter and the Wolf* was also presented and was valuable in helping the children listen to music, as the performers gained experience in useful manual skills, in dramatic interpretation, and in group participation. Performing was strenuous and sometimes hostile attitudes were encountered. Once some eggs hurled from a window spattered onto the tape recorder, and there was a little trouble with hecklers. After that the troupe had police protection.

Among puppeteers who have assisted with Head Start programs in other parts of the country are Josie Robbins in Seattle, Betsy Brown in Los Angeles and Elizabeth Vondersmith in McLean, Virginia.

The value of puppets in Peace Corps activities has been appreciated by some of its leaders, and puppeteers have been asked to assist in training programs. For example, George Creegan, of Steubenville, Ohio, and his wife gave demonstrations of simple puppet making to a group of Peace Corps trainees at Cornell University, and helped them with ideas about using puppets to communicate with the children in the foreign lands to which they were assigned. A puppet project in Panama carried out by two Peace Corps members is described in Chapter IV.

The above examples are only a few of the many puppet activities throughout the United States which are in progress to advance understanding among people and to improve their lot.

Puppets in recreation

It is difficult to draw the line between recreation and education, and much of what has already been said of the latter applies equally to recreation. Siebolt Frieswyk, Head of Program Services for the National Recreation and Park Association, reports an increase in the use of puppets in the United States since 1960, especially for playground and day camp

1. A large puppet by Peter Schumann. Photo Diana J. Davies.

2. *A Bird in the Hand Beats the Bush* from George Latshaw's adult program *Hand in Glove*.

3. Wizard, Wilbur and Natalie Hackenschmidt in *The Wizard in the Well* by George Latshaw.

4. A scene from *Muzzleshy,* a gun safety film made by Basil Milovsoroff.

5. Puppet designs from roots, by Basil Milovsoroff.

6. A scene from *Davy Jones' Locker*, Bil and Cora Baird's Marionettes.

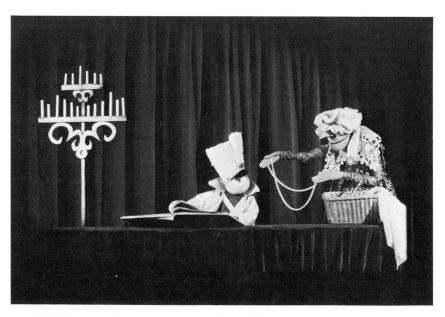

7. The Devil as an Old Woman, from the Baird production of Stravinsky's *L'Histoire du Soldat*.

8. Hungarian Dancers by André Tahon.

9. Papotin, André Tahon's Master of Ceremonies.

10. Kukla, Ollie and Fran in *The Reluctant Dragon,* built by Burr Tillstrom for the Children's Theatre Television Series, NBC.

12. Colonel Crackie and Madame Ooglepuss, Kuklapolitan Players.

11. Kukla as the Little Boy and Fletcher Rabbit as St. George in *The Reluctant Dragon.*

13. Cecil Bill and Mercedes, Kuklapolitan Players.

14. Shari Lewis with Hush Puppy, from her television program for children.

15. Leslie Caron in the film *Lili*, with Carrot Top, made by Walton and O'Rourke.

16. Scene from *The Shoemaker and the Elves* sequence in George Pal's stop motion film, *The Wonderful World of the Brothers Grimm*.

17. *Pas de Voodoo*, with finger puppets by Herb Scheffel.

18. An advertising display, *The Sleeping Bunny*, by George Cregan.

19. Squirrel, Chipmunk and Buzz from Ralph Chessé's television series, *Brother Buzz*.

20. Moses from *The Ten Commandments* by the B. Gay Puppets.

21. *The Nativity* by the Jacoby Marionettes.

29. Scene from *The Painted Eyebrow*, a Chinese shadow puppet production directed by Vernone Tracey and performed by a group of Detroit puppeteers. Photo by the Detroit Free Press.

30. Giant bird by Marjorie McPharlin from *Weapons of Lightning* by Virginia Lee Comer.

31. Part of the underground house of the Tottle family, used in a children's television program *Tottle*, produced by Marshall Izen.

32. Inside view of the Oni tree house, built on a revolving mechanism for *Tottle*.

33. Erica Melchior operates one of her large night club marionettes.

34. Scene from *Fiesta in Miniature* by René.

35. The Hang Ten Trio, marionettes made from gourds by Pat Platt. Photo by Alfred Alden Holston, Jr.

36. Scene from *The Barn-
    yard Frolics* by Bob
    and Judy Brown.

37. Betsy Brown's hand puppets perform
    in front of the Watts Towers, Los
    Angeles.

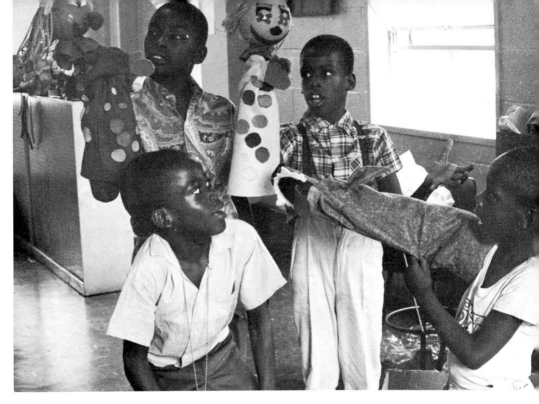

38. Children with their puppets made in a class conducted by Lea Wallace at Carver House, New York City.

39. Children with puppets made in a class at the Cleveland Museum of Art, under the direction of Greta and Henry Sherman.

40. A group of "Quickie" puppets made by adults after Emilie Jaeger's method using styrofoam balls and glued costumes.

41. Mask puppets made by children in an Indian village near Madras.

42. Children and table puppets in Marjorie McPharlin's class in Ankara, Turkey.

43. Song of Freedom from *The Story of Chanukah*. The Puppet Associates.

44. King Ahashverus and Hamen from *The Story of Esther*. The Puppet Associates, Carol Fijan, Director.

45. Farmer and Cat from *The Story of Dick Whittington*, designed and performed by Dick Myers, the Puppet Arts of Woodstock.

46. Scene from a production of *Agamemnon* at the University of Oklahoma, directed by Nat Eek, with nine foot puppets by George Latshaw for the principal characters, and a masked chorus.

47. Marshall Izen in a scene from the puppet opera *La*, performed atop the piano.

48. Lea and Gia Wallace in *Java-nese Suite*, dancer-with-puppet act.

49. Sandra Cerny and foam rubber "Bird".

50. Puppet Theatre in the round, built by Leo and Dora Velleman for the Robert Simpson Company, Toronto, for Christmas shows.

51. Lea Wallace's "Apron Stage" for performing puppet dances.

52. *El Retablo de Maese Pedro* at the University of California, Los Angeles produced by Mel Helstien with puppets and scenery by Mitch Colburn.

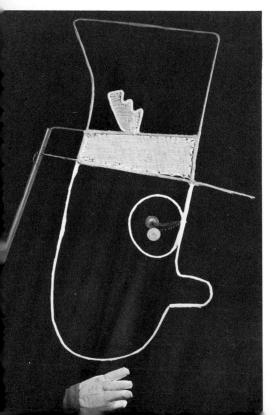

53. *Everyman* with puppets by Diana Jewett, UCLA.

54. *On Patchen* from *Possibilities* at UCLA, puppet by Larry Klingman.

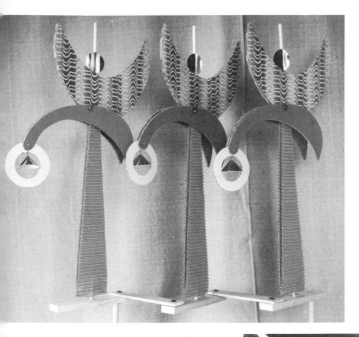

55. Abstract rod-puppets of paper and cardboard with different color arrangements on the two sides, operated by a multiple controller. Marjorie Mc-Pharlin.

56. Marionettes by the Berkeley Marionettes for *Coyote*, a Northwest Indian story.

57. Pink foam rubber Bull with magenta tongue and sequin eyes by Marjorie McPharlin.

58. Don Roldan and Don Gayferos from *Master Peter's Puppet Show*, built by Arlyn Kuthan and Luman Coad.

59. The Hero Falling Before the Night Vision, the Spectral Shadow of Fear and Self Aggression, from *The Legend of Longeth*, a production of the Unstrung Puppet Theatre of Bud and Marlene Wertheim.

60. Another scene from *The Legend of Longeth*, puppet and scenery of welded metal.

61. Giant masks by Peter Schumann in a Peace Parade in New York City.

programs. Puppet making and performances are included in children's theatre operations within the Association, and in some places shows are sponsored by professional or qualified amateur performers. An increase in the use of puppets is likely in the future, but more trained people are needed, because of the present dearth of qualified drama specialists. These may be forthcoming because "park and recreation agencies are becoming more deeply committed to the development of cultural life in their respective communities." Here we can cite only a few examples of recreational puppetry to suggest the kind of programs offered and where they take place.

Many city recreation and park departments include some puppet activity.

Betty Puckle, Research Specialist for the Recreation Department of Phoenix, Arizona, gives workshops and demonstrations as in-service training for the staff, and for numerous groups throughout the city to stimulate interest in puppet making and production. Puppet kits are loaned like library books to leaders of groups, and a direction booklet with several types of simple puppets is included. The Phoenix Guild of Puppetry and the Phoenix Arts Council work closely with the Department. In many cities, the recreation department sponsors shows which visit the playgrounds. Peg Blickle and Dora Rosenfeld spent the summers of 1950 and 1951 on such a tour in Columbus, Ohio. Usually performing out-of-doors, they were often interrupted by dog fights, train whistles, and adverse weather. A marionette workshop for children was sponsored by the Topeka (Kansas) Recreation Commission in 1955 and 1956. This production traveled by show wagon, visiting twenty playgrounds twice during the season. By the end of the second year, it had chalked up 94 performances.

In 1953, a program of puppet shows, which became the Vagabond Puppet Theatre, was inaugurated by the Oakland (California) Recreation Department. Joyce Lobner, who had taught puppetry for many years, directed the project. From 1954 to 1960, Lettie Connell Schubert was supervising specialist of puppetry. She produced marionette and hand-puppet shows which toured in a gaily painted trailer to playgrounds and school yards throughout the city of Oakland. With two assistant puppet specialists and some teen-age volunteers, she gave from forty to eighty free performances to 5,000 to 12,000 children and adults each summer. The program was meant not only to entertain, but to stimulate interest in live entertainment and to encourage dramatic activities on the playgrounds. A recreation leaders' workshop was given at the beginning of the summer by the three puppeteers, who also served as advisors for puppetry projects. They wrote scripts, built from two to four plays each summer, and performed them. Some of the titles were *Punch and Judy, Peter and the Wolf, Winnie-the-Pooh, Mrs. Witherspoon's Busy Day, The Tale of the Terrible Tiger,* and *Beauty and the Beast.* Many members of the staff started as teen-age volunteers, became directors, and then went on to larger theatre jobs. For instance, Frank Osnowicz and Jerry Juhl ran the project after Lettie Connell Schubert left, and then went on to work with Jim Henson's Muppets in New York. Dahl Delu became technical director with the Tyrone Guthrie Theatre in Minneapolis, and Robert Darling has designed sets for off-Broadway shows and for operas in Europe and San Francisco. The Vagabond Theatre, with Ruth Sicular as its head, is still performing.

For several years, children in Montreal parks were treated to puppet shows given by André Fayard in his mobile puppet theatre, decorated in the style of an old-time medicine show wagon. Lewis Mahlmann has done revue-type shows at Yosemite National Park and in parks of the San Francisco Bay area. Tommy Trent spends two weeks each summer giving shows in the parks and playgrounds of Miami Beach. In 1958 Rod Young established an annual summer series of shows sponsored by the County of Westchester (New York) Department of Parks and Recreation. For ten years he performed thirty shows each summer in parks and play areas, first with a trailer theatre, then with his regular stage set up outdoors.

The longest-lived puppet theatre sponsored by a park and recreation department is in New York City. In 1939, Commissioner Robert Moses decided to have a traveling marionette theatre to perform in the five boroughs of New York. Four recreation leaders were assigned the job of organizing it. Ascanio Spolidoro, who was one of Remo Bufano's assistants, became director, and Dorothie Fisher was manager. Several months later the first production, *Jack and the Beanstalk,* was ready to tour. From that day to the present, the Park Marionette Theatre has played to thousands of children, outdoors in the parks during the summer, indoors during the winter. The Swedish Cottage, a part of Sweden's educational exhibit at the 1876 Centennial Exposition in Philadelphia, had been purchased by the City and set up in Central Park. In 1947, Dorothie Fisher persuaded the Department to turn the Cottage over to the Marionette Project for its headquarters and workshop. She also worked to get an annual appropriation from the city budget, and to have the title of Puppeteer established in Civil Service. The examination for this position was made up by Shirley O'Donnol and Frank Paris, and the first applicants were tested in 1963. During its long history, many people have worked in the Marionette Theatre. With Miss Fisher's death in 1964, and the resignation of Spolidoro in 1966, new people have led it.

Some parks have permanent puppet theatres. The Toronto Metropolitan

Parks Commission built the Toronto Island Puppet Theatre, which is open from May 24 through Labor Day. Among those who have performed there are Leo and Dora Velleman, who have given shows during part of the summer for the past three years. Balboa Park in San Diego has a puppet theatre built three years ago. The Padre Puppeteers (Marie Hitchcock and Genevieve Engman), who were first sponsored by the Park and Recreation Department to play in the Public Library, are among the regular performers. For the first summer season, Pat Platt organized and participated in a program given by members of the San Diego County Guild of Puppetry. A similar series is given each year.

The Oakland (California) Park Department built a puppet theatre in Children's Fairyland, and in 1956 Frank Hayward was named director. A few months later he passed away, and his wife Dorothy was appointed to carry on the work. To meet the coming summer schedule, Roberta Mack stepped in "like a fairy godmother." She offered her puppets, and built all the props for *Karnival Kapers,* a variety show with trick marionettes. That autumn, a puppet fair was held, with gay exhibit booths set up in the vicinity of the puppet theatre, and performances were given by many local puppeteers. The fair was repeated nearly every year thereafter. For 1968, in addition to the puppet fair, there will be one for toys, with examples from the past hundred years. Tony Urbano joined the theatre staff in 1958 and remained as director until 1961. Luman Coad, who had previously worked at the puppet theatre in Happy Hollow Children's Park in La Jolla, came in 1963 and directed a long list of plays based on well-known stories, including *The Shoemaker and the Elves, Sleeping Beauty,* and *Red Riding Hood.* Less familiar stories, such as *The Story of the Blue Willow Plate, Guignol and the Lemonade Stand,* and *A Dog's Tale,* were also presented. Lewis Mahlmann succeeded Coad in 1967. Puppet playing at Fairyland is a rigorous business, for six shows a year have to be built and performances given the year round—three times daily, seven days a week during summer vacation, five days a week when school is in session. The unusually long season is possible because of the mild California climate. For many years the Milk Drivers and Dairy Employees Union, Local Number 302, maintained the Fairyland performances; now the Oakland Park Department is co-sponsor.

The Playland Puppet Theatre at Rye Beach, New York, was operated for three summers by Rod Young in the Casino Building's small permanent theatre. He functioned as performer, ticket taker, sweeper (between shows, to remove candy wrappers, etc.), and he even advertised the performances, dressed in a clown suit and a sandwich board. The first summer, eight shows a day, four days a week were given with hand-puppets; subsequently the schedule was cut down to weekends only. Young terms the venture "an artistic success and a commercial failure," because the location was wrong and sponsorship was lacking.

In the Nassau County Park there is a puppet theatre which seats 200 people. From October to May, performances are given on weekends and holidays. Jacqueline Razzano, the Director, writes the five plays used each season, and makes hand-puppets for them. Two mobile trucks also troupe around the county in the summer. At Cain Park, in Cleveland Heights, Ohio, the Alma Puppet Theatre, designed by J. Frances Crothers in 1942, gave puppet shows until about five years ago.

Throughout the United States and Canada there are hundreds of youth organizations which utilize every recreational resource, including puppetry. The Boy Scouts, the Girl Scouts, the Campfire Girls, the Boys' Clubs are national in scope, and these are augmented by a multitude of local groups sponsored by churches, synagogues, schools, and civic organizations. Puppets may be used in camps or after-school projects; they may take part in special events, programs for holidays, and dozens of other activities. Generally, the idea of active participation in the programs is stressed, for it is the making of puppets and presentation of shows which are considered valuable experiences for young people.

O. W. (Bud) Bennett has for many years been a staunch promoter of puppets in the Cub Scout program, and has written a handbook containing suggestions for their use (see Bibliography). He has also conducted training courses for leaders. Helen Lee Denison described her experiences from 1924 to 1931 in an article, "Pioneering Camp Puppetry" (*Puppetry Journal,* January–February 1954), which points out that the problems and opportunities then are similar to those of today. From 1945 through 1962, Dorothy Gleason directed children in the Rhythm Puppets Summer Theatre at Noyes Junior Camp in Portland, Connecticut.

Much puppet activity goes on at community centers, where children or adults make puppets and present their shows, with an audience always at hand. Hull House in Chicago has been for years a place where underprivileged children are given opportunities they would otherwise not have. Hans and Ruby Schmidt have held classes in puppetry there, given shows and lectures and published a book on simple puppet making (see Bibliography). In Ames, Iowa, the Octagon Center for the Arts includes puppet work conducted by Veronika Ruedenberg, sponsors shows by leading puppeteers and has puppet exhibits. Pioneer Craft House, a community center in Salt Lake City directed by Mrs. Beeley, has promoted puppetry for many years, and workshops are given, such as the one-day session with Lewis Parsons, Ron Bowers, Margaret Hamilton and Elliott Airmet participating.

A continuing puppet program was conducted by John Zweers at the

Scattergood Center of the Pasadena Y.M.C.A., first with a group of boys up to twelve years of age, who formed the Junior Club. Some of its members wanted to continue after they passed the age limit, so a Senior Club was formed. During the fourteen years of their existence, the clubs met regularly on Saturdays the year round in their own building. The clubs performed at the Pasadena Art Fair, and each year *The First Christmas* was presented as a gift to the community. The Senior Club members staged classics (*Theseus and the Minotaur, Robin Hood,* and *Peter Pan*), original plays including *Geraldine in Jeopardy,* and their own versions of such stories as *The Shooting of Dan McGrew.* In addition, the clubs built furniture and equipment for their workshop, and edited the *YMCA Puppet Club News.* Harry Burnett assisted in the program for a year, and other volunteers helped from time to time. In addition to his work with young people, Zweers has given many performances with his own puppets, and has built up a large collection of puppets from all over the world.

Under the Department of School-Community Recreation in Madison, Wisconsin, a puppet program was started four years ago with a group of junior high school students who worked on Saturdays with an art teacher. At first only those in one school were involved; then the program was expanded, and two centers were established. In the beginning classes, puppets are made and plays developed from them with improvised dialogue. By March these are ready for performance and the students take them to Saturday school play centers. Those who return from the first year work, rehearse their productions, develop additional material, and give at least ten performances. In the third year, the students form a concert group which experiments with new and more elaborate production techniques, such as 36-inch puppets for *Tom Sawyer,* which was performed on three stages. For the past two years, all the groups have gone by bus to present an afternoon of puppetry for the Uplands Arts Council at the Gard Theatre in Spring Green. Kert Bliss, assistant director of the Department, has been successful in obtaining funds for the project and for a staff consisting of a supervisor, two beginning instructors, two traveling group instructors, and a technician.

Cultural and recreational programs for people not in school are supported by the Department of Education in Ontario. From 1950, when he arrived from England, George Merten has been puppet advisor. As a result of his work, several thousand adults became interested in puppetry, and groups in over 200 communities have held area festivals.

In almost every community, the library offers recreation for children. A summer reading program may have a reward of a puppet show for all those who complete it. *Weapons of Lightning,* with script by Virginia Lee Comer, based on Navajo Indian creation stories, was built by Marjorie

McPharlin and presented for young readers at the Mesa Library in Los Alamos, New Mexico. Nancy Staub regularly builds shows to tour the libraries of New Orleans. These include *Placide and the Alligator*, an original story about bayou animals; *Tall Tales*, with actors in half-masks interpreting folk heroes; and *The Tongue-Cut Sparrow*, which had fourteen performances in the summer of 1967 as part of the summer reading program.

Sometimes library staffs give shows for children, as was done for some years in Salina, Kansas. Every Saturday morning during the school year, Sherman Ripley acted as Master of Ceremonies, with a few magic tricks to start things off. Eleanor Owens and other staff members would then present a puppet play—a new one each week. Kay Kitchen used table-top puppets to interpret fine literature in San Diego libraries, and Mollie Falkenstein has given free shows in return for a library membership in the Puppeteers of America. For Book Week at the San Francisco Library in 1955, Lettie Connell Schubert built *The Magic Teakettle* and *The Real Princess*. In 1947 Tom Tichenor began giving weekly marionette shows at the Nashville Public Library, with traditional fairy tales and original stories making up his repertoire. He continued these for ten years, then divided his time between Nashville and Memphis until he went to New York in 1961. For sixteen years he has been Consultant and Director of Children's Entertainment for the Library, and he also designed the Story Room, with a puppet booth in the form of an old English cottage.

Puppets in therapy

As in education and recreation, the usefulness of puppets in therapy is based upon the many different manual and mental activities involved in the production of a puppet show. Many performances are given to relieve boredom and cheer patients in hospitals and sanatoriums, but puppets are also called upon for therapeutic treatment of a wide variety of physical and mental ailments. Therapy involves close supervision by qualified medical personnel and is sometimes limited because an institution may not be able to afford a trained puppet specialist. There is also reluctance to spread information about using puppets for fear that people without medical background or adequate guidance may use them poorly. However, in some places, instruction in puppetry is given in occupational therapy courses, for example, at Mount Mary College, Milwaukee, and at the Richmond Professional Institute. Emma Warfield, who once taught puppetry at the Philadelphia School of Occupational Therapy and who has been for many years Consultant for the Puppeteers of America, reports that she receives many inquiries about puppetry from people who are working for degrees in occupational therapy or are writing articles about it. Virginia Tooper, who has her own puppet show and has been a teacher and occupational therapist, has used puppets with patients in tuberculosis hospitals, children's hospitals, and at the Child Guidance Home in Cincinnati. She is now working with mentally retarded children as part of her preparation for a doctorate.

Hundreds of people have given performances to bring a little laughter and brightness to shut-ins, both children and adults.

For Dr. Esther Cheatle, now a well-known Chicago therapist, a childhood interest in puppets continued through high school, college and medical school, where her shows helped pay expenses. Then, as an intern at Wesley Memorial College, she gave shows for children with only a suitcase of puppets for equipment. Inga Strehlow, a librarian, became a regular part of the "therapeutic entertainment" program at the Kaiser Foundation Hospital in Oakland, California. At first she simply told stories as part of the Oakland Public Library reading program, but later introduced puppets. With them she told stories designed to allay the fears of children and to give them advice as well as to amuse them. She also trained student nurses in the use of puppets. The Jervis family, Ida, Sidney and their two children Nelson and Alice, have entertained crippled children at the Anderson Orthopedic Clinic in Arlington, Virginia, with Happy Joe's Puppets. Plays, skits, novelty numbers and songs (with Ida in front of the stage to sing them) were included in the performances. Even children have given shows. In 1951, David Mehlin, then age 10, a Boy Scout and Junior member of the Puppeteers of America, performed for children in the North Adams Hospital and Daniel Scherer, also age 10, entertained at the Cerebral Palsy Center, Roosevelt, Long Island, in 1960.

Many organizations sponsor shows. The National Capital Puppet Guild has a Children's Hospital Benefit Show committee, and its chairman, Elizabeth Vondersmith, has presented monthly performances in the children's ward at Alexandria Hospital for the past three years. Many Junior League groups are active in hospital work, giving performances and providing puppets and kits for children to use. In 1960, the Ladies' Auxiliary of the Boston Floating Hospital distributed Peppy, a hand-puppet, to all the children in the hospital. It took fifteen groups of women to do the necessary work, but the lift in morale was evident. The children at Quincy Hospital were also recipients of puppets given by its Ladies' Auxiliary.

In the more serious work of using puppets as a therapeutic aid, people like Roberta Mack have made a career for themselves. She began in 1932 by helping a child with speech difficulties, and ever since she has given innumerable workshops and demonstrations, written articles and helped set up therapy programs. She recognizes that play is a necessity for every child, and much of her therapy work has been in developing techniques for helping handicapped and mentally disturbed children overcome their various difficulties. She has developed relaxing exercises led by a marionette, helped retarded children reveal themselves through a play called *Secrets,* worked out puppet scenes to help children overcome fear of doctors and dentists, prepared "scissors-type" puppets for children with weak muscles, used vegetable puppets for dietary problems and encouraged senior citizens to work with puppets. In the treatment of cerebral palsy, Patricia Griswold of the Indiana University Clinic has found puppets of value in helping children to remember, to understand size, number and sequence of events. *The Three Bears* and *The Three Pigs* are used, and a clown, Simon, leads the children in imitative actions, such as washing the face, getting dressed and eating.

Many ways of helping people with speech difficulties have been worked out. In the Speech Clinic at Mount Mercy Hospital in Pittsburgh, Joan Halloran has used puppets, as has Edythe Benson at the Parmly Hearing Institute in Chicago. Louise Kingman specialized in using puppets for speech correction at Boston University. From 1952 to 1963, she worked in several departments including the Speech and Hearing Center, the School of Education and the School of Fine and Applied Arts. Her methods were feasible for both college students and for children in the public schools, who were reached through the student teachers she supervised. Puppets were quickly made from vegetables, especially potatoes, with a handkerchief for a costume. Plays were developed and recordings made as dialogue progressed. Speech deficiencies showed up at once, and the business of correcting them went forward. Playing a part helped stutterers and shy people, those with articulation problems, the hard of hearing and even the blind. Miss Kingman also worked with foreign students whose English was not fluent. They made up puppet plays about children in their respective countries, and these were given for children in Boston hospitals. The United States Information Agency sent out a release on her work, "American Teacher Uses Puppets for Speech Therapy," which was published in newspapers and magazines in eighty countries.

In the area of mental therapy, puppets function in many ways. In a report given in Baton Rouge at the 1965 Southern Regional Convention of the Child Welfare League of America, Betsy Kimbree pointed out that mental illness is characterized by conflict with the commonly accepted world. Puppets may reach people suffering from mental illness and help them restore their harmony with the world through the release of emotion in the puppet play and through communication with others in the group. Some may even become interested in puppetry as a hobby, and performing helps bridge their relationship to the community. Whenever the attention of a patient can be focused on a puppet, there is likely to be involvement with it, and the resulting words and actions are so revealing that psychiatrists use puppets in their analyses. For example, Dr. P. Kors at Pontiac State Hospital and Isidore Shapiro of the Child Guidance Center, Hewlett, Long Island, found that children using puppets revealed problems in family relationships.

An experiment in puppet therapy was carried out by three members of the Larchmont (New York) Junior League at the Westchester ARC School in Pelham, which cares for emotionally disturbed, brain-damaged, and retarded children. Under the direction of the teachers and the school psychiatrist, plays were especially written and presented to help the children grasp spatial concepts and resolve conflicts, and to prepare them for situations they might encounter. The children were also allowed to work with the puppets and develop their own plays. At the request of Dr. Gladys Holmes of the Montana State Hospital for the Insane, three women from the Butte Junior League taught marionettes for a year to both men and women. Despite very slow progress and many difficulties (even a violent attack by one of the women patients), a show was presented. During the year the hospital staff was given instruction so the work could be continued.

Puppetry with retarded children is a valuable experience for them. Dorothy Rankin, of Peabody, Massachusetts, has recently given demonstrations at the Hawthorne School for the Mentally Retarded in Salem. She helped the children work finger-puppets, which was a great effort for many of them. An undersea play gave a chance to show them all kinds of puppets in colorful costumes, and a large dog talked to them. Margaret Fickling had many years of experience working with retarded children in California. In that state, such children are integrated into the regular school system, but work in separate rooms with no more than eighteen pupils. Mrs. Fickling found the puppet show a successful way to develop academic skills, such as reading and arithmetic, as well as abilities in art, manual work and music. Even more important, the presentation of a puppet show to the whole school brought acceptance by the normal children and a feeling of equality with them. The use of creative approaches in puppet and playmaking offered a maximum opportunity for each child to use whatever capacities he had.

Puppets are sometimes used in the schools for special classes, such as those for slow learners whom Ruth Bolick taught in Dayton, Ohio. She found that puppets helped in emotional adjustments and character building, as well as academic subjects including language arts, arithmetic and social studies. Manual skills and artistic expression were also developed, and interest in music inspired.

In the School of Occupational Therapy at the Richmond (Virginia) Professional Institute, Clark Sabine uses a therapeutic clown in his course in Physical Dysfunction. A fully articulated marionette is hung from a special controller set into a solid stand. The strings pass over spools and a ring attached to the end, so that the patient can activate the figure and exercise his fingers, strengthening them and improving coordination. The basic fascination of puppets for children is here utilized to lessen the boredom of exercise. In another course, Pediatric Techniques, taught by Eleanor Wolfe, the students make hand-puppets and present a play to patients in the pediatrics ward of a local hospital. Puppetry is only one of a group of techniques which include arts and crafts, literature, music and games.

Not all mental problems are abnormal ones. It is now recognized that most children encounter difficulties of one sort or another in their adjustment to the world and the people around them. Some attempts are being made by the mass media—especially television—to present and resolve such problems. An unusually successful puppet program was developed by Marshall Izen with the Tottles, a family of woodland creatures who experience all sorts of situations familiar to children. More will be said of them in Chapter III.

Puppetry classes

Where do people learn puppetry? Knowledge is disseminated in many ways. Books help, as a glance at the Technical Section of the Bibliography will show, but classes and workshops for both children and adults frequently provide beginners with the necessary skills to develop their interest in the field.

Many children are taught puppetry in school, especially in art classes. For sixteen years Vernone Tracey taught puppetry in the Art Department of Greenfield Park School in Detroit to children in grades three through eight, with production as the major aim. From 1934 until her retirement in 1963, Galene Myers taught fifth grade, first in Excelsior, Minnesota, then in Redondo Beach, California, where puppets became an indispensable teaching tool. Leona Madsen has taught puppetry in her art classes at many grade levels in the New York schools, always with an eye alert to new creative approaches. One production with high school students, *The Night Before Christmas,* had music by the school choir and special choreography for the hand-puppets who performed on a large stage.

For many years Vivian Michael included puppet projects in her art classes at Everett Junior High School in Columbus, Ohio, and produced excellent shows with the students. A student of Tony Sarg, she used marionettes until her daughter Gayle developed a new design for hand-and-rod-puppets. With these, her students were able to reach a more professional level of performance, and their shows were presented throughout central Ohio. More imaginative puppets and more original plays, often done with improvised dialogue, supplanted the older classic adaptations, because this freer approach appealed to the students.

Esther Heydt, who teaches in San Diego, has recently developed new techniques in shadow-puppetry. The figures are made of household gelatine and painted with vegetable colors. A special light with a dimmer, designed by her husband Wilson, makes possible many interesting effects. Used in a cultural arts program in some of the city schools, the shadows evoke a delighted response from the children. She has also worked out a method for transposing second-grade children's drawings to simple shadow-puppets which are then used in dramatizing stories. Each semester she lectures on puppetry to the Creative Dramatics classes at San Diego State College to give the students an awareness of the possibilities of puppet theatre "beyond the potato head and papier-mâché-on-a-light-bulb stage."

For twenty years Claire Zeidelman has been an active puppet educator in Philadelphia. With about thirty children, ages twelve to sixteen, she has produced an annual puppet play at the Penn Treaty Junior High School. The group works as a Marionette Club, with some sessions on school time and additional ones after hours. She writes the scripts and does much of the designing and construction, aided by the children, who also do the production. The plays are often based on stories of other lands—*In a Persian Market* (a musical interpretation); *The Willow Plate; The Nuremburg Stove; Ali Baba and Thief Number 40; Carmencita; Japanese Farewell;* and *Remi*, a French story. Some plays have historical significance, such as *The Man Without a Country* or *Salute to Kensington*, the story of William Penn's treaty with the Indians, which was signed at a spot near the school. One year they did a play for the United Fund which was also televised. Claire Zeidelman also has a program of short scenes and variety which she has performed many times.

Classes for children are held in many places outside the schools. Arthur Scheller had classes at his Wooden Tots Puppet Studio in Rochester, New York, as did Vera Leeper, at her Montrose, California, home. Harry Burnett and George Latshaw have taught puppetry at the Idyllwild Summer School maintained by the University of Southern California, where many classes in the arts are conducted for children. For the past twenty years, both children and adults have been able to study puppetry under the direction of Emma Warfield at the Community Arts Center in Wallingford, Pennsylvania. Here the students design their own puppets and make their own scripts. The Puppet Associates of Great Neck, Long Island, have operated a school since 1958, where they teach a special methodology to bring the puppet to life. Believing that puppetry is a *performing* art, they present it as a means of creative vocal expression. Adults as well as children and teen-agers study here, and they learn all phases of puppet making and production. The school staff consists of Carol Fijan, director; Shirley Roman, designer, and Sy Roman, writer. Several teen-agers assist with manipulation, lights and sound.

From 1950 to 1960, Lea and Gia Wallace directed the Village Dance and Puppet Center in Greenwich Village. Children came on Saturdays from ten in the morning to three in the afternoon for studies in the performing arts, especially dance and puppetry. Some weekdays there were classes after school, and adults worked in the evenings. The elements of mime and drama were also taught with puppets. In June, recitals representing all departments of the school were given.

For many years after J. Frances Crothers started puppet work at Cain Park (Cleveland Heights) in 1942, puppet performances and classes were held there in the summer. Many people have been associated with this work at one time or another, including Helen Haiman Joseph in the forties, and more recently, George Latshaw, Shirley O'Donnol, and others. Regular puppet performances given by the staff and apprentices were also a part of the program, as were performances by child actors. Puppetry has not been included for the past five years, and the park closed in 1967, but may reopen.

Classes in puppet making have been offered in the summer program of the Casper (Wyoming) Children's Theatre. Shirley O'Donnol had charge of them in 1951, and Rod Young in 1954 and 1955. The latter taught six- to twelve-year-olds, who met morning and afternoon for three weeks and then presented a play for the local library. Scripts were developed by Young from the characters which the children created.

The Mott Foundation, of Flint, Michigan, administered by the city Board of Education, has a strong adult education program which includes many classes and workshops in speech and drama, coordinated by Helen Hardy Brown. A summer drama school, established in 1962, presents a dance-drama and a play for children at the annual Fine Arts Festival. The Children's Theatre Enrichment Program includes Creative Drama, Teen Theatre, and Puppet Theatre. These classes are conducted in the various community schools of the city and have been growing steadily during the past fifteen years. Eighteen puppet classes meet after school and on Saturday, with ten summer classes extending over a six-week period. Puppet demonstrations are also given at Tot Lot centers in elementary schools,

involving hundreds of children. Five puppetry teachers, supervised by
Jennie Trojanowski, keep this work going, and others are trained in the
three divisions of drama during spring and fall workshops in Children's
Theatre. The Mott puppetry program is notable because of its creative
theatre approach, which includes not only puppet making and presentation, but experience in creative drama, dramatic literature, and playmaking. A special puppet class at the Durant-Tuuri-Mott Elementary
School is conducted for orthopedic and hearing-conservation pupils, in
which the problems of poor hearing and of puppeteers performing in
wheelchairs or on crutches are overcome, with resultant gains in the self-
confidence of the children.

Puppets have an important place at the Children's Centre for Creative
Arts at Adelphi University, Garden City, Long Island, where they have
been used for over fifteen years. This "integrative program for children
and adults where the arts are related to living" began with drama and art,
and its moving spirit and director was—and still is—Grace Stanistreet.
Creative expression was little understood then, but those children who
came to the Centre for after-school or Saturday meetings responded with
enthusiasm. Acting, poetry, music, puppetry and other arts were added,
and by 1968 there were ten artist-teachers with thirty-four volunteer student leaders to help. One hundred children are now enrolled in the Saturday classes, with another group of twenty teen-agers in a Tuesday evening
acting workshop. Also on Saturday morning after the regular classes, there
is a special class in music for both children and staff and another in dance
for boys. Parents and other interested adults are drawn into the program
through special workshops for them, and for an activity called Creative
Arts in Action, children and adults in equal numbers make up the groups.
This heterogeneous grouping works in situations where the emphasis is
upon problem solving through individual thinking, spontaneity, and the
courage to try. All the programs at the Centre are based upon individual
development rather than set goals of achievement: drama is not the production of formal plays, but creative drama; music is not learning to play
an instrument but experiencing sound and rhythm and using them expres-
sively; so it is also with poetry, dance and puppetry.

Ludwig Riemenschneider relates his puppet work to all the other
activities at the Centre and stresses creativity in his whole approach.
While many of the classes are for children from six to twelve years, he
has been successful in interesting teen-agers in a play form involving the
interplay of the puppets' world with that of the real child. A variety of
situations are enacted in which the puppets represent a person's tiny inner
voices, both good and bad, who help or hinder the undecided persons in
front of the booth in the solution of their "conscious troubles." Thus the

puppets are equal partners with live actors, and these "Dramas of the Inner Self" lead to further uses of puppets in creative acting classes.

Adults are able to learn puppetry in a variety of ways. Almost everyone who has had any experience in the field communicates his enthusiasm and knowledge to other people. Innumerable workshops, demonstrations and classes are held for teachers, community leaders and others engaged in group activities.

Emilie Jaeger has demonstrated her Quickie Puppets to Jo Lawrence's storytelling classes at Phoenix College; to librarians; to park, recreation, Scout and Campfire leaders; at children's theatre and puppeteers' conventions. Betsy Brown conducted workshops for a Confraternity of Christian Doctrine Convention, and a demonstration for teachers at Barnsdall Park Children's Art Center in Los Angeles. In 1965 and 1966, Leo and Dora Velleman taught a course in Instant Puppets at the Ontario College of Art, a teacher-training course sponsored by the Department of Education. It also has in-service courses in art, with an optional unit in puppetry which has been led by the Vellemans, George Merten, Joicey Horne, Roy Hughes and Kenneth McKay. In the 1967 Toronto program, about eighty students were involved, working in groups of twenty for eighteen hours over a six-day period. Workshops for leaders of puppetry in the Junior League are held at intervals by Alfred Wallace and Jean Starr Wiksell, as well as by many local puppeteers.

Many museum programs and those of the Puppet Guilds include demonstrations and workshops. These are also an integral part of the annual Puppeteers of America Puppet Festivals. Technical aspects of puppet making and staging, problems of production, playwriting, creative approaches, manipulation, and many other subjects have been covered. In 1954, following the Festival at Dartmouth College, an eight-day Institute was held, with a choice of (1) a basic course in puppet making and show production, (2) variety and trick puppets especially for night club acts and (3) creative puppetry "for advanced puppeteers, art teachers and the creatively inclined."

From 1960 to the present, Isabel Tolman has conducted many workshops—for puppeteers, teachers, nurses, therapists, Scout leaders, music teachers, and the general public. They have been held at museums, regional festivals, university summer schools and other centers. At Chautauqua she held summer classes from 1962 through 1967, for three- to six-week periods, and she gave shows for school children in the Boston area under the name of the Penguin Puppeteers from 1958 to 1963. A play, variety, and a demonstration of puppet making were included on the program. She has also made a set of stock characters for the Frank Laubach Literacy Program to be used in Nigeria.

Professional puppeteers have sometimes conducted classes. Cedric and Mabel Head (the Kingsland Marionettes) held a summer workshop from July 1 to Labor Day at Lake Dunmore in Vermont from 1935 to 1955. A new show was built each year, and about 200 puppeteers were trained during the twenty-year period. At the Stevens studio in Middlebury, Indiana, a number of young puppeteers have "learned by doing" while assisting with the building of productions. The Stevens Correspondence Course, which covers the whole process of puppet making and show production in twenty sessions, was offered for sale in 1957 and is still in demand. Frank Paris and many other puppeteers have had classes in their studios, or admitted one or more people for intensive training.

Puppet teaching in colleges and universities takes a variety of forms. In most places, puppetry is offered at intervals, either as classes extending over a period of time, such as a summer session or a semester, or as short-term workshops of a few days or weeks. Some institutions have had an active puppet group for a number of years, then discontinued it when its "moving spirit" was no longer present. A few places have regular puppetry courses in the department of theatre arts, speech, drama, or art education.

For several summers Trenton State College offered a graduate course in puppets and playmaking under the direction of Henry W. Ahrens and Hilda S. Wagner, chairmen of the Departments of Art and Speech respectively. Pennsylvania State University first offered a puppet course in 1958, which was taught by Walter H. Walters. In 1961 and 1962, George Latshaw took over and also gave two performances. The next year Ellis Grove conducted the work. It was not offered again until 1967, when Irwin Sirota gave a course based on the glove-puppet in all its variations. The class of twelve students studied sculpture and caricature, made puppets, wrote scripts, designed booths, painted scenery, worked on publicity and gave a performance. This was an all-student puppet carnival, for which each student prepared his own show. As part of the Summer Theatre Festival, Sirota presented *Punch and Judy, Jack and the Beanstalk* and *The Magic Axe*.

At San Francisco State College, Ralph Chessé taught puppetry for two years, 1950 and 1951. Nancy White has had a spring semester class for the past five years, with a three-week session every other summer. The plays produced were mostly children's classics. Lewis Mahlmann is currently teaching there and working on a production of *Gulliver* with a dance-pantomime class for a puppets-people show. In the autumn of 1967, Arizona State University offered two puppet classes through its Extension Department, under the direction of Tamara Nijinsky. Frank Paris has had classes at Columbia and at New York University, and Sue

Hastings spent part of her time for ten years teaching at the University of Miami.

When William Duncan became director of the Leonard Theatre at Western College, most of his time was spent with live actors, but occasionally puppets appeared with them. He also included puppet history and demonstrations in his theatre classes. With his wife Ruth, he sometimes gave shows, especially that perennial favorite, *The Glowing Bird,* which has had more than 2,500 performances. Another Duncan program, *Meet the Marionettes,* presented by Ruth Duncan, is flexible in content. It can be for entertainment, or have an educational approach with emphasis on construction, manipulation, and puppet history, or it can stress the use of puppets in teaching, therapy and other fields. At present the Duncans are living in Santa Fe, and their puppet work is limited by their involvement in other activities.

Virginia Lee Comer and I conducted workshops in puppetry and creative dramatics at the University of New Mexico and at New Mexico Highlands University, where we developed the techniques described in *Puppets and Plays, A Creative Approach.* A new course in creative puppetry taught by Betsy Brown began with the spring semester of 1958 at the Los Angeles Valley College. Shirley O'Donnol became assistant professor of drama at Sacramento State College in 1964, where she has classes in puppetry and children's theatre, costuming, and make-up. She also directs puppet shows which are presented as part of the season's drama schedule.

Ken Moses, technologist for the Regent Theatre of Syracuse University, recently began a puppet program. Students in the drama department have built *Puss in Boots* and *A Midsummer Night's Dream,* which are presented with the same attention to sets, lighting, costume and acting as the plays given with human actors. Although *Dream* was conceived as serious adult drama, Moses has trouble overcoming the "puppets are for kids" attitude—a common enough complaint among puppeteers.

Caroline S. Lutz, English professor at Westhampton College, University of Richmond, worked for many years to build adult interest in puppets. Performances were given back in 1931 in connection with her English classes, and later, regular courses were introduced. She accumulated a large collection of puppets, which were used for exhibits and lectures designed to demonstrate the artistry of puppets and their long history. A number of well-known puppeteers have been technical directors of this work, including Shirley O'Donnol from 1950 to 1953, and Rod Young from 1954 to 1957. During these years, many different types of plays were presented with all kinds of puppets. In due course Caroline Lutz retired, and her death in August 1967 ended a long career of prosyletizing the art of puppetry. Her collection, bequeathed to the University of Richmond, is to be housed in the new art building.

With the strong impetus given to puppetry by artists and its widespread use in education, it is not surprising to find it firmly established at Wayne State University in Detroit, in the Department of Art Education. Here, since 1936, Fern Zwickey has taught classes in puppet making, presented shows and generally advanced knowledge and appreciation of puppets through lectures, demonstrations and workshops. She stresses a creative approach to puppet production, with emphasis on the dramatic qualities inherent in puppets. One feature of the work is an annual Christmas performance in which the lively imagination of the students is given full sway.

Sister Corona Sharp believes puppetry is a serious theatre art. During the past two decades she has developed a strong program at Brescia College, London, Ontario, which features the comedies of Shakespeare. *A Midsummer Night's Dream, Twelfth Night* and *The Merry Wives of Windsor* have been performed with hand-puppets. While one group of actors reads the lines, another operates the puppets. Fast action is accomplished by tossing the puppets from one part of the open four-level stage to another. The performances have won acclaim from Shakespearean scholars. The Brescia Puppets also have a large repertoire of children's shows, in which most of the characters are animals.

At UCLA, puppetry was introduced into the Department of Theatre Arts by Melvyn Helstien in 1954. Children's shows were built, and toured in the region. In 1966 several graduate students participated in puppet productions of *Everyman* and *The Ancient Puppet Play of Johannes Doctor Faustus*. Puppets for the former were designed by Diana Jewett, with Lewis Segal directing. Carl Richard Mueller provided the translation of the Faust play, for which Mallory Pearce built the puppets, and Lorna Ross directed. The 1967 productions were the de Falla-Lorca opera, *El Retablo de Maese Pedro*, with puppets and settings by Mitch Colburn, and Dr. Jan Popper as conductor, and *The Love of Don Perlimplin for Belisa in the Garden*. Antoinette Botsford and Mel Helstien played the leading roles, and he designed the puppets. Such productions are now a part of the drama presentations of the department.

Glenn Hughes organized the University of Washington Puppeteers in 1934. They made extensive tours to schools within a 100-mile radius of Seattle with hand-puppet shows. In addition, an elaborate marionette production was produced annually and performed in one of the University theatres. A week before the opening of *The King of the Golden River* in 1941, Mel Helstien, who had the part of Schwartz, was called into service. Aurora Valentinetti was "lured" into the puppet workshop and soon found herself metamorphosed into Schwartz. Other parts for her in the puppet company followed, and upon graduation in 1943, she began teaching puppetry, and has continued to this day. Over the years she has gradually changed the pattern from emphasis upon production and touring to educational puppetry. By 1959 the student touring shows had been abandoned, and class work concentrated on the needs of the students, many of whom came from other departments, such as education and therapy. However, there was still interest in puppet productions, and this need was met by the organization in 1948 of the Valentinetti Puppeteers, who were students with several years of experience. They had enough interest in puppetry to devote time to it without much thought of monetary gain. So the group has worked and experimented, performing when and where they chose, with constantly revised scripts. Most of these are designed for children, but many also have adult appeal, and others, such as Alfred Jarry's play, *Ubu Roi*, are meant to capture adult interest. Seasonal performances such as *The Nativity, Santa's Dilemma, The Lost Easter Egg* and *Easter Fashions* are part of the repertoire, while *Punch and Judy* is an old stand-by. Three classes in puppetry are offered, in both the day and evening schedules, and an extension course off-campus began in 1968. Beginning students make puppets for use with and for children; intermediate classes are fitted to individual interests, and the advanced class is for production. Puppetry is also part of the Introduction to Children's Theatre class.

In all of her work, Aurora Valentinetti makes it clear that puppetry is a theatre art, a demanding one even for a simple show. She stresses puppet history with slides and actual figures, thus insuring a proper attitude of respect, but at the same time suggesting the creative and stimulating aspects of the art. The students have many opportunities to participate in community programs. There are local puppet festivals with performances and workshops; television programs; community development projects and Girl Scout encampments, where shows, demonstrations, exhibits, and talks are offered for entertainment and education.

Educating the public is a problem which concerns all serious puppeteers. They believe that puppetry is an art worthy of adult attention, but they have difficulty getting beyond the general concept in this country that puppets are primarily for children. The lecture-demonstration is one of the most widely used methods for acquainting people with the significance of puppets and their long history. Most puppeteers are quite willing to reveal what they know about the technical side of puppetry, and to talk about historical puppets and what is going on in various parts of the world.

Nola Bucknell gives talks on past and present puppetry, with samples of different kinds of puppets. For two weeks in the spring and fall, she and her husband Bruce open their workshop for demonstrations and lectures to Campfire Girls, Cub Scouts, and Girl Scouts. Rod Young has presented "The Art of Puppetry" on the lecture series of Western and Earlham Colleges, and a simpler talk for assembly programs in schools. In the Miami area, Jero Magon visits schools to demonstrate and talk about puppetry, with similar programs for art clubs and other groups.

The School Art League of New York City sponsored four programs in March 1964, designed to give junior high school students some background in puppetry. Judy and Bob Brown did their *Fantasy on Strings*; Roberta Paine showed films of Chinese and Japanese puppet theatres at the Metropolitan's Junior Museum; Jim Henson presented his Muppets, and Lea Wallace talked on "Puppetry as a Theatre Art." She has also given her talks for many groups, including the Pen and Brush Club of New York City.

Along with his performances, Daniel Llords has held puppet seminars in universities and colleges in the United States, including Hawaii, and in the Philippines, Germany, and Korea. With a representative exhibit of puppets from around the world, Marjorie McPharlin gives occasional presentations of "Puppets on the International Stage." Ruth Duncan's *Meet the Marionettes*, which has had about 500 performances, is also basically educational.

For twenty years Dorothy Rankin has been active in puppet production, and has developed an unusual program, *Adventures with Wooden Actors*. It is a survey of the theatre of stock characters, mimes, masks, and puppets. There is also a performance with some of the large cast of puppets, and sometimes she turns the stage around to show the audience how it is done. With her rich stock of demonstration material, she can adapt a program for any kind of audience, child or adult, and of any length. She has performed for women's clubs, lodges, high school and college students, magicians, bankers, life insurance agents, advertisers, and a host of others.

Puppets for advertising

The growing use of puppets as an advertising technique has been closely associated with the expansion of television during the past decade. More of this will be said later. Here we will consider only those situations in which live puppets are used for advertising or promotional purposes. From time immemorial, they have been "attention getters" and so they are today. Many puppeteers do an occasional advertising show and a few make a specialty of it.

George Creegan is an "entrepreneur of the department store and shopping center circuit," with a varied background in music, puppet films, television, script writing and promotional work. With his wife Joann, who provides voices for the puppets, he builds elaborate and fanciful displays which incorporate plays given by hand-puppets, mechanically animated scenery, and all sorts of special effects. They are engineered for easy operation, and despite their elaborate appearance, they can be moved into any spot where "family traffic building" is desirable. Some of the shows promote direct sales, such as *Rudolph the Red-Nosed Reindeer*, who has about 500 products bearing his name. Creegan has also used animated products such as Corningware for merchandising, with a coffee pot named Perky and a whole cast of similar characters. Larger displays are made for shopping centers. Fort Christmas is an American fort with Santa in a covered wagon, elves making candy and the puppets presenting their show. A similar "display spectacular" is Snow White's Enchanted Cottage with mechanical displays and the appropriate puppet play. Another Creegan innovation is his line of "Talking Displays That See," such as a Christmas tree with a face. Its mouth moves and the tree "talks" with the onlookers through the hidden operator, who in this case looks out through a one-way mirror. There is also a Talking Mailbox, a Talking Gingerbread Train and a Talking Humpty Dumpty. Appearances on television, radio, and in person with his displays are part of the promotion. Creegan often appears as Sir George, dressed in chain armor and a real eighteenth-century dress helmet. He and his wife toured the United States for Volkswagen, with a puppet and magic show built into a Volkswagen bus. Featured was the play, *Sir George and the Dragon*, with Creegan in the title role doing battle with a large latex dragon made in Germany.

Otto and Caroline Kunze have devoted a large number of productions to promotion. In 1948 they made a film, *Broken Strings*, for the Savings Banks Association of New York State, in which lessons in thrift were presented by Mr. Wise Owl, who explained banking procedure with the aid of the Bee Bank for Savings. The film was shown to school children throughout the state, and was also used by a Swedish banker and by the U.S. Army in Japan, with appropriate sound tracks. Another Kunze production was *Take It from George*, built for the National Association of Purchasing Agents and presented by the organization's Committee on Education at a national meeting in Cleveland. In 1962 the Pepsi-Cola Company had a six-week exhibit of Toys from All Over at the company's exhibition hall in New York City. The Kunzes performed *Hakeem the Wise One* to more than 300 school classes. Re-engaged the next summer, they played six shows a day for 107 days.

For a promotion sponsored by the Dairyman's Association, Helen Hubbard toured schools in the Buffalo area in a station wagon fitted up with a backdrop representing a barnyard. Children from the audience were costumed as animals to lend authenticity to the scene. There were magic acts and cowboy and cowgirl numbers by Helen Hubbard, who made lightning costume changes. The children sang, and finally the barn door opened to reveal a marionette stage, where trick figures performed. She appeared at the end in a white gown, symbol of milk. A cardboard bank in the shape of a barn was given to each child, and a larger one was left with the teacher.

There have been, and still are, many promotional shows at fairs, shopping centers, conventions and schools. Some of them are large and some small. They may operate in a limited area or the whole country and promote an infinite variety of products. Ruth Quinn of St. Louis has built shows for Maritz, Inc., the Ford Motor Company, Studebaker-Packard and the Advertising Clubs of Kansas City and St. Louis. The Paul Ashley Puppets helped attract crowds to the Eastman Kodak Exhibit in Grand Central Station in New York by performing every fifteen minutes. Erica Melchior, with her large marionettes, has done much department store promotion, including regular appearances at the May Company in Cleveland, assisted by her daughter Peggy. After Tom Tichenor produced his film, *The Tale of Truthful George*, for the Gas Pavilion at the New York World's Fair, the animal characters were manufactured in plush by Bantam-United States Toys, Inc. To promote them he gave shows in department stores throughout the country. All kinds of advertising projects have engaged the attention of Pat and Betty Percy who have been specializing in this field for more than twenty years.

Puppets may help in fund-raising. Typical are the presentations of Lewis Mahlmann for the United Crusade, Creegan's for the Leukemia Society and Tony Williams' for Christmas Seals. Using the arts for their own sake has become widespread in the advertising field. Exhibitions of painting, sculpture and handicrafts are an integral part of the pavilions built by various countries at world's fairs, and so are the performing arts. Puppets have their place in all this display of culture. The Lytton Savings and Loan Association of Hollywood maintains an art gallery which has stimulating shows, one of which was an extensive puppet exhibit, and Macy's of San Francisco had an important showing of puppets from Germany.

Puppets often appear as art creations in shop windows. When Frank Paris' twenty-four marionettes were displayed in the windows of Henri Bendel in New York, and Max Leavitt's for *The Emperor's Nightingale* in those of Lord and Taylor, they held their own with the costumed mannequins, and demonstrated the high artistic quality of the best designed puppets. The seasonal puppet performances so frequently seen in store windows are often delightfully imaginative and decorative. Because window display in the large stores has become a highly developed art, the puppet show may be part of a general theme, such as the Dickens window of Abraham and Straus in 1959, which included Sky High-Chief's show that closed with an 1860 stagecoach drawn by two white horses, a coachman on the box and a couple as passengers. Lewis Mahlmann designed *Christmas Around the World* for the San Francisco Macy's and the next year he did a *Nursery Rhyme Christmas*. One year Bamberger's in New York chose a Renaissance window theme. Bob Brown built *The King's Christmas Party* with an all-animal cast. The set was a lavish Renaissance banquet hall where the Lion King and his court were entertained by animal versions of juggling, tightrope walking and jousting. At the Adam and Eve Shop, Elek Hartman had a seven-minute show, *Mink Kastle*, a story about two wealthy minks. Alfred Wallace regularly produced department store shows and exhibits in New York and Montreal, and Tom Tichenor has presented musicals for Macy's Christmas windows. Thus puppets delight the public and add to Christmas cheer or Easter gaiety all across the land.

Puppet toys and commercial products

Throughout his long history, Mr. Punch has appeared in many places other than his puppet booth. It was not surprising, therefore, to find Punch and Judy banks, popular in the nineteenth century, again offered for sale by Bloomingdale's in New York. In 1955 a Punch and Judy silk-screened wallpaper was offered by Katzenbach and Warren, and in 1963 men's ties showing scenes of Punch in action were available. Macy's once carried a line of Fieldcrest sheets, pillow cases, blankets and towels with puppet show designs in color.

Many other puppet characters have lent their names to commercial products, or been made into simple toys for children to operate. James Gamble used Wally the Weathergator on a television program in the Denver area. Wally gave weather forecasts with such charm that he became a favorite character and soon there were Wally Donuts, Wally Coloring Books and Wally T-shirts. Walt Disney's characters have become puppets in many forms, and so have those popularized by Shari Lewis.

Children have plenty of opportunities to acquire ready-made puppets from department stores or mail order houses. Toy shops such as F.A.O. Schwartz in New York carry a full line of American and foreign toy puppets, including the Pelham Puppets from England and the Steiff animal puppets from Germany. One year Macy's offered exquisite French marionettes, ten inches high, representing Pierrot, Columbine and several French peasants. Fur-cloth puppets, a by-product of the New York Fur Company, have been marketed, and Creative Playthings has a hand-puppet family which is advertised for therapy, the characters being obtainable either as white or Negro. Variations of the toy paper theatre continue to appear, such as Shirley Temple's Magnetic TV Theatre, with a stage, characters for three stories, and little puppets operated by magnets. With the perfection of rubber casting, puppets can be cheaply produced and almost anyone or anything may appear, from Dennis the Menace to a crocodile and the whole gamut of wild and domestic animals. Various composition materials are also used for marionette dragons, break-away skeletons, fairies, clowns, everyday people and space-age explorers.

There are puppet-making kits of many kinds. The Indianapolis Children's Museum once offered everything needed for a Chinese shadow production of *The Legend of the Blue Willow*. The Topstone Rubber Toy Company sold Paint-a-Puppet sets for making hand-puppets. Some companies offer kits as premiums. One could get a set of cardboard circus puppets from the Texcel Cellophane Tape Company, which had a full-page advertisement in *Life* Magazine about them. The U.S. Envelope Company offered four sets of puppets for home shadows, one in each package of self-seal envelopes. The Hallmark Greeting Card Company put out Merry-O-Nettes in 1966 (not as premiums), which were well-designed interpretations of Alligator, Bird, Fish and Walrus in accordion type honeycomb paper. One company even packaged its bubble bath in a tiny puppet theatre box with cardboard cut-out puppets to be used in it!

Magazines with large circulation sometimes offer articles about puppets, with patterns for their construction and plays for them. *House Beautiful* (December 1960) featured a Christmas show with a religious theme, which included full-size patterns for stage and puppets. *Good Housekeeping* has had patterns for puppets especially designed for small hands. *Better Homes and Gardens* published patterns for three puppets designed by Bil Baird, and for *Woman's Day* he wrote "Making and Staging Marionettes" in collaboration with Otto Kunze, which was published in October 1951. His puppet play, *The Magic Onion*, published in the June 1961 issue of the same magazine, is still a favorite. The wide-reaching effect of magazine articles was recently illustrated when Bob and Judy Brown's *The Barnyard Frolics* appeared in *Woman's Day* (July 1967). The text of the play, a scene from it and pictures of the puppets, all in bright colors, were included, with the offer of a complete booklet of directions to be ordered for 75¢. Within a month 5,000 copies had been sold and they were still in demand in the autumn. As a result, these two puppeteers were sent by the magazine to show the puppets at Expo '67.

Few puppeteers devote themselves exclusively to designing or making toy puppets, but many of them do so upon occasion. Sallie Sellers Hayes made up a Spool Puppet Kit in 1950, which she still sells. Mollie Falkenstein and her daughter Jan at one time made a great many felt hand-puppets which were sold at the Laguna Art Festival and through her studio. Pat Platt began making puppets from gourds some years ago, and developed simple hand-puppets which she sells locally and in Virginia Curtis' shop in Los Angeles. Mrs. Williams G. Burnett, of Wantagh, Long Island, offers Peckery Puppets, made to order. These are gaily and beautifully dressed marionettes, twenty inches high, which have the strings attached with hooks for easier untangling.

Other puppeteers have designed puppets for commercial manufacture which have had wide distribution. The S. S. Kresge Stores distributed Bil Baird's Bilygoons in 1958. These were sleeve puppets of a goony bird, a dragon and an alligator. One of his television characters was Charlemagne the Lion, which appeared as a toy. Of professional size, with a rubber head, movable mouth, a thick yarn mane, good modeling and coloring, Charlemagne was an excellent commercial puppet. Jim Henson's large frog, Kermit, and his dog, Rowlf, have recently been available through mail-order houses. They retain some of the imaginative quality which distinguishes his puppet design. On the novelty side, bedroom slippers and mittens, designed either to be worn or worked as animal puppets, have been available in ten-cent and variety stores during the Christmas season, some of them well-designed.

Most toy puppets are subject to the vast turnover of the toy industry, or the momentary promotion of an advertising gimmick, but some have survived for many years. Such a fortunate one is Clippo, the winsome clown marionette designed by Virginia Austin in 1936. He was featured by Marshall Field's in Chicago for many years, and was first manufactured by the Effanbee Doll Company. Since 1943 he has been made by Curtis Crafts, founded by Virginia and her husband George. In New York they had their factory in an old house on West Broadway, but later moved to Pasadena. After George's death in 1964, she continued limited production, and in 1966 opened a shop at 24 Olvera Street, where she teaches marionette manipulation and sells Clippo and a group of other characters added through the years. Clippo has gone to countries around the world and has not only delighted children, but has provided them with a well-balanced, well-constructed puppet with which they can learn manipulation. With a big Clippo working a little Clippo and other numbers, Virginia toured for many years on the theatre-vaudeville circuit and from 1958 to 1966 she played club dates on the West Coast.

Among the puppets displayed year after year are the Hazelle Marionettes, which have been manufactured since 1932 in Kansas City, Missouri. What began as a small enterprise has grown into a flourishing business under the guidance of its originator, Hazelle Rollins. She says it was all a matter of chance, the result of helping a neighbor boy make puppets for a school show. Then she grew impatient with all the work entailed by making puppets, and thought it would be easier for children to put on shows if they could have the puppets at hand. Thus the puppet factory came into being. Her husband, J. Woodson Rollins, an engineer, handles business and mechanics, and twenty-five employees make about 250,000 puppets per year, including marionettes of different sizes and prices, hand-puppets, finger-puppets, and stages. The various lines include a broad selection of human and animal characters, but many special puppets for television, advertising, and religious presentations are also made. Recently, large shipments went to missionaries in Africa and South America.

Wolo is a man who has devoted a good part of his life to enterprises for children. A writer of children's books, he made his first puppet to fend off stage fright when he had to give a talk to 500 librarians. This little squirrel, a character in one of his books, was followed by others, and Wolo soon found himself giving puppet shows up and down the West Coast. After working for the United States Information Service in Europe during World War II, he returned to California where the television business claimed his attention for a number of years. About 1957, he opened a studio-shop in San Francisco called Happy Things, which he stocked with toys and other items decorated in his colorful style, puppets, and imports. Lettie Connell and Gage Schubert helped him, and in due course Schubert bought the shop. In 1959 Lettie did a show in the window for the Street Fair, and it attracted so much attention, she continued performances almost every night. Featured was Struppke, a dog hand-puppet (made by the Hohensteiner Puppets in Germany), who not only drew traffic-stopping crowds but also sold lots of puppets. Lettie and Gage were married in January 1961, and the next year opened a second shop called Schubert's Toy Square. In 1963 Happy Things was closed.

Wolo is now writing plays, and he recently designed the Sandman's Theatre, a variation of the toy theatre, to stimulate interest in reading. One child reads the story (also by Wolo), while another holds up the puppet characters as they appear.

II

Puppet Programs

We shall here consider some of the turns and plays which constitute present-day programs, in order to give a general picture of the kinds of programs which have evolved in the past twenty years.

Variety

In America there is a long tradition of puppets performing all sorts of short numbers designed to amuse the audience and impress it with the technical skill of the puppeteer. Sometimes an entire program consists of such acts; at others, they may be combined with a play. Such variety programs may be offered at night clubs, in movie theatre programs, in department store promotion, on school assembly programs, on television and numerous other places. Variety is generally non-dramatic and depends for its effect upon action, song, dance, and acrobatic tricks. However, some acts may be developed into pantomimes which express a mood, an idea, or a dramatic situation. Actually, the line between a variety number and pantomime is often very thin. Tony Urbano, for instance, wrote a "pseudo-Elizabethan folksong" about a minstrel and a "wanton she" who seduces him and poisons his beer. He discovers her perfidy when he drops his flagon against a willow tree which promptly withers. With many "fa-la-las," he slays her with his lute. In one of Bil Baird's shows, there was a romantic bit done with gloved hands and wooden balls on the index finger. This pair painted faces on each other, put on ridiculous hats, and courted. One sketched a lake on a blackboard, the other brought in a canoe and together they paddled back and forth, with a loud kiss at the end.

Almost anything may appear in variety, but some themes occur repeatedly, having been used by generations of puppeteers. To this body of traditional material, original acts are constantly being added. Thus there are dancers of every persuasion: ballet, tap, Oriental, gypsy, Hawaiian; there are portraits of famous dancers such as Rufus Rose's Fred

Astaire and Ginger Rogers, or Frank Paris' Carmen Miranda. As styles in dance come and go, puppets interpret them in their own way. Even abstract objects or parts of machines are turned into puppet dancers, such as Baird's dancing trapezoids and rhomboids. Then there are the puppet instrumentalists. Hundreds of variations of the piano player have been presented in the past and are still popular. Puppets play the guitar to accompany sad cowboy laments, or the maracas in Mexican rhythms; they beat drums or toot horns. There are jazz combos, too, or humorous ones, such as Pat Platt's Hang Ten Trio, made from large gourds, who play their instruments and sing with gusto, for they have large gaping mouths.

Puppets often satirize human performers: the soprano with heaving bosom has been popular for a long time, and endless fun is poked at the orchestra conductor with his long hair and elaborate gestures, which puppets can exaggerate so well. Puppet imitations of the strip-teaser have been and continue to be presented in endless variations. Puppets can also do many things which are impossible for human beings. Of these, the breakaway skeleton is seen most often, and may be jolly or a bit macabre, as was the Proctors' act with a group of skeletons. The white figures rose from a greenish graveyard, danced, rattled their bones, which flew off in all directions and then reassembled.

Animal acts are legion. Sometimes animals are substituted for human beings, and imitate or satirize them, but it is in the *Circus* that puppet animals are put through some of their most interesting routines. Puppet monkeys juggle, tumble, and perform on the trapeze; French poodle puppets vie with their live counterparts, and puppet snakes are duly charmed. For the amateur puppeteer as well as the most skillful professional, the circus offers almost infinite opportunities. With a ringmaster to give some continuity, the puppets are seen as tightrope walkers, trapeze artists, cyclists, jugglers, skaters, "stretch" figures and clowns, as well as all the animals. Out of the circus have come some famous characters, such as Togo, Rufus Rose's lovable clown, who bumbles through his act and comes to grief when he blows up a balloon which carries him aloft. A little pin prick from the operator, and poor Togo lands in a heap on the stage. His bewilderment is truly touching.

For Frank Still, the puppet circus became the focal point of his life work. For many others, including Nancy Cole, Rod Young, Lewis Mahlmann, George Cole and Gia Wallace, a circus has been included at one time or another in their repertoire.

At the Puppeteers of America Festival in 1956, Fritz Holzberlein presented his *Circus Shadows*, in which the adventures of two children at a circus provided a framework for a succession of acts, including a ballerina, a maharajah on his elephant, a unicycle rider and a high wire balancing act, all done with figures of colored plastic. Holzberlein continued his experiments with shadows until his death in 1966.

An unusually lavish circus produced by Bob Baker Productions had its premiere at the Laguna Beach Art Festival in 1961 and played there during July and August. Every attempt was made to simulate a real circus as the following notes (from a description by Lewis Mahlmann) will suggest. There was a decorated tent with posters and a box office, and inside a 24 by 40-foot stage floor where the operators worked the marionettes in the open. Bleachers for the audience surrounded this ring on three sides. At the back of the stage was a striped canvas wall with a curtained opening. When this parted, a painted backdrop showing a circus band and conductor with "live" arms projecting through the curtain were revealed. Following the overture, this curtain opened, and eight monkeys played a trumpet fanfare in front of a red curtain. This curtain parted to show another painted backdrop of a circus tent and the audience. The ringmaster entered and the show was on. A beautiful girl rode a horse, clowns rushed out to do their special acts, a mother seal and her baby did a teeter-totter and horn-blowing number. More clowns came on, then a parade of wild animals, and Captain Wilbur with a trained elephant and wild lion. Three ostriches danced—right into the audience. Both lovely and sumptuous in tones of ivory, pink and fuschia was the Oriental parade directed by a swami: two umbrella boys, a camel, a tiger, a horse with rider, another camel, two bearers with a sedan chair in which sat a cymbal-banging monkey, a Hindu boy with a bird of paradise and, to climax all this, a huge elephant with a girl in a howdah, fanning herself. More clowns appeared, the last one a man in a slicker with an umbrella spouting water for a head, pulling a toy duck and her little ones. For the finale, the circus-tent drop was rolled down to reveal the ceiling of the actual tent, from which two trapeze artists were lowered for their act. And so the puppet circus, whether large or small, remains one of the mainstays of traditional puppetry in America.

While most American puppeteers include some variety in their work, a good many specialize in it. Some concentrate upon the night club-movie theatre circuit, although they may also perform anywhere a fast-moving, sophisticated show for adults is appropriate.

Tommy Trent's career on the theatre and vaudeville circuit with variety and *Punch and Judy* began in the thirties when his act "was the hottest thing in show business." After World War II, he gave up professional puppetry for architectural engineering. Now living in Miami Beach, he still performs his original show in hotels and clubs in the area.

Two weeks each year he entertains children in city parks, sponsored by the Recreation Department.

Paul Walton and Mickey O'Rourke, with a cast of elegant, glamorous marionettes, have been going the rounds for years, and have traveled extensively abroad. In a gentler mood they created the puppets for the film *Lili*. Although not exclusively night club performers, Bil and Cora Baird have done their share of it, and something of the style of this type of show is evident in all their work. Stan Kramer and his father, with his mother assisting at times, has played *Les Jolies Poupettes* for more than fifteen years. Marion Myers used to perform in Philadelphia, and Robert Longfield played from coast to coast, from Canada to Mexico, between 1946 and 1952. His *Puppets by André* were three-foot marionettes which he worked on an open, semi-circular stage. Vic Charles, the Kurtis Marionettes, Carl and Faith Simpson, Paul and Reta Page have entertained club habitués, while the Martin Brothers' *Spice O'Life* was featured at Radio City Music Hall and other places. The work of Bob Bromley and Frank Paris, both specialists in the night club field, is described elsewhere. Penny and Paul appeared at the Palace Theatre, New York, in 1954 with their Peop-ettes. This type of puppet is a body hung around the operator's neck, and his head forms the head of the puppet. Dressed in black, the operator uses his hands to move the puppet, and decorates his face with mustaches, eye glasses, hats, jewelry, wigs, and so on. In this particular act, the puppets mimed to recorded voices of television stars.

Jerry Hartnett's *Marionette Musicale* plays in night clubs and theatres, especially in the New York City area, and he has also taken his puppets abroad and on Caribbean cruises. Milton Halpert also works in the New York region.

Erica Melchior's Marionettes appear in night clubs in a sophisticated program, but she also has shows which are appropriate for fairs, department store promotion, conventions and many other situations. Barclay Shaw's program is strictly for adults, and includes a comic bit by Mr. Magoo, who is shown as a lecherous old man, and a "foul-mouthed chicken," which does a variation on the traditional egg-laying routine. In contrast, there is a sad clown who wins the sympathy of the audience. When André Tahon came from Paris to the United States in 1959, he brought a new flavor to television and night club shows. An account of his years in this country appears in Chapter IV.

The puppet revue is a more elaborate variety show, and may be almost as large and spectacular as a performance with human actors. *Les Poupées de Paris* is such a one. Sid Krofft, with a long record of night club performances, and his brother Marty based *Les Poupées* on the *Folies Bergère*, staged it lavishly with a real waterfall, rain, and other spectacular effects, and provided girls and more girls doing all that their live French counterparts do, and more. It opened in October 1961 at Nat Hart's Gilded Rafters, a well-known Southern California night club. The audience was dazzled by a fast-moving succession of acts: two lovers disport themselves in a real swimming pool as exotic birds fly above; a South American juggler "does his stuff"; a mad doctor brings a monster to life; skeletons jazz about; Liberace plays the piano and introduces a bosomy opera singer; four French girls give an instrumental concert, and so on to the finale with a bevy of girls and fireworks. The following year the revue played at the Seattle Fair, and in 1964 and 1965 at the New York World's Fair. Regular tours followed, and in 1968, *Les Poupées* played at Hemisfair in San Antonio, Texas. Bil Baird's puppet revues, on the other hand, are of quite a different type, being more concerned with commentary and satire.

The puppet variety show is so versatile that it is widely used for all sorts of community entertainment, such as schools, churches, women's clubs, birthday parties, fairs, conventions, department stores, colleges and universities. We can mention here only a few of the hundreds of puppeteers who perform variety.

Jero Magon and William Herrschaft, both retired, present *Bill and Jero's Puppet Show* to many groups in the Miami area. Magon's numbers include *The French Poodle, Miss Goldilocks, Sing Along with Mush, Chimpo the Beatle* and others, while Herrschaft has *Cyclists, Poor Butterfly, Jazz Combo Quartette* and some more. Ruth Quinn's *Varieties* have been known in St. Louis for many years, and Dorothy Gleason's *Puppetown Players* were active in Cincinnati. Elaine Vavrinek Woodall has grouped her numbers into *The Nutcracker Suite* and *A Trip Around the World*. Lea Wallace, in her divertissement, *Around the World*, presents well-choreographed dances from many lands. Bob and Judy Brown have two variety programs: *Fun with Puppets* includes a demonstration of puppet making, while *Small World* is a group of marionette specialties.

René is a Mexican, born in San Salvador, who came to the United States when he was three years old. His early interest in puppets has developed into a profession, and he is now a popular West Coast entertainer. His variety, which includes a wide range of animal and human characters, often has a theme. For instance, *Fiesta in Miniature* has a Mexican setting in which sleepy Mexicans in sombreros, raucous birds, dancers, and an animated guitar perform. Or it may be *Toyshop Fantastique*, with Cyrano, a fluffy cat; an ice ballet; Romeo, a sad dog; Aurora, a ballet dancer; a clown; a parade of wooden soldiers and a *Punch and Judy* sequence. René performs in the open, with set pieces for the scenery, and lighting to focus attention on the puppets. He performed Tchaikovsky's *The Nutcracker Suite* at the Seattle World's Fair.

Bruce and Nola Bucknell, Cedar Rapids, Iowa, have made a successful career with their *Variety Show on Strings*. Since their marriage in 1945, they have worked together as a team and separately. Bucknell usually spends part of the year on tour while his wife plays in their home region. One year he toured for nine months on a school assembly program from Iowa to the East Coast. Their acts are traditional, their marionettes are carefully constructed to give natural movement, and the costumes are realistically detailed. The three Bucknell children are all interested in puppets. Elaine created her own show and paid part of her college expenses with her performances. Like her father, she also did a school assembly tour. Delbert also has his own show and Curt is in the process of building one. Sometimes there are four Bucknell shows performing simultaneously in different places, and all of the Bucknells occasionally combine their talents.

Puppets and magic acts are often combined. John Zweers is equally skilled as a puppeteer and a magician, and Johnny Sisson not only performs magic himself, but makes his puppets do likewise. Doug Anderson, with his wife Gayle, has a puppet and magic program which is widely performed in the New York metropolitan area, on television, and aboard ships cruising in the Caribbean.

Puppet plays

The situation with puppet plays has not changed radically since 1948. The old favorite stories are still a substantial part of the puppet repertoire; the supply of published scripts is still very limited, and most puppeteers write their own plays. These are often adaptations of fairy tales, folk stories, myths, legends and fables, or plays based on classic or modern children's stories. Many original plays are also written for presentation to a general audience, for special occasions, or for such purposes as therapy or religious education.

Punch and Judy is still popular. George "Pinxy" Larsen entered show business in 1908, and was active until his retirement in 1956. His interpretation of the Punch story was one of the finest in America. A master wood carver, he made puppets and ventriloquial figures for showmen all over the world. Jay Marshall, who learned his first routine from Larsen, played *Punch and Judy* for thirty years in department stores, night clubs, on television, for the USO and even in a circus. Now he operates the Punch and Judy Bookshop in Chicago and sometimes plays club dates. Larry Benner, an entertainer who has performed in many parts of the world, may impersonate a clown or other characters, play *Punch and Judy*, or be a magician or ventriloquist as the occasion demands.

Some years ago Ray Palmer left England to live in the United States where *Punch and Judy* was part of his puppet program. He and his wife are now back in England. Ken Wyndham is still an enthusiastic Punch man, having learned the art twenty years ago before he left England.

Penelope Corrin reports that *Punch and Judy*, which she and her husband Dick have been presenting since 1935, is still more popular than other plays they have done. They have performed on television and to varied audiences throughout the Midwest. Their study of this old play has resulted in an extensive library. Before 1948 and for many years thereafter, *Punch and Judy* was part of the May Day celebration at the University of Richmond.

Many Punch performances by Junior League women have been given, and are continued today. Other woman puppeteers who include *Punch and Judy* in their repertoire are Nancy Cole, Mary Williams, Virginia Tooper, Frances Meharg, Dorothy Rankin and Gia Wallace. The Berkeley Puppeteers and the Valentinetti Puppeteers have *Punch and Judy*, and so have John Zweers, Bil Baird, Bob Mueller, Irwin Sirota, Rod Young, Thomas Miller and many others. Tony Urbano has a different Punch presentation, done as a musical with lively songs and actor Albert Rome as "bottler" to relate the puppets to the audience.

Although not so frequently as in the past, Punch still appears at outdoor fairs and celebrations. Gordon Bennett built a show for the Old Sturbridge Village, Massachusetts, where he has performed on the village green to more than 80,000 people in a single season. Punch was on hand at Expo '67 performing in the Belgium Village. Norman Ernsting, a young student of business economics at the New School for Social Research, was the showman. He became fascinated by the Cruikshank editions of *Punch and Judy* and decided to revive the play. His version has the ribaldry and slapstick humor of the old shows, and the text, music and songs are those used by the Italian puppeteer Piccini, who played in London 200 years ago. Ernsting's show was seen at the Roosevelt Field Shopping Center on Long Island, and is likely to pop up almost anywhere. Thus, in new ways and old, this most durable of puppet plays keeps its popularity in a changing world.

Puppeteers interested in appealing to adult audiences often turn to classic drama. There have been many adaptations of Shakespeare's work during the last two decades. Sister Corona Sharp's work at Brescia College has already been mentioned. *Romeo and Juliet* and *A Midsummer Night's Dream* are favorites; *Hamlet* was produced by Jero Magon; *Macbeth* and

The Taming of the Shrew by Martin and Olga Stevens. Among the celebrations for the Bard's 400th birthday, there was a Shakespeare Puppet Festival in New England. On a brightly-lighted, arena-type stage, the puppets were operated by Ruth Brand, with Eleanor Boylan seated in front as narrator. *Romeo and Juliet* and *Macbeth* were presented as whole plays, with two scenes from *The Merchant of Venice*.

The Faust story appears at regular intervals on the puppet stage. Among the recent productions was *The Ancient Puppet Play of Johannes Doctor Faustus* at UCLA. Marlowe's *Doctor Faustus* has been presented by Peter Arnott, formerly of the University of Wales and since 1958 a professor at the University of Iowa. He is the most determined exponent of puppet interpretations of classic drama, and he has published his theories in *Plays Without People*. Working alone on an open stage, he has given marionette performances of Greek plays, such as Sophocles' *Oedipus the King* and Euripides' *Medea*. The medieval morality play *Everyman*, Racine's *Phèdre* and Ben Jonson's *Volpone* represent other periods of drama he has performed.

The Berkeley Puppeteers include Molière's *Le Malade Imaginaire* in their repertoire. Shirley O'Donnol built a production of the Indian poet Kalidasa's *Shakuntala*, and Schnitzler's *Gallant Cassian*. The latter was a curtain raiser for a 1956 off-Broadway presentation at the Tempo Playhouse of Genet's *The Maids*. Barrie's *Peter Pan* was recently adapted by George Creegan, and O'Neill's *Emperor Jones* was revived in 1957 by Ralph Chessé and Blanding Sloan, who produced it back in 1928.

A modern play, *Ubu Roi* by Alfred Jarry, has been produced by a number of European companies during the past several years, and the Valentinetti Puppeteers performed it at the Northwest Drama Conference in Seattle, February 1967. Peter Schumann gave his own interpretation of the same play at the Puppet Festival in 1963.

The scarcity of published puppet plays is due, in part, to the fact that writers are not generally attracted to the puppet theatre, nor are publishers enthusiastic about issuing plays for which there is not much demand. Bil Baird believes that growth of the American puppet theatre depends upon attracting the best talent to write plays, to compose music and to design for it. This is an avowed purpose of his theatre in New York City.

From time to time attempts have been made to stimulate playwriting. In 1955, the Department of Theatre Arts of the Detroit Institute of Arts conducted a playwriting contest. Adolph Cavallo, then Curator of the Department, in an article in the *Puppetry Journal* (September–October 1955), wrote: "In order to encourage thinking and to suggest that works of art may lead to the creation of original images and characterizations, we stipulated that the scripts submitted be based on some object, painting, print, drawing, sculpture, furniture, glass, textile, metal in the collection of the Detroit Institute of Arts."

Other conditions were that the play be suitable for children four to twelve, run from 20 to 50 minutes and be written by a resident of Michigan. Fifty-five scripts were received. The jury included Fern Zwickey in the Department of Art Education at Wayne University; Margaret Brayton, Director of the Children's Museum in Detroit; and Leonard Leone, Director of the Wayne University Theatre. Daniel G. Waldron of Detroit was awarded first prize for *The Bear That Played the Bijou.* It was inspired by *The Trappers Return,* a painting by George Caleb Bingham, dated 1851, which depicts two fur trappers floating down a river in a canoe with a bear cub chained to the deck. Iva N. Wood of Flint won second prize, and honorable mentions went to David Gibson, Mary Harris, Stuart McLeod and Frances Patterson. Performance of the prize play was guaranteed. Clark Eastham of Royal Oak and painter Charles Culver of Vellaire were commissioned to provide music and designs for the show. On April 4 and 6, 1956, under George Latshaw's direction, Waldron's play was given by the Junior League Puppeteers at the Institute. It was repeated for the Puppet Festival at Evanston, Illinois, that same summer. Unfortunately, despite the success of this project, no further contests have been sponsored by the Institute.

Original puppet plays are written about a great many subjects. Some are based on historical characters, such as *Pocahontas* (at the University of Richmond); *Cleopatra* and *Joan of Arc* (produced by Martin and Olga Stevens) and *A Flag for the Brave,* about Betsy Ross (by the Cole Marionettes). Among plays written for special occasions are *Alice and the Dormouse,* which Nelly Mendham presented for a St. Louis YWCA anniversary, and *Sokar and the Crocodile* for the St. Louis Art Museum during an exhibit of objects from the tomb of Tutankhamon.

Every holiday season, especially Christmas, brings a spate of puppet plays. Many are based on well-known stories or religious themes, but even more are designed to fit a special program for church, school, department store, or party. Selected at random are these titles: *Christmas Fantasy, A Magic Christmas, The Unexpected Guest, Christmas Eve at Puppet House, Arizona's First Christmas, Where Did the Toys Go?,* and *Mercy Me, It's Christmas.* Jeanne Charlton has a play which can be changed to suit various occasions. It may be *The Dancing Dragon and the Enchanted Birthday Cake* or *The Magic Christmas Tree,* or whatever may be appropriate.

The space age has inspired the kind of play for which puppets are especially suited. A few of these are: George Latshaw's *The Runaway*

Rocket and *U.F.O.;* Judith Lawrence's *An Adventure in Outer Space;* Marshall Wynnychuk's *Muk Luk the Man from Outer Space;* Rod Young's *The Royal Space Ship* and *Jack and the Space Beans.* The moon has inspired such plays as Ed Johnson's *Beyond the Moon,* Virginia Tooper's *First Goose on the Moon,* Jeanne Charlton's *Mystery of the Moon Coneys,* and Henry and Greta Sherman's *Secret on the Moon.*

The following titles suggest the type of original plays which have been produced during the past twenty years:

The Toymaker by Martin Stevens, widely performed by many puppeteers.

How the Dragon Got a Dime and *The Cook and the Mischievous Mouse* by Spence and Alan Gilmore.

The Magic Flyswatter, one of the Children's Fairyland plays.

Bucktooth Bill and the Red Devil, produced by Mollie Falkenstein with a group of children.

The Wishing Pot; Snipp, Snapp, Snupp and the Red Shoes and *Kangaroo Makes Friends,* in Judith Lawrence's repertoire.

The Magic Onion by Bil Baird, published in *Woman's Day* and frequently performed by various puppeteers.

Wilbur and the Giant, Show and Tell (A Fable of the Future) by George and Patricia Latshaw.

The Yellow Haired Witch, most recent production by Luman Coad and Arlyn Kuthan (Coad Canada Puppets).

Mrs. Witherspoon's Busy Day and *Grover the Great* by Lettie Connell Schubert, written for her hand-puppets.

The Cave of Jewels and *The Ghastly Ghost in the Haunted House* by John Zweers.

The Blue Unicorn, The Golden Phoenix and *The Queen of Hearts Flower Show* by Dora Velleman.

Over the years, a great deal of puppet work has been done by Junior League groups, and many original plays have been written. Among them are: *The Magic Sneeze, Nestor the Talking Horse, Nestor and the Alligator, The Mystery of Crinkle's Nose, The Stranger, Millie Presents* and *Kentucky: a Bear.*

The above plays have been given for audiences of children, although some of them have considerable adult interest.

A few of the plays written specifically for adults are:

The Net by Bill Cassady, performed by the Berkeley Puppeteers. This play considers man's entanglement in the Net of Illusion and his efforts to escape from it.

American Guignol is a group of seven plays by Ralph and Catherine Moreno for their Opera Pupi theatre for adults, consisting of comedy situations, satires, and commentaries on man's problems.

Punch at the University, a play of farce and satire by Irwin Sirota.

A Cat Happening by Bernice Silver is a "slightly hysterical" satire for adults.

In some plays people and puppets have appeared together. Martin Stevens is visible at times behind a scrim in his performance of *The Toymaker;* Margo Rose (seen from the knees down) represented Mrs. Noah in *The Mouse in Noah's Ark,* thus contrasting the human and the mouse world. Marionettes are sometimes used in *A Midsummer Night's Dream* for the fairies, to give a convincing relationship between them and the mortals. This was done in Luman Coad's production at the San Jose State Children's Theatre in 1961. George Latshaw has written and published a version of *Pinocchio* for human actors, in which only Pinocchio and Punchinello appear as puppets. In *Quillow and the Giant* all the actors except the Giant were Latshaw puppets. Eleanor Boylan, director of a children's community theatre group, the Young Newton Players, in Newton Falls, Massachusetts, combined child actors and puppets in *Gulliver's Travels.* In the first act, Gulliver was a boy and the Lilliputians were hand-puppets made by Ruth Brand. In the second act, Gulliver was a puppet, with children as the Brobdingnagian giants.

Nancy Staub, Children's Theatre Director at the Gallery Circle Theatre in New Orleans, regularly combines live actors and puppets. For *Tall Tales,* actors in half-masks played American folk heroes Paul Bunyan, Stormalong and Pecos Bill. Ordinary people were played by rod-puppets, which were also used for a whale, insects and hobby horse. There was a score for banjo, with many folk songs and sound effects. *Placide and the Alligator,* an original play about bayou animals, included a little girl played by Leslie, Mrs. Staub's daughter. A masked actor was the Wolf in *The Wolf and the Kids,* and two actors represented magicians who acted as narrators in *Beauty and the Beast.* In her 1967 production, *The Tongue-Cut Sparrow,* an actor in Kabuki costume and make-up narrated the story as it was performed with puppets. A special feature was a dragon, with a large mask for a head and two people for a body, which danced among the audience, in the manner of a Chinese dragon in a street parade.

An awareness of social problems appears to be increasing among puppeteers. Although they have always been concerned with the underlying moral implications of the plays presented to children, a more active concern for serious content, at least in the work of certain producers is evident.

"Puppets with a Purpose" has been the slogan of the Puppet Associates (Carol Fijan, Director) since its organization in 1950. Everything this group has done has had the theme of Peace, Brotherhood and the Dignity of Man, whether in teaching or performing. *The Adventures of Wee and Uss* deals with integration. Wee, a white puppet, and Uss, a Negro, share adventures in a space ship and on Mars; they encounter a magic pearl and buried treasure. They always have to fight a witch adversary, but are saved by the Star Fairy (a Negro puppet) and learn that only by working together can they achieve happiness. These plays are in the form of "pupp-o-rettas," with songs taught to the children who sing them during the performance. As part of the poverty program, the Puppet Associates perform in the summers on the streets of Harlem, with a play in which both white and colored puppets are included.

Satires for adults are also produced by this company, under the general title, *Show of Hands*. These performances have been seen on election trucks, at rallies, union halls, on television, in churches, synagogues, schools and night clubs. Some of them have anti-war themes; others take a dig at conformity, Suburbia, smoking, pollution, modern art or the race to the moon. The last is a pantomime. On the stage a rounded mound is seen against the sky. Up floats a U.S. spaceman, who plants a flag, then a Russian spaceman does likewise. They fight, then reach an agreement by drawing a line dividing the moon. Each rules his side, but neither can resist the impulse to steal the other's flag, and there is more fighting. Now the mound rises slowly, revealing the Man in the Moon, who looks in wonder at the two Earthmen. Disgusted, he takes a flyswatter and brushes the spacemen into space, plucks the flags from his head and returns to his place.

Underlying the work of Lea and Gia Wallace in their poverty program classes is a concern for the miserable condition of some of New York City's residents, and this is reflected in many of the plays they develop.

Puppets lately have had a good deal to say about the war in Vietnam. Luman Coad produced *The Reluctant Giant* for the Society of Friends, and student protests have included puppet shows.

Peter Schumann's Bread and Puppet Theatre regularly engages in peace marches and protest demonstrations, although he asserts that this is not primarily a theatre of protest, but rather one in which to say things which need to be said. Theatre is a means of probing, exposing, and presenting ideas so that they get to the people. Schumann's masked actors and giant puppets, which may be eight, ten or even eighteen feet high, have a powerful impact upon the crowds in a street, and not infrequently cause violent reactions.

Schumann came from Germany to the United States about 1961, taught art in Vermont, then moved to New York where he opened the Bread and Puppet Theatre in a loft on the Lower East Side in 1963. He believes that puppet theatre should be as basic as bread. His wife bakes it, and it is served at his theatre where it has a ritualistic function. George Denison, writing in *The Village Voice* (June 2, 1966), describes how an actress in a dark robe passed out programs and pieces of bread. Everybody looked at his piece, popped it into his mouth and began to chew. "And so there we all sat, chewing our bread and glancing at our neighbors, very comfortably aware of and joined to each other by this homely yet deeper-than-articulate little action of chewing, consuming the one communal loaf."

This theatre is composed of poets, artists, musicians and a varying number of actors. Sometimes many persons may participate, as in the street parades and in *Bach Cantata*. Other shows require only a few actors. Performances at the theatre have a small admission charge, and contributions are accepted for outdoor appearances, but finances are slim, and Schumann and his helpers often do odd jobs. Ideas for plays may come from music, or from the puppets—trying their movements, studying their expressions, then building a story and presenting it with improvised dialogue. A drawing may develop into a play. One of these became an hilarious stab at bureaucracy and was presented as a "movie" on an East Side sidewalk. A long drawing passed through a scroll machine, which showed a man who finds a rat, takes it home, feeds it, and is horrified to see it grow into a monster which threatens his baby. He calls the police department which responds, "Wrong number." The fire department asks if the rat is on fire, and the health department if it is sick. Bureaucracy fails, but an angel swoops down and saves the baby.

In one peace parade, long lines of people wearing masks of women and swathed in white robes carried branches as they marched down Fifth Avenue. In a protest against the war in Vietnam, giant heads represented blindfolded women chained together, while a mock airplane of wood with shark's teeth dived out of the sky, and a band of skull heads blew tunes on improvised instruments, and played a dirge on gasoline tins filled with nuts and bolts. One play, *A Man Says Goodbye to His Mother*, a protest against the war, is frequently performed. A narrator wears a skull mask and carries a bag of properties, and a trumpeter is similarly masked. A woman in a grayish silver mask and her son, in Army fatigues, say goodbye. The narrator recounts how the Son is going to a far land, and how he is wounded. The Woman dons another mask representing an Oriental type, and becomes a Woman of the Village. The village is a dangerous place, where one needs a gun, which is given to the Son. Then he gets an airplane. The Woman stops working to look at the sky. She is given a plant, but the narrator says that the Son poisons the vegetation, and a cloth is placed over the plant. The people must hide in their houses, and a cut-out house is handed to the Woman, who holds it in front of her face. The Son starts to burn the house but the action is interrupted by the narrator, who reminds everyone that New York fire regulations forbid the burning of houses in this building, so instead, the Son rips the house into bits. The Woman is given a Child, which the Son kills. She takes a pair of scissors and stabs him through the heart. The narrator looks at the Son, covers him with a sheet. After a long, silent pause, he and the Woman carry away the body.

Another presentation, called *Fire*, is a memorial to three Americans who immolated themselves because of their country's involvement in Vietnam; it uses masked actors and life-size puppets, robed like Buddhists and Vietnamese peasants. The action takes place in nine brief scenes. In the first seven, named for the days of the week, the dead perform everyday actions such as passing food from one to another, or undoing the rope which binds one of them. The eighth scene uses the style of Picasso's *Guernica* to portray an air raid, and in the last, an old woman stands in a wire enclosure, fastening red strips to her garments, working from the feet upward. As the strips pass across her features, she sinks to the ground, leaning against the wire. Throughout, the tolling of a bell and other musical sounds are heard, sometimes coming from offstage, at others played by the masked figures. This is not so much a play of protest as a revelation of "our feelings about death and the basic human dependencies which the fact of death makes vivid to us." (George Denison, in *The Village Voice*, June 2, 1966)

Schumann has also produced religious plays, based on the themes of the Crucifixion and the Nativity, but incorporating modern ideas, which have been performed in a number of leading churches. Many huge puppet heads and the choir of Judson Memorial Church were combined in *Bach Cantata*, in which 100 people participated.

During the summer of 1966, Schumann and his group conducted a workshop for children sponsored by the New York City Parks Department and the Council for Parks and Playgrounds; they made puppets, and then (with assistance) devised plays for them which were given in several parks. Other workshops go on from time to time with experimental plays and music sessions. In the summer of 1967, performances were given at the Newport Folk Festival, and at Expo '67 in Montreal. During the autumn of that year, tours to colleges on the eastern seaboard were made, and performances given at Bennington, Mount Holyoke, Duke, the University of North Carolina and others. In addition, three plays were filmed by National Education Television.

Schumann describes his theatre as "a continuous workshop in sculpture, painting, mime, dance, story-making, puppet-building and operation, music and instrument making." His emphasis on social themes might be explained by his question, "How can we live at this time and not be concerned?"

Interpretations of music and pantomime

Music has always been an integral part of puppet shows, but in recent years it has been the dominant feature in many productions. Back in 1931, when Stravinsky's *Oedipus Rex* was given by the Philadelphia Orchestra with a chorus and Remo Bufano's nine-foot puppets miming the action, such performances were unusual. In the past two decades they have been increasingly common.

Beginning in 1958, the Detroit Puppet Theatre and the Detroit Symphony Orchestra collaborated on a number of performances given for the Young People's Concert Series, with puppets by George Latshaw. The first was Aaron Copland's *Billy the Kid,* with nine-foot puppets to represent the fourteen characters of the story. The large figures not only suggested the vastness of the American West, but also showed up adequately on the large stage of the Ford Auditorium. Gil Oden, then curator of Theatre Arts at the Detroit Institute of Arts, was producer, and Valter Poole conducted the orchestra. Performances took place on March 15 and April 5, and the production has been repeated at various times in Cleveland and other cities. The following year, Debussy's *La Boîte aux Joujoux* was presented with smaller puppets, operated in the manner of the Japanese Bunraku by people costumed in colorful ponchos who formed part of the stage setting. In 1964, a double bill included Richard Strauss' *Till Eulenspiegel* and selections from Kabalevsky's *Comedians,* which were produced by Audley Grossman, Jr., present Theatre Arts curator at the Institute. Bunraku-type puppets were used for the former, and the three sections of the Kabalevsky music were interpreted by abstract forms. The first, says George Latshaw, "was a dance of squares; the second was linear in ever-changing forms; the third was a fluid dance of sculptural forms, which suggested but did not represent, animals. The audience was able to supply the missing visual links . . . so there was communication, surprise, understanding and laughter with no words of explanation."

Here are some additional performances which puppets have given with orchestras:

Stravinsky's *Emperor's Nightingale,* with thirty-inch marionettes by Max Leavitt, at Hunter College, New York, April 1956, Thomas Scherman conducting the Little Orchestra Society.

Ernst Toch's *Circus Overture,* given in 1956 by the Portland (Oregon)

Junior Symphony, conducted by Jacob Avscholomov. The puppets were made and operated by the Portland Junior League.

Prokofieff's *Peter and the Wolf* is an excellent piece for puppets and it has been done countless times with recordings. Two live performances were Hope Bennett's with the New Jersey Symphony in 1963, and the elaborate production for the Toledo (Ohio) Orchestra Junior Concerts in February 1958, built by the Toledo Puppet Workshop of the American Association of University Women.

Ravel's *Mother Goose Suite* was performed on March 1, 1959, by the Oakland Symphony Orchestra, Piero Bellugi conducting, with twenty marionettes by Tony Urbano. The actress, Sylvia Cirone, played the Mother, and Julie Wakefield the Little Girl. A number of the Bay Area's well-known puppeteers assisted, including Marian Derby and Robert Smith, who helped with production, and Dorothy Hayward, Pat Levin, Sally Henson, and Frank Osnowicz, who manipulated. Rod Young performed the *Suite* in 1964 with the Westchester Symphony Orchestra, using hand-puppets, marionettes, and rod-puppets.

Saint-Saëns' *Carnival of the Animals*, with the Baird Marionettes and the Little Orchestra Society, was performed at Hunter College in 1962.

Many orchestral works are included in the repertoire of Llords "International," which he performs in regular symphony subscription series in America and abroad.

Stravinsky's *L'Histoire du Soldat*, with the Philadelphia Chamber Society and the Baird Marionettes, was performed on January 8, 1967, at the Academy of Music as part of an all-Stravinsky program. About forty-four puppets appeared in a booth at the center of the stage, with Morris Carnovsky as narrator seated at the left, and seven players at the right, led by Anshel Brusilow. The piece is a commentary on forced recruitment in the reign of Tsar Nicholas I, and is an appropriate vehicle for puppets. A soldier on leave exchanges his fiddle for a magic book proffered by the devil, and has some exciting adventures: Prancing horses turn into skeletons, he marries a princess, and plays a card game with the devil in which huge cards literally "get out of hand" and fight each other. At the end, a greatly magnified devil sweeps the soldier off to his fate, while the musicians play the old chorale, *A Mighty Fortress Is Our God*, to point out the moral of the tale: "Don't desire more than you have."

For Larry Berthelson, creating a visual counterpart to operatic and symphonic music has become a specialty. Formerly of New Haven, Connecticut, he began with the Symphony Orchestra of that city, and he still appears with it almost every year, although he has been in New York for sixteen years. His Pickwick Puppet Theatre has collaborated with the Cleveland Symphony in Prokofieff's ballet *Cinderella* and Ibert's *Diver-*

tissement. He has also appeared with the Baltimore, Annapolis, and Hartford Symphonies and the Brooklyn Philharmonic. Many of these performances have been taped and are shown in schools in the New York area. Several of Berthelson's most important shows have been commissioned by Thomas Scherman, who conducts the Little Orchestra Society in Young People's Concerts at Philharmonic Hall. Ravel's *L'Enfant et les Sortilèges,* presented in February 1968, used actors, rod-puppets and puppeteers inside life-sized objects. Tchaikovsky's ballet, *Sleeping Beauty,* was given in November 1966, and was also performed with the Detroit Symphony Orchestra. Berthelson has also given many shows for government programs, such as Higher Horizons, for museums, schools, clubs and on television.

Opera is also included in children's entertainment, but some puppet performances of opera also have adult appeal. One of the most popular is the García Lorca-Manuel de Falla opera *Master Peter's Puppet Show* (*El Retablo de Maese Pedro*), which was first performed in 1923 at the Paris salon of the Princess de Polignac, who had an elaborate marionette theatre. It is based on the episode in Cervantes' *Don Quixote* in which the Don visits an inn where a puppet show is given for entertainment of the guests. He is enthralled by the adventures of Melisandra, a Christian princess who is captured by Moors. Her husband, Don Gayferos, does not immediately dash off in pursuit, but when he is chided by Charlemagne, he finally makes his way to the tower where Melisandra is imprisoned. Rescuing her, Don Gayferos places her on his horse and they gallop off, pursued by a band of Moorish horsemen. Don Quixote, fearing the two will be overtaken, draws his sword and demolishes the Moors.

The Cleveland Junior League presented *Master Peter* in 1955 with George Latshaw's puppets. Singers and musicians performed it at the Peabody Conservatory in Baltimore in 1957, with Bernard Paul's puppets enacting the show-within-a-show. It was done by Ralph Chessé in collaboration with Lettie Connell Schubert in 1957 with the San Francisco Symphony, Enrique Jorda conducting. Leo and Dora Velleman performed the opera with the St. Louis Symphony in 1965, and in Washington, D.C., Manuel Merono's puppets were used in a 1966 performance. The first production of the Coad Canada Puppets was *Master Peter's Puppet Show,* presented with the Vancouver Symphony Orchestra for the 1967 Vancouver Festival. They used strongly designed hand-and-rod-puppets.

The Festival of Opera at Laguna Beach, California, in the summer of 1967 included *Master Pedro's Puppet Show,* for which Tony Urbano designed and staged the puppet action. The thirty-one marionettes were constructed by Bea Kienitz and Jaro Jenski. Many of the lavish costumes were made from Urbano's sketches by the ladies of the Opera Guild.

Under the title *Master Peter's Puppets*, the opera was presented in October 1967 by the Department of Theatre Arts at UCLA. The parts were sung by students of the Music Department and the conductor was Jan Popper. Mitch Colburn built the hand-and-rod-puppets and the abstract scenery and Melvyn Helstien directed.

In the same year Larry Berthelson produced the opera for Thomas Dunn and his Festival Orchestra, which performed it for adults at Philharmonic Hall, New York. Don Quixote and his companions, as well as his horse and Sancho Panza's donkey, were large rod-puppets, the tallest being seven feet high. They were worked from behind by operators dressed in black. The puppet show took place on a simple draped stage, with three-foot-high flat cutout figures designed and constructed by Berthelson's associate, Penny Jones. Behind the brightly-lighted playing area for the puppets was the orchestra, hardly visible.

Another Berthelson production, commissioned by Thomas Scherman, was Mozart's *Magic Flute*, performed in February 1965. Haydn's *Philemon and Baucis* and Mozart's *Bastien and Bastienne* have been done by Frank Paris. This Mozart opera was also presented by the Valentinetti Puppeteers and the Seattle Symphony Ensemble, Milton Katins conducting, on May 17, 1959.

With the growth of musical comedy in the United States, it was inevitable that this form should influence the puppet theatre. Usually there is a semblance of plot and some dialogue, although the principal interest is in spectacle and music, both vocal and instrumental.

Bil Baird's *Davy Jones' Locker* is sometimes referred to as a "marionette musical" for children, and his puppets played an integral part in the Broadway production of *Flahooley* in 1951. Tony Urbano's productions are likely to lean towards musicals, for he has a natural flair for the catchy tune. *Mary Louise, Little Red Riding Hood* (one of the Children's Fairyland productions) and even his *Punch and Judy* are notable for their music. Rod Young built *A Mouse Named Pocahontas*, a marionette musical presented outdoors in Richmond, Virginia, in the summer of 1957.

For many years Bobby Clark was known for his marionette night club shows. In 1963 he turned to the musical show and produced *Pinocchio*, a "fresh and grandiose kind of entertainment for children." It had more than a hundred puppets from two-and-a-half to six feet tall, which were moved around on a mammoth stage with a proscenium twenty feet wide and eight feet high. There was lots of scenery, glitter, and as much music as a Broadway musical. Arthur Miller wrote six songs and appropriate tunes for the entire show, including dances. *Pinocchio* opened in December 1964 at the Pabst Theatre in Milwaukee, and was booked into more than seventy major theatres the first season by an enterprising publicity man.

The show was advertised as a "Broadway Musical for Children," with due emphasis upon its size and cost. Another show, *The Lad . . . Aladdin*, was built in 1966, with more puppets, a bigger stage, more exotic settings, more songs—and of course at a greater cost. It was indeed a super spectacle.

In April 1961, the musical *Carnival* opened on Broadway. It was the most recent incarnation of a story by Paul Gallico, first published as "The Seven Souls of Clement O'Reilly." The story inspired the film, *Lili*, and was later expanded into a short novel, *The Love of Seven Dolls*, before reaching Broadway as *Carnival*. Jerry Orbach played the bitter puppeteer in a French circus, Pierre Olaf was his assistant, and Anna Maria Alberghetti was Lili, the orphan girl who wanders by and is hired to converse with the puppets. The director, Gower Champion, chose Tom Tichenor to make the four puppet characters: Marguerite, an aging prima donna; Carrot Top; Reynardo the Fox and Horrible Henry, the Walrus. They symbolize the conflicting elements of the puppeteer's character, and through them, Lili reaches him with her love and transforms him. With book by Michael Stewart, songs by Bob Merrill, imaginative settings and lighting, the story came through with all its warmth.

After the show was released for amateur production, Jim Menke built the puppets for a presentation at the Clarence (New York) Central High School, February 1964. Every department of the school became involved, for there was a cast of ninety and a thirty-piece orchestra. Professional theatre people designed settings, plotted the lighting and directed. George Latshaw made the puppets for a production of *Carnival* at the University of Oklahoma, November 14–19, 1966. No doubt there are, and will continue to be, many other presentations by amateur groups and professional road shows.

There are also many plays in which music is more than incidental but which are not musicals. Lewis Mahlmann's production of *Bluebeard* with Bela Bartok's music and *The Stone Flower* from Timothy Thompson's story are examples. Robert and Diane Mueller have arranged music and dances for several classic puppet plays, as well as some original ones, such as *The Magic Harp* and *The Dragon School*. *The Pink Siamese*, presented by the Puppeteens, a group of young people connected with the Department of Theatre Arts of the Detroit Institute of Arts, was a musical play with story and lyrics by Susan Otto and Seymour Barab respectively. Tony Urbano designed the marionettes, Gene Scrimpsher did the scenery and lighting, and Gil Oden directed.

Dick Myers, who has been in and out of puppetry for a good many years, returned to it in 1966 with a one-man production of *Dick Whittington*. Preceding it was a long period of preparation: the rod-puppets were made of plastic wood with costumes painted on and inner control mechanisms; the script was built carefully with the parts enacted by Myers; the scenery which comes and goes before the eyes of the audience was made, and the music was carefully selected to move the play along, to accompany the scene changes and to give the performance its special quality. Myers' feeling for the power of music to coordinate and illuminate the action of the puppets leads him to regard his show as a "musical art form." With the addition of *Cinderella,* now under construction, he hopes to play concert dates.

"Significant gesture without speech" is the dictionary definition of pantomime, and it is sometimes used effectively in the puppet theatre. Years ago Basil Milovsoroff began using pantomime through dance in such ballets as *Color Fantasies, The Fables, The Nutcracker* and *Sinbad the Sailor,* in which color and design also contributed to the dramatic effect. He believes that the play derived from the theatre of human actors is not the puppet's best medium, but that "the dance motion inherent in inanimate objects or artistically designed animal, insect, or vegetable images introduces new esthetic, and delightfully humorous possibilities in the ballet" (from a brochure). Lea and Gia Wallace have combined their own dance-pantomime with that of puppets in such numbers as *Circus Suite.*

Visitors to Knott's Berry Farm in Southern California have enjoyed sitting under an awning on low benches and watching Tony Kemeny perform his puppets on a wagon similar to the horse-drawn vehicles in the old country. Someone would drop a quarter in a slot, the music would begin and Tony would go into action. Using commercial Steiff puppets, he performed expressive pantomimes. He grew up an orphan in Budapest, spent half a lifetime in Nazi or Communist prisons and finally came as a refugee to the United States.

Frank Osnowicz, formerly of California, where he produced his own shows and was director for a time of the Vagabond Theatre in Oakland, is now part of the New York scene. He performed a group of satirical pantomimes at the 1964 Puppet Festival. In *The Man,* a confused gentleman in a battered top hat, with one white gloved hand, tries to locate a small bug. He beckons, cajoles, and is in despair when he accidentally crushes it. *The Reader* is trying to get the news by stealing glances at a fellow commuter's paper and his furtive actions are played for their fullest comic effect. In *Help,* a small figure, just a styrofoam ball on a bare hand, tries to awaken an inert hand, which does not respond until he places his own head on it, thus giving life. For these numbers, piano accompaniment was provided by Eve Titus.

George Latshaw, in his adult program *Hand in Glove,* makes use of satirical or comic situations, which suggest a great variety of moods.

Although he uses some puppets, many of the numbers are done with his hands, either bare or "costumed" in various colored gloves. In *The Taming of the Shrew,* the basic character relationships of Katherine and Petruchio are suggested. *A Bird on the Hand Beats the Bush,* in which a glove with a tall feather and beak portrays a sprightly bird, who plucks blossoms off a bush suggested by another glove, is a clean-cut bit of whimsy. In *Three from Tennessee,* a critter something like a crocodile impersonates a Tennessee Williams-type character. A satire on private-eye whodunits is carried off with hammers and other hardware in *This Hammer for Hire.* In another number, Professor Alberti, a boring musician, refuses to heed Wilbur's admonition to "cut it short," whereupon Wilbur literally reduces his long hair to a crew cut. Music and spoken commentary in Latshaw's many voices are used in the dozen or more numbers which make up this sophisticated and imaginative program.

George Merten's *Mood, Music and Mimes* included three numbers, *Man with a Rose, The Witch* and *Pierrot,* in which he created a strong emotional quality through pantomime.

Elizabeth Merten made a specialty of selecting musical compositions and developing pantomimes from them. Directions for one of these, *The Comedians* by Kabalevsky, have been published (see Bibliography). Delibes' *Sylvia Ballet* was the basis for a whimsical pantomime, *The Missing Maestro,* who conducts an imaginary orchestra, and is carried off by two zanies who hide him in a blue drapery. Many strange things happen and a variety of characters run in and out with props and scenery, while the maestro hobbles in at intervals, still entangled in the blue drapery. A green dragon carries off the zanies and is overcome by St. George in armor, who turns out to be the missing maestro. *Blue Lady,* in flowing chiffon costume, and *Hansel and Gretel* were also in her repertoire, with *Four Animal Songs* for contrast. One was the Flanders and Swann duet, "Mud, mud, nothing quite like it for cooling the blood," mimed by a pair of velveteen hippopotamuses.

Nancy Hazell, who often assisted Elizabeth Merten, worked out many pantomimes of her own. *Raggle Taggle Renard* was a fantasy with music. *The Jester and the Alchemist, Spirit of the Candy Cane* and a number with penguins, entitled *Walking on Ice,* were short items in her repertoire.

Lettie Connell Schubert began developing pantomimes in 1957 with her *Masques for Small Mimes.* The following year she built a new version, *Moods for Small Mimes.* These dramatic sketches are done with a variety of characters manipulated with precision to convey the pathos of the Troubadour singing to Columbine who never appears on her balcony, or the playfulness of a little boy with his dog, or the strangeness felt by moon people meeting Earthlings, and many other experiences.

The world of music provides the satirist with a great deal of material. Victor Borge and Alec Templeton, among others, have poked fun at their own profession, while opera singers, orchestra conductors and instrumentalists exhibit mannerisms which may be hilarious when imitated and exaggerated, as they have been with puppets. Now there is Marshall Izen, a concert pianist who devotes part of his program to musical satires which illuminate the foibles of the concert and operatic world. He uses the closed top of the piano as a stage where the opera *La* is enacted with puppets. Izen sings all the parts, accompanies with a free hand (if he has one), and operates a tape recorder by remote control foot pedal to fill in for duets and trios. In other interpretations, Izen may use his right hand to operate Jakamoe Unstoc, concert pianist, and his left to play the Rachmaninoff *Prelude in C Sharp Minor*. He may also don appropriate hats or other costume accessories, and make use of his own facial expressions to gain his effects. Whether he is playing music seriously, or spoofing some of its conventions, Marshall Izen's broad musical and theatrical training are always in evidence.

III

Where Puppets Meet Their Public

Puppets still perform in the same places they did in the period before 1948—at fairs, in permanent puppet theatres, and in traveling shows. In the past twenty years, however, television has become increasingly important, and now many puppets may be seen right in one's own living room.

Puppets go to the fair

Traditionally puppets are found in the midst of those places where people gather for entertainment and trade: the carnival, the market place, the fair. So today they appear, exercising their crowd-drawing talents to advertise, educate or provide diversion. Throughout the country every year there are numerous fairs—local, county and state. Agricultural products, livestock, arts and crafts, machinery, commercial displays, horse races, carnivals, theatrical entertainment and almost anything else may be seen. Puppets may pop up anywhere.

Some shows, such as *Stove Talk* and *Porgy Wins a Prize*, commissioned by the Cincinnati Gas and Electric Company and produced by Sally Sellers Hayes, were used for advertising. The Three Puppeteers (Julie Neagle, Dorothy Quinn, and Anne-Marie Cecil) have appeared at the Easthampton, the Southampton and the St. John's of Lattingtown Fairs. Erica Melchior has covered the "fair circuit" in New England, Ohio, Indiana, Illinois, Michigan, and Pennsylvania, performing in numerous small towns as well as at the big Ohio State Fair. Bob Mueller has presented his Peacock Puppet Theatre at New Jersey fairs and Bob Longfield spent the summers from 1952 to 1959 playing fairs on weekends while working at a regular drafting job. The summer of 1958 found Marge Kelly playing for six weeks at Western Canadian fairs to packed grandstands. Jack and Jackie Shafton found performing at county fairs much to their liking. In the 1958 season, for instance, their itinerary covered the Yolo County Fair near Sacramento, the Stockton, Bishop, and San Jose Fairs. Their variety included the kinds of acts which have been current in

546

America for a hundred years: the egg-laying ostrich, a soft shoe dancer, a "hayseed trio." Some fairs honor special products, such as California's Indio Date Festival and the San Bernardino National Show. For both of these, Bob Baker and Alton Wood played a ten-day engagement in 1960, and then went on to other fair engagements for the whole summer. They have also performed at the New Mexico State Fair in Albuquerque.

Cities often have special fairs. In 1960, the Millbrae (California) Chamber of Commerce had a street fair, with Linda and Christine Moore to provide puppet entertainment. At the Napa City Fair, Calistoga, California, the Leselli Marionettes performed during the week of July 4, 1963. In May 1960, there was an outdoor fair at Rockefeller Plaza in New York, with a puppet show by Jean Knopf, Barbara Gilbery and Jerry Hartnett. The Department of Parks and Recreation of Los Angeles had an All Nations Fair in 1966, and Vera Leeper had her puppets there. For the Upper Grant Avenue Street Fair in San Francisco, Lettie Connell Schubert built and presented her hand-puppet *Masque for Small Mimes* in June 1957.

In recent times there has been a proliferation of international trade fairs in many parts of the world. They are designed to show the industrial, commercial and artistic products of the exhibiting countries.

Puppets, of course, are likely to appear as they did when Bobby Clark presented his marionettes in *A Trip Around the World* in Chicago, and the Vellemans did *Canadian Folk Songs* in Toronto. Department stores sometimes sponsor special showings of imported art objects, textiles, and other products at such events as the Nieman-Marcus Fair in Dallas. Each year, one country or area of the world is represented. Nancy Staub of New Orleans performed there during the week of the French Fair. She also built a show, *Arlecchino and the Ogre*, for the 1964 European Import Fair at the Maison Blanche in New Orleans. The play used the Commedia dell'Arte technique, with a traditional plot, several bits of by-play (*lazzi*), and music of the period. The ogre was played by an actor in thirteenth-century mask and costume.

Puppet shows are often included at festivals of the arts. In the summer of 1963, Marie Hitchcock of San Diego took her musical show, *Down Beat*, to the 8th Annual Festival of Music in Anchorage, Alaska, and returned in time for the Del Mar Fair. Lewis Mahlmann's Lilliputian Players gave performances in their booth at the San Francisco Art Festival in 1963. A regular feature of the Huntington Art Fair is a puppet show by Mildred Berry, who prepares a new one each year. In 1966 it was *Eeyore's Birthday*. Les and Ellie Heath (the Leselli Marionettes) have performed at the Marin Art and Garden Fair, Ross, California, and on the other side of the United States, Punch performs in a green and white striped tent at the

Charlotte (North Carolina) Arts Festival. During the three-and-a-half-day run, thousands of people see the show. In 1965 Blanche Hutto unpacked her puppets, which had been inactive for twenty-five years, dressed herself in a Dutch costume and several helpers in various other national costumes to perform for children at the Talbot Street Art Fair in Indianapolis. Elizabeth Vondersmith has performed at the Annapolis Festival of Fine Arts, with *Jack and the Beanstalk* in 1966, and *Sleeping Beauty* and *Around the World* in 1967. Mollie Falkenstein has performed many times for the Winter Festival in Laguna Beach, California.

Puppets frequently perform at world's fairs. Puppet shows in unusual numbers appeared at the Century of Progress in Chicago, 1933 and 1934. Some were for entertainment and others advertised products with all the old verve of the medicine man. At subsequent world fairs the same pattern has been evident.

At the Century 21 Exposition, held in Seattle from April 21 to October 21, 1962, some puppet shows were included in the performing arts program. René and his Continental Artists, sponsored by the Children's Theatre of America, presented *The Nutcracker Suite,* interpreted as an Insect Ballet. It was hoped that a number of foreign companies would perform, but only the Bunraku Troupe from Japan actually did so. The two-week run, from July 25 to August 5, was the first appearance in America of this famous company. All summer long Sid and Marty Krofft's *Les Poupées de Paris* played for adults in Le Petit Théâtre.

At the New York World's Fair in the summers of 1964 and 1965, Bil Baird's Marionettes presented the *Show-GoRound* for the Chrysler Corporation. This was a mammoth puppet revue featuring a chorus line of Motor Blockettes, and a cast of hubcaps, differentials, and carburetors which danced and sang and, of course, put in a word for the sponsor's automobiles. Continuous showings for twelve hours a day necessitated four alternating crews of twelve puppeteers and additional technical personnel. There were four stages on a revolving seventy-two-foot drum, each of which faced an auditorium seating 600 people. A different segment of the show, lasting eight minutes, was set on each stage and the drum revolved to present it to each audience. Eighty-eight shows per day were given. *Les Poupées de Paris* played in the amusement area, and numerous other puppets were selling, promoting, demonstrating around the Fair. At the Indonesian Pavilion, daily performances of traditional puppets were given, and a puppet film on religion was shown at the Protestant and Orthodox Church Center.

October 12, 1964 was Columbus Day and Puppet Guild of Greater New York Day at the Fair. Twelve groups of puppeteers performed at the New York State Pavilion, with the Manteo Sicilian Marionettes to open and close the program. Other participants were the Maema Marionettes (Alice-May Hall), the Haggerty Puppets, the B. Gay Puppets, Frank Paris, Larry Berthelson's Pickwick Puppet Theatre, the Lea Wallace Puppets, Rod Young, The Three Puppeteers (Dorothy Quinn, Anne-Marie Cecil, Julie Neagle), Doug Anderson, the Wonderland Puppets (Alice Swann and Nancy Schmale), and Bud Wertheim's Unstrung Puppet Theatre.

The next year, June 18 was Guild Day at the U.S. Commission Building, and a number of puppeteers turned out to show their specialties. Alice-May Hall, dressed in a Colonial costume, circulated among the audience with a portable stage around her neck, and harriet was an organ grinder with her chimp. Junior puppeteer Marshall Katzman performed, and so did Nat Norbert, Jerry Hartnett, Frank Paris, Doug Anderson and Marlene McCauley's Popcorn Puppet Playhouse. On July 18, the Guild presented an afternoon of twenty puppet items at the New York State Exhibit. Doug Anderson, as for other Guild programs at the Fair, was Master of Ceremonies, and also presented variety with Gayle Anderson. Most of those who performed in June again appeared, and in addition there were Florence Crosby, Ginger Brearton, Eleanor Haggerty, the Wooden Tots Puppet Studio (Arthur Scheller, Richard Dipasquale), Jewel's Street Puppeteers (Mary Hoffman, Edna Torrence, Alice-May Hall), Rod Young Puppets, the Macbeth Trio (with Jewel Street personnel plus Louise Manzone), Milton Halpert, Rose Perlman's Marionettes, Arena of the Catspaw (Louise Marie Pizzaia, Nadine Smyth, Frank Smyth), Jean Rapicano Marionettes (Ann Rapicano, Anna Bell Green), Bernice Silver, and Edna Torrence Puppets. Most of these people were from the New York area, but some came from other parts of the state and from New Jersey and Pennsylvania.

Expo '67, held in Montreal for six months, was the most truly international fair to be held in America, and this was reflected in the puppet shows. In addition to shows scattered through the Pavilions of the Nations, an International Puppet Festival was held at the Youth Pavilion from July 9 through 16. Each day was devoted to the work of one country. Jacques Chesnais of France presented his Wooden Comedians in *Circus, Pantomimes and Mimodramas*. The next day German puppeteer Madame Burke showed *A Chinese Poem* and *The Afternoon of a Little Faun;* Felix Mirbt gave *The Thousand and One Nights*, and Albrecht Roser with Ina Vacano performed *Varieties*. On July 11 and 13, Czechoslovakia was represented by the Marionette Theatre of Spebjl and Hurvinek in short numbers featuring these well-known characters invented years ago by Josef Skupa. Micheline Legendre represented Canada with *Once Upon a Time* and *The Nightingale and the Emperor of China*. July 14 was United States Day, with the Rufus Rose Marionettes in *Pinocchio* and the Puppet

Arts of Woodstock, directed by Dick Myers, in *The Story of Dick Whittington*. All through the week, performances were interspersed with puppet films, and on closing day, there was a lecture by Jacques Chenais.

The Youth Pavilion was also the scene of less conventional activities, such as Happenings, total theatre, karate demonstrations, the latest in painting and sculpture, and all forms of music, from rock-'n'-roll to classical. Into this milieu the Bread and Puppet Theatre of Peter Schumann fitted perfectly, and he was there with a program of anti-war plays.

John Keogh did a six-scene travel review in the horseshoe theatre of the Brewery Association of Canada, with rod, hand, and string-puppets. The performance was fast paced and spectacular. Leo and Dora Velleman had a tent show in the Children's World, where they presented *Laurentian Parade* in May and *Undersea Fantasy* in July on a round stage eight feet in diameter, with the audience clustered all around it.

The fixed playhouse

The fixed playhouse for puppets is not common in America, although at various times and places there have been some which have operated successfully. Usually it is not economically feasible for a puppet showman to depend upon audiences drawn from a given locality, unless he has a subsidy, devotes part of his time to other forms of puppetry, or has more lucrative sources of income. Puppet theatres in parks which are used, mostly in summer, for children's recreation have already been discussed.

In 1940, Herbert Hosmer, Jr., opened a little country toy shop in South Lancaster, Massachusetts, and the next year instituted puppet performances in the Toy Cupboard Theatre. 1968 was the twenty-eighth season of shows for children presented during July and August. They are now given once a month during the year, with performances on holidays or for special groups. An added attraction is the Museum, which has been growing all these years.

About the same time, another very different puppet theatre was installed at the Kungsholm Restaurant in Chicago. Ernest Wolff and his mother Esther had used small rod-puppets, for which they had a patent, in productions of the Victor Puppet Opera Company at the New York World's Fair in 1939. When this was over, the Opera toured for a while and then came back to Chicago, where it appeared at Kimball Hall. Meanwhile, Fredrik Chramer had opened the Kungsholm Restaurant in the old McCormick mansion about 1937. He converted the fourth floor ballroom into a movie theatre where invited guests could see films of his famous friends, many of whom were opera stars. He saw the Victor Puppet Opera and offered to install it in his movie theatre. An agreement was reached with Esther Wolff (Ernest had been inducted into the Army), and opera performances began on February 23, 1942. In time various difficulties arose over the puppet patents and other matters, and the Wolff-Chramer association ended.

Interwoven with Kungsholm is the career of William Fosser, who as a child became fascinated with opera. He produced opera with various kinds of puppets and finally gravitated towards rod-puppets. He read about the puppet opera at Kungsholm, went to see Chramer and was hired as a puppeteer—at the age of fourteen. After a summer and fall there, he left because the work interfered with school. When the war came to an end, Ernest Wolff returned to Chicago and rebuilt his opera as the Tivoli. Fosser worked with him in the summer of 1947. That same year the whole Kungsholm establishment went up in flames. Fosser recalls that he stood by Chramer, who wept as the fire consumed his beloved Opera. The restaurant was rebuilt, with a new auditorium for the Puppet Opera, which reopened about 1952. Fosser's work with Wolff was short-lived, and he came back to Kungsholm for a couple of years. The Opera, with its several thousand rod-puppets, all richly costumed, and its elaborate scenery done in meticulous nineteenth-century style, became a mecca for the Chicago elite. In 1957, Chramer, broken in health, leased the Kungsholm to the Fred Harvey Company. He died in 1960.

Fosser had become an art director in the commercial motion picture field, and had built a stage and puppets for a small repertoire of operas. He went to Detroit in 1961 and performed his *Opera in Focus* at the Impresario Restaurant for three years. After this he toured with his show for the Mott Foundation, but felt that this kind of program was not well suited to child audiences. Back to Kungsholm as director of the Opera was the next venture. He wanted to change the nature of the performances from full-length affairs to excerpts, and to replace the puppets with his own, but this did not work out, and after two years he left. While there, however, he did a condensed version of *Kismet,* and now other musicals have been introduced into the Kungsholm repertoire, which is still being presented under the direction of David Peneton. Fosser is preparing at this writing to open *Opera in Focus* at Riccardo's Restaurant in Chicago.

On March 31, 1966, the last performance at the Turnabout Theatre took place. For fifteen years, no visit to Los Angeles was complete unless one attended the Yale Puppeteers' little theatre on La Cienega Street, where puppets performed at one end of the auditorium and live actors at the other. During intermission, the street car seats were reversed—thus the audience was "turned about." The theatre was open continuously during its lifetime, except for one six-week tour, and 5,400 performances were given. The puppets played musicals, some of which antedated the Turnabout period, for which Forman Brown wrote the music and Harry Burnett made the puppets. Included were *The Pie-Eyed Piper, Mister Noah, Caesar Julius, Bearding Bluebeard, Uncle Tom's Hebb'n, Tom and Jerry* and *The Brash Monkey*. The list of human actors who performed at Turnabout includes Elsa Lanchester, who was there for twelve years, right from the beginning, and Lotte Goslar and Frances Osborne for about ten years, while a long procession of artists came at intervals to sing, dance, or do pantomimes, dramatic numbers or comic bits. Some of them were Queenie Leonard, Marais and Miranda, Gilda Gray, Leota Lane, Corinna Mura, Inesita, the Duncan Sisters, El Brendel, and Odetta, who started her professional career at Turnabout. Harry Burnett often played, as did Dorothy Neumann, the other permanent partner, who costumed and directed the live revues. As the years went by, the walls of the theatre filled with the names of celebrities who visited it, and those who had come more than ten times were given a key to a sugar box in the anteroom until about 500 were in circulation. In the fifteen years of the theatre's existence, the olive trees in the patio grew from bushes to tall trees which topped the walls.

For thirty years the talents of Forman Brown and Harry Burnett were combined in the activities of the Yale Puppeteers, along with general manager Richard Brandon's business ability. Now the "three B's" maintain a house full of puppets and mementoes of their long career. They are not idle either, for Brown continues his music writing, Burnett has been teaching puppetry to young people, and Brandon still "manages."

Geniiland is a place of fantasy in Los Angeles where children may have the kind of birthday parties which only a genie could conjure up. Jean Cease (Mrs. Leonard Wohler) began her puppet work in 1957. At first she went to people's houses and other places with her shows, but decided that magic and make-believe were hard to achieve except in specially designed theatrical surroundings. She opened the first small Geniiland Puppet Theatre in 1959, moved to a larger place in 1960, and again in 1962. Located at 14837 Besemer Street, Van Nuys, California, since 1967, Geniiland has everything needed for a party. The theatre is reserved in advance and no tickets are sold. The children arrive and play games until show time, when they are escorted to front row seats, with the guest of honor seated on a mushroom throne on the stage. It is a large stage, with open playing space for marionettes, and imaginative backgrounds which include areas for hand-puppets and rod-puppets to perform. Genie herself provides the forty-five minutes of storytelling and musical variety, with lots of puppet characters—a singing mouse, a dancing rabbit, a talking tree, etc.—and short scenes such as *Please Don't Eat the Daisies*. Then, in the Partyroom, everybody eats birthday cake and ice cream, gifts are opened (with the help of the puppets), and balloons are popped. The theatre is also used for adult birthday parties, baby showers, or performances for fund-raising campaigns. There is also a touring stage, with which shows are given in clubs and churches by three puppeteers. Geniiland in Miniature is a one-girl set-up for nursery schools and other places where only a small show can be used.

Occasionally the puppet theatre has an "angel" who believes in it and spares no effort (or money) to realize an idea. Such a person was Louisa Mustin of Augusta, Georgia. She wanted a permanent place where puppets could perform, and in due course, the Puppet Playhouse was built, after designs by Phil Molby, and opened in 1951. The stage was designed for all types of puppets, and the most efficient equipment was installed. The front of the theatre facing Broad Street was yellow tile, with a large multicolored abstract design in the center. O'Neill's *Emperor Jones* was the first production for adults, with *Jimmy in the Land of Mer* for children. In 1953 the Playhouse company toured Georgia and North and South Carolina with *The Mikado* and *Beauty and the Beast*. At that time the staff included Louisa Mustin, William Tennent, chief puppeteer, Barbara Lucas, Charles Hardman and Yvonne Somers. Unfortunately, there were many difficulties and this experiment ended not long afterwards.

Bob Baker, Alton Wood and Helen Crail have been entertaining children and their parents since 1963 in a beautiful puppet theatre in old Los Angeles. White iron gates lead to a courtyard with painted green grass from which oversize wooden daisies grow. Inside, the spacious, high-ceilinged auditorium with rich red carpet and proscenium curtains is lighted by three sparkling crystal chandeliers. Children are seated on the floor at the sides and back, with chairs for adults behind them. The red curtains open to reveal the set, and from it come the marionettes. They play in the entire open space and move freely among the children in the first rows—dancing, singing, sometimes commenting, as their operators bring them to life. The whole presentation has a fairy-tale quality, with excellent lighting to enhance the gaiety, the scariness, the fantasy, the weirdness or the humor of the puppets. At every performance, there is at least one Birthday Child, who wears a gold or silver crown and receives a birthday kiss from the puppets. Afterwards, everybody has refreshments in the patio, which has seasonal decorations. Adults are invited to inspect the workshop, where everything needed for puppet making is neatly arranged. Baker insists he does this because nobody realizes that "it takes all this stuff just to make puppets." The program is basically musical variety, but sometimes a theme provides continuity, as in *Something to Crow About,* which has a barnyard scene for a background and the operators dressed in overalls, with all sorts of animal puppets in action.

Bob Baker has been in the puppet business since the forties, when, at the age of nineteen, he started a puppet manufactory, which he built into an enterprise with forty employees. Later he had his own television show, built productions for department stores, and gave performances at birthday parties for the children of movie stars. In 1947 he produced an elaborate circus, which took twenty-five people five and a half months to build. Then in 1961 he again built a circus, which is described in Chapter II.

At present the theatre staff includes Roy Raymond, Shirley Hibbard, Reed Johnson, Danny Baldwin and Russell Turner. In past years, many people have been associated with the Bob Baker Marionettes. One of them, Mrs. Malcolm Wilkes, specialized in portrait puppets and costuming. Many West Coast puppeteers employed her to dress their finest puppets because of her rare skill in this difficult art. Bob Mason, longtime puppeteer on the night club circuit, worked with Baker and was one of the operators for the 1961 circus.

In 1954 Sidney Kittinger established the Pixie Players in a fifty-seat theatre in a converted store in New Orleans, with Nancy Staub as partner and assistant puppeteer. His original plays, *The Lemonade Clown* and *The Near-Sighted Princess,* were featured. After he left the theatre, Mrs. Staub continued it, converted to hand-puppets and changed the name to the Punchinello Puppets. She gave weekly performances and had special engagements, including some on television, but closed the theatre in 1960. Lois Larson installed her Mount Joy Puppet Theatre in a carriage house at Dane, Wisconsin. Aided by her husband and son, she uses both hand-puppets and marionettes, her 1966 production being *The Happy Prince.* She also has a portable stage for touring. Ralph Geddes and François Martin, whose work goes back to 1924 when they helped Ellen Van Volkenburg with *A Midsummer Night's Dream* in San Francisco, built the Tantamount Theatre in Carmel Valley about 1960.

James Gamble spent four summers at Santa's Workshop, North Pole, Colorado, where he built a puppet playhouse in Bavarian gingerbread style. Nearby Pike's Peak was another attraction for tourists, and in those summers more than a million people saw Gamble's puppet shows. With variety and "a few hundred *Punch and Judy* thrown in" he totaled over 2,000 performances, at the rate of eight fifteen-minute appearances per day. After Gamble went on to other projects, the puppet house was transformed into a magician's until 1967, when Hollis Keller and his wife returned it to puppetry.

For two years Pat Platt has maintained the Puppet Playhouse at 3903

Voltaire Street in San Diego. Performances are given on weekends from the repertoire of *Heidi, The Brave Tailor, The Magic Ring, Small One, Red Riding Hood, The Three Wishes* and *Wizard of Oz.* Many of her puppets are made from gourds of various sizes, which provide interesting basic shapes for heads and bodies, both human and animal. They are grown at the W. F. Bradley Gourd Farm at National City, California, and have become popular with the puppet makers of the region.

Recently, Tamara Nijinsky, daughter of the famous dancer Nijinsky, opened the Tamara Nijinsky Puppet Theatre in Phoenix, which plays for both children and adults. The first production was a ballet, *The Spectre of the Rose,* an adaptation for puppets of a ballet performed by her father and Tamara Karasavina in Paris in 1911. Also in Phoenix is Jo Lawrence's Tumbleweed Theatre. At Green Gables, a lavish Phoenix eating place, built in the form of a castle, a puppet jester appears at a stained glass window to tell customers when their table is ready. He has a quick tongue and is likely to heckle the guests and engage in verbal exchanges with the live entertainers. If there is a children's birthday party, the puppet may present a small gift to the guest of honor.

For a long time, Linalice Carey tried to interest someone in Austin, Texas, in puppet production, with no success until Alix Whitaker from Pennsylvania came along. They built a portable stage and prepared *Punch and Judy* and *The Three Musicians of Bremen.* In January 1967, they performed at The Catacombs, a small theatre used by a professional theatrical group called the Bijuberti Players. It was decided at once that the puppets should perform there regularly, and so the Bijuberti Puppeteers became the troupe name. Until May they played every alternate Saturday morning, and then migrated, along with as many Texans as could do so, to the cool lakes in the area, where they played all summer. Back they came to The Catacombs in the fall, with *The Lobster's Lament* and *Six Aesop's Fables* added to the repertoire. Mrs. Carey now has plans to convert a barn on newly-acquired property into a puppet theatre to seat about fifty children.

In Denver, the Norwood Puppet Theatre began presenting shows seven years ago. Its director, Elton Norwood, has ambitions for a permanent puppet theatre for Denver, having played for a time at the Trident Theatre. Although he found that live and puppet theatre do not mix too well, because of the necessity of clearing the stage after each performance, the advantages of being in one place were considerable. The puppets for a recent production of *Lord of Gooseberries,* a Japanese tale, are life-size, and some are operated like the Bunraku, including a warrior and a girl who dances and plays the koto. *Puppets in Potpourri* consists of a group of numbers also done with large marionettes. Among these are Fatima the Happy Hippo, a gargoyle in a chest, a unicyclist, Brunhilda and her trapeze, the Gloworm and a dance to *A Night on Bald Mountain*.

The Lovelace Marionette Theatre in Pittsburgh opened in May 1963. With twenty-one marionette shows in the repertoire, the bill is changed every four weeks, and examples of ancient and modern puppets are on view in the theatre. Margo Lovelace, the director, has worked with all types of puppets since 1947 and has studied with Cedric Head and with Obraztsov in Moscow. Department store work and television programs are also part of the Lovelace presentations.

In addition to barns, carriage houses, and garages which puppeteers have turned into puppet theatres, many others are to be found in living rooms or studios. Puppets are often at their best in such intimate sur-roundings where the small audience may savor the full subtlety of puppet art.

Rufus and Margo Rose have a good-sized theatre in their Waterford, Connecticut, home, and the Stevens "Mousetrap" in Middlebury, Indiana, has a large enough living room to accommodate a small audience. An ele-gant studio theatre is emerging at 12 Gay Street, New York, where Frank Paris and Ted Lewis have their living quarters and workshops. Bud and Marlene Wertheim live on a farm near Livingston Manor, New York, and sometimes they give performances there.

Having successfully done battle with zoning laws and regulations, and having received a grant from the National Foundation for the Arts and Humanities, Bil Baird's Marionette Theatre opened in New York on January 27, 1967. This is an auspicious beginning, for the theatre is meant to be a showcase for good puppetry, and the grant is to help develop adult audiences. Perhaps it marks a new era.

The traveling show

Although many puppeteers manage to do most of their work in one place by concentrating on television or maintaining a regular perform-ance place, most showmen travel. Some still make long annual tours through large areas of the country as they have done for many years, but others may troupe their shows within a city or a limited area. The arrival of a traveling puppet show at school, community center or park still cre-ates the excitement of anticipation. In addition, a show presented directly to an audience has a theatrical impact which many showmen find more satisfactory than television or films. They are willing to put up with the ardors of travel to give children this experience. Many kinds of shows in many different styles are found, and to illustrate, we shall mention here the work of a few puppeteers, all of whom present plays, sometimes with variety added.

Romain and Ellen Proctor, for instance, produced traveling shows for over thirty years, and took them to all parts of the United States. Cedric Head retired in 1959, after thirty-one years of touring such shows as *Alice in Wonderland, Robin Hood,* and *Snow White.* About 100,000 miles were clocked annually in these nine-month journeys throughout the country. Frank and Irene Still, although nominally retired in Florida, continue some tours. For thirty-five years they have been known principally for their *Circus of Marionettes,* which has worn out and been rebuilt three times. This program, together with several plays, has been presented mostly to school children. In 1956, a fire in their Florida studio destroyed 200 puppets and the scenery for five plays. The *Circus* escaped because it was in their trailer. Now they have another studio and puppet building goes on. In his book *Charming Children* (see Bibliography), Still has recorded some of his technical methods and experiences.

Robert and Edith Williams celebrated their twenty-fifth anniversary season in 1953–1954. Traveling out from Puyallup, Washington, each year they went on tour with a show designed for children six through twelve years of age. Still active, the Williams Marionettes are the result of a lifetime of experimentation in puppet design, playwriting, and acting. The Rufus Rose Marionettes made long tours throughout the country until the early fifties, when he began work on the *Howdy Doody* television show.

Although they began work in 1934, George and Lucile Cole did not become professional puppeteers until 1945. At that time, there was little entertainment for children in the public schools in the Chicago area, so the Cole Marionettes filled a need and are now an accepted part of the school auditorium program. Their longest run has been thirty consecutive years in the Decatur, Illinois, school system. Their five companies tour under the School Assembly program and play to a quarter of a million children annually. The repertoire includes a circus and favorite stories, such as *King Midas, The Hearty Tin Soldier, Dick Whittington, The Pied Piper of Hamelin* and many others.

Like the Coles, Meredith Bixby, of Saline, Michigan, found there was little touring entertainment for young children. He began producing plays for them in 1932, and has continued to this day. Since 1948, some of his shows have been *Pinocchio, Caliph Stork, The Enchanted Birds* and, in 1967, *The Wizard of Oz.* All the plays of the Bixby Marionettes are retained and repeated about every seven years. They tour from September to June to 300 schools and other organizations in the larger cities of the Midwest.

Working with marionettes has been a long-time business for Ed Johnson, of Milford, Michigan, who began in 1928. He has been associated with a number of professional groups, but is best known for his development of the one-man marionette play which he began in 1938. Except for the interruption of World War II, he has continued his presentations to date, and he was also a pioneer in the use of puppets on television. While he was stationed in the Philippines, Johnson became aware of the richness of folklore and natural phenomena as a source for puppet plays which would not only entertain but also teach. Since 1947, he has written eleven scripts, all based on stories from various lands, beginning with the Philippine *Wonder Mountain* and going on to *Magic Light* (Greenland Eskimo), *Neptune's Kingdom* (the sea bottom), *The West Wind* (American Indian), *Voyage to Nowhere* (sailing ships and the sea), *The Grass Forest* (life in an ant colony), *The Magic Sword* (a lesson in self-confidence), *The Secret* (ancient Egypt), *The Magic Man* (India), *Beyond the Moon* (rockets and space travel), and *The Human Planet* (size relationships from the solar system to the atom). Play number twelve, "involving apathy, caring enough to do one's best, and patriotism," is in preparation for 1968.

Lewis Parsons came into puppetry about 1950 with a musician's background. His interest is in playwriting and acting rather than construction, which is done for him by various artists. Thera Knudson (Mrs. James Liska) made some of his lovable animal marionettes; Bob Mills, Henry Sherman, and Eileen Thompson made other casts of characters. Ron Bowers, who has been with Parsons for eight years, is chief puppet and scenery maker and also helps on tour. Their work is almost entirely in elementary schools, with a varied program including hand-puppet plays of favorite stories, musical activity with piano and solobox, and marionette variety. The latter is performed in full view to demonstrate manipulation. Free shows are given in hospitals, schools for handicapped children, and homes for the aged. Each summer Parsons returns to his headquarters in Pentwater, Michigan, where he prepares the next season's show, composes and records music and sound effects, leaving the dialogue to be given live. Much of his work is in Texas, with engagements all along the way, and he has also played in Mexico.

From its base in Maywood, Illinois, the Coleman Puppet Theatre tours each year, as it has since 1948, to play for children in elementary schools, as well as for numerous organizations, clubs and churches. A new show is usually prepared for each season by Fay and Barbara Coleman, whose repertoire includes well-known stories, and some less commonly presented, such as *The Magic Dog of Fuji* and *The Amazing Voyage of Nicky Noodle. Aladdin, Snow White* and *Pinocchio* have been popular revivals.

The theatre has toured in twenty-eight states, mostly in the Midwest and along the Atlantic Seaboard. Many schools in the Chicago area have sponsored a Coleman show annually for the past twenty years. Fay Coleman has also taught puppetry, mostly for community recreation projects and YMCA groups. Both he and Barbara have also done many floor shows with marionettes. They were among the first to use tape-recorded sound, with the 1950 production of *Tom Sawyer*.

About 1935, Dorothy Zaconick and Ruth Wacksman organized the Suzari Marionettes and played extensively in schools and department stores, for industrial exhibits and television, sometimes with several troupes in operation. The company split up about six years ago. Dorothy Zaconick's half became the Dozari Marionettes. Nick Coppola became company manager for Mrs. Wacksman's Nicolo Marionettes, which is still active, with headquarters in New York.

The touring puppet show is a strenuous business, as these details contributed by Ron and Jane Herrick indicate. Every year before they leave from their Kingston, New York, home, they buy a new car and by the time they return, it has clocked about 35,000 miles. They cover New England and go south to Virginia and North Carolina, playing in elementary schools during the week and on weekends for organizations, industrial accounts, colleges, museums and little theatre groups. They keep eight shows working all the time and two different programs of variety. In addition they often give workshops, and have found time to film two of their shows for Educational Television. By the time the season is over, they are ready for relaxation, and often seek it in travel to foreign countries. The Herricks began puppetry as a hobby, but soon found themselves transformed into professionals in 1935, and they have been performing ever since.

Les and Ellie Heath (the Leselli Marionettes) are also veterans of the road, for they started touring with plays and variety before 1948 across the whole U.S.A. They now live in San Rafael, California, and do much of their work in the western states, sometimes spending the summer playing at the many fairs which are regular events up and down California. Over the years a good many shows have gone out from the Stevens studio in Middlebury, Indiana. These are booked through the School Assembly Programs and are performed by puppeteers whom Stevens has trained.

Robin and Edith Reed, of Wales, Wisconsin, became professionals in 1950 and have toured since then under the sponsorship of civic organizations, college concert programs, art festivals, and theatres. Their repertoire consists of plays adapted from standard stories, such as *The Wizard of Oz, Pinocchio, Through the Looking Glass* and *The Emperor's Nightin-*

gale, which they stage in various ways to eliminate waits for scene changing. At one time they used two wagon stages moved back and forth on a thirty-three foot track to fill an eleven-foot proscenium; another device was a canvas conveyor belt which moved the scenery along as needed. Now they have two curtains in a wide proscenium so that scenes can alternate between two parts of the stage or the whole playing space can be used. A complete theatrical lighting system has an automatic control console with forty circuits and dimming programmed on a punch-card.

From Toronto, the touring company of Leo and Dora Velleman travels to schools in Quebec, Ontario, and the northern United States with a program of original plays written by Dora. They have tried many innovations in staging, the most recent being a completely round stage which has been used in department store shows and at Expo '67. So that all the people surrounding it may see, two sets of puppets are used in coordination, with the action mimed to a tape recording. In other experiments, they have freed the puppets' movement by increasing the proscenium length to fifteen feet, or by using a large open proscenium stage with three playing areas. All the Ledo productions are carefully designed, with stylized puppets and settings.

Among those who play more or less within a local area, one finds great variety in the productions. Luman Coad recently moved from California to Vancouver, British Columbia, and formed the Coad Canada Puppets for touring. Arlyn Kuthan is his associate and does most of the designing. She has experimented with carved foam rubber puppets, presented handpuppet plays, and taught puppetry for the Vancouver Adult Education Board. Jim Menke has been active in puppetry for twenty years, but as a professional only since 1954. He has toured in the Midwest and Southeast for School Assembly programs, but now does his own booking, and plays for PTA and similar groups. He has also done television programs, performed in foreign countries, and has developed a traffic safety show for Kar Service Centers, which has been presented in many western New York schools.

Dorothy Quinn, Anne-Marie Cecil and Julie Neagle combined their various talents and formed The Three Puppeteers. They produced shows for children which they toured in the New York area to churches, fairs, schools and many organizations. They have also worked with the New York Junior League Puppeteers. Like many puppeteers, these women have other commitments and are "retired" for the moment.

Edna Torrence has worked in the Morristown, New Jersey, region since 1948, although she was interested in puppets long before. A group from the Morristown Little Theatre to which she belonged produced benefit shows for hospitals and other worthy causes. She has had many classes for

Scout leaders and in children's camps. Lecture demonstrations and shows for clubs, church fairs, schools, and birthday parties, plus a back-to-school safety show for the Kresge Department Store in Newark, are other activities. She studied with Frank Paris, and in 1963 passed the civil service examination for the New York Parks Department Marionette Theatre where she worked as a puppeteer until a back injury forced her to give up this strenuous job. Now she has time to do puppets with her grandchildren and to organize her puppet memorabilia.

Nancy Schmale and Alice Swann, of Southampton, Pennsylvania, have been performing puppet plays since 1961 as the Wonderland Puppet Theatre. They play for emotionally disturbed and retarded children, or at schools for the deaf and blind; for Head Start groups and assembly programs; for audiences in museums and cultural centers. Their programs include such plays as *The Valiant Tailor* and *The Lion and the Mouse*, pantomimes for *The Sorcerer's Apprentice* and *The Carnival of Animals*, and demonstrations of puppets from other countries using material in their own collection.

Roger Dennis and his Portmanteau Puppet Theatre work largely in the Cleveland area presenting shows for children, the latest being *St. George and the Dragon*. Gordon Westphal began the Pinwheel Puppets in 1957. He has developed an individual style for his hand-puppets and written original plays for them, including *The Polka Dot Cake*, *Knight for a Day*, *The Tattletale Tulips* and *The Mouse in the Moon*. These are played mostly for children and family groups in Detroit. He has also been on television and performed for trade shows. When United States Steel put on its *Rhapsody of Steel* sales promotion, Westphal presented *The Stainless Thief or Who Stole Mrs. Stover's Steel* to advertise stainless steel cooking ware.

Mildred Berry began puppet work as a hobby and became semi-professional. Active in the Detroit area, she presents shows for a wide variety of organizations, including annual book fairs held by the Jewish Community Center; the Twelfth Annual Detroit Children's Book Fair in 1965, and the Huntington Woods Art Fair. Marilyn O'Connor also began puppetry as a hobby and is now a professional, trouping her show to Detroit schools five days a week. Since 1964 she has worked largely with folk singer Rowena, who sits outside the stage and sings to the accompaniment of various folk instruments, while the puppets on stage mime the action or present plays based on folk tales. Lately they have been using Carl Orff's Schulwerk rhythm instruments, many of which the puppets can play. In 1967 they collaborated with Philip Molby in a small puppet theatre in a Birmingham, Michigan, gift shop as a promotion feature, which ran from February through May.

Philip Molby and John Sutton, both Detroiters, joined forces to produce school shows and played *Beauty and the Beast* during the 1967–1968 season. Molby has been active in puppetry for many years, having been associated with a number of professional puppeteers. He has also toured with his own company. Sutton was an actor with the Grosse Pointe Children's Theatre, and had his puppet apprenticeship with Molby's company. He has also worked with several touring companies and assisted in the 1967 television productions of Jim Henson's Muppets.

Emeline Goulsby Dobbins was puppet director for the South Carolina State Parks Commission of Forestry from 1946 to 1950. Since then, she has been continuously busy with workshops and performances for many different types of audiences in Atlanta, Richmond, and her present home, Kansas City, Missouri.

Nellie Mendham, a St. Louis puppeteer, has worked with all kinds of puppets for many years. Formerly a drama teacher at Idaho State University where she also directed plays, she later turned to puppet production and teaching. She has introduced puppets in art and adult education programs, conducted classes for adults and children, especially for the presentation of religious plays and for programs at church art fairs. She is a shadow-puppet enthusiast and has worked with them for many years, using a variety of techniques in plays for children, church groups, and museum presentation.

Harry and Cleo Fowler built shows in their Apple Tree Workshop in Chicago Heights and performed in the area from 1953 to 1965, with original scripts and adaptations of fairy tales. Gregg and Marie Samanisky call themselves the Balalaika Puppeteers because they use Russian music as their theme. Since 1953 they have been giving shows in the Twin Cities region, some with music by Gregg. They also give demonstrations for children and adults, and exhibit their collection of puppets from time to time. Marie has been conducting a puppetry workshop for children at the Minneapolis Public Library for a year and a half. Currently they are working on *Androcles and the Lion* and *The Mikado*.

Many puppeteers on the West Coast find ample opportunity for giving shows without going very far afield. Some are mentioned elsewhere; we here add a few more. The Mitchell Marionettes, based in Whittier, California, perform widely in theatres, at fairs, at country and yacht clubs in the western states. Howard and Marjorie Mitchell met in high school and began performing magic and puppet shows, which they continued after their marriage and expanded into a professional activity, featuring original routines and trick marionettes. Their two daughters often help with the shows, and sometimes there are two or more units on the road, especially during holiday seasons.

Margaret Fickling's educational and therapeutic work has been mentioned, but she was also a performer. She and Peggy Manchester presented shows in the Los Angeles metropolitan area for more than fifteen years until Mrs. Fickling's death in 1966. Both were active in Guild and Regional puppet activities.

Shirley McManus is one of those who have recently become puppeteers, having made her first puppet in June 1966. Her program of variety and plays, called *Puppets Please*, has been given for Head Start and Poverty Programs, in schools and community centers. She usually performs alone, but for her presentations in the Balboa Park Puppet Theatre in San Diego, she commandeers the assistance of her family. Her husband helps work the puppets, and, she adds, "Terry, our daughter, age seven, plays Christopher Robin, and David, age four, collects tickets while Grandma sells 'em."

Helga and Bill Cassady (the Berkeley Puppeteers) not only perform widely in California, but are also active in organizing exhibits at art festivals and libraries, teaching, and participating in other forms of theatre, such as the construction of masks for *The Tree of Night* produced by the Contemporary Dancers. Cassady played the leading role in Pacifica Radio's production of C. J. Zemalis' *Land of Green Pyramids*. He is also a photographer and a writer who has contributed to a number of periodicals. The Berkeley Puppeteers have produced some plays for adults, and have done considerable work in colleges, but the bulk of their production is for children. However, they are concerned with the possibilities of the puppet theatre, and are working to realize some of them. Research in Mexico, the Southwest, at the New York Museum of Natural History and the Metropolitan Museum of Art has been undertaken to broaden their background and thus help their productions.

Puppetry in museums

Considerable puppet activity is sponsored by museums in many parts of America. Some have collections which are exhibited at intervals; some present occasional performances, and others have a regular series of shows; some have workshops for children and adults as part of their educational program.

Several museums are noted for their emphasis upon puppetry. At the Detroit Institute of Arts, theatrical presentations were a part of its entertainment program for many years. With the acquisition of the Paul McPharlin collection of theatre arts materials, presented in 1952 by his parents, Mr. and Mrs. W. H. McPharlin, and his wife, Marjorie Batchelder McPharlin, its activities were greatly expanded. The collection included over eight hundred books and periodicals on puppet theatre, ballet, opera, theatre design and history; puppets from America and abroad; correspondence from Gordon Craig and puppeteers around the world, as well as playbills; photographs, and data collected for his publication of *Puppetry: A Yearbook of Puppets and Marionettes.* The Theatre Arts Collection soon became a permanent section of the Institute and was administered for a time by Francis Robinson. In 1954, the post of Curator of Theatre Arts was created, and Adolph Cavallo was named to it. Gil Oden was appointed in 1956, and upon his resignation, Audley Grossman, Jr., took over the work.

From the original bequest of 274 puppets, the collection doubled within a few years, aided by the income from a purchase fund given by Mr. W. H. McPharlin, and by contributions. Among these were three giant puppets designed by Robert Edmond Jones and made by Remo Bufano for the League of Composers' production of Stravinsky's *Oedipus Rex,* a gift of Mr. and Mrs. Cedric Head; the foyer of a marionette theatre designed by Fabrizio Clerici, the gift of the Italian Government; and a group of puppets by the vaudeville performer, John Lewis, presented by the local Goodwill Industries. The collection is still growing, with acquisitions of puppets by Walter Deaves and Daniel Meader, famous nineteenth-century American showmen, a Victorian hand-puppet stage complete with characters and scenery, and many gifts from puppeteers.

The books and archives are now available for research in the Institute's Library, and the puppet collection may be visited by special arrangement. Some puppets are on exhibition at all times, and upon occasion loans are made to other museums. Television programs also make use of puppets from the collection; in one program, Gary Jennings used "Punch" Irving's nineteenth-century *Punch and Judy* cast to explain modern art.

The Institute has been host to a number of important puppet events for which special exhibits were arranged. On November 5 and 6, 1954, the Detroit-Toronto Festival was held, with American and Canadian puppeteers participating. The Detroit Puppeteers Guild, which works closely with the Institute, and the Toronto Guild were co-sponsors. The McPharlin Memorial Conference, January 24 and 25, 1958, included a talk by Marjorie McPharlin and a panel discussion, "Towards Exciting Puppet Theatre," with Helen Haiman Joseph, George Latshaw and Dick Myers. Harro Siegel's troupe from Braunschweig was in the United States at that time, and gave a performance of *Comic Interludes* and *Doctor Faust.* Siegel presented an illustrated talk, "European Puppetry Today." In 1960, the Puppeteers of America Festival was held at the Institute, and again in 1965. For the latter, "Puppet Cavalcade," a spectacular puppet exhibit, was arranged in the Great Hall by Audley Grossman and his staff. The walls were hung in black velvet, and at the far end, the Bufano *Oedipus* figures towered, and row upon row of pedestals, each with a single puppet spotlighted from above, displayed figures of all styles and types. On either side of the entrance foyer were large Latshaw puppets which had appeared in the Institute performances of *Billy the Kid* and *Till Eulenspiegel.*

In 1954, the *Detroit News* made the first of its annual grants to establish and maintain the Detroit Puppet Theatre. Eight puppet shows are sponsored each year. A typical series was that of 1963–1964 which included *Cinderella* by the New York Park Marionette Theatre; *Snow White and the Seven Dwarfs* by the Coleman Marionettes; *A Christmas Story* by Leo and Dora Velleman; *The Enchanted Birds* by the Meredith Bixby Marionettes; *The Mousetronaut* by the Nancy Cole Puppets; *The Runaway Rocket* by the George Latshaw Puppets; *The Emperor's New Clothes* by the B. Gay Puppets; *The Emperor's Nightingale* by the Reed Marionettes and *Neptune's Kingdom* by the Ed Johnson Marionettes.

Workshops for children and sometimes for adults are part of the Detroit Puppet Theatre program. The first was given in 1954 by Vernone Tracey. A group of young people formed The Puppeteens, and they assisted with a number of productions, including *Gammer Gurton's Needle* and *The Pink Siamese.* Also, performances of the prize-winning play in the 1955 playwriting contest, described earlier, were given. Local puppeteers have been commissioned to take their shows to institutions for ill or under-privileged children, and there have been a number of cooperative projects with the Junior League. Impressive performances have been staged with the Detroit Symphony Orchestra, with local puppeteers as manipulators. Youth Workshops in Theatre are also sponsored, and one of these produced Latshaw's version of *Pinocchio.* Shows by foreign puppet companies are sometimes given, and some with adult appeal have been included, although most of the performances are primarily for children.

A varied program of activities began at the Museum of the City of New York in 1962 when an exhibit called "Punch's Progress—Heroes of the Puppet Stage" was installed. Intended to be temporary, it proved so popular that it has been retained as a permanent feature. Many puppets have been added to the Museum collection, and others have been loaned, so that a representative cross-section of world puppetry may be seen. In addition, workshops are given at intervals by well-known puppeteers, and in the small auditorium puppet shows are a regular part of the weekend programs given from October to April.

On June 21, 1963, the International Puppet Museum and Theatre was dedicated at Stony Creek, Connecticut. Since the thirties, Grace Weil had been collecting puppets, specializing in the Sicilian type for the past few years. Over sixty of these three- to four-foot figures were on display, many of them made by Sebastian Zappala, one of Sicily's greatest nineteenth-century craftsmen. Some of the puppets, operated by James Weil and Salvatore Macri, were used to perform scenes from romances of chivalry. It was planned to give regular performances of these Sicilian plays, but with the death of Grace Weil, the high hopes for the museum and theatre faded, although a few performances were given.

Some museums have a strong educational program. The Des Moines Art Center stresses the creative aspect of puppetry in Theatre I, II, and III, in which various types of puppets are made and used in original plays developed with improvised dialogue. Through knowledge of puppet history, as well as the technical aspects of puppet making, the children in these courses are made aware of puppetry as an art form. In a film promoting the Art Center, one advanced group appeared with Fran Allison; there have been television programs, and the puppets helped to launch a creativity seminar at Iowa State University given by Peggy Patrick, the Associate Director of Education for the Center. For the annual Junior Art Museum exhibition, puppet plays are used to bring alive art cultures of the past. Mrs. Patrick notes that "the results have been educational, dramatic and just loads of fun."

The Cleveland Museum of Art has included puppetry in its children's program for a long time. During the past ten years Henry and Greta Sherman have taught classes for seven- to fourteen-year-olds. They use a creative approach to puppet making, using simple materials such as wooden spoons, rubber balls, plastic bottles, and fabric draped over coathangers for costumes. The resulting puppets are strong and clear in design. Music is essential and often sparks creativity. Children learn their lines, because the Shermans believe that correct speaking is very important. So is the discipline of the theatre, which the children accept as the corollary of creativity, and the whole experience leads to the satisfaction of a complete performance.

At the Mint Museum of Art in Charlotte, North Carolina, there is an active puppet program. It began about 1958, when Jacqueline Crutchfield's interest in puppetry was given impetus by the Puppeteers of America Festival at Chapel Hill. The director of the Museum asked her to set up a workshop. She invited George Merten to conduct it; later, Elsie and Tom Harrison and Nancy Cole assisted her. Weekly meetings in the Crutchfield home during the spring and summer have kept the workshops going. Since 1960, two productions a year have been presented at the Museum. A permanent room was especially designed for the puppets, in which the stages are set up, and the puppets stored, some in wall showcases. Mrs. Crutchfield's interest in adult puppetry resulted in a spoof called *The Seven Lively Arts*. However, the need is for entertainment for children of three to six, and most programs are designed for them. For the past four years a *Punch and Judy* has been presented for Charlotte's Festival in the Park. During this week, about eighty-five performances are given to an audience of approximately 200,000 persons. With the new facilities, plans are in progress to have three puppet groups: one to conduct two children's workshops per year, one to develop and present two shows at the Museum, and one to use a portable set-up to entertain underprivileged children, those in hospital wards and some schools, as well as to present the Park shows.

The Children's Museum in Detroit is a part of the public school system. Sets of puppets are made by the Technical Department and sent out to the schools as a stimulus for the children to make up their own plays. Years ago an art teacher made sets of small hand-puppets for dramatizing fairy tales, and they were so successful the Museum began providing similar sets. Sometimes the puppets are made for a specific purpose, such as the group of Doctor, Nurse, Family with Mr. Soap, Mr. Comb, Mr. Brush, Mr. Tooth. This "tell-it-yourself" approach to health problems proved more effective than cut-and-dried teaching plays. Workshops are also given at the Museum for teachers, in which they are shown how to make simple puppets from available materials. An exhibit, "Puppet Actors," which includes typical puppets from various parts of the world, is available for display in the schools. Through them the children are inspired to learn about the countries of their origin, and to put on their own puppet shows.

The Lake Erie Junior Nature and Science Center in Cleveland is in its eighteenth year of puppet classes for children. Eight-week sessions are held each autumn, winter and spring. Kay Geffine is instructor, and she reports that the classes are kept lively by making each one different. Sometimes only one puppet will be made in a term, at others a quick puppet will be created each week, or impressions of television personalities will be translated into puppets, or one character may be made from many different materials and the play put on in the various ways the materials suggest. The plays are tuned to the puppets—or vice versa—but they are always important. The Center has excellent physical equipment: a new building, a stage for television, two lightweight portable stages for class work, and a dual-purpose one which was a gift from the Kiwanis Club many years ago.

Kay Geffine sums up the therapeutic, educational and recreational values of puppetry thus: "A child seems to be able to release inhibitions, hostilities, joys or nearly the whole gamut of emotions through a puppet. He can transfer these things to an inanimate object which he can make 'alive.' Shy children, nervously disturbed, overly aggressive, as well as uncomplicated children, seem to be able to find a personal pace and a release in creative concentration—an escape into the wonderful world of imagination. Yet with it all they seem to keep respect and admiration for their fellow puppeteers. A sharing and consideration develop especially during the production of a play. The 'play's the thing,' not the individual, and nearly all conform to this, for they have expressed their particular individuality through the creation of their own puppets." The children have ample opportunity for puppet playing, since they give shows throughout the area for all kinds of audiences under all kinds of circumstances. Thus, all the benefits inherent in puppetry, from craft work to puppet history to dramatic expression, are realized in this program.

Some of the many other museums which have used puppets in their educational program are: the Rochester (New York) Museum of Arts and Sciences, the Junior Museum at the Tucson (Arizona) Art Center, the Brooklyn Museum, the Junior Museum of the Pasadena Art Institute and the Deland (Florida) Children's Museum.

Performances and exhibits have also aided in the general appreciation of puppetry. The Metropolitan Museum of Art in New York presents shows from time to time in the Museum auditoriums, or outdoors in the Cloisters or Central Park. Sometimes a special show is commissioned to illustrate a museum theme. When the New York *Times'* Third Annual Boys' and Girls' Book Fair was held at the American Museum of Natural History in 1949, the Milovsoroff and the Rose puppets provided entertainment. Gustave and Jane Baumann gave a series of performances at the Museum of International Folk Art in Santa Fe in June 1959, in which Indian and Spanish themes prevailed. Frank Dreusike and Jack Stackpole produced two programs at the San Francisco Museum of Art. *Aladdin* played Saturdays and Sundays from May 12 through June 1962 and *Beauty and the Beast* from October 5, 1962 through February 9, 1963. The puppets were made by William Jones, and Lettie Connell Schubert assisted in manipulation. She also presented her hand-puppets for the annual Children's Christmas Party in 1963.

In November 1949, an exhibit of puppets called "Small Wonders" at the Cooper Union Museum for the Arts of Decoration, New York, included figures of all types from the museum collection, as well as loans from many puppeteers. The Museum's eighteenth-century marionette stage with Commedia dell'Arte puppets and a group of rare shadow figures from the Théâtre Seraphin (1776–1870) were part of an exhibit, "Theatre Design" in May 1965.

Another exhibit in which puppets took their place as part of the larger theatrical scene was "Harlequin and the Arts," held at the Denver Art Museum in 1957. It traced the history of the Commedia dell'Arte from

Greece and Rome through the Middle Ages to its flowering in Renaissance Italy, and its continuing influence in ballet, theatre, and art. Masks, puppets, prints, and sculpture from ancient to modern times told the story. In 1951 the Denver Museum and the Puppeteers of America collaborated in an extensive exhibition of puppets.

Museums do not have a monopoly on showing puppets to the public, for many organizations have exhibition galleries. The American Craftsman Council in New York City displayed "The Fabulous Punch" in 1951, to show the historical significance of this most famous character of the Western puppet world. Lytton's Art Centre, a small gallery maintained by the Lytton Savings and Loan Association, Los Angeles, assembled a large puppet exhibit in 1964 with Josine Ianco Kline as curator. Alan Cook, Betsy Brown and Roberto Lago were advisors. Some famous puppets were there: Edgar Bergen's Charlie McCarthy and Mortimer Snerd, many Disney characters, and the hand-puppets by Walton and O'Rourke for the film *Lili*. American puppeteers, both past and contemporary, were represented, and there was a good selection from foreign countries. The walls were gay with posters painted by children on the theme "Come See the Puppets." Bob Bromley was on hand to show how to manipulate puppets, and in the small adjoining auditorium, Bob Towers, dressed in Punch costume, told puppet stories with a real Punch on his hand and introduced puppet movies from many lands. The next year, some of this material was shown in Palo Alto under the title "The Greatest Show on Strings—An International Puppet Exhibit."

Many American museums, universities and individuals have important puppet collections. Unique is Pauline Benton's group of shadow-puppets from China and other Oriental countries. For many years she presented authentic Chinese shadow plays with figures from North China and suitable musical instruments. Now she is cataloguing the collection of about 500 figures. Rosalynde Osborne Stearn assembled a variety of puppets, illustrative material, and toy theatres, which she presented to McGill University in Montreal, together with her large library of puppet titles. The Ontario Puppetry Association also has a puppet collection. In 1960, the Brander Matthews Museum at Columbia University marked its fiftieth anniversary. A repository of miscellaneous theatre material, the collection includes a large group of puppets from many countries and periods.

At UCLA, the Museum and Laboratories of Ethnic Arts and Technology was recently organized by the late Ralph Altman. Already it has acquired many puppets, including a rare set of shadows from Taiwan, which are quite different from the well-known Chinese type. On the same campus, Melvyn Helstien is adding to the puppet collections of the Department of Theatre Arts, and there are fine Indonesian puppets in the

Institute of Ethnomusicology. Eventually all these may be housed in a single museum.

Puppet films

Although puppet films in America generally have not reached the high degree of artistic excellence found in those of some European countries, some notable ones have been produced, and a great many are made for television or distribution to schools and organizations.

Occasionally puppets appear in Hollywood films. The motion picture, *Lili,* starring Mel Ferrer as the puppeteer and Leslie Caron as Lili, had puppets made by Walton and O'Rourke. A short puppet sequence in *The Sound of Music,* an incidental bit in the film, was provided by Bil Baird's marionettes.

Closer to puppetry than such films, however, is the animated cartoon, popularized by Walt Disney and others. One of these "others" is George Pal, from Cegléd, Hungary. He had studied architecture in Budapest, but opened a motion-picture studio when the building business slumped. He soon changed from the flat cartoon film to the three-dimensional figures animated by stop-motion, which became famous as the Puppetoons. Soon after he came to Hollywood in 1939, he won his first Academy Award, and has continued production of his imaginative films to the present time. In 1959, fifty Puppetoons were combined with a cast of human actors in *Tom Thumb,* which appeals to adults for its sly humor and to children for its miniature effects. With the coming of Cinerama, puppets and actors took on a new dimension in the Metro-Goldwyn-Mayer production of *The Wonderful World of the Brothers Grimm.* Scenery and live action were filmed in Germany, with the Pal puppet sequences produced in Hollywood by Project Unlimited, Inc. This film was the result of Pal's lifelong interest in Grimms' fairy tales and the story of the brothers who preserved them. The reality of the brothers' struggle and the reality of the characters who people the stories are happily portrayed by combining human and puppet actors.

Late in 1954, a very elaborate film of *Hansel and Gretel,* adapted by Padriac Column from the Humperdinck opera, started its rounds. Its producer, Michael Myerberg, had worked with Walt Disney on *Fantasia,* and concluded that there must be a better way to do this kind of film. For about fifteen years he pondered and experimented with plastics and electronic devices. On meticulously jointed armatures the bodies of the stop-motion puppets were modeled of rubber plastic which looked, felt, and behaved like human tissue. The body movement of the "minikins," as Myerberg called them, was done by hand in the usual stop-motion technique, but for close-ups, an electronic control panel with twelve dials was used to produce thousands of changes of expression. Never before had this kind of puppet reached such realism, which was carried through costumes, settings, and lighting. Some critics (and a good many puppeteers) wondered why people could not have been used just as well. Nevertheless, it has had wide circulation and has reputedly earned more than a million dollars.

For the past twenty years the name of Lou Bunin has been associated with the production of stop-motion films. Back in 1945 he began to mull over the possibility of doing *Alice in Wonderland* with puppets and a live actress for Alice. Two years later he and twenty assistants (with their families) moved to France, where the puppet scenes were made. Authentic rooms at Oxford were reproduced for those scenes in which Lewis Carroll appeared. The sound track of music and voices was done in London with English actors, and J. Arthur Rank built a laboratory to process the finished film, which was released in 1951. Costly, elaborate, realistically true to the Tenniel illustrations, *Alice* was received with mixed reactions. Nevertheless it sometimes attained the fanciful heights dreamed of by the author, and marked an important historical moment in puppet films. As head of Punch Films, Inc., Bunin has produced a long list of puppet movies for children. *Homer the Horse Who Couldn't Talk* won first prize at the 1958 Brussels World's Fair, and *The Dingo and the Kangaroo* was a prize winner in the Karlovy Vary International Film Festival, 1962. A series of comical films, *Schultz and Dooley*, won first and second prizes at the Venice Film Festival in 1963. Bunin has always been interested in "mixed media" films, and has long been looking for the ideal script which would reveal fully the wonders of stop-motion. At this writing he believes the search has ended with Ben Lucien Burman's *High Water at Catfish Bend*.

Ordinary hand, rod, string, or shadow-puppets in their settings are used in most American puppet films, instead of the difficult stop-motion figures. Martin Stevens, Rufus Rose and Alfred Wallace are noted for their film work. In 1950 Stevens' *The Toymaker* was made in collaboration with Rose in the part of the creator of two characters, Spots and Stripes, who thought they were different from each other until the Toymaker showed them to be two parts of himself. This was symbolized by showing them as hand-puppets, one on each hand, with the dim figure of their creator in the background. Thus the idea of brotherhood was conveyed. In 1963, Stevens and Wallace made a new film of the story with the former as Toymaker. It has been on the recommended list of films issued by the United Nations and the World Council of Christian Education. Stevens also performs the story live. 1950 was also the year Rose produced *The Ant and the Grass-*

hopper. In 1953 Stevens-Wallace Puppet Films was formed. They made two films for the United States Information Agency, based on the Turkish *Hoja* stories. During the next two years a series of safety education films was produced for the J. C. Penney Company. Two of these, *Stop and Go, the Safety Twins* and *Stop and Go on a Bike* still reach a yearly audience of 40,000,000, through 600 to 800 showings in schools and on television. Well-known puppeteers who assisted in these include George Latshaw, Ed Johnson, Don Sahlin, Shirley O'Donnol and Olga Stevens, with Ernie Dufour as head of the "shooting" crew. Spots and Stripes from *The Toymaker* were featured in *The Santa Claus Suit* and *The King and the Lion,* filmed in 1955.

Wallace and Wango Weng later made *The Magic Pear Tree* with Chinese shadow-puppets, as part of a folk tale series for NBC-TV. Rufus Rose made one-hour color films of *Treasure Island, Rip Van Winkle* and *Aladdin* in 1964, which have had some television showings. There were other puppeteers who did outstanding films. Bil and Cora Baird began making educational puppet films in 1943. The American Telephone and Telegraph Company commissioned several, and 9,000 prints of *Adventure in Telezonia* have been made. The Ford Foundation sponsored a film for use in teaching a new Lebanese alphabet in which 600 characters were reduced to 30. Nine half-hour films comprise *Adventures in Numbers and Space,* which emphasize the fun and fascination of mathematics. In the first film of the series, typical Baird characters, Snarky and Gargle, demonstrate the counting systems of ancient civilizations.

Herman London, of Peekskill, New York, has a special interest in puppet films, and he has made a bibliography, selections from which have been published in the *Puppetry Journal.* He lists a number of how-to-do-it films: *Dolls, Puppets and Diversion* shows Girl Scouts making puppets from simple materials; *The Puppeteers,* from the studio of Canadian puppeteer Micheline Legendre, illustrates the creation of a puppet and a performance; two films, *The ABC of Puppets,* give details of making a puppet and a stage. These are typical of many others which are available.

Another group of films gives glimpses of puppet shows in various countries: England's *Punch and Judy,* a Javanese *Wayang Kulit* (shadow play), a visit to a Polish puppet theatre, and a summary of the shadow theatre by Jero Magon, called *Shadowland.*

A few titles will suggest the stories which may be seen in films. Tom Tichenor's dog story, *The Tale of Truthful George,* has been mentioned; Marshall Wynnychuk recently produced a space fantasy called *Moonicorn;* Mabel and Les Beaton made a number of films, including *The Mayflower Mouse* and *The Spirit of Christmas;* from Canada we have *Kumak, the Sleepy Hunter,* an Eskimo story filmed by Alma Duncan and Audrey McLaren; *Red Riding Hood* by the Leselli Marionettes, and *Sinbad the*

Sailor by Ray and Betty Mount. *Adventures in Christmas Tree Grove* was a series in fourteen episodes made for the Kasper-Gordon Company of Boston by Gordon Bennett. Another type of film, using still puppets, was produced by Viewmaster Stereo, from 1953 to 1959. About ten plays, including *Peter Pan, Twenty Thousand Leagues Under the Sea, The Littlest Angel* and *Bambi* were done in this technique.

A number of foreign films are available. Trnka's *A Midsummer Night's Dream* has been widely shown in America. Other Czech films are *The Emperor's Nightingale* and *The Song of the Prairie.* The Salzburg Marionettes' *Snow White and Rose Red* reflects the complicated techniques of this famous theatre. Lotte Reiniger's shadow films are allied to the early history of animation, and still delight American audiences.

Although puppet films offer many opportunities for experimentation, not much has been done in America. Basil Milovsoroff points out that most puppeteers do not realize that the camera is a creative medium, and most cameramen know little about puppets. In the mid-fifties he made two films which suggested some possibilities. One was *Muzzleshy,* a gun safety film for the New Hampshire Fish and Game Department, in which stylized crows were the actors, and the other, *Poison in the House,* for the medical profession, in which ants vividly showed the dangers of bleaches and other household supplies. Although he is not at present working with puppets, having become a professor of Russian at Dartmouth College, he hopes sometime to pursue his theories.

In such lively centers of experimental film making as the Motion Picture Division of the Department of Theatre Arts at UCLA, perhaps some new ways of using puppets in films will evolve.

Puppets on television

Since the early thirties when puppets first appeared on television, they have pervaded the medium. There is hardly a puppeteer who has not shown his puppets on television or made special ones for it, hence to record all this activity would require an entire book. We can only suggest the kind of programs which puppets present in regular series, in special performances, as guests on network and local shows, for advertising, and for education.

The name of Burr Tillstrom comes to mind whenever anyone mentions puppets on television, for he has been a part of the medium since his first appearances on the *Junior Jamboree* from WBKB, Chicago, in 1947. His contribution to television is discussed in Chapter V.

The children's program, *Howdy Doody,* began in 1947 and lasted for thirteen years. The National Broadcasting Company asked Martin Stone to put on a children's show, and he asked Bob Smith to be master of ceremonies. One of the characters in *Smith's Triple Ranch Show* always said, "Howdy Doody," in greeting people, and this name was given to the program's principal puppet character, which was made by Frank Paris. Paris and NBC could not come to terms over ownership of the show, so he left and filed suit for use of the puppet without permission. After considerable litigation he received damages. Meanwhile, a new Howdy Doody was built and the show continued. From 1952 to 1960, Rufus Rose and Company handled the construction of the marionettes, their direction and manipulation. The mute clown, Clarabell, played by a human actor, who sounded a sweet horn to signify "yes" and a sour one for "no," became an integral part of the show. It was shown daily to an estimated audience of fifteen million, and at the time of its demise in 1960, there had been 2,300 performances—more than any show in the history of network television. Despite the fact that the show reputedly earned around $40,000,000 a year through the sale of Howdy Doody merchandise, it was dropped.

A notable show produced in color was *The Blue Fairy,* based on *Pinocchio,* which ran for 26 weeks from WGN, Chicago. It won the Peabody Award for the best children's television series of 1958. Rufus Rose made the puppets, Martin Stevens wrote the scripts, Urbach and Kane were producer and director respectively.

Bil and Cora Baird have contributed programs such as *Life with Snarky Parker* (1950), in which exciting happenings in the Western town of Hot Rock were shown five days per week. For it, they designed the Scriptanola: the day's script, written on a special typewriter with three-eighths-inch letters, was attached to wide moving rollers set below the stage floor out of camera range, and moved mechanically as the play progressed. *The Whistling Wizard* played during the 1951–1952 season, and *The Bil Baird Show* was presented twice weekly for thirteen weeks in 1953. Bil and Cora appeared in person as disc jockey masters of ceremonies, assisted by Groovy, a screwball rabbit. Three recorded numbers, acted out by puppets of all sorts, comprised each show.

Another series, which had a ten-year run, was produced by Bernard and Edith Paul for Hutzler's Department Store in Baltimore, and aired over WBAL. From January 1948 to March 1958 they presented fairy tales for children every Tuesday and Thursday. On *The Little Bookshop,* a Junior Classic Program, they did *Robinson Crusoe* and *Hans Brinker* in serial form, from December 1954 to April 1955.

Ralph Chessé produced his first marionette television series, *Willie and the Baron,* in 1951 for KGO, San Francisco. In this spoof on interview programs, Willie talked with storybook characters. The next year Chessé created *Brother Buzz* for the Latham Foundation for the promotion of humane education. The story was of an elf turned into a bumble bee who traveled in the animal world as ambassador of kindness to all living things. He learned from the animals he met about how they were treated by human beings, who were given some needed lessons in the proper treatment of animals. This program has continued in various forms to the present, and is now used as an introduction to documentary films produced by ABC for national distribution. Thirteen episodes are filmed annually.

Another program, *Woody Willow*, was presented from 1948 to 1958 on WBS-TV in Atlanta. It was originated by Don and Ruth Gilpin, who developed many ideas including a sequence called *Planet People,* sparked by the flying saucer phenomenon. Fred and Fae Taylor had a children's program in Denver called *The Clubhouse Gang,* for which James Gamble provided puppets. His Wally the Weathergator gave forecasts every day, and became so popular that a Draw Wally Contest drew 50,000 entries, and a number of commercial products were named after him. Some shows are seasonal, such as *The Adventures of Uncle Mistletoe,* a Christmas series in twenty-six episodes by Arthur Lewis Zapel. Leo and Dora Velleman have done several series of puppet shows, such as twenty-six episodes of *Planet Tolex,* which ran during the 1953–1954 season on the Canadian Broadcasting Company's Toronto station. In 1958 they began *Fignewton Frog and Dora,* which went on for a year, and was again aired between 1961 and 1963 over twenty-three stations in Canada. They also produced *A Basket and a Bus* for CBS, and programs for educational television while they were in St. Louis.

Wolo was active in West Coast television during the fifties, first with Peter Abenheim and his program for Red Goose Shoes. Then, having won a CBS Best Puppeteer Contest, he spent two years with KNX in Hollywood. KPIX, San Francisco, aired a series, *World of Wolo,* for which he wrote plays, adapted fairy tales, designed puppets and taught people how to make them. In another series, his puppet, Aloysius, had incredible adventures on the moon, such as finding sad cows in a crater—all those who had tried to jump over the moon and didn't make it. A new show each day meant constant work, and the search for ideas led to such things as catching live fish from a real tank of water, sailboat regattas (with nutshell boats), a farm with real earth from which real potatoes were harvested and real grapes picked from vines.

Most television puppet series have one character around whom the action is built. Thus Kukla, Snarky Parker and Howdy Doody were indispensable to the continuity of their shows, even though other characters were associated with them. Another such puppet is Foodini the Wicked Magician, who has appeared on many shows produced by Hope and

Morey Bunin. An early program was the *Lucky Pup* series, in which a small dog was pitted against Foodini, who was always trying to get his money. In other stories Foodini was a newspaper editor, a cook, or a gardener whose crop turns out to be all ragweed—plants with actual pieces of gay fabrics growing on them.

Mary Chase Drozdoff used Fearless Fosdick from the *Li'l Abner* comic strip as leading character in a twenty-six episode detective series for NBC. Another story, which appeared in 1953, was *Johnny Jupiter,* a witty fantasy with a satirical point of view. A janitor, played by actor Vaughn Taylor, wanted to become a video engineer. Although ignorant of all the mechanics, he tinkered with the dials and switches in the contact room and brought in Johnny and his companions from the planet Jupiter. Through the eyes of these visitors, many comments on conditions and customs on planet Earth were made.

Fantastic puppets of another sort appeared about 1961 from Chicago, when Jim and Bud Stewart used many kinds of gloves decorated and painted to suggest characters in a children's series, which had enough satire to interest adults. Many stories involve animals. Paul and Mary Ritts had a program, *In the Park,* in which actor Bill Sears was the central character who had many adventures with Calvin the Crow, Albert the Chipmunk and other delightful birds and beasts.

In the summer of 1962, an unusual television series called *Tottle* was aired by CBS from WCAU-TV, Philadelphia. All the characters were fictitious "woodland creatures" designed and made by Marshall Izen. The Tottle family—mother, father, son Coslo and daughter Taffy—live in a completely equipped underground house which looks like an illustration from a story book, while the Oni Family has a tree house. There are numerous other characters, all of whom behave more like human beings than animals. In fact, the program was designed to present and solve problems which confront children through the actions of these charming creatures. The stories were developed under the guidance of psychologist Zanvel A. Liff, who did research for each one. The material was made into plots by his wife Sylvia, and then dramatized by Izen, James Damico or Nancy Lawrence, with a final check by Dr. Liff for accuracy. Because the settings and puppets were so appealing, children were enthralled and identified with the situations presented, thus learning about sportsmanship, generosity, fear of the dark, jealousy, as well as about death, world crises, and discrimination. *Tottle* was subsequently shown in other cities, and now plans are being made for a series of films which could be widely distributed.

As guest performers on regular television shows, both local and network, puppets help to satisfy the insatiable demand for talent. For instance, Tony Urbano and his puppets have been on the *Red Skelton Show* and the *Dean Martin Show*, while Elizabeth Merten often had her puppets on *Junior Magazine*, a Canadian program popular in 1956. Early in his career, Jerry Hartnett appeared ten times on Paul Whiteman's *T. V. Teen Club*, and his children's show has been featured on *Captain Kangaroo*. After Hartnett won the All Navy Talent Contest of 1954, he was invited to appear on *The Ed Sullivan Show*. During the many years this weekly program has been on the air, dozens of puppeteers—American and foreign —have been seen by a nation-wide audience.

Jim and Jane Henson began their puppet work in Washington, D.C., where they appeared for several years on local television. Moving to New York, they formed The Muppets, a company which has performed offbeat entertainment spots on such network variety programs as the *Ed Sullivan Show*, the *Perry Como Show*, the *Arthur Godfrey Show*, the *Steve Allen Show, Hollywood Palace*, the *Tonight Show* and the *Jack Paar Show*. The Muppets were on the *Today Show* for several seasons. Special characters were often created, the most famous being the hound dog Rowlf, who appeared first on the *Jimmy Dean Show*, and was a regular on it for three seasons. Like no other puppets on the American scene, the Muppets are imaginative creations which suggest but do not imitate human or animal forms, and are eminently suited to comic and satirical commentary. They are also renowned for their many lively commercial television spots. Henson Associates, Inc., is a newly-formed company which is producing such feature films, both with and without puppets.

Puppeteers with good variety programs are likely to have many guest appearances. Frank Paris has been on more than a dozen leading shows, and so has Bil Baird. The latter has appeared fourteen times with Ed Sullivan, thirty-four times with Jack Paar, eight times with Sid Caesar and the *Today Show*, to mention only a few. Baird's puppets participated in a memorable program on *The Telephone Hour* in 1959, when Maurice Evans read Ogden Nash's verses for Saint-Saëns' *Carnival of the Animals*. He portrayed a ringmaster who introduced a variety of animals which came out of their cages and performed.

Many puppeteers have joined forces with other entertainers on regular shows. *The Looking Glass Lady*, with folk singer Bash Kennett and Lettie Connell Schubert's hand-puppets, was on KRON-TV, San Francisco, in 1954. In 1957 and 1958, her puppets Twinkle and George were part of *This Morning Show*. For two years (1958–1960), Rufus Rose participated in the *Jimmy Blaine Show* on NBC with his puppets José the Toucan, and Rhubarb the Parrot.

Larry Smith was a teen-ager when he made his television debut with puppets on WHIO-TV in Dayton. Since then most of his puppetry work has been in this medium. After three and a half years in Dayton, he joined the *Al and Wanda Lewis Show* on WCPO-TV in Cincinnati, which also had a year's run on the ABC network. After appearing with Burr Tillstrom on Broadway in the fall of 1961, he returned to Cincinnati as host for WKRC-TV's *Rudy and Teaser Show* and *Hattie the Witch and Friends*. During a one-hour show for WCPO he introduced *The Contemporaries*, in which the puppets poked fun at the current scene. He took part in WLW's regional network series, *Jamboree*, beginning September 1964. At present he is producing for educational television.

The work of Doug and Gayle Anderson of New York might be termed "variations on a theme." Basically using variety, they incorporate magic, illusion, ventriloquism, and cartooning with their puppets, making their program adaptable to almost any occasion. Much of their work is for television. They designed and built special puppets for many commercials: a pair of can-can-girl "onions" for Campbell's Onion Soup; a singing and talking milk bottle for the Glass Bottle Blower's Association; the Royal Lion for Royal Puddings and Desserts, and so on. They appeared weekly for a year on the Sealtest *Big Top Show*, with Doug as the Masked Magician. For about five years they worked on the NBC network program for Bonomo's Turkish Taffy. He was the Magic Clown and she was Glamour Gayle, his assistant and puppeteer. Doug was a regular cast member during the first year of the *Captain Kangaroo Show*, and as the Magic Barn Painter used marionettes, cartooning, magic and his ventriloquial dummy, Scoopy. He was also a clown, Mr. Hocus Pocus, and an illusionist, the Masked Merlin, on the NBC *Marx-Magic Midway Show*. The Andersons have also been guests on many programs. For syndicated television they wrote the script and produced a fifty-two segment series, *The Magic Knight*. Doug was the star and writer, and Gayle the puppeteer for a filmed children's series, *Mr. Krackerjacket* (later called *The Magic Corner*) for David Robbins Productions. They also made the puppets and sets for a film based on the Turkish *Hoja* stories, which this same company prepared for the State Department.

The Andersons also tour in the area and play for children in theatres, schools, at fairs and parks, always incorporating their various forms of entertainment. They both work in other fields of art: Gayle is a technical illustrator and advertising artist and now teaches at Bethpage High School on Long Island, and Doug is a cartoonist and illustrator.

About 1954, the *Kartoon Club* appeared on New York's WPIX starring Shari Lewis, who combined music, ventriloquism, and storytelling to entertain and teach children. Later she was part of the NBC *Hi Mom* show which offered advice on the care of young children. Her hand-puppets Hush Puppy, Lamb Chop and Charley Horse became favorites of her child audience, and she varied the program with juggling, singing, and magic. Her own show, *Shariland,* which won four Emmy awards, was presented for several years by NBC, and was also seen by audiences in Germany, Hong Kong, and Australia. She has also written fourteen books for children (see Bibliography). In 1964 her children's show went off the air because she felt it was time to move into new fields, which would give her more scope as a dramatic actress and an entertainer. In her new role she is frequently seen in night clubs as well as on television with a song-dance-comedy act for adults.

Every so often a special puppet program is shown on television. On Christmas Eve, 1948, Dickens' *A Christmas Carol* was presented over ABC with the Rufus Rose Marionettes—the first major marionette television show in the U.S. On one adventure program in 1953, CBS and the American Museum of Natural History collaborated in presenting a talk by Margaret Mead on shadow plays and ceremonial dances in Bali.

The NBC Children's Theatre was established to give children a variety of theatrical productions. On November 3, 1963, *Quillow and the Giant,* a musical adaptation of James Thurber's fable, was presented as the first of four one-hour color specials. Quillow is a toymaker who is considered a dreamer and a fool until he saves his village from the ravages of Hunder the Giant. Win Stracke played the Giant, and the other characters were puppets made by George Latshaw. Seven songs were written by Ralph Blane and Wade Barnes, and music was supplied by the NBC Orchestra in Chicago. The production won the Ohio State University Award and the Monte Meacham Award from the Children's Theatre Conference. Latest in the NBC puppet productions was Burr Tillstrom's production of *The Reluctant Dragon,* with Fran Allison and the Kuklapolitans, March 21, 1968. Ollie with a wig to make him more menacing was the Dragon, Fletcher Rabbit was St. George, Kukla was the Little Boy and Fran was Kukla's Mother.

Gilbert and Sullivan's *H. M. S. Pinafore* was presented complete with an all-puppet cast as a television "spectacular" on April 8, 1956, by WABD, New York. Puppet construction and costuming were designed by Paul Ashley, who also provided dialogue, assisted by Claude McCann, Michael King and George Nelle.

One of Bil Baird's television specials was *Art Carney Meets Peter and the Wolf* (1959). Although the Prokofieff themes were utilized, a number of features were added—a dog named Humphrey, a crafty weasel, and lyrics by Ogden Nash ("Pardon the Warp in my Woof," sung by the Wolf). A later special was *Art Carney Meets the Sorcerer's Apprentice.* Human actors sometimes have difficulty holding their own with puppets, but in both productions, Art Carney proved his ability. *Winnie the Pooh,*

O'Halloran's Luck and *Louisville Courier Journal* were also Baird specials, and his puppets participated in *Heidi* and *Babes in Toyland*. The latter was aired December 19, 1954, with a bevy of television stars and numerous puppets and animated toys.

Regular television is a commercial enterprise, and every program is influenced to a greater or lesser extent by the sponsor. The spot commercial, usually lasting one minute or less, is interspersed in most programs, and here, too, puppets have made their mark. Considerable ingenuity and imagination go into the preparation of these brief sales talks. Kukla, for instance, is a past master, and manages to invest them with credibility. Jerry Hartnett once constructed and operated six life-size marionettes in a minstrel show advertising Molson's Beer; Rufus Rose provided commercials on *Captain Kangaroo* for two years; Bruce and Nola Bucknell created a character, Bill Boulder, who provided sales pitches for Wilson and Company for more than four years. The Gordon Sisters have made films for television in the Chicago area; Peg Blickle and Vivian Michael used their puppets as Santa's helpers for the Lazarus Department Store television advertising program; Tom Tichenor has promoted Sunshine Cookies and Good Humor Ice Cream; Larry Smith and Larry Berthelson have prepared many a commercial along with their other puppet work.

Mary Chase Drozdoff specialized in puppets for film and television. In her New York studio she made, among many others, a marionette of Elsie, the Borden Cow. Two of her hand-puppets helped with the promotion of Johnny Mop, a "foaming action" cleanser, and dog Reddy did plugs for Red Heart Dog Food. Sealtest Ice Cream offered a hand-puppet premium, Bat Masterson, Jr., and the product was advertised by a large rod-puppet of the same character. In a 1968 film for television, her Sheriff Howdy and his two-headed horse, Clyde, were used in commercials for the 7-Up Company. Now residing in St. Louis with her two sons, ages fourteen and twelve, she plans to produce shows for family entertainment with their assistance, for they mean to make a career of the puppet business.

Over the years Bil and Cora Baird have produced or appeared in more than 300 commercials. Some of their sponsors have commissioned numerous spots: Utica Beer, 85; the Borden Company, 36; General Mills, 25.

Sylvia Meredith, who was for many years associated with the Sue Hastings Marionettes, began doing television commercials about 1955. Using the Three Bears theme, she had a show for Maxwell House Coffee; an elephant appeared for the Jumbo half-gallon ice cream pack on the Sealtest Circus show; a Scotty dog spoke for Thom McAn Shoes, and her puppets also worked for Bird's-Eye Frozen Foods, General Electric, Beauty Rest Mattresses, Maillard's Chocolates, Progresso Foods and Oldsmobile. She has appeared in person with her puppets on the *Today Show,* the *Home Show,* and the *Night Owl.* Captain Glenn's *Bandwagon* featured her puppet, Buttercup, and her *Snow White* was presented for a week in serial form on *Captain Kangaroo.* Another series, *The Adventures of Blinky,* had thirty-six episodes in which her Harpy the Witch was featured along with a large cast of characters made by Paul Ashley and others.

In recent years there has been growing dissatisfaction with commercial television, and the number of subsidized programs is increasing. Colleges and universities have their own stations, closed circuit telecasts are given for schools and other institutions, community antenna television serves some areas, and there are many educational television stations.

Here we can mention only a few examples of the ways in which puppets fit into the noncommercial television pattern. Ten years ago Peg Blickle and Vivian Michael presented *The Play's the Thing* over WOSU, Ohio State University's station. In this weekly series, puppets enacted scenes from plays for a panel of experts to guess the title. They also had a semiweekly show for children. In Tacoma, puppets were a regular part of closed circuit programs for preschool classrooms, and Los Angeles' noncommercial station offered four programs by Betsy Brown, which included some puppet history as well as performances. Cincinnati's Community Television Station, WCET, currently presents *The Magic Forest,* a daily 90-minute show for children, in which Larry Smith's puppets have a fifteen-minute spot.

There are 130 stations in the United States which are affiliated with National Educational Television, which sends out only a few puppet programs. Included in a series, *The Creative Person,* is *The Puppets of Kinosuke* which shows this famous Japanese artist at work on his puppets. *The Friendly Giant,* played by a human actor, has animal puppets for his associates, and in *Misteroger's Neighborhood,* Fred Rogers uses puppets to develop stories to help children with such problems as overcoming fear of the dark. The National Educational Television Film Service produced *The Puppeteers,* which tells the story of puppet showmen in early America.

The National Center for School and College Television uses puppets in some of its courses. *Meet the Arts* is a fifteen-lesson series conducted by Sonya Hamlin, which explores the basic elements of all the arts, and the characteristic styles of some periods of Western civilization. For the lesson on Content, Ruth Brand's puppets perform *The Fox and the Crow* and *The Fisherman and His Wife.* Another series of eleven lessons is *All About You,* a course in science and health. With a dancing marionette clown, the nature of muscles is demonstrated. A new thirty-lesson series, *Stepping into Melody* is now in preparation, and puppets will be used in a number of them.

Many more puppets appear on local educational television stations. In 1958, puppeteer Don Gilpin became production manager of WETV, Atlanta, which is owned by the Board of Education. He used puppets in a number of programs and, with his wife Ruth, adapted *The Sorcerer's Apprentice*. Leo and Dora Velleman were Children's Directors of WKNO-TV in Memphis, and they produced several puppet series, one based on the *Raggedy-Ann* stories (1957). They moved to St. Louis, where, at station KRTC-TV, they made fifty-two kinescopes for *A Number of Things* and twenty-six for *Fignewton's Newspaper*, featuring Fignewton Frog. Tom Tichenor also worked in Memphis, where he was Children's Director for three and a half years. *Tales of Poindexter*, a fifty-two-episode film series, was made for National Educational Television, and ten films for *The Adventures of Sir Upton the Earnest*. Vernone Tracey gave shows and demonstrations with children as puppeteers over Detroit's ETV station in 1958 and 1959. At Pennsylvania State University, a series, *Key to the Cupboard*, was taped in 1962. Dr. Mattil, head of the Art Education Department, was host, and Dr. Alice Schwartz demonstrated the use of materials, with children to carry out a variety of projects. Puppetry was included, and George Latshaw helped with it. Another series in which puppets were related to art was *Form and Imagination*, an in-service art course for elementary teachers produced in 1966 by WQED, Pittsburgh, under the direction of Mary Sceiford. There were six half-hour lessons in puppetry. Margo Lovelace presented historical puppets on the introductory program, and there were demonstrations of puppet making, and several performances by children. Throughout the series, puppetry as a creative dramatic art was stressed.

Let's Make Puppets was a 1965 ETV series in which a number of New York puppeteers, including Milton Halpert, Jim Henson, Frank Paris, and Grace George Alexander, participated. Also in 1965, Florence Backus, of Arlington, Virginia, did four programs of favorite children's stories which were shown in the schools. Jim Menke won an Ohio State University award with his *Mr. Whatnot* series, designed for children in kindergarten through the third grade. Nancy Staub in New Orleans is currently working on an ETV series, assisted by her co-worker, June Steinbaugh. Meredith Bixby has two programs, *The Educated Puppets* and *Puppets and Puppeteers*, showing on the NET network. They were produced at the television station of the University of Michigan. Two plays from the Herrick repertoire have been filmed for educational television use.

In Canada, Marshall Wynnychuk and his puppet caterpillar Clarence teach math on television. In 1966, ten programs were shown, and in 1967, fourteen more. They will all be filmed for further distribution. Along with many other puppet activities at the University of Washington in Seattle, many programs have been designed for ETV station KCTS. In 1964 *Puppet Playhouse* featured performances of fairy tales. *Puppet Playhouse Workshop* was begun the same year, continued the next and repeated in the spring of 1968. University students and children take part in these. Aurora Valentinetti, director of puppetry at the University, has also given puppet episodes in such programs as *Looking into Art* with Jerry Conrad, which is shown to fourth-grade classes for a period of five years. She says that if time allowed, much more could be done for ETV. And that is undoubtedly true all over the country, wherever there are active puppeteers.

IV

International Activities and Cultural Exchange

A good many American puppeteers have traveled and performed abroad, and numerous foreign puppeteers have visited this country, thus providing for an unofficial exchange of ideas and techniques. It is only in recent years, however, that the idea of government-sponsored cultural exchange has developed and that the United States government has been concerned with the arts as a means of communication and understanding among people of all nationalities. Although the place of puppets in official exchanges has so far been small, there are indications that such activities may increase in the future.

American puppeteers abroad

Puppeteers who travel usually take along a few puppets, even though they may not be on a performing tour. They ferret out puppet shows, make friends with puppeteers, and may do impromptu shows. Thus contacts are established, and may be the basis for later official exchange programs.

When Burr Tillstrom went to Europe in 1951, Kukla and Ollie went along and performed in Monsieur Hammon's theatre aboard the *Liberté*. They entertained school children in Normandy, and did a show for Americans and Italians in Florence. They went again in 1953. Ascanio Spolidoro was a guest on the WOR radio program *Wonderful City* and won a trip to Italy to visit puppet theatres. During their European tour in 1953, Ellen and Romain Proctor saw hundreds of puppets, made friends with dozens of puppet showmen whose performances they saw, and also managed to see all the tourist sights. Ralph Chessé's European visit in 1959 included Munich and the Puppet Museum there. An exchange of photographs followed. Roberto Lago led a group of teachers to Europe in 1961, and he undoubtedly included puppets in the itinerary. Jim and Bud Stewart were in Africa in 1963, where there seems to have been an interesting encounter between a live and a puppet giraffe. Olga Stevens visited Paris the same year and saw Desarthis' show in the Luxembourg Gardens; in 1965 she went to New Zealand and met puppeteers there. Mollie, Jan and Bob Falkenstein were in Europe in 1963, touring in a Volkswagen to Great Britain, France, Switzerland, Austria and Germany, seeing many shows. Tommy Termite, one of Ruth and Don Gilpin's puppets, went along with them to Ireland and England where he had his picture taken at 10 Downing Street. In 1967 when Ruth Gilpin joined an International Study Tour of Oriental Women in Radio and Television to observe the production methods of puppeteers in Japan, Taipei, Thailand, and Hong Kong, Tommy went too.

Americans stationed in foreign lands may turn to puppets. Dusty Stoughton and her husband were on the island of Yap in the Carolines in 1954. Their current hobbies were beginning to pall when the idea of making puppets occurred. They had never seen a puppet show, but were undeterred. Beginning with a hot pad mitt, they created a number of characters, some of whom got a little out of hand and developed personalities quite different from the original intention. Virginia Hartwell worked in Ecuador with the World Radio Missionary Fellowship and began presenting puppet shows over the Fellowship's television station eight years ago. Performances of secular plays in Spanish were given for children in her studio, and for two years a Bible emphasis program, *The Box of Surprises*, was presented weekly, with the help of missionary children. John Stuck, a fellow missionary, went into the jungle where the Jivaro Indians dwell, made puppets representing characters of this remote tribe, and presented simple stories with them. Elaine Miller accompanied her husband to Bombay, where he had a Fulbright grant. There, she assisted Mrs. Meher Contractor in a puppet workshop and learned a good deal about working with people of a different culture.

Beverly Flanders had been giving puppet shows for children's birthday parties in Atlanta, before she went to Tripoli in Libya, as a draftsman for a construction company. During her stay of nineteen months (1952–1954), she gave puppet shows for local Arab schools. A memorable performance was the one at the Prime Minister's house at the end of Ramadan. All the relatives and many friends were there. It was a special treat for the women, who seldom went to the local movie house, the only source of public entertainment. Her program of variety numbers, as always, overcame language barriers. At home she is also known as a magician, one of relatively few women in this profession, and she finds magic and puppetry a happy combination.

Bud Gambee was a Fulbright Lecturer in Library Science at the American College for Girls in Cairo for the 1952–1953 academic year. With his wife Ruth, he had built a production of *Red Riding Hood,* complete with taped voices and music, which he took along. In foreign countries mechanical details, such as differences in electric cycles, may completely disrupt a tape. This happened shortly before the Gambees' first performance in Cairo, but they retaped, and the show went on. Later they made an Arabic version, and played thirteen shows to more than 2,000 children in Assiut. Another time they participated in a Christmas program given by the Cairo Women's Club, with a diversified membership of Egyptian women—Moslem, Christian and Jewish—as well as those from America, Europe and the Near East. The tape recorder refused to work; this time, the voltage was wrong. Frantic efforts to adjust it were completed just in time, and the show was a success. The puppets were followed by the Vicar of the Cathedral leading his choristers singing Christmas carols, each one carrying a lighted candle set in a Coca-Cola bottle.

We do not have records of all the people who have worked their puppets in the Armed Services, but a few examples will suggest what they do. George Creegan's interest in puppets began when he was stationed in West Germany with the Radio and Television Service of the Air Force. Asked to do a show for children of the military personnel, he decided to use puppets, as he had just met a group of Italian craftsmen and learned puppet making from them. The resulting show was successful, and he eventually toured with it through France, Germany and Austria.

James Gamble is an airline pilot who is also a puppeteer of many years' experience. (His work at Santa's Workshop in Colorado has been noted.) In 1958, a Methodist Youth Caravan was organized to work in Bolivia. Gamble was one of eight college students who contributes his special talents to the Caravan. He gave performances, directed puppet-making, and taught secondary school teachers in the Instituto Americano, which supports the only co-educational high schools in the country. Most of his work was in Cochabamba and La Paz, but sometimes the group went into the jungles and performed for Indians who were a little superstitious about the puppets. This three-month experience also included work in Panama, Peru, and Ecuador. He entered the Air Force Jet Pilot Training Program in 1961, graduated a year later, and was sent to Sculthorpe, England. In his free time, he continued his puppet work, and found his night club variety with large trick marionettes very popular. He also made the acquaintance of a number of English puppeteers. In 1964 he was transferred to Ankara, Turkey. His work kept him busy most of the time, but he was able to perform for the embassies, the military personnel, and the Turkish-American Association. He knew French and learned Turkish, and gave performances in both languages. With his wife Marty, he sought out Kuchuk Ali, one of the last masters of the Turkish shadow play, Karagoz, and saw him perform during Ramadan. Another transfer came in June 1965, when the Gambles went to West Germany. During their fifteen months there, he performed for military clubs and villages near Frankfurt. He met Frau Zink who had given shows with her husband for forty years; afraid that her marionettes would be destroyed after her death, she gave twenty-five of them to the American puppeteer, with books, posters, and other treasures of her puppet theatre.

Jim Menke was inducted into the Army in February 1958, and when he was assigned to Munich, his puppets were also sent. Before long he entered the 1959 All Army Entertainment Contest. The puppets had stiff competition from dancers, magicians, comics, etc., but Menke's act placed. In Washington, further competitions were held among numbers from all over the world, and Menke won second place. Twenty-five people, including Menke, were then selected to tour the world in a musical revue called *Rolling Along of 1959*. With three-and-a-half tons of equipment, all designed to fit through the cargo doors of a regular airplane, they went from Washington to Canada to Alaska. On the way to Okinawa, they were caught in the tail end of a typhoon, and had some bad moments before reaching the island. Some of the performances there were cancelled because the roofs of a couple of the theatres had been blown off. Next came Korea, where the going was rugged; to reach one camp the performers jounced over rough country roads in trucks, but were rewarded by playing to an audience of fifty Korean children who had been adopted by the unit. In Tokyo, special performances honoring the ninetieth birthday of one of the manipulators (probably Bunjoro) were being given by the two leading Bunraku companies, and the Americans saw this famous puppet theatre. On the way back to Hawaii, the troupe stopped at Pacific Island posts, and reached Waikiki Beach for Christmas. Afterwards came a tour of posts in Germany, Italy, and France. For one show, officials and many people from East Berlin were invited; they came and packed the house. In all there were over 200 performances in seven countries, as well as most of the fifty states, in the course of this tour.

American puppeteers have gone to foreign countries under various auspices. One of these is the USO. Among USO entertainers was Marge Kelly, who spent two weeks in Greenland in 1959, and the Wallace sisters, Lea and Gia, who worked several summers with USO camp shows. In 1952, they traveled for four and a half months to Hawaii, Wake Island, Japan, and Korea. During their two-month stay in Korea, they had an interesting exchange of dance ideas with Kim Beck Cho. When she and her group performed, the Wallaces were astonished to see dancing which was basically the Martha Graham technique, except for the hand movements, which were Oriental. It turned out that this Korean dancer had never heard of Martha Graham, but had studied with someone who had once traveled in America. The next year, the Wallaces performed in the Bahamas, and in 1954 went to Alaska and Greenland, where they were interested in the reactions of the Eskimos, who didn't quite know what to make of the puppets. They visited Mexico and the West Coast in 1955. For these USO shows, the program was a combination of puppets and numbers with the sisters in costume, dancing with puppets in *Circus Suite, Javanese Suite* and others.

Many puppeteers have given performances and workshops abroad as part of their regular work. Marjorie Shanafelt has taken her shows to Denmark. Herb Scheffel and his finger puppet, Miss Bubbles Divine, went to Europe as tourists but ended up performing on the *Queen Mary* going over, and in many European capitals. Children on the British European Airways flight from Rome to Nice were entertained by Bubbles. Spence and Alan Gilmore, who toured the United States and played at puppet festivals during the fifties, took their puppets to Europe in 1952. In London they performed at a meeting of the British Puppet and Model Theatre Guild, and afterwards made eleven appearances at the Exhibition and Festival sponsored by this organization.

It is probably not generally known that puppets helped along the Marshall Plan, but they did. Colin Drake was making a brief visit to Paris when he was robbed. Being a puppeteer with Sue Hastings' company, he had no trouble in getting a job with one of the small theatres which play in the public parks. Passing the hat was not very lucrative, so he hit upon the idea of building a marionette show to publicize the Plan, and it was accepted by the United States Information Agency. The show was taped in five languages, and with the help of two assistants, he toured France, England, Denmark, Holland and Belgium.

The extensive tours of Lewis Parsons have taken him into Mexico upon numerous occasions. In an account of an early visit in 1954, he mentions Rusty, a clown who was smuggled across the border and became "an international public relations puppet." At gas stations, restaurants and hotels, in public squares, and by country roadsides, Rusty's appearance brought crowds of sympathetic spectators. Once, in the mountain village of Jacala, a musician played on the crude bull's horn trumpet to accompany the clown's dance, and once a village band played for him—and demanded a round of drinks afterwards. This one puppet brought Parsons rich rewards: people helped him with his Spanish and invited him into their homes; children showed him their singing games, and accepted him without suspicion. Parsons later traveled in Mexico with his show, firm in the belief that "puppets are a means of exploring the world and communicating with people."

Audiences in South Africa, New Zealand and Australia were exposed to a different kind of American puppetry when Bobby Clark toured for twelve weeks with his musical version of *Pinocchio*. Daniel Llords' contribution to the international scene is described in Chapter V. Fern Zwickey on her world tour in 1956 gave a puppet workshop in New Delhi for World Literacy, Inc., and Jean Wiksell gave a demonstration and workshop at the University of Hawaii in 1955. Pauline Benton was in Honolulu the preceding year. With Arvo Wirto she presented about twenty performances and workshops at the Academy of Art during the month of February. George Adam Renz went to Europe to learn, and worked with the Wilispoon Theatre in Amsterdam, Desarthis' theatre in Paris, and the Little Angel Theatre in London, directed by John Wright. During the 1964-1965 academic year, Mel Helstien was at Chulalongkorn University in Bangkok, Thailand, to assist in the theatre program. He and his wife Antoinette sought out Siamese puppet performances, collected some figures, and spent some time in Malaya where they made films of puppet shows. They returned via Europe, and saw a few puppet theatres in Hungary, Czechoslovakia, and Belgium.

Most Americans go abroad, stay for a time, and return home. With Donald Cordry it was different. He went to Mexico in the thirties to collect masks, and has lived there ever since. He developed a business in craft designing in Mexico City and later in Cuernavaca. In the early fifties he made a set of carved wooden marionettes for *Hansel and Gretel* and gave performances in the house which he and his wife Dorothy designed. About this time, several variety numbers were also built, and a start made on a cast for *Beauty and the Beast*. Then illness struck, and his activities were severely curtailed. Through the years the Cordrys have made an extensive collection of Mexican Indian costumes, and their book on the subject has recently been published. He is working on another book, *Dolls of Mexico*, and has published several articles on Mexican textiles, while *House Beautiful* featured a house he designed. All the while, he has been adding to his puppet collection.

Puppeteers with variety shows find it relatively easy to travel, and many of them have gone to foreign countries. Bob Bromley's work is described in Chapter VI. Walton and O'Rourke have also performed extensively abroad. In 1953 they went via Hawaii and the Fiji Islands to Australia, where they had engagements all over the country. Sid Krofft had a long run in Paris beginning in December 1954, and he also played in London. The Trotter Brothers performed for six months in Europe, and another six months in Australia during the 1959-1960 season. Addis Williams played for two weeks at the Caribe Hilton Hotel in San Juan, Puerto Rico, in between engagements at a Long Island department store at Easter time, 1962. Tommy Trent appeared at Havana's Sans Souci for three weeks in 1958. Alfred Wallace did a program for an amusement park called Coney Island in Caracas, Venezuela, which he says was "extremely lucrative." Jerry Hartnett played the Intercontinental Hotels in Caracas, Curaçao, and Santo Domingo about 1963. Hartnett has also filled many engagements with steamship lines, having been on three Mediterranean cruises on the *Queen Elizabeth,* a North Sea journey on the *Mauritania,* and other sailings, all in the last four years. He also played club engagements in London. Other puppeteers who have found shipboard performances both pleasant and profitable include Doug and Gayle Anderson, who have been on several cruises to Bermuda; Frank Paris and Ted Lewis, who have sailed the Caribbean, and Lea Wallace.

When Erica Melchior went with her husband and daughter Peggy on a European vacation, she took some of her marionettes "just in case." She saw an agent in Dusseldorf, who booked her into the Palladium for a week and then sent her to Bern's Salon in Stockholm to substitute for a star who was ill. A week at the U.S. Officer's Club in Wiesbaden followed. Other appearances, including Paris, were offered her, but she declined as it was time for Peggy to return to school. George Prentice is another puppeteer who has performed all over the world with his *Punch and Judy.* Since World War II, when he entertained service men, he has been active at home, on television, and abroad. Lately he returned from tours of Europe and Vietnam, where his six months of performances there won him a citation from General Westmoreland.

American puppeteers on the whole have not shown an avid interest in foreign puppetry, but in the last ten years increased contact with it has changed their attitude considerably. An important event in this development was the First International Festival of Puppet Theatres sponsored by the Rumanian Government, which took place in Bucharest, May 15 to June 1, 1958. More than 300 delegates from twenty-seven countries attended, and saw a cross section of world puppetry in the forty shows presented. Most of these were given in competition for a variety of prizes awarded by a jury of fourteen international judges. (Javier Villafañe from Argentina and I represented the New World on this panel.) UNIMA held its VIth Congress and Romain Proctor attended as the U.S. member of the Presidium. Bucharest was again host in 1960 for the Second International Festival. This time the theatre La Pareja from Cordoba, Argentina, directed by Eduardo and Hector de Mauro, performed, and I was again on the jury.

With the regular UNIMA Congress and the proliferation of international festivals, puppeteers have been able to follow world developments in the puppet theatre. American participation is still limited, but it is increasing. Micheline Legendre presented her Marionettes of Montreal at the UNIMA Congress and Festival in Warsaw, 1962. Fred Putz from Colorado did a short number, and then went on around the world visiting many puppet theatres on the way. Llords' "International" performed in Braunschweig and Colwyn Bay in 1963, and George Latshaw's first foreign appearance was at the latter festival. At the Third International Festival in Bucharest in 1965, Lewis Mahlmann, Luman Coad and Mollie Falkenstein gave short performances, and about twenty people from North and South America were there.

In the fifties, the United States government began setting up exchange programs in theatre, music, dance, and literature with countries of Eastern Europe. Artists in all fields, either singly or in groups, also went into Africa, India, South America, and many other places. American officials, however, were slow to take advantage of the widespread appeal of puppetry, but when the State Department learned that I had been invited to Rumania for the International Festival in 1958, it suggested a visit to Turkey as well, under the auspices of the American Specialists branch of the Bureau of Educational and Cultural affairs. A month's work in Istanbul and Ankara was arranged, including work with teachers at an English language seminar at the American Girls' College in Istanbul and some brief sessions with teachers and children in Ankara. None of these projects was especially successful, but they suggested possibilities for future ones. Persistent efforts during the next two years lead to my four-month tour in 1960: Ankara for six weeks with projects in creative art, including puppetry, for the summer recreational program sponsored by a group of Ankara citizens for children in the poorer sections of the city; Yugoslavia, Czechoslovakia, Poland, Rumania, and Russia, giving talks on American puppetry and creative approaches to puppet and play making, meeting with puppeteers, and seeing many performances. Such person-to-person contacts among people in a given field was the purpose of the American Specialist program.

The next McPharlin venture was the VIIIth UNIMA Congress in Warsaw in 1962 (not government-sponsored), and an amateur festival in Pulawy afterwards. In 1963, a Fulbright grant made possible for me a full year in India, giving workshops in Puppetry and Creative Drama in different parts of the country. The program was arranged by the Indian Theatre Society, Natya Sangh, founded by Kamaladevi Chattopadhyay, one of India's outstanding women leaders, with a long list of accomplishments in the cultural field to her credit. She has a keen interest in puppet theatre and its development in India, and at her request, I made a survey of Indian puppetry as seen during my travels and made a report, together with recommendations to further it. One of these was the appointment of

Meher Contractor to the Natya Sangh staff to conduct puppet projects. As a member of the UNIMA Presidium, Mrs. Contractor has seen many shows, and has put her knowledge to good use in numerous workshops for teachers, as well as performances. My three-month Fulbright grant to Ceylon followed the one in India, and then a return trip home via Indonesia, Cambodia, Thailand, Hong Kong (no puppets were seen there, but a Chinese opera performed in an amusement park, with actors in gorgeous costumes and headdresses with long waving pheasant feathers), and Japan.

Under the Foreign Leaders and Specialists Program, outstanding individuals in various fields are invited for two-month visits to the United States. Kamaladevi Chattopadhyay came in the fall of 1962 to observe community theatres, and she also became acquainted with some puppeteers. Mane Bernardo from Buenos Aires came in the spring of 1963, and extended her stay so that she could attend the Puppeteers of America Festival. A glimpse of modern Polish puppetry was provided by Jan Wilkowski, artistic director of the Lalka Theatre in Warsaw, and designer Adam Kilian. They came to the United States in June 1964 for a brief visit sponsored by the State Department. The visit came about as a result of Lewin Goff's earlier trip to Warsaw, where he saw and liked their work. They spent a couple of weeks at the University of Kansas, attending classes in Prof. Goff's theatre department and giving informal lecture-demonstrations. They brought along an elaborate picture and poster display which hung in the foyer of the University Theatre, and much of this material and two marionettes were left for the theatre collection. They went on westward and stopped in various cities, took in Disneyland and saw the Grand Canyon on the way back. In New Mexico they saw Indian dances which were of special interest, for they planned to do a production about them. The Children's Theatre Conference was held that year at the University of Kansas, and the two Polish artists contributed to the program not only in their lectures but also in personal contacts. Adam Kilian made measurements of the University Theatre stage, and when he returned to Warsaw made designs for a production of three Mrozek plays, which were directed by Janusz Warminski of the Ateneum Theatre in Warsaw. He arrived in the fall of 1964 with the designs, which were executed by the theatre technicians.

The State Department negotiated a major puppet event—a tour of India, Nepal, and Afghanistan by the Baird Marionettes. The Bairds left in January 1962, with 5,000 pounds of equipment, two stages and 150 puppets to present variety, *Davy Jones' Locker* and *The Princess and the Dragon.* Bil and Cora, with eight assistant puppeteers, toured for seventeen weeks, performing in regular theatres in the big cities and outdoors in small villages. They gave numerous workshops to help Indian puppeteers carry on their work. As time allowed, they also saw Indian puppet shows, and were constantly aware of the contribution India has made to puppet art. In previous years a number of puppet companies from Eastern Europe performed in the Orient, most of them with large and impressive shows. It was notable that the Baird troupe held its own with them, and thus built up a favorable image of American puppetry.

The following year the Bairds went to Russia for a ten-week tour. Their show stood up well there also, despite the large number of state-supported puppet theatres and the elaborate quality of the Russian productions. As in their previous tour, the language barrier was not a great problem, because the material presented did not depend too much upon the spoken dialogue. Moreover, a puppet master of ceremonies acted as interpreter. In Russia, it was Pytor Ivanovich, who offered to help when Baird apologized for his ignorance of the language. Pytor's words were provided by an interpreter, but it was Baird's policy to know a little of the language himself.

The cultural exchange program with Russia involves complicated agreements which are renegotiated at intervals. In return for the Baird visit the Russians sent their most famous puppeteer, Sergei Obraztsov and his company to the United States. Under the auspices of Sol Hurok, they played at the Broadway Theatre in New York for eight weeks in the fall of 1963. *An Unusual Concert*, the satirical program which has been regularly performed since its premiere on July 9, 1955, at Obraztsov's Central State Puppet Theatre in Moscow, was given for adults, and *Aladdin and His Wonderful Lamp* for children.

In the fall of 1965, Sergei and Olga Obraztsov returned to the United States with the *Concert* which he performs alone with her piano accompaniment. This time they started from the West Coast and were booked in nineteen cities across the country. When they played at the Detroit Institute of Arts, they visited Fern Zwickey's puppet class at Wayne State University, saw a number of student presentations, admired two zany characters with roving ping-pong eyes, and took them off to Moscow for the Museum as gifts of their creators. They also took along a description of the mime, and a recording of Stan Freberg's *Banana Boat Song*, which inspired it.

The Peace Corps has developed an extensive program of community development in many countries around the world. In the spring of 1965, a group of trainees was recruited from the performing arts, a hitherto untapped source. They spent three months in training at UCLA, where, in addition to rigorous drill in Spanish (they were all headed for Latin America), various techniques in folk dancing, music, creative dramatics and play production were given by the staff of the Department of Theatre Arts, and I gave them some experience in a creative approach to puppet making with available materials, and showed how to develop plays not only for entertainment but for the presentation of ideas concerning health, family planning and other social problems. Nathan Gilgoff and Lynn Odinov were assigned to Panama where they established a shadow-puppet troupe, Los Titiriteros de Panamá. It began with a propaganda piece for rat control, to which have been added many other numbers developed by the young people who comprise the group. The project has the support of government and community agencies, but the problem is its continuance after the Peace Corps volunteers leave. Besides performing in Panama City, the group made a tour to Montijo, Santiago and Sona under the auspices of the Ministry of Agriculture, and it hopes to continue traveling with *Don Quixote,* the new production. The establishment of such "grass roots" theatres offers a whole new field for American puppeteers if such organizations as the Peace Corps can see the possibilities.

Another project is George Latshaw's work in Puerto Rico. In the summer of 1966 he had a six-week seminar for teachers, and a trainee program to launch Miniteatro Infantil Rural. Four performers with a repertory of three one-act and two puppet plays toured schools in the Humacao region with a stage on a pick-up truck. The climax of the first season was a presentation before the legislature in El Capitolio, San Juan. The following summer Latshaw returned to continue the training program for fifteen boys, some of whom were chosen to make up three two-man companies to tour three school regions. The idea for this program originated with Dr. Leopoldo Santiago Lavandero, Director of the Programa Teatro Escolar, which presents a variety of plays, both classic and modern. The Secretary of Education, Dr. Angel Quintero Alfaro, encouraged the puppet program, which is sponsored by the Department of Education of the Commonwealth of Puerto Rico. A seminar for teachers was conducted jointly with Señorita Angeles Gasset, a puppeteer-educator from Madrid, whose plays comprise the MIR repertory. A copy of her book, *Títeres con Cabezo,* was left at each school where a puppet show was given, to encourage the use of puppets in the classroom. Latshaw believes that his function is to help these people to discover their own style and outlook, which will be reflected in their puppetry.

Foreign puppeteers in America

In addition to those already mentioned, a number of puppeteers and companies have performed in America. The Salzburg Marionettes have been here most frequently, traveled the farthest, and been seen by the most people. This theatre, founded in 1913 by Anton Aicher, has been active ever since. His son Herman was ten years old at the time, and in due course he took over the theatre and still runs it, assisted by his wife and children, with others as needed. From the beginning, the operas of Mozart and plays about him have been their specialty, performed by meticulously constructed and costumed marionettes. Equal care is given to settings, lighting, and music, so that all may be perfect.

The company usually spends part of the year on tour, and the remainder in Salzburg, performing in its small theatre and preparing new shows. It has played all over Europe and at various times in Canada, Mexico, and in Central and South America. It toured the United States in the 1951–1952 season, and for the next three years, then the company was not seen here until 1964, when it arrived in New York to play at Town Hall from December 17 to January 8. During the 1965–1966 season there was a more extensive tour in the West, Midwest, and Canada. Some of the Mozart operas which the Salzburg Marionettes have brought to America are: *The Magic Flute, Abduction from the Seraglio, Don Giovanni* and *Bastien and Bastienne.* They have also presented humorous plays, such as *Wolfgang Mozart and the Butcher* and *Mozart Visits the Empress,* ballets and fairy tales, thus pleasing both adults and children.

Other German companies have been to the U.S.A. On November 12, 1959, the Goethe House in New York presented the Hohensteiner Puppets from Essen, an outstanding hand-puppet ensemble of six players. During the Christmas season of 1958, Harro Siegel's troupe from Braunschweig opened in New York for the beginning of a five-week tour. The program included *Dr. Faust,* an Egyptian story, *Tee and Hapshisoot,* and *Comic Interludes,* a group of variety numbers. These were quite elaborate productions, with excellent staging, lighting, and English sound track. The marionettes had the special stylistic quality one finds only in German puppets. Siegel's work has been an important part of the European puppet theatre for many years.

Robert Lago of Mexico City is an integral part of the American puppet scene. Nevertheless, we mention his seven-week tour of the United States in 1956 here, not only because Mexico *is* a foreign country to those living north of the border, but also because his show had qualities different from those usually seen here. Its distinctive Mexican flavor was reflected in the program of folk dances, dramatizations of such folk tales as *El Raton y La Cucaracha Mondinga* and that favorite play of the Mexican theatre, *Don Juan Tenorio.* Written in Spain in 1844, and first presented in Mexico in 1865, it has become an annual event of All Souls' Day. Lago's adaptation to puppets takes full advantage of the supernatural elements of the story, but there is also a good deal of humor. The tour was arranged by the

Department of Theatre Arts at the Detroit Institute of Arts and sponsored by eleven other museums.

Sicilian puppet shows have been a part of the American scene since the latter part of the nineteenth century. Although they have died out to a large extent, they may still be seen now and then. The Manteo family performed at the Guild presentations for the New York World's Fair, and plans are afoot to have the Manteos perform at Bil Baird's theatre. When Grace Weil set up her theatre and museum at Stony Creek, she invited Salvatore Macri from Acrireale to do research and assist James Weil in organizing a Sicilian theatre.

The Stockholm Marionette Theatre of Fantasy, directed by Michael Meschke, came to the United States in 1966. Experimental and avant-garde, the performances of Brecht's *Threepenny Opera* somewhat startled American audiences. For children, *The Wizard of Oz* was presented.

Jan and Ann Bussell with their Hogarth Puppets from England gave shows in Canada and the state of Washington in 1965. During the course of their television performances, they made a popular television hero of Muffin the Mule, a character from a story by Annette Mills. A glance at the Bibliography will show the contribution Jan Bussell has made to puppet literature.

Among the numerous performances of Manuel de Falla's *El Retablo de Maese Pedro*, one given by the Opera Society in Washington, D.C., in April 1966, had authentic Spanish puppets. These were brought from Madrid by Manuel Merono and his stage manager, José Ramon de Aguirre, who came under the auspices of the Spanish government and the Instituto de Cultura Hispanica. The characters displayed a stylized Byzantine quality, and were richly costumed in bright colors. Don Gay-feros, splendid in silver armor and flowing mantle, galloped to the rescue of Melisandra on a green steed. Señor Merono did not bring any pup-peteers, but ten members of the National Capital Puppetry Guild volun-teered to operate the puppets, and succeeded despite the fact that re-hearsals were conducted in a mixture of English, French and Spanish.

American puppeteers have admired and wondered at the performances of the famous Bunraku puppet theatre of Osaka, Japan, known to them only through pictures and the reports of those who saw them. In 1962, however, visitors to the Century 21 Exposition in Seattle could see the Japanese puppets on their first venture outside their own country. Every-thing was there: the three-foot puppets gorgeously costumed, with three operators to work the principal characters; the samisen players and readers seated to one side of the stage; the elegant and unmistakably Japanese settings. This was a theatrical form from a past era, dominated by movement and vocal interpretation long since stylized, and used to portray tragic stories, ritualistic dances, or scenes from domestic life. It was the world of the Japanese block print in animate form. On this trip the company played for two weeks in Seattle, then made brief visits to Vancouver, Los Angeles, and Honolulu. During March and April 1966, the Bunraku troupe made a tour which included Honolulu, Los Angeles, San Francisco, New York and Washington, giving more Americans a chance to see this unique puppet theatre.

For decades, whenever one thought of Italian puppetry, the name of Vittorio Podrecca and his Teatro dei Piccoli came to mind. Visitors to Rome saw his performances, but many saw them on this side of the Atlantic, too, for he crossed the ocean a number of times and toured in both North and South America. The theatre had already circled the globe three times before its first tour in the United States in 1932–1933, and another in 1940. At least one American, Martin Stevens, was inspired to become a puppeteer after seeing these puppet actors. The Piccoli probably had considerable influence on puppetry, for their program of opera, revues, fantasies, ballets, and circus acts parallels much of the work done by American puppeteers. With the cast of 800 puppets and more than twenty-five people to work them, Podrecca's company probably showed most of the variety acts still in use today. In 1959, the theatre began a grand anniversary tour. In Switzerland, Podrecca was stricken by a heart attack while working on the bridge, and died on July 7. The company manager assumed control and the tour continued. From Mexico they came into the United States, and performed in Seattle in the spring of 1963. A small theatre on the Exposition grounds became available and regular performances were given from June 22 through September 5. There were difficulties with the company manager, chiefly financial, and after they went on to Philadelphia, the puppeteers disbanded, and most of them were sent back to Italy at the expense of the Italian Government. One manipulator, Gioaccino Gorno, got a job with the Krofft's *Les Poupées de Paris,* and another, Roberto Gamonet, took a position outside puppetry, both having obtained permanent visas through the assistance of Lois Ludington in Seattle. On November 25, 1959, the Instituto Italiano de Cultura of Buenos Aires paid tribute to Vittorio Podrecca in a commemorative program presided over by Mane Bernardo.

The bad as well as the good in puppetry has been imported, as in the case of the Teatro dei Piccoli Attori. Martin Stevens saw a performance by this group, inevitably confused with Podrecca because of the word Piccoli, and deplored its poor quality. Perhaps this is the tag end of the Italian tradition so brilliantly upheld for so many decades by Podrecca, but which must surely give way to fresh ideas.

At intervals during the past two decades, flashes of imaginative puppetry have come from France. Yves Joly and his three assistants appeared in 1951 in *Les Mains Joly* at La Vie en Rose in New York. They used only their hands, with bits of paper and other materials or colored gloves to suggest the actions of people or moods, and the watching audience created along with the operators, through an act of the imagination. The art of the mime was here displayed in even simpler terms, for ideas usually conveyed by the movement of the whole body, were expressed by only one of its parts. Despite the fact that *Les Mains Joly* was seen on television across the country, few puppeteers attempted to utilize the basic principles upon which the show was built. Several years later, Georges Lafaye's company of four came to New York's Blue Angel, and introduced the technique known as "black theatre." Puppeteers dressed in black worked in front of a black curtain, holding puppets or objects in their gloved hands and moving them freely about. Lights were arranged to illuminate the objects but not the operators. This technique of dis-embodied forms moving in space was used to convey ideas and emotions or to satirize them. Sometimes Lafaye used newspapers made into interest-ing designs. In one number a cello player nods to his instrument and it nods back; two huge hands come out of the darkness to caress it; the hands are routed, but the cello is indignant and disintegrates into a group of angry butterflies which fly about the cellist's head. In another number, *John and Marsha*, which has become famous, the essence of an amorous flirtation is fully explored with only a top hat and a feather boa.

In December 1956, a revue called *Cranks* was presented by Richard Charlton and John Krimsky at the Bijou Theatre in New York. Two numbers were hand ballets. One was an interpretation of the ballad *Elizabeth*, in which four sets of gloved hands suggested the movement of flowers, waterfalls, rain, clouds, wind and so on. The other was *Gloves*. A boulevadier sits at a table, awaiting a rendezvous. He reads a news-paper, becomes bored, and tosses it aside. It rustles and from under it comes a pair of white gloves. They dance, they entwine themselves with his hands, caressing them. His amour appears and the gloves are brushed aside, but they reappear, move over her body and through her feather boa. She is annoyed and leaves, followed by the man. The gloves find the decanter and two glasses, pour wine into them, clink them in a silent toast, and disappear into the dark.

Many variants of the techniques described above have been developed in Europe; by 1965 there were so many "black theatre" performances that people wearied of them. Years before, Obraztsov used his hands with a ball on each forefinger, and later the hands alone, to interpret some of the songs he did in his *Concert*. When he was in the United States, these were included in his program. Some American puppeteers have developed hand techniques; perhaps the most sophisticated program (for adults, of course) is George Latshaw's *Hand in Glove*, matched only by Burr Tillstrom's powerful hand ballets. The "black theatre" technique is used for Ed Sullivan's mouse, Topo Gigio. From behind a black velvet curtain, three people worked this small puppet by means of short sticks.

In August 1961, two Frenchmen, Philippe Genty and Yves Brunier, departed on a tour which lasted four years and took them through Eastern Europe, the Near East, India, Japan, Australia, Central and South America, Mexico and the United States. Known as Expedition Alexandre, the tour was sponsored by UNESCO and the Alliance Française, and its purpose was to make a film of puppet theatres around the world. Michiko Tagawa joined them in Japan, and contributed her skills in puppet making and manipulation, which she had learned as a member of the Takeda Troupe in Tokyo. In due course the Expedition reached South America. A car accident badly injured Michiko's arm, necessitating many operations which were done in Los Angeles, where she stayed for many months, working with various puppeteers as her arm slowly mended. The Expedition went on, and gave performances in various cities. Alexandre, the central character, is a wide-eyed little boy, curious but tender, whose grief over the accidental killing of a butterfly is sensitively portrayed in one of the numbers. Another is a Samurai swordsman of the Bunraku type, which the Frenchmen operate with the same meticulous care the Japanese bestow on their puppets. Other numbers reflect French elegance and sophistication. There are combinations of people and puppets, a brown pelican singing "Hello Dolly," a dancing trumpet, South American cha-cha dancers, and a group of cats, remarkable in their purple, chartreuse and blue colors as well as their movements. Again, music and pantomime proved understandable the world over, as the travelers performed these numbers wherever they went. In August 1965, Genty and Brunier sailed for home; Michiko Tagawa remained, partly because her arm was not yet fully mended, but also because she decided to remain permanently in the United States.

On June 6, 1948, André Tahon gave his first public performance with puppets at a Boy Scout benefit show. He plans to celebrate the twentieth anniversary of this event with a Jubilee in Paris in 1968, for his Compagnie des Marottes has been active during all these years. In June 1959, he came to the United States, and performed here most of the time until December 1966. His individual style is a mixture of sophistication, humor, repartee, and satire; his puppets (marottes) are elegant and richly costumed but simply constructed with stylized heads. Papotin is an engaging master of ceremonies, and Nathalie, a "susceptible French damsel"; there are also chorus lines of Russian dancers, Hungarian dancers, and twelve

Bottle Dancers, with long braided pigtails and little bottles of colored water balanced on their heads. These are all based upon national folk dancers in their brilliant costumes, but Tahon has managed to invest them with a contrasting sophistication. *The Caterpillar and the Snail* has become one of his most popular numbers, with new versions introduced at intervals. There are also mice, lots of them. As many as seventy-two cavorted over a set representing Paris rooftops in one *Hollywood Palace* presentation. They are grey with pink ears, and the lady mice wear frilly white dresses.

Tahon has provided full details of his American tours, which we here summarize because they illustrate the active life of a popular entertainer on the theatre-night-club-television circuit. His first engagement was at the Stardust Hotel, Las Vegas, and lasted twenty-four weeks. He appeared on a number of television shows including Ed Sullivan's, the *Dinah Shore Chevy Show*, and a Victor Borge Special on which Jane Powell taught the mice to sing "Do-Re-Mi" from *The Sound of Music*. Then he joined the *Johnny Mathis Show* and went on tour with it from September 2, 1960 to January 30, 1961. The group played in theatres, civic centers, high school and university auditoriums across the United States, dipped into Canada, and moved westward to Manila and Honolulu. Tahon had six numbers, one of which was Nathalie singing "J'attendrai" with Mathis.

After the tour, the Marottes returned to Europe for almost a year, but came back in December 1961 to open at the Tropicana Hotel, Las Vegas. After this four-month run came twenty-two weeks at Harold's Club in Reno. The year 1963 included more guest appearances; two with Steve Allen who took lessons in puppet making from Papotin, and two runs of *Papotin's Revue* at Disneyland, one lasting two weeks, the other fifteen. He gave some special performances, and in November was guest star in the *Lotte Goslar Show*, a "mad revue produced by Victor Borge," according to Tahon, but President Kennedy's assassination cast a pall over the nation and the show closed. In 1964 and 1965 he made nine appearances on *Hollywood Palace*, each with a different host. For some of them Tahon did parodies such as "Dominique" by the Singing Nun and various numbers by the Beatles. A short tour with Victor Borge, a run at Radio City Music Hall and several performances in between, another tour with Johnny Mathis, and a special Gala performance at the Lisner Auditorium in Washington, D.C., all took place in 1964. The French Embassy sponsored this Gala as an evening of the National Chapter of the Society of Arts and Letters, and featured the *André Tahon Show* with variety numbers and *The Forced Marriage* by Molière.

In January 1965, he played at the Americana Hotel in Miami for twelve weeks, then moved to Radio City Music Hall for the Easter Show. A new number, *Spring Is Here*, was prepared for it, with fifty-eight yellow feathered chickens scattered all over the 100-foot-wide stage. He also gave many single performances: one was at a party given by Victor Borge at the Greenwich Yacht Club to honor the Royal Danish Ballet Company; Papotin did a take-off on dancing schools and prima ballerinas. He was also M.C. in *La Parisienne* at the Golden Hotel, Reno, and told naughty stories during a six-week run beginning in March 1966. The Marottes also played the Latin Quarter in New York, and in August they opened at the Comédie-Canadienne Theatre in Montreal, played for three weeks, and then went on tour with this theatre revue. In October the same show played four weeks in a night club version at the Folies-Royal, and was seen on color television. André Tahon returned to Paris on December 10, 1966.

Puppets in Latin America

In general, most of the trends evident in the United States and Canada are reflected in those Latin American countries which have kept up their puppet activities. Here we include some brief notes of recent activities in Mexico, Brazil, Argentina, and Cuba.

A surge of interest in puppetry developed in Mexico prior to 1948, when shows were sponsored by the National Institute of Fine Arts for entertainment and education. Several companies worked under the general direction of Roberto Lago, who had the assistance of many artists and literary people. In 1947 and 1948, the Teatro El Nahual, having been successful in the great literacy campaign in Mexico, went to Venezuela for a similar effort. From then on, Lago reports, things went along much as they had in previous years and only recently have there been new developments.

After Lago retired as puppet theatre director, Lola Cueto, who had been closely associated with the project since its beginning, became director in 1961. Two theatres still perform widely to school children, and new workshop quarters with a small theatre have made possible an extension of the program. Now many puppet courses are given, and teachers from Mexico City as well as from the provinces take advantage of them. Among recent productions is *Pinocchio*, adapted by Lola Cueto for living actors and puppets.

Some of the older puppet companies are still performing. Lewis Parsons mentions having seen the Rosete-Aranda Company in a tent show several years ago. With hundreds of string-puppets stored in their vans and eight manipulators, these puppeteers played in rural communities, carrying on the tradition of the original troupe which was founded about

1860. After it disbanded, Carlos Espinal took over the name along in the forties, and it is probably this group which Parsons saw.

In Mexico City, Francisca Pulido Cuevas, born in 1861, was still to be seen in recent years, despite her great age, going about with Death and the Devil or other characters attached by strings to a stick. With one hand she animated the puppets on a little wooden platform placed on the ground and with the other played the mouth organ. She was one of a long line of street performers, now almost vanished.

Graciela Amador, one of the group which began the educational puppetry movement, performed on television and had a weekly show until her death in 1960. Likewise, Gilberto Ramírez Alvarado with his theatre Don Ferruco worked on television. One show, sponsored by the Ministry of Health, was *La Familia Tiripitín*. He has also maintained the traditional practice of playing in the open air, and has performed for many years on Sundays in Chapultepec Park or the public squares. Guillermo Torres López, who was one of Lago's assistants, gave performances during the Christmas season, and made regular appearances at the department store, El Palacio de Hierro. He was also in demand for children's parties. His recent death ended a long career of puppet playing in Mexico · City.

Many more government departments now sponsor puppet theatres: Sanitary Education, Social Affairs, Social Security, Audio-Visual Educational Service, Cultural Mission of the National Autonomous University, Teachers' Training College, and so on. Of special interest is the Petul Theatre, directed by Professor Marco Antonio Montero, at the Indian Coordination Center of San Cristóbal de las Casas in Chiapas State. This is part of the Indian Institute's program for incorporating three million non-Spanish-speaking Indians into Mexican life. Petul, a popular puppet, communicates with them, teaches the advantages of vaccination, literacy, respect for the law, and encourages them to come to the Institute for assistance. Like the puppet Chapulín of an earlier day, who could persuade whole audiences of children to use their toothbrushes, Petul has won the confidence of the people.

The University Theatre Center has recently formed puppet groups from students in the various faculties, and awarded a two-year scholarship to Carmen Bassol for study in Czechoslovakia. A great deal of puppet teaching goes on in schools, too, and the work of Virginia Ruano/Vargas is probably typical. She uses puppets in audio-visual programs for teaching many subjects.

In 1951, the Children's Plastic Arts Workshop was founded to develop creative aptitudes, with puppet theatre as the central activity. Roberto

Perez Rangal is Director. A new Children's Center at Tepito opened in 1967 as a result of official interest in promoting all sorts of cultural activities, and at the Children's Theatre Center in Mexico City, Pepe Díaz is active, having had long experience in Lago's theatre. He also teaches and gives workshops for teachers in the city and provinces. Cuca Ramírez, also formerly of El Nahual, recently produced *The Wizard of Oz* at the Center.

In the realm of social, civic and political affairs, the theatre Don Toribio, directed by the Herrera Brothers and sponsored by the Social Security Institute, gives shows in social centers and schools. Upon occasion, they play in the open air on behalf of political campaigns, and attract large crowds with slapstick variety acts.

Lago mentions an exciting performance he saw "under the moon" in front of the Castle of Chapultepec of García Lorca's *El Retablillo de Don Cristobal*. It was put on by a group of university students from the Faculty of Philosophy and Letters under the direction of Victoria Espinosa de Maisonet. Puppets were not used, but the actors imitated hand-puppets. With large papier-mâché heads and short arms, they were visible only from the waist up. Movements, voices and appearance all combined to give the illusion of huge hand-puppets.

Also bringing new ideas to puppetry is Alexandro Jodorowsky, a mime formerly associated with Marcel Marceau. He combines miming with puppetry in a program he calls *The Insane Marionettes*. One of his numbers is *The Puppeteer and the Puppet*, which is powerfully projected. He is also a theatre director who has produced plays in many parts of Latin America, an author, and in lighter moments, the creator of a comic strip in which he often portrays himself as a marionette.

Lago, since his retirement, has traveled widely in Europe and has attended some of the International Puppet Festivals. He also comes to the United States occasionally to perform or to visit, as have other Mexicans, including Virginia Ruano/Vargas.

In recent years, there has been considerable artistic and technical advance in Cuban puppetry, thanks to government sponsorship. One group of eleven people directed by Nancy Delbert produces a weekly television show based on Cuban and foreign stories. Los Solari, working under the Provincial Council of Culture, Havana, performs children's shows, such as Rene Ariza's *The Lesson of the Naughty Cat* and Dora Alonso's *The Wizard Dinghy*. They also do musical comedy-type performances for adults. There are many amateur groups who bring puppet shows to workers in field and factory. Cuban puppeteers sometimes have an opportunity to study in foreign countries. In 1962, Luis Interian and his companion were at the Prague Academy for training. Dr. Renée Potts has attended International Puppet Festivals and was elected to the UNIMA Presidium in 1965.

In 1943, Carol and Roscoe Wood went from the United States to Brazil under the joint sponsorship of the Committee for Inter-American Affairs and the Department of Education of the State of Rio de Janeiro. They toured extensively with a hand-puppet show designed to acquaint school children with life in North America. Cicero de Oliveira collaborated with them, and later introduced puppetry as an educational medium into the schools of Curitiba, capital of Paraná. Madame Helena Antipoff, founder of the Pestalozzi Society of Brazil, initiated country-wide programs of educational puppetry in Rio and Belo Horizonte. She was assisted by a group of artists and writers, including the poetess Cecilia Meirelles, who wrote puppet plays based on Brazilian folklore, and Luis Cosme, who provided special music. Another group, under the direction of Michel Simon of the French Lycée in Rio, staged plays by García Lorca, Pushkin, Shakespeare and others.

Courses for teachers and puppet performances have been sponsored by local Departments of Education. In 1958 a section on puppets, galantys and masks was introduced in the Theatre School of the University of Bahia, with the help of Olga Obry. That same year the first Festival of Puppet Theatres was held in Rio, sponsored by the Brazilian Association of Theatre Critics.

At the Escolinhas de Arte, founded by Augusto Rodrigues, children make puppets and produce shows with the same creative approach they follow in painting. Nieta Lex directed courses for teachers in the State of São Paulo, sponsored by the Theatre Commission. A well-known dancer, she also performed with puppets and with masks similar to those used in ritual dances of the Indians. Performances for children and adults have been presented by José Lima at the Museum of Modern Art in Rio.

The puppet theatre is being widely promoted throughout Brazil. Plays, such as *Pluft, the Little Ghost* by Maria Clara Machado, are being written; television programs, such as those prepared by Madame Yolanda Rebello, Carmosina Araujo and others, are presented, while Washington Pinto continues his loyal support of the Pestalozzi Society Puppet Theatre.

Argentina has a long history of puppet playing. Javier Villafañe retired from his active puppet career but was honored at the First International Festival of Puppet Theatres in Bucharest in 1958, as a member of the international jury for the competition held at that time. Alfredo Bagalio has continued to use puppets in educational work during the past twenty years. He gives performances, works with teachers in schools, gives radio and television programs and participates in puppet festivals. He went in 1960 as a delegate from the Asociación de Titiriteros de la Argentina (ATA) to the International Festival of Glove Puppets at Piriapolis, Uruguay. In 1965 he assisted with National Puppet Week, organized by ATA in Azul. On April 4 during this meeting, a memorial to the puppeteer Otto Alfredo Freitas was set up in a public park. Bagalio made a trip to Europe in 1962 for a study of the puppet theatre in various countries. New editions of his books have been printed, and he has edited a volume of puppet plays. Lately he has been experimenting with hand-puppets for mentally retarded children.

Mane Bernardo, a well-known painter and teacher of art in Buenos Aires, has been active in the puppet theatre since 1943, and in recent years she has devoted most of her time to it. With Sarah Bianchi and her company, she performs a great variety of plays with puppets and hand pantomimes with musical accompaniment. While Mane Bernardo was president of the Asociación de Titiriteros, the first International Puppet Exhibit in Argentina was organized in Buenos Aires. Work from over twenty foreign countries, seventy Argentine puppet theatres and many individual collections was displayed for a month beginning November 17, 1958. During this time there were performances, lectures, film showings and round table discussions. Then the exhibit was moved to the National University of La Plata, and performances were given during January.

On November 25, 1959, a commemorative program for Vittorio Podrecca was held by the Italian Cultural Institute, with a performance and talk by Mane Bernardo. She has traveled in England, France, Italy and Spain, presenting lectures and films about her puppets. In 1963, she came to the United States under the Foreign Leaders and Specialists Program sponsored by the Department of State. For two months she visited puppeteers and saw shows, then attended the Puppeteers of America Festival and presented some of her hand pantomimes, assisted by Blanca Cappagli. She has also written a number of books about puppetry.

From this glimpse of puppetry South of the Border, it is evident that much work is done for children and that a great many people are involved in it. There is some experimentation going on, and puppeteers have considerable contact with other countries through travel, books and exhibits.

V

Some Careers in Puppetry

Many people working in puppetry today have been active twenty years or more, and their careers are summarized in the "List of Puppeteers." For the sake of continuity some of these are here brought up to date. Others who have come more recently onto the puppet scene are also included because they shed further light upon the varied activities which constitute the profession of puppetry; several others illustrate many years of work within a specific range of puppet activity. Together, these careers suggest both the similarities and the differences which exist in the work of American puppeteers, and they tell a good deal about what it means to be a puppeteer in America.

Bil and Cora Baird

The multi-faceted business of puppetry is nowhere more completely exemplified than in the work of Bil and Cora Baird. From their New York workshop has come a steady stream of productions in almost every medium to which puppets are adaptable. There have been "spectaculars," touring shows, performances with symphony orchestras, educational films and large-scale advertising shows at world's fairs. Their puppets have appeared in Broadway musicals, in night clubs, vaudeville, at Radio City Music Hall and in a Hollywood film. Much of their work is known to nation-wide audiences via television, for they have produced hundreds of commercials, appeared as guest artists on popular programs, and had long runs of a number of children's shows. Some Baird designs have been made into commercial toys, and articles on puppet making have appeared in such magazines as *Woman's Day*. It is not surprising, therefore, that the Baird name appears frequently in this account of American puppetry since 1948.

All the Baird shows have the mark of his individual style. The puppets are designed with a strong sense of caricature, for his intention is not to imitate, but to interpret people through satire and burlesque. He makes full use of non-human characters, too, and many of his animals have become real personalities, while abstract objects are often used to ridicule human foibles. Music is integral to all his shows, and dominates in some of them. In the puppet theatre, imagination may have full sway, and so it does in the Baird shows. Back of it all is a technical knowledge developed over a period of thirty years, which enables him to bring into being anything he can imagine, and to stage his shows with lavish costumes, settings and lighting. Evident also is a sense of showmanship, which enables him to weld together all the ingredients of the theatre.

In 1962, the Bairds were sponsored by the U.S. State Department for a seventeen-week tour of India, Nepal and Afghanistan. With a ten-man company, a large stage for theatre use and a smaller one for playing in the villages, they traveled 10,000 miles. On the program were *Davy Jones' Locker, The Princess and the Dragon* and a selection of variety numbers. This proved to be one of the greatest successes of the Cultural Exchange Program, and so they were sent the next year to spend ten weeks touring six Russian cities.

Such tours brought awareness of what is going on in the puppet world outside the USA. No doubt part of the inspiration for the writing and publication of his book *The Art of the Puppet* came from Baird's contacts with puppets in the countries he visited. This book, lavishly illustrated, was published in 1965, with French and Italian editions in 1967. He also became interested in UNIMA (Union Internationale des Marionnettes), attended the Conference in Leningrad in 1964, and the Third International Festival of Puppet Theatres in Bucharest in 1965. He is now a member of the UNIMA Presidium. (Cora Baird died in 1967.)

For several years Bil Baird has lived and worked in a six-story building at 59 Barrow Street in New York City. After many delays and difficulties, they opened the Bil Baird Theatre in February 1967. This was a significant event and is linked to an important development in American cultural life, which was given its first impetus by President John F. Kennedy. Subsequently, on September 29, 1965, Congress passed Public Law 90–209 which established the National Foundation on the Arts and Humanities. Roger Stevens became the Chairman of the National Council on the Arts, the purpose of which is to assist artists and associations engaged in many cultural activities, including the performing arts. So it came about that a grant of $20,000 was made to the American Puppet Arts Council, Inc. This organization, of which Bil Baird is executive director, is dedicated to the art of the puppet, but specifically covers the activities of the Baird Theatre. It is hoped that the interest in puppetry as a serious art which is notable in many European countries may be fostered in this country by developing shows for adults by the Baird company, and by the use of the theatre as a showcase for the work of other puppeteers, both foreign and American. As Baird says, "Our first step must be to keep the house filled and make it a popular thing for adults to attend live puppet theatre." Then other companies can be invited. To attract this kind of audience, the best talent in playwriting, designing, and musical composition must be drawn into the puppet theatre. If this can be accomplished, the quality of puppetry all over the country should be improved.

Financial backing for the American Puppet Arts Council has also come from a Billy Rose Foundation grant, and contributions from the Charlpeg Foundation, the New York State Council on the Arts, and the Hecksher Foundation for Children. If this venture proves worthy, it may bring about increasing support for puppet theatres in other parts of the country, and thus the whole art may be advanced.

The Baird Theatre is organized as an Equity repertory company. Favorable status was worked out with the Union by Cora Baird. This required considerable negotiation because puppeteers are scene shifters, builders and maintainers as well as actors. In the present company are Frank Fazakas, Carl Harms and Frank Sullivan, who have been with it for twenty years. Cora Baird, whose death in December 1967 left a void which cannot be filled, had been active co-partner in all the Baird activities. Now Phyllis Nierendorf and Robin Brooks have joined the company, and so have Fania Sullivan and Byron Whiting. Other people are associated with the theatre in various capacities, and the two Baird children also participate in the business.

In the repertory at present are *Ali Baba, Davy Jones' Locker, Man in the Moon, Winnie the Pooh,* Stravinsky's *L'Histoire du Soldat* and *People Is the Thing That the World Is Fullest Of.* The last was the adult attraction at the opening of the Baird Theatre. It is a musical revue, produced by Arthur Cantor, directed by Burt Shevelove. Although conceived by Baird, it was written by "divers hands" and some of the songs were composed by Buster Davis, with musical arrangements by Alvy West. Done with the typical Baird flair for satire, color, and movement, the show is likely to be "on" for a long time, for it can be revitalized periodically by new material. Some of the numbers are: *Conformity, Man and Woman, Lover, Science Fiction, Pollution, Africa, The Family Danced* and *Population Explosion.* Not only people-puppets but abstract and animal figures are used to show off the special talents of puppet actors. In addition to the people mentioned above, Jerry Nelson and Robin Kendall manipulated, Will Steven Armstrong was design consultant and Peggy Clark was light consultant.

A Pageant of Puppetry is also part of the repertory. Characters from many countries perform in variety numbers, with comments and demonstrations by the puppeteers. Now in preparation is *The Wonderful O,* adapted from the James Thurber story by Louis Solomon.

Baird is negotiating an exchange with Sergei Obraztsov—one of his technicians to work in New York, one of Baird's to work in the Central State Puppet Theatre in Moscow. Puppeteers are also being trained at the Baird Theatre under the Mobilization for Youth program and he is working with Montreal to establish a permanent puppet theatre there. All these activities going on at 59 Barrow Street are directed toward building recognition of puppetry as a significant form of theatre.

Bob Bromley

Today Bob Bromley continues to perform the type of variety he began in the thirties, working in full view of the audience. During the past two decades he has played in the United States, with extensive tours abroad. He appeared at the Lido Cabaret in Paris for five engagements, each lasting a year. In between he played in Johannesburg and Cape Town and toured South Africa for a year. For eight months he was part of a musical show in Melbourne and Sydney, which had for a finale thirty-two portrait marionettes of the stars, each of whom worked his own miniature image. He made two six-month tours of Scandinavia, played in famous London night clubs and those on the Riviera.

By 1960 he was touring South America, then returned to the United States to perform in the Hilton Hotel Ice Show for eight months. Returning to South America in 1962, he toured the principal cities. In Buenos Aires he went on television with *Mundo Marvellioso,* combining puppets and people, and won the Gold Palm Leaf Award. Then in Santiago, Chile, he staged a ballet called *Puppet and Peasant,* which ran for six months. Back in Paris in 1963, he took part in experimental television shows produced by Giles Margaritis. At the Cirque Medrano he had a trapeze-performing marionette worked from below, and a three-foot-tall puppet ballet dancer who rode a live horse at a gallop around the ring! In recent years he has lived in Studio City, Los Angeles, and presents shows mostly in Southern California.

Bromley points out that a mere record of activities can't convey the emotional impact of performances, the excitement of audience response, and the thrill of such never-to-be-forgotten events as the Gala Performance for the wedding of Grace Kelly and Prince Rainier of Monaco, the command performance at the Palladium for England's royal family, and the month-long participation in the Hans Christian Andersen Anniversary in Copenhagen.

Betsy Brown

For more than thirty years Betsy Brown has been active in puppetry—in designing, construction, hunting continuously for good, meaningful scripts and music, performing and teaching. She is a serious educator who has enlisted the help of husband Bert and daughter Penny, in her undertakings. While much of her work is based on religious subjects, her basic concern is with the broader applications of moral principles underlying present day preoccupation with understanding among nations and people of all races and colors.

In 1960, inspiration for new and more elaborate puppet shows came with her collaboration with Forman Brown, who wrote words and music for many plays, some based on stories of the Saints, others on favorite children's stories. One of these, *Noah's Ark*, was for a half-hour film on the television program, *The Hour of St. Francis*. She has also used material from the United Nations to encourage better interracial attitudes among children, and recordings of her daughter's harp music have been especially useful in performances she has given for Head Start groups. Her broadening horizons have been reflected in her television programs on puppet history, her participation in the assembling of the puppet exhibit at Lytton Center of the Visual Arts, and in visits to European puppet museums and festivals.

Mrs. Brown's many teaching projects have culminated in the course in creative puppetry which she is currently giving at Los Angeles Valley College. To it she brings a background in art acquired from such teachers as Glen Lukens in ceramics, and Sister Corita of Immaculate Heart of Mary College, whose creative approach to art is well known.

Puppetry is only one of Betsy Brown's activities, for she is a liturgical sculptor and has done many decorations for churches. A recent one is the 6 x 24-foot mosaic she designed for the front of the new auditorium of the Carmelite Sisters of Santa Teresita Hospital. The Sisters spent all their recreation time for months glueing the thousands of pieces into place.

Ralph Chessé

From 1928, when his first show, *Hamlet*, was produced, until 1940, when he went into war training, Ralph Chessé was active in the puppet theatre. In 1949, he resumed puppet work with *Oliver Twist*, produced under the San Francisco Adult Education Program. The next year he began teaching puppetry at San Francisco State College, and continued for three years. He produced television commercials, and in 1950 began his first marionette series. Chessé has also performed with the San Francisco Symphony, acted in plays and films, and lately has returned to painting. His trip to Europe in 1958 gave him a chance to see many European puppet theatres.

Nancy Cole

With a degree in drama from Carnegie Institute of Technology and a Master's degree from Stanford University, Nancy Cole brought sound theatrical knowledge to the puppet theatre. Her interest in the French character, Guignol, hero of the Lyon puppet theatre and the subject of her graduate studies, led to her show, *Salut Guignol.* It also took her to France for firsthand observations, and there she attended the UNIMA Congress and meeting of French puppeteers in 1959. Guignol, Kasperle and Commedia Piccola were international "festival" shows which she presented in her Theatre of the Little Hand for three seasons at the Commercial Museum, Trade and Convention Center in Philadelphia. Featured were popular folk puppet heroes and plays. She has given in-store performances for department stores in New York and other cities from New Orleans to Minneapolis. Commercial television advertising is also a speciality, and she has appeared on the *Today Show, Captain Kangaroo* and many others. Nancy Cole keeps about seven shows in repertory, with one built and one retired annually. Among her titles are: *The Magic Box, Punch and Judy, Puss in Boots, The Mouse Next Door* and *The Juggler of Notre Dame.* They have been seen in such places as the Christmas 1962 season at the Phoenix Theatre, the summer repertory in Sterling Forest Gardens Park, the Museum of the City of New York, the Detroit Institute of Arts, and in Washington, D.C., under the auspices of the French Expositions in the U.S. and the French Embassy. At present she is teaching puppetry in the Educational Theatre program of the Graduate School of Education at New York University, as well as performing.

Sue Hastings

A long career in puppetry, begun in 1924, has extended into the sixties. Sue Hastings retired and moved to Miami in 1945, but for some years her touring company continued under the direction of Lynn Roberts. As many as eight troupes performed during busy seasons, with an active cast of 600 marionettes and 1,000 more in reserve. There were also many commercial shows, live and on television, as well as films. Soon after she moved to Florida, she began teaching at the University of Miami and continued until 1957. She has also given shows on television and for recreation at Miami Beach. For the *Jackie Gleason Show* she made all the figures and costumes for a puppet cast, for which Gamma Ward did portrait heads. In 1967 she claimed she had *really* retired.

William Herrschaft

Early in the thirties William Herrschaft opened his Marionette Workshop in Hartford, Connecticut, where he experimented with tiny puppets as well as twelve-foot "mobile figures" operated by rods from below. In the mid-1930's he became interested in light and built a color organ with which he gave performances in Color Music until 1960. He also used projected scenic effects on his puppet stage. Now, having retired to Miami, he is expanding his puppet work and has plans to experiment in shadow-puppetry. His wife Elena assists with the productions, which have been used for both entertainment and promotion.

Otto and Caroline Kunze

Ever since Otto Kunze came to the United States from Germany in 1932 and married Caroline Sutherland shortly thereafter, the Kunzes have been presenting marionette and hand-puppet shows in the New York City area. Some of their early productions are still being given, and many commercial shows have been built. In 1951 Kunze worked with Bil Baird on *The Complete Manual for Making Marionettes* which was published by *Woman's Day*. Thousands of copies were sold and it inspired many a puppeteer. At their studio, a life-time collection of puppets, books and theatre memorabilia share the spacious rooms, with a rehearsal stage and all the puppets and settings which the Kunzes have built.

David Lano

The story of the Lano family in America has already been told (Pp. 201–220). David, of the third generation, retired from show business in 1952, but set down his memoirs in *A Wandering Showman, I*. His death ended a unique chapter in puppet history.

George Latshaw

With a background in theatre firmly established by his training in the Drama Department of Yale University, George Latshaw regards puppetry as a theatre art, which is subject to the same disciplines as the theatre of human actors. Attracted by the medieval idea of the guilds and training through apprenticeship, he set about learning the profession of puppetry by working with a number of professionals, including Cedric and Mabel Head, Helen Haiman Joseph, Martin and Olga Stevens, Alfred Wallace, Burr Tillstrom and Walton and O'Rourke. Each gave him insights which proved valuable when he launched his own company early in the fifties. His work has been marked by creativity in puppet design, innovations in staging and originality in his dramatic material.

The Latshaw traveling shows are: *The Wizard in the Well* (1952); *The Runaway Rocket* (1953); *Rumpelstiltskin* (1956); *Wilbur and the Giant* (1957); *Hand in Glove,* for adults (1958); *The Pied Piper of Hamelin* (1959); *Shipwreck at Swordfish Bay* (1962); *Show and Tell* (1964); and *The Emperor's New Clothes* (1966).

He has done many special puppet projects. In 1955, he designed and directed de Falla's opera *Master Peter's Puppet Show,* a joint undertaking of the Cleveland Music School and the Junior League. Three performances were given at the Cleveland Music Hall, March 7, 8, and 9. The twelve Sicilian-type rod-puppets about four feet high were made of light weight Celastic, paper and cardboard. Live singers played Don Quixote, the Boy and Master Peter. Several commissions were given Latshaw by the Department of Theatre Arts at the Detroit Institute of Arts. In 1956, he directed the prize-winning puppet play, *The Bear That Played the Bijou.* He built four shows as visual interpretations of musical works played by the Detroit Symphony for its Young People's Concerts. Another project, the annual children's pilgrimage to Trinity Cathedral, is described in Chapter I. In the fall of 1966 he spent two months at the University of Oklahoma, where he produced *Agamemnon.* For this he built nine-foot puppets for the principal characters and combined them with masked actors for the Chorus. He also gave a lavish production of *Carnival,* for which he made the puppets, trained the actors who manipulated them, and played the contrasting roles of Marguerite and Horrible Henry. While working at the University of New Hampshire, he staged two Kafka stories and a mime, *Adam and Eve,* done with hands, apple and serpent.

Latshaw taught puppetry at the Cain Park Youtheatre for six weeks each summer from 1954 to 1960. In addition to giving puppet classes and a performance each season, he also directed young people in a number of plays. As director of the junior school division one year, he introduced new approaches to class programming in dance, puppetry and foreign cultures. For three summers he had a puppet class at Pennsylvania State University and he has conducted puppet workshops at Towson State College, Texas Western College, and Texas Women's University. In 1966 he taught a children's class in puppetry at the Idyllwild School of Music and the Arts in California.

Television programs have been interspersed with Latshaw's other activities. He had a weekly ten-minute spot on *The Merry Go Round* over WXEL, Cleveland, from 1952 to 1955. In 1959 he produced and did puppet host spots for a thirteen-week series of half-hour shows over WJW-TV, Cleveland, in which various activities in the creative arts at Cain Park were featured. While teaching at Pennsylvania State University in the summer of 1962, he showed puppet sequences on the thirteen-week *Key to the Cupboard* series. A special production of *Quillow and the Giant* for NBC's Children's Theatre was done with Latshaw puppets in 1963, and *The Bird Who Came in From the Cold* was a half-hour color special for Christmas on WJW-TV, for which he wrote the script and performed, assisted by Pat Latshaw and Ernest Mauer. With the same assistants he presented *The Convertible Crocodile,* which was one of a seven-part series on the arts called *Inner Feelings, Outer Forms,* aired by CBS. His script for this show brought him membership in the Writers Guild of America.

He has done some department store presentations: pre-Christmas window shows for the J. L. Hudson Company, Detroit, for several years, and in 1967 for Higbee's in Cleveland. For the latter he used only four animal characters and with them created a show which reached a cross-section of the city's population and involved people in the audience through personal exchange. If a mother brought her children back a second or third time, she would be personally greeted by the puppets, much to her delight, for Latshaw believes that people need to be touched as individuals, and puppets can do this supremely well. The animals became real characters whose personalities he had a chance to develop fully because there were no distractions of elaborate scenery or multitudes of puppets. In such situations the power of the actor behind the puppet becomes evident.

Latshaw keeps in touch with the world of human theatre through his job as Children's Theatre Consultant for the Association of the Junior Leagues of America. For the Association he wrote the *AJLA Children's Theatre Manual* as a guide for groups engaged in this community activity. He is also trying to bring the areas of Children's Theatre and Puppetry closer together, and as one step he wrote a chapter on puppets for *Children's Theatre and Creative Dramatics in the United States.* His version of *Pinocchio,* with human actors and two puppets, written and performed at the Cain Park Youtheatre, has also been published. Other productions written by Latshaw for human actors at Cain Park were *The Prince with the Elephant Spell,* later produced with puppets at the Detroit Institute of Arts; *The Pied Piper of Hamelin,* also done with puppets, and *Noah and the Floating Zoo.*

Latshaw's participation in projects in foreign countries includes the educational work in Puerto Rico described above, and a performance at the 1963 International Puppet Festival at Colwyn Bay, Wales. A second appearance there took place in May 1968.

Daniel Llords

Puppets sometimes instill an unquenchable enthusiasm in people. So it is with Daniel Llords. He has been in some form of theatre or music ever since his professional debut at the age of seven playing the Mozart D Minor Concerto with the Los Angeles Philharmonic Orchestra under Otto Klemperer. He has also been an actor and singer in films, has a degree in theatre arts. His studies abroad, and teaching at university level gave him experience which he brought to the puppet theatre. Now a resident of Los Angeles, he had a permanent playhouse on Cannery Row in Monterey, California, from 1959 through 1962, where he played puppet programs to adult audiences.

A long list of symphonic works, beginning with Stravinsky's *Firebird Suite* in 1958, are a part of his repertoire of interpretations with puppets which he has performed with orchestras throughout Canada and the United States. Dr. Roger Peter Dennis wrote *Concerto for Puppets and Orchestra* in 1961 under commission from Llords. It was first performed by the Victoria Symphony Orchestra, British Columbia.

In 1962 he began a world tour which lasted twenty-two months, and in 1965 he again circled the globe, returning in June 1966. To date, he has played in forty countries, and more will be added during his 1968–1969 tour. He has performed at three International Puppet Festivals: Braunschweig, the German Federal Republic, in March 1963; at Colwyn Bay, Wales, in May of the same year, and in Munich, June 1966. During his travels abroad, he has participated in exhibits, given seminars at universities, and been an ambassador of good will for his country. His international activities include extensive correspondence with puppeteers throughout the world, a task performed by his personal manager Jones, who accompanies him on all his tours.

His program is known as Llords "International," a Concert theatre for Adults. It is a technical *tour de force* of staging, manipulation and music, with the performer visible. He built all the puppets and the ingenious stage, and executes all the staging, lighting and effects. His performance begins with the national anthem of the country in which he is playing, with a spotlight on the appropriate flag among the Flags of the Nations which decorate the stage. A great variety of musical interpretations, dances and dramatic scenes representing many different countries may appear on the program, some serious, some humorous, some glamorous. There may be *Capriccio Espagnole,* a Spanish village scene with a religious procession at dawn to a fiesta at night, done to Rimsky-Korsakov's music. Or a *Fantasy on Faust* may portray the highlights of the story, mimed to Gounod's music. There may be short numbers, such as *Minuet at Versailles, Lotus Land, Changing of the Guard at Buckingham Palace,* Hawaiian hula dancers whose performance ends with a volcanic eruption, waltzers who dance around a fountain spouting real water or a "ballet buffa" performed to the Overture of Offenbach's *Orpheus in the Underworld.*

Although Llords manages to speak some lines in the native tongue wherever he performs, such a program is independent of language. Thus it is enjoyable for audiences in countries around the world, as was the program of Walter Deaves, that enterprising American puppet showman who played in far corners of the world during his global travels between 1908 and 1914.

Jero Magon

From his first production in 1931, which used a sliding wagon stage for scene changes, Jero Magon has been especially interested in problems of puppet staging and lighting. After many years of teaching in New York City, he retired to Miami. He was inactive in puppetry for ten years, then became reinspired by the Puppeteers of America Festival in Miami in 1964. Since then he has organized the Puppet Guild of Greater Miami, given lecture-demonstrations for both children and adults, and appeared on television programs. He and William Herrschaft give many performances of their joint variety show. A film, *Shadowland,* was produced under Magon's direction by Brandon Films.

Lewis Mahlmann

Although Lewis Mahlmann has been active in puppetry since 1952, it was not his exclusive occupation, for he is also a real estate man in San Francisco. Recently, however, the puppets have taken precedence, as engagements for his shows have increased. In addition, he has the full-time job of director of the puppet theatre at Children's Fairyland in Oakland. All forms of theatre interest Mahlmann. He has studied piano, singing, acting, dancing and creative playwriting. For the Opera Ring, a musical house in the round, he sang and danced leading roles, and appeared in *The Threepenny Opera* and *The Golden Apple.* It is not surprising, therefore, that his puppet work has great variety. Especially notable have been performances of musical works, such as Gian-Carlo Menotti's *The Unicorn, Gorgon and Manticore,* the Ravel-Colette *L'Enfant et les*

Sortilèges and Stravinsky's *L'Histoire du Soldat*. An experimental ballet-pantomime, *Le Boeuf sur le Toit* by Darius Milhaud, was performed with hand-and-rod puppets in 1965. His 1967–1968 production was Gilbert and Sullivan's *Patience*. Music also forms an integral part of most of his plays, including *The Stone Flower* from the story by Timothy Thompson, *The Emperor's Nightingale* of Von Henze-Andersen, and *Bluebeard*, with music by Bela Bartok, all of which have special appeal for adults.

Mahlmann approaches puppetry with an experimental attitude, trying many kinds of "theatre with puppets." He has used all types of puppets, with various methods of staging, sometimes with human actors, at others with the "black theatre" technique, and even with moving scenery as part of the show. A group of talented designers, composers, writers, actors, singers and manipulators in the Bay Area assist in his productions.

He has presented many shows for children, appeared with variety at national parks, taught puppet classes at the YWCA and city parks, and performed at the Third International Festival of Puppet Theatres in Bucharest in 1965. When Macy's of San Francisco organized an exhibit of 150 puppets from the Munich Museum in 1966, Mahlmann acted as curator, and presented fifteen-minute shows to illustrate the history of puppetry.

Frank Paris

During his forty years' experience as a puppeteer, Frank Paris has produced shows for many purposes. He is known especially as an exponent of the variety genre, which he has developed to a high degree of technical perfection. He has played in night clubs across the country, in Cuba, Rio de Janeiro, and aboard ship on Caribbean cruises. In New York City, he has had many engagements at Radio City Music Hall; he has played at Madison Square Garden to an audience of 27,000 and appeared many times at the Strand, Roxy, Palace, Paramount and Loew's State theatres.

He has had his own shows on television, and appeared frequently as guest on those of others, including Perry Como, Jackie Gleason, Laraine Day, Milton Berle, Don Ameche. Of late years puppeteers have performed with symphony orchestras in increasing numbers; Paris has done so often, having worked with the Rochester, Connecticut, and New Haven orchestras, as well as numerous performances with New York's Little Orchestra Society. In advertising, he has prepared commercials for more than thirty sponsors of such diverse products as International Business Machines, Smirnoff Vodka, Crazy Foam, Jumping Jack Shoes and Ronzoni Macaroni. Promotional shows have also been done for such institutions as the Willowbrook State Hospital for the Mentally Retarded, the Pestalozzi Foundation of America and the Veterans' Hospitals.

During the past decade Paris has been active in educational work: he taught a puppet class at New York University for three years and is now in his fifth year at Columbia University Teachers College. Herb Scheffel, in a *Puppetry Journal* article (March–April 1958), "Paris Label," described one of the end-of-semester shows given by Paris' students at New York University. It was a Mardi Gras hand-puppet revue in which originality, fresh ideas and new materials were displayed by these students who were not afraid to experiment. Several numbers, Scheffel felt, could be of professional caliber with further rehearsal. Lydia Ressner used a Dorothy Parker monologue and worked it around two ridiculous caricatures on a dance floor; a spoof of *Rapunzel* was given by Mary Duane Hoffman; Leatrice Lawrence's Signor Stromboli, mentalist, came alive through her voice projection and manipulation, and Alice May Hall had a miniature Arabian Nights extravaganza. Over the whole performance the "extravagant theatrical craftsmanship and design" of the "Paris label" was apparent. This may also be said of each of his class presentations.

With his large collection of masks and puppets, Paris gives numerous lectures on puppetry in its historical and modern aspects for museums and many organizations. He has also lent material for a dozen or so exhibits in museums and community centers.

Within the framework of recent government-sponsored programs, Paris and Ted Lewis worked for Head Start, and also trained a group of teenagers to build and perform a traveling puppet show for the Clark Center for the Performing Arts, in the summer of 1965.

In 1956, Paris bought an early nineteenth-century house at 12 Gay Street in New York, complete with a ghost which is described in Hans Holzer's *Yankee Ghosts*. With his partner, Ted Lewis, he has converted the ample quarters into puppet workshops where he holds classes, living quarters which also house a collection of antiques, and a small theatre in the basement. Not the least of the pleasant activities in this house are the lavish parties which take place there during holiday seasons.

Bernard and Edith Paul

From Bernard and Edith Paul's well-equipped studio in Linthicum Heights, Maryland, have come a long series of puppet plays, advertising and display puppets, and television programs, for they have been in the puppet business for over three decades. Both are graduates of the Maryland Institute of Art, where Paul gave his first puppet show and where he still teaches a class in puppetry. Paul's Puppets have performed in all sorts of places, from the White House to a backwoods church and the Peabody Conservatory of Music. Edith adapts stories from the classics and writes original scripts and also attends to the costuming of the puppets, while Bernard does the construction. Both are interested in research, and each production is preceded by careful studies of people and how they live, for they try to convey a sense of realism in all their shows. Among the first to use puppets extensively in advertising, they divide their work about evenly between puppetry for commercial purposes and for entertainment. They also have contributed to Head Start and Rural Art Enrichment Programs in the schools, and given many performances for retarded and handicapped children.

Romain and Ellen Proctor

Long before 1948 the Proctor Puppets were an established part of the American puppet scene, touring extensively season after season. Their repertoire included variety, circus acts and favorite children's classics: *Sleeping Beauty, Hansel and Gretel, Little Red Riding Hood, The Three Pigs, Jack and the Beanstalk, Rumpelstiltskin, The Three Bears, The Three Wishes*, and *The Spinning Fairies*. A regular part of their work was a Christmas show at the Scruggs-Vandervoort-Barney department store in St. Louis. After Romain died in 1961, Ellen continued for three years, and this rounded out twenty-five years of appearances there. For the Pre-School Opening at Ayres' in Indianapolis, the Proctor Puppets gave annual performances for seven years.

Romain Proctor's contribution to the promotion of interest in UNIMA is mentioned in Chapter VI, and he was also a devoted supporter of the Puppeteers of America. His collection of puppets, books and everything pertaining to the puppet theatre was quite extensive.

Ellen Proctor has been on the Cultural Enrichment Program, government sponsored, in the inner-city schools of Detroit the past two seasons. She has presented a puppet show at the Children's Christmas Carnival for the City of Detroit, and she also has a lecture-demonstration for clubs, colleges and conventions. Currently working in the Department of Theatre Arts at the Detroit Institute of Arts, she assists with puppet presentations and the McPharlin Memorial Collection.

Josie Robbins

Some careers in puppetry have been built upon teaching, writing, and the persistent promotion of puppets over a long period of time. Such has been the work of Josie Robbins of Seattle. She has written a number of little books on simple puppets and puppetry to help her in her work as leader of the Girl Scouts, Cub Scouts and Y-Teens, as entertainer in hospitals, as a Vice President of the National Story League, and as a teacher for ten years at the Cornish School. With puppets of all types she has produced numerous short shows, based on well-known children's stories, which have been widely used for entertainment and to stimulate interest in puppetry. During the past two decades, she has collected many puppets and books, which have been put to good use in her work and that of others. The Robbins crusade for puppetry, speech, and drama has been conducted on television; with talks, demonstrations and workshops for children and teachers; with the local puppet guild, and the colleges and universities in the area. In 1966 she organized a large exhibition of puppets, many from her own collection, which was on view for three months at the Museum of History and Industry, where she gave demonstrations every Saturday.

Rufus and Margo Rose

From 1931, when Rufus and Margo Rose formed the Rufus Rose Marionettes, they regularly toured the whole United States until 1961 when fire destroyed 250 marionettes and part of their studio-theatre at Waterford, Connecticut. Since then, *Pinocchio, Rip Van Winkle, Treasure Island, Snow White* and a group of variety numbers have been rebuilt and are in the regular Rose repertoire. In recent years, the company has done much work in film and television.

The three Rose sons, who grew up surrounded by puppets, have been interested in them at various times. When the family theatre at Waterford was opened in 1943, James, the oldest son, then eleven years old, worked as a puppeteer in *Pinocchio* and *Rip Van Winkle.* In 1947 he built *Princess Morning,* a hand-puppet show which he performed in his home area and at puppet festivals in Detroit and Oxford. He continued to work in the company until he went off to college, where he gave some performances and made a few television appearances. He majored in theatre, then received his M.A. from Yale, taught a couple of years at the University of North Carolina, and is now head of the theatre department at Antioch College.

Rufus, Jr. (Bunnie) also helped with the family shows from about 1944. Both he and Jim helped on the television special, Dickens' *A Christmas Carol,* which ABC telecast on Christmas Eve, 1948. Bunnie had the famous line, "God bless us every one." For some years he worked with the puppets, then other interests developed. Now he is a Lieutenant Commander in the Navy.

Christopher went along on tour as a small child and helped a little backstage or sat in the audience and told everybody what was coming next. In 1963, when the Roses revived their shows, Christopher helped and became an excellent puppeteer. He went out with a one-man show for Martin Stevens' School Assembly tour in the fall of 1965. The following July he joined the Army, where he had training in photography, which is now his prime interest.

Don Sahlin

It is quite possible for a puppeteer to have a career in puppetry by working for other puppeteers. Prior to 1948 Don Sahlin produced a number of shows and in that year toured with the Stevens' School Assembly Show and worked with Stevens on five films. In 1949 he was with Bob Baker in Hollywood. In 1950, he not only produced his own *St. George and the Dragon*, but also helped Remo Bufano in New York and Burr Tillstrom in Chicago. Service in the Army took up a couple of years and then he worked as an animator in Michael Myerberg's film, *Hansel and Gretel*, and assisted Stevens with more films. In 1955 he worked with Tillstrom on the television spectacular *Alice in Wonderland,* and two years later was again with Bob Baker. Then came George Pal's *Tom Thumb*, for which he was an animator, and this work continued in 1959 with Pal's *Time Machine.* Again in New York, Sahlin helped Tillstrom in his Broadway show *Kukla, Burr and Ollie* in 1960, and continued to make new characters for the Kuklapolitan Players and to assist with television commercials until 1963. He also spent some time in 1962 working with Pal on his Cinerama production of *The Wonderful World of the Brothers Grimm.* Since 1963 Sahlin has been with Jim Henson as prop maker and chief puppeteer for the Muppets. He created the famous hound-dog puppet, Rowlf. An extra job in 1965 was the building of a 25-foot marionette Knight-Giant, assisted by Kermit Love, for George Balanchine's ballet *Don Quixote.*

Now he is interested in the kite and model rocket business, and has aspirations for "revolutionizing the kite industry."

Marjorie Shanafelt

For Marjorie Shanafelt, puppets have been a creative avocation. She first used them in 1931 to attract people to the Museum of the University of Nebraska, where she was a staff member. Later, she played throughout Nebraska, as well as at puppet festivals. In 1949 she visited Copenhagen, where she performed in the Tivoli Gardens. After a memorable appearance at the Palace, a leading night club, she was urged to tour the country but she refused, because she felt puppets would not be fun if they demanded three or four shows a day. She has taught puppetry on television and had classes through the extension department of the University of Nebraska, for which she wrote and published numerous booklets on technique. All these years she collected puppets, which were displayed in her home—a veritable museum. There, too, she gave informal performances to small groups and continued her studies of the history of puppetry. Although frail health made a move to Oregon necessary, she was able to attend the puppet festival in San Diego in 1966, her lively interest in puppets and puppeteers undiminished.

Blanding Sloan

Back in the yeasty days of the Puppet Revival, Blanding Sloan was associated with some exciting events. From about 1928 to 1931, his Puppet Theatre in San Francisco was the scene of such productions as *Emperor Jones* and *Hamlet*, with Ralph Chessé, and the famous Erskine Scott Wood *Heavenly Discourse*. For the puppet festival in 1957, he and Chessé revived *Emperor Jones*.

The puppet theatre was only part of his artistic activities, the extent of which was shown in an exhibition of fifty years of his art (1909–1959) held in Altadena, California, in November and December 1959, where his paintings, prints, monotypes, drawing, illustrations, sculptures, and his puppets and stage designs were on display. He has also been a teacher: at the Chicago Academy of Art, in private schools, at the University of California at Carmel, and in his own studio. Another interest is the research foundation, Origins of Art.

In the late forties he formed the East-West Film Company for making sixteen millimeter animations in color and sound. He has not done much with puppets in recent years, but from 1953 to 1959 he made all the sets and props for a series of plays for Viewmaster Stereos, which were done with still puppets made by his associates Warren Cheney, Wah Chang, and Martha Armstrong. Sometimes he writes about puppets. "My First Puppet Production," published in the *Puppetry Journal* (March–April 1966), is a hilarious account of a misadventure with a broken glass tank and a bucket of goldfish—long ago in 1924.

Burr Tillstrom

The persuasive ways of Burr Tillstrom's Kukla became evident during the World War II years when he was a master salesman for U.S. Savings Bonds. It is said that he would order the Michigan Avenue bridge to open to provide a captive audience for his sales campaign conducted from his booth outside Chicago's Wrigley Building. When, in 1947, Burr Tillstrom agreed to do a daily one-hour show for NBC's WBKB, Kukla began his rise to television stardom. This character, with the winsomeness of a small boy and the wisdom of a sage, appeared for ten years with the Kuklapolitans, a group of friends, each of whom represents a facet of human nature. Ollie the Dragon, Madame Ooglepuss, Colonel Crackie, Cecil Bill, Beulah Witch, Mrs. Olivia Dragon (Ollie's mother), Dolores Dragon, Mercedes, Paul Pookenschlagl, Mrs. Buff-orpington, Hubert, and Fletcher Rabbit—all of these are projections of Tillstrom's knowledge of people and understanding of their relationships.

The format of *Kukla, Fran and Ollie* was set at the very beginning, when Fran Allison agreed to be in the show. She would stand outside the little booth, exchange repartee with the characters and sing with them. The program was entirely improvised, with only the general idea agreed upon beforehand. The musical numbers were provided by Jack Fascinato for the first seven years, and then by Carolyn Gilbert for one season and Caesar Giovanni for two. At first a local program, it was the first to be sent from West to East when network telecasting began in 1949. In 1954, the show moved to ABC and continued until 1957. During these ten years, *Kukla, Fran and Ollie* had a wide audience appeal. Little children watched it and sent presents to Kukla and his friends; adults watched it and adjusted their social and domestic activities so that nothing would interfere with their viewing. This was a show of social commentary built upon daily happenings, presented with a basic philosophy which demonstrated the amicable resolution of difficulties. Under it all lay the idea that each person has his own "villain" within himself. Thus, no one character represented the villain in the usual sense. Numerous awards to *Kukla, Fran and Ollie* paid tribute to its excellence.

The last performance of the Kuklapolitans was noted with sadness in many newspapers and periodicals. The description by *The New York Times* ended thus, "Fran smiled, Kukla waved his little hand and Ollie his magnificent tooth. It won't be like television anymore without them."

Of course it was not the end, for they have made many appearances since. Perry Como and Jack Paar have been frequent hosts to the Kuklapolitans, they have been on the *Today Show* and with Merv Griffin and Mike Douglas. Kukla has kept his hand in with countless commercials. There have been various teaching projects, and some involvement in politics when the Kuklapolitans gave their views of the 1956 nominating conventions in Chicago and San Francisco.

The Kuklapolitans also appeared in some special programs. In 1953, Arthur Fiedler, conductor of the Boston Pops Orchestra, commissioned and presented *St. George and the Dragon,* an opera by Jack Fascinato. Tillstrom and Fran Allison (who played the part of the Princess) managed to sing all the parts, Kukla overcame the Dragon by stuffing a dish mop into his mouth, and St. George demanded only that everybody be baptised in the Christian faith as reward for subduing the Dragon. Town Hall was the scene of a concert given by Oliver J. Dragon on Thanksgiving Day, 1953. With the assistance of Kukla, Fran and all the others, he presented native songs, ballads and spoofs. *St. George* was also performed. At Christmas time, 1954, ABC-TV aired Tillstrom's production of James Thurber's *Many Moons,* using a two-level set on which the puppets performed the fantasy with their own distinctive humor and satire. In the fall of 1955, the Hallmark Hall of Fame opened its television season with *Alice in Wonderland.* Maurice Evans was producer and host, Eva LeGallienne and Elsa Lanchester played the White and Red Queens respectively, Gillian Barber was Alice and Reginald Gardiner was the White Knight. Burr Tillstrom played the Cheshire Cat and Mock Turtle. He also operated the Oysters as finger-puppets, a technique he had used many years ago.

Inevitably, he went on to New York. *An Evening with Kukla, Fran and Ollie* was a live production which played in Princeton, Washington and New York City in 1957. For a brief time he gave performances in the Emerald Room at the Astor Hotel, which brought critical acclaim. A new development in recent years was the hand pantomime. In 1951, when Tillstrom was in Paris, he saw a performance in which four puppeteers with their hands alone created powerful dramatic effects, and he was much impressed. Sometimes in the television studio he would practice bits of business for *Kukla, Fran and Ollie* without the puppets and ask the production crew to guess which character was acting, but he did not use this technique seriously until he joined the weekly satirical show, *That Was the Week That Was.* The hand pantomimes which he developed for it include one on old age, *Power,* and *The Berlin Wall.* The latter won him both an Emmy and a Peabody Award.

In the fall of 1966 he returned to Chicago and was associated for a time with Field Communications, which had a new UHF television station and where, with Kukla and Ollie, he commented on current events. A 1967–1968 CBS program, the *Children's Film Festival,* had Kukla, Fran and Ollie as hosts, and for NBC the Kuklapolitans gave their version of *The Reluctant Dragon* on the 1968 Children's Theatre Series.

Tony Urbano

In 1949, when he was thirteen, Tony Urbano worked in Ralph Chessé's production of *Oliver Twist.* He then built his own shows and gave them for the Armed Forces personnel at camps and hospitals. After graduation from high school he moved to Southern California and worked for the Yale Puppeteers at the Turnabout Theatre, which proved a valuable experience in playwriting and puppet production. He also danced in the Turnabout live show, and went on tour with it. Then, in 1957, he built *Mary Louise* for the puppet festival at UCLA. It had a musical format, with puppets, book, lyrics and music by Urbano. His production assistants were Jack and Elva Aiken.

He worked at the Children's Fairyland Puppet Theatre for four years beginning in 1958, where a variety of plays were produced. These were basically for children, but many parents attended, so the dialogue was clever and sophisticated. Each play, even though based on a familiar story, was done in an original manner, such as *Red Riding Hood* in the style of a Gilbert and Sullivan operetta, and *Mother Goose: or Simple Simon and the Magic Mountain,* a hand-puppet extravaganza, as an English pantomime with a transformation scene from the Baron of Gorn's dank castle to the pink and white palace of the Queen of Hearts. Fairyland was excellent training and Urbano kept the productions from having a feeling of sameness by involving himself in different phases of the work for each one.

He has conducted workshops at the Detroit Institute of Arts; in one of them the marionettes for *The Pink Siamese* were constructed. He has also performed there on the regular Puppet Theatre series, and at puppet festivals. A different sort of production was Ravel's *Ma Mère d'Oye* with the Oakland Symphony Orchestra, and his most recent production was also musical—de Falla's *Master Peter's Puppet Show,* with Marylin Interlandi as the Boy, at the Laguna Beach Festival of Opera in 1967.

From 1961 to 1964, he built marionettes "with the regularity of a factory machine" for Sid and Marty Krofft's *Les Poupées de Paris,* manipulated part of the time, and staged some numbers, including one with colored shadows made of laminated Cinemoid shown on a screen nine feet high and twenty feet long.

Since 1966 he has had his own studio in Santa Monica. His activities have included television appearances, making puppets for other puppeteers, and presenting shows. His versatility accounts for the great variety in his puppet work.

Leo and Dora Velleman

Like most puppeteers, Leo and Dora Velleman have engaged in many puppet activities, and they work in both Canada and the United States. Their first productions were shown at Morgan's Department Store in Montreal, in schools and colleges, and at service clubs. They toured through Quebec and New England, and later in the northern and western parts of the United States. Based in St. Louis and Memphis, they spent five years in this country working on educational television and performing.

Their work has been almost equally divided between live shows and television, and their contributions to puppetry are reflected in the many references to them in this supplement. Original plays or adaptations written by Dora, innovations in stylized puppet design, and new methods of staging mark them as creators in the puppet theatre.

They are interested in education, too, and have undertaken to train young puppeteers by apprenticing them to their own company so that they may learn all the intricacies of puppet making and presentation, acting, and manipulation. While their workshops and demonstrations acquaint children and adults with some aspects of puppetry, this apprentice system brings the aspiring puppeteer face to face with the realities of puppet production.

The Vellemans now reside in Toronto.

Lea and Gia Wallace

The Wallace sisters are known throughout the New York City area both for their collaborative and their individual work as puppeteers.

Lea has an art and dance background, having studied at the New York School of Industrial Arts, with Martha Graham and other modern dancers. She performed with the Humphrey-Weidman and Helen Tamiris Concert Groups, and has studied ballet, jazz, and ethnic dance. With a degree from Brooklyn College, an M.A. from Hunter in speech and theatre education, she still takes courses in theatre whenever she has time.

Puppetry was first a hobby, then a profession. Before 1947, she had much experience in adult revues performed across the country in leading night clubs. In that year she returned to the dance and was a member of José Limón's Dance Group, but two years later returned to puppets and opened the Village Dance and Puppet Center with her sister Gia. A new development in her solo puppet act was the invention of the apron stage designed as part of her costume. The apron is easily raised and held in place by a cord around her neck, leaving room to perform two hand-puppets. Many of her numbers are based on the ethnic dances with which she became familiar years before. She has been guest artist on many television programs with her apron stage, and has appeared at the New York Palace.

In 1960 she set up a showcase for puppeteers at the Greenwich Mews Theatre. Here performances by different showmen were presented at a central location so that bookers and agents, as well as the general public, would become aware of available talent. After one season the project had to be abandoned for it proved economically impractical. Always interested in experimental work, Lea saw to it that the Puppet Guild of Greater New York included a committee to explore new ideas in puppet theatre, and offered her studio as a meeting place. She has also produced shows with puppet and human actors combined, as in Edna St. Vincent Millay's *Aria da Capo* and Frederico García Lorca's *El Retablo de Don Cristóbal.* In her teaching she has had many opportunities to approach puppetry with a creative attitude: in the Washington Irving High School's speech department and in such projects as the summer work at Carver House. Lately she has opened classes in her studio, and presents puppetry as a theatre art. She also lectures on this subject as often as possible.

Gia Wallace also has had training in art and dance. Over the years she has gravitated toward projects with underprivileged children and is now working for her Master's degree at New York University in Recreational Therapy with a strong emphasis on puppetry. The Village Dance and Puppet Center continued from 1949 to 1960. It was during many of these summers that the sisters toured abroad for the USO. At this time they had two titles: the Gialea Theatre for their concert work, and the Wallace Sisters for theatres and clubs. They combined puppets and dancer-with-puppet acts based on the circus, Javanese dance and other ideas. They also ran the Wallace Puppet Theatre for children, and played on weekend afternoons for ten years.

Beginning in 1960, the sisters worked individually. Gia gave weekend shows during this season at the Hotel Albert, and at the Jan Hus Theatre in 1961–1962. She presented children's programs of favorite stories, such as *Sleeping Beauty, Cinderella, Puss in Boots,* as well as *Punch and Judy,* which she has also given for schools, parties, organizations, television, the New York Historical Society and the Museum of the City of New York. From 1960 to 1966 she taught puppetry to underprivileged children in many community centers under a program sponsored by the American Guild of Variety Artists and the New York Youth Board. In the summer of 1967 she conducted a puppetry class for emotionally disturbed boys, nine to sixteen years of age, at Children's Village, Dobbs Ferry, New York, which proved very successful. Lea and Gia combined their efforts again in the summer of 1966 to build a mobile puppet theatre with teen-agers, under the Self Help Against Poverty Program, which is described elsewhere.

Rod Young

Persistence and determination, training, hard work, and a certain amount of luck may be necessary to make a career in puppetry, as they were in the case of Rod Young. Involved with puppets from the age of nine, by 1949 he was assisting backstage at Pauline Benton's Red Gate Shadow Puppet Theatre in New York. In the fall of 1950 he went to Atlanta, where he worked with the Gilpin Marionettes on their daily television show. He started his own program in 1952, with a solo mario- nette as co-host with a live actor on *Tea for Two*. Then, in Richmond, Virginia, in 1956 he and the elf, Sassafras, presented "soap opera" style adventures for about six months. However, television was not to be Young's principal activity, although he later appeared from time to time on educational and commercial programs.

Interspersed with his puppet work between 1953 and 1958 were periods of study: at Emory University and the Atlanta Art Institute, at Miami University, at the Richmond Professional Institute of William and Mary College, from which he received his Bachelor of Fine Arts Degree in 1958.

He spent two summers, 1954 and 1955, as director of the Casper (Wy- oming) Children's Theatre. In the fall of 1954 he became instructor in puppetry and director of puppet shows at Westhampton College, at the University of Richmond, where he remained for three years, directing from three to five plays annually, teaching puppetry, and doing free-lance shows for schools, churches, the Hampton Institute Book Bazaar, and dental health. During this period he also worked part-time in the summers for the Richmond Parks and Recreation Department with both puppets and live actors.

In the fall of 1958 he returned to New York and set about earning his living with his one man hand-puppet show called the Rod Young Puppet Theatre, and filling in part-time with the Suzari Marionettes. Summers from 1958 to 1967 he produced a series of adapted and original plays for the County of Westchester Department of Parks and Recreation, a project which is described in Chapter I. For two summers he performed at the Playland Puppet Theatre in Rye Beach, New York, another project men- tioned elsewhere, which added to his experience in the park recreation field.

Although he had an agent, bookings in this area were difficult, and in the autumn of 1960 things looked pretty gloomy. At this point, luck stepped in and he heard about a position in the Marionette Theatre of the City of New York, sponsored by the Department of Parks. He was ap- pointed, and thus began a six-year association, first as chief puppeteer and then, from June through December 1966, as director of the whole project. He was asked to institute a new program, the Creative Puppetry Workshop and Show. During the winter of 1967, the program was developed, tours made to the schools, and it has been in progress ever since. All the while, Young has done other programs at intervals: workshops for children at the Brooklyn Museum, the Museum of the City of New York and Macy's branch stores; Saturday shows for children during one season; and lectures at various colleges. In the spring of 1965 he produced an adult show of *Carmen* at the Amato Opera Theatre. With an assistant and a lighting designer, and using a four-track stereo recording with Maria Callas' voice, he experimented in utilizing a variety of forms, not to present the opera *per se*, but to interpret its meaning through color and movement. At times Carmen was a sequined red cloth, whirling madly; a chorus line of cigarette girls was made from cigarette boxes; shadows were painted on a screen, washed off, and applied again. Over it all was the Rose, fluttering, falling and crushed. "Rather violent and offbeat, but interesting to see," remarked Young.

Avocations in puppetry

Puppetry as a hobby or avocation calls into play so many activities it is likely to be completely involving and may lead no telling where. Of the hundreds of people known to be associated with puppetry in America, a majority are amateurs or part-time practitioners. Some bring to it a high degree of artistic and dramatic talent, others may be content with shows important only for their own satisfaction, while many contribute to the religious, recreational and educational activities of their communities. Quite often people begin puppetry as a sideline, only to find it turning into a full-time profession. Conversely, a person's interest may center on puppets for a time and then shift to another field.

Consider the Williams family of St. Paul, Minnesota. Lem did about 500 shows between 1941 and 1954, mostly to build good will for the Nickel Plate Railroad for which he worked. An ardent festival-goer, his wit created good will there, too. His wife, Mary, with *Punch and Judy* and variety, has given several hundred performances and has taught puppetry to children. Their son Tony fell heir to this interest, and he began performing with a Pinocchio puppet at age five. He demonstrated puppets suitable for Cub Scouts at an Institute of Puppetry at the University of Minnesota, promoted the sale of Christmas Seals in 1953 with television performances, and has given about 100 shows during the past twelve years, sometimes assisting his mother, at others with his own show.

Herb Scheffel was a commercial artist by profession, but he was also a prolific water color painter who had numerous exhibitions throughout the eastern United States. He wrote many articles for the *Puppetry Journal* on various aspects of puppet production, as well as reviews and biographical accounts of puppeteers. He designed puppets for Bill Schuring, director of the Pied Piper Puppeteers of Waldwick, New Jersey. Hand-, rod- and shadow-puppets were used in 1955 on a three-bill program of *The Drum Dance, Triple Talk,* and *The Death of Tintagiles.* He became interested in finger-puppets and built some notable shows, such as *Pas de Voodoo,* with strobe light effects. A still unpublished manuscript on this less practiced form of puppetry had been completed at the time of his death in 1962.

Dorothy Gleason's Puppetown Players of Cincinnati presented variety with hand-puppets from 1936 to 1962. She also had several television series, worked at a summer camp in Connecticut, and perfected a method of making puppets with liquid latex. All this activity has been in addition to her job as housewife. Now her chief interest is lecturing to garden clubs on flower arrangements, including "avant-garde constructions of plant materials . . . also mobiles, stabiles." Her puppets occasionally perform for her fellow garden-club enthusiasts.

People doing office work find puppets a welcome change. Ruth Quinn, University City, Missouri, is an executive secretary, but for twenty years she has given variety for elderly people and underprivileged children, for church groups, clubs and parties. At times she has performed on television, made puppets for sales promotion, given demonstrations for Scout troupes and participated actively in the Puppet Guild of St. Louis. Louise Ewing, of St. Louis, is also a businesswoman who has found time to provide children's entertainment, to work with Sunday school classes, and to lecture on the history of puppetry to adults. Under the name of the Edlo Puppeteers she has worked with Edith Finney and Genevieve Albers.

What should be done when the television gives out, the children get bored, and the repair bill is too high for the budget? Don Avery found one answer. Take the children to the library and get a book on puppets. In this way he began the fulfillment of an idea he had in high school. The Avery family of Don, Ella and three children have found puppets a rewarding avocation ever since their first show was built in 1959. The play was based on a hymn and given in their church in Dearborn, Michigan. Other performances in other churches followed, more plays were staged, and in 1965 they were invited to Buffalo to play for a large religious youth meeting. They now live in St. Louis, where they continue to be "happy puppeteers."

Joe and Mary Owens, of Scotia, New York, have been enthusiastic amateur puppeteers for many years. Until recently, they made a point of attending puppet festivals where they often performed their variety, a favorite number being their cigarette smoking, singing cowboy.

Archie Elliott, of Cleveland claims to be the only puppeteer who is a non-puppeteer. He has made an avocation of promoting the Puppeteers of America: as Festival Chairman, as President, as Business Advisor. He has also done some production, such as the vaudeville show, with puppets by Shirley O'Donnol, which was specially prepared for the 1965 Puppet Festival. "Love of puppets and the people who create them" is his abiding interest.

Henry Weber was a showman who entertained with music, ventriloquism, magic and *Punch and Judy* for forty years. By 1948 he had become inactive, but his interest never waned, and with his wife Florence, he regularly attended both the national puppet festivals and the meetings of the Detroit Puppeteers Guild. During these years his eyesight failed, yet even when it was gone he liked to be with puppeteers and seldom missed a chance to be where they were in action. Until his death in 1967, interest in everything connected with puppetry was an avocation, and for Florence it continues to be.

One day Mrs. Jack Davis and her three children heard about a puppet show at a nearby camp. They went, came home and began making puppets. They kept happily busy all summer, and for Mrs. Davis puppets became an avocation which she has put to good use, giving shows and workshops for a variety of organizations in Winter Park, Florida.

The delicate hand skills of the dentist may be turned to the equally precise work of the magician and the puppeteer. Macy H. Goode was a member of the International Brotherhood of Magicians, and he developed a puppet demonstration which he presented to various Rings. Along with his work as a dentist, he taught puppetry to children at the Long Branch (New Jersey) Community Center, and was interested in cartooning. These varied activities were ended by his death in 1965.

ABC Television in Chicago had a show, *The Little Revue*, for which William Weber staged two or three puppet numbers each week during 1949 and 1950. He also had a variety show which he played in the area until 1952. Then he went off to college and the puppets were packed away. They remained packed during his Navy duty from 1955 to 1958. He works at the Chase Manhattan Bank in New York, which sent him to Paris and the Virgin Islands for a time. The puppets went along and performed at intervals. Will he "activate the troupe" again? Perhaps.

Gary Wilmott became interested in puppets as a teen-ager and built a number of shows which have been presented for his own pleasure and that of others at schools, churches, community organizations and libraries. He also taught puppetry from 1949 to 1950 at the Children's Center for the Creative Arts at Adelphi University. The students made the puppets first and developed plays from them, with the avowed purpose of producing something worthy of their attention in terms of good puppetry. Now a busy educator, he has little time for puppets but maintains a display case for them in his office.

Puppetry is an absorbing avocation for Lanelle and Edgar Rice, of Wellesley, Massachusetts, both of whom work full-time at other jobs. For twenty-five years they have been interested in puppetry, but in 1959 they began to work intensively when they made and manipulated marionettes for productions of *The Mikado, The Adventures of Alice* and *Robin Hood,* for which the Wellesley Community Chorus provided the dialogue and music. With these performances their puppet technique improved so much that they began making marionettes for other puppeteers in the United States and Canada. With a good stock of puppets on hand, they planned a demonstration called *The Puppetry Sampler,* using different kinds of puppets, with short scenes to show them in action. Now they are at work on a demonstration of shadow-puppets, which range from black and white ones to the colored figures of Asia, modern ones of plastic, and even three-dimensional objects. Except for a Christmas show for children, the Rices concentrate on adult shows, which are given for women's clubs, family groups, such as church couples' clubs and Winterfest, Boston's Festival of the Arts.

Probably Robert and Diane Mueller, of Roosevelt, New Jersey, would consider their Peacock Puppet Theatre more a supplementary source of income than an avocation. He is an artist, an engineer and a writer who regards the puppet theatre as a serious art form. In his latest of four nonfiction books, *The Science of Art: The Cybernetics of Creative Communication,* he examines the interaction between science and art to illuminate the idea of art as communication. In one chapter, "Vivifying with Words," he discusses the interrelationships between language and literature, television, movies, and the theatre, of which dance and puppetry are a part. The Muellers have tried many approaches to puppetry, including a stint as itinerant puppeteers with no bookings. Now they play periodically for a set fee, or gratis for various poverty programs. *St. George and the Dragon, Rumpelstiltskin, The Dragon School* and *The Magic Harp* have been arranged with music and dance sequences, which come naturally since she plays piano and has had dance training, while he plays the flute.

Some retired people have both time and energy which they put to good use. Emilie Jaeger, a former grade school teacher, whose present role as grandmother keeps her lively, does all sorts of things with puppets. Several years ago she developed a method of making puppets from socks, which turned out to be comic characters because of their large movable mouths. Not long ago she was asked by the Phoenix Junior League to do a workshop for the Arizona Foundation for Blind Children. The children made simple puppets with styrofoam balls into which they stuck golf tees for eyes and glued on squares of cloth for costumes. They experienced the feel of the puppet on the hand, and in a week good movement was achieved, with conversation and song. Mrs. Jaeger further developed this method into the Quickie Puppet, with costumes glued instead of sewed. (She has published a booklet to describe it.) Since then, she has given countless workshops, made puppets for her daughter to use in Sunday school classes, and presented plays at the local library. Before moving to Phoenix she was active in the Detroit Puppeteers Guild and worked in David Gibson's group, which created paper sculpture figures for several shows. Now she works with the Phoenix Guild and helps with the annual Art Festival. When Jo Lawrence presented *Arizona's First Christmas* on television, Mrs. Jaeger helped her and they later used the same marionettes for *Barn Dance at Bumble Bee*, shown at the Chris Town Shopping Center. In October 1967, she and several other delegates attended the National Federation of Grandmothers Clubs in Miami Beach. They appeared at the reception wearing long sleeved green dresses and tall hats crowned with white flowers to represent the Saguaro cactus, Arizona's state flower—designed by Mrs. Jaeger, of course.

When a man is a sculptor first and a puppeteer second, the result is likely to be interesting. This is the case with Bud Wertheim, of Livingston Manor, New York. He began to articulate small sculptures around 1952, and later became involved in the idea of environment for sculpture. Using a whole room was too expensive, but the puppet stage proved ideal. Gradually his Unstrung Puppet Theatre came into being. Much experiment has gone into it, for he subjects his characters to the stimulus of sounds, smells, tactile sensations produced in a variety of ways including electronic music and oscillators. As the puppets react to these, and thus become involved with the environment, so does the audience. He has made a ballet tightly choreographed to electronic music called *The Legend of Longeth,* with puppets of steel and bronze, scenery of steel sculpture, and "visions" of foam rubber and cloth. Longeth, a knight in armor, flees from Day Vision, represented by a moving ball of light cloth which symbolizes "the unknown quantities of knowledge and committed love," and falls before Night Vision, a dark, forbidding mass which pursues him as a "spectral shadow of fear and self-aggression." Wertheim, assisted by his wife Marlene, plays mostly for adults, but finds that his productions also appeal to the imaginative sensibilities of children. Now he is experimenting with light as a three-dimensional element and with the use of translucent materials to conduct it, hoping to be able to make a complete stage setting with light alone.

VI

Organizations

The Puppeteers of America

During the past twenty years the Puppeteers of America, a national organization founded in 1937, has grown from 178 members to about 900. Only a handful of these are professionals, but many are part-time showmen who might be termed "semi-professionals." Hundreds of amateurs work in their communities, and they provide most of the puppet work in schools, churches, hospitals, and organizations. There are also the Juniors, people under sixteen, many of whom get a start in puppetry through the Puppeteers of America.

Since the organization's membership is scattered throughout the United States, Canada, Mexico and some foreign countries, the office of Executive Secretary was established in 1950 to provide continuity and serve as headquarters. William I. Duncan served from 1950 to 1954, when Rena Prim took over until 1966. Olga Stevens is the present incumbent. Another unifying force is the *Puppetry Journal,* begun in 1949 and published bimonthly. George Latshaw was Editor for the first year, and upon his resignation, Vivian Michael and Peg Blickle were named Co-editors. After some time the latter became Associate Editor and Advertising Manager, serving until 1960. Vivian Michael has remained its faithful editor for the past eighteen years (with the exception of one year, 1967–1968, when Herman London served as editor). The *Puppetry Journal* continues to offer articles—historical, technical and theoretical; eight pages of pictures, and a news column which has been compiled for varying periods of time by George Latshaw, Rod Young and Martin Stevens. Since 1949 the *Journal* has been the principal record in America of puppet activity.

In June 1961, members voted to incorporate the organization under the laws of the State of Ohio. Willis E. Bauer, Jr., long-time member and well-known variety showman, took care of the considerable amount of work connected with this change in status, which became effective in the late summer.

The annual Festival of the Puppeteers of America is held in a different part of the country each year. The First American Puppetry Conference and Festival was organized by Paul McPharlin, and was held in Detroit, July 8–11, 1936. Plans for establishing a national organization were discussed, but it was not until the next year that the Puppeteers of America was founded, during the Second American Puppetry Festival, held in Cincinnati, June 28–July 1, 1937.

Except for the years 1942–1945, a festival has been held every year since then, as follows:

1938 Third American Puppetry Festival, Chicago, June 27–30.
1939 "Puppets on Parade," Fourth Annual Festival of the Puppeteers of America, New York City, June 27–30.
1940 "Puppets Are Stealing the Show," Fifth Annual Festival, St. Paul, June 25–28.
1941 Sixth Annual Puppetry Festival, St. Louis, June 24–27.
1946 National Puppetry Festival, Waterford (Conn.), June 27–30.
1947 The St. Louis Puppetry Festival, St. Louis, June 25–28.
1948 The Puppeteers of America Festival, Oklahoma City, June 22–25.
1949 National Festival, Detroit, June 28–July 1.
1950 National Festival, Oxford (Ohio), June 27–30.
1951 National Festival, Oxford, June 26–29.
1952 National Festival, Baton Rouge, June 24–27.
1953 Festival of Puppetry, Minneapolis, June 23–26.
1954 National Festival, Hanover (N.H.), June 23–26.
1955 National Festival, Bowling Green (Ohio), June 28–July 1.
1956 National Puppetry Festival, Evanston, August 6–11.
1957 National Puppetry Festival, Los Angeles, August 5–10.
1958 Puppetry Festival, Chapel Hill, August 4–9.
1959 The Puppeteers of America Festival, Oxford, August 3–8.
1960 Puppetry Festival, Detroit, August 1–6.
1961 Festival, Asilomar (Calif.), June 19–24.
1962 Puppeteers of America Festival, Oxford, June 25–30.
1963 Puppeteers of America Festival, Hurleyville (N.Y.), June 24–29.
1964 Festival, Miami Beach, June 29–July 5.
1965 Puppetry Festival, Detroit, June 24–28.
1966 Puppetry Festival, San Diego, June 25–30.
1967 Puppeteers of America Festival, Waterloo (Ontario), July 3–7.
1968 Puppetry Festival, St. Louis, August 19–23.

While performances, exhibits, demonstrations, talks, and workshops provide inspiration and assistance, puppeteers also prize the personal contacts with their fellow workers. Many regard festival week as a vacation, and return year after year. Only one person, though, has attended every festival, a unique honor held by Emma Warfield. The custom developed of having an auction of miscellaneous items contributed by puppeteers. In 1960 the Festival Store was substituted and became a regular feature, with Vivian Michael as the manager. She assembled a stock of books, plays, and supplies to augment the items puppeteers contributed, and kept them available throughout the year. The store has been profitable both for puppeteers and for the organization.

Performances of plays and variety are given at the festivals, and they reflect the state of puppetry in America. A program of *Potpourri* affords young showmen a chance to show their work, and others to display a new puppet or act. Puppet films, both foreign and American, are a regular feature of festival programs, and through them some idea of foreign puppetry is gained. One of these films, showing bits from the International Festival of Puppet Theatres in Bucharest in 1965, was especially revealing. Occasionally foreign puppeteers perform. Mane Bernardo's appearance at the 1963 Festival brought a glimpse of modern puppetry from Argentina. Sometimes festival-goers have seen the Manteos of New York City, who brought the age-old folk puppetry of Sicily when they migrated to the New World. Roberto Lago has performed with his Mexican puppets at three festivals. The 1967 meeting in Waterloo, Ontario, was memorable for the large representation of foreign puppeteers. Lenora Shpet and Viktor Afanasiev came from Russia, Henryk Jurkoswki from Poland, and there were performances by Jacques Chesnais' company from France and the Spebjl and Hurvinek Theatre from Czechoslovakia.

Through the years, the festival workshops have been primarily devoted to the technical aspects of puppet making and staging, for this reflects the primary interest of most puppeteers. There have been some attempts to relate puppetry to theatre in "presentation workshops" dealing with acting, pantomime, and characterization. Sessions have also been given on playwriting, play analysis and new approaches to playmaking. In general, the festival programs have been devoted to puppetry with little emphasis upon the other arts. Recently, however, there have been panel discussions on "Puppetry as a Theatre Art," on "New Designs for the Puppet Theatre," on "Creative Approaches to Puppet and Play Making." Puppets related to other forms of theatre have been seen in such programs as the group of dances inspired by puppets in the Detroit Institute of Arts and developed by the Wayne University Dance Workshop. One was *The Death of Tintagiles* by Maeterlinck, danced by Harriet Berg and Luis Ybarrondo with Fern Zwickey as Commentator and Roy Etherington and Nelson Rabe operating Marjorie Batchelder's rod-puppets. On the same program, Lea and Gia Wallace gave some of their dancer-with-puppet numbers. At the Dartmouth Festival at Hanover, New Hampshire, in 1954, there were two experimental hours. At the Waterloo Festival, a number of experts in theatre gave talks and demonstrations. Included were "Stage Movement and Stage Grouping" by Betty Carey of the Hamilton School of the Dance, with her students; "Elements of Drama in the Theatre," by Dr. James Reaney, University of Western Ontario, and Mrs. Kay McKie Guelph of the Little Theatre Company; and "Composing Music for Puppets" by Frank Haworth.

Local Puppet Guilds

Local organizations are important in keeping alive enthusiasm generated at national festivals, and providing regular contacts among puppeteers. When John Zweers was President of the Puppeteers of America in 1960–1961, he inaugurated a regional division of the country, each with a director, promoted the organization of new guilds, and encouraged affiliation with the national organization. In several cities, notably Chicago, Minneapolis-St. Paul, Detroit and Seattle, there was an active organization long before the dates of their charters as listed below:

1. Quaker Village Puppeteers, 1940
2. Columbus Guild of Puppetry, 1940 (inactive)
3. Houston Guild of Puppetry, 1956 (inactive)
4. Los Angeles County Guild of Puppetry, 1957
5. San Diego County Guild of Puppetry, 1958
6. Detroit Puppeteens Guild, 1960 (inactive)
7. San Francisco Bay Area Puppeteers Guild, 1960
8. Rocky Mountain Guild of Puppetry, 1961
9. New England Guild of Puppetry, 1961
10. Chicagoland Puppetry Guild, 1961
11. Seattle Guild of Puppetry, 1961
12. Orange County Guild of Puppetry, 1961 (inactive)
13. Phoenix Guild of Puppetry, 1961
14. Twin City Puppeteers, 1962
15. Empire Guild of Puppetry, 1962
16. Detroit Puppeteers Guild, 1963
17. Puppet Guild of St. Louis, 1963
18. National Capital Puppetry Guild, 1964
19. The Puppet Guild of Greater Miami, 1965
20. The Puppet Guild of Greater New York, Inc., 1962
21. The Puppet Guild of Long Island
22. The Red River Guild of Puppetry, 1966

The pattern of guild activities is much the same everywhere: regular meetings with talks, performances by members or visitors, workshops, discussions and business. The sessions are also social occasions, with refreshments and a special dinner or picnic once a year. Most meetings are open and guests are welcome. Visiting puppet companies are entertained, and the guilds support their performances. This is a particularly happy function in the case of foreign puppeteers, who have a chance to see something of American puppetry. Thus, Mane Bernardo and Blanca Cappaglia, Argentine puppeteers who visited the United States at the invitation of the State Department, were entertained with a show and banquet by the Los Angeles Guild, and other guilds also assisted in their program. Roberto Lago's tour of the country was punctuated by pleasant meetings with local guilds and exchange of information about puppetry. When Podrecca's Piccoli Theatre played in Seattle for several months in 1963, the guild there "adopted" the puppeteers, worked in their show as manipulators, and helped them in many ways.

Osaka, Japan, and Seattle are sister cities, and so it was appropriate for the Bunraku puppet troupe to be honored by the guild when it played at Century 21 Exposition in 1962. On a later tour, the Japanese puppeteers were entertained by other guilds, including those of Los Angeles and New York. The latter twice had pleasant exchanges with Sergei Obraztsov from Moscow. On November 11, 1963, a reception was held at the World Affairs Center by the guild for the Russian company. There was an exhibit set up like an American fair and a program of performances, including the puppets of Nat Norbert, the B. Gay Puppets, Lea Wallace, Larry Berthelson, Frank Osnowicz, the Manteos, and Burr Tillstrom with Kukla, Fran and Ollie. Obraztsov and his wife Olga reciprocated with some famous numbers from his solo *Concert*. He and some of his group also visited the North Shore Community Art Center at Roslyn, where junior puppeteers directed by Carol Fijan presented a show for them. In 1965 the Obraztsovs returned for a tour with the *Concert*, and again they were entertained by the guilds in several cities.

A Newsletter is sent out by each guild to its membership, which may number anywhere from fifteen to ninety. There is also a regular column in the *Puppetry Journal* called "Regional Ramblings" which was started by John Zweers, continued by Lois Ludington and presently compiled by Lanelle Rice.

It is impossible to mention all the projects which the guilds have undertaken, but a few will suggest the range of activities. In 1950, when the McPharlin collection was presented to the Detroit Institute of Arts, it was the Detroit Puppeteers Guild which helped organize and renovate it. Since then, members have given workshops and helped with performances and festivals given in Detroit. Some experimental work has been done by guild groups. David Gibson conducted one in which paper sculpture puppets were used in *The Carnival of the Animals* and *The Twelve Days of Christmas*. Vernone Tracey was the leader of another which presented a program of experimental puppets at the festival in Bowling Green in 1955. There were abstract puppets, interpretations of poems by Edith Sitwell with music by William Walton, and other unusual numbers. Another activity by the Detroit group was a summer program of Puppet Wagon Shows for parks and recreation, directed by Nancy Henk in 1963.

The Quaker Village Puppeteers is an active group which sometimes inspires its members to be imaginative by suggesting a theme, such as "green" or "tooth," upon which acts are developed. They also have workshop meetings, in which experiments such as colored tissue paper for shadow-puppets are tried.

The Experimental Committee of the Puppet Guild of Greater New York has been active since the autumn of 1964. Bud Wertheim was chairman, and at the first meeting he gave a demonstration of the visual and psychological relationships of abstract shapes—circle, square, triangle and so on—which in subsequent meetings were developed into mobiles or shadow-puppets to enact situations drawn from the Commedia dell'Arte. In one of these, the eternal triangle of Harlequin (diamond), the fickle Columbine (circle) and the soulful Pierrot (tear drop) were supplemented by a mermaid and a merman of flexible wire. Leona Madsen later became chairman. An interesting session was held at a meeting of the Puppet Guild of Long Island, at which she talked about experimenting with forms. To illustrate this, Lea Wallace, Bruce Madsen and Luigi Samuels gave a ten minute "romp" called *Flow and Flex at Arthur's Discoteque*, with feathers, foam rubber and styrofoam masks. At this same meeting, Jim Henson spoke of the unlimited scope of puppetry, and showed some of his films. There was another film, *The Organized Brain*, with an electronic music score, a discussion on "Anatomy of a Script," a talk by Rod Young on his creative puppetry workshops, and a couple of numbers performed by Jean Knopf.

At another New York Guild meeting which lasted all Sunday afternoon and evening, everybody created puppets out of miscellaneous materials and presented them in improvised scenes, and at a picnic, "instant puppets" were made and performed to music. Further ingenuity was displayed in the masks made by guild members for the ball at Fraunces Tavern, May 22, 1965, to commemorate the first puppet show in New York.

Guilds sponsor or participate in many activities—exhibits, fairs, and art festivals. The Los Angeles County Guild was co-sponsor with the Los Angeles County Museum of a comprehensive exhibit of puppets in 1959, entitled "The History of Puppetry," for which an illustrated catalogue was published. This guild also exhibits and performs each year at the Long Beach Hobby Show, as well as at regional and national festivals, and it assists at the puppet fairs held at Children's Fairyland. September

1, 1956 was a gala day, with shows and demonstrations to celebrate the park's sixth birthday. The contribution of the New York Guild to the world's fairs has already been noted, and there are many smaller ones. The Chicago group started an annual Puppet Fair about 1962. This is an annual collaborative project of the Chicagoland Puppetry Guild and a civic or service organization which finds an auditorium, attends to promotion, and ticket sales. For the fair held the weekend of October 1, 1966, for example, there were performances by Robin Reed, the Colemans, Hans Schmidt and Michiko Tagawa. The St. Louis Guild held its twenty-sixth annual Puppet Carnival in 1966, and the San Francisco Bay Area Puppeteers Guild participated in the Marin County Festival of Performing Arts in 1962.

The recent trend toward a closer relationship with other arts is illustrated in the last-named event, for here the puppet group was associated with many others. Realizing the advantages of such contacts, the Puppetry Guild of Greater Miami has become one of twenty-two groups in the Greater Miami Cultural Arts Center, Inc., which is working toward an "all-encompassing building or group of buildings dedicated to the arts" (from *The Key*, published by the Center). Likewise, the guild in Phoenix is affiliated with the Phoenix Arts Council and contributes to the Annual Youth Arts Festival at the Civic Center. This reaching out is evident in many guild programs, such as the "cultural excursions" arranged by the Los Angeles group, the demonstration of Origami by Lillian Oppenheimer for the New York puppeteers, and the joint projects of the Red River Guild of Puppetry and the Junior League, which performed *The Star Polisher*, an original play by guild member Jane Wylie. Another member has written a puppet play which is destined for League production, and a firm relationship with the Manitoba Theatre Centre has been established. Puppetry in this new guild thus promises to be a part of the larger field of the performing arts.

The guilds assist the national festivals; in fact, these are often scheduled in cities where there is a strong local group. In recent years, the importance of regional festivals has been stressed, and a number of guilds have sponsored them. The Northeastern Region has had two, both organized by the New England Guild of Puppetry. The first was a one-day meeting at Sturbridge, Massachusetts, on September 15, 1962, coordinated by Gordon Bennett. Talks, demonstrations, and performances went on all day and far into the night. A similar one took place at Newton Centre, Massachusetts, on February 13, 1965, where the public "was given massive doses of puppetry in all forms by an extensive list of practitioners." (*Puppetry Journal*, March–April, 1965) Syracuse had a Festival of Marionettes in 1962 at the Everson Museum of Arts, with an exhibit and shows. In the

Southeastern Region, two conferences were held in New Orleans in 1962 and the Miami Guild sponsored regional festivals in 1966 and 1967.

Beginning in 1960, California has had a regional meeting every year. San Francisco had the first, followed by Laguna Beach, San Francisco again, San Diego, and Pasadena. In 1965, the Asilomar Conference Grounds at Pacific Grove was the site, and it has been chosen for subsequent festivals.

A significant development in regional meetings took place at the University of Washington, Seattle, February 9–11, 1967, when the Northwest Drama Conference and the Seattle Guild of Puppetry joined forces in a program called "Theatre Potential." This was the annual regional meeting of the American Educational Theatre Association, which includes the Children's Theatre Conference, with the assistance of the Seattle Junior Programs, Inc., the Seattle Repertory Theatre, the Puppeteers of America, and the Junior League. Over 600 people were there, double the usual number. Although many of the AETA and puppet events were concurrent, the latter attracted their full share. The workshop, planned for forty, was expanded to sixty-five and ended up with eighty. Puppet performances had to be repeated. There was a puppet exhibit, too, and through this program about 3,600 people came into contact with puppets —most of them non-puppeteers.

In addition to the groups affiliated with the Puppeteers of America, there are many others, small and large, which promote puppetry. The Toronto Guild of Puppetry offers courses and has performances in a 150-seat theatre. The Ontario Puppetry Association draws members from the entire province. One of its activities is the collection of historical and contemporary puppets, playbills, and posters from which loans to various institutions are made.

The Association of Junior Leagues of America

The Junior Leagues are composed of young women between the ages of twenty and forty, who are trained volunteers serving their community in "Health, Welfare, Education, Radio and Television, Children's Theatre, Puppetry and the Arts." In 1950, forty-five Leagues had a puppet program; in 1967 there were 133. A large number of amateur puppeteers are involved, and their work has considerable impact. Although the Wichita (Kansas) League has done puppet work continuously since 1937, in most Leagues there is a large turnover of people interested in it. Consequently, puppet groups come and go.

The basic aim is to familiarize children with theatre and to provide meaningful entertainment, especially for those who would not otherwise have it. Shows are trouped to schools, hospitals, libraries, orphanages, settlements, churches and synagogues, retirement homes and Head Start centers. In a few communities, performances are centralized in a museum or library and occasionally in a civic auditorium. Much of the puppet work is educational, either directly or in a broad sense, and many plays promote safety and health. One year the Detroit League presented sixty performances of *Patrick and the Poison Punk* to 12,500 children in public schools and libraries, made a film of it, and gave a live performance on television as part of the Poison Control Project. Interesting children in local history was successfully undertaken with a series of plays by the Lincoln League presented at the Nebraska State Historical Society. *Percy the Prairie Dog* was given in Tulsa to educate children in the geological side of the oil business. Other scripts have been based on art, music, nature and children's poetry.

More than a hundred play titles are listed in the 1965–1966 Puppetry Chart. To supply the large demand for scripts, the League maintains a library containing adaptations of children's stories and original plays by members and a few by well-known puppeteers. An original script built around music and performed with the Portland Junior Symphony was *Three Cool Cats*. Original music was part of *The Hungriest Dragon in Town* with which the Salt Lake City League chalked up 110 performances to a total audience of 34,300 during the 1965–1966 season. Other League statistics for that year indicate that some plays were performed only once or several times, many had twenty-five to fifty showings, and a good number had more. Likewise, audiences varied greatly. Some plays were shown to fewer than a hundred persons, but 108 had audiences of 1,000 or more, many totaled between 5,000 and 15,000. Although most puppet work is for children, some adult programs have been given to promote community enterprises. Puppet shows were used in Oklahoma City to enlist support for a bond issue for a new library and bookmobile, and League puppeteers had a "Get Out the Vote" campaign in Galveston. Television is also used to promote League or community programs, and some shows are taped or presented to schools and hospitals via closed circuit.

A great many workshops in puppet making have been given by League members for children, and those recuperating in hospitals have been especially benefited. Another type of workshop may be given for the community in which demonstrations of simple puppet construction and staging techniques suitable for recreation groups and organizations are conducted.

Assistance for its various programs is provided by the Association through a group of consultants. Jean Starr Wiksell, an active puppeteer, became a puppet consultant in 1937. By 1948 the League work had increased so much, her own performances were curtailed. During the next years she directed a number of plays for the Leagues in New Orleans and Oklahoma City, and made the puppets for some of them. In 1948, Alfred Wallace became a puppet consultant because so many Leagues had puppet projects one person could not handle them all. Help was given through correspondence, especially on play scripts and technical details, and workshops were conducted when requested. One of the consultants would go in person to help with the selection and preparation of the script and the technical aspects of production, direction, and manipulation. As of March 31, 1968, the puppetry consultants' services were discontinued except as individual Leagues might request and pay for them. Many factors were involved in this curtailment, including inevitable developments occasioned by new conditions. That the program continued to grow for three decades is evidence of its importance, and it is to be hoped that it will be continued.

Jean Wiksell has also contributed a play to the League's list, made a film in color on hand-puppet and marionette construction, directed the Baton Rouge Children's Theatre, given demonstrations at the University of Hawaii, and attended the Puppeteers of America Festivals as the Association representative. Alfred Wallace has designed portable stages and equipment for League puppeteers, and conducted many workshops. His own puppet work is described elsewhere.

UNIMA (*Union Internationale des Marionnettes*)

Founded in 1928 in Prague, Czechoslovakia, UNIMA was the first attempt by puppeteers to consider the international scope of the puppet theatre. Thereafter, a number of Congresses were held at intervals. Interrupted by World War II, they were resumed in 1957:

    I. Prague, Czechoslovakia, 1929.
   II. Paris, France, 1929.
  III. Liège, Belgium, 1930.
  IV. Ljubljana, Yugoslavia, 1933.
   V. Prague, Czechoslovakia, 1957.
  VI. Bucharest, Rumania, 1958.
 VII. Bochum and Braunschweig, German Federal Republic, 1960.
VIII. Warsaw, Poland, 1962.
  IX. Munich, German Federal Republic, 1966.
   X. Prague, Czechoslovakia, 1969. (Scheduled at this writing)

Each Congress has a theme pertinent to the puppet theatre, and papers are delivered by people who are outstanding in the field. For instance, at the Warsaw Congress, the relation of the puppet theatre to other forms of art was considered, and at Munich, the significance of the puppet theatre in our day was the central argument. In addition, business is transacted, including the election of officers, and a festival of puppet theatres, international in character, is held.

While it does not sponsor them directly, UNIMA is represented at all international puppet festivals, which have greatly increased in number since 1957. Bucharest, which sponsored the First International Festival of Puppet Theatres in 1958, held the second in 1960 and the third in 1965. Braunschweig's festival in 1957 had an international flavor, and its subsequent ones in 1960, 1963, and 1966 have established them as important international puppet events. Budapest, Rome, Sofia, Mechelen and Colwyn Bay, Wales, have also held festivals with performances by companies from many countries. In fact, many national meetings, such as the annual festivals at Bochum, held since 1958, attract people from foreign countries, and thus the tendency toward world participation grows. In 1964, even the Czech Festival of Amateur Puppet Theatres, after thirteen years of annual meetings in Chrudim, took on international significance through the participation of other countries.

Prior to the reactivation of UNIMA at a 1957 meeting in Paris, American puppeteers were not much concerned with puppetry in foreign countries. However, Romain Proctor, then President of the Puppeteers of America, was elected to the UNIMA Presidium, and devoted much of his energy to stimulating interest in world puppetry. The following year he attended the First International Festival of Puppet Theatres in Bucharest. Marjorie McPharlin was also there as a judge for the puppet theatre competition. More and more European festivals were held, and gradually Americans began to attend, although distance and expense still keep the delegations small. After Proctor's death in 1961, Marjorie McPharlin was elected to the Presidium, and in 1966, upon her resignation, Bil Baird became the United States representative. Meanwhile, Mollie Falkenstein became interested in UNIMA affairs, and succeeded Nancy Cole as co-ordinator of American members. Following the pattern of many European countries, UNIMA U.S.A. was organized in 1966, with a long list of officers, including Mollie Falkenstein as Executive Secretary. In 1967, membership totaled 159, including people from Canada, Mexico, the United States, and two from Korea.

VII

Puppetry in Print

Various aspects of puppetry have been dealt with in books, theses, and articles, the general trends of which are discussed in this chapter. More specific references will be found in the Bibliography.

Books

Few new books have come along, and most of the old standbys are out of print. Publishers are reluctant to take on books with such specialized appeal. Those which have been published in recent years deal mostly with construction methods for educational purposes. However, Plays, Inc., has a growing list of reprints. Some historical works long since out of print are again available, together with a variety of technical books, and it is the purpose of this publishing house to keep them on the list.

Historical and theoretical works have little appeal to puppeteers unless they are brilliantly illustrated, as is Bil Baird's *The Art of the Puppet,* which is now distributed by Plays, Inc. Although he does not claim this to be a history of puppetry, the principal traditional puppet theatres of the world, as well as modern ones, are discussed. Baird also brings in his theories about the art of puppet theatre which have evolved during his long career in the field. Peter Arnott in *Plays without People* states his theories and explains how he puts them into practice. A brief analysis of puppetry as an art form is included in Robert Mueller's *The Science of Art.* Virginia Lee Comer and I conducted experimental workshops in Puppetry and Creative Drama, based upon the theory that puppetry is primarily a dramatic art having qualities distinct from those of other theatre forms. This resulted in *Puppets and Plays, A Creative Approach,* which sets forth new ways of making puppets and building plays for them.

At regular intervals, new technical books have appeared, most of which perpetuate old and elaborate construction methods, although they purport to be suitable for children. However, stimulating, unhackneyed ideas are beginning to appear in a few books, which are noted in the Bibliography.

There is a dearth of published puppet plays, although one or more are often included in technical books, and a few titles have been issued in America. Tom Tichenor's *Folk Plays for Puppets You Can Make* is for young children, but has play ideas and simple construction methods which could be adapted for other groups. *Eight Plays for the Puppet Theatre* by George and Elizabeth Merten has plays for older children and adults. Other collections by Vernon Howard, Lisl Beer and foreign authors are listed in the Bibliography.

Theses

Records of theses with puppet subjects are incomplete, and we are glad to refer the reader to J. Frances Crothers' Bibliography. A few typical areas of investigation may be noted here. Aurora Valentinetti prepared a series of puppet plays for her Master's thesis at the University of Washington and Susan Smith at the University of Georgia wrote an original play. Shirley O'Donnol adapted Kalidasa's *Shakuntala,* produced it at the University of Richmond and won an M.A. in 1952. She supervises graduate work at Sacramento State College, and one of her students, Anthony J. Damiani, presented *The Value of Puppetry at the Elementary Level* in 1966. Another, Evon Morrison Ray, produced *Alice in Wonderland* in 1967. Gordon Bennett worked on *Puppetry in the Elementary and Secondary Schools* for his M.A. degree at Emerson College, Boston, 1962. *The Effect of Puppetry on the Development of Creativity* was Margaret Bennington's thesis title for her work at Illinois State University. Elaine Miller worked on *A Justification of Puppetry as an Art Form* at Kansas State University and won her M.A. in 1964. Leona Madsen did part of her research in Europe, and received her M.A. from New York University in 1960, while Lois Ludington received hers at the University of Washington.

Studies of traditional puppet theatres have been made by a number of people. Nancy Cole presented *A Study of Guignol of Lyons* for her thesis from Stanford University in 1958. At UCLA, Diana Jewett designed a production of *Everyman,* and Mallory Pearce, *The Ancient Puppet Play of Doctor Faustus* which were presented in 1965 as part of their graduate work. Currently, Antoinette Helstien is working on the relationship of Ghelderode to the Belgian folk puppet theatre in preparation for her doctorate, and Conrad Young has access to a remarkable set of shadow-puppets from Taiwan, complete with scenario-scripts, acquired by the Ethnic Collection of the University, which will form the basis for his Ph.D. dissertation. Virginia Tooper is working in Special Education and Guidance on her Ph.D. from the University of Cincinnati. She incorporates puppetry in her work with the mentally retarded as part of her research.

Articles

The professional and amateur activities of puppeteers have brought forth many articles in the press, most of them for publicity purposes. Very little critical evaluation takes place, although intelligent reviews occasionally appear. For example, Joe R. Mills, Radio and Television Editor of the *Columbus Dispatch,* wrote a sensitive article, "Tillstrom and Pantomimes," and Richard R. Shepard discussed "Obraztsov and the Bairds" in the *New York Times.* When Baird's new theatre opened in 1967, both Norman Nadel and Dan Sullivan of the *Times* wrote thoughtful reviews. Generally though, puppets are mostly ignored by drama critics, for the puppet theatre still has to win a significant place in the performing arts. *Variety* and other trade publications, of course, mention current performances and night club acts, but it is notable that the now defunct *Theatre Arts* rarely published articles about puppets, especially in its later years. Recently, however, two issues of *World Theatre* have been largely given over to articles about present-day puppets and those of countries outside Europe. In 1955, *The UNESCO Courier* devoted its June issue to puppets, with thirteen articles and an editorial which laments the idea that puppets are merely for children, and points out some of the ways they appeal to adults.

During the period of Paul McPharlin's *Yearbook,* Helen Reisdorf, a librarian in Detroit, used to compile a list of periodicals with puppet articles which was published in it. Since then there has been no comparable record for handy reference. However, there has been a considerable body of writing by puppeteers upon all aspects of their work, and the articles published in the *Puppetry Journal* from 1949 to date are typical. Most of them are short, but some have been more detailed. A good many deal with historical subjects, such as puppets in India, Korea, and Japan. One gave some details about puppets in primitive Pacific societies. Puppetry in Rumania, Czechoslovakia, Slovenia, Russia and Bulgaria has been described in articles, some written by people from those countries. The results of Daniel Keller's research on Spanish puppets and plays have appeared, as well as his "Puppets and Politics in Mexico's Past." Glimpses of past history have been given in Doug Anderson's notes on Jewell's Manikins, and Jero Magon summarized developments in the United States since 1915 in "Golden Jubilee." The stories of the Turnabout Theatre, Bob Baker's Theatre, and the Tatterman Marionettes have been told. Articles about foreign puppet theatres include the Sicilian Theatre, Die Hohensteiner Puppenspiele, Podrecca's Teatro dei Piccoli, and the English Toy Theatre. Guignol of Lyons and Karagoz of Turkey have been described, while Peg Blickle contributed a detailed study of Mr. Punch. In two articles "Craig and the Marionette Theatre," Cleveland Haubold discussed the theories and work of this man whose influence has been so great.

Many articles have been about puppeteers. We can mention only a few of them: Sarg, Proctor, Tillstrom, Paris, Baird, Kunze and the Ritts from the United States; the Vellemans from Canada; Obraztsov, Siegel and Roser from Europe; Bramall, Hogarth and the Lanchesters from England; Takeda of Japan. Other glimpses of the work of individual showmen or theatres of a given country have been brought to *Journal* readers through the accounts of visiting puppeteers. Many have gone to Europe, some to South America and Mexico, a few to the Orient and several all the way around the world. Since 1958, accounts of International Puppet Festivals and UNIMA have increased as more Americans have planned their foreign trips to attend them. Romain Proctor was the chronicler of UNIMA Congresses and Festivals until his death in 1961, and I wrote three articles on the First International Festival of Puppet Theatres (1958), and two on the second one in 1960. Other accounts have come from Jan Bussell ("The Tenth Amateur Czech Festival"), David Lodwig ("Bochumer Figurentheaterwoche"), and the Third International Festival in Bucharest was reviewed by Mollie Falkenstein, Lewis Mahlman, Margaret Fickling and Alan Cook. The Children's Theatre in the United States has also entered the international scene, and Sara Spencer's article "Assitej Children's Theatre" gave puppeteers an account of its founding and purpose.

Because the *Journal* is the official organ of the Puppeteers of America, a good deal of space is devoted to its activities. In 1953 Peg Blickle wrote three articles on the history of the organization, and in 1960 Romain Proctor contributed "Twenty-Five Golden Years" as an anniversary tribute. Plans for the annual Festival and reviews of the shows and workshops bring a spate of articles. The problem of critical evaluation has always been a touchy one, for Festivals are regarded by many as a happy time for renewing friendships rather than a serious meeting for the analysis and discussion of puppet shows. The *Journal* has reported panel discussions on evaluation, published outlines for it and articles by individuals deploring the lack of constructive criticism, yet for the most part the reviews of Festival performances have remained glowing accounts rather than impartial analyses. Puppeteers are less inhibited in their reviews of performances outside the Festival, although most of them have been motivated by a surge of enthusiasm experienced by the reviewer. Herb Scheffel wrote a number of telling reviews for the *Journal* in which he did not hesitate to blame as well as to praise. Martin Stevens issued a strong protest against a poor show in "Teatro dei Piccoli Attori." The Salzburg Marionette Theatre and Obraztsov's *An Unusual Concert* were carefully reviewed by harriet for the New York Guild Newsletter. Some puppet exhibits have been reviewed in detail. Erna Albu wrote her impressions of the Lytton Puppet Exhibit in "That Magic World of Puppets" and George Latshaw described the 1965 Festival Exhibit at the Detroit Institute of Arts in "Puppet Cavalcade." Book reviews in the *Journal* have been infrequent. Many brief references to the publication of puppet books may be found in it, but only a few analyses, such as Bill Cassady's discussion of Peter Arnott's *Plays without People* and my extensive study of *The Puppet Theatre of the Modern World*.

Through the years, there have been a surprising number of articles in the *Journal* which have considered the theoretical aspects of the puppet theatre: its nature, its function, its future development. Basil Milovsoroff has a clear-cut image of what the puppet theatre should be, an image quite different from the American reality. In a series of articles published in the fifties he explained his ideas, and they were put into practice in a creative puppetry workshop he conducted at the 1954 Festival. Lewis Parsons reported on this in a *Journal* article. Jero Magon has suggested the use of symbolism, expressionism, and fantasy in the puppet theatre, and George Latshaw has stressed the need for seeking inspiration from the broad field of all the arts, as well as from other puppeteers, in order to create rather than to imitate. A discussion of artistry in the puppet show was contributed in 1950 by Walter Wilkinson, and some of Obraztsov's ideas on the unique quality of puppet theatre were published in 1963. Burr Tillstrom explained his philosophy in *Journal* articles, a philosophy he has consistently illuminated in all his work. A number of puppeteers, including Helen Haiman Joseph and Sister Corona Sharp, have emphasized in their writings that puppetry is a theatre art. Gil Oden made penetrating analyses in "Elements of Theatre" and "The Place of Puppetry in Theatre Arts." At the 1963 Festival a panel chaired by Lea Wallace discussed this subject, with Lewis Mahlmann, Rufus Rose, Virginia Terrell, Vera Warsager, Lisl Beer and Davis Alan representing various elements of theatre. A report appeared in the *Journal*.

The 1966 Festival triggered a series of articles which reflect what may turn out to be a decisive change in attitudes towards the puppet theatre. For so long, American puppeteers on the whole have been conservative, and worked within their own little realm. Now, the influence of our changing world is being felt by the puppeteer, bringing new problems, and also new possibilities. Several young inquiring people came to this Festival, took a critical look at the performances they saw there, and dared to put their observations in writing, and the *Journal* printed them. Paul Vincent Davis wrote a short but incisive commentary, "A Critical Analysis of Puppetry," and G. William Ludwig set down his "Personal Impressions of

a First Festival," which were both appreciative and critical. During 1966
and 1967 other articles appeared. Davis discussed puppet theatre theory
in "New Directions," Ludwig analyzed the puppet theatre in "Manifesto
of a Novice," Valentine Bean wrote "In Puppetry Circles" to discuss theoretical questions, and Robert E. Mueller contributed "A Renaissance for
Puppetry." Marjorie McPharlin, in a series of seven articles, took a critical
look at the American puppet theatre, and developed a plan for an experimental approach to new ideas for the puppet theatre.

The many roles of the puppet have been discussed in Chapter I; it is
necessary only to mention here that many *Journal* articles have been
written to explore the fields of education, therapy, recreation; of advertising, television, night club and film. So also, the many aspects of puppet
play production have been considered in *Journal* articles. There is the
business side of puppetry and economic factors which influence it, such
as booking and publicity, which have been covered by articles on photography, preparing brochures, and a series by Marge Stevens called "Puppets for Fun and Profit." Recently, a new element in the economic picture
is government subsidy for Head Start and other programs, as well as
grants being made by the National Foundation on the Arts and Humanities, one of which went to Bil Baird's puppet theatre.

Playwriting is an ever present problem for the puppet showman because the supply of published plays is so limited. A good many articles
have therefore been written on the subject. The requisites of a good
puppet play were discussed in such articles as "What Is a Puppet Play?"
by Alfred Wallace; "Puppets and a Child Audience" by Winifred Ward,
whose long experience in Children's Theatre qualifies her to speak au-
thoritatively, and "Writing Your Own Script," an account by Jean Starr
Wiksell of a session she moderated at the 1956 Festival. "Script Writing for
Puppets" by Clem Easly, an exposition of the Aristotelian principles expressed simply and concisely, was reprinted in 1967. Martin Stevens, for
whom Easly wrote many scripts, used his basic plan for many workshops
in playwriting at Festivals, and added some pointed remarks in several
Journal articles. Other puppeteers, including Robert Williams and Kathryn Robb, explained their ways of constructing a play, and Arthur L.
Zapel considered "Scripting a TV Puppet Series for Children."

Sources for play ideas were explored: from poetry to Elizabethan
comedy, from American folklore to satire. In 1967, William Ludwig continued his examination of the meaning of puppet theatre by writing
"Source Material—Gathering of Friends," in which he suggested a wealth
of plays, stories, fables, spoofs, children's books, documentaries, ideas and
images which are potential dramatic material for puppets. John Tag-
liabue's "Puppets and Terror: Some Notes in Hope of a New Puppet

Theatre" was published in the *Journal* in 1955. Now more probings are taking place in such articles as Valentine Bean's analysis of "Puppets and G.B.S." and "Letter to a Young Puppeteer." And, in "Basics for the Beginning Playwright" by Stanley Richards, the *Journal* editor went outside the realm of puppetry to that of the theatre of human actors for an analysis by a professional playwright.

Not as many articles on puppet construction have appeared in the *Journal* as one would expect, considering that this has been the central interest of puppeteers. However, new developments in materials for puppet making have been duly recorded, from gourds to celastic; from rubber to fiberglas; from Shreddi-Mix to Fender Mender, and many others. There have been articles on specific details of construction: the tricks of knife-throwing and egg-laying, animal marionettes, construction of hands and feet, wigs, cloth puppets, make-up, painting with plastic paint or encaustic, etc. Other articles have discussed certain kinds of puppets, such as the hand-and-rod, humanettes, finger-puppets and even Mag-Nettes—little figures of foam rubber propelled by magnets, and used in hospital shows.

Articles on stages ranged from descriptions of Bob Baker's Theatre in the Round to architectural stages. Lighting for the stage, for transformations, and "Black Light and Fluorescent Colors" were discussed. Some old hands at costume designing, like Alfred Wallace, Walton and O'Rourke, and Shirley O'Donnol wrote about it. Nor were effects for smoke, fire, and various sounds neglected. With the coming of tape recording, a good many articles emerged, some for, some against. "New Sounds for the Puppet Theatre" by Marian Derby suggested creative uses of the tape recorder to produce electronic compositions and hitherto non-existent sounds. Technical matters were discussed in two especially pertinent articles. "Did You Hear the Puppet?" was contributed by Rod Satory, a physicist at the Physics and Engineering Laboratory of New Zealand, a specialist in acoustics and also a theatre man, who gave some practical suggestions about tape recorders and sound amplification systems. Donald Coleman in "The Abducted Princess" presented some useful hints about fuses, line loads, and how to prevent oneself from being electrocuted on today's popular aluminum stages.

Music, so important to the puppet show, was discussed by Ed Johnson in "Stereophonic Recording," and by Verna Arvey in "Music for the Marionette Theatre." Lewis Parsons, whose work is almost as much with music as with puppets, wrote about "Music Problems," "Music and the Puppet Show," and "Resources of Sound."

Every puppeteer knows that all the elements of a show have to be thought about in relationship to each other, and that this involves the difficult job of production. A panel discussion chaired by Rod Young at the 1960 Festival entitled "New Designs for the Puppet Theatre" was reported in the *Journal*. Several puppeteers gave their views on the various aspects of design—puppets, scenery, lighting—which need to be coordinated. How different puppeteers plan and build a show formed the subject of a number of *Journal* articles. Jim Menke told how he built a production of *Carnival* with high school students; Raymond Mount, Jr., explained how he began with the selection of the play, and used old puppets to try it out before beginning construction; the Vellemans told of building *The Blue Unicorn* with rod-puppets and how they designed several experimental stages; Bob Brown described the problems he encountered in building a department store window show; Mollie Falkenstein, in "Building a New Show," stipulated that it was "for amateurs only" and went on to tell all the steps involved in working out the action for a recording of *Peter Rabbit*. Several people described projects with children, and Kay Geffine told how shows were organized at the Lake Erie Junior Nature and Science Center. There were also articles on showmanship, choreography, and musical pantomime; on voice projection; on manipulation, timing, and many more.

Marge Stevens proposed a creative way of thinking about all the problems of puppet production in her *Journal* article entitled, "Play Your Way to Originality" in which she applied the rules of brainstorming to them: (1) Forget for the moment what you know about conventional methods, and (2) Allow your mind complete freedom to play the game, no matter how silly or impossible the various ideas may be. Then you keep asking the question, "What if . . . ?" What if stages didn't have to be square or rectangular? What if you named the show first and built the puppets to fit the title? What if you discarded all your numbers and started afresh?

With this attitude, who knows what exciting things might happen in the puppet theatre and set it on new paths? On the basis of ideas which are already coming into the consciousness of puppeteers, we might ask some questions about the future:

What if puppeteers became less conservative and more creatively experimental in exploring the potentialities of puppet theatre?

What if the best talent in music, dance, writing, acting, and puppetry could be combined to build puppet productions compelling enough to interest adults and imaginative enough to delight children?

What if the talent of the puppet theatre to entertain were directed also to plays which could give to children and to adults a dramatic experience to touch their emotions and not merely to excite their senses?

What if the power of the puppet to satirize, to ridicule, to provoke laughter, as well as to arouse sympathy, anger or indignation, were directed towards social problems—to illuminate them and perhaps point to solutions?

If puppeteers should seriously work along these lines, the puppet theatre could become a *unique* theatre where audiences could experience a kind of art to be found nowhere else, expressed in old dramatic forms, as well as new ones, with imaginative ways of presenting them—in short, an important area of the performing arts in America.

Bibliography

This is a selected list of published material on all aspects of puppetry: History and Theory, Puppet Making and Production, and Plays for Puppets. In addition, there are listed important puppet periodicals, bookshops and other sources for obtaining puppet books, and companies which have puppet films available.

The principal books in English and currently in print are stressed, but some out-of-print titles (designated by *) which are likely to be found in libraries are included. Certain standard works in foreign languages or published abroad, many of them dealing with important puppet theatres in various countries, are also mentioned, especially for the benefit of those interested in historical research.

A section of this bibliography is devoted to books and articles on Art and Theatre, including Dance, Music and Sound, Creative Drama, Television and Film, to help relate puppetry to current developments in other art forms, and to provide ideas for the construction and use of puppets.

BIBLIOGRAPHIES

Crothers, J. Frances (Comp.). *The Puppeteer's Library Guide: The Bibliographic Index to the Literature of the World Puppet Theatre.* 6 vols. Metuchen, New Jersey: Scarecrow Press. In preparation.

A comprehensive work which includes books and articles on all phases of the puppet theatre, the result of more than fifteen years of research.

Ransome, Grace Greenleaf (Comp.). *Puppets and Shadows.* Boston: F. W. Faxon Co., 1931.

Books and articles, published before 1931, from many countries, are arranged in classified lists.

Bibliographies found in many puppet books may be helpful; *Subject Guide to Books in Print, U.S.A.,* and *Books in Print, U.S.A.,* published annually by R. R. Bowker Co., New York, can be found in most libraries, and will give information on books currently available.

Puppet Theatre History and Theory

A Selection of Books in English

Arnott, Peter D. *Plays Without People*. Bloomington, Indiana: Indiana University Press, 1964.

How the author performs serious drama with marionettes and his theories of their use in revivals of classic plays, with notes on staging his one-man shows and some historical notes are all included.

Baird, Bil. *The Art of the Puppet*. New York: Macmillan Co., 1965. Now distributed exclusively by Plays, Inc., Boston.

A beautiful and lavishly illustrated book with many fine color plates, dealing with important puppet theatres of the world, past and present, and the author's personal theories about puppets and puppetry.

*Batchelder, Marjorie. *Rod-Puppets and the Human Theatre*. Columbus, Ohio: Ohio State University Press, 1947.

History and technique of the rod-puppet from ancient times, with a section on the aesthetics of the puppet theatre and an extensive bibliography.

*Beaumont, Cyril W. *Puppets and Puppetry*. New York and London: Studio Publications, 1958. New edition of *Puppets and the Puppet Stage* (1938).

Brief notes on history, types and uses of puppets, with about 400 illustrations, mostly from America and Europe.

Boehn, Max von. *Dolls and Puppets*. Philadelphia: David McKay Co., 1932. New edition issued by Charles T. Branford Co., Newton Centre, Mass., 1956. Now available in reprint from original edition from Cooper Square Publishers, New York.

Dolls, automata, Christmas cribs, tin soldiers are included, as well as puppets from antiquity to modern times in Europe; shadows and marionettes in the Orient.

*Brown, Forman. *Punch's Progress*. New York: Macmillan Co., 1936.

The story of the Yale Puppeteers from the beginning of their association until they went to Hollywood in 1933 and made the puppets for the film *I Am Suzanne*.

*Bussell, Jan. *The Puppets and I*. London: Faber and Faber, Ltd., 1950.
*———. *Puppet's Progress*. London: Faber and Faber, Ltd., 1953.
*———. *Through Wooden Eyes*. London: Faber and Faber, Ltd., 1956.

These three books deal with the author's own work, his views about puppetry, and accounts of his travels in foreign countries from Europe to the Far East.

Craig, Edward Gordon. *On the Art of the Theatre.* New York: Theatre Arts Books.

This and other writings by Craig explain his views, which are important for their influence on the puppet theatre.

*Efimova, Nina. *Adventures of a Russian Puppet Theatre.* Translated by Elena Mitcoff. Birmingham, Michigan: Puppetry Imprints, 1935.

Contains not only the story of this important Russian puppet theatre, but also technical information on the type of puppet originated by Efimova and now used throughout Eastern Europe and other parts of the world.

*Haar, Francis. *Japanese Theatre in Highlight.* Rutland, Vermont: Charles E. Tuttle Co., 1952. Revised edition, 1954.

A well-illustrated book with brief descriptions of the Noh, Bunraku and Kabuki Theatres.

Hironaga, Shuzaburo. *Bunraku, Japan's Unique Puppet Theatre.* Tokyo: Tokyo News Service, Ltd., 1964.

With eight plates of color photographs and a number in black and white, this book deals largely with synopses of 98 plays, but also includes some historical notes, names of present Bunraku reciters, samisen players, and operators.

*Joseph, Helen Haiman. *A Book of Marionettes.* New York: Viking Press, 1929.

The first history of puppets in English, and a standard reference.

Keene, Donald, *Bunraku: The Art of the Japanese Puppet Theatre.* Rutland, Vermont: Japan Publications Trading Co., 1965.

This is the most complete study of Bunraku, with historical notes and detailed information about the puppets, plays, narrators and musicians. There are color pictures of scenes and individual puppets. Many black and white illustrations show poses of puppets, facial expressions, operation of heads, scenes from plays, and puppets from various regions. A collector's item.

Lano, David. *A Wandering Showman, I.* Lansing, Michigan: Michigan State University Press, 1957.

An account of his tours into the by-ways of America by this third generation puppeteer whose grandfather emigrated from Italy.

*McIsaac, F. J. *The Tony Sarg Marionette Book.* Illustrated by Tony Sarg. New York: B. W. Huebsch, Inc., 1921; Viking Press, 1940.

One of the earliest books in America to reveal the secrets of puppet making, this little book is historical, too, for it has an account of Sarg's work and a chapter on puppet history.

*McPharlin, Paul (ed.). *Puppetry, A Yearbook of Puppets and Marionettes.* 16 vols. Birmingham, Michigan: Puppetry Imprints, 1930–1947.

Historical and technical developments around the world are described and illustrated; work of puppeteers is recorded. Some of the volumes are still in print and information may be had from the Department of Theatre Arts, the Detroit Institute of Arts.

*March, Benjamin. *Chinese Shadow-Figure Plays and Their Making.* (Handbook IX) Birmingham, Michigan: Puppetry Imprints, 1938.

Historical and technical details of Chinese shadows, with many illustrations and the texts of a trilogy of plays, make this an authoritative study.

*Martinovitch, Nicholas N. *The Turkish Theatre.* New York: Theatre Arts, Inc., 1933.

The three types of popular Turkish theatre—Orta oiunu, Meddah and Karagöz—are described, with stories or plays typical of each. There are colored illustrations of the shadow-puppet characters of the Karagöz play.

Niculescu, Margareta, and others (eds.). *The Puppet Theatre of the Modern World.* Translated by Ewald Osers and Elizabeth Strick. Boston: Plays, Inc., 1967. First published as *Puppentheater der Welt.* Berlin: Henschelverlag, Kunst and Gesellschaft, 1965.

An editorial board of UNIMA (Union Internationale des Marionettes), headed by Margareta Niculescu, compiled this book of "Opinions and Assessments" of contemporary puppetry by seventeen authorities. Their comments, together with 238 plates of excellent illustrations in color and black and white, present the most comprehensive world view of present-day puppetry yet published.

Obraztsov, Sergei, *The Chinese Puppet Theatre.* Translated by J. T. MacDermott. London: Faber and Faber, 1961. Distributed in the United States by Plays, Inc., Boston.

Obraztsov's visit to China resulted in the publication of *The Chinese Theatre,* and then his historical notes, analyses and illustrations of all types of Chinese puppets were published as a separate book.

*———. *My Profession.* Translated by Ralph Parker and Valentina Scott. Moscow: Foreign Language Publishing House, 1957.

An account of the author's development as a puppeteer; a penetrating view of the nature of puppetry and its place in the theatre.

Oden, Gil. *Puppets Past and Present: A Picture Book of the Puppetry Collection in the Detroit Institute of Arts.* Detroit: Institute of Arts, 1950.

Philpott, A. R. *Let's Look at Puppets.* London: Frederick Muller, Ltd., 1966.

The origin, history, and types of puppets.

Saito, Seijiro, with Yamaguchi Hiroichi and Yoshinage Tahao. *Master-*

pieces of Japanese Puppetry. English adaptation by Roy Miller. Rutland, Vermont and Tokyo: Charles E. Tuttle Co., 1958.

A beautifully printed limited edition with 32 fine color plates of Japanese puppet heads and notes on the characters they represent. There is also an historical sketch of the Bunraku and its performances.

Scott, A. C. *The Puppet Theatre of Japan*. Rutland, Vermont: Charles E. Tuttle Co., 1963.

The origins of the Japanese Puppet Theatre, with notes on puppeteers, readers, narrators, stage and puppet anatomy. The plots of ten plays are summarized, and there are a few illustrations.

*Sibbald, Reginald S. *Marionettes in the North of France*. Philadelphia: University of Pennsylvania Press, 1936.

Originally presented for his doctoral dissertation, Sibbald has sketched the general history of marionettes in France from antiquity through the eighteenth century as background for his discussion of the theatre of chivalric romance in Amiens, Lille and Roubaix.

Spatháris, Sotíris. *Behind the White Screen*. London: Alan Ross, 1967. Distributed by Secker and Warburg.

A small paperbound book in which this master of the Greek Shadow Theatre recounts the story of his puppet work from 1909–1947. The few illustrations do not do justice to this lively popular theatre.

Speaight, George. *The History of the English Puppet Theatre*. London: G. G. Harrap, 1955. Distributed in the United States by Plays, Inc.

A carefully documented and scholarly work which is the definitive study of this subject. The origins, as well as the development to contemporary times, are recounted.

———. *Juvenile Drama, The History of the English Toy Theatre*. London: Macdonald and Co., Ltd., 1946.

Many colored illustrations of puppets and scenes enliven this careful historical account of the toy theatre, a favorite home entertainment for generations of English children.

The UNESCO Courier, VIII, No. 2 (1955). New York: The United Nations, UNESCO Department of Communications.

This issue is devoted to puppets, and has thirteen articles and an editorial.

*Wilkinson, Walter. *The Peep Show*. London: Geoffrey Bles, 1929.

*———. *Puppets in Wales*. London: Geoffrey Bles, 1948.

*———. *Puppets in Yorkshire*. London: Geoffrey Bles, 1931.

*———. *Puppets into Scotland*. London: Geoffrey Bles, 1935.

*———. *Puppets Through America*. London: Geoffrey Bles, 1938.

*———. *Puppets Through Lancashire*. London: Geoffrey Bles, 1936.

*————. *A Sussex Peep Show*. London: Geoffrey Bles, 1933.

*————. *Vagabonds and Puppets*. London: Geoffrey Bles, 1930.

Wilkinson's accounts of his travels on foot, pushing his theatre on a kind of barrow, are more than amusing anecdotes about puppets, for they reveal his astute observations about people and places. In America he had to forego hiking, but he saw much of the country, and nothing escaped his keen eye.

Wilson, Albert E. *Penny Plain, Twopence Coloured*. London: G. G. Harrap and Co., Ltd., 1932.

A well-illustrated account of the English toy theatre, its plays, and the people who made its history.

*Wimsatt, Genevieve. *Chinese Shadow Shows*. Cambridge, Mass.: Harvard University Press, 1936.

Discussion of history, description of a performance in a Chinese courtyard, notes on puppet construction, on musical instruments, on sources of the plays, with action and dialogue for *The Lotus Flower Temple*.

World Theatre (International Theatre Institute). Vol. XIV, No. 5 (1965), "Puppets Outside Europe." Vol. XV, No. 2 (1966), "Present Day Puppets." Paris: Imprimerie Michel Brient & Cie. American distributor: Theatre Arts Books.

Illustrated articles on puppets in Africa, Brazil, Cuba, Mexico, Japan, Indonesia and Vietnam are included in Volume XIV. Volume XV has an editorial on modern puppetry, and discussions of puppets through new channels, new functions, new materials, new drama and an account of the Third International Festival of Puppet Theatres, Bucharest.

A Selection of Puppet Books Published Abroad

These are important books dealing with puppetry in various countries. Out-of-print titles are not here indicated, but those not published in recent years are unlikely to be in print. Some may be obtained through libraries, or from book dealers listed below under Sources for Puppet Books.

Altherr, Alfred. *Marionetten*. Erlenbach-Zurich: Eugen Rentsch, [c. 1927].

Illustrations of some of the strongly stylized puppets and scenery of the Zurich Marionette Theatre are included, with three reproductions of lithographs by Pierre Gauchat.

Baty, Gaston, et Chavance, René. *Histoire des Marionnettes*. Paris: Presses Universitaires de France, 1959.

Benegal, Som (ed.). *Puppet Theatre Around the World*. New Delhi: Bharatiya Natya Sangh, 1960.

One of the first books to deal with international puppetry. Articles on Indian showmen of special interest.

Bridhyākorn, Prince Dhaninivat Kromamün Bidyalababh. *The Nang*. ("Thailand Culture, New Series," No. 3, 3rd edition.) Bangkok: The Fine Arts Department, 1962.

This pamphlet has illustrations of shadow-puppets with notes on history and production techniques. In the same series, Number 6 on *The Khon* and Number 7 on *Khon Masks*, are also of interest to puppeteers. They were obtainable at the Museum in 1964, and probably still are.

Chesnais, Jacques. *Histoire Générale des Marionnettes*. Paris: Bordas, 1947.

This work has a good general historical background, with accounts of French puppet characters, and puppeteers active before 1947.

Craig, Edward Gordon. *The Marionette, Tonight at 12:30*, Vol. I, Nos. 1–12, Florence, Italy: 1918.

These little volumes contain many illustrated articles on all phases of puppet theatre, and they are among the early writings of the puppet theatre revival.

Eudel, Paul. *Les Ombres Chinoises de Mon Père*. Paris: Edouard Rouveyre, éditeur, [c. 1885].

This is a collection of plays, but the illustrations give a good idea of the style of the "Chinese Shadows" popular in the nineteenth century.

Gasch, Sebastian. *Títeres y Marionetas*. Barcelona and Buenos Aires: Libreria Editorial, Argos, S.A., 1949.

An account of the principal Spanish puppeteers before 1949.

Gauchat, Pierre. *Marionettes*. Erlenbach-Zurich: Eugen Rentsch Verlag A. G. 1950.

There are eight handsome color lithographs, 10¼″ x 14½″, of marionette characters. Edwin Arnet's astute observations about puppet theatre and Gauchet's notes on performances at the Zurich Marionette Theatre comprise the text. There are also many excellent black and white illustrations and sketches. A collector's item.

Gervais, André-Charles. *Marionnettes et Marionnettistes de France*. Paris: Bordas, 1947.

This book is important for its account of French puppeteers in Paris and the provinces, some of whom are still active, and for its extensive bibliography of puppet books in French.

Guiette, Robert. *Marionnettes de Tradition Populaire*. Brussels: Éditions du Cercle d'Art, 1950.

A valuable account of the traditional rod operated puppets of Belgium. A general introduction is followed by a description of puppetry in various cities such as Anvers, Brussels, Liège, with the text of a characteristic play from each. There are 53 plates of illustrations.

Hadamowski, Franz. *Teschner und sein Figurenspiegel.* Wien-Stuttgart: Eduard Wancure Verlag.

A study of Teschner's famous rod-puppet theatre.

Hansmann, Claus. *Puppenspiel in der Welt.* West Berlin: F. A. Herbig Verlag, 1966.

With illustrations of world puppets.

———. *Schattenspiel aus Szetschuan.* München: Ehrenwirth Verlag, 1964.

With text and some colored illustrations of shadow-puppets.

Jacob, Georg. *Geschichte des Schattentheatres im Morgen und Ubendland.* Hannover: Orient Buchhandlung Heinz Lafaire, 1925.

Jacob is a leading authority on the shadow theatre. In this and his other books, he presents a scholarly analysis of the principal shadows of the world. There is a 57-page bibliography.

Jeanne, Paul. *Les Théâtres d'Ombres à Montmartre de 1887 à 1923.* Paris: Les Presses Modernes, 1937.

The shadow theatre of the Parisian cabaret, the Black Cat, was famous for the artists, poets and musicians who produced its shows, and this is an account of it and other theatres which it inspired.

deKleen, Tyra. *Wayang (Javanese Theatre).* ("Publications of the Ethnographical Museum of Sweden," New Series, No. 3.) Stockholm: Bokforlags Aktiebolaget Thule, 1937.

A description of the various forms of Javanese Theatre (Wayang), notes on plays and a summary of *The Story of Arayana* are contained in this handsome volume. There are 18 full page plates of the author's paintings in color of the rod-puppet characters for this play, and 20 of dance poses illustrating her discussion of the Serimpis. A collector's item.

Kolar, Erik. *Puppetry in Czechoslovakia.* Prague: Orbis, 1957.

There have been a number of editions of this book, which is updated from time to time. It deals with both past and present puppetry.

Kuřsová, Květa. *Le Théâtre en Tchécoslovaquie.* Prague: L'Institute du Théâtre, n.d. [but c. 1964].

An excellent pictorial survey of modern Czech puppetry, with an introduction by Kuřsová and articles by a number of leading puppeteers.

Magnin, Charles. *Histoire des Marionnettes en Europe depuis l'antiquité jusqu'à nos jours.* Paris: Michel Lévy Freres, 1852. Second edition, 1862.

This is the work to which all puppet historians are indebted, for Magnin was the first scholar to set down the development of the puppet theatre in the Western world, and he did a thorough job. A collector's item.

Maindron, Ernest. *Marionnettes et Guignols*. Paris: Félix Juven, 1900.

Although there are chapters on puppets in some European countries, and the shadows of Turkey, Java and China, this book deals primarily with important French puppet theatres.

Malik, Napsal Jan. *Joseph Skupa, Národní Umělec*. Prague: Státni nakladatelství krásné literatury a umění, 1962.

This noted Czech puppeteer provides notes on Czech puppet history, and tells the story of Skupa, this country's most famous puppet showman. There are many illustrations and sketches.

Mignon, Paul-Louis, Moulen, Jean-Pierre, and Dalain, Yvan. *J'aime les Marionnettes*, Lausanne: Éditions Rencontre, 1962.

One of the most important modern publications, this book has an excellent pictorial record of French puppetry with equally good articles on its history, and that of the puppet theatre in general. There are also notes on well-known puppet characters from many countries, and an international glossary of puppet terms.

Neuville, Lemercier de. *Histoire Anecdotique des Marionnettes Modernes*. Paris: Calmann-Levy, 1892.

———. *Les Pupazzi Noirs*. Paris: Ch. Mendel, 1896.

———. *Souvenirs d'un Montreur de Marionnettes*. Paris: M. Bauche, 1911.

———. *Théâtre des Marionnettes à l'Usage des Enfants*. 2 vols. Paris: Bornemann, 1904.

The writings of this author have much historical interest. His *Souvenirs* is the story of his puppet work, with many references to famous people of his time. In addition to the above books, he published several volumes of plays (see Ransome, *Puppets and Shadows*).

Niessen, Carl. *Das Rheinische Puppenspiel*. Bonn: Fritz Klopp Verlag G.M.B.H., 1928.

The traditional rod-puppet theatre in Cologne has existed for more than 100 years, and this is a scholarly history of it, with texts from some of its plays centering around the character of Hänneschen.

Od Szopki do Teatru Lalek. Edited by a group of Polish puppeteers, with articles by Jan Sztaudynger, Henryk Jurkowski and Henryk Ryl, Wydawnictwo Lodzkie. [c. 1962].

An excellent collection of pictures of modern Polish puppets and scenes, and biographies of some leading Polish puppeteers.

Pinon, Roger, and Dewez, León. *Quand les Marionnettes du Monde se donnent la Main.* Liége: Commission du Folklore de la Saison Liégeoise, 1958.

There is a wealth of information in this 500-page volume: the catalogue of the International Exhibit of Traditional Marionettes; notes on theatres which performed during its display; texts of talks given by eminent puppeteers at the International Congress of Traditional Marionettes which ran concurrently.

Purschke, Hans R. *Liebenswerte Puppenwelt.* Hamburg: Marion von Schröeder Verlag, 1962.

With text and 184 pages of illustrations of many puppet theatres.

————. *The Puppet Theatre in Germany.* Darmstadt: Neue Darmstadter Verlagsanstalt, 1957.

Reinfuss, Roman. *Szopki Krakowskie.* Krakow: Wydawnictwo Artystyczno-Graficzne RSW "Prasa," 1958.

This small book contains eight color and many black and white pictures of the traditional Polish puppet theatres used for performances at Christmas, with a historical account of their origin and development.

Ritter, Hellmut. *Karagös, Türkische Schattenspiele.* Hannover: Orient-Buchhandlung Heinz Lafaire, 1924.

A collection of translations into German of Karagös plays. Eight fine color plates and many in sepia wash of the characters are included in this large, beautifully printed volume. A collector's item.

Siyavusgil, Sabri Esat. *Karagöz.* Ankara, Turkey: Saim Toraman Basimevi, 1955, The Turkish Press, Broadcasting and Tourist Department, Publisher.

The author, a professor at the University of Istanbul, presents an excellent historical account of the Turkish shadow theatre, with notes on its characters and its mystical, satirical spirit. There are 22 large plates reproduced in not very accurate color from paintings of characters and scenery pieces, which are adequate for identification.

Tilakasiri, J. *Puppetry in Ceylon.* ("Arts of Ceylon Series," No. 1.) Colombo: Department of Cultural Affairs, 1961.

This little book has information about the relatively unrecorded puppets of Ceylon with a few illustrations.

Vermorel, Jean. *Quelque Petits Théâtres Lyonnais des XVIII et XIX Siècles.* Lyon: Cumin et Masson, 1918.

Visan, Tancrède de. *Le Guignol Lyonnais.* Paris: Bloud et Cie., 1910.

Both the above books deal with the Guignol theatres of Lyon, and the latter contains a good bibliography.

Warsage, Rodolphe de. *Histoire du Célèbre Théâtre Liégeois de Marionnettes.* Brussels: Librairie Nationale d'Art et d'Histoire, G. Van Oest and Co., 1905.

The special character of the puppet theatre of Liége is here described, historically and technically. There is also a list of fifty-four puppet theatres operating in 1902, and the text of *The Nativity.*

PUPPET MAKING AND PRODUCTION

Many technical books on puppetry have been published in the United States during the past two decades, the majority designed for educational use. Most of those in print are here listed, together with a few British titles. Some out-of-print books are included, designated by *.

Nearly all the books stress puppet construction with less said about the dramatic uses of puppets or their importance as a creative art, but some of the more recent ones have a balanced treatment of all phases of production. Many suggestions which purport to be suitable for children are too difficult, and they reiterate traditional methods which tend to be fussy and stilted rather than broad and creative. Stages are almost invariably too small for adequate freedom of movement.

To suggest ways of bringing puppet design and production closer to modern practices in art education, creative drama, dance, and music, the reader is referred to the titles listed under *Art and Theatre.* Along with the recent spate of puppet books for children, some dealing with professional puppetry are listed.

Ackley, Edith Flack. *Marionettes: Easy to Make, Fun to Use.* New York: Frederick A. Stokes Co., 1929. Now published by J. B. Lippincott Co.

Directions for making and using cloth marionettes are presented in this early technical book, which is still sound in its basic principles, although sewing is not as easy for children as some other methods.

Adair, Margaret Weeks. *Do-It-In-a-Day Puppets for Beginners.* New York: John Day Co., 1964.

Utilizing creative techniques, easy construction methods are described, with directions for preparing scripts, staging and performing. Nicely illustrated with color photos and patterns.

*Batchelder, Marjorie, and Michael, Vivian. *Hand-and-Rod-Puppets.* Columbus: Ohio State University Press, 1947.

Diagrams and directions for making and using this versatile type of puppet, invented by Nina Efimova and dedicated to her.

————, and Comer, Virginia Lee. *Puppets and Plays, A Creative Approach.* New York: Harper & Row, 1956.

New techniques for puppet and playmaking, staging, production, with emphasis on puppetry as a dramatic medium, and puppet theatre as a distinctive form of theatre.

————. *The Puppet Theatre Handbook.* New York: Harper & Row, 1947.
   A comprehensive technical manual for the construction of all types of
puppets, staging, play selection, and production. This book presents
both simple and advanced methods.

*Beaton, Mabel, and Les, *Marionettes, A Hobby for Everyone.* New
York: Thomas Y. Crowell Co., 1948.
   For those interested in realistic productions, this book offers clear construction diagrams and photographs, with complete directions for
making marionettes, stages, properties, scenery; for planning lighting,
and production. Text of *Beauty and the Beast* included.

Bennett, O. W. *Skits, Puppets and Ceremonies.* ("Pow Wow Series," No.
4390A). Boy Scouts of America.
   Directions for making simple puppets of several types, notes on
stages, manipulation and plays, all directed to the use of puppets for
Scout or other groups.

Binyon, Helen. *Puppetry Today.* London: Studio Vista, Ltd., 1966. In the
United States, Watson-Guptill Publications.
   An important book with a contemporary outlook which stresses new
approaches and experimentation. Information about historical and present-day puppets is presented, along with suggestions for making marionettes, hand-puppets, rod-puppets and shadows, the last being the most
stimulating. There are excellent illustrations of traditional and modern
puppets, and clear marginal diagrams of technical details of puppets
and stages.

*Blackman, Olive. *Puppets Into Actors.* London: Rockliff, 1948.
   The author, one of England's leading puppeteers, gives directions for
marionette making, and stresses production details, such as rehearsals.
The illustrations are stimulating and more "contemporary" than one
would expect in 1948.

*————. *Shadow Puppets.* London: Barrie and Rockliff, 1960. American
edition, Harper and Row, 1960.
   The first part of this book is an excellent history of shadows, the
second is a practical guide to making and staging shadow shows, with
suggestions for suitable plays. A good bibliography and a list of museums with important shadow-puppet collections are included.

Bodor, John. *Creating and Presenting Hand Puppets.* New York: Reinhold
Publishing Corp., 1967.
   Lists of materials are given at the beginning of each chapter, with
step-by-step instructions for preparing the script, puppets, properties,
special effects, lights, stages, performances. The head construction of
styrofoam balls covered with plaster of Paris seems cumbersome, and

the procedures somewhat cut and dried, doubtless so planned to fit into tight school schedules. Clear photographs illustrate processes.

Bramall, Eric, and Somerville, Christopher C. *Expert Puppet Technique.* London: Faber and Faber, Ltd., 1963. Published in the United States by Plays, Inc.

One of the few books dealing with production, this one has valuable notes on design, script writing, manipulation (based on the vertical controller), settings, lighting, rehearsal and performance.

————. *Making a Start with Marionettes.* London: G. Bell, 1961.

Written for the adult amateur beginner, two methods of constructing relatively simple marionettes are described, together with production notes.

Bufano, Remo. *Remo Bufano's Book of Puppetry.* New York: Macmillan Co., 1950.

Based on an earlier Bufano book, *Be A Puppet Showman,* this one has a historical introduction, directions for making hand-puppets with wooden heads and hands; also animals and notes on a puppet theatre. Marionette making with stuffed bodies, papier-mâché or wooden heads, notes on acting and plays, with the text of four plays of varying lengths are all included.

*Bussell, Jan. *The Puppet Theatre.* London: Faber and Faber, Ltd., 1946.

In addition to sound construction methods for different types of puppets, the author has a good chapter on production and another on "new spheres" for puppets, which were just becoming evident in 1946.

Cassell, Sylvia. *Fun with Puppets.* Nashville: The Broadman Press, 1956.

Small, fussy puppets made from peanuts, dried raisins and things are not quite adequate, but other ideas for simple puppets are usable. There is also a section on Puppetry in Religious Education.

Creegan, George. *Sir George's Book of Hand Puppetry.* Chicago: Follett Publishing Co., 1967.

For those interested in using Celastic, complete instructions are given, with clear illustrations. Brief production notes are included.

Cummings, Richard. *101 Hand Puppets.* New York: David McKay Co., Inc., 1962.

Many good ideas for simple, even "instant" puppets and stages are in this book, with the usual plastic wood and papier-mâché methods for professional puppets. Plays suitable for various puppet types are included, but there is more stress on construction than production.

Curry, Louise H., and Wetzel, Chester M. *Teaching with Puppets.* Philadelphia: Fortress Press, 1966.

An excellent analysis of the value of puppets as a teaching tool, with many suggestions for their use, based on current educational philosophy. Construction details given are less satisfactory and so are the two play examples which are narrative rather than dramatic. The basic elements of drama are outlined and ways to develop it creatively are given. Graded lists of story sources and a bibliography drawn from various sources as well as puppetry add to the book's usefulness.

*Dwiggins, W. A. *Marionette in Motion.* (Handbook XII.) Birmingham, Michigan: Puppetry Imprints, 1939.

Many professional puppeteers have found this well-balanced construction system basic to good movement.

Ficklen, Bessie A. *A Handbook of Fist Puppets.* New York: Frederick A. Stokes Co., 1935. Now published by J. B. Lippincott Co.

This is still a basic source for hand-puppet construction and presentation.

French, Susan. *Presenting Marionettes.* New York: Reinhold Publishing Co., 1964.

An exposition of a somewhat difficult construction method, suitable only for skilled puppeteers, clearly illustrated, with notes on staging, lighting and scenery for the story of *Persephone,* but with no comparable emphasis on production or drama.

Goaman, Muriel. *Judy's and Andrew's Puppet Book.* London: Faber and Faber, Ltd., 1942. American edition, Plays, Inc., 1967.

A simple enough way for children to make hand-puppets is described, with the text of *Punch and Judy.* Marionette construction from wire with heads of "fire cement," however, is not simple. The stages suggested are small and cramped, only slightly larger than those of the toy theatre.

Hopper, Grizella H. *Puppet Making Through the Grades.* Worcester: Davis Publications, 1967.

This recent book is in line with the creative work in art now often found in school programs. Many simple ways to make puppets are described. These allow for imagination and direct designing with materials, other than the traditional papier-mâché method, which is also included. Puppetry as dramatic play is explored and creative drama is suggested as a basis for play making. Although table top performances are mentioned, the stage pictured is the usual small booth in which little freedom of movement is possible. The illustrations of children's work are delightful.

Inverarity, R. B. *A Manual of Puppetry.* Portland: Binfords and Mort, 1936. Second edition, 1938.

Basic principles of puppet construction and presentation are here supplemented by an anthology of excerpts from famous works relating to puppets.

Jagendorf, Moritz. *Puppets for Beginners.* Boston: Plays, Inc., 1966. Originally published under the title *The First Book of Puppets* by Franklin Watts, New York, 1952.

Most of the construction methods here shown are simple enough for children. Staging shows on tables, in doorways, behind furniture are suggested as well as the usual small puppet booth. The pictures, including some of puppets in various parts of the world, are colorful and stimulating.

Jaeger, Emilie. *Quickie Puppets.* Phoenix: Arizona (753 East Montecito St., 85014).

With styrofoam heads and costumes glued instead of sewed, this method takes much of the tedium out of puppet making and allows for individual imagination. Complete instructions for these hand-puppets are given, with suggestions for stages, manipulation and plays.

Lanchester, Waldo S. *Hand Puppets and String Puppets.* Leicester: Dryad Press, 1937. Eleventh edition, 1965.

This little book has been in print for over thirty years, and still is useful for its descriptions of plaster casting, papier-mâché, and several construction methods for hand-puppets, marionettes and stages. A detailed, full-size diagram sheet for an eighteen-inch marionette is included in the last edition.

Lee, Miles. *Puppet Theatre, Production and Manipulation.* London: Faber and Faber, Ltd., 1958.

This book stresses those aspects of puppet production which are not usually given adequate consideration, such as theory of the puppet theatre, its artistic and educational uses, detailed notes on movement, grouping, light plots, speech and acting. Primarily for professional puppeteers, everyone working with puppets would benefit by a careful reading of it.

Lewis, Shari, and Oppenheimer, Lillian. *Folding Paper Puppets.* New York: Stein and Day, 1962.

———. *Folding Paper Masks.* New York: Dutton and Co., 1965.

———. *Folding Paper Toys.* New York: Stein and Day, 1963.

Lewis, Shari. *Making Easy Puppets.* New York: Dutton and Co., 1967.

Based on Origami, the folded paper designs in these books offer stimulation for imaginative puppet designing, even though they are meant for young children. In the last named book, the author has presented ways of making puppets from many simple materials, added notes on how to use them, and a short history of puppets.

MacNamara, Desmond. *Puppetry*. New York: Horizon Press, 1966.

There is considerable emphasis upon rod-puppets, with some workable construction methods for them. Less satisfactory is the wire and papier-mâché marionette. One chapter is devoted to nodding heads and movable features. There are notes on glove-puppets and a good plan for an open proscenium stage for puppets worked from below.

*McPharlin, Paul. *Animal Marionettes*. (Handbook X.) Birmingham, Michigan: Puppetry Imprints, 1936.

Basic construction for many animals, with indications of scale, are included.

*Merten, George. *The Hand Puppet*. New York and Toronto: Thomas Nelson and Sons, 1957.

*———. *The Marionette*. New York and Toronto: Thomas Nelson and Sons, 1957.

The basic principles of marionette and hand-puppet construction are covered in these two books.

*Mills, Winifred, and Dunn, Louise M. *Marionettes, Masks and Shadows*. New York: Doubleday, Doran and Co., 1927.

*———. *Shadow Plays and How to Produce Them*. New York: Doubleday, Doran and Co., 1939.

These two books were among the early technical studies published in the United States, with ideas which are still valid.

Morton, Brenda. *Needlework Puppets*. Boston: Plays, Inc., 1967. First published in Great Britain, 1964.

For anyone skilled with the needle, this book offers many ideas for attractive puppets which children can operate, even though sewed puppets are not the easiest kind for them to make.

Mulholland, John. *Practical Puppetry*. New York: Arco Publishing Co., Inc., 1968.

An excellent general purpose book, with a thoughtful introduction. A variety of construction methods, simple and advanced, are described, with many clearly illustrated details for joints, stage hardware, scenery supports and special control devices. A number of stages, including two round ones for hand- or rod-puppets are fully described, and a valuable chapter, Visibility on the Puppet Stage, considers sight lines.

Myers, Galene J. *Puppets Can Teach Too*. Los Angeles: Augsburg Publishing House [c. 1966].

The author discusses puppets in religious education and gives some ideas for constructing them. Best of these are large flat felt profile puppets, least practical are the directions for marionettes.

*Nelson, Nicholas, and Hayes, James J. *Trick Marionettes*. (Handbook VI.) Birmingham, Michigan: Puppetry Imprints, 1935.

Explanations given for stringing marionettes to perform many of the traditional tricks.

Pels, Gertrude. *Easy Puppets.* New York: Thomas Y. Crowell Co., 1951.
Hand-puppets which children can make from a variety of common materials are described and illustrated, with notes on stages.

Philpott, A. R. *Modern Puppetry.* London: Michael Joseph, 1966. American edition published by Plays, Inc.
The reader is urged to experiment. Exercises in movement with a variety of materials and objects are suggested to stimulate ideas for puppets to be made. Many construction details are given in the discussion of the basic puppet types. The author is a well-known English showman.

Rasmussen, Carrie, and Storck, Caroline. *Funtime Puppets.* Chicago: Children's Press, Inc., 1952.
Obviously intended for children, some of the construction ideas are unsuitable, such as a wooden marionette joined with opened screw eyes, or the head modelled directly in plastic wood. Other ideas for simple puppets are workable, some stages are described, and the book has colorful illustrations.

Riemenschneider, Ludwig. *A Puppetry Manual.* Garden City, New York: Adelphi University, 1968.
The making of ten simple puppets is described, using oak tag, paper and cloth, with patterns and not very appealing diagrams. There is no mention of plays, production, or the relationship of puppetry to the other programs at the Children's Centre for Creative Arts at Adelphi University.

*Rossbach, Charles Edmund. *Making Marionettes.* New York: Harcourt, Brace Co., 1938.
The essentials of marionette construction are presented, with nicely drawn illustrations, and the texts of three plays.

Schmidt, Hans. *The Puppet as an Actor.* Chicago: Coach House Press, Inc., 1959.
There is a thoughtful introduction about puppet playing, with directions for making papier-mâché heads on electric light bulbs, and some production suggestions.

Slade, Richard. *You Can Make a String Puppet.* London: Faber and Faber, Ltd., American edition published by Plays, Inc., 1966.
The method described here includes papier-mâché heads, wooden and cloth bodies, dowel rod legs and arms—processes satisfactory only for an experienced craftsman. Excellent photographs show construction details.

Snook, Barbara. *Puppets*. Newton Centre, Mass.: Charles T. Branford, 1966.

Planned for school use, this book describes some simple puppet heads, and the usual papier-mâché method. There are construction suggestions for hand-puppets and string-puppets; instructions for special stringing; diagrams for some animal characters (Owl, Cat, Turkey, Pig, Walrus, etc.) for specific plays or poems; a few suggestions for stages and scenery.

Stevens, Martin. *Stevens Correspondence Course in Puppetry*. Middlebury, Indiana 46540.

All phases of construction and production are covered in 20 lessons.

Still, Frank. *Charming Children with Puppets for Thirty-Five Years*. Jacksonville, Florida: Paramount Press, Inc., 1967.

This long-time traveling puppeteer recounts some of his experiences and presents his methods of construction with not-too-clear diagrams and photographs.

Wall, L. V., White, G. A., and Philpott, A. R. (eds.). *The Puppet Book*. London: Faber and Faber, Ltd., 1960. Published in the United States by Plays, Inc., Boston. Revised edition of *The Complete Puppet Book*, 1950.

A number of English puppeteers have contributed to this book on educational puppetry which covers all aspects of production.

Whanslaw, H. W. *Animal Puppetry*. London: Wells Gardner, Darton & Co., Ltd., 1939.

————. *The Bankside Book of Puppets*. London: Wells Gardner, Darton & Co., Ltd., 1935.

————. *A Bench Book of Puppetry*. London: Wells Gardner, Darton & Co., Ltd., 1957.

————. *Everybody's Marionette Book*. London: Wells Gardner, Darton & Co., Ltd., 1935.

————. *Everybody's Theatre and How to Make It*. London: Wells Gardner, Darton & Co., Ltd., 1923.

————. *A Second Bench Book of Puppetry*. London: Wells Gardner, Darton & Co., Ltd.,

————. *Shadow Play*. London: Wells Gardner, Darton & Co., Ltd., 1950.

————. *Specialized Puppetry*. London: Wells Gardner, Darton & Co., Ltd., 1948.

For several decades Whanslaw has been writing excellent technical books on puppetry, which are full of detailed information. Some are still available from the publisher.

*Wynnychuk, Marshall. *Puppetry for Magicians*. Calgary, Alberta, Canada: Micky Hades, 1962.

For showmen who want to combine magic and puppets, this book offers suggestions by a well-known practitioner of both techniques.

PLAYS FOR PUPPETS

Books dealing with puppet making and production often contain one or two plays, but few volumes of collected puppet plays have been published. Most puppeteers must write their own plays. For children's programs, good children's books, such as the Caldecott and Newbery Award winners suggest ideas, and a list of stories suitable for adaptation is found in *Puppets and Plays* (Batchelder and Comer). Creative playmaking is also explained in this book. For adult interest, several titles which appeared years ago are included in the following list, but little is published currently to interest adults in puppet drama. For those concerned with the repertories of foreign theatres, many titles are listed in Grace Ransome's bibliography, *Puppets and Shadows*, in the bibliography of Paul McPharlin's *A Repertory of Marionette Plays*, while a further source is J. Frances Crothers' *The Puppeteer's Library Guide*.

Baumann, Hans. *Casper and His Friends*. Translated by Joyce Emerson, London: Dent [c. 1967].
   Ten puppet plays for children from German sources are included.
Beer, Lisl. *The Silver Series of Puppet Plays*. Boston: Bruce Humphries, 1961–1966. The last two published by Brandon Press, Boston, which now handles all the titles.
   The eighteen plays in this series, published in separate volumes, represent a variety of original and adapted stories from foreign literature. They vary in suitability for puppet production.
Bramall, Eric. *Puppet Plays and Playwriting*. London: G. Bell, 1961.
   Essentials of the puppet play and making it from stories or original themes are discussed, with examples of scripts to illustrate. A section on "pure puppetry" deals with ideas which cannot be portrayed by human actors.
*Brown, Forman. *The Pie-Eyed Piper and Other Impertinent Puppet Plays*. New York: Greenberg, 1933.
   These five are representative of the gay, witty, musical plays which characterized the work of the Yale Puppeteers through the years at the Turnabout Theatre and before.
*Bufano, Remo. *Magic Strings*. New York: Macmillan Co., 1939.
   Some of these plays are not suitable for children but there are several which are usable.
Bussell, Jan. *Plays for Puppets*. London: Faber and Faber, Ltd., 1951.

————. *Twelve Plays for Pelham Puppets.* Marlborough, Wilshire: Pelham Puppets, Ltd., n.d.

Both of these collections, the second one graded, contain good plays in a variety of styles, mostly with unhackneyed subjects, suitable for a variety of audiences.

*Collier, John Payne. *Punch and Judy.* London: S. Prowett, 1828.

This was the first edition of this famous play, with illustrations designed and engraved by George Cruikshank. Five editions followed, the sixth in 1873, with substantially the same text and illustrations. Many other versions of the play have also been published. In 1937, it was issued by the Limited Editions Club, edited with an introduction by Paul McPharlin, and 24 sketches in color by Cruikshank never before printed. See below for a modern edition.

*Dwiggins, W. A. *Millennium I.* New York: Alfred A. Knopf, 1945.

An imaginative and serious puppet play for adults, with machines as the dominant characters who almost obliterate Man.

Emberley, Ed. *Punch and Judy.* Boston and Toronto: Little Brown and Co., 1965.

A recent edition, with sprightly ink and color illustrations. Four action sketches appear on the left hand page with text on the right, and there is a frontispiece and "curtain call" showing all characters on stage.

Jagendorf, Moritz. *Penny Puppets, Penny Theatre and Penny Plays.* New York: Bobbs-Merrill Co., 1941. New edition published by Plays, Inc., 1966.

Construction methods described here are not of the best for children, but there are a number of usable plays.

Joseph, Helen Haiman. *Cinderella, Snow White and the Seven Dwarfs, Pinocchio, Hansel and Gretel, Jack and the Beanstalk, Sleeping Beauty.* Puppetry Journal Publications, Ashville, Ohio 43103.

Separate scripts which are useful dramatizations of these classical stories.

*Kreymborg, Alfred. *Puppet Plays.* With a preface by Gordon Craig. New York: Samuel French, Inc., 1926.

The modern producer interested in drama for adults might find inspiration in these poetic, rather static plays for his own compositions, using words and moods in fresh ways.

Latshaw, George. *Pinocchio.* Chicago: Coach House Press, 1957.

Written for live actors and two marionettes, the staging is in the manner of the Commedia dell'Arte.

*Maeterlinck, Maurice. *Alladine and Palomides, Interior, The Death of Tintagiles.* London: Duckworth and Co., 1899.

Words are more important than action in these plays, and are used to create strong suspense. They are tragedies, pervaded by a sense of doom. For those interested in deeper content for puppet plays, these offer ideas in the use of language, of suggestion, and of the power of impersonality. This edition is out of print, but the plays may be found in the author's collected works.

*McPharlin, Paul. *A Repertory of Marionette Plays.* New York: Viking Press, 1929.

A collection of fourteen plays from various countries, written by well-known authors such as Goethe, Maeterlinck, Craig, or drawn from traditional puppet theatre repertoires, such as those of Duranty, Mourguet, Bonneschky. There is an excellent bibliography, including plays in many languages.

*Merten, George, and Elizabeth. *Eight Plays for the Puppet Theatre.* Toronto: Thomas Nelson and Sons, Ltd., 1958.

Seven excellent original plays, written especially for puppets, take advantage of their special abilities; the eighth is a detailed action pattern for a musical interpretation done in the Commedia dell'Arte manner.

Philpott, A. R. (ed.). *Eight Plays for Hand Puppets.* London: J. Garnet Miller, Ltd., 1968. American edition published by Plays, Inc.

These plays, suitable for grade school children, are written by members of the Educational Puppetry Association of England, or by children under the direction of their teachers. A brief but good introduction to playmaking and production is included.

*Sand, Maurice. *Plays for Marionettes.* Translated by Babette and Glenn Hughes. New York: Samuel French, Inc., 1931.

Written for performance in the Théâtre des Amis between 1860 and 1880, these five comedies by George Sand's son are still interesting, especially to adults.

Stahl, LeRoy, and Preston, Effa E. *The Master Puppet Book.* Minneapolis: T. S. Denison and Co., Inc., 1964.

This 400-page volume has a great variety of original plays. Many have irrelevant interpolated songs and end with rather meaningless dances. Detailed instructions for the costumes and settings are included, the latter somewhat elaborate, with painted backdrops and wings which would overpower the puppets if not very carefully handled.

Tichenor, Tom. *Folk Plays for Puppets You Can Make.* Nashville: Abingdon Press, 1959.

Suggestions for very simple puppets which children can make are included with the texts for five plays based on favorite stories.

Whanslaw, H. W. *A Book of Marionette Plays.* London: Wells Gardner, Darton and Co., Ltd.,

Another useful book in the series written by this long-time worker in the English puppet theatre.

PUPPET PERIODICALS

A few of the important puppet periodicals are here listed. In addition, the Newsletters of some of the Puppetry Guilds have sufficient content to be classed as periodicals.

Československý Loutkář. Dr. Miroslav Česal, Editor. Prague II, Vinohrady, Vinohradská 3, Czechoslovakia.

This is probably the oldest puppet periodical in existence, having first appeared in 1917 and continued, with some interruptions, to the present. It records puppet activities not only in Czechoslovakia, but in other parts of the world. Published monthly, it is to be found on newsstands.

Figuren Theater. The Deutches Institut für Puppenspiel, Bergstrasse 115, Bochum, German Federal Republic.

Marionettes. UNIMA-France, 86 rue Notre Dame des Champs, Paris, 6ᵉ, France.

This has grown into a well illustrated and printed publication with editorials, articles, and reviews.

Perlicko-Perlacko. Dr. Hans R. Purschke, Editor and Publisher. 6 Frankfurt/Main, Postfach 135, German Federal Republic.

Het Poppenspel. Louis Contryn, Editor. Auwegemvaart, 87, Malines, Belgium.

A good publication, with articles, illustrations and a puppet play in each issue.

The Puppet Master. The British Puppet and Model Theatre Guild, c/o Harold Aidalberry, Treasurer, 46 Northumberland Ave., Wanstead Park, London, E. 12, England.

The Puppet Post. The Educational Puppetry Association, 23A Southampton Place, London, W.C. 1, England.

Published quarterly.

The Puppetry Journal. The Puppeteers of America, Olga Stevens, Executive Secretary, Box 1061, Ojai, California 93023.

Published bi-monthly by the Puppeteers of America for its members. Contains news, articles, reviews, and illustrations.

Teatr Lalek. Lódz, ul. Piotrkowska 116, Poland. Distributed by Ruch, Warszawa (Warsaw), ul. Wilcza 46, Poland.

The Polish puppet theatres utilize modern techniques of design and staging, which are well illustrated in this periodical. Puppet theatres in other countries are also considered.

Le Théâtre en Pologne. The Polish Center of the International Theatre Institute, Varsovie (Warsaw), ul. Moliera 1, Poland.

With French and English text, this periodical is useful to puppeteers for its stimulating accounts of the Polish Theatre, and especially for the issues devoted to the puppet theatre which appear about once a year. Published monthly.

ART AND THEATRE

This selection of books is included to provide inspiration for the puppeteer from the whole field of the plastic, graphic and performing arts.

Art

For ideas useful in designing puppets, there are many fine books on painting and sculpture. Among these, the catalogues of exhibits at the Museum of Modern Art (11 West 53rd Street, New York, N.Y. 10019) are recommended to those interested in stylization. Art teachers in the public schools have access to many books which stress the creative use of materials, and some of those on the list, *Books for Art Education,* available from Davis Publications, Inc., would be stimulating to puppeteers. Many other publishers of educational books have similar lists. Also, many illustrated children's books have a style quality which would be suitable for puppets and scenery.

Baranski, Matthew. *Mask Making, Creative Methods and Techniques.* Revised edition. Worcester: Davis Publications, 1966.

Several construction methods, from paper bag masks to professional types, are described in detail and illustrated with diagrams and photographs. There are interesting "body masks" for bird and animal characters.

Betts, Victoria Bedford. *Exploring Papier Mâché.* Worcester: Davis Publications, Inc. [c. 1962].

Most puppet books explain head-making with papier mâché, but this one extends the technique to many other uses.

Cole, Natalie Robinson. *The Arts in the Classroom.* New York: John Day Co., 1942.

————. *Children's Arts from Deep Down Inside.* New York: John Day Co., 1966.

The first Cole book deals with the value of the various arts and how they can be related to a broad creative program, and the second is a further exploration of children's art.

D'Amico, Victor. *Creative Teaching in Art.* Scranton, Pa.: International Textbook Co., 1953.

Although he has not worked directly with puppets, D'Amico has long been a proponent of art teaching techniques which stimulate and guide creativity. What he says of art is basically sound as applied to puppet making and presentation. If followed, his ideas could do much to free educational puppetry from the stilted approaches too often used.

Fabri, Ralph. *Sculpture in Paper.* New York: Watson-Guptill Publications, 1966.

Basic forms are explained and illustrated, directions for making human and animal shapes are included, as well as insects, birds, sea creatures and imaginary beasties. Some inanimate objects, mobiles, stabiles, and ideas for holiday decorations are shown. Ten color pictures, although gay and brilliant, show designs which are not quite as satisfactory as the clean-cut quality of many others in the book.

Frankels, Lillian, and Godfrey. *Creating from Scrap.* New York: Sterling Publishing Co., 1962.

At the present time, much stress is placed upon the imaginative use of common materials in art programs. This and similar books offer many suggestions for the puppeteer.

Hughes, Toni. *How to Make Shapes in Space.* New York: E. P. Dutton and Co., Inc., 1955.

The several ways of making three-dimensional shapes here explained could be useful for making imaginative puppets and scenery pieces.

Johnson, Pauline. *Creating with Paper.* Seattle: University of Washington Press, 1958. Available in regular edition and popular edition (paper over boards).

Of the many books dealing with paper as a medium for creating all sorts of objects as well as sculptural forms, this one is especially valuable for the handsome photographs which stress the clean-cut beauty of white paper. Fundamental principles are explained, and many applications of them are suggested.

Johnston, Mary Grace. *Paper Sculpture.* Revised edition. Worcester: Davis Publications, Inc., 1965.

A smaller volume than the preceding, but with many stimulating ideas especially useful for work with children.

Lord, Lois. *Collage and Construction.* Worcester: Davis Publications, Inc., 1958.

Some of the techniques here described could be used in puppet construction and the principles of collage applied to scenery could be effective.

Lowenfeld, Viktor, and Brittain, W. L. *Creative and Mental Growth*. 4th
Edition. New York: Macmillan Co., 1964.

This has long been a standard work on the nature of creativity in
children, which could well be considered in educational puppet work.

Lynch, John. *How to Make Collages*. New York: Viking Press, 1961.

Another educator explains collage and its uses. He has also written
books on mobiles and metal sculpture, which would be of interest to
puppeteers.

Mearns, Hughes. *Creative Power: The Education of Youth in the Creative
Arts*. 2nd revised edition. New York: Dover Publications, Inc., 1958.

Ever since its publication in 1929, this has been a favorite book
among those interested in creative education, for it illuminates the
subject with insight and charm.

————. *The Creative Adult*. Garden City, Long Island, New York:
Doubleday and Co., Inc., 1940.

Pauli, Anna E., and Mitzit, Margaret. *Paper Figures*. Peoria, Ill.: Chas. A.
Bennett Co., Inc., 1967.

More ideas and techniques for using the versatile medium of paper.

Penrose, Roland. *The Sculpture of Picasso*. New York: Museum of Modern
Art, 1967.

No modern artist has presented such a variety of work in painting,
sculpture and other media as Picasso. This handsome volume, containing illustrations of his recent New York showing of sculpture, should
point the way to imaginative concepts of form in puppet design. Alfred
A. Barr, Jr., in 1946, prepared an equally informative catalogue of an
earlier Museum exhibit entitled *Picasso, Fifty Years of His Art*.

Rasmusen, Henry, and Grant, Art. *Sculpture from Junk*. New York: Reinhold.

Read, Carl, and Orze, Joseph. *How to Make Things from Scrap*. Worcester: Davis Publications, Inc., 1960.

These two books, one emphasizing sculptural form and the other a
variety of objects, give further ideas for the creative use of common
materials.

Weiss, Harvey. *Clay, Wood and Wire*. New York: William R. Scott, Inc.,
1956.

With these three media, a variety of forms can be made, many of
which are applicable to puppetry.

Creative Drama

Siks, Geraldine Brain. *Creative Dramatics: An Art for Children*. New
York: Harper & Row, 1958.

Slade, Peter. *Child Drama*. London: University of London Press, Ltd., 1964.

————. *An Introduction to Child Drama*. London: University of London Press, Ltd., 1958.

Ward, Winifred. *Playmaking with Children*. New York: Appleton-Century-Crofts, Inc., 1947.

Of the four titles above, the most penetrating is Slade's *Child Drama*, although Winifred Ward's book is better known in this country, for she is a pioneer in all aspects of children's theatre, and her influence has been immeasurable.

Dance

Modern dance is one of the liveliest of the arts, and its developments are described in the *Saturday Review's* regular section on Dance. *Newsweek, Time, Dance Magazine* and other periodicals also run articles, and they reflect the growing popularity of this art.

Andrews, Gladys. *Creative Rhythmic Movement for Children*. New York: Prentice-Hall, Inc., 1954.

Useful ideas for movement work with children which can be applied to puppetry.

Cohen, Selma Jeanne (ed.). *The Modern Dance: Seven Statements of Belief*. Middletown: Wesleyan University Press, 1966.

"The Great Leap Forward," *Time* (March 15, 1968), 44–48.

A cover story, featuring Robert Joffrey's ballet *Astarte*. Also included are color pictures and notes on many other avant-garde choreographers and their productions which illustrate the creativity of modern dance.

Haskell, Arnold. *The Wonderful World of Dance*. Garden City, New York: Doubleday and Co., 1960.

This is a lovely book for children which considers dance forms the world over, with colored illustrations and a clear, simple text.

Laban, Rudolf. *Modern Educational Dance*. London: MacDonald and Evans, Ltd., 1963.

This book, and the Cohen title listed above, have fundamental ideas about the nature of modern dance, which is of prime importance to puppeteers interested in significant puppet theatre.

Martin, John. *The Modern Dance*. Brooklyn: Dance Horizons, Inc., 1965.

First published in 1933 this was one of the first attempts to analyze modern dance in America, and it provides a good background for the understanding of the latest developments. Many other titles by this outstanding critic illuminate various phases of the dance.

Sorell, Walter. *The Dance Through the Ages.* New York: Grosset and
Dunlap, 1967.
   Lavishly illustrated, this is a recent addition to the many books on the
history of the dance. It has a section on modern developments.

Theatre

   Books about the history and technique of the theatre are so numerous
that no attempt is made here to list a representative selection. For the
puppeteer, technical works on stage lighting, scenery and staging offer
basic ideas which can be adapted. Masks, especially those used in ceremonies, have stylistic qualities which the puppet designer would find
useful, and there are a number of books to which he can refer. Many
are exhibited in museums. Modern developments, such as Happenings,
Environments, Mixed Media or Total Theatre draw together the various
arts, and the references included below relate to Art, Dance, Music and
Communications as well as Theatre.

Brecht, George. *Chance-Imagery.* New York: Something Else Press, Inc.,
1966.
Cage, John. *Silence.* Cambridge, Mass.: M.I.T. Press, 1966. (Paper)
   A series of observations by this writer and composer who is actively
connected with the most modern developments in theatre and dance.
He works with Merce Cunningham and his dance company, Happenings, tape music and is also a lecturer.
The Drama Review. School of the Arts, New York University, 32 Wash-
ington Place, New York, N.Y. 10003. (Formerly *The Tulane Drama
Review*)
   Published quarterly, this is a magazine of the avant-garde theatre
which sometimes has special issues such as the one on Bertolt Brecht
(T 37, 1967), Happenings (T 30, 1965) and Genet/Ionesco (T 19), as
well as articles on a wide variety of theatrical subjects—even an inter-
view with Peter Schumann about his Bread and Puppet Theatre (T 38,
Winter, 1966).
Ewen, Frederick. *Bertolt Brecht: His Life, His Art and His Times.* New
York: Citadel Press, 1967.
   An understanding of the work of Brecht is important to an under-
standing of much that is happening in the theatre today, and this book
is illuminating as a supplement to the reading of his plays.
Hansen, Al. *A Primer of Happenings and Time/Space Art.* New York:
Something Else Press, Inc., 1965.

Janis, Harriet, and Blesh, Rudi. *Collage.* Philadelphia and New York: Chilton Company, 1962.

Basically an art technique of superimposed images, the principle of collage is also used in music and sound, in film, in the dance, and in Happenings and other modern theatre forms.

Kaprow, Allen. *Assemblage, Environment and Happenings.* New York: Abrams, 1966.

———. *Some Recent Happenings.* New York: Something Else Press, Inc., 1966.

Happenings were first popularized in 1959 by Kaprow, who continues to be active in their production.

Kirby, Michael. *Happenings.* New York: E. P. Dutton and Co., 1965.

Lippard, Lucy R. *Pop Art.* New York: Frederick A. Praeger, 1966.

The glorification of everyday objects, which is the basis of Pop Art, is also to be found in the performing arts in such works as Murray Louis' *Junk Dances,* which reveal its banality, and in Happenings which make full use of both the trivial and the momentous events of life.

Priestley, John B. *Wonderful World of the Theatre.* Garden City, New York: Doubleday and Co., Inc., 1959.

A book about the theatre in the Wonderful World series for children, this is a companion volume to Dance and Music listed above.

Rubin, Joel E., and Watson, Leland H. *Theatrical Lighting Practice.* New York: Theatre Arts Books, 1954.

This is more specialized than the usual books on stage lighting and implies a knowledge of basic principles. A short chapter on puppet stage lighting suggests some of its special problems.

Seitz, William G. *The Art of Assemblage.* New York: The Museum of Modern Art, 1961.

Simon, Bernard and Avivah. *Simon's Directory.* 3rd edition. New York: Package Publicity Service, Inc., 1966.

A valuable reference book which has a bibliography of theatre books and booksellers specializing in them. It lists addresses of periodicals, film distributors, puppeteers (a few), stage equipment, costume materials, and other theatrical supplies.

The Theatre of Bauhaus. Middletown, Conn.: Wesleyan University Press, 1961.

The roots of many modern developments in the arts may be found in this short-lived German school in which noted artists, architects, sculptors and theatre people taught and experimented.

"Theatre Outside the Theatres," *Theatre Design and Technology* (October, 1967), 48.

The Tulane Drama Review. See *The Drama Review.*

Film, Television, Communications

There are many books on animation and other phases of film making to which the interested puppeteer may refer. Likewise, the literature on television is too extensive to be adequately summarized here, for, like film, it is part of the vast field of communications. We suggest only a few titles to point the way to others.

Benešová, Marie. *Od Spalíčku Ke Snu Noci Svatojanské.* Prague: Orbis, 1961.
    A well-illustrated history of Trnka's film work. Czech puppet films are among the best, thanks to Trnka and many others.
Bocek, Jaroslav. *Artist and Puppet Master.* Prague: Artia.
    Also about Trnka.
Hazard, Patrick D. (ed.). *TV as Art.* Champaign, Ill.: National Council of Teachers of English, 1966.
    A series of thoughtful essays by a number of educators and television producers. Marshall Izen's program, *Tottle,* is discussed.
McLuhan, Marshall. *The Medium Is the Massage.* New York: Random House, 1967.
    Also available in paperback by Bantam Books, Inc., New York.
——. *Understanding Media.* New York: McGraw-Hill Book Co., 1964. Also available in paperback by Signet, 1966, New American Library.
    McLuhan's stimulating and controversial writings on communications cannot be ignored by anyone engaged in this field, which includes the puppet theatre. There is an excellent bibliography in the latter book.
Mueller, Robert. *The Science of Art: The Cybernetics of Creative Communication.* New York: John Day Co., 1968.
    Written by a man who is an artist, a writer, a puppeteer and an engineer, this is a mind-stretching book which considers the nature of creativity, the communicative basis of all the arts, including puppetry, and their relationship to science.

Music and Sound

As in the other arts, new developments are taking place in music, not only in form, but also in the technology of recording and presentation, such as the tape recorder and the music synthesizer. These open up a whole new realm of sound and music which should be inspiring to puppeteers, and we list a few writings and recordings to point the way. In addition, some children's records are imaginative, while the rich gamut of sounds from the Far East may provide unusual effects. The creative use of the tape recorder offers unlimited opportunities, and we have therefore included some references to electronic music. Two sources for assistance in sound are: Experiments in Art and Technology, 9 East 16th Street, New York, N.Y. 10003 and Stereo Spontaneous Sound, 6245 Santa Monica Blvd., Los Angeles, Calif. 90028. Puppeteers might find the Rhythm Ace useful. Made by the Ace Company in Japan, it plays popular dance rhythms at the touch of a button, and by manipulating these buttons a variety of rhythm effects in varying speeds can be obtained.

With all this technology, the creative use of simple sound instruments and the human voice, especially in working with children, should not be overlooked, nor should the familiar realms of classical and popular music.

Books and Articles

"Art and Science Proclaim Alliance in Avant-Garde Loft," *The New York Times* (October 11, 1967), p. 49.

"Art and Science: Two Worlds Merge," *Bell Telephone Magazine* (November–December, 1967), p. 12.

"Art and Technology," *Art in America* (January–February, 1968), pp. 28–47.

A special section including "The New Combine" and "Towards Play" by Douglas M. Davis; conversations with Gyorgy Kepes, Billy Klüver and James Seawright.

"Art and Technology Make It Official," *The Wall Street Journal* (October 11, 1967).

Britten, Benjamin, and Holst, Imogen. *Wonderful World of Music*. Garden City, New York: Doubleday and Co., 1960.

Another Wonderful World book for children, with pictures and text about the music of many peoples. Out of print.

Browning, Jon. "Engineer-Artist Teams Shape New Art Forms," *Chemical Engineering* (February 26, 1968), p. 102.

Dolan, Robert E. *Music in Modern Media*. New York: G. Schirmer, Inc., 1967.

Hiller, L., Jr., and Isaacson, L. *Experimental Music*. New York: McGraw-Hill, 1959.

Jenkins, Ella. *This Is Rhythm*. New York: Oak Publishers, 1962.

A helpful book for work with children.

Judd, F. C. *Electronic Music and Music Concrete*. Chester Springs, Pa.: Dufour, 1961.

Powell, Mel. "Electronic Music and Musical Newness," *American Scholar*, Vol. 35, No. 2 (Spring, 1966).

"Theater and Engineering: An Experiment," *Artforum* (February 1967), p. 26.

Recordings

Alakazam the Great. Vee Jay, LP 6000. (Vee Jay Records, 1449 South Michigan Avenue, Chicago, Ill.)

Cage, John. *Fontana Mix—Feed.* Columbia. MS 7139.

Electronic equipment is used for this recording, which also includes electronic music by Karlheinz Stockhausen, Sylvano Bussotti, Earle Brown, and Morton Feldman. Consult the *Schwann Long Playing Record Catalog*, available at all record stores, for listings of other works by Cage, Stockhausen, and other avant-garde composers.

———. *The 25th Retrospective Concert of the Music of John Cage.* KO8P. Six sides.

(From George Avakian, 10 West 33rd St., New York, N.Y. 10012). Performed at Town Hall, May 15, 1958, released in 1959.

Contact with the Godz. ESP 1036, 1037. (ESP-Disk, 156 5th Ave., New York, N.Y. 10010.)

Dr. John, the Night Tripper, Gris-Gris. Atco. SD 33-234. (Atco Records, 1841 Broadway, New York, N.Y. 10023.)

Electronic Music. Folkways. Folk 3435.

Folkways Records has many avant-garde composers on its list.

Electrosonics. Philips. Phi S600047.

A recording of electronic music.

The In Sound from Way Out! Vanguard. VSD 79222.

Electronic pop music.

Orff, Carl. *Music for Children.* Angel. 2-Ang. 3582.

Shankar, Ravi. *Prabhāti; Swara Kāhali* (based on Ragas—Gunkali; Til-ang). Angel S36418.

One of the most interesting influences on modern music is the music of India, especially as popularized by Ravi Shankar. In this recording, Shankar performs with violinist Yehudi Menuhin. The *Schwann Supplementary Catalog*, available at record stores, gives complete listings of international popular and folk music, as well as children's records, Latin American, and imports available in the United States.

Sound effects. Folkways, Elektra, Audio Fidelity, and other record companies have sound effects records of all types, including such records as *Sounds of Science Fiction* (Folkways 6250), *Sounds of Animals* (Folkways 6124), *Circus Carnival Calliope* (Audio Fidelity 5958), *Authentic*

Sounds (Elektra S7), *Sounds of the South American Rain Forest* (Folkways 6120). The Schwann Catalog lists many more.

Varèse, Edgard. *Poème electronique; Hyperprism.* Columbia MS 6146.

   Direct Magnetic Tape Creation. See the Schwann Catalog for other titles by this composer.

Sources for Puppet Books and Films

   Those wishing information about puppets in specific countries may find assistance through the sources listed here. Useful also is the consulate or embassy of a given country, for most of them have a cultural affairs office, and some have films and other material pertaining to art and theatre. The United States embassies also have cultural affairs officers, who usually know about characteristic cultural activities in the country to which they are assigned and who could direct the puppet researcher to suitable sources of information. The countries of Eastern Europe have Ministries of Culture under which the puppet theatres operate. UNIMA has branch organizations in many countries through which information can also be obtained. In addition, museums in all parts of the world may have publications relevant to art, theatre and puppetry.

Puppet Books

Artia, Prague I, Nové Město Ve smečhách 30, Czechoslovakia.

British Book Centre, Inc., 122 East 55th St., New York, N.Y. 10022.
   Books published in Great Britain can be ordered here.

Buchhandlung Lehmkuhl, Konzertvorverkauf und Schallplatten, 8 München 23, Leopoldstrasse 45, German Federal Republic.
   Has puppet books, and issues a list of them from time to time.

Dance Book Gallery, 50 West 53rd St., New York, N.Y. 10019.

Davis Publications, Printers Bldg., Worcester, Mass. 01608.
   Art books useful in puppet design.

R. Roland Dearden, P. O. Box 245, Jenkintown, Penna., 19046.
   Specializes in books of the theatre.

Drama Book Shop, Inc., 150 West 52nd St., New York, N.Y. 10019.
   A good source for all types of books about the theatre.

K. R. Drummond, Bookseller, 30 Hart Grove, Ealing Common, London, W. 5, England.
   Periodically issues catalogue of puppet books, current and out-of-print titles.

Educational Puppetry Association, 23A Southampton Place, London, W. C. 1, England.

Can supply books in print. Also publishes various leaflets on puppet making.

European Publishers Representatives, Inc., 36 West 61st St., New York, N.Y. 10023.

Subscriptions to *Le Théâtre en Pologne* and *Teatr Lalek* can be placed through this company.

Ifan Kyrle Fletcher, 22 Buckingham Gate, London, S. W. 1, England.

Handles puppet books, especially rare and out-of-print titles.

Lee Freeson, P. O. Box 922, Hollywood, Calif. 90028.

Does not stock many puppet books, but deals in books about the theatre, especially rare and foreign titles.

Gotham Book Mart, 41 West 47th St., New York, N.Y., 10036.

A good source for books on puppetry and theatre. Catalogue issued from time to time.

Jay Marshall, Bookseller, Punch and Judy Bookshop, 5082 North Lincoln Ave., Chicago, Ill. 60625. By appointment only.

Punch and Judy items, as well as other puppet books and materials.

Orbis, Prague II, Vinohradská ul. 45, Czechoslovakia.

Handles exports of books from Czechoslovakia, and subscriptions to the periodical, *Ceskoslovenský Loutkář*.

Plays, Inc., 8 Arlington St., Boston, Mass. 02116.

Publishes a growing list of puppet books, mostly reprints, and is distributor of Baird's *The Art of the Puppet* and American publisher of Niculescu et al. *The Puppet Theatre of the Modern World*. Catalogue.

The Puppet Centre, 39 Henley St., Stratford-upon-Avon, Warwickshire, England.

Operated by Waldo and Muriel Lanchester, who have books, puppets and other items.

Martin Secker and Warburg, Ltd., 14 Carlisle St., Soho Sq., London, W. 1. England.

Distributor for Spatháris, *Behind the White Screen*, possibly other titles.

Stechert-Hafner, Inc., 31 East 10th St., New York, N.Y. 10003.

Foreign books can be ordered here.

Theatre Arts Books, 333 Sixth Ave., New York, N.Y. 10014.

Distributor for *World Theatre*, published by the International Theatre Institute, and publisher of selected books on the theatre.

Theatre Institute (L'Institut du Théâtre), Prague I, Valdstejnské/Nám 3, Czechoslovakia.

A source for books on Czech puppetry.

Charles E. Tuttle Co., Inc., Rutland, Vermont 05701.

An excellent source for books on Oriental arts and culture, including some puppet titles. General catalogue number 8 (50¢) entitled *Books to Span the East and West* also lists Americana.

Madame S. Zlatin, 46, rue Madame, Paris, 6ᵉ, France.

Books on theatre, dance, music, circus, marionettes. Catalogue.

Puppet Films

Only a few of the many film distributors who handle puppet films are listed; for further information consult the catalogues of companies which have educational films.

Association Instruction Materials (A division of Association Films, Inc.), 347 Madison Ave., New York, N.Y. 10017. Also 1621 Dragon St., Dallas, Texas 75207.

Handles Bil Baird's series, *How Man Learned to Count,* nine half-hour programs.

Bailey Films, Inc., 6509 DeLongpre Ave., Hollywood, Calif. 90028.

Has *ABC of Puppet Making* in two parts, as well as some films on the dance, suitable for educational use. Catalogue.

Contemporary Films, Inc., 330 West 42nd St., New York, N.Y. 10036. Also 1211 Polk St., San Francisco, Calif. 94109.

Stevens' *The Toymaker* and puppet animations by Jiri Trnka (*The Hand*) and Starevitch (*Carrousel Boreal* and *Nez au Vent*). Catalogue.

Films Incorporated (A Subsidiary of the Encyclopedia Britannica Educational Corporation), 38 West 32nd St., New York, N.Y. 10001. Also offices in other parts of the country.

A number of catalogues are available, including a general one of 16mm films and one of films for children. Puppet subjects include *Lili,* Disney's *Alice in Wonderland* and George Pal's *Tom Thumb.*

Jim Henson Associates, 303 East 53rd St., New York, N.Y. 10022.

Has a film on the Muppets, and is producing feature films, both puppet and non-puppet.

Seymour Hymowitz, 41 West 47th St., New York, N.Y. 10036.

Has Bunin's *Alice in Wonderland.*

International Film Bureau, Inc., 332 South Michigan Ave., Chicago, Ill. 60604.

Their catalogue of Art Films and Filmstrips lists many titles of interest to puppeteers, including animation techniques, creative methods, such as paper sculpture, and Norman McLaren's drawings done directly on film, such as *A Chairy Tale* with a ballet between a young man and an uncooperative chair, a surrealistic film, *A Phantasy* with synthetic sound, and others.

Marshall Izen, 411 West End Ave., New York, N.Y. 10024.

Has several films from his production of the *Tottle* television program, including one in color, *The Red and Gold Uniforms*.

Museum of Modern Art Film Library, 11 West 53rd St., New York, N.Y. 10019.

Punch Films, Inc., 250 West 57th St., New York, N.Y. 10019.

Lou Bunin, known for his *Alice in Wonderland,* has also produced many films for children, available from this company. In them, puppets and other forms of animation are used. Catalogue.

Index (1524–1948)

Index to Supplement (since 1948)